MARKETING MODELS

Gary L. Lilien
Penn State University

Philip Kotler
Northwestern University

K. Sridhar Moorthy
University of Rochester

Prentice Hall, Englewood Cliffs, New Jersey 07632

Library of Congress Cataloging-in-Publication Data

Lilien, Gary L.
    Marketing models / Gary L. Lilien, Philip Kotler, K. Sridhhar
Moorthy.
        p.   cm.
    Includes bibliographical references and index.
    ISBN 0-13-544644-9
    1. Marketing--Management.   I. Kotler, Philip.   II. Moorthy, K.
Sridhar.   III. Title.
HF5415.13.L52   1992
658.8--dc20   91-34512
                                                                  CIP

Acquisitions Editor: Jennifer Young
Editorial/production Supervision and
   Interior Design: Barbara Grasso, Lisa Kinne
Copy Editor: Sally Ann Bailey
Cover Design: Ben Santora
Prepress Buyer: Trudy Pisciotti
Manufacturing Buyer: Robert Anderson
Editorial Assistant: Ellen Ford
Production Assistant: Renee Pelletier

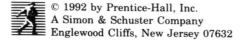

© 1992 by Prentice-Hall, Inc.
A Simon & Schuster Company
Englewood Cliffs, New Jersey 07632

Printed in the United States of America

10   9   8   7   6   5   4   3   2   1

ISBN 0-13-545641-X

Prentice-Hall International (UK) Limited, *London*
Prentice-Hall of Australia Pty. Limited, *Sydney*
Prentice-Hall Canada Inc., *Toronto*
Prentice-Hall Hispanoamericana, S.A., *Mexico*
Prentice-Hall of India Private Limited, *New Delhi*
Prentice-Hall of Japan, Inc., *Tokyo*
Simon & Schuster Asia Pte. Ltd., *Singapore*
Editora Prentice-Hall do Brasil, Ltda., *Rio de Janeiro*

To wife, children and parents
Dorothy Lilien
Amy, Melissa and Jessica Kotler
S. Krishnamoorthy and Rajalakshmi Moorthy
with love

CONTENTS

PREFACE

The battle for markets will increase in intensity in the coming years. Sales in many markets have been flat or declining. Competitors have been growing in number and in desperation. Products and brands are exhibiting shorter life cycles. These developments underscore the need for more sophisticated marketing decision making.

At the same time many company executives despair of putting marketing on a more scientific basic. They see marketing processes as lacking the neat quantitative properties found in production and finance. In marketing, human factors play a large role, marketing expenditures affect demand and cost simultaneously, and information is rarely adequate. Furthermore, the effects of marketing decisions are typically delayed, nonlinear, stochastic, and difficult to measure.

Yet the truth is that the tools and models now exist for improving marketing-decision effectiveness. Recent scientific, computer, and data-base developments have already enabled leading companies to increase their marketing productivity, to get "more marketing bang for the buck." This book examines the more promising scientific and data-base developments that assist managers in arriving at cost-effective marketing strategies and budgets and describes some of the important developments in marketing theory that are enabling marketers to understand and control markets more effectively.

Companies are increasingly applying the modeling approach to marketing decision making. Several trends are driving the process:

1. Marketing decision-support systems are being developed. The amount of data is exploding, the reporting of data is becoming more timely, and the quality of marketing data is improving. The development of new data sources and computer-based systems require marketing models to summarize, interpret, and make normative use of these data.

2. Quantitative MBAs are becoming marketing managers. The new generation of marketing managers is trained in and receptive to quantitative decision support.

3. Marketing theory is improving. More experiences are being shared through the marketing literature, and theoretical developments are being systematically codified, leading to improved theories and better models.

4. The value of marketing models is being reported. Throughout this book there are situations where not only was implementation reported but the value of implementation was reported as well. As such reports continue the use of marketing models will accelerate.

UNDERLYING DISCIPLINES FOR MARKETING MODEL BUILDING

Four major disciplines provide a foundation for the model-building approach to marketing decision making.

Consumer Behavior. Psychologists, behavioral scientists, and economists have produced a vast literature on buying behavior and buying motives. This behavior must be understood before it can be used for marketing plans. Consumer behavior theory provides a theoretical base upon which to build models of market size, growth, and behavior.

Economics. The economic theory of the firm and household consumption provides a starting point for developing models that can be used to understand markets and guide optimal marketing decision making. It provides useful building blocks in forming models of marketing systems as well as a valuable paradigm for building theoretical models.

Management Science/Operations Research (MS/OR). Management science is the application of scientific theories, empirical knowledge, and mathematical methods to the modeling and solution of management problems, including those in marketing.

Statistics/Econometrics. Research into marketing problems often generates a large amount of data. The fields of statistics and econometrics provide methodology for understanding these data.

These four disciplines—consumer behavior/behavioral science, economics, management science/operations research, and statistics/econometrics—provide the structure and the tools that are needed to develop and implement a model-building approach in marketing.

ORGANIZATION OF THE BOOK

Our view is that there are essentially three purposes for modeling in marketing: measuring marketing actions and outcomes, developing operational support for marketing decisions, and explaining marketing observations or phenomena. We call these modeling approaches measurement models, decision support models, and theoretical models, respectively. This book deals with decision support and theoretical models in detail and discusses measurement models to a lesser degree, as they are dealt with in-depth in many other texts. (In Chapter 1 we point to other sources that have developed measurement models in considerable detail.)

The book is organized as follows:

Chapter 1 provides the overview and philosophy of the book, dealing with theory and models in marketing.

Chapters 2 and 3 develop models of consumer and organizational buying, providing the "equations of motion" that our marketing systems obey.

Chapters 4 to 9 deal with the elements of the marketing mix—price, product, advertising, promotion, sales force, and distribution. Each of these chapters links to the others by focusing on the interactions among these variables.

Chapters 10 and 11 integrate and build on the earlier developments, dealing with new product models and marketing strategy models.

Chapter 12 deals with a current view of integrating computer-based tools in organizations to implement marketing models. We discuss successful implementation of marketing models and review some of the newer developments in expert or rule-based systems that are providing a different definition for what decision models will mean in marketing in the years to come.

In addition, we include five appendices covering some basic analytical tools that are used throughout the book: Appendix A, mathematical bases for marketing models; Appendix B, methods for developing objectives and utilities; Appendix C, the types and functional forms that models come in; Appendix D, methods for calibrating models; and Appendix E, concepts in non-cooperative game theory.

APPROACH WITHIN EACH CHAPTER

Most chapters start with a review of the basic concepts and theory in the area, followed by in-depth analyses of a small number of models. The complete details of a few models will suggest how to approach problems. Any model must be customized for a particular situation, and we prefer to develop a few models in depth; each model we discuss gives insight into the problem-solving process. Following the in-depth analysis is a short review of other model-based work in the area. The theoretical and decision support model developments are intertwined in each chapter.

Each chapter ends with a set of discussion questions and problems. The best way to learn about models is to push some numbers through existing models and to build some new models. Both types of problems are provided at the end of each chapter.

USES OF THE BOOK

The book is designed to be a text for graduate students and as a reference for practitioners and marketing academics.

The student should have some knowledge of calculus, probability and statistics, and matrix algebra to follow the complete exposition in the book. Not many marketing or business students have such a background. The text therefore provides, in the appendices, a review of the mathematical tools needed to carry on marketing model building.

The book can be used over a one-term or a two-term sequence. A one-term course is appropriate for students who are motivated and have the necessary quantitative and marketing background. A two-term sequence is appropriate where the students' mathematical skills need building. The instructor might cover the material in the appendices, and perhaps Chapters 2 and 3 in the first term, supplemented by several computerized or model-based cases to provide a flavor of application.

The book can also be used as a background reader in a case-based course in analytic marketing. A sufficient number of analytical cases are available to provide substance for such an advanced case course in marketing: this book is well suited to provide preparatory/supplementary material and background readings.

ACKNOWLEDGMENTS

Many colleagues and students contributed to the development of this book. The bibliography at the end of the book is testimony to the many influences in the field, all of whom cannot be cited here.

Much of the work on this book was done while one of us (Lilien) was on sabbatical leave at the Australian Graduate School of Management in Sydney, Australia. Our colleagues there (Grahame Dowling, David Midgley, John Roberts and John Rossiter) were tremendously supportive of the effort needed to bring this book about. Two fine AGSM PhD students, Lawrence Ang and Pam Morrison, provided considerable research support.

A number of our colleagues provided substantial suggestions and corrections on earlier drafts, including Kalyan Chatterjee, Dennis Gensch, Eitan

Gerstner, Srinath Gopalakrishna, Jim Hess, Dan Horsky, Shlomo Kalish, Lakshman Krishnamurthi, Vijay Mahajan, John McCann, Scott Neslin, John Rossiter, and Seenu Srinavasan.

Two colleagues provided feedback and input of a particularly substantial nature. Josh Eliashberg thoroughly reviewed the manuscript several times and told us what he thought of it. Hopefully, we have responded well to his suggestions (although we may never get it right).

John Roberts, principal co-author of chapter 2, had substantial suggestions about the structure and content of the book, and contributed more than he ever dreamed he would.

A number of students provided very valuable research support, including Nam Kim, Nipun Ramaiya, Brent Johnson, Paul Fields, and Michel Claessens (of the University of Liége).

The chapter problems came from several sources, including a marketing models course at MIT. Several of the problems were created by Gilles Laurent, John Little and Manu Kalwani, but their individual contributions have been lost to time.

Finally, Carmella Letzeisen and Mary Wyckoff handled the U.S.-based typing while Fiona Reay provided support in Australia. Their work involved countless hours and unrealistic deadlines and was always performed both capably and with good humor that neither the work nor its producers deserved.

1 | THEORY AND MODELS IN MARKETING

What are models? How do they relate to theories in marketing? What kinds of models are there? What are they good for? And what is the common ground among science, marketing, and models? These are the questions we consider in this chapter.

SCIENCE AND MARKETING MODELS

Science is a process of inquiry. It is a procedure for answering questions and solving problems and for developing more effective methods for answering questions and solving problems. Too often, we mistake science for the body of knowledge it has produced. In our development of an understanding of science in marketing, we will concentrate on the process that generates that knowledge—the modeling-and-inquiry process—rather than on the knowledge itself.

EXAMPLE

Consider the PIMS (profit impact of marketing strategy) project to be discussed in Chapter 11. This study is aimed at collecting product, market, and company financial data on a large number of businesses and deriving efficient operating rules from a careful study of what has been tried and what has worked. The project has produced regression models that provide norms for marketing strategy. Is this modeling effort scientific? The knowledge base produced by the project has been questioned by some. (Does high market share cause high profitability?) But as an inquiry process, the PIMS project is clearly scientific, producing better models and better analysis procedures as the base of observations and the analysis of past results have grown.

EXAMPLE

The recognition that sales of new, frequently purchased products can be modeled by a trial-repeat process was a scientific discovery. That discovery provided an explanation of the typical sales curve for new consumer products—with an overshoot prior to steady state—illustrated in Exhibit 1.1. This separation of curve (c) into its factor curves, (a) and (b), provides both an explanation for the shape of curve (c) and a means for diagnosing new product problems and forecasting results. (See Chapter 10 for details.)

Then what of the intuitive manager, who takes his gut feeling, his experience, and flies by the seat of his pants in making decisions? Is he scientific? Or, alternatively, is he using common sense? The distinction between common sense and scientific inquiry is not one of quality but degree.

> Science is, I believe, nothing but trained and organized common sense, differing from the latter only as a veteran may differ from a raw recruit; and its methods differ from those of common sense only so far as the guardsman's cut and thrust differ from the manner in which a savage wields his club. *(Huxley, in Wiener, 1953, p. 130)*

Or, again,

> Scientific statements, no less than those of common experience, are opinions—only enlightened (grounded and testable) opinions rather than arbitrary dicta or unchecked gossip. What can be proved beyond reasonable doubt are either theorems of logic and mathematics or trivial (particular and observational) statements of fact, such as "This volume is heavy." *(Bunge, 1967, p. 5)*

It is generally recognized that as a process of inquiry becomes more scientific, we are more likely to obtain correct answers to questions and better solutions to problems. This is not to assert that better results always occur when scientific approaches are used but that we are more likely to achieve superior results with a scientific approach.

In fact, even a systematization of managers' actions seems to provide superior results. Bowman's (1963) managerial coefficients theory is based on the interesting and challenging assertion that a model calibrated on a man-

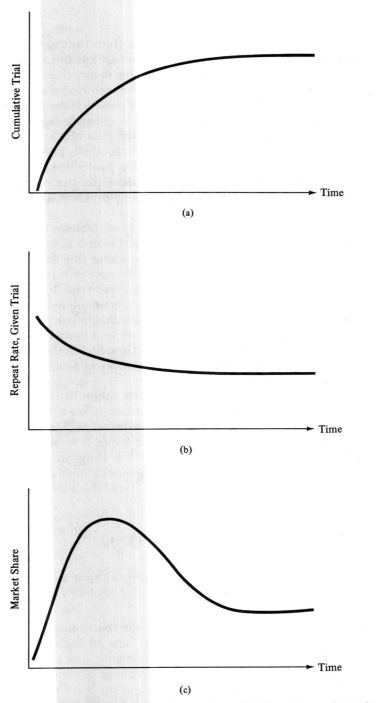

EXHIBIT 1.1 The time path of market share (c), modeled as the product of trial (a) and repeat (b), a scientific discovery.

ager's past actions will perform better than that manager in future, similar decision situations. Bowman's argument is that the calibration procedure separates the signal from decision-making noise, leading to a more consistent decision-making process. He and others (see Kunreuther, 1969, for example) have shown that this systemization of past actions has wide applicability.

The scientific process of inquiry is superior because it is controlled. "A process is controlled to the extent that it is efficiently directed toward the attainment of certain objectives" (Ackoff, 1962, p. 3). Every inquiry process in marketing and elsewhere has some controlled, as well as some uncontrolled, aspects. Marketing is scientific when the research effort has, along with the objective of solving a particular problem, the objective of improving the procedures employed.

Two things should be noted here. First, by our discussion, there are clearly many degrees of inquiry, not just scientific and nonscientific. So our objective will generally be to see how we move along this continuum in the scientific direction. Second, even where a scientific approach leads to better results than those of common sense, it is not always preferred. In many small, fragmented markets the cost of an advertising experiment may be many times the potential profit from discovering the optimal advertising policy. Many small businesses cannot justify the fixed cost of a model-building effort and must rely on common sense and rules of thumb. Furthermore, marketing emergencies often arise where a timely answer is preferred to one that is better but too late to use.

Physical experimentation is often taken to be synonymous with scientific research: "In scientific experimentation, we control everything that happens" (Giddings, 1924, p. 55). But controlled inquiry may clearly occur without physical manipulation. The astronomer does not manipulate the objects of the study. The astronomer's control is the conceptual manipulation, with models and mathematics, of the phenomena under study. We will discuss such thought experiments in greater detail as "theoretical modeling" shortly.

THE COMPLEXITY OF MARKETING

Several characteristics of the marketing environment make it difficult to predict and control the effect of marketing actions:

Sales Response to a Single Marketing Instrument.   Marketing managers are frequently trying to understand "how advertising affects sales." But the relationship between the market's response and the level of a given type of any marketing instrument like advertising is typically unknown. Summarizing individual buyers' behaviors into a measure of total sales response is a challenging task.

Marketing Mix Interaction.   Marketing effort, far from being a homogeneous input, is a composite of many different types of activities, including (1) pricing and price promotions; (2) promotional activities such as advertising, personal selling, and public relations; (3) distribution activities related to the availability of goods and servicing of orders; and (4) product-development and product-improvement activities. The market's response to variations in the level of any one marketing input is conditional on the level of the other activities. Furthermore, the variation of two or more marketing activities at the same time can have effects that are greater or less than the sum of the separate effects.

Competitive Effects.   The market's response to the marketer's actions is related to competitors' actions as well, and the firm rarely has good knowledge of or control over competitors' actions.

Delayed Response.   The market's response to current marketing (especially advertising) outlays is not immediate but in many instances may be delayed by weeks or months.

Multiple Territories.   The firm typically sells in several territories with different rates of response to additional marketing expenditures.

Multiple Products.   Most companies market a number of products and need to allocate limited marketing funds among them.

Functional Interactions.   Marketing decisions cannot be optimized without joint decision making in the production and financial areas.

Multiple Goals.   A company tends to pursue multiple and often contradictory goals. Company presidents often say that they seek maximum sales at minimum cost. The firm must clearly state its objectives to guide the choice of a marketing strategy from a potentially large number of alternatives.

MODELS

Because marketing systems are too complex to manage in all their detail, people deal with models of them. Everyone builds models all the time. When you give a colleague directions to your office, you are providing a verbal model of the (physical) route. When you draw a map, you are using a pictorial model. When selecting a sales pitch for a specific customer ("Our Ectozorch is the highest-tech solution to your problem in the market today" versus "Our Ectozorch has been used by seven of your major competitors in similar applications for over a year"), you choose the message that you think will work best given your model of customer response based on your experience.

So, marketing managers, like everyone else, use models all the time. The only difference between those who say they use models and those who say they don't is how systematic and formal that model building is. It is helpful to think about models in terms of their *methodology* and in terms of their *purpose*.

Methodology

There are two basic methodologies for modeling in marketing: verbal and mathematical. Verbal models, as the name suggests, are cast in prose form. Most of the models in the so-called "behavioral literature" in marketing are verbal. The variables, the relationships among them, and the arguments are all verbal. For example, Howard and Sheth's (1969) theory of consumer behavior is a verbal model of consumer behavior. Another example is Lavidge and Steiner's (1961) model of advertising: "advertising should move people from awareness . . . to knowledge . . . to liking . . . to preference . . . to conviction . . . to purchase." Often, verbal models are expressed graphically for expositional reasons. Note that verbal models are not unique to behavioral marketing. Many of the great theories of individual, social, and societal behavior, such as those of Freud, Darwin, and Marx, are verbal theories. So is Williamson's (1975) transaction-costs theory of economic behavior.

Mathematical models use symbols to denote marketing variables and express their relationships as equations or inequalities. The analysis—when done correctly—follows the rules of mathematical logic. Examples of mathematical models are Bass's (1969a) model of diffusion of durables, Little's (1975) BRANDAID model, and McGuire and Staelin's (1983) model of channel structure.

Exhibit 1.2 shows a new product growth model verbally, graphically, and mathematically.

Purpose

There are essentially three purposes for modeling in marketing: measurement, decision support, and explanation or theory building. We will call the corresponding models, measurement models, decision support models, and theoretical models, respectively.

Measurement Models.   The purpose of measurement models is to measure the "demand" for a product as a function of various independent variables. The word "demand" here should be interpreted broadly. It is not necessarily units demanded but could be some other variable that is related to units demanded. For example, in conjoint measurement models, the demand variable

Verbal Model

New-product growth often starts slowly, until some people (early triers) become
aware of the product. These early triers interact with nontriers to lead to acceleration of sales growth. Finally, as market potential is approached, growth slows
down.

(a)

Graphical/Conceptual Model

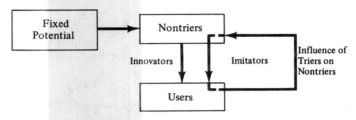

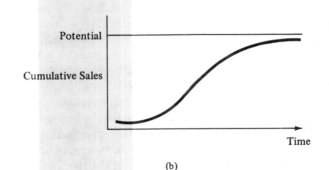

(b)

Mathematical Model

$$\frac{dx}{dt} = (a + bx)(N - x)$$

where x = number of purchases by t
N = market potential
a, b = constants

(c)

EXHIBIT 1.2 Illustration of three model structures describing the same phenomenon.

is an individual's preference for a choice alternative. In Bass's (1969a) model of diffusion of new durables, the demand variable is "sales to first adopters." In Guadagni and Little's (1983) model, the dependent variable is whether or not an individual made a purchase of a given brand on a given purchase occasion.

The independent variables in measurement models are usually marketing mix variables—again interpreted broadly to mean any variables the firm controls—but they could include variables to account for seasonality, consumer characteristics, and competitors' actions. In conjoint measurement models, for example, the independent variables are usually the attributes of the choice alternatives. Bass's model has two independent variables, "cumulative sales since introduction" and the square of cumulative sales since introduction. Guadagni and Little's model has several independent variables including whether or not the brand was on deal at a given purchase occasion, regular price of the brand, deal price (if any), brand loyalty of the individual, and so on. These examples suggest that measurement models can deal with individual (disaggregate) demand or aggregate (market-level) demand.

Once the demand function has been specified, it is then "calibrated" to measure the parameters of the function. Calibration reveals the role of various independent variables in determining demand for this product: which variables are important and which are unimportant. Also, once the demand function has been calibrated, it can be used to predict demand in a given situation by plugging in the values of the independent variables in that situation. A variety of methods are used to calibrate demand functions: judgment, econometric techniques, experimentation, simulation, and so on (see Appendix D). For example, Bass uses multiple regression to calibrate his model; Srinivasan and Shocker (1973) use linear programming to calibrate their conjoint model; Guadagni and Little use maximum-likelihood methods.

The book by Hanssens, Parsons, and Schultz (1990) deals almost exclusively with measurement models.

Decision Support Models. These models are designed to help marketing managers make decisions. They incorporate measurement models as building blocks, but go beyond measurement models in recommending marketing-mix decisions for the manager. The methods used to derive the optimal decision vary across applications. Typical techniques are differential calculus, operations research techniques such as linear and integer programming, and simulation. Little and Lodish's (1969) MEDIAC model for developing media schedules (Chapter 6) is an example. They develop an underlying measurement model here, relating sales in each segment to advertising exposure level. That model is calibrated by managerial judgment. The estimated sales-response function is then maximized to develop an optimal media schedule using a variety of maximization techniques—dynamic programming, piecewise lin-

Measurement Module   **Optimization Module**

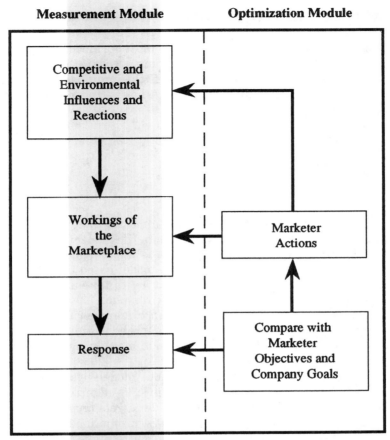

EXHIBIT 1.3   A decision support system, showing measurement and optimization modules.

ear programming, heuristic methods—and incorporating various technical and budgetary constraints.

Exhibit 1.3 shows a decision support system. Note the arrow leading from "marketer actions" to "competitive reactions." This is to recognize that, unlike other environmental variables, competitors' actions could be affected by "our" actions. Later in this book we will show how game theory can be used to model such competitive interactions.

The next section develops decision support models in detail.

Theoretical Models.   The purpose of these models is to explain marketing phenomena. Theoretical models can be verbal or mathematical, but here we are concerned mainly with mathematical theoretical models. We discuss theoretical modeling in detail later in this chapter.

DECISION SUPPORT MODELS

Many managers feel threatened by models. Models require (1) systematic thinking, (2) specification of assumptions, (3) data (judgmental or otherwise), and (4) exposure to new and often difficult-to-understand concepts.

In a decision-making situation a marketing manager often wants support for his position:

in black-and-white terms

in simple, concrete language

as soon as possible

at no cost

The decision support modeling approach may lead the manager to difficulty because it may be hard to explain the model to superiors and the model may yield solutions that are difficult to implement.

So why do we increasingly use model-based decision making? The answer is simple: managers can't afford *not* to take a model-building approach in their fast-moving, competitive environment.

First, the amount of information a manager can obtain is growing exponentially. Therefore, if he is to comprehend this information, he needs a model to relate the data to his decision-making needs, and then use a computer to analyze the data.

Second, while manager A (without models) gets reports on what things are—data points for sales, shares, prices, advertising expenditures—manager B, using models to interpret his data, gets reports on how things react—price elasticities, advertising responses, promotional-effectiveness indicators. Manager B is clearly in a better position to make better informed decisions.

The last point calls for a look ahead, with new models and methodology leading to better decision making. In a Darwinian sense, the fittest organizations tend to survive. The development and proven value of model-based aids to marketing-strategy development will provide more profitable, healthier environments for those organizations using the tools correctly.

EXAMPLE

During the course of this book, we will present a number of examples showing the value of decision support models, such as the following, given by Shapiro (1976). H. J. Heinz, in promoting one of its products, began an analysis of promotional effectiveness in 1972. A preliminary study indicated that promotional effectiveness, in terms of effect on market share, was different for different package sizes within a district and varied across districts. A model, based on the results of the initial study, showed wide variation in promotional effectiveness across markets. That model, a simple regression model, linked share of features and promotions by size to market share. The market response model was embedded into an optimal allocation-of-effort model and showed that a budget reallocation might be in order. Specifically,

> For the first fiscal year 1973–1974, the total number of promotions was reduced by 40% from what it had been the previous year. At the same time, by concentrating mostly on those promotions which proved themselves to be effective, market share was increased by more than three share points. *(Shapiro, 1976, p. 86)*

This example of marketing modeling and analysis makes several important points:

> Standard business practice (the prior promotional policy) may be less than optimally cost-effective.
>
> Marketing models do not have to be complex to be valuable.
>
> Models may help isolate situations where profitability can be increased by reallocation of resources or by cutting spending.
>
> Models help focus on the key variable of interest (the market-varying, promotional-response parameter) and help serve as vehicles for analyzing its impact.

Model results were implemented here because it was clearly cost-effective to do so. As our marketing systems respond more quickly and become increasingly complex, more marketing managers will use model-based analyses because it will be too costly to ignore them.

Postscript. The analysis just detailed did not lead to a regular, model-based, monitoring-and-control procedure (e.g., redoing the analysis on an annual basis). Heinz management was convinced that new market-specific spending norms had been developed and that further analysis was not needed. This view is a manifestation of what we will call modeling myopia—the feeling that once model-based analysis is done, it does not need to be done again, ever. Some causes and cures for this syndrome are discussed in Chapter 12.

THEORETICAL MODELING IN MARKETING

A theoretical model is a set of assumptions that describes a marketing environment. Some of these assumptions will be purely mathematical, designed to make the analysis tractable. Others will be substantive assumptions with real empirical content. They can describe such things as who the actors are, how many of them there are, what they care about, the external conditions under which they make decisions, what their decisions are about, and so on. It is these latter assumptions that will participate in explaining the marketing phenomenon in question. Note that the concept of a model in theoretical modeling is different from the concept of a decision support model. There, a

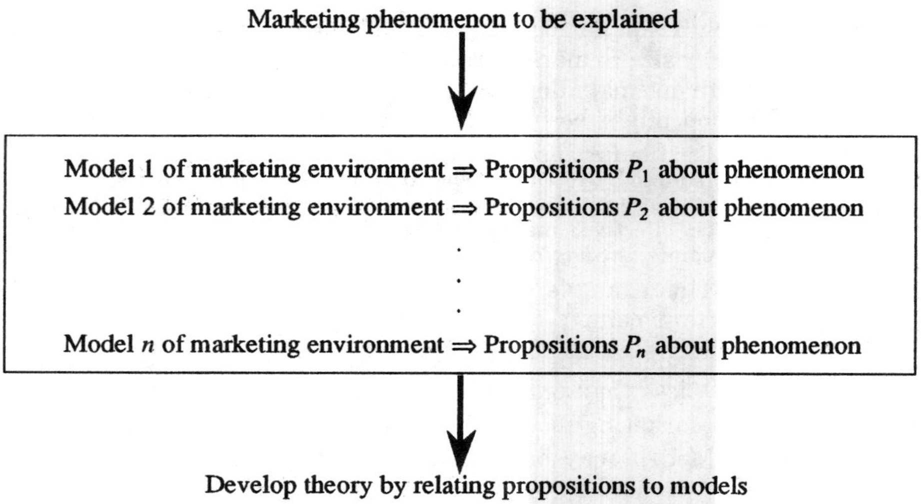

Marketing phenomenon to be explained

$\downarrow$

Model 1 of marketing environment $\Rightarrow$ Propositions P_1 about phenomenon

Model 2 of marketing environment $\Rightarrow$ Propositions P_2 about phenomenon

.

.

.

Model n of marketing environment $\Rightarrow$ Propositions P_n about phenomenon

$\downarrow$

Develop theory by relating propositions to models

EXHIBIT 1.4   Overview of the theoretical modeling process.

model is defined as a "mathematical description of how something works." Here it is simply a setting in which the inquiry takes place.

Once a model has been built, the researcher analyzes its *logical* implications for the phenomenon being explained. Then another model, substantively different from the first, is built—very likely by another researcher—and its implications are analyzed. The process may continue with a third and a fourth model, if necessary, until all the ramifications of the explanation being proposed have been examined. By comparing the implications of one model with those of another, and by tracing the differences to the different assumptions in the various models, the researcher develops a theory about the phenomena in question (see Exhibit 1.4) This is as if a logical experiment were being run, with the various models as the "treatments." The key difference from empirical experiments is that, whereas in empirical experiments the subjects produce the effects, here the researcher produces the effects by logical argument and analysis. Let us try to illuminate this abstract discussion with an illustration:

Using Theoretical Modeling to Understand Sales Force Compensation Schemes.   Firms use a variety of ways to compensate their sales forces, including salaries, commissions, quotas, sales contests, free vacation trips, and so on. A natural question to ask is: "Why is there such a variety of compensation schemes and what function does each compensation component serve in a compensation package?" Let us focus only on salaries and commissions. The agency theory literature on this subject originates from economics where the problem is viewed as that of a "principal" designing a compensation package for an "agent" whose contributions to the welfare of the principal, the principal cannot observe. We will discuss this theory in detail in Chapter 8; here we focus on the model structure.

We first construct a "super" model, specifying the overall environment in which the action takes place. Later, we will construct other models as submodels of this supermodel. The analogy to behavioral experiments is that the supermodel specifies the boundaries of the experiment and the submodels are the various treatments in the experiment.

The assumptions describing our supermodel (the environment) are:

Assumption 1: There is a sales manager, representing the firm, designing a compensation package for a salesperson working alone.

Assumption 2: The sales manager designs a compensation package for the salesperson and commits to it. The compensation package can consist of a salary and/or commissions on the gross profits of the firm. The salesperson can accept or reject the compensation package offered. If he rejects it, then he will work somewhere else and get expected utility U_o.

Assumption 3: If the salesperson accepts the compensation package offered to him, then his utility from income I and work W is given by $U(I, W) = V_I(I) - W$. $V_I(\cdot)$ is an increasing, twice continuously differentiable concave function of I. The salesperson will decide how much work to put in by maximizing his expected utility.

Assumption 4: The manager designs the compensation package in order to maximize the firm's expected net profits, anticipating the salesperson's reaction. The net profits are given by $\pi - I$, where π denotes the gross profits of the firm.

Assumption 5: The gross profits of the firm are a function of W, the work put in by the salesperson, and ε, a random variable representing the uncertainty in the resulting sales. ε is independent of the gross profits generated by any other salesperson in the firm, and neither the manager nor the salesperson observes the resolution of this uncertainty. Both can verify the gross profits obtained, however. As the salesperson works harder, he shifts the distribution of π such that higher gross profit outcomes are more likely.

Assumption 6: Assumptions 1–5 are common knowledge to the sales manager and the salesperson.

We now study a series of models, each with a set of special assumptions added to assumptions 1–6, restricting the environment further, and state their logical implications for salesperson compensation. Exhibit 1.5 shows the experimental design and results.

Model 1. (Salesperson is risk-neutral, and his effort is observable.) This is

**Salesperson
attitude
toward risk**

	RISK NEUTRAL	*RISK AVERSE*
OBSERVABLE	Model 1 Any combination of salary and commission	Model 2 All Salary
UNOBSERVABLE	Model 3 Pure commission	Model 4 Specific mixture of salary and commission*

**Observability
of
salesperson
effort**

*Under some technical conditions.

EXHIBIT 1.5 The "experimental design" for theoretical models for optimal sales force compensation.

the simplest model. Here, where we assume that the salesperson's utility function is linear in income, it is immaterial whether the package is all-salary, all-commission, or any combination, as long as the package yields the same expected income to the salesperson. Furthermore, given that the salesperson's work is observable, the manager can design the compensation package such that if the salesperson doesn't work "hard," then he will be penalized severely. The salesperson's expected income, if he works hard, will yield him utility U_o, the utility he will get from the alternative job.

Model 2. (Salesperson is risk-averse, and his effort is observable.) Here an all-salary plan is optimal and an all-commission plan is not. The reason is that with all-commission plan, the salesperson's income will fluctuate, so for any effort level, his expected utility will be lower than if he were given the same expected income in salary. In other words, if the manager asks the salesperson to put out effort W and have an expected utility level of U_o, he would have to pay him more compensation on average with all commissions than with an all-salary plan.

Model 3. (Salesperson is risk-neutral, and his effort is unobservable.) Under these circumstances, a pure commission compensation scheme is optimal for the firm and the salesperson will work as hard as he did under model 1. The commission scheme, however, can't be the same as in model 1. Now the commission rate will be such as to give the salesperson *all* of the firm's gross profits. But how will the firm make any money then? By having the salesperson pay a lump-sum amount equal to the firm's net profits under model 1. Here the manager is essentially selling the firm to the salesperson! Both the firm and the salesperson will be as well off here as they were in model 1.

Model 4. (Salesperson is risk-averse, and his effort is unobservable.) In this case, under some technical assumption about the distribution of π (Grossman and Hart, 1983; Holmstrom, 1979; and Basu et al., 1985), we can show that the optimal compensation package must involve both salaries and commissions. Furthermore, the salesperson will not work as hard as he did under model 2, and with some other assumptions (Chapter 8), we get the following results:

1. The greater the gross profit varies with selling effort, the less the salesperson works, the less his expected income, the less the firm's expected profits, and the greater the proportion of salary to expected income.

2. As the salesperson's work-effectiveness increases, the greater the firm's expected profits and the harder the salesperson works.

3. As the expected utility from the alternative job increases, the less the salesperson works, the more his expected income, the less the firm's expected profits, and the greater the proportion of salary to expected income.

As shown in **Exhibit 1.5**, the four submodels can be seen as a 2×2 experimental design with two factors and two levels of each factor. Comparing the implications of model 1 versus model 2 and model 3 versus model 4, we see that the salesperson's risk preference—whether he is risk-neutral or not—has a "main effect" on the optimal compensation plan: with risk neutrality, salaries are not needed; with risk aversion, salaries are needed. Similarly, comparing model 1 with model 3 and model 2 with model 4, observability of the salesperson's effort has a main effect on the optimal compensation plan: if the salesperson's work is observable, then commissions are not needed; otherwise they are. There are also interaction effects. For example, for the dependent variable "how hard the salesperson works," there is an interaction effect between risk aversion and observability: lack of observability results in less work if the salesperson is risk-averse, but with risk neutrality, observability has no effect on how hard the salesperson works.

Issues in Theoretical Modeling. The foregoing discussion illustrated a role that theoretical modeling can play in marketing. Here we address in turn the following issues: division of modeling labor, validity, and usefulness for theoretical modeling.

Division of Labor. We presented the results in the example as if they were the result of the work of a single researcher. Indeed, a number of researchers (Borch, 1962; Wilson, 1969; Harris and Raviv, 1979; Ross, 1973; Holmstrom, 1979; Basu et al., 1985; and others) worked on them for a period of over 20 years. This means that the theoretical experiment may not be finished in a single piece of research.

Validity and Realism. The internal and external validity of theoretical models are legitimate concerns, as they are in empirical experiments. Internal validity is generally quite high in theoretical models (assuming that the mathematics is performed correctly). In our example the models formed a factorial design, and our analysis clearly showed the main effects and interactions. But this high degree of internal validity comes at the cost of realism. This lack of realism happens in two ways: first, it is easier to infer cause and effect relationships if other distracting forces are not there. Thus, our model world (like most laboratory experiments) is rather sparse and unrealistic. Second, to infer cause and effect, conditions must vary, and all of the models analyzed here certainly cannot simultaneously be "realistic." Moorthy (1990) discusses the external validity issue in detail.

Usefulness. The main purpose of theoretical modeling is pedagogy—teaching us how the real world operates—and that purpose is well served by internally valid theoretical experiments. But what about the practical use of such work for marketing managers? Such models are of direct value to managers when they uncover robust results that are *independent* of the unobservable features of the decision making environment. Under these circumstances, the models have two uses: (1) as direct *qualitative* guidance for policy ["in our situation, we need low (high) proportions of sales force compensation in commissions"] and (2) as the basis for specifying operational models and associated decision support systems that can adapt the theory to a particular environment and generate *quantitative* prescriptions.

FOCUS AND STRUCTURE OF THIS BOOK

The foregoing discussion suggests that all three directions in the development of marketing models—measurement models, decision support models, and theoretical models—have significant values for practitioners and researchers. As the area of measurement models is covered in other places, we deemphasize their role here and give major coverage to both the decision support models and theoretical models.

The book is structured as follows:

Chapters 2 and 3 develop models of consumer and organizational buying. These provide the background or equations of motion that describe how and why markets operate.

Chapters 3–9 deal with the elements of the marketing mix—price, product design, advertising, promotion, sales force, and distribution. Each of these chapters links to others by focusing attention on the interactions among these variables.

Chapters 10 and 11 integrate and build on the earlier developments, dealing with new product models and marketing strategy models.

Finally, Chapter 12 deals with a view toward the development of computer-based tools to help implement the results of marketing modeling activities.

The book also includes five appendices, outlining (1) some of the mathematics that is useful in understanding marketing models, (2) methods for developing objectives and utilities, (3) the types and functional forms that models come in, (4) procedures for calibrating models, and (5) key elements in game theory.

As you proceed through this book, with its extensive catalog of mathematical models, bear in mind that whether one's goal is understanding (as with theoretical models) or better decision making (as with decision support models), a major benefit of marketing models is the systematic and careful thought that goes into their construction and analysis. While the effort (and the level of technical expertise) may be high, the outcome will pay handsome returns.

PROBLEMS

1.1. What is the value of theory in marketing?

1.2. Give examples of descriptive, predictive, and normative models that are applicable to marketing, providing a brief statement of their content and purpose.

1.3. The Tempus Company is a small producer of a laundry bleach that has successfully competed against its larger competitors selling laundry detergents that claim to have bleaching power. Tempus management has just learned that its competitors are considering the introduction in the near future of a detergent with soaking characteristics. Management at Tempus must decide whether or not the firm should also develop and market such a soak product. Carry out a brief analysis of the problem faced by Tempus management in this situation, following the list of steps through which the operations researcher should go in analyzing a problem.

1.4. Differentiate between experience-based response and the response specified through a descriptive/predictive model. Give an example of each.

1.5. The ABC Company has been making standard-grade paper towels and bathroom tissue and selling them at prices slightly below those of its competitors. Sales have been stagnant over the last two years. ABC Company wants to increase growth and is considering the following options:

a. Introduce some new products (napkins, disposable cloth kitchen wipes, etc.)

b. Introduce higher-grade items of the products it is already producing, advertise them heavily, and sell them at premium prices

c. Invest heavily in an advertising campaign that shows "equal quality at discount prices" for its existing products

Develop a verbal model and an associated graphical/conceptual model that can aid in deciding among the three options given and a fourth, do-nothing option.

1.6. "A model is situation-specific and must be customized to any individual situation." Is this statement true? If so, why should we study models in other situations? Give examples.

1.7. Assume that regional sales for an instant breakfast food have been related to advertising as follows:

$$S = 27 + 2.1A - 0.025A^2$$

where

A = advertising dollars, 1,000s
S = sales dollars, 1,000s

What is the optimal advertising level? Assuming that current advertising is $15,000, what is the marginal value of increasing advertising spending by $1,000? What is the interpretation of the 27 in the formula?

1.8. Models $f(X)$, $g(X)$, and $h(X)$ all fit historical data equally well. What criteria should be used to determine which model is best? Give a specific example.

1.9. What is a model? What is a law? What is a theory? What is a hypothesis? How are these concepts related?

2 | CONSUMER BEHAVIOR*

At the heart of marketing's equations of process and outcomes are models of consumer behavior. Understanding the household consumer (and, in the next chapter, the industrial customer) is the starting point for all marketing planning and action. The marketing philosophy has been defined as seeing our products and services through the eyes of the customer. In this chapter we show how we can understand the customer's viewpoint (his or her needs, values, perceptions, and actions) so we can see the world through his or her eyes.

CHAPTER OVERVIEW

The literature on consumer behavior and related models is vast. It studies both internal influences on the consumer (using theories from psychology) and external influences (using theories from sociology). Our objective in this chapter is first to review some of those basic theories (and their associated complexities) and derive a framework for studying models of consumer behavior. We then use them to see how they relate to our mathematical models.

By developing a framework of consumer purchase processes, we tie together individual-level models of consumer behavior and discuss their uses and limitations. These basic building blocks may be combined in different ways to study complex problems and to deal with different managerial needs.

*John Roberts was principal co-author of this chapter, drawing from Roberts and Lilien (1992).

Models of behavior in consumer markets differ drastically in their objectives and forms. We can define a market as the set of all individuals and organizations who are actual or potential buyers of a product or service. Alternatively, rather than concentrating on the buyer side, we can define a market in terms of the products that are offered (the seller side, which we call the "industry" or "competition"). Obviously, a marketing transaction occurs when these two elements are brought together.

EXAMPLE _____

To illustrate the range of purchase decisions that we will encounter, let us visit with the Smith family on a typical day. The washing machine has been making a clunking noise, and Fred Smith, a lawyer, had promised to visit some downtown major appliance stores during his lunch hour to look at possible replacements. The whole annoying episode has forced him and his wife Sally to think about what they really value in a washing machine. He was also hoping to find time for a haircut. Sally, a physician who works mornings at a health clinic, plans to pick up some groceries on the way home. Other than regular supplies such as milk, fruit, cheese, bread, and meat, the household is low on a number of things. For example, the family needs breakfast cereal, and Sally poured the last of the peppercorns into the pepper mill last night. Also, she'll be in trouble with her teenage son, Bob, if she doesn't put some soda in the fridge because it is almost out. Chances are that if there are some good specials available she will pick up some other products as well, although she has no plans to do so. Last week, for example, she bought coffee that was offered on a special price deal that was too good to pass up. After school Bob intends to try to return his skateboard to the store where he bought it last week. It broke on its first tryout. He felt that he should have known that it would be no good because it had not been made by a well-known manufacturer. The other member of the family, Debbie, is 4 years old. After preschool she will help Sally unpack the groceries, which gives her a chance to express an opinion on household purchases from breakfast cereal to bathroom cleaner.

We will revisit the Smith family throughout this chapter to illustrate the range of purchase behavior that we must capture with our models.

The Foundations of Consumer Behavior Models

The engineer builds on well-established laws of physics that have been derived by theoretical analysis and tested by empirical investigation. Similarly, consumer behavior models are based on consumer behavior theory and then tested in the marketplace. In this section we briefly review the theoretical bases for consumer behavior models, referring the interested reader to more complete treatments where appropriate. As we work through models of purchase decisions, we will see evidence of the empirical validation that these theories have undergone.

The field of consumer behavior provides a rich foundation on which to build quantitative marketing models. Before introducing a framework to classify these models, it is useful to examine the major traditions of consumer behavior research.

Behavioral Learning.   One of the earliest theories of consumer behavior and one that is still influential is that of behavioral learning (Skinner, 1938). Under this theory, consumers' prior experience is the primary determinant of future behavior. The theory provides no model of the internal mental process of choice, but specifies that past conditioning explains future actions. The best known theories in this category are Pavlov's theory of classical conditioning (in which events that repeatedly occur together tend to be associated in the future, with a stimulus leading to a response) and Skinner's theory of operant conditioning (in which reward is provided after a desired behavior is undertaken.) Peter and Nord (1982) provide a useful discussion of the difference between these two techniques and their implications for marketing practitioners.

EXAMPLE

The last two times he found no soda in the fridge, Bob made a fuss and threatened to "take the car to get some." As he only has his learner's permit, Sally does not want him driving unnecessarily and will surely remember soda on this shopping trip. (Bob has "conditioned" her.)

Personality Research.   A second major tradition of behavioral research revolves around personality. For example, Freud's psychoanalytic theory has been used to explain the aspects of consumer behavior that are unconsciously motivated. Also, attribution theory—where the consumer attempts to reconcile his or her behavior, the behavior of others, and the state of his or her environment with his prior beliefs—has proved useful when trying to explain personal and social normative beliefs (see Folkes, 1988).

EXAMPLE

Bob attributes the reason for his skateboard breaking to his choice of a private label, versus the better known and more expensive national brand. (This is called "object attribution.")

Information Processing. A third area of consumer behavior, that of information processing, is exemplified by the work of Bettman (1979). It studies both the idiosyncratic structure of individual consumers' decision-making processes and also how their beliefs change as they learn more about the behavior concerned. The theory has clear implications for how we ought to mathematically describe information integration strategies.

EXAMPLE

When Sally empties any package in her kitchen (in this case, the peppercorn box), she considers placing the now out-of-stock item on her shopping list. (This is based on an "information processing protocol.")

Attitude Models. A fourth major consumer behavior research tradition, the one that has had the most profound impact on the modeling of consumer behavior, is the field of attitude research. (For an in-depth review, see Ajzen and Fishbein, 1980.) In this paradigm, the consumer's intention regarding performing a behavior such as purchasing a product is viewed as a function of his or her attitude toward the behavior and beliefs about the social norms regarding the behavior. That attitude, in turn, is composed of beliefs about the consequences of performing the behavior and an evaluation of how the consumer will feel about those consequences. The attitude model approach provides the theoretical underpinnings of much of the research in marketing modeling, which views product attributes as the drivers of the consumer decision process.

EXAMPLE

In beginning to evaluate alternative washing machines, Fred and Sally are compiling a list of important attributes, which may include capacity, reliability, number of wash cycles, quietness, energy use, price, and so on. (Attitude models specify how individuals form judgments and preferences about objects based on their perceptions of how those objects perform on the key attributes.)

The Nature of Consumer Behavior Models

The models outlined differ in their emphasis on the external environment, the internal cognitive processes of the consumer, and in the way they deal with past behavior, individual differences, and evaluation processes in determining choice. We argue in Chapter 1 for pluralism in marketing science. This holds for consumer behavior models: rather than regarding these models as competitors, we take a contingent view and suggest that there are some circumstances in which one of these views (or models) may prove valid or useful, while others might apply in other situations.

The consumer model that we use will depend on the objectives of the model builder, the important phenomena in the marketplace, and the availability of relevant theories and data to support the analysis.

When we consider the purchase decisions made by the Smith family on a typical day, we note that there are a number of differences between the way they went about them. The diversity of consumers, of choice processes, and of decision contexts explains many of these differences.

Consumers Are Different.   Consumers vary according to their personalities, values, preferences, and a range of other characteristics. These differences mean that a model that is appropriate for describing the behavior of one particular consumer may be inadequate in explaining the behavior of another.

Choice Decisions Differ.   Not only do consumers differ from one another, but even for a given consumer, a model that might describe his or her behavior for a specific purchase decision may not work in describing another. There are a variety of reasons for these differences. The level of involvement that the consumer has in the decision will determine the amount of cognitive effort and search that he or she is prepared to invest in it. Phenomena associated with low involvement decisions (often called routinized response behavior) include habit, low risk, and lack of search. As the level of involvement grows through limited problem solving to extended problem solving, other phenomena such as brand perceptions and evaluation rules become important.

The Context of Purchases Differs.   Consumers vary in their decision-making rules because of the usage situation, the user of the good or service (for family, for gift, for self), and purchase situation (catalog sale, in-store shelf selection, salesperson-aided purchase). Each such context may invoke a different decision-making strategy. For example, a consumer buying a watch for herself may value consistency with her other jewelry, image, and aesthetics, but when buying one as a gift for a friend, may treat price and manufacturer reputation as the most important attributes.

EXAMPLE _____

Fred and Sally are busy developing a list of important attributes before Fred goes to several major appliance stores to gather further information leading to evaluation and purchase of a washing machine. (This is a multiperson, extensive problem-solving situation.)

Sally bought some coffee last week, but the coffee was not on her shopping list. (This was a limited problem-solving situation: Was the deal attractive enough to make an unplanned purchase?)

This week, peppercorns are on Sally's shopping list, and she may or may not spend time thinking about whether to change brands or sizes. (This may be a routinized rebuy situation if she and her family were satisfied with the brand and the size, or it may be a limited problem-solving situation if someone expressed dissatisfaction with the last purchase. In either case, this purchase is planned.)

One thing is certain: Sally will buy Bob's favorite brand of soda, because she knows he makes quite a fuss when she substitutes the less expensive store brand. (This is a routinized rebuy situation where the purchase is for another family member who has strong preferences.)

Sally will also buy some soda for Fred, who drinks soda from time to time but does not strongly prefer one brand to another. (This is another routinized rebuy situation, this time for a family member with weak preferences.)

This example focuses on consumer-related differences that would suggest a range of consumer behavior models. But models are also important managerial tools, and differences in managerial problems may also drive us toward different consumer behavior models. For example, if management is interested in a pricing strategy, then a model that emphasizes the consumer's evaluation process and the role of price in that process may be most appropriate, whereas if management is interested in making consumers aware of a new product launch, then a model that focuses on information search and perception formation may be best. A model that deals with all aspects of consumer behavior in complete detail may be theoretically sound but hopelessly complex in terms of its data requirements and potential for calibration. In searching for the best model in a given situation, the manager or analyst has to trade off richness in capturing the important phenomena against parsimony in making the model simple to understand and possible to calibrate and use.

To achieve this parsimony it is useful to consider consumer behavior as a staged or phased process. That is, we can think of consumers as going through a number of steps as they move from recognizing a need to purchase and postpurchase behavior. This view enables us to break down a complex problem into a sequence of simpler problems and also provides a mechanism for understanding and classifying model-based developments in this field.

UNDERSTANDING THE STAGES OF CONSUMER CHOICE

In the previous section we argued that a variety of models is necessary to explain different forms of consumer behavior and to meet different managerial objectives efficiently. Here we build a framework to understand the types of consumer behavior for which different models are appropriate. We will classify models on the basis of two characteristics: the stage of the consumer decision process and the consumer's level of involvement in the purchase decision.

In our quest to build parsimonious models, different stages of the process will offer us varying degrees of insight in different consumer decision situations and for different managerial problems.

A Five-Stage Model of Consumer Behavior

In describing the consumer decision process we assume that the consumer goes through up to five steps in the purchase cycle: need arousal, information search, evaluation, purchase, and postpurchase feelings. Our framework suggests that the consumer choice process may start well before the actual purchase and that in each phase marketers can do certain things to facilitate or influence the process. We describe these phases in turn. (See Exhibit 2.1.)

Need Arousal.   The buying process starts with need arousal. A need can be activated through internal or external stimuli. In the first case, one of the person's normal drives—hunger, thirst, sexual desire—rises to a threshold level and becomes a drive. In the second case, need is caused by an external stimulus or triggering cue (an advertisement, sight of an acquaintance's product, etc.). Consumers must then determine the type of product that could possibly satisfy the need.

Information Search.   If an aroused need is intense (e.g., hunger) and a well-defined gratification object is at hand (e.g., a candy bar), the person is likely to gratify the need right then. In most cases, however, the consumer cannot satisfy an aroused need immediately. The need enters the consumer's memory as an item requiring satisfaction. Depending on the intensity of the stored need, the consumer enters one of two states. The first is called *heightened attention* where the individual becomes alert to information bearing upon the need and its gratification. Under conditions of more intense need, the indi-

Need Arousal	Stochastic Models of Purchase Incidence Discrete Binary Choice Models
Information Search	Individual Awareness Models Consideration Models Information Integration Models

Evaluation
  (a) Perception
  (b) Preference
	(a) Perceptual Mapping
	(b) Attitude Models
	     Non-Compensatory
	     Compensatory

Purchase	Multinomial Discrete Choice Models Markov Models
Post-Purchase	Variety Seeking Models Satisfaction Models Communications and Network Models

EXHIBIT 2.1 A Framework for classifying consumer behavior models

vidual enters the second state, that of *active information search*, where the consumer seeks information from personal, commercial, and public sources.

Following the search process, the consumer has a group of brands that he sees as being possibly suitable to satisfy the identified need. This group of products has been called the *evoked set*, the *consideration set*, and the *relevant set* (although the last term is also used to include products that have been searched and rejected). The consideration set is the group of brands that enter the next stage, the evaluation phase. As evaluation progresses, further brands may be eliminated: the consideration set is dynamic. When a consumer is just about to make a purchase, the remaining set of brands is the *choice set*.

Evaluation. Evaluation has two components. First, consumers must establish their beliefs about the features of the alternative products that they would consider (*perceptions*), and, second, they must determine, based on those perceptions, their attitudes toward the products (*preferences*).

Perception Formation. Incoming information helps the consumer clarify and evaluate alternatives and therefore form attitudes and perceptions about product alternatives. There is no simple, single evaluation process used by consumers in all buying situations; there appear to be alternative processes.

Most current models of the consumer evaluation process are cognitively oriented—that is, they see the consumer as forming product judgments largely on a conscious and rational basis. This stage is not so important with low-involvement products, however, where consumers undertake less information processing.

Certain basic concepts help us understand consumer evaluation processes. The first is the concept of *product attributes*. The fields of psychology (Fishbein, 1967) and economics (Lancaster, 1966) both suggest that the consumer sees a product as having several attributes. Consumers perceive a particular product in terms of where it lies in the space spanned by the set of attributes relevant to its product class. For example, in the aspirin category important attributes might be speed of relief, reliability, side effects, and price. While these attributes may be of general interest, individual consumers vary as to which attributes they consider most relevant. The market for a product can be segmented by the attributes that are of primary interest to a target group of buyers.

Consumers are likely to develop opinions about where different brands stand on each attribute. The set of beliefs that consumers hold about a particular brand is known as its *brand image*. Consumers' beliefs or perceptions may vary from the "true" attributes because of consumers' particular experience and the way consumers gather and process information. It is consumers' perceptions of a product's characteristics that influence their behavior, not the "true" characteristics.

Preference Formation. The consumer must then turn these perceptions into brand preferences in the second half of the evaluation phase. Most models assume consumers have a utility function for attributes, which describes how the consumer's valuation of the product varies with alternative levels and combinations of attributes. The consumer arrives at an attitude (judgment, preference) toward the brand through some evaluation procedure. Starting with his consideration set, he compares products and ends up with an order of preferences.

Purchase Decision. In the evaluation stage the consumer forms a ranked set of preferences for the alternative products in his evoked set and an intent to purchase the product he likes best. But a number of additional factors often intervene before a purchase can be made (Sheth, 1974). The first factor is the attitude of others. The extent to which the negative attitudes of others will reduce a consumer's favorable attitude depends on two things: the intensity of others' negative attitudes and the consumer's motivation to comply with the others' wishes (Fishbein, 1967). A consumer's purchase intention is also influenced by changes in anticipated situational factors. The consumer forms a purchase intention on the basis of such factors as expected family income, the expected total cost of the product, and the expected benefits of the product.

Furthermore, when the consumer is about to act, unanticipated situational factors may intervene to prevent him from doing so (such as the lack of availability of a preferred product). Thus, preferences and purchase intentions are not completely reliable predictors of actual buying behavior: while they guide purchase behavior, they fail to include a number of additional factors that may intervene. For that reason, we include a distinct purchase phase in our framework.

Postpurchase Feelings.   After buying and trying the product, a consumer will experience some level of satisfaction or dissatisfaction. What determines the level of postpurchase satisfaction? A major theory holds that a consumer's satisfaction is a function both of expectations and the product's perceived performance (Swan and Combs, 1976). If the product meets his expectations, the consumer is satisfied; if it exceeds them, the consumer is highly satisfied; but if it falls short, the consumer is dissatisfied. Consumers form their expectations on the basis of messages and claims sent out by the seller and other communication sources. If the seller makes exaggerated claims for the product, the consumer experiences disconfirmed expectations, which lead to dissatisfaction. The amount of dissatisfaction depends on the size of the difference between expectations and performance. Psychological theories have been advanced suggesting that consumers may either magnify or diminish the importance of the differences between expectations and performance (Anderson, 1973). For example, contrast theory says that the amount of dissatisfaction will be larger than the performance gap, while cognitive dissonance theory says that the amount of dissatisfaction will be less than the gap because the consumer will try to reduce the dissonance by imputing higher performance (Festinger, 1957).

The relevance of postpurchase feelings to the consumer decision process is twofold. First, satisfaction with a product will influence a consumer's choice on a subsequent purchase occasion. Second, consumers are likely to communicate their feelings about the product to other potential consumers who are seeking information. The former is a more powerful influence in frequently purchased goods where own-experience is critical for repurchase and repurchase rates are high, while the latter is a more important consideration for durable products.

Level of Involvement

The second major dimension along which we classify consumer behavior is the level of involvement that the consumer has with the decision process. We have suggested that consumer decisions vary by level of involvement. Low-involvement decisions, such as Sally's purchase of milk, involve little effort and can thus be described by relatively simple models. High-involvement decisions, such as the washing machine purchase, involve considerable effort and often require more complex models. Understanding this level of involvement can be important. For example, Gensch and Javalgi (1987) show that for fertilizer purchases by Iowa farmers, estimating separate models for consumers with different levels of involvement yields improved model fits and better managerial insights. Our use of the involvement construct is based on consumer behavior research: see Zaichkowsky (1985); Greenwald and Leavitt (1984); and Celsi and Olson (1988).

Most of the models we review here may be applied to situations in which the purchasing process is assumed to require complex decision making or brand loyalty. But as pointed out by Kassarjian and Kassarjian (1979), many purchase decisions are better described by low-involvement conditions. High levels of involvement are associated with extended problem solving, while low involvement entails routinized response behavior (or routine problem solving) (e.g., see Howard, 1989). Intermediate levels of involvement and cognitive effort are called limited problem-solving decisions.

While a typical high-involvement purchase is assumed to follow the process illustrated in Exhibit 2.1, low-involvement decisions may not include all these stages, may have the stages in a different order from that shown, or may have a set of causal factors different from those in a high-involvement situation. For a product like flour, for example, the consumer may receive information through a TV commercial, where the ad may not even really be perceived in the sense that it is comprehended. Petty and Cacioppo (1986) argue that there are two routes to persuasion: the central route and the peripheral route. In the first, an appeal is made to the consumer on the basis of the valued attributes of the brand. In the second, the advertisement may gain the awareness and liking of the consumer by using some indirect medium (for example, the endorsement of a sports celebrity) and hope that favorable attitudes are transferred to the product. Petty and Cacioppo show that peripheral persuasion is more effective for low-involvement products.

The level of consumer involvement also determines the factors that will influence attitudes and behavior at any stage. For example, the role of several elements in the marketing mix will differ depending on which of these decision processes is predominant. In a low-involvement situation, the role of advertising is to create awareness and familiarity through repetition (Rothchild, 1979). A small number of points should be emphasized in the ads; repetition creates a relationship between advertising symbols and brand use. In a high-involvement situation, advertising seeks to go beyond awareness, to influence the consumer through a persuasive message. The content of the message, rather than repetition, is the key. Messages are likely to be more complex, more varied, dealing more directly with desired product benefits (see Arora, 1985, or Rossiter and Percy, 1987, for a review of different advertising strategies for low- and high-involvement products). The level of involvement has implications for price and promotional strategies too. Since little prepurchase evaluation occurs for low-involvement products, brand choice is frequently made in the store, and in-store conditions become critical.

In summary, the stages in Exhibit 2.1 vary in relevance depending on level of involvement and other situation-specific factors. Some authors have suggested that it is useful to categorize models specifically on the basis of consumer involvement (e.g., Howard, 1989). We have not done so for two reasons. The first is that the five stages in Exhibit 2.1 fit a range of both low- and high-involvement situations, although with the stages in a different order in some instances. The second and more important one is that involvement is not a unidimensional construct. Arora (1982) and Laurent and Kapferer (1985) both demonstrate the discriminant validity of different aspects of involvement. Moreover, Laurent and Kapferer (1985) indicate

> knowing the involvement level on one facet (e.g., perceived importance, the classical indicator of involvement) is not sufficient. The full profile must be known because different facets have different influences on selected aspects of consumer behavior.

It is because of this complexity of consumer behavior that we sometimes see simple stochastic models being used for apparently complex high involvement behavior (e.g., Morrison et al., 1982) and quite complex discrete choice models applied to packaged goods, generally thought to involve low involvement (e.g., Guadagni and Little, 1983).

Use of the Framework: A Range of Models

While our taxonomy will help categorize much of the work on consumer behavior models, other dimensions can be used to differentiate between these models. Three such dimensions are breadth of phenomena, level of aggregation, and level of detail.

The Breadth of Phenomena Addressed.   This dimension refers to the degree to which a model unifies theories in mapping the whole or a part of a decision-making process. In our framework, this dimension refers to how many of the decision-making stages a model spans.

The Level of Aggregation.   A dichotomy in consumer behavior models exists depending on whether the unit of analysis is the individual or groups of individuals. In this chapter we deal primarily with models of the individual (although often with a view to aggregating them to make statements about the total market). In other chapters we look at the response of the market as a whole. Those macromarket models relate market changes in sales and share to marketing activities (e.g., advertising and price), without resorting to microlevel models, relying solely on aggregate, market-level data. An area of continuing research is the relationship between individual response models and aggregate market models (see, for example, Ehrenberg, Goodhardt, and

Barwise, 1990, for an example of the use of stochastic models to understand aggregate market share data, and Chatterjee and Eliashberg, 1990, for an example of the use of individual-level information integration models to understand diffusion dynamics).

The Level of Detail of the Model.   Ideally, a model would behave as follows:

1. Identify and measure all major variables making up a behavioral system.

2. Specify fundamental relationships between the variables.

3. Specify exact sequences and cause and effect relationships.

4. Permit sensitivity analysis in order to explore the impact of changes in the major variables.

For the sake of parsimony, most consumer behavior models only attempt to do a portion of this job.

From Understanding to Equations.   This introduction has helped, we hope, to motivate and justify our use of Exhibit 2.1 as a unifying framework for understanding consumer behavior models. We now proceed, section by section, through the Exhibit 2.1 framework.

STOCHASTIC MODELS

Our framework in Exhibit 2.1 suggested that there are multiple approaches for modeling consumer choice behavior. Later sections of this chapter deal with choice situations when the focus is on the *determinants* of choice, but with uncertainty in the model arising because of missing variables, simplified specification, measurement error, and the like.

However, in many situations, particularly for low-involvement products where little conscious decision making takes place, a stochastic model—concentrating on the random nature of the choice process rather than on a deterministic explanation—may be more appropriate. The following example suggests why.

EXAMPLE _____

Recall that Bob likes soda. After his tennis match at the high school, he went to the soda machine to buy a drink. His choices were Coke, Diet Coke, Sprite, Diet Sprite, and Fanta Orange. He chose Sprite, not his favorite soda, but one that he likes occasionally. In fact, if we kept tabs on his purchasing behavior, it would appear that, given the choice set just presented, he chooses Coke about 60% of the time, Sprite 25% of the time, and Fanta Orange the remaining 15% of the time. (As a growing teenager, he has no use or need for diet beverages.) When asked why he makes these choices, he replies, "I don't know. Sometimes I just feel like one or the other."

What this example suggests is that there may be no discernible pattern to one's purchasing behavior beyond that which can be explained by a stochastic model. (Here, that model might be a multinomial process with $p_1 = 0.6$, $p_2 = 0.25$ and $p_3 = 0.15$, $p_4 = 0$, $p_5 = 0$ for p_i where $i = 1$ (Coke), 2 (Sprite), 3 (Fanta Orange), 4 (Diet Coke), and 5 (Diet Sprite).

Partly because frequently purchased consumer packaged goods are often low-involvement items and partly because a large quantity of brand-switching data is available for such products, much of the focus of stochastic choice modeling has centered on such goods.

Stochastic choice models differ in a number of ways, as illustrated in Exhibit 2.2. For example, they can be classified as to whether or not they consider brand choice, purchase timing, store of purchase, and the impact of marketing variables. They also differ as to how they handle customer heterogeneity: some models try to segment customers into homogeneous subsets and analyze them separately. Most models use the concept of a mixing distribution—an explicitly probabilistic characterization of the way a characteristic (usually represented by a model parameter) varies across the population. (See Appendix A.) This distribution enables us to aggregate over individual members of the population and make statements about the behavior of the market as a whole.

Purchase Incidence Models

In this section we deal with purchase incidence models first. Later we deal with brand choice models as well as models that integrate both aspects.

The NBD Model. Following Morrison and Schmittlein (1988), the negative binomial distribution (NBD) model has three main assumptions: Poisson purchasing behavior, gamma heterogeneity (mixing distribution) and stationarity.

Poisson Purchasing. If the likelihood of purchase during any period of short duration is constant and independent of when the last purchase was made, the time until the next purchase will be exponential:

$$f(t|\lambda) = \lambda e^{-\lambda t} \tag{2.1}$$

where

t = time to next purchase

Brand Choice	Which brand will be chosen next? How many alternatives are considered (us versus them)?
Purchase Timing	When and how frequently will purchases occur?
Impact of Decision Variables	What will be the effect on choice of price, advertising, and so on?
Heterogeneity	Is the population considered homogeneous or heterogeneous with respect to purchase probability, consumption, or response?
Stationarity	Do the probability laws change over time or as a result of consumer- or marketer-controlled actions? If so, what is the probability law?
Store Bought from	Where was the purchase made?
Measures of Interest	Does the model compute expected brand shares, penetration, market structure, and so on?

EXHIBIT 2.2 Characteristics of stochastic models

λ = purchase rate (no. units/time period)

and the probability that the number of purchases in a period of unit length will be Poisson:

$$P_p(X = x|\lambda) = \frac{e^{-\lambda}\lambda^x}{x!}, \qquad x = 0, 1, 2 \ldots \tag{2.2}$$

where

X = the number of purchases, a random variable
λ = exponential purchase rate

We assume that different households have different λ's (that is, λ is implicitly subscripted by a household index, i).

Gamma Mixing Distribution. The gamma distribution has a flexible, two-parameter form that can take on a variety of intuitively reasonable shapes and is defined on $\lambda > 0$:

$$g(\lambda|r, \alpha) = \frac{\alpha^r \lambda^{r-1} e^{-\alpha\lambda}}{\Gamma(r)}, \qquad \lambda > 0 \tag{2.3}$$

where r and α are the gamma parameters. (Note that if $r = 1$, g is exponential; if r is an integer, g is called an Erlang distribution. See Appendix A.)

If we can assume that the purchase rate parameter, λ, governing an individual household's purchasing pattern is gamma distributed, we can aggregate (or "add up") across all households to find the average probability of purchase for a random population member.

We do this by combining (2.2) and (2.3) to get

$$P_{NBD}(X = x|r, \alpha) = \int_0^\infty P_P(X = x|\lambda)g(\lambda|\alpha, r)\, d\lambda \tag{2.4}$$

$$= \binom{x + r - 1}{x} \left(\frac{\alpha}{\alpha + 1}\right)^r \left(\frac{1}{\alpha + 1}\right)^x \tag{2.5}$$

for $x = 0, 1, \ldots$, and $r, \alpha > 0$, and r integer. If the period of time is t, the scale parameter α in (2.5) is replaced by α/t but r remains the same.

Useful moments of these distributions are

$$E(\lambda) = E(X) = \frac{r}{\alpha} \tag{2.6}$$

$$\text{Var}(\lambda) = \frac{r}{\alpha^2} \tag{2.7}$$

$$\text{Var}(X) = \frac{r}{\alpha} + \frac{r}{\alpha^2} \tag{2.8}$$

Equation (2.8) can be interpreted as follows: the variance in purchasing for an arbitrary individual with the NBD is the sum of the within-individual (Poisson) variation (the variance of a Poisson distribution equals its mean) plus the across individual purchase rate variability.

NBD parameters are typically estimated using the method of moments, fitting the observed mean and variance of the number of purchases across buyers with their theoretical values: if M and s^2 denote the observed mean and variance of x, then

$$\hat{\alpha} = \frac{Mt}{(s^2 - M)}, \text{ and} \qquad\qquad (2.9)$$

$$\hat{r} = \hat{\alpha}\,\frac{M}{t} \qquad\qquad (2.10)$$

(See Morrison and Schmittlein, 1988, for some other estimation methods.)

Morrison and Schmittlein argue that the most managerially useful insights from the NBD model are derived by considering conditional expectations: $E(X_2|X_1 = x)$ or the expected number of purchases in period 2 given x purchases in period 1.

This expectation is

$$E(X_2|X_1 = x) = \frac{r}{\alpha + 1} + \left(\frac{1}{\alpha + 1}\right)x \qquad\qquad (2.11)$$

A major use of the NBD model is as a before-and-after tool: to predict what would have happened and to compare it with what did happen. Suppose a brand runs a promotion and sees a sales increase. Did this increase come from (1) nonbuyers (the intent of the promotion) or (2) from previous heavy buyers (borrowing from future sales, perhaps). Note that (1) is a good thing while (2) does not represent incremental consumption. (Chapter 7 describes methods for assessing the value of a promotion.) An example (Exhibit 2.3) from Goodhardt and Ehrenberg (1967) illustrates the point: column (e) shows that 132 of the 140 added units of sales can be attributed to the previous nonbuyers (the zero class).

Morrison and Schmittlein (1988) provide an excellent overview and summary of the development of the NBD model and several key extensions developed by replacing some NBD assumptions:

1. *Purchases more regular than Poisson.*   Clearly, at the limit, the Poisson assumption breaks down—one would not expect the maximum probability of purchase to occur immediately after the previous purchase, as suggested by the Poisson. Chatfield and Goodhardt (1973) provide some empirical support for purchasing behavior more regular than Poisson and argue for an Erlang distribution for interpurchase times, yielding a "condensed" negative binomial model (CNBD). Morrison and Schmittlein (1981) and Schmittlein and Morrison (1983) show that the CNBD gives a more regular sales pattern than the NBD model, and, in particular, it gives an *increasing* slope to the zero class (as opposed to the linear conditional expectation found in equation (2.11)). (See Exhibit 2.4.)

(a)	(b)	(c)	(d)	(e)
$X = x$	n_x	T_x	$NBD\widehat{T}_x$	$(c) - (d)$
0	880	185	53	132
1	53	57	48	9
2	24	45	41	4
3	14	31	35	(4)
4+	29	165	166	(1)
Total	1000	483	343	140

Where

x	=	number of purchases in period 1
n_x	=	number of individuals making x purchases in period 1
T_x	=	actual total purchases in period 2 made by the n_x individuals that made x purchases in period 1
$NBD\widehat{T}_x$	=	predicted value of T_x using the NBD model calibrated from data in the first period.

EXHIBIT 2.3   The main source of additional period 2 sales is identified as the "zero class" $(X = 0)$ using the NBD model

2. *Dealing specifically with the zero class.*   Especially if there exists a class of individuals who will never buy (i.e., for $\lambda = 0$), then the proper mixing distribution has a mass point representing that proportion of the population at $\lambda = 0$ and then a (gamma, say) distribution for the remaining population proportion. Here, relative to the NBD, an NBD with spike at zero gives conditional expectations that are linear for $x \geq 1$, but with a slope that is less steep than for the NBD and an overall concave shape (see Exhibit 2.4).

3. *Nonstationarity.*   A most difficult and perplexing problem for all stochastic models is nonstationarity, because it can occur in so many different ways. Morrison and Schmittlein (1988) argue that, at least for one form of nonstationarity (in which λ goes up in period 2 when it is low in period 1 and vice versa—light buyers may discover that product, heavy buyers get bored with the product), nonstationarity will enhance the regression-to-the-mean effect.

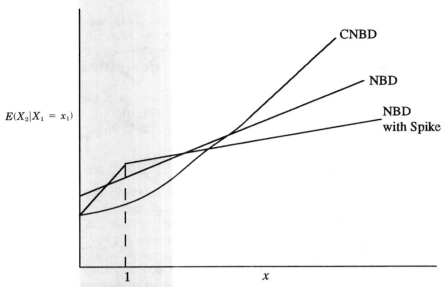

$E(X_2|X_1 = x_1)$

CNBD

NBD

NBD
with Spike

1   x

EXHIBIT 2.4   The NBD conditional expectations compared with those from relaxing
two assumptions: the condensed NBD (CNBD) gives a steeper slope
(higher expected purchases at x_2 when x_1 is high) and a *convex* shape;
the NBD with spike at zero gives a lower slope than NBD and a *concave* shape

Issues to bear in mind when dealing with the NBD model include

1. Is the item of interest (X) purchase occasion or units purchased? We
have assumed that these quantities are the same here. The basic NBD
model is reasonable if one is focusing on the number of units in a given
time period (versus interpurchase time, when there would be a number
of "zeros"). See Morrison and Perry (1970) for a procedure for explicitly
modeling this situation.

2. Are the purchases of a brand or a product category? Morrison and
Schmittlein (1988) outline the (technical) conditions when NBD at the
brand level leads to NBD at the product class level and vice versa. In
most empirical applications, if NBD works well in one area (brand or
product category) it works well in the other.

The NBD model has a number of advantages (see, especially, Ehrenberg,
1988), and its mathematics allows for calculations of some appealing quantities such as the "penetration" —the number of buyers in a time period; the
number of "lost" buyers (those who bought in t but not in $t + 1$); the number
of new buyers—(those who bought at $t + 1$ but not at t); and the quantities
purchased by new buyers. Ehrenberg (1972), in popularizing the model, ar-

gues that these simple rules and analyses explain far more about a brand's purchasing behavior than do assumptions about loyalty, marketing effects, and so on. "The fundamental finding in the study of buying behavior is that there are simple and highly generalizable patterns" (p. 1). Morrison and Schmittlein (1988) argue that the value of the model is that it provides a sensible benchmark that can be included (with zero cost in terms of incremental data) in econometric/logit models; indeed, they argue that the relevant criterion for model performance ought to be discrepancies from the NBD baseline (Wagner and Taudes, 1986).

EXAMPLE _____

Schmittlein, Morrison, and Colombo (1987) develop a model based on the NBD that can be used to determine how many of a firm's current customers are "active" determined by transaction activity in the last year. Such information is valuable when one is monitoring the size and growth of the firm's ongoing customer base, evaluating a new product's success based on trial and repeat purchases, and targeting a subgroup of customers for a promotion. Such a model is appropriate for brokerage firms, credit card users, catalog lists, and so on.

They develop a model based on the following assumptions:

At the individual customer level,

1. Poisson purchases: When alive, every customer purchases in Poisson fashion with parameter λ.

2. Exponential lifetime: Customers remain alive for a lifetime that is exponentially distributed with parameter μ.

At the population level,

3. Gamma heterogeneity for purchasing and death rates. Both μ and λ are distributed across the population via (independent) gamma distributions.

The authors maintain that these assumptions have proven reasonable using data from Merrill Lynch. The Poisson purchasing and gamma heterogeneity assumptions imply an NBD model of purchasing behavior for active customers. Exponential death rates with gamma heterogeneity yield a Pareto distribution of the second kind:

NDB Purchasing.

$$P(X = x|r, \alpha, \tau > T) = \binom{x + r - 1}{x}\left(\frac{\alpha}{\alpha + T}\right)^{r}\left(\frac{T}{\alpha + T}\right)^{x} \quad \textbf{(2.12)}$$

where

x $= 0, 1, 2, \ldots,$
τ $=$ time of "death"
r, α $=$ gamma distribution parameters for interpurchase time rate

Pareto Lifetime.

$$f(\tau, | s, \beta) = \frac{s}{\beta}\left(\frac{\beta}{\beta + \tau}\right)^{s+1}, \qquad \tau > 0 \qquad \textbf{(2.13)}$$

where

s, β $=$ gamma distribution parameters for lifetime length

Using Bayes's theorem at the individual level, the authors show that the probability that an individual is alive at T is

$$P(\tau > T | \lambda, \mu, X = x, t, T) = \frac{1}{1 + [\mu/(\lambda + \mu)][e^{(\lambda + \mu)(T-t)}]} \qquad \textbf{(2.14)}$$

where

t $=$ time of last purchase
T $=$ current time
X $=$ number of purchases the customer made in $(0, T)$

The authors then calculate

$$P(\text{alive|parameter estimates}) = P(\tau > T | r, \alpha, s, \beta, X = x, t, T) \qquad \textbf{(2.15)}$$

which is the weighted average over λ and μ of the individual level probabilities from equation (2.14). Although the algebra is tedious, the explicit formula in equation (2.15) tells the key story. It tells whether an average customer is active at T given his or her history [number of purchases, x, in $(0, T)$ and the time of last purchase].

This so-called NBD/Pareto model can then be used to

• estimate the number of active customers over time. This measure allows management to track the health of the brand franchise.
• identify the P(alive|parameters) at the individual level. Management can then rank order them to determine which customers should be deleted from active status (removed from a mailing list, say).

• predict future transaction levels. This use of the model—as a baseline prediction—can be used either by itself, as a forecasting tool or as a benchmark as discussed above when evaluating promotional programs.

In a typical application, Wellan and Ehrenberg (1990) use the NBD model to segment the soup market into those customers who buy all year round and those who are seasonal, buying only in the winter.

Stochastic Models of Brand Choice

In the preceding section, we developed category stochastic purchase incidence or purchase timing models. We now develop brand choice models before integrating the timing and choice processes in the following section.

Brand choice models can usually be distinguished by how they deal with (1) population heterogeneity, (2) purchase-event feedback, and (3) exogenous market factors.

As developed here and in Appendix A, the mixing distribution is the most popular approach for moving from many models of individual behavior to one overall model for the population as a whole. It deals with population heterogeneity by having each individual in the population make a random choice from some distribution of response. Although conceptually difficult, this approach has a distinct advantage: the identification and the measurement of specific discriminating characteristics of households need not be done explicitly, and most model developments use this approach.

Models differ according to how they deal with purchase-event feedback, the influence of present purchase behavior on future purchase probabilities. Models that assume no purchase-event feedback are called zero-order models: the name refers to the fact that the purchase probability of the brand on the $(n + k)$th occasion, p_{n+k}, is equal to the purchase probability on the nth occasion, p_n. On the other hand, Markov models assume that only the previous brand choice affects the present purchase probability, while learning models assume that the entire purchase history affects current choice, with more recent purchases having the most effect.

Market factors are the third determinant of brand choice behavior and are most frequently accounted for in one of two ways: (1) explicitly including the influence of specific market factors in the model and (2) postulating that the effects of all such forces can be accounted for with a time trend or structural shift in the model. Models whose parameters do not change over time are referred to as stationary-in-parameters models; such models do not necessarily include stationary purchase probabilities, which may change because of purchase feedback.

		Brand Bought on Occasion 2			
		A	B	C	Total
Brand	A	137	47	19	203
Bought on	B	41	179	12	232
Occasion 1	C	22	10	46	78
	Total	200	236	77	513

(a) Purchases of brands A, B, and C over two purchase occasions: 137 of 513 people bought brand A on both purchase occasions.

		Brand Bought on Occasion 2			
		A	B	C	Total
Brand	A	0.267	0.092	0.037	0.396
Bought on	B	0.080	0.349	0.023	0.452
Occasion 1	C	0.043	0.019	0.090	0.152
	Total	0.390	0.460	0.150	1.00

(b) Joint-probability matrix: 137 of 513, or .267 of the population, bought brand A on both purchase occasions.

		Brand Bought on Occasion 2			
		A	B	C	Total
Brand	A	0.674	0.232	0.094	1.00
Bought on	B	0.177	0.772	0.051	1.00
Occasion 1	C	0.283	0.125	0.592	1.00

(c) Conditional-probability matrix: of the 203 people who bought brand A on the first purchase occasion, 137 or .674 (137/203) bought it on the second occasion.

EXHIBIT 2.5 Brand-switching habits of 513 consumers over two purchase occasions.

Much of the information used in a number of popular brand choice models can be extracted from a brand-switching matrix. The elements in this matrix are obtained from purchase information on two choice occasions separated in time, where the time between the two purchases may differ considerably for different consumers.

Exhibit 2.5 gives some data on the brand-switching habits of 513 consumers over two purchase occasions. In this exhibit, parts (b) and (c) show transition probabilities expressed as joint and conditional probabilities, respectively. Let

$p(i|j)$ = conditional probability that a customer will purchase brand i on the second-purchase occasion given that brand j was purchased on the first occasion

$p(i, j)$ = joint probability that a consumer will purchase brand i on the second-purchase occasion and brand j on the first purchase occasion

These purchase probabilities are related as follows:

$$p(i|j) = \frac{p(i, j)}{p(j)} \qquad \textbf{(2.16)}$$

where $p(j)$ = probability of purchasing brand j on the first-purchase occasion; so $p(j) = m_j$, the market share of brand j. It also follows from the definition of joint and conditional probabilities that

$$\sum_j p(i, j) = m_i \qquad \textbf{(2.17a)}$$

$$\sum_i p(i|j) = 1 \qquad \textbf{(2.17b)}$$

In the example in Exhibit 2.5, the joint and conditional probability measures are obtained from information in part (a).

Zero-Order Models. We review several zero-order models here that differ in (1) the assumptions they make about consumer preferences and choice and (2) the number of brands they consider.

The heterogeneous Bernoulli model assumes that (1) in a population of customers, each has a (constant) probability p_i of buying one of the two brands in the market (brand 1) and (2) p is distributed as $f(p)$ in this population. Exhibit 2.6 illustrates this second assumption. In the exhibit, distribution 1 represents a relatively homogeneous population with almost all consumers having nearly the same probability of purchasing brand 1; distribution 2 represents a situation where there is substantial heterogeneity, with probability of purchase distributed widely across the population; and, finally, distribution 3 represents an extremely heterogeneous population where, in effect, there appear to be two distinct market segments, one loyal to each of the two brands.

In Appendix A, we show that if $f(p)$ has a beta distribution with parameters α and β (which can take any of the shapes in Exhibit 2.6) and if we

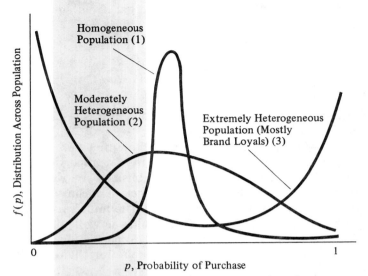

EXHIBIT 2.6   Three types of population-heterogeneity distributions.

observe that an individual makes r purchases of a brand out of n purchase occasions, then the (posterior) distribution of p is also beta with parameters $\alpha + r$ and $\beta + n - r$.

A *simple multiple-brand model* is the next zero-order model we consider. On the basis of extensive empirical research, Ehrenberg (1972) postulated that the joint probability of a consumer purchasing brands i and j on successive purchase occasions is given by

$$p(i, j) = km_i m_j \tag{2.18}$$

where $\{m_i\}$ are the market shares of the respective brands. With equations (2.17) and (2.18) it is easy to show that

$$p(i, i) = m_i - km_i(1 - m_i) \tag{2.19}$$

Then summing equation (2.19) over brands, we get an equation for k:

$$k = \frac{1 - \sum p(i, i)}{1 - \sum_i m_i^2} \tag{2.20}$$

Noting again that $p(i) = m_i$, we get, from equations (2.16), (2.18), and (2.19),

$$p(i|j) = \begin{cases} km_i, & j \neq i \\ 1 - k(1 - m_i), & j = i \end{cases} \qquad (2.21)$$

which shows that the conditional probabilities of purchasing brand i are independent of brand j.

Kalwani and Morrison (1977) show that two assumptions—(1) a zero-order process applies and (2) switching is proportional to share—are sufficient to derive the results shown. Alternatively, Kalwani (1979) shows that if the purchase probability density function of consumers in a choice category is given by the Dirichlet distribution (the multivariate extension of the beta distribution), then equation (2.18) holds as well. Bass, Jeuland, and Wright (1976) have shown that equation (2.18) can be derived by starting with individual consumer preferences and combining them with Luce's (1959) choice axiom.

Using the data from Exhibit 2.5, we construct, in Exhibit 2.7, the theoretical brand-switching matrix following equations (2.18), (2.19), and (2.20). The observed and expected switching proportions are quite close, suggesting that this model adequately describes this switching behavior.

There have been a number of other models and studies dealing with zero-order behavior. See Massy, Montgomery, and Morrison (1970) for an historical perspective and the Jeuland, Bass, and Wright (1980) model discussed shortly. In an interesting study Bass and colleagues (1984) demonstrated that, across a range of 10 frequently purchased consumer products, between 57% and 83% of (stationary) families switching show purchase sequences that are consistent with the zero-order hypothesis. They conclude that, while a significant fraction of individuals (at least for packaged goods) may be zero order, a mixture of processes exist including higher-order process and nonstationary processes. Their results both suggest why models such as the NBD frequently do well, and why higher-order and/or nonstationary models are needed for more complete descriptions of the market.

Markov Models.   While zero-order models assume that brand choice is independent of past purchase behavior, other models assume purchase-event feedback; that is, they specifically model the effect of postpurchase behavior on future brand choice. Markov models (of the first order) assume that only the last brand chosen affects the current purchase. Specifically, there are two properties that characterize a stationary (probabilities do not change) first-order Markov process. Let Y_t denote the brand chosen on the tth purchase occasion and N denote the number of brands. Then the stationary Markov process satisfies the following conditions:

Brand	Shares (m_i)	$m_i (1 - m_i)$
A	0.390	0.238
B	0.460	0.166
C	0.150	0.513

Where $k = \dfrac{1 - \sum_i p_{ii}}{1 - \sum_i m_i^2} = \dfrac{0.294}{0.614} = 0.479$

and $p(i \mid j)$ is given from equation (2.21).

Expected/Observed Brand-Switching Matrix
Brand Bought on Occasion 2

		A	B	C
Brand Bought on Occasion 1	A	0.275 / 0.267	0.086 / 0.092	0.028 / 0.037
	B	0.086 / 0.080	0.341 / 0.349	0.033 / 0.023
	C	0.028 / 0.043	0.033 / 0.019	0.089 / 0.090

Note: Theoretical switching values are in the upper left in each box; observed switching values are in the lower box.

EXHIBIT 2.7 Computations of theoretical switching levels using the Ehrenberg (1972) model.

$$p(Y_t = k|Y_{t-1}, Y_{t-2}, \ldots, Y_0) = p(Y_t = k|Y_{t-1}) \tag{2.22}$$
(one-period memory)

$$p(Y_t = k|Y_{t-1}) = p(Y_1 = k|Y_0) \tag{2.23}$$
(stationary for all t, k)

All the information needed to characterize brand choice in a Markov model is contained in the probability transition matrix (Exhibit 2.5). Let us denote such a matrix as $\mathbf{P} = \{p_{ij}\}$, where p_{ij} is the probability of purchasing j next, given i was last purchased. As a so-called stochastic matrix, $\mathbf{P}$ has the following properties:

$$0 \le p_{ij} \le 1 \tag{2.24}$$

$$\sum_i p_{ij} = 1 \tag{2.25}$$

Given current market shares, a Markov model can be used to predict how market shares change over time. Suppose we know $\{m_{it}\}$, the market share of brand i at time t; then market shares for all brands at time $t + 1$ can be calculated as

$$m_{j,t+1} = \sum_{i=1}^{n} p_{ij} m_{it}, \quad j = 1, \ldots, n. \tag{2.26}$$

EXAMPLE ——————————————————————————————

Consider a two-brand example, A and B, with the following switching matrix:

		$t + 1$	
		A	B
t	A	0.7	0.3
	B	0.5	0.5

where $m_{At} = 0.5$ and $m_{Bt} = 0.5$.
By equation (2.26), we get

$$\hat{m}_{At+1} = m_{At} p_{AA} + m_{Bt} p_{BA} \tag{2.27}$$

$$= (0.5)(0.7) + (0.5)(0.5) = (0.6)$$

Similarly,

$$\hat{m}_{Bt+1} = 1 - 0.6 = 0.4$$

$$\hat{m}_{At+2} = \hat{m}_{At+1} p_{AA} + \hat{m}_{Bt+1} p_{BA}$$

$$= (0.6)(0.7) + (0.4)(0.5) = 0.62$$

and so on, until

$$\hat{m}_{A\infty} = \text{long-run market share} = 0.625$$

This example demonstrates two uses of the Markov model. First, it shows that forecasting of market shares can be performed by using the transition matrix. Second, it shows how the effect of a change in market structure can be evaluated.

Suppose in this example that the transition matrix was calculated following a price shift. What is the effect of the shift on brand A? In the long run, it can be expected to lead to a share change of $\hat{m}_{A\infty} - m_{At} = 0.625 - 0.50 = 0.125$. That increase in share can then be evaluated for cost-effectiveness.

As with other stochastic models, the calculation of transition probabilities is usually based on panel or Universal Product Code (UPC) data.

Several critical assumptions are present in this development, including purchase timing (one purchase per time period), homogeneity, and stationarity. This last assumption is often unrealistic; a firm losing market position will take corrective action. A number of models in the literature, including Maffai (1960a), Harary and Lipstein (1962), Ehrenberg (1965), and Montgomery (1969), allow for varying transition probabilities. The Montgomery (1969) model—addressing time-varying transition probabilities via a diffusion process—represents a potentially fruitful research direction other researchers have ignored. Other researchers—such as Telser (1962); Hartung and Fisher (1965); Lee, Judge, and Zellner (1970); and Horsky (1976, 1977)—relate the transition probabilities to decision variables.

EXAMPLE _____

Morrison and colleagues (1982) develop a Markov model characterizing the account activity of Merrill Lynch customers. In particular, Merrill Lynch classifies its customers as "prime" and "not prime" (defined on dollar volume of business) with each customer moving between prime and nonprime states according to a (heterogeneous) Markov process:

$$
\begin{array}{c}
 & t+1 \\
 & \begin{array}{cc} 1 & 0 \end{array} \\
t \begin{array}{c} 1 \\ 0 \end{array} & \left[\begin{array}{cc} p & 1-p \\ kp & 1-kp \end{array} \right]
\end{array}
\tag{2.28}
$$

where 1 = "prime," 0 = "nonprime," and $p = Pr$ (prime at $t + 1$|prime at t and remained in the Merrill Lynch system). They assume that p is distributed across customers via a beta distribution. In addition, they assume that each customer has a (constant) probability, q, of leaving Merrill Lynch each year. In addition, the parameter k in equation (2.28) is also assumed constant across customers and can be interpreted as a "recency" effect—it is a measure of the influence the current state has on the future of that customer. To see this, note that the long-run probabilities of being in states 1 and 0 are

$$\Pi_1 = \frac{kp}{1 - p + kp} \qquad\qquad \textbf{(2.29a)}$$

$$\Pi_0 = \frac{1 - p}{1 - p + kp} \qquad\qquad \textbf{(2.29b)}$$

so that, if $k = 0$, the current state has maximum influence (i.e., if a customer gets into state 0, he stays there) while if $k = 1$, the process becomes Bernouilli, with probability p of being in state 1 (i.e., zero memory).

The authors estimate k, p and α and β (the parameters of the beta heterogeneity distribution) from historical Merrill Lynch records and some managerial judgment. While the data and results are disguised for proprietary reasons, a representative set of the forecast resulting from the analysis is:

Conditional Probability	Actual	Model Forecast
P(Prime '80|Prime '79, Prime '78)	0.632	0.626
P(Prime '80|Prime '79, not Prime '78)	0.456	0.432
P(Prime '80|not Prime '79, not Prime '78)	0.138	0.177
P(Prime '80|not Prime '79, not Prime '78)	0.063	0.066

These forecasts look quite good and gave management enough confidence to use the model for two-year and five-year forecasts. The model was used as a baseline against which to test various marketing and promotional activities. In addition, this modeling activity (and its benefits) led to a reorganization of its (previously accounting-oriented) data system to make analyses like these easier.

Although quite flexible, the one-period learning effect and implicit homogeneity of most Markov models have limited their use somewhat. See Morrison (1966) for a discussion of the problems of including heterogeneity in a general Markov structure. Also, more flexible mechanisms for incorporating learning may be desirable. We deal with one such mechanism next.

Learning Models. To express the reinforcement effects of past brand choices, Kuehn (1962) applied a learning model, developed by Bush and Mosteller (1955), to a consumer choice problem. Learning models are based on the idea that, at the individual level, each purchase of a given brand enhances the likelihood of future purchases of the brand.

To understand the model in its simplest form, consider a two-brand market where

$$Y_t = \begin{cases} 1, & \text{if the brand of interest is purchased on occasion } t \\ 0, & \text{otherwise} \end{cases}$$

and

$$p_t = \text{probability of purchasing the brand on occasion } t$$

$$[\text{i.e., } p_t = p(Y_t = 1)]$$

The basic equations of the simple linear learning model are a pair of operators called the acceptance operator and the rejection operator:

$$p_t = \alpha_1 + \lambda_1 p_{t-1}, \qquad \text{if brand } i \text{ is purchased at } t \tag{2.30}$$
$$\text{(acceptance operator)}$$

$$p_t = \alpha_2 + \lambda_2 p_{t-1}, \qquad \text{if brand } i \text{ is not purchased at } t \tag{2.31}$$
$$\text{(rejection operator)}$$

The updating process of the model is displayed in Exhibit 2.8. The horizontal axis represents the probability of choosing brand j in period t, and the vertical axis represents the probability of choosing brand j in period $t + 1$. The figure contains a positively sloped 45° line as a norm. The figure also contains two positively sloped lines representing the acceptance and rejection operators from equations (2.30) and (2.31).

For example, suppose the probability that a consumer purchases brand j this period is 0.60. Suppose it is actually what he buys. The probability that the buyer will buy brand j again, assuming that he is satisfied, is found by running a dashed line up from the horizontal axis at 0.60 to the purchase-operator line (because brand j was purchased) and going across the vertical axis and reading the new probability. In this illustration the new probability is 0.78. If the buyer had not purchased j, the dashed line from 0.60 would

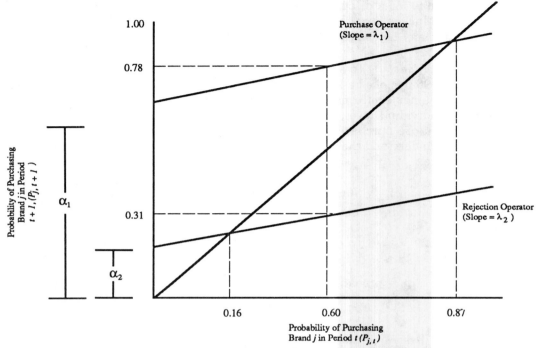

EXHIBIT 2.8 An illustration of the purchase and rejection operation in simple linear learning models. (*Source:* Adapted from Kuehn, 1962.)

have been run up only to the rejection operator and been read on the vertical axis. In that case the probability of the person buying *j* next time would have fallen from 0.60 to 0.31.

If the consumer continues buying brand *j*, the probability of buying brand *j* approaches 0.87 as a limit. This upper limit, given by the intersection of the purchase-operator and the 45° lines, represents a phenomenon known as *incomplete habit formation*. No matter how much brand *j* is bought, some probability still remains that the consumer may buy another brand. On the other hand, if the consumer does not buy brand *j* for a long time, the probability of buying this brand falls continuously but never to zero. This is the phenomenon of *incomplete habit extinction*. There is always some positive probability that a consumer may buy a previously neglected brand.

The incomplete-habit-formation aspect of this model is seen by successive substitutions of equation (2.30):

$$p_t = \alpha_1 + \lambda_1 p_{t-1} = \alpha_1 + \lambda_1(\alpha_1 + \lambda_1 p_{t-2})$$

$$= \alpha_1 + \lambda_1\alpha_1 + \lambda_1^2\alpha_1 + \ldots \qquad \textbf{(2.32)}$$

$$= \alpha_1(1 + \lambda_1 + \lambda_1^2 + \ldots)$$

$$p \to p_u = \frac{\alpha_1}{1 - \lambda_1} \qquad \text{upper limit of } p \qquad \textbf{(2.33a)}$$

Similarly, when the brand is never bought,

$$p \to p_L = \frac{\alpha_2}{1 - \lambda_2} \qquad \text{lower limit} \qquad \textbf{(2.33b)}$$

For a two-brand market, if $\lambda_1 = \lambda_2 = 0$, the linear learning model reduces to a Markov model with constant transition probabilities.

Applications of the learning model have been reported by Kuehn (1962) with data on the purchase of frozen orange juice, by Carman (1966) with dentifrice data following the American Dental Association's endorsement of Crest, by Kuehn and Rohloff (1967a) in the context of evaluation promotions, and in a modified form by Haines (1964). Applications also include those of Lawrence (1975) and Wierenga (1974). In the latter work the linear learning model produces results superior to those of the homogeneous and heterogeneous, zero-order and first-order Markov models. In another study Massy, Montgomery, and Morrison (1970) show that the linear learning model may account for population heterogeneity; the approach works essentially through the introduction of a mixing distribution on the initial probability levels, as reviewed earlier.

In the form just described the linear learning model does not contain any decision variables. Lilien (1974a) introduces price into the model:

$$p_{t+1} = (1 - c)(\alpha + \beta Y_t + \lambda p_t) + c\Phi(\delta_{t+1}) \qquad \textbf{(2.34)}$$

where

c = price consciousness of consumer
δ_t = price measure
$\Phi(\cdot)$ = price-response function

He uses the model to measure the effect of price on brand choice/learning behavior and to derive pricing policies under given assumptions about competitive behavior in the marketplace. His results in the gasoline market are generally supportive of this model form.

The linear learning model and its derivatives generally face three problems. First, the model is well suited for two-brand markets (us versus them) only; when more detailed market descriptions are needed, it is not easily extended. Second, the model is structured to give only positive feedback for brand purchase and, hence, may not be useful in new product situations. Third, the model is analytically more complex than the others cited here, limiting its

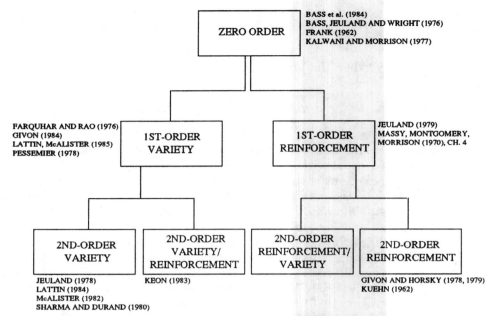

EXHIBIT 2.9 Taxonomy for variety-seeking/reinforcement models. (*Source:* Kahn, Kalwani, and Morrison, 1986a, p. 93.)

accessibility. Indeed, Leeflang and Boonstra (1982) suggest that limited degrees of freedom for parameter estimation using micro data and the infeasibility of estimation with macro data will continue to limit the model's applicability.

Other Forms of Stochastic Purchase Feedback. Kahn, Kalwani, and Morrison (1986a) propose a taxonomy for defining and measuring alternative forms of purchase reinforcement and variety-seeking behaviors. They define *reinforcement behavior* as an *increase* in repeat-purchase probability after buying a brand and *variety seeking* as a *decrease* in that repeat-purchase probability. They also characterize models as first or second order; that is, a second-order variety-seeking model would have an individual more likely to switch brands after two consecutive purchases than after one. And they introduce mixed models—for example, a second-order reinforcement/variety-seeking model has one purchase of a brand increasing the repurchase probability, but two consecutive purchases decreasing that probability. Exhibit 2.9 gives their taxonomy of models and references to those models that are consistent with each of the assumptions.

In an empirical assessment of a general model that incorporates these models as special cases, they conclude that variety seeking and reinforcement tendencies differ across product classes and even across brands in some product classes. For example, they conclude that breakfast cereals show variety-seeking behavior but that for soft drinks, some cola drinkers are loyal and some seek variety while noncola drinkers more uniformly seek variety.

Their models do not deal with marketing-mix variables, multi-item purchasing on the same trip (which may confuse the purchase-sequence data) and multiple consumers within the household (where aggregation tends to derive the observed behavior more toward zero order—see Kahn, Kalwani, and Morrison, 1986a).

Combining Brand Choice and Purchase Timing.

Multinomial/Dirichlet Model. Jeuland, Bass, and Wright (1980) develop an integrated brand choice–purchase timing model with the following assumptions:

> *Purchase timing.* The authors assume that interpurchase times have an Erlang (or gamma) distribution of order r (Appendix A), with the interpurchase time parameter (λ) of the Erlang distribution having a gamma mixing distribution across the population.
>
> *Brand choice.* The authors assume a zero-order process, with individuals having a multinominal brand choice distribution and with population heterogeneity characterized by a Dirichlet distribution. The multinomial/Dirichlet assumptions here are a direct extension of the two-brand beta/binomial assumptions (Appendix A) to the multibrand case.

Using these assumptions and the assumption that these processes are independent the authors relate the following key market descriptors to model parameters:

> **1.** *Market share*, by brand, over time
>
> **2.** *Penetration*, the proportion of the population that buys the brand at least once during a given time interval
>
> **3.** *Duplication*, the proportion of the population that buy any pair of brands, X and Y
>
> **4.** *Brand switching*, the proportion of purchase occasions on which a different brand is purchased
>
> **5.** *Repeat buying*, the proportion of time any brand is bought on two consecutive purchase occasions

While the development of this model is somewhat technical, it clearly has potential to provide a set of useful market descriptors and a baseline against which to check actual market performance. This basic model has been applied to the analysis of store choice as well: Keng and Ehrenberg (1984) find that, by analyzing the foregoing statistics, store penetration, repeat buying of a grocery product at the same store, and multistore buying are all consistent with the zero-order model assumptions: over time, people spread their purchases to other chains of stores in line with market shares.

Other models that integrate purchase incidence and brand choice include those of Zufryden (1978) and Dalal, Lee, and Sabavala (1984). Zufryden's model assumes a linear learning model for brand choice and Erlang interpurchase times; Dalal, Lee, and Sabavala assume Poisson interpurchase time and a Bernoulli brand choice process. However, they assume that the Poisson and Bernoulli parameters can vary in an arbitrary way across the population. In particular, they do not assume that brand choice and purchase timing distributions are independent.

Incorporating Explanatory Variables.   Most of the models developed here have ignored the effect of explanatory variables on the purchase process. Lilien's (1974a, b) model was an attempt to incorporate explanatory variables in the framework of a linear learning model and that model was extended to the multiple-brand case by Leeflang and Boonstra (1982). Wagner and Taudes (1986) develop a model in which the mean purchase rate (following a Poisson process) can be influenced by marketing-mix variables and by time.

EXAMPLE

Givon and Horsky (1990) provide a useful illustration of a two-state Markov model that incorporates explanatory variables. In their model the two-state transition matrix has the following form:

$$
\begin{array}{c}
\begin{array}{cc} A_t & \quad\quad B_t \end{array} \\
\begin{array}{c} A_{t-1} \\ B_{t-1} \end{array}
\begin{bmatrix} \alpha_t + \beta & 1 - \alpha_t - \beta \\ \alpha_t & 1 - \alpha_t \end{bmatrix}
\end{array}
\quad\quad \textbf{(2.35)}
$$

Each consumer in the market is assumed to follow the process shown, with β, the "brand feedback" effect constant across customers. The effect of controllable variables, α_t, is modeled as follows:

$$
\alpha_t = a_0 + \gamma(X_t + \lambda X_{t-1} + \lambda^2 X_{t-2} + \cdots +) + \delta R_t + \varepsilon_t \quad\quad \textbf{(2.36)}
$$

where

$$
\begin{aligned}
a_0, \gamma, \lambda, \delta &= \text{constants} \\
X_t &= \text{advertising level at time } t \\
R_t &= \text{(relative) price of brand } A \text{ at time } t
\end{aligned}
$$

ε_t = random error term

The authors note that

$$m_t = \alpha_t + \beta m_{t-1} \tag{2.37}$$

where

m_t = market share of brand A at time t

Substituting (2.36) into (2.37) yields

$$m_t = a_0 + \gamma(X_t + \lambda X_{t-1} + \lambda^2 X_{t-2} + \cdots) + \delta R_t + \beta m_{t-1} + \varepsilon_t \tag{2.38}$$

Transforming equation (2.38) by first considering $m_t - \lambda m_{t-1}$ and then $m_t - \beta m_{t-1}$ yields

$$m_t = a_0(1 - \lambda) + (\beta + \lambda)m_{t-1} - \beta\lambda m_{t-2} \tag{2.39}$$
$$+ \gamma X_t + \delta R_t + \delta\lambda R_{t-1} + \mu_t$$

where

$$\mu_t = \varepsilon_t - \lambda\varepsilon_{t-1} \tag{2.40}$$

In an empirical application of this model in four product categories (after dealing with some tricky aspects of estimating the model with temporally aggregated data), the authors found the following:

a. There was no advertising carryover ($\lambda = 0$) for all products.

b. There was a strong dynamic effect resulting from purchase feedback ($\beta > 0$).

c. The coefficients of current advertising effects (λ) and price effects (δ) had the expected signs.

The authors conclude that at least in these product categories, and for monthly and bimonthly measurement periods, purchase reinforcement dominates the carryover of advertising in affecting the evolution of market share.

Note that this model does not deal with population heterogeneity or with purchase timing. Horsky (1977) has also developed a Markov-type model that looked at advertising, and Zufryden (1986) has developed a first-order Markov model that models the transition probabilities as functions of the controllable variables in a logit specification.

Another approach to incorporating controllable variables in stochastic choice models is a semi-Markov model (a Markov process where the timing of stay in a particular state is a state-dependent random variable) developed by Hauser and Wisniewski (1982a, b). In their model they deal with multiple brands and multiple states per brand (e.g., unaware, aware and not using, aware and using) with the state transition probabilities functions of marketing variables. Models by Urban (1970) and Urban, Hauser, and Roberts (1990) are similar in spirit, modeling customer flows across states as function of both that state and controllable marketing variables.

More complete stochastic models, incorporating timing, choice, heterogeneity, marketing variables, feedback, and so on (Exhibit 2.5) face two problems. First, the inclusion and linking of these additional phenomena lead to models that are analytically complex and difficult to communicate. Second, these models require more data and more subtle estimation procedures than are often available for practical applications. Hence, developments in this area have tended to trade off model completeness on the one hand with applicability (in terms of understanding, data availability and estimation) on the other. The balance of these forces will continue to direct the development of the field in the years to come.

PROCESS-ORIENTED MODELS OF THE CONSUMER CHOICE PROCESS

The stochastic models just described have the advantage of parsimony, which allows models of individual consumers to be aggregated and enables us to describe the characteristics of the population as a whole. As the complexity of the purchase situation increases, we may wish to include more phenomena into our models and allow consumers to vary across a wider range of characteristics. This increased richness in explanation comes at some cost: we can no longer aggregate over the sources of heterogeneity in the population and describe it as a whole. What we obtain in return is the ability to include a range of causal variables into the purchase decision. We now develop a series of models to describe the consumer behavior identified in the five stages of our framework (illustrated in Exhibit 2.1).

Need Arousal

Binary Choice Models of Need Arousal.   In this section we deal with need arousal, that is, when a need will reach a level such that the consumer will seek gratification. Model building in this area is based on two major traditions in consumer behavior (see Zaltman and Wallendorf, 1979, for details).

The first tradition is Maslow's hierarchy of needs. This theory suggests that needs can be prioritized in a hierarchy and that consumers satisfy higher-order needs before they satisfy those lower in the hierarchy. For example, the need for shelter will be addressed before the need for intellectual stimulation. The second tradition is that of McClelland, which suggests that needs are learned. This approach emphasizes the importance of contextual variables in consumer choice.

Need arousal corresponds to the category purchase decision. In the purchase stage of our framework, we will examine *which* specific product or brand the consumer chooses. The models at both stages are similar: the choice of when to buy and the choice of what to buy. The area is called discrete choice theory (in contrast to other models of demand in economics in which the good is infinitely divisible). In the case of divisible goods, the choice becomes how much to buy rather than whether to buy or not. Many of the models to choose between different brands in the purchase section may equally well be used for the choice between purchase and nonpurchase.

When there are exactly two choices (buy in category/don't buy in category, as in our need arousal models) discrete choice models are called *binary choice models* and have been applied to a wide variety of classification problems within marketing and in other areas. Ben-Akiva and Lerman (1985, Chapter 4) have an excellent exposition of these models, their derivations, and methods of estimating them.

Assume that the utility that consumer i expects to get from the category at the time of the purchase decision is U_{Bi}, while the utility of not buying within the category is U_{Ni}. Furthermore, we assume that we can divide these utilities into two components: a systematic part, V_i, and a random component, ε_i.

Thus,

$$U_{Bi} = V_{Bi} + \varepsilon_{Bi} \tag{2.41a}$$

and

$$U_{Ni} = V_{Ni} + \varepsilon_{Ni} \tag{2.41b}$$

that is

Buy/not buy utility = True value + assessment error

Specification of the Systematic Components, V_{Bi} and V_{Ni}.   A key question that arises in specifying the systematic component in equation (2.41b) is how to determine the utility of not buying within the category, V_{Ni}. Various authors have suggested different benchmarks against which the utility of buying within the category can be compared. For example, budget constraints compare the utility (net of price) that the category in question gives to that of other durables and a composite good of nondurables. This will result in an ordering that consumers can use to purchase durable products.

EXAMPLE

The Smith family, for example, have to work out how the utility they will derive from a new washing machine fits in with their current plans to take the family on a vacation to Australia this year, to buy a snow blower, to buy a personal computer, and to buy a new car for Fred. Their current list of priorities looks something like this.

Priority Number	Cost ($)	Cumulative Cost ($)	
1 Personal Computer	6,500	6,500	
2 New car	11,200	17,700	
			← Budget constraint ($18,000)
3 Australian Vacation	4,400	22,100	
4 Snowblower	1,100	23,200	

Their durable budget constraint ($18,000) suggests that the vacation and the snowblower would have had to have been deferred this year. The unforeseen increased utility of a new washing machine at an expected cost of $1,200, which they now place as their top priority, suggests that the new car may have to wait as well.

APPLICATION

Hauser and Urban (1986) derive and test a decision rule where they posit that consumers undertake this budgeting process, called the value priority algorithm. Under the value priority algorithm, consumers select the durables of highest utility per dollar, or highest utility net of price, first and proceed down the list ordered on that basis until they meet their budget constraint. Hauser and Urban's value priority algorithm is consistent with Coursey (1985, 1988) who appeals to the economic theory of Lancaster to suggest that (1988, p. 407)

> consumers sequentially satisfy higher ranked activities in their preference ordering up to the point that their monetary and time resources were exhausted.

The order of acquisition literature suggests that this preference order is homogeneous throughout the population. For example, Kasulis and colleagues (1979) used Guttman scalogram analysis to show an acquisition order of first TV, first vehicle, refrigerator, range, stereo or tape player, drier, second vehicle, dishwasher, second TV, freezer, and microwave for 1,747 residents in Oklahoma City. The error of classification was 12.9%.

Hauser and Urban derive their utility ordering of durables by examining the utility maximization task facing a household considering the purchase of a number of durables. That problem may be expressed as the following linear program (assuming linear, additive utilities of durables):

$$\text{Maximize} \quad u_1 g_1 + u_2 g_2 + \cdots + u_n g_n + u_y(y)$$

$$\text{Subject to} \quad p_1 g_1 + p_2 g_2 + \cdots + p_n g_n + y \le B$$

$$\text{and} \quad g_j \ge 0 \qquad \text{for all durables } j$$

where

u_j = the expected utility of durable j

p_j = price of durable j

g_j = $\begin{cases} 1, & \text{if durable } j \text{ is purchased and} \\ 0, & \text{otherwise} \end{cases}$

B = budget that the consumer has to spend, of which

y = spent on products other than durables, giving a utility of $u_y(y)$

An equivalent problem for the consumer is to minimize the dual linear program, that is, to solve the following problem:

$$\text{Minimize} \quad B\lambda + \gamma_1 + \gamma_2 + \cdots + \gamma_n$$

$$\text{Subject to} \quad c_j \ge u_j - \lambda p_j, \quad \text{for all } j$$

$$\text{and} \quad \lambda = \partial u_y(y)/\partial y$$

The behavioral interpretation of this problem is that γ_j is the shadow price of the constraint $g_j \le 1$. That is, γ_j is the forgone value of not having durable j or the value of relaxing the constraint that durables are discrete. The rule of complementary slackness from linear programming theory says that net utility or consumer surplus, $u_j - \lambda p_j$, is greater than zero if and only if durable j is purchased.

Hauser and Urban fit the model by combining four measures of purchase intent: the reservation price of the durable, the stated probability of purchase, and two different orders of preference for the durable in a lottery. Both value per dollar and net value (assuming the consumer maximizes net utility) predict individual budget plans adequately for the majority of consumers: 60% have a correlation between predicted and actual plans of greater than 0.5 with the former and 84% for the latter.

In addition to other durables goods, benchmarks against which the new purchase might be compared include the utility of existing stock in consumer marketing (Hauser, Roberts, and Urban, 1983) and the utility that purchase of the product will provide in business to business marketing (the present value of future income streams; see Mansfield, 1961). Alternatively, the utility of the category after adjusting for price may be compared to the utility of not having purchased, that is, zero. If the net category utility exceeds zero, the product will be purchased and is said to offer a consumer surplus to the purchaser equal to its net utility.

Having specified the value of not buying within the category, V_{Ni}, let us consider the determinants of the expected value of buying within the category, V_{Bi}. This can be done in two ways. First, buying within the category can be characterized by the value that a typical new washing machine would offer in terms of the anticipated attribute levels. Thus, relative to having a washing machine that was not working well, Sally and Fred may have evaluated the idea of a new machine on the basis of how well it would wash, its noise, the relative risk of it breaking down, and its aesthetics, balanced against its cost. Sally and Fred are thinking of the category's utility, V_{Bi}, as a function of a vector of attributes, x. Alternatively, when they consider the purchase of a new car, a category with a wide range of prices and styles, the Smith family may find it difficult to think in terms of the value of a "typical" new car. In that case it is possible to estimate the expected utilities of all the new car brands that they would consider. From the utilities of the individual cars that they would consider, they can gain an estimate of the utility of the category as a whole. For example, if a logit model could be used to describe their brand choice, then the expected utility that they would obtain from the category would be

$$V_{Bi} = E[\max(U_j)] = \ln (\Sigma_{j \in C} \exp V_j) \tag{2.42}$$

where

V_j = their expected utility for the jth brand in their consideration set, C (Ben-Akiva and Lerman, 1985, p. 105).

Specification of the Error Component. A consumer will choose to purchase (the aroused need will be gratified) if

$$V_{Bi} > V_{Ni} \tag{2.43}$$

that is, if the utility of purchasing the product exceeds the utility of doing without it. Thus, we are interested in

$$
\begin{aligned}
\Pr(U_{Bi} > U_{Ni}) &= \Pr(V_{Bi} + \varepsilon_{Bi} > V_{Ni} + \varepsilon_{Ni}) \\
&= \Pr[V_{Bi} > V_{Ni} + (\varepsilon_{Ni} - \varepsilon_{Bi})]
\end{aligned}
\tag{2.44}
$$

We can now consider the appropriate form for the distribution of ε_{Ni} and ε_{Bi} or for $(\varepsilon_{Ni} - \varepsilon_{Bi})$. Basically, varying the assumptions about the distributions of ε_{Ni} and ε_{Bi} (or of their difference) leads to different choice models. However, as Ben-Akiva and Lerman (1985, p. 65) point out, it makes little sense to think about the specification of the distribution of the ε's independently from the specification of the V's, since a major source of the random component will arise as a result of specifying V as a function of the attribute vector.

Binary Probit. One logical assumption for the ε's is to treat them as the sum of a large number of unobserved influences. If we can assume independence of those influences, then the sum of all of these factors will tend to be normal by the central limit theorem. If we assume that $(\varepsilon_{Ni} - \varepsilon_{Bi})$ is distributed as $N(0, \sigma^2)$ (with the corresponding assumed normality but not necessarily independence of ε_{Ni} and ε_{Bi}), then we can derive the probability of consumer i buying within the category, P_{Bi}, as a function of the expected utility components, V_{Bi} and V_{Ni}:

$$
\begin{aligned}
P_{Bi} &= \Pr[V_{Bi} > V_{Ni} + (\varepsilon_{Ni} - \varepsilon_{Bi})] \\
&= \Pr[(\varepsilon_{Ni} - \varepsilon_{Bi}) < V_{Bi} - V_{Ni}]
\end{aligned}
\tag{2.45a}
$$

$$
= \int_{-\infty}^{V_{Bi}-V_{Ni}} \frac{1}{(\sigma \sqrt{2\pi})} \exp\left[\frac{-(x/\sigma)^2}{2} \right] dx \tag{2.45b}
$$

Equation (2.45b) is called the binary probit model.

Binary Logit. The binary probit, while intuitively appealing, lacks a closed algebraic form. To overcome this problem, a model that relies on a slightly different error theory is often used; the binary logit. The binary logit assumes that the difference $\varepsilon_i = \varepsilon_{Ni} - \varepsilon_{Bi}$ is distributed logistically; that is

$$F(\varepsilon_i) = \frac{1}{1 + \exp(-\mu\varepsilon_i)} \tag{2.46}$$

From equation (2.46) we can show that the probability of purchase is given by

$$P_{Bi} = \Pr(V_{Bi} - V_{Ni} > \varepsilon_i)$$

$$= \frac{1}{1 + \exp[-\mu(V_{Bi} - V_{Ni})]}$$

$$= \frac{\exp(\mu V_{Bi})}{\exp(\mu V_{Bi}) + \exp(\mu V_{Ni})} \tag{2.47}$$

It may be seen that under the binary logit, the probability of purchase is its share of the utilities after exponentiation. If the benchmark comparison for nonpurchase is $V_{Ni} = 0$, then the binary logit becomes

$$P_{Bi} = \frac{\exp(\mu V_{Bi})}{1 + \exp(\mu V_{Bi})} \tag{2.48}$$

The binary logit can also be derived by assuming that the distributions of ε_{Bi} and ε_{Ni} are double exponential (extreme value, Appendix A) and independent (see Amemiya, 1981).

Other Binary Choice Models. There are a number of other binary choice models available, the most common of which are the linear probability model (assuming a uniform distribution of ε_i) and the arctan (assuming an arctan distribution). (See Ben-Akiva and Lerman, 1985).

APPLICATION _____

Nooteboom (1989) used the logit model, as specified in equation (2.48), to study the decision to adopt computing equipment by independent retailers in the Netherlands. He posited that the utility from having computers was a function of organization size (S_i) and that this did not change over time. The other variable he considered was risk (α_t), which he assumed was not a function of firm size, but did change over time. While he measured size directly, he imputed risk. Thus his model was

$$P_i = \frac{1}{1 + \exp(\alpha_t' + \beta S_i')} \tag{2.49}$$

where

$$\alpha_t' = \log \alpha_t \quad \text{and} \quad S_i' = \log S_i$$

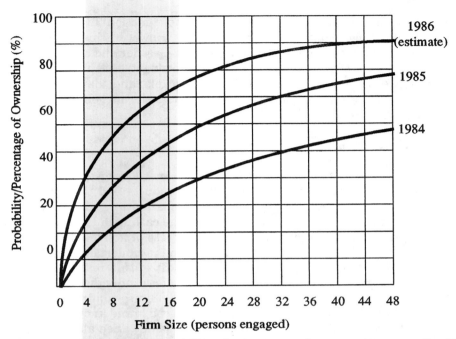

EXHIBIT 2.10 Change in probability of category purchase over time, as a function of company size. (*Source:* Nooteboom, 1989, p. 120.)

Because Nooteboom had details of when retailers first introduced computers, he was able to look at the adoption or otherwise at various points in time. He found that size was statistically significant in nine out of ten of his cross-sectional regressions. He also found the level of risk, or the intercept in equation (2.49), decreased monotonically with time. Thus, each year the probability of purchase increased for a company of a given size, while for a given year, it was higher in larger firms than for smaller ones. This result is illustrated in Exhibit 2.10.

One point that this application demonstrates is the dynamics of the probability of purchase. If we think of $\alpha'_t + \beta S'_i$ (the utility of having or buying a computer) as a consumer's level of susceptibility, we can see that, at a given point in time, susceptibility is higher for larger customers than smaller ones, while susceptibility for all customers increases over time. See Bodnar, Dilworth, and Iacono (1988) and Robinson (1985) for similar applications.

Issues in Binary Choice Models of Need Arousal. The relative performance of these and other binary choice models has been reviewed by Gessner and colleagues (1988) who suggest that in the absence of major violations to their assumptions, all of the choice models they examined (probit, logit, linear probability, and two types of discriminant function) fit and predict reasonably well, giving qualitatively similar results. However, this is not the case if there are major violations to the assumptions. Gessner and colleagues conclude that the choice of model should be data dependent, that there is little difference between the binary logit and probit models, and that users of these models should test for data inadequacies and transform their data where necessary to avoid them.

Information Search

The decision to buy within a category (need arousal) leads customers to a state of heightened awareness about products and their attributes. Buyers will be more receptive to product information in such a product category. If the need is particularly acute, as was the case with the Smith family's washing machine, they will undertake a process of active search.

The amount of search that consumers undertake has attracted considerable attention among researchers. Most of this research has concentrated on different types of search behavior across individuals for a given product class. For example, Punj and Staelin (1983) use confirmatory factor analysis to show that high cost of searching and good brand knowledge were associated with less search activity for new automobiles. (See also Johnson and Russo, 1984.) High search activity, in turn, led to larger savings off the sticker price of the car. Claxton, Fry, and Portis (1974) used cluster analysis to classify types of searchers for furniture and appliances as "thorough" or "nonthorough" depending on the effort that they invested in gaining information. For the symbolic product of fashion clothing, Midgley (1983) identified five types of information seeking: peer assisted, spouse assisted, extensive search, and minimal search (deliberate and decisive). Urbany, Dickson, and Wilkie (1989) show that the amount of search is related to two dimensions of customer uncertainty: uncertainty about what alternatives exist and uncertainty about which alternatives to choose.

We organize the process of consumers gathering information about potentially suitable brands prior to evaluation into three steps: awareness, consideration (the searched set of brands among the aware set), and information integration (the updating of attitudes and beliefs about searched brands).

Models of Brand Awareness.   Whether by passive search or active (including direct experience), consumers become aware of brands that could satisfy their need. Rossiter and Percy (1987) define awareness as "the buyer's ability to identify (recognize or recall) the brand within the category in sufficient detail to make a purchase." Most of the literature on awareness relates the reaction function of awareness to advertising at the aggregate level, and many models have no individual level interpretation. Mahajan, Muller, and Kerin (1984), for example, review five common awareness forecasting models, all of which relate the proportion of the total *population* that is aware of the brand to advertising. (See Chapter 6.) Some awareness and exposure models, estimated at the aggregate level, do have individual level interpretations.

APPLICATION

Blattberg and Jeuland (1981) use a Bernoulli advertising exposure process and an exponential forgetting process to model awareness. The Bernoulli assumption implies that if there are n advertisements during a period, then the probability that a consumer will be exposed x times is

$$P(x\ exposures) = \left\{ \frac{n!}{[x!(n-x)!]} \right\} q^x(1-q)^{n-x} \qquad \textbf{(2.50)}$$

where q is a parameter (Appendix A). Exponential forgetting suggests that if the last advertisement was seen by the consumer at time t_1, the probability of his remembering it (still being aware) at time t, p_t, is given by

$$p_t = \exp[-\alpha(t - t_1)] \qquad \textbf{(2.51)}$$

where α is a parameter (the retention rate).

The probability of a consumer being aware at time t, $f(t)$, may be calculated in terms of the probability of the consumer having seen the most recent advertisement (at time t_1) times the probability of having not forgotten it, plus probability of having seen the previous advertisement (at time t_2) and not forgetting that (given that he did not see the most recent advertisement), and so on. Mathematically, we may write

$$f(t) = q \exp[-\alpha(t - t_1)] + q(1-q) \exp[-\alpha(t - t_2)]$$

$$+ q(1-q)^2 \exp[-\alpha(t - t_3)] + \cdots \qquad \textbf{(2.52)}$$

$$= \Sigma_r\, q(1-q)^{r-1} e^{-\alpha(t - t_r)}$$

At the aggregate level, the interpretation of $f(t)$ is the expected proportion of the target population that is aware.

To translate awareness at a given time into sales over a period of unit length, Blattberg and Jeuland assume that sales during period k, $s(k)$, are proportional to the level of awareness of the product:

$$s(k) = c_1 + c_2 \int_k f(t)dt \qquad \textbf{(2.53)}$$

Assuming n_k placements of ads in period k, they are able to derive the sales advertising equation at the aggregate level by substituting equation (2.52) in (2.53):

$$s(k) = c_1 + \left(\frac{c_2 q}{\alpha}\right) \cdot \frac{(1 - e^{-\alpha/n_k})}{(1 - \lambda_k)}$$

$$\cdot \{n_k - \lambda_k(1 - \lambda_k^{n_k})/(1 - \lambda_k) + (1 - \lambda_k^{n_k}) \cdot \gamma_{k-1}\}$$

(2.54)

where

$$\lambda_k = (1 - q)e^{-\alpha/n_k}$$

and

$$\gamma_{k-1} = \lambda_{k-1}^{n_k} - 1 \cdot \lambda_{k-2} + \lambda_{k-1}(1 - \lambda_{k-1}^{n_k} - 1)/(1 - \lambda_{k-1})$$

This nonlinear model not only has a microlevel interpretation, it allows the separate effects of reach and frequency to be identified. Blattberg and Jeuland show that the carryover effect (the effect of this period's advertising on next period's sales) depends on previous advertising as well as on the current reach and frequency of advertising. They use simulation to demonstrate how the model explains a number of anomalies in aggregate advertising response: abnormally long lags, higher lagged coefficients when moving from monthly to quarterly data, and higher apparent advertising effectiveness from the previous period's advertising than the current one's.

In a more general form of this type of model, Leckenby and Kishi (1984) derive the Dirichlet multinomial distribution (DMD) to model the proportion of the population that will be exposed to 1, 2, 3 ..., mn of the n insertions in each of m media vehicles. This model comes from the assumption that exposure to the mn advertisements for any individual consumer is multinomial, while individuals' parameters are distributed Dirichlet across the population. Leckenby and Kishi find superior performance of this model (estimated using a variety of algorithms) over other similar models.

A major challenge in this area is to develop and calibrate models that improve our understanding of how advertising, word of mouth, and usage drive awareness at the individual level.

Models of Consideration Set Formation.   Many empirical studies show that consumers do not search and evaluate (consider) all the brands of which they are aware. The consideration set may be defined to be all those brands that the consumer will evaluate or search for a given purchase. Study of the com-

Published Studies		ASSESSOR database	
Category	Mean (or median) consideration set size	Category	Mean (or median) consideration set size
Antacid*	3.0	Analgesic	3.5
Autos* (USA)	8.1	Antacid	4.4
Autos* (Norway)	2.0	Air freshener	2.2
Beer	3.0	Bar soap	3.7
Beer (USA)	2.6	Bathroom cleaner	5.7
Beer* (Canada)	7.0	Beer	6.9
Coffee	3.3	Bleach	3.9
Coffee	4.2	Chili	2.6
Deodorant*	3.0	Coffee	4.0
Dish washing liquid	5.6	Cookies	4.9
Fast food restaurant	5.4	Deodorant	3.9
Food product	2.9	Frozen dinners	3.3
Gasoline	3.0	Insecticides	2.7
Laundry detergent	5.0	Laundry detergent	4.8
Margarine	4.3	Laxative	2.8
Over-the-counter medicine*	3.0	Peanut butter	3.3
Pain reliever*	3.0	Razors	2.9
Shampoo*	4.0	Shampoo	6.1
Skin care product*	5.0	Shortening	6.0
Soft drinks	5.0	Sinus medicine	3.6
Table napkins	5.0	Soap	4.8
Tea	2.6	Soda	5.1
Toothpaste	3.1	Yogurt	3.6

* Median

EXHIBIT 2.11   Consideration set sizes—empirical findings. (*Source:* Hauser and Wernerfelt, 1990, p. 394.)

position of the consideration set is important for two reasons. First, lack of consideration may be important in its own right. For example, a company wishing to be invited to tender for a contract may wish to know the determinants of the consideration set (the list of invited tenderers). Second, consideration may be important as a part of the overall study of the consumption process. Recent research has shown that better fits, superior forecasting ability, and richer management diagnostics may often be obtained by including a consideration stage in a choice model (e.g., Gensch and Svestka, 1984). A summary of typical consideration set sizes reported by Hauser and Wernerfelt (1990) shows a range of typical average consideration set sizes from 2.0 to 8.1 (Exhibit 2.11).

A key question that arises in modeling consideration is whether the process should be compensatory (in which shortcomings in one attribute may be traded off against benefits on another) or noncompensatory (in which certain thresholds exist for different attributes and the brand must meet some combination of those thresholds, irrespective of its levels on other attributes). Narayana and Markin (1975) suggest that nonconsidered brands can be classified as "inept" or "inert." For inept brands there is something that specifically precludes consideration, that is, something wrong with them. This corresponds to a noncompensatory representation of the consideration process. Inert brands are those for which there is nothing specific wrong; rather, they are just not good enough. This corresponds to brands that would be considered if any of a number of attributes were improved: representing elimination by some compensatory process. Narayana and Markin found some categories for which inept criteria dominated the inert criterion (e.g., toothpaste) and some where the reverse was the case (e.g., beer).

EXAMPLE

Roberts and Lattin (1991).   Models of noncompensatory processes are described later in this chapter. Here we illustrate one compensatory model of consideration, derived by Roberts and Lattin (1991). If we assume that the consumer will choose from the consideration set according to a logit choice model at the purchase stage, we can estimate the expected utility that he or she will derive from buying within the category, given a consideration set of C, as:

$$E_{B|C} = \ln \left[\Sigma_{j \in C} \exp(U_j) \right] \qquad \textbf{(2.55)}$$

If the consumer now becomes aware of a new brand, N, with search costs c_N and utility U_N, we can use equation (2.55) to estimate whether or not it will be considered. It should be considered if the incremental expected benefit from the new consideration set $E_{B|C \cup N}$ more than offsets the cost of search, c_N; that is,

$$E_{B|C \cup N} - E_{B|C} > c_N \qquad \textbf{(2.56)}$$

Substituting the expression for expected category utility from equation (2.55) and rearranging terms, we can derive the minimum utility that the brand needs to justify entry into the set, or alternatively, the maximum search costs that it can afford to be included:

$$E_{B|C \cup N} - E_{B|C} > c_N$$

if

$$\ln \left[\Sigma_{j \in C \cup N} \exp(U_j) \right] - \ln \left[\Sigma_{k \in C} \exp(U_k) \right] > c_N$$

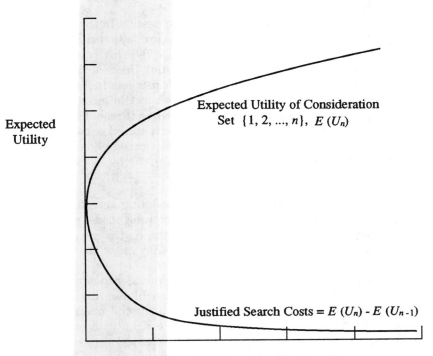

EXHIBIT 2.12 Maximum search costs to enter the consideration set as a function of set size.

that is,

$$U_N > \ln \{[\Sigma_{k \in C} \exp(U_k)][\exp(c_N) - 1]\} \qquad \textbf{(2.57a)}$$

or

$$c_N < \ln \left[\frac{1 + \exp(U_N)}{\Sigma_{k \in C} \exp(U_k)} \right] \qquad \textbf{(2.57b)}$$

Roberts and Lattin show that with equal search costs for each brand, the consumer will pursue a greedy algorithm in composing his consideration set (that is, he will choose the brand of highest expected utility first, followed by the second highest, and so on).

Equation (2.57) suggests that even if all brands are of equal utility $(U_k = U)$, as the number of brands already considered increases, the maximum search costs that an additional brand can justify decrease. That is illustrated in Exhibit 2.12.

Roberts and Lattin test their results in three ways. First, they show that their threshold utility model predicts inclusion in the consideration set at the individual level with a 75% hit rate (compared to just over 50% using a random allocation rule). Second, they show that the model, calibrated on the existing market predicts inclusion of new product concepts in the consideration set, both at the individual and aggregate levels. Third, they find that their utility threshold model, combined with a logit choice model, outpredicts both stated consideration combined with a naive choice model and a sophisticated choice model with no consideration phase.

In an alternative approach to modeling consideration set composition, Hauser and Wernerfelt (1990) assume a probit model at the choice stage rather than logit. They distinguish between the cost of search and the cost of evaluating and deciding between brands. They show that low search cost brands are more likely to be considered.

Large consideration sets for individual consumers are associated with lower search and evaluation costs and a higher variance of brands' utilities across consumption occasions. To establish the market level implications of consideration, Hauser and Wernerfelt concentrate on testing their model at the aggregate level. They show that observed distributions of consideration set sizes, order of entry effects, asymmetric advertising effects, and level of promotional activity in a number of packaged goods markets are consistent with their model.

In addition to industrial and consumer products, the concept of consideration has also been applied to retail outlets. Fotheringham (1988) suggests that consideration sets are not dichotomous, but rather fuzzy sets (whether because consideration is not a discrete process to consumers or because as researchers we are not capable of measuring it). Thus he suggests that brands will be taken into the evaluation and choice phase only with some probability. For the problem of retail choice, he makes that probability a function of the closeness of other stores in the awareness set. If closeness leads to a positive effect on the probability, he terms this an agglomeration effect. If it decreases the probability, he calls that a competitive effect.

Application of consideration models has increased in recent years, both for durables and packaged goods (Shocker et al., 1991). One point we must remember in their application is that the consideration set is dynamic. If consideration sets are calibrated well before the consumer enters the need arousal stage, then the results may not be a good indicator of later behavior (Day and Deutscher, 1982).

Information Integration.   Brands of which the consumer is aware and which merit consideration will be searched. Research has been conducted both into

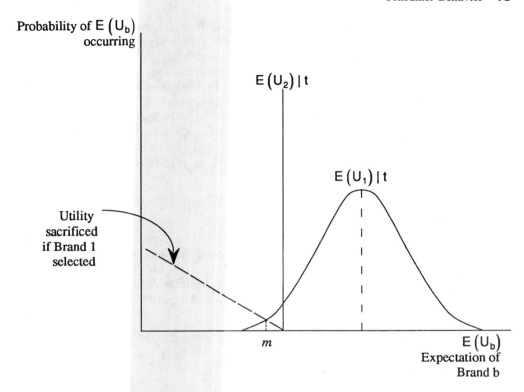

EXHIBIT 2.13 Utility distributions when considering sampling information from brand 1. (*Source:* Hagerty and Aaker, 1984, p. 232.)

whether more search should be conducted and where, as well as how the information discovered during search should be integrated into consumers' perceptions.

Hagerty and Aaker (1984) develop a model for information search strategies based on the sequential sampling literature which looks at the expected value of sample information (EVSI). They assume a utility-maximizing consumer who will search the piece of information with the greatest difference between the expected value of the information and the information processing cost next.

To illustrate how the EVSI is calculated, let us assume that the consumer is currently considering three brands: 1, 2, and 3. Associated with each brand j is the expected utility of the brand, $E(U_j)$, which has some uncertainty associated with it, σ_j^2. Hagerty and Aaker assume that the distribution of beliefs about the utility of each brand is distributed normally, as illustrated for brand 1 in Exhibit 2.13. If the consumer does not gather any more information, he will choose brand 1, since it has the highest expected utility. To estimate the value of additional search of brand 1, consider the expected utility of brand 1 after the new information has been gathered.

Search will change only the consumer choice and thus alter the utility that he realizes if, based on the new information, brand 1 has an updated expected utility, m, of less than $E(U_2)$. In that case the expected utility that would be forgone by not undertaking the search is $E(U_2) - m$, represented by the dashed line in Exhibit 2.13. What search enables us to do is to reduce the chances of incurring that loss by giving us a better fix on the true value of $E(U_1)$. The expected value of search is $E(U_2) - m$ integrated over the probability distribution of different values of m, $p(m)$, from $-\infty$ to $E(U_2)$:

$$\text{EVSI} = \int_{-\infty}^{E(U_2)} [E(U_2) - m]p(m)dm \qquad (2.58)$$

Since prior beliefs are normally distributed, if we assume that new information is normally distributed, the posterior mean (the utility of brand 1 after updating, m) will also be normally distributed, with variance σ_m^2. From this, Hagerty and Aaker show that in the multibrand case, the expected value of sample information from searching brand j may be rewritten:

$$\text{EVSI} = \sigma_m \Phi\left(\frac{\delta_y}{\sigma_m}\right) \qquad (2.59)$$

where

$$\delta_y = \begin{cases} E(U_1) - E(U_j), & \text{for } j \neq 1 \\ E(U_1) - E(U_2), & \text{for } j = 1 \end{cases}$$

Φ = integral of the standard normal distribution

The extension of this formula to all brands is analogous to equation (2.59). The problem of the consumer in deciding which piece of information, y, to process at time t then becomes

$$\text{Maximize} \qquad \text{EVSI}_t^y - c^y \qquad (2.60a)$$

$$\text{Subject to} \qquad \text{EVSI}_t^y - c^y > D \geq 0 \qquad (2.60b)$$

That is, maximize the value of the next piece of information minus processing costs as long as the search has a value of greater than D, a threshold below which it is not worth the effort of searching.

Hagerty and Aaker use this framework to show that more information will be processed if there are large reductions in EVSI, brands are close in terms of utility, and there is high initial uncertainty. The type of information that will be searched is that which leads to the greatest reduction in information uncertainty, is associated with attributes with large importance weights, and is uncorrelated with information that has already been discovered.

They also use the framework to predict when attribute processing will take place and when brand-based processing will occur. Attribute processing is examining all brands on the basis of one attribute and then moving on to search the next attribute. Brand-based processing examines all the attribute values of a brand before examining the next brand.

Included in Hagerty and Aaker's model of optimal information search is a rule that specifies how consumers incorporate new information into their existing belief structures. This is an area that has recently attracted increasing attention. Updated perceptions are generally a weighted average of consumers' beliefs and the sample information discovered. In the information updating part of Meyer and Sathi's (1985) model of consumer choice during product learning, they suggest that updated beliefs about attribute k's level in alternative i after n pieces of information y_{ik}^n is a function of baseline beliefs y_{ik}^0 and the mean value of the attribute suggested by the new information $\bar{y}_{ik}$:

$$y_{ik}^n = \Sigma_p b_p \bar{y}_{ik}^p + (1 - \Sigma b_p)^{y_{ik}^0} \tag{2.61}$$

where

b_p = weight given to the pth piece of information (relative to a weight of one for prior beliefs)

A more formal updating rule is given by Bayesian analysis. Bayes' rule says that if prior beliefs about attribute k are normally distributed with mean y_{ik}' and variance $\sigma_{ik}'^2$ and new information is received also distributed normally (mean $\bar{y}_{ik}$ and variance σ_y^2), then beliefs after updating will be normally distributed with mean y_{ik}'' variance $\sigma_{ik}''^2$ (DeGroot, 1970) where

$$y_{ik}'' = \frac{\sigma_y^2 y_{ik}' + \sigma_{ik}'^2 \bar{y}_{ik}}{\sigma_y^2 + \sigma_{ik}'^2} \tag{2.62a}$$

and

$$\sigma_{ik}''^2 = \left[\frac{\sigma_y^2}{(\sigma_y^2 + \sigma_{ik}'^2)} \right]^2 \sigma_{ik}'^2 + \left[\frac{\sigma_{ik}'^2}{(\sigma_y^2 + \sigma_{ik}'^2)} \right]^2 \sigma_y^2$$
$$= \frac{\sigma_{ik}'^2 \sigma_y^2}{\sigma_y^2 + \sigma_{ik}'^2} \tag{2.62b}$$

The prior and sampling distribution are called a normal-normal conjugate pair. Other conjugate pairs of distributions include the beta-binomial, gamma-Poisson, and gamma-exponential. (See Oren and Schwartz, 1988, for an application of beta/binomial updating.) Studies testing the assumption of

Bayesian updating in consumer decision processes have had mixed findings (see Roberts and Urban, 1988, p. 173, for a review). However, in the absence of an obvious alternative contender, Bayes' rule has had considerable popularity in dynamic models.

We have discussed the way in which attribute perceptions (and uncertainty) change over time in this section. In the next section we will look at the structure of perceptions and how they relate to underlying consumer preferences.

Perceptual-Evaluation Models

A set of useful consumer behavior models describe consumer beliefs about brands in a marketplace. Beliefs about products (perceptions) can be measured directly by asking consumers how much of a feature they perceive a certain product to contain, or they can be inferred, by asking consumers how similar certain products are and then inferring what discriminates between different products.

Because we search for parsimony in our description of consumer decision making and also because evidence suggests that consumers do not process large numbers of attributes in practice, we often try to capture the difference between products with fewer dimensions than those used in data collection. There is debate as to whether these reduced space dimensions are actually used by the consumer or if they just form a useful approximation of decision process; in either case, we can derive managerially useful information from looking at perceptions in this way.

The two analytical approaches most frequently used to derive evaluation criteria and build perceptual maps are decompositional methods, based on nonmetric multidimensional scaling (NMS), and compositional methods, based on factor analysis (FA). NMS procedures infer dimensions that discriminate between consumers' evaluations of different products based on brand interrelationships, while FA methods take explicit attribute data and distill them into underlying dimensions or factors. It is beyond the scope of this chapter to present these procedures in detail, but we sketch the main ideas next.

Multidimensional Scaling. Multidimensional scaling (MDS) is a set of procedures in which a reduced space depicting product alternatives reflects perceived similarities and dissimilarities between products by the interproduct distances. Different types of multidimensional scaling may be distinguished on the basis of

- The type of data input to the model
- The number of modes
- The geometric model used to analyze the data

The type of data determines the type of algorithm appropriate for analysis. Ordinal data, such as those obtained when pairs of products are ranked from most similar to least similar are analyzed using *nonmetric* methods. Interval- or ratio-scaled data, based on a rating of how similar a pair of products are (on a 9-point similarity scale, for example) are analyzed using *metric* multidimensional scaling. Recent research suggests that the results from these two approaches tend to be consistent.

The number of modes refers to how many different characteristics the input data have. Single-mode data have one dimension; for example, a single respondent's dissimilarity ratings on pairs of products. Two-mode data might have respondents and products as its two modes; for example, a ranking of different respondents' preferences for a number of products. Three modes might include individuals, products, and product attributes.

The geometric model refers to the algorithm used to analyze the data and how the results are presented. Green and Rao (1972) provide a review of the classical techniques available.

Single-Mode, Nonmetric Scaling.　Exhibit 2.14 gives an example of the input and output of an NMS study of the Smith family's washing machine purchase. The dimensions, as seen from that exhibit, might be interpreted as "efficiency" (ability to get the wash clean) and "capability" (tub capacity, wash cycle options, etc.). The idea behind MDS is to have the interproduct distances in Exhibit 2.14(b) have the same rank order as the direct similarity judgments in (a).

Let δ_{ij} denote the perceived dissimilarity between product alternatives i and j, which can either be obtained directly or be derived from distances using attribute rating scales. Then, with NMS, we find a configuration of points (the product alternatives) in a space of lowest dimensionality such that the ranking of interpoint distances d_{ij} is as close as possible to the ranking of the original dissimilarities δ_{ij}. This result is called a monotonic relationship between the d_{ij}'s and the δ_{ij}'s. To reach its objective, NMS algorithms minimize a quantity called stress:

$$\text{Stress} = \left[\frac{\Sigma_{i<j}\,(\hat{d}_{ij} - d_{ij})^2}{\Sigma_{i<j}\,d_{ij}^2} \right]^{1/2} \tag{2.63}$$

where $\hat{d}_{ij}$ is a distance as close as possible to the d_{ij} but is monotonic with the original dissimilarities δ_{ij}.

For a given dimensionality the configuration retained is the one that minimizes the stress function. The resultant map shows the relationship between the various products in the market. It may be arbitrarily reflected or rotated to aid interpretability.

Two-Mode Multidimensional Scaling.　Most of the ideas behind single-mode

	BS	WE	WB	WF	KM	KS	AP	PC	AF
Blanco "Style"	16	17	2	19	10	13	21	22	
White "Econowash"			1	11	15	14	25	31	30
White "Basic"				8	7	9	27	32	34
White "Featurest"					12	3	20	24	26
Kanji "Mid Range"						4	29	35	36
Kanji "Super Family"							23	28	33
ACE "Premium"								5	18
ACE "Power Clean"									6
ACE "Full Cycle"									

(a)　Similarities between pairs of considered washing machines
(1 = most similar pair, 36 = least similar pair)

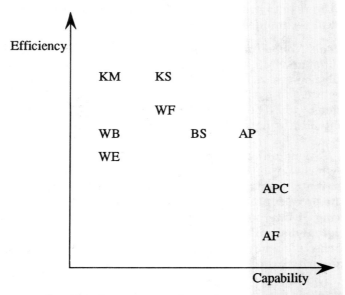

(b)　Resultant perceptual map from analyzing similarity data in (a)

EXHIBIT 2.14　Nonmetric multidimensional scaling analysis of Fred and Sally's perceptions of the washing machine market.

multidimensional scaling also apply to two-mode analysis. Two-mode maps are often called joint spaces because they allow two types of data to be plotted on the same graph. So, if we collect different respondents' preferences for a variety of products, we can work out both the implied positioning of brands that best reproduces the respondents' preference ordering, and we can also plot a respondent's preferences in the form of an ideal point. Two-mode analysis enables us to compare one brand's position to that of another, to view the different preferences of consumers for a segmentation study, and to examine the relation between individuals' preferences and products in the market. The process of deriving these two mode maps is called *unfolding*. There may be substantial differences in a consumer's perceptions of brand interrelationships at the perception and preference stages of the decision process, so the results of single-mode MDS based on similarity data and two-mode MDS based on preference data may vary.

There are also a number of other ways in which two mode data can be presented. Brands can be represented as points, while respondents' preferences may be represented as vectors. This is called a *projection model* and is more appropriate when the dimensions are monotonically increasing in preference ("more is better" for each dimension). An individual's preference for brands can be obtained by projecting the brand onto the individual's ideal vector.

Models that measure brands' similarity or ordering in this way are called *direct models*. We can also derive MDS maps from attribute data on brands, indirectly. If we have a respondent's perceptions of the attribute levels of a number of products, we can construct a two-mode map in which products are again represented by points and the attributes by vectors. This is a very popular way to work out what the dimensions should be called (following a technique called PROFIT, developed by Carroll and Chang, 1964).

APPLICATION _____

Moore and Winer (1987) provide an example of the use of multidimensional scaling to a management situation and its integration with other decision-making tools. Building on the work of DeSarbo and Rao (1986) whose GENFOLD2 model showed how linear constraints could be used to incorporate marketing-mix variables into MDS models, they start with an unfolding model based on "pick any" data. "Pick any" data are provided when respondents are not constrained in how many objects they can choose from a set of stimuli. "All the brands you have ever purchased" is one example of a "pick any" process. Moore and Winer construct joint spaces at five points in time from cross-sectional choice data showing the preferences of households clustered into segments (homogeneous with respect to their ideal points), and average product positions (Exhibit 2.15).

Segment-level response functions were estimated over time by relating the distance of each brand from each segment's ideal point as a function of the marketing mix (price and advertising) and feedback effects (previous period's market share).

Market share was then estimated by the distance of each product's perceived position from the relevant market segment's ideal point.

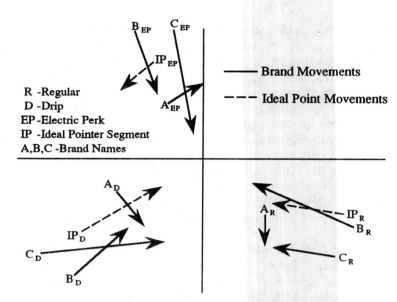

R -Regular
D -Drip
EP -Electric Perk
IP -Ideal Pointer Segment
A,B,C -Brand Names

——— Brand Movements

– – – Ideal Point Movements

EXHIBIT 2.15 Consumer perceptions of brands in the coffee market and ideal points of segments, including movement over time. (*Source:* Moore and Winer, 1987, p. 31.)

Algebraically,

$$RD_{ijk} = \alpha_0 + \alpha_1 MS_{ijk-1} + \alpha_2 RP_{ijk} + \alpha_3 AS_{ijk-1}$$

$$+ \alpha_4 B_1 + \alpha_5 B_2 + \mu_{ijk} \qquad (2.64)$$

$$MS_{ijk} = \beta_0 + \beta_1 RD_{ijk} + \beta_2 B_1 + \beta_3 B_2 + \varepsilon_{ijk} \qquad (2.65)$$

where

RD_{ijk} = relative distance between brand i and the ideal point of segment j in period k,

MS_{ijk} = market share of brand i in segment j in period k

$RP_{ij}k$ = relative price of brand i to segment j in period k

AS_{ijk} = advertising share of brand i in segment j in period k

$\mu_{ijk}, \varepsilon_{ijk}$ = error terms

B_1 and B_2 are brand dummies and the α's and β's are parameters. In fitting the model for equation (2.64), lagged market share, relative price, and the B_2 dummy were all significant at the 10% level at least, giving an R^2 of 0.29. The fit of relative distance of a brand from the ideal point in explaining market share (equation 2.65) was strong, explaining 87% of the variation, with all variables significant at the 1% level.

Moore and Winer conducted a successful test of the model using an advertising campaign for Pepsi Cola. The power of this approach is that it not only combines two powerful sets of tools—MDS and market response analysis—it is able to do so using a single data source, making it easy to apply.

New approaches to MDS are leading to a revival of its use. These approaches include the incorporation of asymmetric relationships, development of an error theory, and the use of alternative data sources and formats. The benefits of asymmetric MDS (for example, DEDICOM, applied by Harshman et al., 1982) are that it greatly improves the fit for a given number of dimensions and there are interesting managerial insights from allowing asymmetric similarities. The cost of unraveling these interesting asymmetries is that we can no longer represent them in Euclidean space, and we lose our ability to draw perceptual maps. If a traditional MDS analysis is first conducted, then a map can be constructed and asymmetric analysis can follow, pointing to key areas of unequal effects, allowing an evaluation of the adequacy of a symmetric model, and also providing supplementary insight on the market structure.

A second form of advance in MDS techniques is provided by MacKay and Zinnes (1986). They show that when there is measurement error, deterministic MDS models can be unstable. They derive maximum-likelihood estimation techniques to construct maps that are more robust and provide an error theory that enables hypothesis testing on perceptual maps.

Another recent advance in MDS involves its application to a variety of alternative data sources. Holbrook, Moore, and Winer (1982) demonstrated the use of Levine's procedure to marketing to allow the analysis of two-mode "pick any" data to construct maps of interbrand and interrespondent relationships. Both DeSarbo and Hoffman (1987) and Elrod (1988) provide excellent literature reviews (Table 1 in both cases) of work that has been performed in deriving maps from individual-level choice data. Katahira (1990) uses this combination of analysis of choice data with multidimensional scaling to show different preference functions can be incorporated into the mapping process.

Several issues need to be considered in the use of multidimensional scaling:

Number of products needed: Klahr (1969) shows that at least eight products are needed for a good two-dimensional map. Green and Wind (1973) suggest that the number of dimensions should be less than one-third of the number of products. Given that five seems to be a median for the size of consumers' consideration sets in most categories, consumers may not have sufficient familiarity with enough brands to complete the task adequately. Conversely, n brands lead to $n(n-1)/2$ dissimilarity judgments, and so the task can become onerous if the number of considered brands is too large.

Determining the number and names of dimensions: As in factor analysis, discussed shortly, there is little theory to guide the selection of the number of dimensions. However, the stress measure (equation 2.63) can be plotted against k (the number of dimensions) to determine when marginal changes in stress are becoming small. Naming can be assisted if attribute perceptions are available using the technique proposed by Carroll and Chang (1964).

Reliability, validity, and robustness: The stability of the techniques has been subject to considerable scrutiny. Moore and Lehmann (1982) showed that MDS spaces are relatively stable as new products are introduced. They found less movement for the new brand over time if the name was descriptive of the product attributes. Malhotra, Jain, and Pinson (1988) tested the robustness of MDS to incomplete data. Even with 60% of the data missing, correlations between map positions based on incomplete data and those based on complete data were still over 0.4. Finally, in a test of the reliability and validity of MDS, Malhotra (1987) found that at the individual-level correlations of interpoint distances derived from both dissimilarities and from a semantic differential were of the order of 0.4 to 0.5.

Factor Analysis. Factor analysis was originally developed in connection with efforts to identify the major factors making up human intelligence. Educational and psychological researchers did not believe that every test in an educational battery measured a different facet of intelligence. In fact, test scores for certain pairs of tests were highly intercorrelated, indicating that a more basic mental ability underlies test performance. Factor analysis was developed to explain these intercorrelations. It identified three basic factors: verbal ability, quantitative ability, and spatial ability. Since that time, factor analysis has been applied to many other problems and is a frequently used technique in performing product-evaluation analyses in marketing.

The basic factor analysis model assumes that original perceptual ratings about a product are generated by a small number of latent variables, or factors and that the variance observed in each original perceptual variable is accounted for partly by a set of common factors and partly by a factor specific to that variable. The common factors account for the correlations observed among the original variables. This model can be written as

$$x_{ijk} = a_{k1}F_{ij1} + \cdots + a_{kR}F_{ijR} + d_k y_{ijk} + \varepsilon_{ijk} \qquad (2.66)$$

where

R = number of factors common to all items

x_{ijk} = person i's rating of product j on attribute k

a_{k1} = effect of common factor 1 on attribute k (called a loading)

F_{ij1} = person i's score of product j on factor 1

d_k = weight of unique factor y_{ijk}

y_{ijk} = unique factor of product j on item k for person i

ε_{ijk} = error term

Thus, in common factor analysis, the perceptual model has each observed variable being described in terms of a set of $R(R < k)$ common factors plus a factor unique to the original observed variable. Generally, the original items are standardized [if x_i^* is an original score, then $x_i = (x_i^* - \bar{x})/\sigma_x$ is used], so that certain relationships hold:

The *loadings* $\{a_{kr}\}$ represent the correlation (ρ) between (hypothetical) factor r and the variable k, and a_{kr}^2 represents the fraction of variance in variable k accounted for by factor r:

$$\rho(F_r, x_k) = a_{kr} \tag{2.67}$$

The *communality* h_k^2 expresses the percentage of the variance in variable k accounted for by the R common factors:

$$h_k^2 = \Sigma_r a_{kr}^2 \tag{2.68}$$

The *eigenvalue* λ_r represents the contribution of each factor in the total variance in the original variables:

$$\lambda_r = \Sigma_k a_{kr}^2 \tag{2.69}$$

In a specific application it is not uncommon to extract a small number of factors that account for the major part of the total variance (80–90%). However, the larger the number of attributes, the smaller will be the explained variance of a given number of factors. In these cases factor analysis is deemed successful in having identified a small number of composite dimensions that underlie the set of given variables (or item ratings).

Another useful aspect of factor analysis is the construction of a perceptual map—the matrix of factor scores—that describes the factor scores as a linear function of the original ratings:

$$F_{ijr} = b_{r1}x_{ij1} + \cdots + b_{rK}x_{ijK} + \text{error} \tag{2.70}$$

where $r = 1, \ldots, R$ for each individual i.

The perceived position of product j is usually constructed by averaging the F_{ijr} over the respondents, i:

$$\{F_{*j1}, \ldots, F_{*jR}\} = \{(\Sigma_i F_{ij1})/I, \ldots, (\Sigma_i F_{ijR})/I\} \qquad (2.71)$$

By inputting the original items (x's) into equations (2.70) and (2.71), the average positions of a product (or set of products, if multiple products are being evaluated) in a reduced factor space can be constructed.

An alternative form to common factor analysis is principal components factor analysis. Principal components factor analysis is the same as that expressed in equation (2.66) with the exception that the unique factors, y_{ijk}, are omitted. All the variation between the ratings of stimuli are attributed to the underlying factors (F_{ijr}). Studies comparing principal components and common factor analysis generally find similar results.

APPLICATION _____

Hauser and Shugan (1980) analyzed the views of scientists and managers at Los Alamos Scientific Laboratory on telephone and personal visits and three new product concepts in communications. They generated 25 items (attributes), using focus group–type procedures, a selection of which appears in Exhibit 2.16.

They ran a common factor analysis with the ratings of each of five products by 41 managers on the 25 scales. Exhibit 2.17(a) gives the factor loadings relating the resulting two factors to the 25 attributes following a varimax rotation. By underlining the heavy loadings (those with correlations of 0.40 or larger) and examining the relationships among the heavy loadings, the authors interpreted those factors as "effectiveness" and "ease of use." The product map is produced by using the matrix of factor score coefficients shown in Exhibit 2.17(b). Suppose that, when standardized, individual 1's ratings for the telephone are $X_{1,1} = 1.5$, $X_{1,2} = 0.8$, ..., $X_{1,25} = -1.3$. Using equation (2.70), the estimate of the effectiveness factor, E, for the telephone becomes

$$F_{1,E} = -0.10 \times 1.5 - 0.08 \times 0.8 + \cdots + 0.07 \times (-1.3) = 0.3$$

where the b_{i1}'s come from the first column of Exhibit 2.17(b).

When averaged across individuals, these factor scores produce a perceptual map as shown in Exhibit 2.18. The map has a reduced number of dimensions characterizing the way individuals perceive products in the space. As indicated in Exhibit 2.18 the space provides room for a new product opportunity, a point we will return to in Chapter 11.

Hauser (1984) shows how this analysis, when related to preference, can be used for product redesign and segmentation strategies.

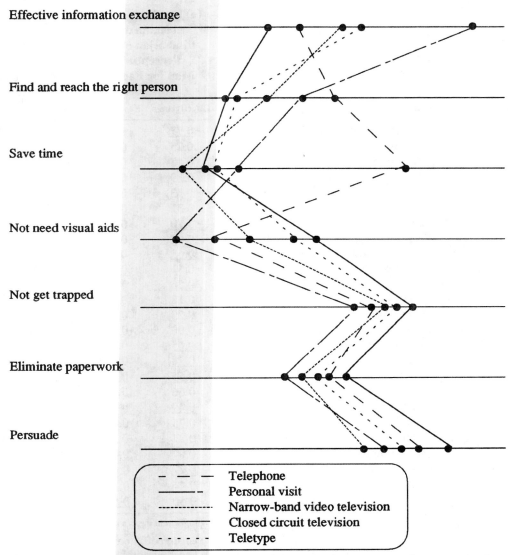

EXHIBIT 2.16   Partial snake plot of scientists' and managers' perceptions of communications options. (*Source:* Urban and Hauser, 1980, p. 191.)

A series of analytical issues that must be addressed in factor analysis includes the following:

The Number of Factors.   There is no well-developed theory here; judgment and intuition are most frequently combined with the following criteria:

Attributes†	(a) Loadings Used to Name the Dimension of the Perceptual Map for Factor Analysis		(b) Factor-Score Coefficients Used to Estimate Product Positions in Perceptual Map	
	Effectiveness	Ease of Use	Effectiveness	Ease of Use
1. Effective Information Exchange (-)	- 0.77	- 0.17	- 0.10	- 0.04
2. Find and Reach Right Person	0.25	0.43	- 0.08	0.11
3. Save Time	0.17	0.47	- 0.05	0.26
4. Not Need Visual Aids	0.39	- 0.16	0.06	0.04
5. Get Trapped (-)	- 0.33	- 0.20	0.07	0.06
6. Eliminate Paperwork	0.31	0.43	0.02	0.18
7. Persuade (-)	- 0.70	- 0.20	0.13	0.01
8. Focus on Issues	- 0.04	- 0.07	0.01	- 0.00
9. All Forms of Information	0.65	- 0.18	- 0.02	- 0.05
10. Real Hassle (-)	- 0.11	- 0.83	0.07	- 0.29
11. Control Impression	0.56	0.07	0.03	- 0.04
12. Security	0.18	0.11	- 0.00	- 0.02
13. Plan in Advance (-)	0.23	- 0.44	0.04	0.00
14. Eliminate Red Tape	- 0.00	- 0.21	0.00	0.01
15. Monitor People, Operations, Experiments	0.65	0.15	0.05	0.01
16. Interaction	0.78	0.05	0.25	- 0.07
17. Solve Problems (-)	- 0.55	- 0.27	- 0.02	- 0.09
18. Express Feelings	0.66	0.17	0.13	- 0.05
19. Misinterpret (-)	- 0.49	0.00	0.00	0.05
20. Group Discussion	0.75	0.05	0.20	- 0.08
21. Inexpensive	- 0.27	0.52	- 0.04	0.09
22. Quick Response	0.07	0.71	- 0.04	0.20
23. Enhance Idea Development	0.77	0.09	0.22	- 0.05
24. Commitment	0.44	0.32	0.06	0.05
25. Maintain Contact	0.50	0.52	0.07	0.18

†(-) indicates question was worded so that a high attribute rating would mean a poor evaluation

EXHIBIT 2.17 Factor loadings and factor score coefficients from communications options study. (*Source:* Urban and Hauser (1980), pp. 200–205.)

1. Stop extracting factors when the eigenvalue drops below 1 (such a factor explains less variance than an average item).

2. Stop extracting factors before the plot of explained variance versus the number of factors levels off, a "scree" test.

3. Stop factoring when you see a similar result with a random data set in a Monte Carlo simulation.

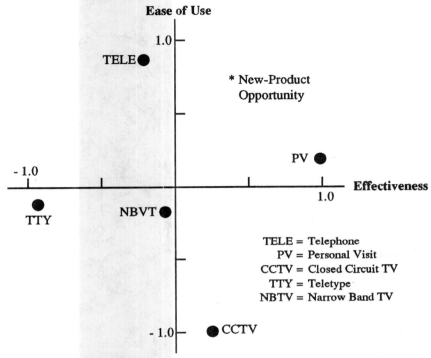

Ease of Use

1.0

TELE●

* New-Product
Opportunity

PV ●

- 1.0

Effectiveness

1.0

NBVT●

●
TTY

TELE = Telephone
PV = Personal Visit
CCTV = Closed Circuit TV
TTY = Teletype
NBTV = Narrow Band TV

- 1.0

●CCTV

EXHIBIT 2.18 Perceptual map for communications options. (*Source:* Hauser and Shugan, 1980, p. 303.)

4. Select the number of factors that gives the most interpretable factor
solution.

Factor Naming. A combination of intuition plus examination of the factor
matrices will generally allow meaningful interpretations.

Rotation. In most studies the factor loadings are rotated to a factor matrix
in which each variable has loadings mainly on one factor. This aids interpretability. A number of analytical definitions of simple structure exist, with
the varimax criterion possibly being most widely used in marketing applications.

There are several other difficulties associated with factor analysis. Note
that in the Hauser-Shugan study, regression estimates of factors are used in
place of actual factors (factor scores that one cannot determine since they are
elements of theoretical constructs). These factors are interpreted, post hoc here,
by reference to their loadings.

Problems also arise because we normally collect data for different respondents' evaluations of different products according to different attributes.
As Srinivasan, Abeele, and Butaye (1989) point out, there are a number of

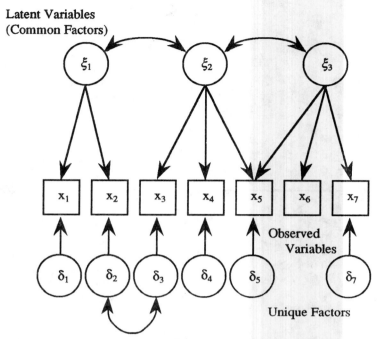

Latent Variables
(Common Factors)

Observed
Variables

Unique Factors

EXHIBIT 2.19 Example of a confirmatory factor analysis model. (*Source:* Long, 1983, p. 14.)

ways that we can analyze the variations between these measures. We can look *within* products to examine how different respondents perceive the same product or groups of products, we can look *among* products to find out how a respondent or group of respondents evaluate different products, or we can look at the *total variance* across respondents and products. Differences may also be accommodated by grouping respondents. Dillon, Frederick, and Tangpan-ichdee (1982) show how to test for differences between respondent groups.

Confirmatory Factor Analysis. The form of common factor analysis dis-cussed so far is called exploratory factor analysis. It places no constraints on which variables load on the various factors and assumes that all unique fac-tors are independent. In confirmatory factor analysis, the researcher imposes constraints motivated by theory as to which common factors are correlated, which observed variables affect which factors, and which pairs of unique fac-tors are correlated.

Thus, if we represent the relationship between the variables that we observe (x's) and the underlying common factors (F's) and unique factors (y's) in Exhibit 2.19 then the relationship between ξ_1 and ξ_2 would not have been permitted in exploratory factor analysis and all the relationships between the factors (F) and observed variables (x) would have had to be included.

In confirmatory factor analysis we can constrain some of the a_{kr}'s in equation (2.66) to zero and test that assumption; we can also allow the unique factors $\{y_{li}\}$ to be correlated. If we assume that the common and unique factors are normally distributed, then we can test hypotheses concerning the appropriateness of alternative structures. Confirmatory factor analysis provides a unique maximum-likelihood estimate of a predetermined structure and also provides a chi-squared statistic to test the number of factors necessary to account for the correlation matrix. The seminal work in this area was developed by Jöreskog and Sörbom (1979). An excellent source for the fundamentals of the approach is Long (1983). (Appendix D provides additional details.)

Comparison of MDS and Factor Analytic Approaches.   A number of studies have compared the application and performance of multidimensional scaling and factor analytic methods of building perceptual maps. Shocker and Srinivasan (1979) provide a detailed review of the use of these techniques in new product development and concept evaluation. In comparing the performance of factor analysis with multidimensional scaling, Hauser and Koppelman (1979) conclude that factor analysis is superior from the standpoint of predictive ability, interpretability, and ease of use. However, the difference in nature between the two techniques will lead to differences in the prevalence of their application. In markets that are relatively new and in which the cognitive structure of consumers is not well understood or well developed, multidimensional scaling on dissimilarity data might be preferred because it makes fewer assumptions about the criteria on which consumers will evaluate products. Where there is a solid, historical structure for the product category, factor analysis may be preferred since it will add diagnostic richness on which attributes are causing the positioning of products on the perceptual map. In the absence of a well-developed theory of the formation of evaluation criteria, the researcher might well be advised to perform both analyses in search of a convergent picture of the market.

Several other methods have been applied to modeling perceptual spaces, particularly multiple discriminant analysis and correspondence analysis. Multiple discriminant analysis (MDA) is a method of determining which variables explain the groups that different stimuli belong to. For example, MDA could be used to determine which combination of intelligence, age, education, and income best predicts innovators in a population. The analysis also extracts the second most successful (independent) combination of discriminating variables. This forms another method of distilling perceptual data. We can construct perceptual maps using the resultant discriminant functions that are combinations of the underlying attributes, in this case constructed on their ability to differentiate between group memberships.

Categorical data are common in marketing, partly because they are easy to collect. Correspondence analysis is a method that summarizes both the rows and columns of such data collections in a lower-dimensional space (e.g., what are the underlying types of brands in the category and what are the factor dimensions underlying product attributes). The flexibility of data format is achieved at a cost of not being able to interpret interpoint distances (see Hoffman and Franke, 1986).

Models of Attitude and Preference Formation

The previous section dealt with the issue of *perceptions*—what we believe about products. This section discusses *attitudes*—how favorably disposed we feel toward those same products. The basic concept behind attitude measurement and modeling is that the way we feel about something determines how we act when we are presented with a purchase opportunity. Advertising expenditures are often justified on the basis that such investments can modify perceptions and attitudes and, hence, behavior.

An attitude can be defined as an overall tendency to respond consistently favorably or unfavorably toward an object. Most models of attitude formation assume that choice behavior, as well as attitudes, are determined by judgments on specific attributes of the choice object (perceptions). These models transform consumer judgments based on attribute evaluations to a single-dimensional scale of brand attitude, frequently after first distilling the attribute information using the perceptual mapping techniques described in the previous section.

The product attributes must be salient; that is, they must be the ones that are considered important by consumers and ones on which the various brands or products are perceived to differ. Thus, the major challenge in this section is to take the perceptions that we studied in the previous section and understand their relationship to the consumer's overall attitude toward the product. (See Hughes, 1974, for an overview of methods for attitude identification and measurement.)

Models of attitude structure can generally be classified by whether they are compensatory or noncompensatory. In a compensatory model the weakness of a brand on one attribute can be compensated for by strength on another, and the attributes are summed to determine the favorability or unfavorability of the attitude toward the brand. In noncompensatory models usually only two or three attributes are used to evaluate a product, and shortcomings on any one attribute cannot be compensated by more favorable levels on another. A third alternative is that both types of rules could be used in sequence, called a phased decision rule (Wright and Barbour, 1977).

We review models of preference by first examining simple linear single equation models in which consumers are assumed to maximize their expected utility based on their perceptions of the attributes that considered products will offer. Next, we consider an extension of confirmatory factor analysis that enables us to look at the structure of preferences and beliefs using multiequation models. Then, we relax the assumption of linear utility, allowing for general forms of risk aversion and interdependence of attributes. After this review of compensatory preference functions, we describe some of the major types of noncompensatory preference models.

Compensatory Models.

The Fishbein Model.   Fishbein (1963) developed a theory of attitude formation and change based on behavioral learning theory, which can be summarized as

$$A_o = \Sigma_i b_i a_i \tag{2.72}$$

where

A_o = attitude toward any psychological object
b_i = belief (subjective likelihood) that object possesses attribute i
a_i = evaluation (goodness or badness) of attribute i

In this model the overall attitude toward a brand is viewed as the product of the beliefs about a brand along a particular attribute and the value of the attribute, summed over all attributes. For example, consider a facial cleanser. We would consider the degree to which a respondent believes a brand supplies moisturizing and the relative goodness or badness of moisturizing as an attribute.

The Fishbein model has seen a number of studies evaluating its relevance to marketing situations. (See Lutz and Bettman, 1977, and Wilkie and Pessemier, 1973, for reviews.) However, marketing researchers have had difficulty in actually applying it in its strictest sense. The use of a probability scale to measure brand attributes proved cumbersome, and so simple scales were proposed as measures of beliefs (e.g., the rating of degrees of moisturizing from 7 = very moisturizing to 1 = not moisturizing). But, as Lutz and Bettman (1977) note, this modification compromises the theory behind the Fishbein model.

Belief/Importance Model.   This model was first proposed in marketing by Bass and Talarzyk (1972). They state that the overall evaluation of a brand is a function of beliefs about the attributes possessed by the brand (b_{oi}) weighted by the importance of each attribute (I_i):

$$A_o = \Sigma_i b_{oi} I_i \tag{2.73}$$

Evidence comparing this model to the Fishbein model is mixed: Bettman, Capon, and Lutz (1975) report superior results from the Fishbein model, while Mazis and Ahtola (1975) report superior results from the beliefs/importance model.

A variety of methods have been advanced for imputing the relative importances of attributes by relating brand preferences to the amount of each attribute that these preferred brands contained. These methods include multiple regression, linear programming, and monotonic analysis of variance. For a review of data collection techniques and the relative advantages of associated estimation methods, see Shocker and Srinivasan (1979), Green and Srinivasan (1978), or Horsky and Rao (1984).

Extended Fishbein Model.   The ambiguous results obtained from using multiattribute models to predict behavior prompted Fishbein and others to reassess the beliefs/evaluation model to make it more relevant to marketing (Fishbein and Ajzen, 1975). The most widely known extension has others, apart from the person making the purchase, influencing the decision in some decision circumstances. In particular,

$$BI = \Sigma_i a_i b_i + \Sigma_j SNB_j MC_j \tag{2.74}$$

where

$$
\begin{aligned}
BI \quad &= \text{behavioral intent} \\
a_i, b_i \quad &= \text{defined as before in equation (2.72)} \\
SNB_j \quad &= \text{social normative belief, which relates what an individual considers is expected of him by an external social group on scale } j \\
MC_j \quad &= \text{motivation to comply with these expectations}
\end{aligned}
$$

The extended Fishbein model has generally been shown to perform better than the original model. In addition, Wilson, Matthews, and Harvey (1975) and others found that attitudes toward the purchase of a brand and behavioral intention were more closely related to behavior than were attitudes toward the brand itself. Thus, it may be more relevant to ask consumers whether their teeth will get white if they use Ultra Brite than to ask whether they think Ultra Brite whitens teeth. Bearden and Etzel (1982) in testing the importance of reference group influences (social normative beliefs) found that they were higher for goods which are publicly consumed rather than privately, and for goods which were more luxuries than necessities.

Ideal-Point Model.   An offshoot of the belief/importance model, the ideal-point model, requires a consumer's rating of an ideal brand along with his ratings of the actual brands being analyzed (although ideal levels of attributes can be imputed in the same way that importance weights are estimated).

EXAMPLE _____

Lehmann (1971a) modeled television show choice as follows:

$$A_o = \Sigma_i V_i |B_{io} - I_i|^k \tag{2.75}$$

where

A_o = overall attitude (preference for a TV show)

V_i = weight attached to TV show characteristic i (action, suspense, humor, etc.)

B_{io} = belief about show on dimension i

I_i = ideal position on dimension i

k = distance metric

This model was substantially better at predicting behavior than were models based on demographic variables. Attributes should be included in an ideal point form if, beyond some level (the ideal point), there are negative utility returns for further increases in the attribute. With the width of a car, for example, any rational consumer will find some widths too wide and others not wide enough, implying an ideal level between those extremes. With miles per gallon, however, for most consumers it is likely to be the more the better if all other attributes stay the same, so a belief/importance formulation would be more appropriate.

Structural Modeling of Preferences. We have seen how factor analysis can be used in a confirmatory way, as well as to explore the relationship between different measures of a number of variables and their underlying constructs. This framework may be extended to test the relationships between the resultant structures. In the models we have seen in this section so far, there is one measure of attitude of preference, and we have attempted to understand it in terms of underlying product attributes. In structural equation modeling there are several physical and/or psychological states, and we test the relationship between them and a number of external factors. Thus a structural equation model may be

$$y_{ij} = \alpha + \Sigma_\ell \beta_{i\ell} y_{\ell j} + \Sigma_k \gamma_{ik} x_{kj} \tag{2.76}$$

where

$y_{\ell j}$ = consumer's response on construct ℓ for product j

x_{kj} = level of attribute k for product j

α, $\beta_{i\ell}$, and γ_{ik} = parameters

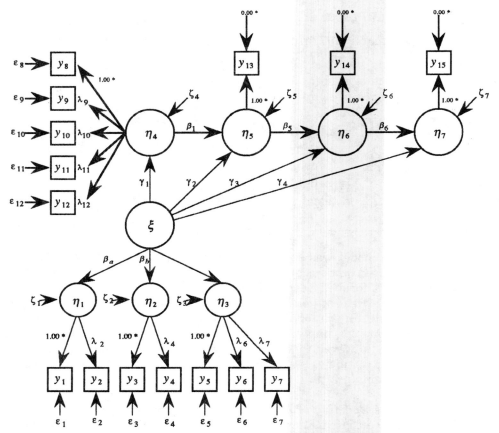

EXHIBIT 2.20 Causal model relating expectancy value model to attitude to the act, behavioral intention, and actual behavior at two points in time. (*Source:* Bagozzi, 1982, p. 578.)

These models lend themselves to diagrammatic representation. For example, Bagozzi (1982) tested the relation between the expectancy value attitude (ξ), measured by three dimensions (η_1, η_2, and η_3), attitude toward the act (η_4), behavioral intentions (η_5), and actual behavior, immediately (η_6) and after a period of four months (η_7) for voluntary blood donations. The model is illustrated in Exhibit 2.20. The relations between the y's and the η's correspond to the confirmatory factor analysis technique of measuring the theoretical constructs, η_1 to η_7. The β's and γ's represent the relationship between the constructs, that is, the structural equations relating the underlying variables in the model.

Incorporating Uncertainty. In some ways the models of this section are related to the determination of objectives in Appendix 3. We have assumed, as in Appendix 3, that we have multiple criteria of varying importance and that we wish to combine them into an overall value or preference function. In the literature on decision theory all these functions would be called value functions. They translate (map) a set of attributes, known with certainty, into a function called value. But there are dangers with this simplified approach. What about a new product? Is it reasonable to use the same model to predict choice when the attributes of some products are known with more certainty than others? Is it realistic to assume constant increases in value for given increases in attribute levels, as is done in equation (2.73)? Can we reasonably assume the value derived from one attribute is independent of the level of other attributes? Here, again, utility theory and the direct assessment of a utility function across attributes are useful, both for testing these assumptions and for developing models when they are violated. Exhibit 2.21 illustrates how risk can be measured in the direct assessment of a consumer's utility function. The methods of Appendix C apply here to test the linearity and independence of attribute utilities. See Keeney and Raiffa (1976) for an axiomatic development of decision analysis, Hauser and Urban (1979) for an application in marketing, Eliashberg (1980) for comparison of utility and value functions and Eliashberg and Hauser (1985) for a treatment of measurement errors in assessing utility functions under conditions of uncertainty.

Noncompensatory Models. The multiattribute models described earlier assume that individuals evaluate brands across a number of different attributes and then determine the most preferred brand by summing across these attributes. Nakanishi and Bettman (1974) suggest that such an evaluation process may be too complex for many consumer goods; consumers may evaluate brands on two or three key attributes and eliminate brands if they are not adequate on any one attribute. We review several of the more common noncompensatory models in the paragraphs that follow.

Conjunctive Model. In a conjunctive model a consumer prefers a brand only if it meets certain minimum, acceptable standards on all of a number of key dimensions. If any one attribute is deficient, the product is eliminated from contention.

Let

y_{jk} = perceived level of attribute k in brand j

T_{jk} = minimum threshold level that is acceptable (negatively valued attributes such as price that have a maximum level can be multiplied by -1)

δ_{jk} = $\begin{cases} 1, & \text{if brand } j \text{ is acceptable on attribute } k \\ 0, & \text{otherwise} \end{cases}$

Instruction to Consumer:

Imagine you can only choose between two health plans, plan 1 and plan 2. In both plans personalness convenience, and value are good (rated 5). You are familiar with plan 1 and know that quality is satisfactory plus (rated 4). You are not sure of the quality of plan 2. If your choose plan 2, then the wheel is spun and the quality you will experience for the entire year depends on the outcome of the wheel. If it comes up yellow, the quality is very good (rated 6); and if it comes up blue, the quality is just adequate (rated 2). Graphically this is stated:

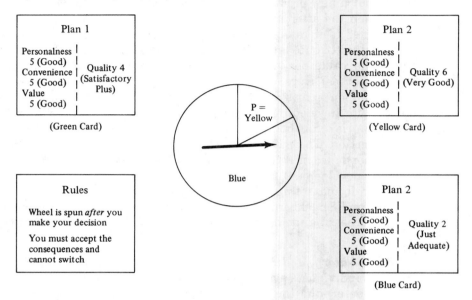

Instruction to Consumer:

At what setting of the odds (size of the yellow area) would you be indifferent between plan 1 and plan 2? (Respondent is given wheel and adjusts it until size of yellow area is appropriate. He is challenged by being given the choice with his setting. If he prefers one plan or the other, the interview iterates the question until a true indifference setting is determined.)

EXHIBIT 2.21 Schematic of lottery question for direct utility function assessment. (*Source:* Urban and Hauser, 1980, p. 274.)

$$A_j = \begin{cases} 1, & \text{if it is a preferred brand overall} \\ 0, & \text{otherwise} \end{cases}$$

Under the conjunctive model, we have

$$\delta_{jk} = \begin{cases} 1, & \text{if } y_{jk} \geq T_{jk} \\ 0, & \text{if } y_{jk} < T_{jk} \end{cases}$$

and

Computer Brand	Memory Capacity	Graphics Capability	Software Availability	Price
A	10	8	6	8
B	8	9	8	3
C	6	8	10	5
D	4	3	7	8
Minimum Requirements (Conjunctive)	7	6	7	2
Minimum Requirements (Disjunctive)	9	None	9	None
Attribute Order (Lexicographic)	3rd	4th	2nd	1st

EXHIBIT 2.22 Ratings of four brands of home computer on a 1–10 scale, with requirements of various noncompensatory models

$$A_j = \Pi_k \delta_{jk} \tag{2.77}$$

Thus, A_j will be nonzero if and only if $y_{jk} \geq T_{jk}$ for all attributes.

EXAMPLE _____

We saw previously that the Smith family is interested in buying a home computer. Exhibit 2.22 gives the attribute ratings of the four brands of computer on which they have sought information. We start by assuming that the Smiths demand minimum levels of 7, 6, 7, and 2 on memory, graphics, software, and price, respectively. Computers C and D are eliminated due to insufficient memory (6 and 4, respectively), while A is eliminated because of insufficient software. The conjunctive model predicts that the Smiths will have the most favorable attitude toward brand B.

_____

Disjunctive Model. In a disjunctive model, instead of preferred brands having to satisfy *all* of a number of criteria, they have to satisfy one of a number of criteria. The conjunctive model is often called the "and" model, while the disjunctive model is called the "or" model. Under the conjunctive model the consumer may insist on a product that has lots of memory *and* software. Under the disjunctive model the consumer may want to settle for either a product with a lot of memory *or* a lot of software.

Mathematically, we can express this as

$$A_j = \min(\Sigma_k \delta_{jk}, 1) \tag{2.78}$$

where A_j and δ_{jk} are defined as before.

EXAMPLE _____

In Exhibit 2.22, the disjunctive model that the Smiths have now decided to adopt requires very high performance on either memory capacity or software (the successful computer must have a 9 on at least one of these attributes). Brand *A* satisfies the memory capability requirement (with 10) and brand *C* satisfies the software requirement (with a 10). Thus, the disjunctive model suggests that two brands, *A* and *C*, are acceptable and another model must be used to choose between these brands.

It may well be that neither the conjunctive nor the disjunctive rules will give a single preferred brand; either may yield zero or more than one brand, leading to a need for further rules.

Lexicographic Model. A lexicographic model assumes that all attributes are used, but in a stepwise manner. Brands are evaluated on the most important attributes first; then a second attribute is used only if there are ties, and so forth.

EXAMPLE _____

In Exhibit 2.22, suppose price is the most important attribute and that it cannot be compensated for by other advantages. Brands *A* and *D* tie on price, so they are next evaluated along the next most important dimension, software, where *D* wins. Thus, the lexicographic model suggests that brand *D* will be the Smith family's preferred computer.

Mathematically, if we assume that the attributes are arranged in order

from most important to least important, then brand j is the preferred brand
if:

$$y_{ji} > y_{jk} \quad \text{for all brands } k, k = 2, \cdots, K \qquad \textbf{(2.79a)}$$

or

$$y_{ji} = y_{jk}^* \quad \text{and } y_{j2} > y_{jk}^* \text{ for some}$$

set of brands $\{k^*\}$ which are a
subset of $2, \cdots, K$

(2.79)

or ...

and so forth

A number of other noncompensatory models have been used. See Bettman (1979) for a more detailed discussion of these and other models.

In general, noncompensatory models require individuals to process information by attribute across brands, while compensatory models require consumers to process information by brand across attributes. Since evaluations are simpler and faster in noncompensatory models, it is likely that they are better representations of decision processes for low-involvement goods or for the screening phase when there are many brands, while compensatory models more accurately describe brand evaluations for high-involvement products in more complex decision-making settings (see Bettman, 1979, for a review of the supporting empirical literature).

In choosing between compensatory models, Lynch (1985) points out that many different rules to transform attribute values into attitudes and preferences will give correlated forecasts. If the validity of the rule is of importance because the process is being studied or the model is to be used outside the range in which it was calibrated, then he suggests ways in which to evaluate the most appropriate underlying model. In choosing between compensatory and noncompensatory models, Bettman (1979) points out that heuristics (noncompensatory simplifications) are more likely to be used when the number of alternatives is large and there are many attributes on which they are to be evaluated, factors shown to affect effort and accuracy by Johnson and Payne (1985) in a series of choice simulation experiments.

Purchase

Previously we developed models to determine the consumer's preferred product from within his consideration set. However, we do not assume that the consumer will always purchase his or her most preferred brand. The consumer may not find the preferred brand available, consumer preferences for brands may vary by usage occasion or by the household member for whom they are purchased, or other variables we have omitted from our model of preference may affect the decision. In addition, if we use our preference measures to forecast purchase, we introduce an additional source of variation in the form of measurement error and changes in the consumer's preferences between the time of measurement and the time of purchase.

EXAMPLE _____

Sally Smith is off to the store to buy breakfast cereal. She ran into a market researcher at the shopping mall last week who determined that her most preferred brand of cereal was Crunchy Bran. Today she bought Wheaties and Special K. She bought Wheaties because her nephew, Alvin, is going to stay next week and she knows that he likes Wheaties. She bought Special K for herself because she found that she was bored with Crunchy Bran.

_____

While attitude or behavioral intent is often a good predictor of future action, it is not a perfect one. Bass (1974a) argued that consumers are inherently stochastic and that there is a random element to their behavior. Whether this random element does indeed exist, or whether the difference between preference and purchase occurs because of omitted variables, is not of great practical importance as long as we are unable to identify and estimate it explicitly. For reviews of the theoretical underpinnings of choice models, see Corstjens and Gautschi (1983), Hutchinson (1986), or McFadden (1986).

We develop models of the brand purchase decision and how purchase relates to preference by starting with an historical model that relates probability of purchase to a brand's perceived utility: the Luce model. This model will help introduce the most commonly used discrete choice model at present, the multinomial logit model (an extension of the binary logit model that we developed previously). Limitations of the logit model have led naturally to a variety of extensions and alternative models, which we review briefly.

Luces's Axiom. Most high-involvement choice models derive from Luce's (1959) axioms and model:

$$P_{ij}(C_i) = \frac{V_{ij}}{\{\Sigma_{k \in C_i} V_{ik}\}} \tag{2.80}$$

where

$P_{ij}(C_i)$ = probability that individual i chooses brand j
V_{ij} = individual i's ratio-scaled preference for brand j
C_i = set of brands in individual i's consideration set

Axelrod (1968) suggested the use of the constant-sum technique for eliciting preference judgments for consumers. Allaire (1973) recommends that these judgments be obtained only from among those brands an individual would actually consider buying. Torgerson (1958, pp. 108, 112) provides a least-squares method for estimating ratio-scale values from paired-comparison data.

EXAMPLE

Suppose there are three brands, A, B, and C, to be evaluated and a consumer is given the following task: "Allocate 20 chips to each pair of brands in a manner that reflects your overall preference for those brands," with the following result:

	A	16	A	16	B	10
	vs		vs		vs	
	B	4	C	4	C	10
Total		20		20		20

This allocation is called a paired comparison.

Ratio-scaled preferences p_A, p_B, and p_C, should satisfy (at least approximately) these relationships:

$$\frac{p_A}{p_B} = \frac{16}{4}, \quad \frac{p_A}{p_C} = \frac{16}{4}, \quad \frac{p_B}{p_C} = \frac{10}{10} \tag{2.81}$$

resulting in one solution of $p_A = 2/3$, $p_B = p_C = 1/6$.

Luce's model is an example of what is referred to as a constant-utility model. In such a model the decision rule is subject to randomness (hence the probability of purchase measure as the dependent variable), but individuals' subjective evaluations of the alternatives are assumed constant. According to these models, choice probabilities are defined by a function of the preference scores of the product alternatives that form the individual's choice set. An approach that has been more popular and seen more marketing applications is that of a random-utility model, in which the preference scores (the product utility values) undergo random fluctuations, while the choice mechanism is deterministic. These models are multivariate extensions of the binary logit models of purchase incidence we developed earlier and evolve as follows: some true utility measure, V_{ij}, is assumed such that

$$U_{ij} = V_{ij} + \varepsilon_{ij} \tag{2.82}$$

where

$$U_{ij} \quad = \quad \text{observed preference or utility measure}$$

$$\varepsilon_{ij} \quad = \quad \text{variation or error in preference measure}$$

These models further assume that individual i will choose the brand with the highest true utility, V_{ij}. If P_{ij} is an estimate of the probability that consumer i will choose brand j, then the random-utility model yields

$$P_{ij} = \text{Pr}(U_{ij} > U_{ik}), \quad \text{for all } k \text{ in } C_i \neq j \tag{2.83}$$

$$= \text{Pr}(V_{ij} + \varepsilon_{ij} > V_{ik} + \varepsilon_{ik}), \quad \text{for all } k \text{ in } C_i \neq j \tag{2.84}$$

This formulation represents the multinomial extension of the two outcome choice models that we saw previously. As we found there, most random-utility models differ in their assumptions about the structure of the error term. We review the assumptions leading to the multinomial logit model here.

Multinomial Logit Model.   The assumptions required for the multinomial logit model are as follows:

1. $\{\varepsilon_{ij}\}$ are independently and identically distributed for all j.
2. The distribution of the $\{\varepsilon_{ij}\}$ is double exponential (extreme value):

$$\text{Pr}(\varepsilon_{ij} \leq x) = \exp(-e^{-\beta x}) \tag{2.85}$$

In the two alternative cases this may be shown to be equivalent to the assumption that $(\varepsilon_{i1} - \varepsilon_{i2})$ is distributed logistically and hence we obtain the binary logit.

Because the ε_{ij} are assumed independent, the joint cumulative distribution for the $\varepsilon_{ij}, j = 1, \ldots, J$, is the product of the J univariate cumulative distribution functions:

$$\text{Pr}(\varepsilon_{i1} \leq x_1, \varepsilon_{i2} \leq x_2, \ldots, \varepsilon_{iJ} \leq x_J) = \prod_j \exp(-e^{-\beta x_j}) \tag{2.86}$$

Now for a given value of ε_{i1}, this equation is the joint cumulative distribution function of $\{\varepsilon_{ij}\}$ for $j = 2$ to J at the values $V_{i1} - V_{ij} + \varepsilon_{i1}$. Integrating ε_{i1} out of the above equation yields

$$P_{i1} = \frac{\exp(\beta V_{i1})}{\Sigma_j \exp(\beta V_{ij})} \tag{2.87}$$

The logit model can be used directly with a linear compensatory value model as follows:

$$V_{ij} = \Sigma_k w_k b_{ijk} \qquad (2.88)$$

where

b_{ijk} = respondent i's evaluation of product j with respect to attribute k

w_k = importance weight associated with attribute k

If we substitute equation (2.88) into equation (2.87), we get

$$P_{i1} = \frac{\exp(\Sigma_k w_k b_{i1k})}{\Sigma_j \exp(\Sigma_k w_k b_{ijk})} \qquad (2.89)$$

Similarly, equations for $P_{i2}, \ldots, P_{iJ}$ can be defined. The importance weights, w_k, can be derived using a variety of different estimation algorithms. In a review of estimation techniques, Bunch and Batsell (1989) advocate the use of maximum-likelihood procedures (see Appendix D). The w_k weights are often called revealed importances because they are revealed by an analysis of choice behavior rather than from direct measurement. They are interpreted in much the same way as regression coefficients.

In most computer packages the statistical significance of each w_k is determined through a t-test based on asymptotic values of the standard errors of the estimates. Chapman and Staelin (1982) suggest a procedure that exploits the information content of the complete rank-order choice set. Note that the probability of purchase derived in the logit model, equation (2.89) is a specific form of Luce's axiom, equation (2.80).

For marketing applications of the logit model, see Berkowitz and Haines (1982), Gensch and Recker (1979), Punj and Staelin (1978), and Guadagni and Little (1983). For more detailed discussion and derivations of other choice models, see McFadden (1976, 1980).

EXAMPLE _____

Suppose that a survey of shoppers has been performed in an area in order to understand their shopping habits and to determine the share of shoppers that a new store might attract. Three existing stores and one proposed store (described by a written concept statement) were rated by respondents on a number of dimensions: (1) variety, (2) quality, (3) parking, and (4) value for the money. The ratings on these dimensions are given in Exhibit 2.23.

Store	Attribute Ratings			
	Variety	**Quality**	**Parking**	**Value for Money**
1	0.7	0.5	0.7	0.7
2	0.3	0.4	0.2	0.8
3	0.6	0.8	0.7	0.4
4 (new)	0.6	0.4	0.8	0.5
Importance Weight	2.0	1.7	1.3	2.2

EXHIBIT 2.23   Ratings and importance data for the store-selection example

By a fit of shoppers' choices of existing stores to their ratings through the logit model, the coefficients $\{w_k\}$ have been estimated:

$$V_j = \Sigma_k w_k X_{jk} \qquad\qquad (2.90)$$

where

$$
\begin{aligned}
V_j &= \text{attractiveness of store } j \\
X_{jk} &= \text{rating for store } j \text{ on dimension } k \\
w_k &= \text{importance weight for dimension } k
\end{aligned}
$$

The data in Exhibit 2.23 come from a group of relatively homogeneous consumers. The share of the old stores with and without the new store, the potential share of the new store, and the draw estimated from this group are given in Exhibit 2.24.

Store	(a) $U_i = \Sigma\, a_d X_{id}$	(b) e^{U_i}	(c) Share estimate without new store	(d) Share estimate with new store	(e) Draw [(c) - (d)]
1	4.70	109.9	0.512	0.407	0.105
2	3.30	27.1	0.126	0.100	0.026
3	4.35	77.5	0.362	0.287	0.075
4	4.02	55.7		0.206	

EXHIBIT 2.24   Logit model analysis of new store share example

Two things should be clear from this example. The first is that the logit model is useful for a variety of applications, such as new product/concept evaluations, as well as for understanding choice between existing products. Louviere and Hensher (1983) and Louviere and Woodworth (1983) provide examples of how the logit model can be combined with experimental design

Store	e^{U_i}	Share Estimate
1	109.9	0.376
2	27.1	0.092
3	77.5	0.266
4	77.5	0.266

EXHIBIT 2.25 Logit model analysis: store example with a change in consideration set

to evaluate hypothetical new product concepts and establish the importance weights of product attributes. However, a very particular form of choice behavior is specified in the logit model. The draw of the new store—(column (e) in Exhibit 2.24)—is proportional to share—(column (c).) Thus the logit model includes special assumptions that may weaken its applicability in certain marketing situations.

Model Limitations and Extensions. There are two main criticisms of the logit model. The first has to do with the (postulated) form of the error function. Although Domencich and McFadden (1975) give some support for the soundness of that particular distributional form, other forms, particularly normally distributed errors, may be more reasonable. The second criticism is that changes in the consideration set, as noted, cause proportional changes in probability estimates. For example, assume that the new store (store 4) was in the same chain as, and right next door to, store 3. With the logit model we would then have the estimates shown in Exhibit 2.25, but it would be more reasonable in this case to expect that store 4 would draw proportionally more from store 3 (its twin) and less from the other stores.

This latter problem is referred to as the problem of independence of irrelevant alternatives (IIA). A number of approaches have been proposed to overcome it. These may be broadly defined as segmenting consumers into homogeneous groups, structuring the market hierarchically into branches that contain products that are similar, and modeling the interactions between products explicitly.

Most applications of the logit model pool data from respondents rather than estimating the model separately for each, in order to obtain sufficient degrees of freedom for the estimation process. Any heterogeneity of consumer tastes can add to the IIA problem because individual customers will have similar brands in their consideration sets. One way to overcome this source of violation of IIA is to segment the population into homogeneous groups and then estimate a separate model for each segment. Gensch (1984, 1985, 1987) calls these models estimated at the segment level *disaggregate choice models*. He shows that a priori segmentation, in one case on the basis of knowledgeability and in another on the basis of strength of preferences, improved forecasts and yielded a much richer set of management implications. In partic-

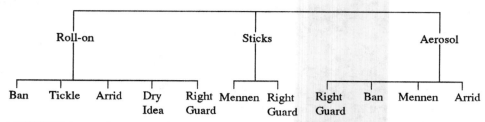

EXHIBIT 2.26   Consumer decision hierarchy for deodorant purchase. (*Source:* Urban and Hauser, 1980, p. 92.)

ular, targeting strategies were able to be refined by an understanding of the differences between segments.

Hierarchical Models of Consumer Choice.   The previous method of tackling the IIA problem was to group consumers into segments that were likely to consider similar brands and have homogeneous importance weights. An alternative approach is to group products into groups that are similar. If we view the choice process as hierarchical and group products that are similar into the same branches of the choice hierarchy, then brands within each branch are more likely to follow the independence of irrelevant alternatives. Thus, in the example of store choice, assume that the consumer first decides on the geographic location in which to shop and then decides the store within that location. The new store, being in the geographic region of store 3, will be forecast to draw customers mainly from store 3. It will still draw some customers from stores 1 and 2 because the store 3/new store geographic area is now a more appealing shopping location, so that at the geographic choice level more customers will shop there, drawing them away from store 1 and store 2's areas.

The Nested Logit Model.   The most commonly applied hierarchical model in marketing is the nested logit. To illustrate its derivation, consider a consumer's choice process for deodorants, using the decision hierarchy illustrated in Exhibit 2.26. The consumer chooses the form of deodorant and then, conditional on that choice, selects a specific brand.

Algebraically, we may write

$$P_{ij} = P_{j|i} \cdot P_i \tag{2.91}$$

where

P_{ij} = probability of choosing brand j and product form i
P_i = unconditional probability of choosing product form i
$P_{j|i}$ = probability of choosing brand j, given product form i

We assume that utility is separable. That is, we assume that we can identify the utility that is common to all members of the product form and the utility that is specific to individual brands. We can write this assumption:

$$U_{ij} = U_i + U_{j|i} \tag{2.92}$$

where

U_{ij} = utility from choosing product form i and brand j
U_i = utility associated with product form i
$U_{j|i}$ = unique utility of brand j (in product form i)

Brand choice, the bottom level of the hierarchy in Exhibit 2.21, can be estimated with a multinomial logit model, as before:

$$P_{j|i} = \frac{e^{U_{j|i}}}{\Sigma_k e^{U_{k|i}}} \tag{2.93}$$

The product form decision may also be modeled using a logit model as long as the error is double exponential and independent of the error at the brand choice stage. To gain some intuition about the equation for the probability of product form purchase, P_i, we note

$$P_i = \Pr(\max_j U_{ij} > \max_j U_{i'j}), \quad \text{for all } i'$$

$$= \Pr(U_i + \max_j U_{j|i} > U_i' + \max_j U_{j|i'}), \quad \text{for all } i'$$

From equation (2.55) we know that $E(\max_j U_{j|i}) = \ln(\Sigma_j e^{U_{j|i}})$. This is termed the *inclusive value* of the brand decision in the product form decision. The equation for the product form probabilities is given by

$$P_i = \frac{e^{\mu[U_i + \ln(\Sigma_j \exp U_{j|i})]}}{\Sigma_i' e^{\mu\{U_{i'} + \ln[\Sigma_j(\exp U_{j|i'})]\}}} \tag{2.94}$$

where

μ = normalizing constant

From equation (2.94) we can see that the individual brand utilities also affect the decision at the product form level through the inclusive value. We can now derive the probability of buying brand j in product form i, P_{ij}, by substituting equations (2.93) and (2.94) into equation (2.91). Bechtel (1990) shows how the nested multinomial logit model can be estimated when individual-level choice data are not available, but only market share data in each period.

For a more comprehensive development of the nested logit see Ben-Akiva and Lerman (1985, Ch. 10).

APPLICATION

The decision hierarchy can involve any number of levels. It can also involve seemingly unrelated decision processes. For example, Dubin (1986) modeled the decision of new home builders in choosing heating as a hierarchy of first the space heating choice, followed by the water heating choice, conditioned on the form of space heating chosen. The water heating choice, given space heating, was related to operating costs, capital costs, an alternative-specific dummy, and a space heating–specific dummy. Operating costs and capital costs were both statistically significant. The relation between the two yielded the implicit discount rate being used by the household: 9.6%. Electricity had a significant alternative-specific constant, reflecting its noncost-related desirability due to cleanness and lack of emissions. The electricity space heating dummy was not significant, while the gas space dummy was, suggesting that if gas was already planned for space heating, electricity's noncost advantages were not perceived as being so appealing.

Dubin related space heating choice to capital cost and operating costs, as well as form specific dummies and the inclusive value of the water heating alternatives. Operating and capital costs were again significant, this time with an implied discount rate of 27%. In order to test whether the nested structure was more appropriate than two separate models, Dubin compared both formulations. A chi-squared test rejected the hypothesis of two independent models at the 1% significance level.

The model was used to forecast trends in the market share of different forms of space and water heating, based on predictions of trends in the prices of gas, electricity, and oil. Dubin also derived a number of other management implications. For example, he suggested that design features that improved operating efficiency would not be highly valued if they were accompanied by substantially increased capital costs, and he proposed creative forms of financing that effectively shifted costs from capital to operating to increase demand.

In the nested logit model the decision whether to buy a specific alternative is made once, at the bottom of the decision hierarchy. In contrast, there are a number of other hierarchical decision models in which the brand is evaluated a number of times on different criteria. Brands in the consideration or choice set are successively discarded until a final choice is made. Models of this type include Tversky's (1972) elimination by aspects model, Hauser's (1986) agenda theory, and Manrai and Sinha's (1989) elimination by cutoffs. These models, while hierarchical choice models, concentrate more on the attribute processing method by which choice occurs than the structure of the market.

Models Incorporating Specific Brand Interactions. We have seen how ensuring that populations are homogeneous and ensuring that products are relatively homogeneous can alleviate problems that the IIA property of the logit model introduces. A further method of addressing those problems is to model brand interactions explicitly. For example, Batsell and Polking (1985) empirically estimate these interactions. Starting with doubles of products $\{i, j\}$ they move on to examine choice probabilities of triples $\{i, j, k\}$, quadruples $\{i, j, k, l\}$, and so on. If the ratio of the probability of choosing brand i to brand j is not the same in the triple $\{i, j, k\}$ as it is in the double $\{i, j\}$, then IIA is violated for this triple and a first-order interaction term is included in the model. Similarly, if the ratio of the probability of choosing brand i to brand j is not the same in the quadruple $\{i, j, k, l\}$ as it is in the double $\{i, j\}$, after allowing for the first-order interaction, then a second-order interaction is included. This process continues until including further interactions does not significantly improve fit. Batsell and Polking suggest that this will usually be achieved reasonably parsimoniously (with only first- or second-order interactions being required).

Ben-Akiva and Lerman (1985, p.127) warn that arbitrarily adding interactions can lead to counterintuitive elasticities. A more axiomatic approach to modeling brand interactions is the generalized extreme value model developed by McFadden (1978). For an application of the generalized extreme value to overcome the IIA problem, see Dalal and Klein (1988).

Multinomial Probit Model. An alternative model to incorporate departures from IIA is the multinomial probit model. This model is an extension of the binary probit developed earlier. It uses a normally distributed error structure and allows the covariance between error terms to be nonzero. But it is not possible to write a general analytical expression for the choice probabilities, and estimation and evaluation are quite complex. However, recent developments have led to practical computer programs for this model (Daganzo, 1979) and its application in marketing (Currim, 1982; Kamakura and Srivastava 1984, 1986; and Papatla and Krishnamurthi, 1991). See McFadden (1991) for a discussion of recent statistical/computational advances related to choice models.

Postpurchase and Purchase Feedback

After purchasing (and experiencing) a product, a consumer's reactions remain important. For frequently purchased products, those reactions will help determine future behavior; for durables, the consumer may tell others about the products (word of mouth) influencing the adoption of the remainder of the population (see Chapter 10). For example, Biehal (1983) showed that, for auto repair services, the outcome of prior experience was more important than external search in choosing the next service provider.

Postpurchase behavior can affect attitude, and in turn affect the consumer's behavior. It can affect how the consumer communicates about the product to others through word of mouth. And a purchase can affect future purchases through variety seeking. In the first two cases, postpurchase experience influences future behavior through learning about the product. In the third, past purchases affect future ones, as the consumer balances consumption over time.

Models of postpurchase effects through learning often include "satisfaction," which is determined by perceived product performance relative to consumer expectations. For example, Bearden and Teel (1983) used structural equation modeling (LISREL) to explain how current expectations, attitudes, and intentions combine with product experience (disconfirmation) to determine satisfaction along with future attitudes and intentions (including complaining behavior in extreme cases) (see Exhibit 2.27). Tse and Wilton (1988) provide a review of the postpurchase feedback literature and compare the predictive performance of different measures.

Word of mouth has been studied extensively in sociology (Rogers, 1983) and marketing (Westbrook, 1987). Biehal (1983) has also tested the impact of product experience on search. In the extreme, dissatisfaction leads to complaints to the supplier or to other consumers (Singh, 1988).

Models of Variety Seeking.   The stochastic learning models we reviewed earlier provide one way to relate past purchase patterns to future behavior. Stochastic models concentrate on the random element of consumer behavior. In contrast, the variety-seeking literature models the effect of current choice on future behavior by understanding the deterministic influences of choice. McAlister and Pessemier (1982) distinguish between several types of behavior by individuals that relate to multiple needs, the acquisition of information, and the alternating purchase of familiar products (variety seeking). They hypothesize that consumers have an ideal point or satiation level for the product's attributes that leads to its decreasing utility after a period of sustained consumption. Thus, if a person drinks six colas there is a good chance that on his next consumption occasion he might wish a lemon soda "just for a change," that is, variety seeking. (Recall how Sally Smith bought Special K as a change from Crunchy Bran.)

APPLICATION _____

Lattin and McAlister (1985) used a Luce model to understand the effect of brand similarities on purchase event feedback. They modeled a consumer's utility for a brand on a given consumption occasion as a diminishing proportion of the value of the features it shares with the brand

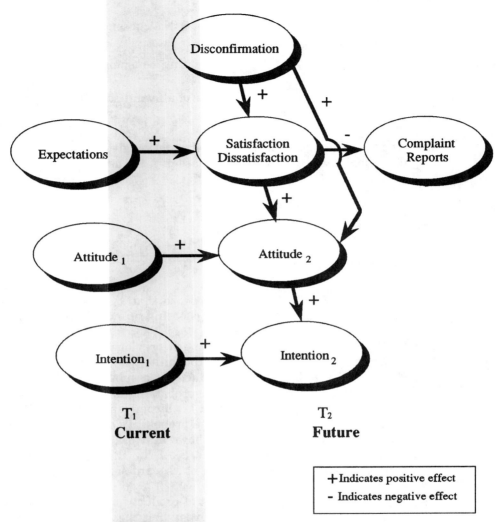

EXHIBIT 2.27   Effect of postpurchase experience on future behavior. (*Source:* Bearden and Teel, 1983, p. 22.)

the consumer chose on the previous consumption occasion via a first order Markov scheme.

Thus,

$$V_{i|j} = V_i - \lambda S_{ij} \qquad (2.95)$$

where

$V_{i|j}$ = utility of i given that j was chosen previously

V_i = unconditional utility of i

λ = discount factor indicating consumer's variety-seeking intensity

S_{ij} = value to the customer of all want-satisfying features shared by i and j

Applying the Luce model to this formulation gives the probability of purchase of i given a previous purchase of j, $P_{i|j}$ as

$$P_{i|j} = \frac{V_{i|j}}{(\Sigma_k V_{k|j})}$$

$$= \frac{(V_i - \lambda S_{ij})}{\Sigma_k(V_k - \lambda S_{kj})}$$

(2.96)

Lattin and McAlister scaled the V_i so that $\Sigma_k V_k = 1$. V_i can then be interpreted as the probability of choosing brand i in the absence of variety seeking.

The authors analyzed how much previous consumption alters the unconditional brand choice probability, V_i; that is, $P_{i|j} - V_i$. $P_{i|j} - V_i < 0$ indicates that product j is a substitute for product i (the consumption of brand j lowers the probability of choosing brand i), while $P_{i|j} - V_i > 0$ suggests that brand j is a complement to brand i (the consumption of brand j increases the probability of choosing brand i). An examination of equation (2.96) shows that brand j will be a substitute for brand i ($P_{i|j} - V_i < 0$) if $V_i < S_{ij}/\Sigma_k S_{kj}$, that is, if product i shares more than a proportional amount of its want-satisfying value with product j.

The asymmetry of the effect of product i on product j, and product j on product i, may be seen by expanding the expression for the effect of product j on i ($P_{i|j} - V_i$) using equation (2.96). $P_{i|j} - V_i$ may be rewritten

$$P_{i|j} - V_i = \frac{\lambda(V_i \Sigma_k S_{kj} - S_{ij})}{(1 - \lambda \Sigma_k S_{kj})}$$

(2.97)

Since $S_{ij} = S_{ji}$, $P_{j|i} - V_j$ is (by symmetry),

$$P_{j|i} - V_j = \frac{\lambda(V_j \Sigma_k S_{ki} - S_{ij})}{(1 - \lambda \Sigma_k S_{ki})}$$

(2.98)

The sign of expression (2.97) depends on whether $V_i \Sigma_k S_{kj} - S_{ij} > 0$. Product j is less likely to be a substitute for product i if product i has a high unconditional utility (V_i) or if product j also shares a large number of features with other products ($\Sigma_k S_{kj}$ is large). The intensity of variety seeking, λ, will magnify the degree of substitution or complementarity.

Lattin and McAlister reported the results of analyzing the soft drink consumption behavior of 27 students over a period of 81 days. They obtained a least-squares fit to equation (2.97) using constrained nonlinear programming, estimating their model at the individual level and averaging across individuals to obtain segment-level estimates. The variety seeking segment consisted of 9 of the 27 respondents with λ's ranging from 0.43 to 0.96. For the other 18 respondents a simple Markov model was sufficient. To illustrate the results of the model, consider the outcome of fitting one respondent, illustrated in Exhibit 2.28.

The estimated shared features show that Pepsi and Coke share common features ($S_{Coke,Pepsi} = 0.109$), while 7-Up and Coke do not. Virtually all of Pepsi's value ($V_{Pepsi} = 0.204$) is in the form of shared attributes (0.109 with Coke and 0.095 with 7-Up), while Coke and 7-Up both have high unique value components. The structure of the market can be seen by examining the negative entries in cross consumption response (marked by the squares in Exhibit 2.28). The three distinct market segments of colas, lemon soda, and fruit flavors emerge. The asymmetric nature of interproduct relationships may be seen by looking at Coke, Pepsi and 7-Up. Coke and Pepsi have an equally strong effect on 7-Up (with a cross-consumption effect of 0.206). However 7-Up has a much stronger complementary effect on Coke than on Pepsi (+0.287 relative to +0.095).

One important implication of the Lattin and McAlister model is that, after allowing for individuals' different preferences, brand-switching matrices do not necessarily reflect substitution effects; brand-switching may well indicate a search for variety or balance.

In other models of variety seeking, McAlister (1982) considers multi-period depletion of inventories of attributes, Lattin (1987) explicitly models different levels of variety seeking for different attributes using a logit framework, and Simonson (1990) examines the contextual determinants of variety seeking.

INTEGRATION: EXAMPLES OF COMBINING MODELS TO SOLVE MANAGEMENT PROBLEMS

We have now examined some of the major tools to understand and predict consumer behavior. In developing our framework, we emphasized the need for parsimony and ease of implementation; thus, we looked at different stages

Product j	Values of features shared by product i and product j (S_{ij})				Total want-satisfying value of product j (V_j)	Cross-consumption response of product i to prior consumption of product j ($P_{iij} - V$)			
	$i =$ Coke	$i =$ Pepsi	$i =$ 7-Up	$i =$ Fruit Flavor		$i =$ Coke	$i =$ Pepsi	$i =$ 7-Up	$i =$ Fruit Flavor
Coke	0.174 (0.110)	0.109 (0.116)	0.000 (0.003)	0.000 (0.017)	0.174 (0.110)	-.163 (.088)	-.067 (.078)	+.206 (.140)	+.024 (.037)
Pepsi	0.109 (0.116)	0.204 (0.090)	0.095 (0.105)	0.000 (0.022)	0.204 (0.090)	-.059 (.096)	-.189 (.079)	+.206 (.144)	+.042 (.032)
7-Up	0.000 (0.003)	0.095 (0.105)	0.556 (0.161)	0.000 (0.047)	0.556 (0.161)	+.287 (.189)	+.095 (.124)	-.489 (.169)	+.108 (.083)
Fruit Flavor	0.000 (0.017)	0.000 (0.022)	0.000 (0.047)	0.065 (0.049)	0.065 (0.049)	+.012 (.030)	+.014 (.021)	+.037 (.032)	-.062 (.042)

(Numbers in brackets are standard deviations)

EXHIBIT 2.28 Model parameters and cross-consumption response for one respondent ($\lambda = 0.954$) using the Lattin and McAlister model. (*Source:* Lattin and McAlister, 1985, p. 334.)

of the decision process separately to concentrate on only those phenomena that are key to understanding behavior and product management. However, there are many situations in which more than one stage and more than one type of model are appropriate.

In this section we give three illustrations of how the building blocks that we have developed can be joined to address particular consumer purchase situations. Our illustrations include (1) the combination of purchase incidence (need arousal) and brand choice (purchase) models, (2) joint consideration and purchase models, and (3) models of information integration and evaluation.

APPLICATION 1

A Model of Brand Choice and Purchase Incidence. Guadagni and Little (1987) examined how a retail store should price, display, and discount products to maximize sales and contribution. To achieve that end, they needed to understand the source of additional product sales: did those sales come from increases in brand share or from additional sales of the category as a whole? The areas of our process model that correspond to these issues deal with the purchase stage (the brand that will be chosen) and the need arousal stage (when a category purchase will occur).

Both phenomena can be modeled using logit models: earlier we developed the nested logit model which provides an integrated framework to understand related logit decision processes. Guadagni and Little used this technique to study purchase incidence and brand choice. They examined the purchase of coffee in Kansas City over a 74-week period using scanner panel data on a sample of 200 households.

Their model of brand choice followed their earlier work (Guadagni and Little, 1983). First, they identified the determinants of *brand choice* for the eight major brand-size combinations of coffee (products) on the market. These determinants were

X_{1ijt} = brand loyalty in period t of customer i to the brand of product j

X_{2ijt} = size loyalty in period t of customer i to the size of product j

X_{3jt} = the presence of a promotion (display) on product j in time t

X_{4jt} = the discount of product j at time t as a proportion of the average category price

X_{5jt} = the regular (undiscounted) price of product j at time t relative to the average category price

and seven product-specific dummies to capture the brand equity of each of the products:

$$\delta_{ijt} = \begin{cases} 1, & \text{for product } j, \quad \text{for all } i, t \\ 0, & \text{otherwise} \end{cases}$$

The logit brand choice model estimated across respondents, products and time periods, is

$$P_{ijt|B} = \frac{e^{(\Sigma_n \beta_n X_{nijt} + \Sigma_m \gamma_m \delta_{ijt})}}{\Sigma_k e^{(\Sigma_n \beta_n X_{nikt} + \Sigma_m \gamma_m \delta_{ikt})}} \tag{2.99}$$

where

$P_{ijt|B}$ = the probability of individual i purchasing product j in time period t given a category purchase

β_n, γ_m = are coefficients of the independent variables and product specific dummies, respectively ($n = 1$ to 5 and $m = 1$ to 7)

Their model of purchase incidence was a binary logit, with the dependent variable being whether a purchase took place or not. Their explanatory variables were

Z_{1Bi} = a dummy variable for the utility that consumer i gets from buying (B) in the category

Z_{2Bit} = a variable to denote whether consumer i made multiple purchases when buying on shopping trip t

Z_{3Bit} = household inventory of coffee

Z_{4Bit} = the category attractiveness

Z_{5Bit} = the average category price

Z_{6Bit} = a dummy variable to account for an announcement of impending price rises due to a crop failure in Brazil

Household inventory, Z_{3Bit}, was imputed from purchase history and average seasonal consumption rates, while category attractiveness is the inclusive value from the nested logit (equation (2.94)). Mathematically, category attractiveness, Z_{4Bit}, is given by

$$Z_{4Bit} = \ln[\Sigma_k e^{(\Sigma_n b_n X_{nikt} + \Sigma_m \gamma_m \delta_{ikt})}] \tag{2.100}$$

To calculate the expected category attractiveness of buying later (of **not** buying in this time period), Z_{4Nit}, and the expected price that consumer i would face if he bought later (and **not** this period), Z_{5Nit}, Guadagni and Little took an average of the attractiveness or "inclusive values" over the previous eight purchase occasions (i.e., the maximum utilities of brand purchases in the category) and the average category prices over the previous eight purchase occasions, respectively. For all other variables (Z_{1Nit}, Z_{2Nit}, Z_{3Nit}, Z_{6Nit}), they set the utility of not buying in period t to zero.

Their final binary logit model of whether category purchase will occur on shopping occasion t or not is

$$P_{Bit} = \frac{e^{(\Sigma_n a_n Z_{nBit})}}{\left[e^{(\Sigma_n a_n Z_{nBit})} + e^{(\Sigma_n a_n Z_{nNit})} \right]} \qquad (2.101)$$

where

P_{Bit} = probability of buying (B) within the category on shopping occasion t

and a_n (n = 1, 2, ..., 6) are parameters

Guadagni and Little estimated the model by first calibrating equation (2.99), the brand choice equation, using maximum-likelihood techniques. The "inclusive value" can then be calculated from (2.100). This enables the purchase incidence binary logit model, equation (2.101) to be calibrated. Results of the brand choice model calibration are presented in Exhibit 2.29a, while the purchase incidence model is described in Exhibit 2.29b.

At the product level (brand choice), both brand name loyalty and product size loyalty are strongly statistically significant. The brand choice decision also responds to store promotions and price cuts, as well as being sensitive to the regular price of the brand relative to the market. Only two product dummies are significant: Folgers small sells significantly more than the benchmark brand (Maxwell House large) and Mellow Roast small sells significantly less. The model fits well, with a U^2 of 0.48 relative to the null model that brands are chosen randomly with probability equal to aggregate brand shares. (A U^2 of 0.0 indicates equivalent fit to the null model, while a U^2 of 1.0 indicates perfect fit. See Hauser (1978) for further details.)

At the purchase incidence level, all variables except the price of the category were statistically significant. This suggests that coffee purchase does not depend on the price of the category as a whole, but the specific brand chosen is price sensitive.

Their combined brand choice/purchase incidence nested logit model allowed forecasts both of brand share and of total brand sales. The effects of individual products' marketing activity were traced through to

Product Choice Model

Variable	Coefficient	t-statistic
Brand Loyalty	3.76	21.9
Size Loyalty	2.97	15.9
Store Promotion	2.04	13.7
Promotional Price Cut	5.26	7.6
Price (Regular)	-5.11	-7.1
Maxwell House Small constant	-0.06	-0.4
Maxwell House Large constant (omitted)	0.00	0.0
Butternut Small constant	0.08	0.5
Butternut Large constant	-0.12	-0.7
Folgers Small constant	0.40	2.4
Folgers Large constant	0.10	0.6
Folgers Flaked Small constant	0.04	0.1
Mellow Roast Small constant	-1.74	-4.7
$n = 1021$	Log Likelihood = .978	$U^2 = .48$

(a) Brand choice model: estimation of equation (2.99)

		Model Number			
	BASE	1	2	3	4
Buy-Now Dummy	-2.52	-1.97	-2.09	-2.10	-2.15
	(-21.3)	(-15.5)	(-16.2)	(-16.2)	(-16.5)
Buy on First Purchase	1.91	1.66	1.77	1.78	1.78
Opportunity of Trip	(15.3)	(13.0)	(13.7)	(13.8)	(13.8)
Household Inventory		-0.164	-0.164	-0.162	-0.170
		(-10.9)	(-10.8)	(-10.6)	(-11.0)
Category Attractiveness			0.099	0.096	0.091
			(8.8)	(8.4)	(7.9)
Category Price				-4.86	-4.34
				(-1.1)	(-0.9)
Crop Failure Dummy					0.440
					(3.9)
U^2	0.0	0.032	0.052	0.053	0.056
Log Likelihood	-2,052	-1,986	-1,945	-1,944	-1,937

(b) Purchase incidence model: estimation of equation (2.101). T-stats in brackets.

EXHIBIT 2.29   Calibration of Guadagni and Little's nested logit model of the brand choice/purchase incidence decision *Source:* Guadagni and Little, 1987, pp. 11–18.

category effects using the "inclusive value" from the nested logit. Additionally, their use of a purchase incidence model enabled them to evaluate the effect of external factors, such as multiple purchases, household inventory, and the crop failure in Brazil.

By approaching the same problem from a stochastic modeling perspective and incorporating explanatory variables into their model, Hauser and Wisniewski (1982b) and Wagner and Taudes (1986) jointly model purchase incidence and brand choice decisions and their determinants. Hybrid approaches combining discrete choice and stochastic models include those of Jones and Zufryden (1981) (with an NBD purchase incidence model and logit brand choice) and Gupta (1988) (with an Erlang interpurchase time distribution and logit brand choice). Gupta also models purchase quantities in his framework using a cumulative logit model.

APPLICATION 2

Integrating Consideration and Choice. Gensch (1987) studied the management problem of influencing the choice process of electric utilities for an industrial durable, in order to design and position the product better. (See Chapter 3 for a discussion of the impact of this modeling effort at ABB Electric.) Gensch noted that there has been a lot of work applying compensatory evaluation rules to examine the relation among product positioning, perceptions, and purchase. But evidence in the consumer behavior literature suggests that consumers often use a two-stage procedure (e.g., see Wright and Barbour, 1977). In our framework this concept corresponds to a screening phase in the information search stage to determine the consideration set, followed by an evaluation and/or purchase stage. Gensch proposed a noncompensatory screening phase, followed by a compensatory evaluation of, and choice between, the surviving alternatives.

Attribute-Based Screening Model. In Gensch's models, products were screened sequentially by attribute on a conjunctive basis. That is, consumer i ensured that his perception of product j on attribute k, y_{ijk}, suitably scaled, does not fall too far short of the best brand's level on that attribute. Starting with the most important attribute, the consumer screens all brands on this basis to come up with an acceptable consideration set. These brands then enter the purchase phase. Mathematically the model may be written as follows.

First, the attribute levels, y_{ink}, are rescaled by

$$x_{ijk} = \frac{\max_n y_{ink} - y_{ijk}}{\max_n y_{ink}} \qquad (2.102)$$

where

$$x_{ijk} = \text{the rescaled perception that consumer } i \text{ has of attribute } k \text{ in product } j$$

Thus, x_{ijk} is the proportion of attribute k that product j has less that of the best product in the category. Gensch then postulated that there are maximum levels of x_{ijk} that the consumer will find acceptable; he called these thresholds T_k. He assumed the utility that attribute k offers is

$$v_{ijk} = \max(0, T_k - x_{ijk}).$$

That is, the attribute offers no utility if it exceeds the maximum allowable difference from the best brand (T_k), and equals the difference, $T_k - x_{ijk}$, if it is above the threshold. Gensch then uses a multiplicative utility function to determine brand j's overall utility to consumer i, V_{ij}:

$$V_{ij} = \Pi_k v_{ijk} \tag{2.103}$$

Equation (2.103) implies that if a brand fails to meet the threshold on any one criterion, then it has zero utility, that is $V_{ij} = 0$ (a conjunctive decision rule). The thresholds, T_k, are estimated from the data to maximize

$$\prod_i \left(\frac{V_{ij*}}{\Sigma_j V_{ij}}\right)^{X_i} \cdot \left(\frac{1 - V_{ij*}}{\Sigma_j V_{ij}}\right)^{1-X_i} \tag{2.104}$$

where

$$j^* = \text{the chosen alternative}$$
$$X_i = \begin{cases} 1, & \text{if } j^* \text{ is not screened out in the consideration phase} \\ 0, & \text{otherwise} \end{cases}$$

Once thresholds, T_k, have been estimated, the consideration set consists of brands such that $V_{ij} > 0$, that is, brands that do not fail any of the threshold criteria. If no brands fulfil this criterion, the brand(s) that was eliminated last (i.e., failed the least important conjunctive criterion) is selected. (Gensch and Svestka, 1984, provide a detailed description of this maximum-likelihood hierarchical model, MLH.)

Logit Discrete Choice Model. Given a consideration set from the previous stage, choice data, and respondent perceptions of suppliers on the salient attributes, Gensch fits a standard logit choice model. The probability of purchase of brand j by consumer i, P_{ij}, is given by

$$P_{ij} = \frac{e^{\Sigma_k b_k y_{ijk}}}{\Sigma_{n \in C} e^{\Sigma_k b_k y_{ink}}}$$

(2.105)

where C is the set of brands surviving the screening process.

Model Testing. Gensch tested the model by examining the ratings of four suppliers by 182 buyers of electrical generation equipment on eight attributes, combined with choice data.

The two-stage model gave superior predictions to either a one-stage logit model or a one-stage MLH model (outperforming the former by a factor of 128 to 53 and the latter by 78 to 34). In addition, two attributes dominated the screening process. Seventy percent of all eliminations occurred on the basis of manufacturer quality, while 26% occurred on the basis of manufacturer problem-solving ability. The one-stage logit model had both of these variables statistically significant. After incorporating a screening phase, both variables became insignificant. This suggests that these variables are important in gaining consideration, but once consideration is gained do not play a significant role in evaluation and choice. The use of this and related models had a major impact on the successful performance of ABB Electric in the 1970s and 1980s (see Chapter 3).

One of the strengths of Gensch's approach is that it only requires attribute perceptions, perceived importances, and choice data, making the data collection task easier than that for the consideration models described earlier. It also means that care has to be taken in interpreting the screening results: we cannot be sure that noncompensatory screening was in fact the process that took place. Rather, we can only conclude that a noncompensatory model screening model combined with a compensatory choice model gives a better fit than does either a single-stage compensatory model or a discrete choice model.

APPLICATION 3

The Dynamics of Perceptions, Preference, and Purchase. Roberts and Urban (1988) developed a dynamic brand choice model to address the problem of forecasting sales of a new consumer durable. With the launch of a new automobile, appeal (perceptions, preference, and choice) is important, but so are the dynamics of how that appeal will change as the product diffuses through the adopting population. GM's Buick Division was interested in how word of mouth (WOM) and information from other sources would affect the sales trajectory.

The modeling task here was combine static choice modeling with a model of information integration to develop an understanding of the dynamics of choice.

Probability of Purchase Model at any Point in Time.   Roberts and Urban used decision analysis theory to show that a (rational) risk-averse consumer with uncertain beliefs will attempt to maximize the expected utility that he will get from the brand minus a constant times the uncertainty involved (Keeney and Raiffa, 1976). They termed this quantity the risk-adjusted preference, x. Thus, the risk-adjusted preference for brand j, x_j is given by

$$x_j = V_j - \left(\frac{r}{2}\right)\sigma_j^2 \qquad (2.106)$$

where

V_j = expected utility from brand j

σ_j^2 = variance of beliefs about V_j

r = consumer's risk aversion

V_j may be further modeled in terms of its constituent attributes, y_{jk},

$$V_j = \Sigma_k w_k y_{jk} \qquad (2.107)$$

to incorporate product positioning.

If x_j is measured with error following the extreme value distribution, we can model the probability of choosing brand j in logit terms:

$$P_j = \frac{e^{x_j}}{\Sigma_{k \in C} e^{x_j}} \qquad (2.108)$$

By substituting equations (2.107) and (2.106) in equation (2.108) we can see how perceptions, expected preference, and the level of uncertainty affect the probability of purchase.

Dynamics of Preference Uncertainty and Choice Probability.   The diffusion of innovations literature suggests that information fills two roles: it reduces uncertainty and it can lead to changes in attribute perceptions and thus preference. To understand how new information about the product affects an individual's perceptions and uncertainty, Roberts and Urban used Bayesian updating theory. Earlier we showed how Bayesian decision makers update their beliefs. Beliefs about expected preference for the brand after search are a weighted average of the prior beliefs and the level of preference that the new information suggests. Uncertainty is reduced by an amount that depends on the faith that is placed in new information. Mathematically,

$$V_j'' = \frac{(\sigma_{wj}^2 V_j' + \sigma_j'^2 \cdot V_{wj})}{\sigma_{wj}^2 + \sigma_j'^2} \tag{2.109}$$

and

$$\sigma_j''^2 = \frac{\sigma_j'^2 \sigma_{wj}^2}{\sigma_{wj}^2 + \sigma_j'^2} \tag{2.110}$$

where

V_j'', $\sigma_j''^2$ = expected preference and uncertainty associated with product j after updating

V_j', $\sigma_j'^2$ = prior expected preference and uncertainty, and

V_{wj}, σ_{wj}^2 = average preference and uncertainty of the incoming word of mouth about product j

By substituting the dynamics of expected preference and uncertainty (equations 2.109 and 2.110) into the equation for risk adjusted preference (equation 2.106) and the probability of purchase (equation 2.108), Roberts and Urban derived a dynamic brand choice model that provides a model of the individual level changes that are driving the aggregate level diffusion process, described in Chapter 10. They assumed that the rate at which new information about product j will become available is proportional to the number of cumulative adopters at time t, Y_{jt}. The variance of word-of-mouth information will be inversely proportional to this rate and thus the cumulative sales of product, j,

$$\sigma_{wj}^2 = \frac{k_j}{Y_{jt}} \tag{2.111}$$

where k_j is a constant reflecting the salience of the new product, j.

Application. Roberts and Urban calibrated their model using 326 respondents' evaluations of the existing U.S. automobile market and a new

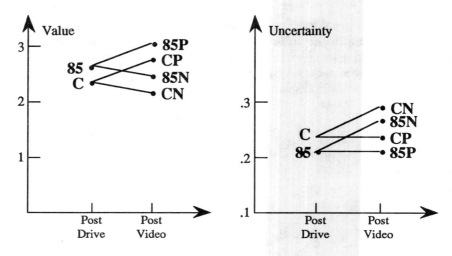

85: New Car Being Tested
C : Control Car (1983 Version of New Car)
P : Positive Videotape Exposure
N : Negative Videotape Exposure

EXHIBIT 2.30   Effects of positive and negative word of mouth on preference for and uncertainty of a new consumer. (*Source:* Roberts and Urban, 1988, p. 18.)

product concept. To test for yea-saying, one-third of the sample saw a control concept that was already on the market. After measuring perceptions, preference, uncertainty, and purchase probabilities with respect to the existing market, respondents were exposed to increasing amounts of information about the new concept car. First, they saw a description, then they took a prototype for a test drive followed by a videotape of owners' reactions to the new car, and finally they were given a consumer report written by an independent testing service. Measures of perceptions, preference, uncertainty, and probability of choice were taken after every information exposure to calibrate the model dynamics.

Respondents were shown either positive or negative information videotapes and consumer reports on a split sample basis to calibrate the effect of different types of word of mouth on the new car's diffusion. Exhibit 2.30 shows the effect of positive and negative word of mouth on preference and uncertainty. They traced the effect of these changes through the risk-adjusted preference to calculate the effect of word of mouth on individuals' probability of purchase and thus the diffusion of the new product, using equations (2.106) and (2.108).

The results of the perceptual evaluation stage of the model (equation 2.107) helped to shape the advertising copy for the car, stressing that the perceived durability did not come at the expense of comfort and style. An understanding of the dynamics of expected sales of the car under conditions of negative word of mouth persuaded management to delay the launch for over six months until a transmission fault was fixed. Finally, although it is difficult to validate durable forecasting models, preliminary indications are that this methodology predicted well (Urban, Hauser, and Roberts 1990).

Meyer and Sathi (1985) proposed a similar model with exponential smoothing updating for beliefs and uncertainty. Recent work has attempted to make these dynamic brand choice models more parsimonious in parameters to allow the aggregate effects of individual level changes to be examined more readily (eg., Oren and Schwartz, 1988; Chatterjee and Eliashberg, 1990; and Lattin and Roberts, 1988).

FUTURE DIRECTIONS FOR CONSUMER BEHAVIOR MODELS

The field of modeling consumer behavior is fast evolving. Changes are being driven by advances in our theoretical understanding of consumer decision processes (e.g., developments in the use of discrete choice models to overcome the independence of irrelevant alternatives), the availability of new data sources (e.g., the new mapping techniques that take advantage of the existence of longitudinal supermarket scanner data at the individual level), and new or more focused concerns of managers (e.g., models of market structure that address problems of market coverage and portfolio management).

Our study of the consumer decision process above also highlights a number of underresearched areas, particularly in terms of need arousal, information integration and postpurchase influences. As the external environment changes at an increasing rate and product life cycles become shorter, equilibrium models of the five stages of our process are likely to become less popular than those incorporating dynamics.

We summarize a number of the major thrusts that we expect in the marketing modeling field in the paragraphs that follow.

Biases and Heuristics. Recent research in the area of psychology into the biases and heuristics that consumers use to simplify decisions is likely to modify the strict utility-maximizing models that we often apply. Tversky and Kahneman (1974) detailed the heuristics and biases that they observed in decision makers (including consumers). The three biases that they identified were representativeness (in which perceived ideas and stereotypes obstruct learning of new information), availability (in which respondents select events or outcomes that are familiar to them, even in defiance of the true probabilities), and anchoring (in which respondents are reluctant to adjust adequately from their preconceived ideas). Subsequently, Kahneman and Tversky (1979) have also studied asymmetric risk aversion to gains and losses from the consumer's current position and the overweighting of low-probability events. Currim and Sarin (1989) developed a method of calibrating and testing these prospect theory models. They show that for paradoxical choices prospect theory (Appendix B) outperforms utility theory, while for nonparadoxical choices there is little difference. Winer (1986) and Lattin and Bucklin (1989) include reference levels in their models of brand choice to account for anchoring, but little work has been done to model and develop an error theory for the simplifying heuristics that consumers appear to use to make decisions.

Modeling the Mental Process.   We predict that formal modeling of mental processes, memory in particular, will see some important advances. The role of memory has been shown to be important in consumer behavior experiments (e.g., Lynch and Srull, 1982). Information once remembered will not necessarily be recalled, and recent work looks at the salience of brands and stimuli (e.g., Nedungadi, 1990).

A considerable body of literature exists on how consumers react when there is incomplete information, or when there is too much information. Huber and McCann (1982) show that consumer inferences affect choice and a number of researchers have developed models to explain this (e.g., Malhotra 1986). Dick, Chakravarti, and Biehal (1990) demonstrate that consumers inference from memory-based knowledge when faced by incomplete external information. Malhotra (1982) and Keller and Staelin (1989) show that information overload also affects choice, though less work has been undertaken to model the simplifying heuristics that the consumer use to overcome the problem.

In addition to the internal elements of consumer behavior that our models ignore, there are also a number of external ones, including context. The range of alternatives available, for example, is important in choice (e.g., Alba and Chattopadhyay, 1985, 1986). The variety-seeking literature also studies one particular form of context. Some very interesting work in context is Thaler's (1985) mental accounting model. Thaler suggests that there are two forms of utility associated with every consumer decision: acquisition utility and transaction utility. The former is the utility modeled in this chapter. Transaction utility reflects the approval or pleasure that consumers gain from the transaction itself. Transaction utility is particularly tied to the concept of fairness and appropriateness. While Urbany, Dickson, and Wilkie (1989) found little evidence of fairness affecting behavioral intentions, there are clearly situations in which transaction utility will be a key determinant of choice.

Matching Models to Market Segments.   Much of the consumer behavior work to date has postulated a single model of consumer response and tested its fit in a given situation against some competing, single model. We expect to see more work on methods for testing for this assumed customer homogeneity, applying models to homogeneous segments. For example, Gensch (1985) showed that prior segmentation of a population into segments homogeneous in perceptions and preferences gave much higher predictive accuracy than when a single model was fit to the entire population. Such segmentation is particularly powerful when it can be done a priori, as Gensch (1987) showed on a population of industrial buyers. In this latter application, more knowledgeable buyers were modeled well within a logit model, while less knowledgeable buyers closely approximated the assumptions of a hierarchical choice model. We expect that further research will lead to a better understanding of what types of models are most likely to be effective a priori, leading to the better application of appropriate, situation-specific consumer behavior models.

Estimating the Appeal of Unfamiliar Products. The problems of decisions involving unfamiliar alternatives (e.g., new technologically sophisticated products) is not well modeled or measured in marketing at present. There is some evidence that novices do not use as rich a mental model as experts (e.g., Alba and Hutchinson, 1987). Management needs in high-technology areas will continue to push for the development of better methods to assess how consumer decision processes evolve in such markets.

A modeling challenge when studying unfamiliar products is that the benchmarks that consumers use in these areas are generally not comparable to the unfamiliar product. For example, consumers might compare a compact disc player to a stereo cassette player. Johnson (1984, 1986, 1988) has suggested that the more consumers are faced with non-comparable alternatives, the more they resort to hierarchical-based processing. That is, he asserts that with noncomparable alternatives, consumers eliminate brands by a very general comparison, rather than a specific attribute-based one. As markets evolve more rapidly and product life cycles shorten, the need for models to understand the adoption of truly new products will become more evident.

SUMMARY

In a field as vast and diffuse as that of consumer behavior and consumer markets, it is difficult to develop a satisfying synthesis. We have drawn from developments in the literature of the behavioral sciences, economics, marketing, statistics, and the like and have categorized models by purchase decision stage. Our models overlap these stages, but this integrating framework provides a useful way of organizing this large, diverse literature.

Buying situations vary from those of routinized purchase behavior (often the case with low-involvement goods) to extensive problem solving (often the case with high-involvement goods). But we note that the same consumer may find a purchase in a product category low involvement in one situation (coffee for everyday use, say) and high involvement for another (coffee for a special, gourmet dinner party). Thus, a major challenge in the area of consumer behavior modeling is to find models that work well for groups of individuals, bearing the limitations of our data and knowledge of the consumer choice process in mind.

We followed our framework from need identification to information search to perception and evaluation and preference formation. From there we went on to purchase and postpurchase feedback models.

Finally, we demonstrated the power of developing models that combined several of the stages in a single framework.

The future of consumer behavior modeling is bright: newer models are richer, more flexible, and more closely attuned to modern data sources. Yet many phenomena are but poorly modeled at the moment. We highlighted the areas of modeling consumer purchase heuristics (and information processing biases), modeling consumer mental processes, matching models to market segments, and modeling choice for truly new or among noncomparable alternatives as fruitful areas that deserve concerted attention in the future.

PROBLEMS

2.1. The market research group for Oligopoly Fidgets has established that each fidget buyer (i) acts on each purchase occasion as if he had a constant probability (p_i) of buying from Oligopoly, independent of his past behavior. It has also been established that these probabilities have a distribution across the market of $f_p(p)$. Thus the chance that a randomly selected fidget buyer has less than a probability of 0.7 (say) of purchasing from Oligopoly is

$$\int_0^{0.7} f_p(p)dp$$

The research group also determined that $f_p(p)$ could be approximated as

$$f_p(p) = \begin{cases} -a + bp, & 0 \leq p \leq 1, 0 < a < 2 \\ 0, & \text{elsewhere} \end{cases}$$

and that the parameter a is related to the level of advertising (in millions of dollars) as

$$a = \begin{cases} 2 - x^{1/2}, & 4 \geq x \geq 0 \\ 0, & x > 4 \end{cases}$$

Suppose total industry sales are \$100,000,000 and are inelastic with respect to advertising expenditures and that incremental company profit is 6% of retail sales. The fixed-cost rate for fidgets is $500,000 per year. Also assume that individuals always purchase the same amount at the same frequency.

  a. What are the maximum and minimum values of Oligopoly's expected market share?

  b. Find the level of advertising that maximizes Oligopoly's expected profit.

  c. What is the expected market share at this advertising level?

2.2. A group of consumers is asked to rate five different brands of coffee according to two characteristics: strength and body. Each brand is rated on a scale from 1 to 7 for each characteristic. Each consumer is also asked to rate his ideal coffee. The brands are rated by the consumers in the following way:

Brand	Strength	Body
A	3	5
B	5	2
C	6	3
D	2	3
E	3	1
I (ideal)	5	5

Assume that the perceptions just presented are typical of the consumer group and that preference falls equally fast in all directions from the ideal brand.

  a. Represent these perceptions in Euclidean two-space, and order the different brands according to their probable market share if product characteristics were the only factor that counted.

  b. Suppose that the consumer is only one-third as concerned with body as he is with the strength of his coffee. Compute the weighted distances, and reorder the brands according to their probable market shares.

2.3. A large marketing research firm pays a large group of households to keep a diary of their weekly grocery purchases. Suppose the record of 20 such households is examined with respect to the purchases of a particular product of which there are three brands: A, B, and C. The accompanying table shows the brands chosen by these 20 households in two successive weeks.

House	1	2	3	4	5	6	7	8	9	10	11	12	13	14	15	16	17	18	19	20
Week 1	A	A	A	A	A	A	A	A	A	A	B	B	B	B	B	B	C	C	C	C
Week 2	A	A	A	A	A	A	A	B	B	C	A	B	B	C	C	C	B	B	C	C

Develop a matrix of brand-switching probabilities on the basis of these two weeks of data.

2.4. Consider this brand-switching matrix:

$$
\begin{array}{cc}
 & \text{To} \\
 & \begin{array}{ccc} \text{A} & \text{B} & \text{C} \end{array} \\
\text{From}\ \begin{array}{c} \text{A} \\ \text{B} \\ \text{C} \end{array} & \begin{pmatrix} 0.7 & 0.2 & 0.1 \\ 0.3 & 0.6 & 0.1 \\ 0.1 & 0.4 & 0.5 \end{pmatrix}
\end{array}
$$

  a. The initial brand shares are (0.10, 0.40, 0.50). What is brand A's expected share next period?

b. What is brand A's ultimate market share if the switching probabilities remain constant?

Using the first-order Markov matrix just shown, determine the following:

c. The probability that A will be purchased in period $t + 1$, given that C was purchased in period t

d. The probability of A_{t+1}, given B_t

e. The probability of B_{t+1} and C_{t+2} given A_t

f. The probability of A_{t+1} and A_{t+2}, given A_t

2.5. Mrs. Smith just moved into town, and on her first trip to the supermarket she enters the store with a 0.4 probability of buying brand B. Suppose she buys brand B this time and also on her second trip. Assume that her learning operators are

$$p_{t+1} = 0.3 + 0.6p_t, \quad \text{for a purchase}$$
$$p_{t+1} = 0.1 + 0.6p_t, \quad \text{for a rejection}$$

a. What is the probability that she will buy brand B on her *third* trip to the store?

b. If she keeps buying brand B, what is her probability of buying brand B in the limit?

2.6. A buyer may choose from three competing brands of laundry detergent, A, B, and C. The unadjusted repurchase probabilities for each brand (i.e., the unadjusted probability that the buyer who has purchased the brand at time t will repurchase that brand at time $t + 1$) are $r_A = 0.70$, $r_B = 0.40$, and $r_C = 0.20$. The relative merchandising attractiveness of each brand is $a_A = 0.25$, $a_B = 0.35$, and $a_C = 0.40$. Construct a model that describes the buyer's switching and staying behavior.

2.7. A frequent exercise among builders of stochastic models of brand choice is to test whether a model fits observed behavior well or to test which of two models fits best. A frequent test of the presence of a homogeneous Bernoulli process is a chi-squared test.

a. We observe, for each customer, two successive purchases of the product. It appears that the same percentage of all buyers buy A on the first and second of those purchases. Suppose this percentage is 70%. Assume that the underlying process is homogeneous Bernoulli.

   i. What is p_A?

   ii. Determine the percentage of the buyers who should have the following sequences of purchases if the process is, indeed, homogeneous Bernoulli: AA, AB, BA, BB.

   iii. We observe 100 consumers for two purchases and find the following sequences of purchases:

Last Purchase	Current Purchase	
	A	B
A	52	18
B	18	12

Do a chi-squared test. Is the homogeneous Bernoulli model fitting?

iv. We now observe 500 customers for two purchases and find the following sequences of purchases:

	Current Purchase	
Last Purchase	A	B
A	260	90
B	90	60

Do a chi-squared test. Is the homogeneous Bernoulli model fitting?

v. Compare the observed frequencies of each sequence of purchase in parts (iii) and (iv). What do you conclude about the chi-squared test?

b. Suppose now we observe the following frequencies for each sequence of purchase:

	Current Purchase	
Last Purchase	A	B
A	42.5%	12.5%
B	12.5	32.5

How does a homogeneous Bernoulli model fit? How does a homogeneous Markov model fit?

c. Suppose that the consumer's population is made up of two subgroups. In subgroup I (which comprises 50% of the consumers), consumers prefer brand A and follow a Bernoulli model: they buy A 90% of the time, regardless of their previous purchase. In subgroup II (which comprises the remaining 50% of the population), consumers prefer brand B and follow a Bernoulli model: they buy B 80% of the time, regardless of their previous purchases.

   i. What is the expected frequency of each of the sequences of purchase (AA, AB, BA, BB) in subgroup I?

   ii. What is the expected frequency of each of the sequences of purchase (AA, AB, BA, BB) in subgroup II?

   iii. Assume a market analyst has data only on the frequency of purchases in the total market and that he does not know about subgroups I and II. What frequencies of purchase should he be expected to observe?

   iv. Compare the results here with the frequencies observed in part (b). Any comments?

2.8. In the linear learning model each consumer has his own probability of purchasing A on his tth purchase p_{At}. This probability depends on the corresponding probability of the preceding purchase, $p_{A,t-1}$, and on whether A was indeed bought on the last purchase, as follows:

$$p_{A,t} = a + b + cp_{A,t-1}, \qquad \text{if A was purchased on occasion } t - 1$$
$$p_{A,t} = a + cp_{A,t-1}, \qquad \text{if B was purchased on occasion } t - 1$$

Assume that $a = 0.0052$, $b = 0.4393$, and $c = 0.5448$.

a. Construct a graph showing on the abscissa $p_{A,t-1}$ and on the ordinate $p_{A,t}$ (the graph should comprise two lines, one corresponding to the case where A was bought on occasion $t - 1$, the other to the case where A was not bought).

b. What is the highest value that p_A can take if it starts from an intermediate value and, because of repeated purchases, increases? Assume a consumer has initially this value for $p_{A,t}$; what is his expected number of purchases before he buys B? How will his p_A change during that time?

c. What is the lowest value that p_A can take if it starts from an intermediate value and, because of repeated purchases, decreases? Assume a consumer has this value for p_A; what is his expected number of purchases before he buys A for the first time? How will his p_A change during that time?

d. Assume a consumer has initially a p_A of 0.5. If one considers his next three purchases, eight patterns are possible: AAA, AAB, ABA, ABB, BAA, BAB, BBA, BBB. What is the probability of occurrence of each of these patterns? What would be the final p_A for each of the patterns? Would you say that the situation of having a p_A equal to 0.5 is stable?

e. Given the results of parts (b), (c), and (d), try to give an intuitive answer to the following question. Suppose we make a histogram of the distribution of initial p_A's over the population. Which one of the following three patterns is more likely to appear? Why?

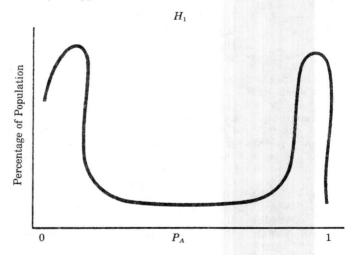

H_1

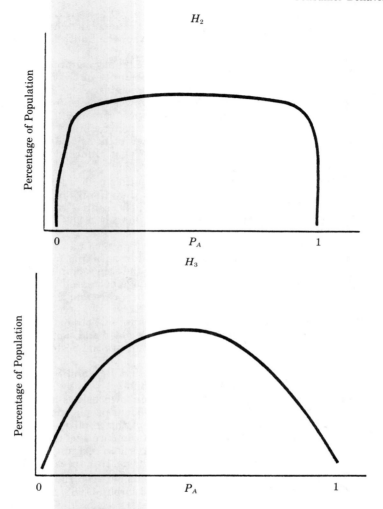

f. The basic assumption of the heterogeneous Bernoulli model is that each consumer has a constant p_A (the p_A's being different from consumer to consumer). Considering your answers to parts (b), (c), and (d), would you say that it is frequent, or not, for a consumer to have a constant p_A during several successive purchases? How well should a heterogeneous Bernoulli model be expected to fit if the true process is a linear learning model and vice versa?

2.9. When the Smith family decides whether to replace their car, they look at the expected value of their current one and the expected value of a new one. Both of these are estimated with uncertainty and a binary logit model can be used to describe the probability of them buying a new car (experiencing need arousal). Currently their existing car (net of its trade in value) is worth 8 points to them (on a measure with ratio scaling), but it depreciates at 30% year. A new car is worth 5 points net of its price. Currently, the Smith family has a 0.2 probability of buying a car in the next year.

    a. What are the sources of variation that explain why we cannot tell for certain from our measurements now whether the Smith family will buy a car in the next 12 months?

    b. What is the scaling constant in the binary logit model (using equation 2.47)?

    c. Calculate and graph how the probability of the Smith family buying a car changes as their existing one depreciates.

    d. The source of the utility of the new car comes from an inclusive value of 7 and value of having to search for new cars of −2. The inclusive value comes from the consideration of four cars using a brand choice logit model (with no scaling factor) which have expected utilities of 6.4, 5.8, 4.8, and 3.8. Recalculate your answer to (c) if a new car is launched which the Smiths consider and assign an expected utility of 6.9.

2.10. The distribution of Bob and Sally Smith's beliefs about the fuel economy that they will get from a new car when they finally replace their old one can be described by a normal distribution. Their best guess (expected value) is 35 miles per gallon, though they agree that there is a 25% chance that it could be as high as 40 mph.

    The distribution of word of mouth can also be assumed to be normally distributed. Bob and Sally agree that after speaking to four new car owners they will only have half the uncertainty that they do now regarding fuel economy (the variance of their estimate will have decreased by half). In fact they speak to nine people who recently bought new cars and the data they get from them is 33, 39, 31, 28, 30, 37, 32, 35, and 32.

    a. What are the mean and the variance of Bob and Sally's prior beliefs about fuel economy? What are the sample mean and sample variance of the average miles per gallon of a new car? What are the posterior mean and variance of their beliefs?

    b. What is the ratio of the weight that Bob and Sally attached to their own beliefs relative to the sample of nine?

    c. Are Bob and Sally weighting their own beliefs appropriately? (Hint: From the weighting that they would give four people and the variance of their prior beliefs, you can get an estimate of the implicit variance that they believe exists in word of mouth. You can compare this to the sample variance.)

    d. Plot the decrease in variance (increase in certainty) of Bob and Sally's beliefs after receiving word of mouth from one, two, three, and so on new car owners.

2.11. The matrix containing the correlations between the ratings of various cars on different attributes from Roberts and Urban (1988) is as follows:

	LUX	*STYLE*	*RELY*	*MPG*	*SAFE*	*MAINT*	*QUAL*	*DUR*	*PERF*
LUXURY	1.000	0.591	0.356	−0.098	0.573	0.156	0.400	0.282	0.519
STYLE	0.591	1.00	0.350	0.072	0.408	0.232	0.414	0.375	0.484
RELY	0.356	0.350	1.000	0.380	0.382	0.517	0.611	0.512	0.467
MPG	−0.098	0.072	0.380	1.000	0.062	0.424	0.320	0.346	0.167
SAFETY	0.573	0.408	0.382	0.062	1.000	0.303	0.401	0.308	0.455
MAINT	0.156	0.232	0.517	0.424	0.303	1.000	0.479	0.463	0.311
QUALITY	0.400	0.414	0.611	0.320	0.401	0.479	1.000	0.605	0.574
DURABLE	0.282	0.375	0.512	0.346	0.308	0.463	0.605	1.000	0.557
PERFORM	0.519	0.484	0.467	0.167	0.455	0.311	0.574	0.557	1.000

To examine the underlying structure of perceptions, both two- and three-factor common-factor analyses were performed with factor loadings after Varimax rotation:

	TWO-FACTOR SOLUTION			THREE-FACTOR SOLUTION		
	Factor 1	Factor 2	Commonality	Factor 1	Factor 2	Factor 3
LUXURY	0.91	−0.03	0.82	0.04	−0.09	0.93
STYLE	0.64	0.19	0.45	0.31	−0.03	0.45
RELY	0.39	0.65	0.57	0.18	0.54	0.24
MPG	−0.10	0.62	0.40	0.09	0.58	−0.19
SAFETY	0.61	0.20	0.41	0.03	0.18	0.59
MAINTENANCE	0.18	0.65	0.46	−0.03	0.72	0.14
QUALITY	0.48	0.64	0.63	0.51	0.29	0.13
DURABLE	0.37	0.63	0.54	0.73	0.16	−0.11
PERFORMANCE	0.62	0.40	0.54	0.73	−0.10	0.18

Eigenvalues for the first through to fifth (unrotated) factors are 4.43, 1.54, 0.72, 0.55, and 0.48.

   a. Evaluate the two-factor solution. Based on the factor loadings, what would you call both factors? How well has the factor analysis captured each attribute? How much of the variance of the attributes overall is explained? How clearly do the attributes load either onto factor 1 or factor 2 (but not both)?
   b. Calculate the commonalities of the three-factor solution.
   c. Interpret the three-factor solution. Based on interpretability, a scree test of the eigenvalues (looking for where there is an "elbow" in the eigenvalues), and fit, which of the factor analyses do you prefer?
   (Thanks to Prof. James Lattin for this question.)

2.12. Members of a group of car enthusiasts discuss their perceptions and preferences with respect to cars on the market. They find they have the same view of the market (homogeneous perceptions), but because they value different features in a car they have varying preferred makes (heterogeneous preference). Their perceptions of a group of cars is as follows:

		Style (out of 10)	Reliability (out of 10)	Price	Country of Manufacture
1.	Kyoto Coupé	5	9	13	Japan
2.	Seoul Sedan	4	7	10	Korea
3.	Michigan Motorer	9	8	16	United States
4.	Tallahassee Tourer	8	6	12	United States
5.	Bavarian Buggy	7	9	22	Germany

Individuals made the following comments on the cars:

John: I would prefer to buy an Italian car but I am prepared to buy one from somewhere else if it is stylish enough (style ≥ 9).

Sarah: A car must be at least moderately stylish (≥ 6) and must be extremely reliable (≥ 9). After that, I don't care.

Jane: I am prepared to trade off reliability against style. Reliability is twice as important to me as style though. Nothing else is really important.

Andrew: All the cars on the market are pretty good. Given that, it boils down to price. I buy the cheapest.

Kathryn: I'm not interested in cars over $15,000. Once I find a car that meets that criterion, I trade off reliability, price, and style. For example, I would rate cars 1, 2, and 3 equally.

a. Describe the decision rule that each person is using.

b. Apply it to the data and work out their preferred car(s).

c. Draw a graph showing where each car falls on style and reliability. Draw lines on the graph to demonstrate each person's preference structure.

2.13. The Smith family is planning their vacation. They are considering Australia, New Zealand, the Caribbean, or a visit to Bob's parents in Florida, a trip to Disneyland, or a camping trip around the national parks in Utah. The first three will be expensive and something of a luxury, while the lasts three are more like the vacations the Smith family usually takes.

The travel agent's marketing analyst has elicited the attribute perceptions of each of these destinations, together with estimating their importance weights from a logit analysis. The results are as follows:

	Economical	Interest	Relaxing	Easy for Kids
Importance weight	0.20	0.35	0.25	0.20
Australia	1	10	6	4
New Zealand	2	8	4	4
Caribbean	4	4	7	5
Florida	8	1	5	5
Disneyland	5	4	5	8
Utah	7	7	5	4

a. Calculate the preference for each location.

b. Calculate the probability of each location being chosen.

c. Calculate the inclusive value of going on vacation (the expected preference that will be derived from the best location that is finally selected).

Assume now that the Smith family makes a hierarchical choice: first whether to vacation within the United States or not, and then the specific destination (with all of the perceptions remaining constant). The preference for vacationing within the United States is just its inclusive value, as is the case for an overseas vacation.

d. What is the probability of each vacation being chosen now? What is the probability of vacationing in the United States under two models?

e. If a civil war that suddenly erupts in Australia leads the Smith family to no longer consider it, how do the probabilities of the other destinations change using first the model in part (b) and second in part (d)?

2.14. A consumer considers shopping in two stores, but sometimes feels that the service in one store is dropping off. Therefore, he always gives 50% weight in his judgment of that store to his most recent experience and 50% to his judgment before entering the store last time. His choice of store is adequately described by a logit model. His valuation of good service at this store is 8 points and bad service 2. The other store performs consistently at 5 points (ratio-scaled for the logit model).

a. If his most recent judgment of the store in which we are interested was 6 before he suffered bad service, what was the change in his probability of visiting it on his next shopping occasion?

b. How many visits to this store will he have to undertake before his judgment is restored to its level before the poor service? What is the expected number of shopping trips for this to occur?

c. Compare this model to a linear learning model.

d. If we now allow degrees of service between 2 and 8 in the store of interest, given a starting judgment of 6, plot the probability of his visiting the store on the next occasion as a function of the service level.

e. Festinger's theory of cognitive dissonance reduction suggests that disconfirming evidence will be ignored if it is not too compelling. Assume the consumer can rationalize away shortfalls in service relative to his expectations of up to 0.15. Redo the graph in part (d) on this basis.

3 | ORGANIZATIONAL BUYING MODELS

It is quite common to differentiate, as we do here, between consumer behavior models and organizational behavior models. This somewhat artificial distinction reflects several key differences between the way individuals buy and the way organizations buy.

First, organizational demand is *derived* demand. Products are purchased by organizations to meet the needs of their customers. Impulse buying is far less common; objective criteria—such as meeting production needs and schedules with a minimum-cost product—often drive the choice process.

Second, more than one individual and often many individuals are involved in the purchasing decision process; as Wind (1976) points out, purchasing managers rarely make a buying decision independent of the influence of others in the organization.

Third, because of (1) the often high dollar volume involved, (2) the number of individuals affected, and (3) the technical nature of the products under consideration, the purchasing process may take a long time and involve extensive bargaining and negotiation processes. This extended purchase process, which may take months (or sometimes even years), and the interactive nature of the resulting negotiations make it difficult to determine a functional relationship between marketing effort and buyer response.

Finally, as Hudson (1971) and others have noted, organizational buyers are not as interested in a physical product as in the satisfaction of a total need. Thus the offering may include such items as technical support, training, delivery dates, and financial terms. This method of satisfying the total need is part of the trend toward systems selling (Mattssons, 1973).

On the other hand, consumer and organizational buying behavior have two attributes in common: a purchase is the usual outcome of the process and the decision is the result of decision-making activities.

There have been a number of debates in the literature (e.g., Fern and Brown, 1984) surrounding the question of whether consumer and organizational buying are really similar or really different. For example, one can view a consumer purchase of a hot water heater as derived demand (i.e., driven by the family need for hot water); the purchase of household durables and "important" products are often the result of family decision making, involving multiple individuals and negotiations. In addition, many consumers have long-term relationships with suppliers (auto dealers, insurance suppliers, legal council and the like) that are similar to the long-term buyer-seller relationships commonly ascribed to organizational buyers.

EXAMPLE

Gensch (1984) used a multinomial logit model, as discussed in Chapter 2, to determine "switchability" or customer loyalty in the electrical equipment market (aimed at electric utility customers). He estimated individual customers' choice probabilities and then tested for significant differences, classifying customers into one of four groups:

Our loyal	Customers who perceive "our firm" vastly superior to competitors
Competitive	Customers who prefer "us" to any competitor, but for whom that difference is not statistically significant
Switchable	Customers who prefer a competitor to "us" but for whom that difference is not statistically significant
Competitor loyal	Customers who perceive a competitor vastly superior to us

In a test of the methodology, the firm reallocated sales force efforts to emphasize the "competitive" and "switchable" customers and stressed those attributes specifically important to those groups. The result: in a one-year, three-territory test, sales were up by 18% and 12% in two territories following the recommendations and down by 10% in a third territory that followed the "old" procedure. In the same period, total industry sales were down by 15%.

Note that, while this is an organizational buying example, the same methodology would be appropriate for a high-involvement, multiattribute consumer product where the purchase was a highly rational decision.

What we will attempt to do in this chapter is to focus on two aspects of buying behavior that are more common in an organizational setting than in a consumer setting: models of group decision making and bargaining models. To put these two categories of models in perspective, we first review several general models of organizational buying behavior.

GENERAL MODELS OF ORGANIZATIONAL BEHAVIOR

Webster (1984) cites three general models of the organizational buying decision process, which are described in the paragraphs that follow. These models focus on the entire process and are applicable to a wide spectrum of industrial products; they identify the most important variables in the process and suggest the relationships between these variables.

The Sheth Model

Sheth (1973b) adapted the Howard-Sheth model of consumer buying behavior for industrial organizations. It is an overall model, focusing on the important elements in the decision process and their interactions. The form of the model, shown in Exhibit 3.1, is a block or flow model in which the variables and their effects are suggested, but functional relationships are not identified.

The model assumes there are three major elements in the organizational buying process: (1) the so-called psychological world of the individuals involved in the buying process, (2) the conditions that precipitate joint decision making, and (3) when the purchasing process is a joint decision, the process of conflict resolution. In addition, Sheth identifies situational factors that influence the final choice of supplier or brand.

Psychological Characteristics. A primary component of the psychological aspect of the Sheth model is the concept of expectations, which he defines as "the perceived potential of alternative suppliers and brands to satisfy a number of explicit and implicit objectives in any particular buying situation" (Sheth, 1973b, p. 52). Because many individuals, including the purchasing agent, may be involved in the buying process, Sheth identifies several factors that cause individual members of the buying process to hold different expectations. These include the background of the individuals, their information sources, their individual attempts at active search, perceptual distortions, and satisfaction with past purchases.

Background variables include education, role orientation, and life-style. Sheth notes that different educational backgrounds of the purchasing agents,

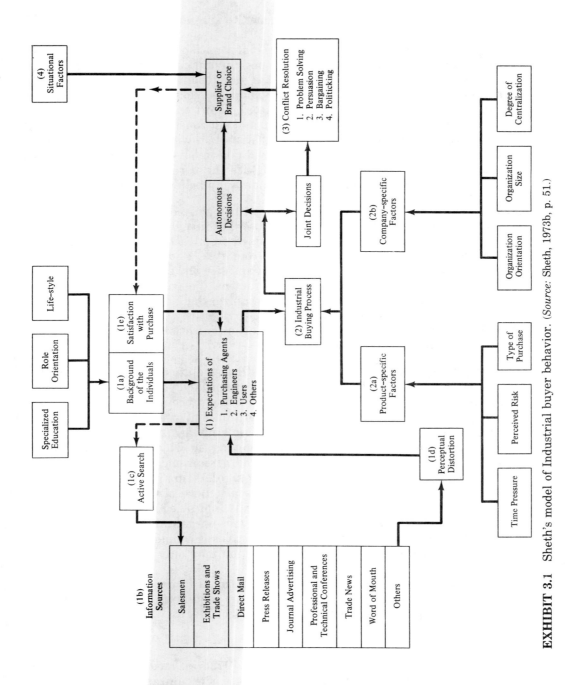

EXHIBIT 3.1 Sheth's model of Industrial buyer behavior. (*Source:* Sheth, 1973b, p. 51.)

engineers, and plant managers may generate substantially different goals and values.

Sheth's second and third factors, information sources and search processes, create unique expectations among buying center members. This concept is consistent with the notion of the gatekeeping function or the delegation of responsibility to certain individuals to search and gather relevant information. The fourth factor, perceptual distortion, is the interpretation of incoming information by individuals to make it consistent with their existing knowledge and beliefs. The last factor, satisfaction with past purchases, causes different expectations among the individuals involved; for example, production personnel may have been pleased with the performance of a previously purchased item, but purchasing personnel may believe it was too costly.

Joint Decision Making. Sheth distinguishes between purchasing processes that involve only one individual and those that involve a group of people. The number of persons involved is determined from factors classified as either product specific—time pressure, perceived risk, and type of purchase—or company specific—company orientation and size and degree of centralization. According to the model, the more nonroutine the purchase, the higher the perceived risk, and the less the time pressure, the more likely it is that the decision process will include more people. Similarly, the larger the organization and the more highly centralized the organizational structure, the more likely is joint decision making.

Conflict Resolution. The process of conflict resolution is relevant in a joint decison-making process when goals, perceptions, and value systems vary. Following completion of early phases of the buying process, including need identification, information gathering, and evaluation of suppliers, the participants will become involved in a conflict-resolving task. Sheth posits two types of rational conflict resolution: problem solving, in which information acquisition and deliberation play key roles, and persuasion, where an attempt is made to influence dissenting members by highlighting incongruities between purchase criteria and overall corporate goals. Both of these techniques can be utilized when all parties agree on goals and objectives. However, when fundamental differences exist, trade-offs and bargaining may be necessary, and when disagreement in goals and objectives is coupled with disagreement on decision-making styles, conflict resolution may only result from politicking.

Finally, Sheth notes that ad hoc situational factors, beyond the control of participants, such as changes in economic conditions, reorganization, and strikes, may influence the purchasing decision.

Webster-Wind Model

A key contribution of the Webster-Wind (1972a, b) model is its view of organizational buying behavior as a special case of organizational decision making. In their view a buying situation is created when members of the organization perceive a problem that can be solved through purchasing action. To address the buying problem, then, they introduce the concept of a buying center, which consists of those members of the organization who will be involved in the buying decision process.

Webster and Wind's model, represented in block diagram form in Exhibit 3.2 considers four sets of variables: environmental factors (E), organizational factors (D), group factors (G), and individual factors (I), all influencing buying behavior (B):

$$B = f(E, D, G, I) \tag{3.1}$$

These four sets of variables are developed as follows:

1. *Environmental factors* include legal, cultural, technological, economic, and physical-environment variables, serving primarily as constraints on action.

2. *Organizational characteristics*, given special prominence in this model, are divided into four sets of variables: technology, structure, goals and tasks, and actors. Technology affects what is purchased and the nature of the buying process itself. Organizational structure is defined in terms of five subsystems—communication, authority, status, reward, and work flow—that shape the buying process. Goals and tasks are associated with the phases of the decision process and the possible roles of the actors involved.

3. *Interpersonal variables* are defined within the structure of the buying center. These variables include task (related to the specific buying situation) as well as nontask variables (related to the general structuring and functioning of the group).

4. *Individual variables* are critical, since Webster and Wind assert that in the final analysis all organizational buying behavior is individual behavior. The variables affecting the individual's decision process include motivation, cognitive structure, personality, learning, perceived roles, and preference structure.

In evaluating a product, Webster and Wind realize that the organizational buyer makes a decision over multiple attributes. They examine several classes of decision models—conjunctive, disjunctive, lexicographic, and compensatory—and conclude that buyers may use any one of them in their individual decision processes.

The Choffray-Lilien Model

Building upon the conceptual work just cited, Choffray and Lilien (1980) developed a model of the organizational adoption process for new capital equip-

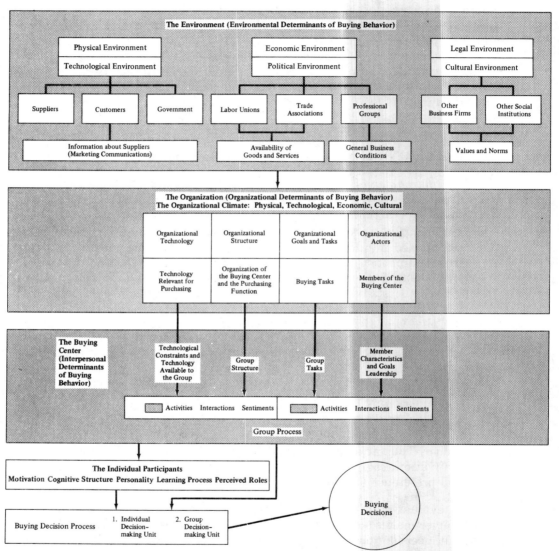

EXHIBIT 3.2 A model of organizational buying behavior. (*Source:* Webster and Wind, 1972b, p. 15.)

ment. Relative to the Webster-Wind and Sheth models, it is short and simple, focusing on those variables with a consistent, major influence across decision classes and organizations.

The model deals explicitly with the links between the characteristics of an organization's buying center and the major stages in the industrial purchasing decision process though the following:

1. The elimination of evoked product alternatives that do not meet organizational requirements
2. The formation of decision participants' preferences
3. The formation of organizational preferences and choices

It handles three types of customer heterogeneity:

1. *Need-specification heterogeneity.* Potential customer organizations may differ in their need-specification dimensions, that is, the criteria used to specify requirements. For example, company A uses payback period as a criterion, while company B uses initial cost only. Furthermore, they may also differ in their specific requirements: company A requires a three-year payback, while company C finds four years satisfactory.

2. *Buying center heterogeneity.* Potential customers may differ in the composition of their buying centers. Who is involved? What are their responsibilities? For instance, company A has a purchasing agency and an engineer involved in the buying process for industrial cooling equipment, where the engineer screens alternatives and the purchasing agent buys. Meanwhile, in company B top management is also involved.

3. *Evaluation criteria heterogeneity.* Decision participants may differ in their sources of information, as well as in the number and nature of the criteria they use to assess alternatives: engineers are concerned about reliability, while purchasing agents are concerned about price.

The consideration of these sources of heterogeneity requires members of the buying center be grouped. To this end, the model assumes the following:

1. Within potential customer organizations the composition of the buying center can be characterized by the job categories of participants involved in the purchasing process.
2. Decision participants who belong to the same job category share the same set of product-evaluation criteria and the same information sources.

The operational sequence of measurements and models are specified in Exhibit 3.3. The first two stages define the market technically and perform a first-level segmentation, called macrosegmentation, that characterizes or-

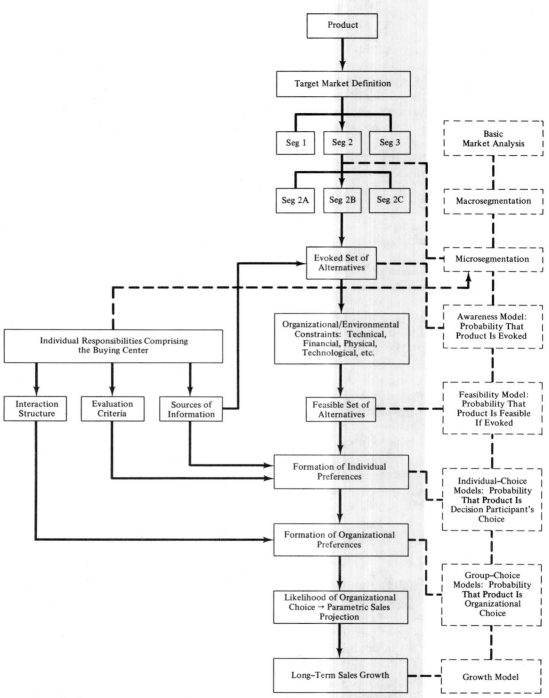

EXHIBIT 3.3 General structure of industrial market analysis model. (*Source:* Choffray and Lilien, 1980, p. 36.)

ganizations likely to react differently to the product offering because of their industry or other observable characteristics.

The next step is called microsegmentation. Here macrosegments are divided into smaller groups with similar decision process structure. A survey tool, called a decision matrix, is used to measure the involvement of different categories of individuals in a particular organization at each stage of the purchasing procedure. Organizations with similar structure across individuals and decision process phases are grouped together.

Following this target market definition, there are five submodels: an awareness model, a feasibility model, an individual choice model, a group choice model, and a growth model. The procedure assumes that organizations in a microsegment (having similar decision-making units) use the same dimensions for screening product alternatives. Similarly, the model assumes that individuals with similar backgrounds and job responsibilities structure preferences in the same manner.

Stated analytically, the probability that product a_0 in evoked set A is the organization's choice at time t (given that the organization is in the market to purchase a product in the class) can be written as

$$p(a_0 = \text{organizational choice})$$

$$= p(a_0 = \text{group choice} \mid \text{interaction, feasible, evoked}) \qquad (3.2)$$

$$\times\ p(a_0 = \text{feasible} \mid \text{evoked}) \times p(a_0 = \text{evoked})$$

As seen in equation (3.2) and in Exhibit 3.3, the procedure is sequential and operational. The authors suggest a variety of procedures and functional forms for determining the likelihood that the product is evoked by the firm, the likelihood that the product meets the firm's evaluation criteria, and, finally, the likelihood that the individuals involved in the decision-making process choose a given supplier. (We develop some of the group choice models later in this chapter.)

EXAMPLE _____

The Choffray-Lilien model and procedure was used to assess the market potential for solar powered cooling systems.

Microsegmentation.   The authors conducted a market survey to develop data for the model. Analysis of survey responses lead to the identification of four microsegments. Exhibit 3.4 gives the sizes of these microsegments, as well as the key decision participants in the equipment-selection phase of the decision process. Companies in segment 4 are smaller, more satisfied with their current cooling system, and more concerned with the economic aspects of cooling. They are characterized by a more

Item	Segment 1	Segment 2	Segment 3	Segment 4
Microsegment size in potential market	12%	31%	32%	25%
Major Decision Participants in a/c equipment selection decision (frequencies of involvement)	Plant managers (1.00)	Production engineers (0.94)	Production engineers (0.97)	Top Management (0.85)
	HVAC consultants (0.38)	Plant managers (0.70)	HVAC consultants (0.60)	HVAC consultants (0.67)
Satisfaction with current a/c system	Medium/ High	Low	Medium/ Low	High
Consequence if new a/c less economical than projected	Medium/ High	Low	Medium/ Low	High
Consequence if new a/c less reliable than projected	Medium/ High	Low	High	Medium/ Low
Company Size	Medium	Large	Large	Small
Percentage of plant area requiring a/c	Medium/ Large	Small	Large	Medium
Number of separate plants	Medium/ Large	Small	Large	Medium/ Small

Note: Abbreviation a/c means air conditioning.

EXHIBIT 3.4   Microsegments of organizations in the potential market for solar air conditioning

frequent involvement of managerial functions and rely on external sources of expertise (HVAC, heating, ventilating, and air conditioning consultants) to assist them. Segments 1 and 3 do not differ much by size of firm, but segment 3 companies have more plants, have larger cooling needs, and are more concerned with reliability of cooling than segment 1 is. Thus companies in segment 3 rely on engineering functions for air conditioning assessment, while those in segment 1 rely on management functions. Finally, segment 2 consists of large companies with a small number of plants. Such companies tend to have decisions made at the plant level, as indicated by the high frequency of involvement of plant managers and engineers.

Market-potential assessment. The authors parameterized individual preference models and tested if different decision participant categories

	Dimension A	Dimension B	Dimension C
Plant Managers	*"Benefits"* Energy Savings/ Protection Modernness Low Operating Cost	*"Risk"* Reliability/ Field Tested Modularity Noise Level	
Production Engineers	*"Benefits"* Energy Savings/ Protection Low Operating Cost Modernness Reduced Pollution	*"Noise"* Noise Level Modularity	*"Risk"* Complexity Field Tested/ Reliability
Top Managers	*"Benefits"* Energy Savings/ Protection Low Operation Cost Modernness Protection against Power Failure	*"Risk"* Reliability/ Field Tested Initial Cost Complexity	*"Noise"* Noise Level
HVAC Consultants	*"Benefits"* Energy Savings/ Protection Modernness Reduced Pollution	*"Risk"* Reliability/ Field Tested	*"Cost"* Initial Cost Noise Level

Adapted from Choffray and Lilien (1978), pp, 220-221.

EXHIBIT 3.5 Perceptual dimensions of air conditioning systems by participants in the buying decision

had the same perception and preference structure. Exhibit 3.5 shows that not only the structure but the number of preference dimensions differed by decision participant category (with preference structures varying as well). Discussions with decision makers in the industry suggested that the use of a weighted probability model (see Section 3.2) to evaluate the interaction process between participant categories would be generally acceptable. Thus to get conditional probability of choice given feasibility, we use the following equation:

$$p_G(a) = \sum_i w_i p_i(a) \qquad (3.3)$$

where

Segment	Size	Conditional Probability of Group Choice Given Feasibility $(p_1w_1 + p_2w_2)$
1	0.12	0.44 x 0.72 + 0.15 x 0.28 = 0.359
2	0.31	0.50 x 0.57 + 0.44 x 0.43 = 0.474
3	0.32	0.50 x 0.62 + 0.15 x 0.38 = 0.367
4	0.25	0.45 x 0.56 + 0.15 x 0.44 = 0.318

EXHIBIT 3.6   Microsegment response in solar cooling study

i = decision-participant category

$p_i(a)$ = fraction of responding individuals indicating first preference for solar and

w_i = importance weight for decision-participant category i

Exhibit 3.6 gives the conditional probability of group choice for each segment.

The model suggests putting these pieces together as

Penetration potential = choice level given feasibility

$\times$ feasibility given awareness $\times$ awareness

For awareness the study showed that 15% of company people and 41% of HVAC consultants were aware of solar cooling. Thus the probability that the group will be aware is $1 -$ (no one is aware), or $1 - \Pi(1 - p(\text{aware}))$. Hence we get awareness by segment:

Segment 1: $1 - 0.85 \times 0.59 = 0.50$

Segment 2: $1 - (0.85)^2 = 0.28$

considering only the two major decision participant groups for each segment.

To develop total market response, we take feasibility = 0.02, as calculated from the study, and calculate likely response as 0.32%. (See Exhibit 3.7.) A similar calculation assuming 100% awareness (perhaps on the basis of a heavy media campaign) would yield an expected share of 0.77%.

This example does not incorporate the final part of the model—the growth

Segment	Size	x	Awareness	x	Feasibility	x	Group Choice	= Response
1	0.12	x	0.50	x	0.02	x	0.359	= 0.00043
2	0.31	x	0.28	x	0.02	x	0.474	= 0.00082
3	0.32	x	0.50	x	0.02	x	0.367	= 0.00117
4	0.25	x	0.50	x	0.02	x	0.318	= 0.00080
							Response	= 0.0032

EXHIBIT 3.7   Calculation of expected response in solar cooling study

model—but it does point out two of the important characteristics of organizational buying, market-customer heterogeneity and group response, that must be incorporated appropriately in organizational buying models if they are to be of operational use.

General models of organizational buying have identified at least the following issues that demand additional research.

1. Multiple individuals are involved in the decision process (Lilien and Wong, 1984; Patton, Puto, and King, 1986; and Morris, Stanton, and Calantone, 1985). The values and goals of those individuals may conflict (Ryan and Holbrook, 1982); they may use different sources of information (Moriarty and Spekman, 1984; Deshpande and Zaltman, 1987); and the individuals may exert power or influence because of their position, their expertise or their reputation (Thomas, 1984). The next section deals with specific models of group decisions.

2. The organizational buyer process is generally more diverse than that for most consumer purchases. It involves varying levels of information gathering, and a more formal sequential process (Cardozo, 1983) and may be driven by the way the organization rewards work activities (Anderson and Chambers, 1985).

Thus, a wide range of modeling approaches may be appropriate to model that behavior (e.g., Keeney and Lilien, 1987).

We deal with models of bargaining, in detail, as one modeling approach that may pay important dividends in understanding organizational buying.

GROUP CHOICE

In family/household decisions as well as in the purchase of products and services by organizations, several and possibly many individuals may be involved. While the organizational buying models discuss the group decision-making problem qualitatively, there has been little work in the marketing area dealing with formal, descriptive models of group choice. (See Appendix D for some results in decision analysis concerning how groups *should* make decisions, i.e., normative group choice models.)

Few published studies have examined how buying centers—those individuals involved in the buying process—resolve preference differences to reach group choice (Corfman and Gupta, 1991; Rao and Steckel, 1991; Steckel, 1990; Davis, 1973; Corfman and Lehmann, 1987; Krishnamurthi, 1988; and Curry, Menasco and Van Ark, 1991), with the last four focusing more specifically on family decision making).

Following Choffray and Lilien (1980), one can view most proposed models of group buying as one of three categories: *nonquota schemes*, where there is no prespecified minimum number of group members who must favor an alternative for it to be related; *agreement quota schemes*, where the group deliberates until a prespecified number (or proportion) of the group selects a given choice; and an *individual decision scheme*, where one group member chooses for the group.

Some analytic models that fall into these categories are given next. Models 1–4 are nonquota models.

1. The *weighted probability model* assumes that the group, as a whole, is likely to adopt a given alternative, say, a_j in the choice set A, proportionally to the relative importance of those members who choose it. Let

$P_G(a_j; A)$ = probability that the group chooses a_j, $j = 1, \ldots, k$ alternatives.

w_i = relative importance, on the average, of decision participant i, $i = 1, \ldots, r$ in the choice process. So,

$$\sum_{i=1}^{r} w_i = 1$$

Then the weighted probability model postulates that

$$P_G(a_j; A) = \sum_{i=1}^{r} w_i P_i(a_j; A), \qquad j = 1, \ldots, k \tag{3.4}$$

Model forms similar to the weighted probability model have been suggested by March (1966) and utilized by Shiflett (1979) to model small group productivity (Steckel, Lehmann, and Corfman, 1988). Corfman and Lehmann (1987) studied a version of the weighted probability in the context of family decision making. Rao and Steckel's (1991) model adds an intercept term to accommodate group polarization. Steckel and colleagues (1988), Kriewall (1980), and Krishnamurthi (1981) examined the weighted probability model in dyadic (husband-wife) and family decision making.

2. The *equiprobability model* takes form (3.4) with $w_i = 1/r$ for all i. Davis (1973) and Buss (1981) both found support for the equiprobability in family and group choice settings.

3. The *voting model* states that the probability that the group will choose alternative a_j is equal to the probability that a_j is selected by the largest number of decision participants. Let

$$X_{ij} = \begin{cases} 1, & \text{if individual } i \text{ chooses } a_j \\ 0, & \text{otherwise} \end{cases}$$

Then

$$\Pr(X_{ij} = 1) = P_i(a_j; A).$$

If we define

$$Z_j = \sum_{i=1}^{r} X_{ij}$$

then

$$P_G(a_j; A) = \Pr[Z_j = \max(Z_k)] \tag{3.5}$$

Davis, Hoppe, and Hornseth (1968) found that a model similar to this one predicted group choice well under risky conditions.

4. The *preference perturbation model* assumes that if a group does not reach unanimous agreement, it is most likely to choose the alternative that "perturbs" individual preference structures least. Let

θ_{iw} = event that individual i has preference ordering w, $i = 1, ..., r; w = 1, ..., k!$, where a preference ordering means, for example, $a_1 >> a_2 >> a_3$ and $>>$ means "is preferred to"

λ_μ = set of preference orderings across decision participants = $\{\theta_{1w_1}, \theta_{2w_2}, ..., \theta_{rw_r}\}$ where $w_i = 1, ..., k!$ for $i = 1, ..., r$ and, hence, $\mu = 1, ..., rk!$

$Q(a_j|\lambda_\mu)$ = "perturbation" associated with the set of preference orderings λ_μ; that is, the sum of the number of preference shifts that are required to make option a_j the first choice of all decision participants

To see how Q evolves, consider a two-person, three-product decision, with

$$\lambda_\mu = (\theta_{1,w_1}, \theta_{2,w_2}) = [a_0 \gg a_1 \gg a_2; a_2 \gg a_0 \gg a_1]$$

Here $Q(a_0|\lambda_\mu) = 1$, $Q(a_1|\lambda_\mu) = 3$ and $Q(a_2|\lambda_\mu) = 2$; that is, a_0 needs to move from second to first choice for participant 2 to give $Q(a_0|\lambda_\mu) = 1$, a_1 must move from second to first for participant 1 *and* move from third to first for participant 2 for $Q(a_1|\lambda_\mu) = 3$, and so on.

Assuming that individual preference distributions are mutually independent:

$$\Pr(\lambda_\mu) = \Pr(\theta_{1,w_1}, \theta_{2,w_2}, \ldots, \theta_{r,w_r})$$

$$= \prod_{i=1}^{r} \Pr(\theta_{i,w_i}), \mu = 1, \ldots, rk! \tag{3.6}$$

where the $\{i, w_i\}$ are suitably mapped to the appropriate μ. The model postulates that the ratio of probability of group choice equals the ratio of needed preference perturbation to achieve first preference within the group:

$$\frac{P_G(a_j|\lambda_\mu)}{P_G(a_e|\lambda_\mu)} = \frac{Q(a_e|\lambda_\mu)}{Q(a_j|\lambda_\mu)} \tag{3.7}$$

Moreover if

$$Q(a_e|\lambda_\mu) = 0,$$

then

$$P_G(a_e|\lambda_\mu) = 1$$

and

$$P_G(a_j|\lambda_\mu) = 0, \qquad \text{for } j \neq e$$

(This is a case of unanimous first preference.)

As the total number of possible preference shifts is fixed, these conditional probabilities are uniquely determined. Hence, the unconditional probabilities of group choice are given by

$$P_G(a_j; A) = \sum_{w} P_G(a_j|\lambda_\mu) \cdot \Pr[\lambda_\mu] \tag{3.8}$$

A form of this model appears in studies by Davis and colleagues (1970a) as the "equal distance compromise model" and as the "city block distance model" of Kemeny and Snell (1962).

Models 5 and 6 are agreement quota models.

5. The *majority rule model* is a special case of the voting model when there is a quota (say, 50% or more) of the group required to agree for an alternative to be chosen.

Formally, we have

$$P_G(a_j; A) = \Pr\left[Z_j = \max(Z_k)|Z_k > \frac{r}{2}\right] \qquad (3.9)$$

As operationalized by Choffray and Lilien (1980), the majority rule model differs from the voting model only in how the group resolves ties (their voting model randomizes the vote while the majority rule model must reject ties given the form of equation 3.9). In groups larger than three, the two models can generate significantly different results.

Davis, Hornik, and Hornseth (1970b), Laughlin and Earley (1982), and Castore, Peterson, and Goodrich (1971) provide empirical tests of this model.

6. The *unanimity model* is another special case of the voting model with

$$P_G(a_j; A) = \Pr[Z_j = \max(Z_k)|Z_k = r] \qquad (3.10)$$

Davis (1973) has studied the predictive ability of this model, but most of the empirical research with this model has a normative focus, studying the quality of the group solution and the group members' satisfaction with that solution (Thompson, Mannix, and Bazerman, 1988; Mannix, Thompson, and Bazerman, 1989).

7. The *autocracy model*, an individual decision model, is no different from any of the models studied in the previous chapter. However, there can be several mechanisms for a single member of a group to decide for the group. For example, the individual can have the most power, the most expertise, the most time, and so on.

The *autocracy model* uses the most influential decision participant's preferences as those of the group:

$$P_G(a_j; A) = P_{i*}(a_j; A) \qquad (3.11)$$

where $i*$ is the index representing that individual for whom $w_{i*} = \max_i(w_i)$.

Where w_i are the weights from equation (3.4). Einhorn, Hogarth, and Klempner (1977) studied a model comparable to equation (3.11).

One can clearly develop more models or combinations of these models (see Corfman and Gupta, 1991). These represent a reasonable and constructive cross section of possibilities, however.

Given the range of possible models of group decision making, what guidelines exist for their use? Wilson, Lilien, and Wilson (1991) suggest a contingency approach, with two contingent dimensions: perceived risk and buying task nature (new task versus rebuying). Their framework suggests that as perceived risk increases, responsibility sharing for the buying decision will take place (e.g., compromise or agreement quota versus individual schemes) and as the buying task nature becomes more unusual for the firm (new task versus rebuy), agreement quota schemes will be used more frequently than compromise schemes. An empirical test of their contingency framework in a wide range of 104 procurement decisions gave the correct predication of organizational choice in 49% of the cases, while the best single model overall predicted choice in 20% of the cases. Three other interesting results were

- The voting model is quite robust and seems to predict group choice very well across a wide range of procurement situations.
- The autocracy model (akin to the "key informant" approach—using a single respondent's preference to represent the organization) did well for low-risk, rebuy situations, but did very poorly for other types of buying situations.
- The weighted probability model—the group choice model that has been proposed and studied most frequently—gave the poorest single prediction of first choice by the organization.

To conclude here, this range of models and the limited empirical testing of those models suggests that (1) modeling group decisions requires more subtlety than does modeling individual decisions, (2) in complex, high-risk situations, buying groups share responsibilities and studying only a key informant or "the" major purchase influences may give misleading results (Anderson, 1985), and (3) considerably more research is needed to develop and test group decision models that are descriptively sound (predict well), that are normatively sound (produce good results for the organization), and that can be readily calibrated and used by marketers (Steckel et al., 1991).

BARGAINING MODELS

In the past chapter and until here in this chapter, we have assumed that there is significant asymmetry in the market between seller(s) and buyer(s). In other words, we have assumed that sellers offer goods with given properties and prices, and buyers "shop" among those goods, selecting some (or none) in accordance with some value or preference functions.

In organizational markets (and in consumer markets with products of high utility and significant product diversity—such as for houses, automobiles, and many durable goods), the price and quantity produced and, indeed, often the nature of what is produced are determined by a bargaining process. "Most major purchases by institutions, government agencies, and commercial businesses and negotiated" Reeder and colleagues (1987, p. 475).

Definition. Bargaining or negotiation is a communication process where two (or more) parties with both *common and conflicting interests* consider a form of *joint action* (which may be an exchange or sale).

"Common and conflicting interest" in the foregoing definition refers to what makes bargaining a rich area for study. Common interest—expanding the pie in what is known as "integrative bargaining"—is one element of many bargaining problems while conflicting interests—dividing the pie in "distributive bargaining"—is the other major element.

"Joint action," or the search for agreement, is the essence of the bargaining process. Unlike the typical consumer transition, the search for agreement is active, with both (or all) parties actively involved in the search for mutually agreeable joint actions.

Raiffa (1982) provides a taxonomy of bargaining situations that we translate into a marketing framework next. These characteristics help to dictate what types of models are appropriate for a particular situation.

1. Are there two or more than two parties? While negotiations with distributors and/or suppliers (and intrafirm negotiation) may involve more than two parties, most marketing negotiations involve a (potential) buyer and seller—two parties.

2. Are the parties monolithic? Many bargaining situations, especially in the business marketplace where team buying and selling is becoming more common, may involve several individuals on both the buyer and the seller side. Those individuals may differ both in their backgrounds and their values.

3. Is the negotiation repetitive? Repetitive negotiations lead to reputations that impact on the process and outcome of future results. Concern for reputation often conditions negotiators' behavior.

4. Are there linkage effects? We interpret this question as asking if there are precedents that relate one agreement to another. For example, a deal with one customer may restrict pricing flexibility with a second.

5. Is there more than one issue? Simple bargaining models usually consider price only. In real marketing negotiations, multiple-issue bargaining (involving trade-offs) is the norm except for certain commodity-like products.

6. Are threats possible? In marketing negotiations, (credible) threats provide a mechanism for the development of power and may be important in an analysis of bargaining situations.

7. Are there constraints or time-related costs? The costs of negotiators' salaries and expenses are a nontrivial part of any business marketing negotiation. In addition, especially in cross-cultural negotiations, variations in the perceived personal cost of time may be significant.

8. Are the contracts binding? Contracts can be binding in three ways: through legal means, through group norms and through "self-enforcement." Legally binding contracts are generally understood; however, group norms, where "traditional" behavior or precedent leads to enforcement, may provide an efficient form of binding. ("You have my word on this deal.") A self-enforcing contract (Telser, 1980) is one that remains in force as long as both parties believe they are better off than they would be by ending the contract.

Raiffa (1982) also considers issues such as whether agreement and/or ratification are required, whether the negotiations are public, the nature of group norms, and whether third-party negotiation is possible.

Several definitions and concepts are important to understand bargaining models. We have already discussed differences between distributive and integrative bargaining. Some other important concepts are

Reservation price. The minimum (maximum) a seller (buyer) will settle for in the negotiation. Although framed in "price" terms, a reservation price can have utility or other dimension.

Zone of agreement. The region (if it exists) between the buyer's and the seller's reservation price.

Complete/incomplete information. Bargaining with complete information assumes all reservation prices are common knowledge. In marketing negotiations, incomplete information is the norm (with buyer and seller knowing their own reservation prices only).

Buyer/seller surplus. A buyer's or seller's surplus is the difference between the contract price and the individual's reservation price.

Exhibit 3.8 illustrates several of these concepts. Another concept that is important in studying bargaining situations is that of efficiency.

Efficiency. Several concepts of efficiency have been proposed for different levels of information available to the players. In our context, we deal mainly with what is called *ex post efficiency*, that is concluding an agreement whenever an agreement benefits both parties.

Bargaining models in marketing generally focus either on the outcome (using various equilibrium concepts—see Appendix E) or on the negotiation process. We discuss each form of modeling in the paragraphs that follow.

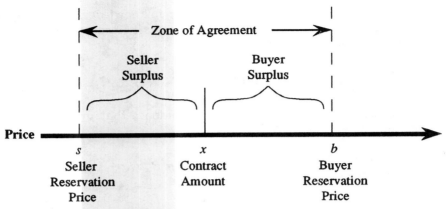

EXHIBIT 3.8 Concepts of a simple distributive bargaining situation. (Note that if $b < s$, no zone of agreement exists.)

Models of Bargaining Outcomes

Nash (1950) introduced a set of axioms that leads to a specific outcome for a simple bargaining (following Neslin and Greenhalgh, 1983, p. 370):

1. *Individual rationality.* The solution to the game should leave both players better off than they would be if they did not achieve a settlement.

2. *Feasibility.* The solution to the game should be a feasible outcome chosen from the set of all possible outcomes to the negotiation.

3. *Independence of utility function scale.* The solution to the game should not depend on the *scale* or orgin used to measure the utility functions of the participants.

4. *Pareto optimality.* The solution to the game should be such that no other settlement exists that would be preferred by *both* players.

5. *Independence of irrelevant alternatives.* If x is the solution to a game consisting of a given set of alternative settlements, x should also be the solution to any game consisting of some subset of these settlements, provided that x is present in the subset.

6. *Symmetry.* Suppose the set of possible settlements is entirely symmetric. This means that for every settlement having utility x to the first player and y to the second player, a settlement exists that has utility y to the first player and x to the second. Second, assume that utility functions must be scaled so that the player's utilities for no settlement are equal. In this case, the solution of the game should have *equal utility* to both players.

Following these axioms, assume that b and s (the buyer's and seller's reservation price, respectively) are common knowledge. Also assume that $\mu_s(.)$ and $\mu_b(.)$ are commonly known von Neuman-Morgenstern utility functions, so that payoffs for agreement, x, are

$$\mu_s(x - s) \quad \text{and} \quad \mu_b(b - x) \tag{3.12}$$

respectively. Finally, assume for convenience that $\mu_s(0) = \mu_b(0) = 0$. If we define

$$\text{Seller's surplus: } R_s = x - s$$

and

$$\text{Buyer's surplus: } R_b = b - x$$

then an efficient solution has

$$R_s + R_b = b - s \tag{3.13a}$$

with R_s and R_b satisfying

$$\max_{R_s, R_b} \lambda_s \mu_s(R_s) + \lambda_b \mu_b(R_b) \tag{3.13b}$$

subject to equation (3.13a) and where λ_s (λ_b) is the weight the seller's (buyer's) utility has in the solution.

Forming the Lagrangean

$$\max \lambda_s \mu_s(R_s) + \lambda_b \mu_b(R_b) - \gamma[R_b + R_s - b + s] \tag{3.14}$$

and solving yields

$$\frac{\lambda_s}{\lambda_b} = \frac{\mu_b'(R_b^*)}{\mu_s'(R_s^*)} \tag{3.15a}$$

$$R_b^* + R_s^* = b - s \tag{3.15b}$$

The symmetry requirement (6) can be translated as meaning that there is a set of weights for the utility functions at the solution point that gives the bargainers equal utility increments over their disagreement values (call these weights $\bar{\lambda}_s$ and $\bar{\lambda}_b$):

$$\bar{\lambda}_s \mu_s(R_s^*) - \bar{\lambda}_s \mu_s(0) = \bar{\lambda}_b \mu_b(R_b^*) - \bar{\lambda}_b \mu_b(0) \tag{3.16a}$$

or, recalling that $\mu_s(0) = \mu_b(0) = 0$,

$$\bar{\lambda}_s \mu_s(R_s^*) = \bar{\lambda}_b \mu_b(R_b^*) \tag{3.16b}$$

Further, the symmetry requirement (6) requires that $\bar{\lambda}_s = \bar{\lambda}_b$ and $\lambda_s = \lambda_b$ in (3.15a) and (3.16b), yielding

$$\frac{\mu_b(R_b^*)}{\mu_s(R_s^*)} = \frac{\mu_b'(R_b^*)}{\mu_s'(R_s^*)} \tag{3.17}$$

The solution (R_b^*, R_s^*) to (3.17) is the solution to

Find R_b^*, R_s^* to

Maximize $\mu_b(R_b)\mu_s(R_s)$ $\qquad\qquad$ (3.18)

The Nash bargaining solution, then, maximizes the *product* of the utilities (in equation 3.18) (Exhibit 3.9).

The predictive ability of the Nash bargaining solution has been studied in several marketing contexts. Neslin and Greenhalgh (1983) showed that the Nash solution held *on average* in an experiment involving the purchase of media time; however, in later work (Neslin and Greenhalgh, 1986) they showed that the results of 37 out of 64 negotiations (also media time purchases) were rejected (at $p < 0.01$) as being Nash solutions. They conclude that while the Nash solution may be a useful benchmark, it should be compared with other solution concepts and, most important, expanded to incorporate situational contingencies and personal preferences (see Weitz, 1981, and Roth, 1979). Eliashberg and colleagues (1986) tested Nash's bargaining solution against one that maximized a group utility function (Appendix C) and found that the Nash solution outperformed the group utility function in predicting outcomes of an experimental marketing channels negotiation. (Also see Roth, 1985, for a treatment of this subject.)

Note that the assumptions resulting in the Nash solution assume complete information and disregard power, influence, negotiating skills, and so on. Roth's (1979) relaxation of the symmetry assumption yields a solution that maximizes

$$\mu_s^p(R_s^*)\mu_b^q(R_b^*) \tag{3.19}$$

The values of R_b^*, R_s^* that maximize (3.19) have been termed the "weighted

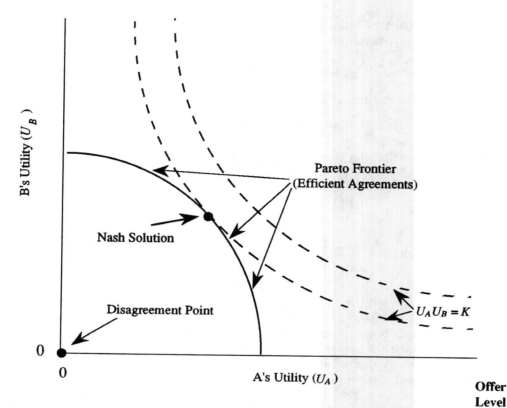

B's Utility (U_B)

Pareto Frontier
(Efficient Agreements)

Nash Solution

Disagreement Point

$U_A U_B = K$

0

0   A's Utility (U_A)

Offer
Level

EXHIBIT 3.9   A simple integrative bargaining situation.

(or asymmetric) Nash" solution. Neslin and Greenhalgh (1983) were not able to find a statistical improvement in predicative power at the aggregate level for the weighted Nash versus the unweighted Nash solution.

Chatterjee (1986) reviews a number of other solution concepts, derived from relaxing and/or modifying Nash's axioms.

As noted, the Nash solution derives from an assumption of complete information. Bargaining models incorporating incomplete information offer more realistic representations of marketing contexts. In addition, incomplete information models offer an explanation for inefficiency in bargaining.

EXAMPLE _____

Chatterjee and Samuelson (1983) analyze the following simple bargaining situation: b and s are drawn from a distribution that is uniform on [0, 1], with b known only to the buyer and s known only to the seller.

Buyers and sellers make offers simultaneously, as b' and s', and the agreed-upon price is

$$\text{Price} = \begin{cases} kb' + (1 - k)s', & \text{if } b' > s', \quad \text{for } 0 \le k \le 1 \\ \text{No agreement}, & \text{otherwise} \end{cases} \tag{3.20}$$

Note that if $k = 1/2$, the resulting price is a "split-the-difference" arrangement.

Chatterjee and Samuelson (1983) show that, in the split-the-difference case, the optimum (equilibrium) offers are

$$b' = \frac{2}{3} b + \frac{1}{12} \tag{3.21a}$$

and

$$s' = \frac{2}{3} s + \frac{1}{4} \tag{3.21b}$$

From (3.21) we see that the optimal offers are *not* "honest" (in the sense that an "honest" offer would be $b' = b$ or $s' = s$). We also note from (3.21) that, on average $b' = 5/12$ and $s' = 7/12$ (since $E(b) = E(s) = 1/2$, given the uniform distribution they are drawn from). This bargaining situation, with honest revelation, would have agreements 50% of the time. Following the strategies in (3.21) the authors show that agreement will take place in 9/32 of the cases. Therefore the "optimal" strategy is only $(9/32)/(16/32)$ or 9/16 efficient. Chatterjee (1982) shows that this lack of efficiency is a general property of bargaining problems of incomplete information.

Chatterjee (1986) provides a valuable introduction to the results and limitations of bargaining theory. He indicates that extensions of Nash's theory and the examination of models of incomplete information are likely to provide fruitful routes for development in this area, especially when focusing on explaining efficiency of solutions. Some exciting developments in this area include models that specifically incorporate reference outcomes (e.g., Gupta, 1990 and Gupta and Livne, 1988) and those that specifically deal with multiple issues (Gupta, 1989). One motivation for these developments and others (Fogelman-Soulie, Munier, and Shakun, 1983; Rao and Shakun, 1974; and England, 1975) is that all the equilibrium/outcome–focused models either ignore or downplay the dynamics of the process and how the process of negotiation (the offers/counteroffers, the selection of a strategy, individual characteristics, perceived time pressure, etc.) affect both the outcome and the process. An early attempt to address this lack is developed next.

Process Models of Negotiation

As noted, most models focusing on negotiation outcomes ignore the issues of most concern to marketers—the bargaining process. How can the preparation and strategy (set of offers/counteroffers) that a salesman or purchasing agent makes affect the outcome? An interesting approach to modeling this problem has been developed by Balakrishnan and Eliashberg (1990), building on some concepts of Pruitt (1981). Specifically, Balakrishnan and Eliashberg (1990) model the negotiation process as an alternating series of offers and counteroffers on a single issue, over time with all communication taking place within the framework of those offers. Let us assume for simplicity here that the issue is "price." They assume each negotiator's behavior is guided by two opposing forces: a "resistance curve," representing the negotiator's *disinclination* to concede, and a "concession curve," representing the negotiator's *inclination* to concede.

Analytically, their model has a seller ($i = 1$) making price offers in periods with an odd index and the buyer ($i = 2$) making (counter) offers in periods with an even index. The seller's problem is to maximize the price offer, X_t subject to

$$\rho_1(X_t) - \phi_1(X_t) = 0 \tag{3.22a}$$

(resistance curve, ρ is in balance with concession curve ϕ) and

$$\mu_1 \leq X_t \leq \tau_1 \tag{3.22b}$$

(offer must be between the reservation price μ and aspiration level τ).

Similarly, the buyer tries to minimize his buying price offer, Y_t subject to

$$\rho_2(Y_t) - \phi_2(Y_t) = 0 \tag{3.23a}$$

$$\tau_2 \leq Y_t \leq \mu_2 \tag{3.23b}$$

where

X_t, Y_t = offers made by seller/buyer, respectively, in period t
ϕ_i = party i's concession curve ($i = 1$ is the seller, $i = 2$ is the buyer)
ρ_i = party i's resistance curve
τ_i = aspiration level for party i (target point)
μ_i = reservation price for party i

The authors propose the following functional forms for the ρ_i and Φ_i curves:

$$\rho_{1,t} = \Pi_1(\tau_1 - X_t) \tag{3.24}$$

$$\rho_{2,t} = \Pi_2(Y_t - \tau_2) \tag{3.25}$$

$$\phi_1 = \alpha_1(X_t - \beta_{1,t}) \tag{3.26}$$

$$\phi_2 = \alpha_2(\beta_{2,t} - Y_t) \tag{3.27}$$

Equations (3.24–3.27) introduce the focal point, $\beta_{i,t}$ for both buyer and seller. The authors interpret this quantity as

β_{it} = party i's projection of j's ultimate offer, given what has occurred up until time t

and model it recursively as:

$$\beta_{1,2t} = \beta_{1,2t-2} + \theta_1(Y_{2t-1} - Y_{2t-3}) \tag{3.28}$$

$$\beta_{2,2t+1} = \beta_{2,2t-1} + \theta_2(X_{2t} - X_{2t-2}) \tag{3.29}$$

where

θ_i = the coefficient of party i's tendency to reciprocate ($-1 \le \theta_i \le 1$) and

$Y_{2t-1} - Y_{2t-3}; X_{2t} - X_{2t-2}$ = most recent concessions made by the buyer and seller respectively.

Note that if $\theta_i < 0$, the bargainer is acting in a reciprocative manner (tit-for-tat) while if $\theta_i > 0$, the bargainer is attempting to exploit concessions of the other party.

Note also the time indices in equations (3.28) and (3.29) suggest that party 1 acts during periods with an even-t index while party 2 acts during periods with an odd-t index.

After some algebra, equations (3.24–3.29) yield

$$X_{t'+2} - (K + 1)X_{t'+1} + KX_{t'} = 0 \tag{3.30}$$

where

$$K = \frac{\alpha_1 \alpha_2 \theta_1 \theta_2}{(\Pi_1 + \alpha_1)(\Pi_2 + \alpha_2)} \tag{3.31}$$

Equation (3.30) is a second-order difference equation, which can be solved using Z-transform methods (Miller, 1968),

$$X_{t'} = \frac{X_1 - KX_0}{(1 - K)} + K^{t'}\left[\frac{X_0 - X_1}{1 - K}\right] \tag{3.32}$$

where X_0 and X_1 are the seller's first and second offers, respectively.

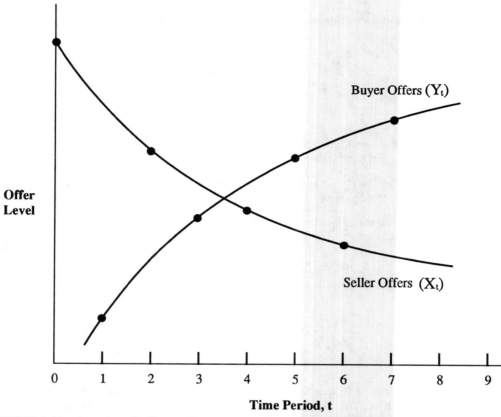

EXHIBIT 3.10 A series of offers and counteroffers resulting in agreement in period 4 (i.e., $X_4 < Y_3$).

An equation similar to (3.32) holds for $Y_{t'}$, and an agreement is said to occur at the first time, t, where $Y_{t+1} > X_t$ (that is, where the buyer is willing to meet the seller's demanded price). By studying the individual- and dyadic-level dynamics associated with equation (3.32), the model predicts if and when an agreement will take place and what the pattern of offers and counter offers looks like.

For example, Exhibit 3.10 shows a process of offers (monotonically increasing for the buyer, decreasing for the seller) that results in an agreement. Sufficient conditions for Exhibit 3.10 to characterize the negotiation are

1. Party 1 and 2 start with a concession: $(X_0 > X_2$ and $Y_1 < Y_3)$.
2. Both parties have a similar strategy of reciprocity: sign (θ_1) = sign (θ_2).
3. $X_2 - KX_0 > Y_3 - KY_1$

The authors also specify the conditions under which offers oscillate, when no agreement will take place, what the agreement point is most likely to be, and when that agreement will take place.

The authors conducted a lab experiment and a field survey to evaluate the predictive validity of the model. The results were generally encouraging, although the authors conclude that it is difficult to develop precise enough measures of the model's micro-level constructs to provide truly conclusive tests.

Even these early results are an encouraging indication that we may be able to model (and, ultimately, control) the nature and dynamics of the negotiation process. This model suggests what behavioral constructs must be known, assumed or inferred—the nature of the competitor's negotiating style (cooperative/competitive), the competitor's reservation price, his aspiration level and the like—in order to use the model predictively. Even if the model does not ultimately turn out to predict well in a wide range of situations, it may stimulate additional research in operational process models of negotiation. In particular, to the extent that this model "seems" like a real negotiator (as seen in the Balakrishnan and Eliashberg survey) it could serve as the basis for building a computerized partner (stooge) in negotiation training (Gauvin, Lilien, and Chatterjee, 1990; Rangaswamy et al., 1989). Of course if a negotiator is able to foresee the results of the model, he or she may act so as to make the model assumptions untrue—a continuing problem when trying to operationalize interactive models of any sort.

We view the area of negotiations as one that will pay important dividends for marketing modelers and practitioners in the years to come. The impact of electronic communications and computerized laboratories are permitting much better data capture, allowing the calibration and testing of models like Balakrishnan and Eliashberg's (1990) in a less obtrusive manner. And, as we develop a better behavioral base and understanding of the process (Campbell et al., 1988; Clopton, 1984; McCall and Warrington, 1984; Lehmann and Corfman, 1989), our models will become richer, more complete and more valid.

RESEARCH NEEDS IN ORGANIZATIONAL BUYING MODELS

While there have been some useful and exciting developments in the area of organizational buying models, the research needs in this area are vast. Some important questions are

How can we model interorganizational relationships in a manner that is distinctly different from interpersonal relationships? Exchange, in an organizational context, is often a manifestation of a long-term relationship between buying and selling firms. The interaction process itself has become the focus of significant research in this area (Ford, 1980; Hakansson and Wootz, 1979; Hakansson, 1982, Turnbull and Valla, 1986; Ford, Hakansson, and Johansson, 1986); but much of that research is still qualitative and descriptive. The development of models and methods of analysis for organizational networks may prove useful here (Easton and Araujo, 1986, and Wasserman and Iacobucci, 1986, 1988) as may decision system analysis (Vyas and Woodside, 1986).

What does "influence" mean? How can we determine, validly and reliably, *who* is involved (or likely to be involved) in a decision process and *what influence* those persons are likely to have? Research in this area must encompass the dynamics of the structure of influence over time, must relate it to the stages of the buying process and must deal with the multiple-respondent nature of the supporting data (Krapfel, 1982; Moriarty and Bateson, 1982; Silk and Kalwani, 1982; Anderson, 1985; Corfman, 1991).

Related to the concept of influence is a need to know how individuals in organizations become aware and knowledgeable about product information. Operational models relating personal and impersonal marketing communications strategies to information flows within organizations are needed to determine the role of informal communications on organizational purchasing behavior.

Are there product, market, and environmental characteristics that can predict, across industries, the structure of the buying process (Who will be involved? How many individuals?) within purchasing organizations (Morris, Stanton, and Calantone, 1985)? Such research would provide a means of developing much more carefully targeted marketing programs.

With the key unit of measurement being the group, or buying center, what research tools—decision matrices, network models, buying panels, protocol studies, gaming/laboratory procedures—can be developed to measure and reflect the richness of industrial buying situations?

Finally, with so much of organizational buying representing negotiated outcomes in a long term relationship, how can we blend the theoretical insights from the game-theory-based outcome models with the operational, situation-specific needs of negotiators?

SUMMARY

Organizational buying represents a complex set of activities by a number of individuals in the buying organization. The process takes place over time, has a number of phases, and is influenced by a number of individual, group, organization, and environmental factors.

Organizational buying models have generally been one of two types: they have focused on a limited aspect of the buying process and studied that aspect in depth, or they have attempted to characterize the process as a whole, models of the latter type provide more perspective, structure, and understanding than operational guidance.

The multiperson nature of organizational buying and the bargaining process that characterized much organizational exchange have seen some important developments in recent years. Much work needs to be done to develop either important, robust theoretical results or truly usable decision support models in either of those areas.

Future work in this area should focus on modeling interorganizational relationships, measuring influence, developing operational models of group buying, and bargaining dynamics.

PROBLEMS

3.1. Compare the Sheth, Webster-Wind, and Choffray-Lilien models in terms of comprehensiveness and operationality.

3.2. Are industrial buyers more rational than consumer buyers? If so, what are the implications of this observation for modeling industrial-buying behavior.

3.3. The Merton Company, which sells bearings, has identified three individuals who influence decisions in a given customer firm. Let the influence of these three individuals on the purchase decision be denoted by $a_i f(t_i)$. The probability of receiving an order is then given by

$$p = \Sigma \, a_i \, f(t_i)$$

where $f(t_i) = 1 - e^{-b_i t_i}$ $(i = 1, 2, 3)$ and t_i is the time devoted to the ith decision influence.

a. What is the optimum allocation of salesperson time to each decision influence?

b. Suggest a procedure for measuring the parameters $\{a_i\}$.

c. How would you interpret a high value versus a low value of b_i?

d. Does the model in its present stage incorporate a brand loyalty component? If not, develop the extension to the model to include this component.

3.4. The Widget Fittings Manufacturing Company has classified its customers according to whether they are current or prospective customers. Current customers are characterized by the phenomenon of source loyalty, and for an average customer the probability of retention is given by

$$R(t) = 0.2 + 0.8(1 - e^{-2t})$$

where t is the time per month spent with the account. For new accounts the relation between time spent and the probability of conversion is given by

$$S(t) = 0.43t + 1.5t^2 - t^3$$

a. What time should be spent with a new account to maximize the conversion probability per time spent [i.e., the ratio $S(t)/t$]?

    b. Assuming new accounts and current accounts are equally profitable, what time should be spent with an existing account so that the marginal returns from existing accounts are equal to those from new accounts?

3.5. Those involved in organizational-purchasing decision processes are often referred to as decision participants. Suggest a valid measure or set of measures for the following:

    a. Whether a particular individual is involved in a decision process

    b. The level of involvement (importance) of a particular decision influence

3.6. An industrial-source loyalty study was conducted in the chemical feedstocks market. A sample of 400 companies was classified in terms of total annual sales (1 = low to 5 = high) and source loyalty (1 = low to 4 = high). The following data were collected:

Annual Sales	Degree of Source Loyalty				Total
	1	2	3	4	
1	11	9	18	27	65
2	8	15	25	31	79
3	15	28	25	28	96
4	28	24	20	8	80
5	33	20	19	8	80
	95	96	107	102	400

Is there a relationship between the size of the company and source loyalty?

3.7. Is the nature of the product or the nature of the customer more fundamental in distinguishing between consumer and industrial marketing?

3.8. A buyer and a seller are negotiating over the price, p, of a car. The buyer has seen another car that he likes just as well for $9,000. The seller has an offer in hand for $8,000.

    a. Sketch the Pareto frontier for this bargaining problem.

    b. Suppose both buyer and seller are risk-neutral. What is the Nash bargaining solution?

    c. Suppose the seller is afraid to lose the sale and is risk averse, with utility function

$$\mu_s = k[1 - e^{-0.005(p-8,000)}]$$

What is the Nash bargaining solution in this situation?

    d. Suppose the seller is a more skilled negotiator than the buyer and thus $p = 2$ and $q = 1$ in equation (3.19). What is the weighted Nash bargaining solution, from (c)?

    e. Discuss the difference between the solutions in parts (b), (c), and (d). When will they apply? What other solutions can you think of?

4 | PRICE

We can now begin our study of models of the marketing mix or marketing decision variables. We define *marketing decision variables* as those variables under the firm's control that can affect the level of demand. They are distinguished from *environmental* and *competitive-action* variables, which also affect demand but are not under the control of the firm, at least not totally and directly.

One can classify the marketing decision variables by the "four P's," the marketing mix (Exhibit 4.1): (1) price, (2) product, (3) promotion, and (4) place. This chapter deals with price; subsequent chapters deal with the other marketing-mix variables.

We focus on price before discussing product because product decisions must anticipate subsequent pricing decisions: not knowing how to price a given product or set of products makes it difficult to determine just what product or products to offer.

PRICING

Pricing is one of the most important elements of the marketing mix. It is the only marketing variable that directly determines revenue. In addition, because price affects quantity sold, it affects costs as well. Thus, few marketing

Price variables
Allowances and deals
Distribution and retailer markups
Discount structure

Product variables
Quality
Models and sizes
Packaging
Brands
Service

Promotion variables
Advertising
Sales promotion
Personal selling
Publicity

Place variables
Channels of distribution
Outlet location
Sales territories
Warehousing system

EXHIBIT 4.1   Marketing-Mix Instruments: The Four P's

(or investment) decisions within a firm have more critical consequences than do pricing decisions.

A number of factors must be taken into account in pricing decisions:

1. The objectives of the organization
2. Consumers' willingness to pay for the product
3. The costs of producing and marketing the product
4. Competition
5. Changes in 2, 3, and 4 over time

It is because of the number of factors involved that it is hard to develop general formulas for optimal pricing decisions. The manager must evaluate his particular situation to determine which factors are important and then assess what the best prices should be given those factors. In this chapter we begin with the case of a profit-maximizing firm that operates in a static environment with no competition, that is, we begin with a specific objective for the firm in an environment where factors 4 and 5 are irrelevant. Then we discuss pricing under different objectives, competition, and dynamic conditions. We conclude with an assessment of the current status and future of price modeling.

A MICROECONOMIC VIEW OF PRICING

As we noted, prices are central to the study of microeconomics. In this section we develop some of the main ideas that microeconomic price theory has produced.

Simple Monopoly Pricing in a Static Environment. In determining its profit-maximizing price, the firm must consider consumers' willingness to pay for its product—their *reservation prices*—as well as the firm's costs of manufacturing and selling the product .

The usual way of recognizing consumers' willingness to pay is via the demand curve, which shows the number of units that can be sold at various prices. Exhibit 4.2 shows a linear demand curve:

$$Q = a - bP \qquad (4.1)$$

where

Q = quantity sold
P = price
a = constant denoting quantity sold when price is 0
b = constant denoting the slope of the demand curve

Thus at price P, $a - bP$ units will be sold. The slope of the demand curve is negative, indicating that consumers will buy less of the product as its price increases. Another way of drawing the demand curve brings out its connection to consumers' willingness to pay more directly. If we plot prices on the y-axis and quantity sold on the x-axis, then the prices represent the maximum price consumers are willing to pay for a given unit of the product. For example, if we were to represent the linear demand curve in Exhibit 4.2 as $P = (a/b) - (1/b)Q$, then $(a/b) - (1/b)Q$ is the maximum price consumers are willing to pay for the Qth unit.

A firm facing a downward-sloping demand curve should be concerned with the question: Would revenues go up or down if I were to change my price? The answer is that it depends on the slope of the demand curve—how price-sensitive consumers are—and the price level from which a change is being contemplated. A summary measure of these two considerations is price elasticity, defined as the percentage change in quantity sold divided by the percentage change in price. In symbols,

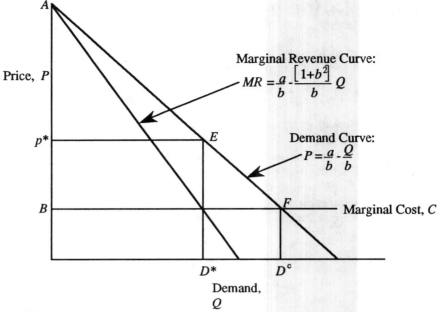

p^* = Optimal Linear Price

D^* = Demand at p^*

F^c = Area ABF = Fixed fee under optimal two-part tariff (when unit price = C)

F^* = Area Ap^*E = Fixed fee under non-optimal two-part tariff (when unit price = p^*)

EXHIBIT 4.2 The optimal linear price and the optimal two-part tariff in a static monopolistic market.

$$\text{Price elasticity, } \eta = \frac{dQ/Q}{dP/P} = \frac{dQ/dP}{Q/P} \qquad (4.2)$$

Dixit (1979), among others, has developed a theoretical basis for this model and Monroe (1990) and Simon (1989) report a number of empirical studies in a range of markets and industries where the linear form has empirical support. Price elasticity is a negative number because demand curves slope down. But it is convenient to omit the negative sign when referring to price elasticity. Thus, when we say that demand function Q_1 is more price elastic than demand function Q_2 at a specific demand level, what we mean is that the absolute value of the price elasticity of Q_1 is greater than the absolute value of the price elasticity of Q_2 at that demand level.

An increase in price results in a revenue increase if the price elasticity is less than 1; an increase in price results in a revenue decrease if the price elasticity is greater than 1. To see this, note

$$\text{Total revenue} = R = PQ(P)$$

So

$$\text{Marginal revenue, } \frac{dR}{dP} = P\frac{dQ}{dP} + Q \tag{4.3a}$$

$$= Q\left[1 + \frac{P}{Q}\frac{dQ}{dP}\right] \tag{4.3b}$$

$$= Q[1 + \eta]$$

Thus, $dR/dP > 0$ if and only if $|\eta| < 1$. If the firm were only concerned about revenues, then it will keep increasing price until the marginal revenue, dR/dP, drops to zero. This will happen at the point on the demand curve where price elasticity is exactly 1.

Now consider costs. Let V denote the (constant) variable cost of manufacturing and selling a unit of this product and F the fixed costs. Then $F + VQ(P)$ is the total cost of manufacturing and selling the product when the price is P. The firm's profit function is

$$\pi = PQ(P) - VQ(P) - F \tag{4.4}$$

Differentiating this expression with respect to P and setting the resulting expression equal to zero we get

$$PQ'(P) + Q(P) - VQ'(P) = 0 \tag{4.5}$$

Note that this equation doesn't have fixed costs in it, because we are implicitly assuming that these costs don't change in the range of prices being considered. Reshuffling the terms, this equation can be written as

$$PQ'(P) + Q(P) = VQ'(P) \tag{4.6}$$

which is the well-known marginal revenue equal to marginal cost rule of pricing. If the marginal revenue were greater than the marginal cost, then the firm could increase its profits by raising price; if the marginal revenue were less than the marginal cost, then the firm could increase its profits by reducing price. At the profit-maximizing price, therefore, marginal revenue equals marginal cost. Note the absence of fixed cost, F, in equation (4.6). Fixed costs have no role to play in determining the profit-maximizing price; they come in only on the decision of whether or not to offer the product. If, at the profit-maximizing price, the profit calculated in equation (4.4) (which contains F) is negative, then it is more profitable not to offer the product at all.

A popular shape for the demand function is based on the notion of constant price elasticity. This function is

$$Q = aP^{-b} \qquad\qquad (4.7)$$

The exponent b (> 0) is the price elasticity, which is constant for all prices. This form of demand function has been popular among analysts because it represents elasticity parametrically, making it easy to manipulate it mathematically. It also has empirical support (see Simon, 1989, for example).

The relationship of price elasticity to time and to stage of the life cycle are two important topics of recent work. Furthermore, both behavioral research and industry experience suggest that price elasticities are likely to be different for price increases than for decreases and for the degree a given price is away from the average market price.

Another important elasticity concept is *income elasticity*. If a substantial price reduction occurs on an item, it amounts to an increase in real income for those households consuming it in substantial quantities. With the greater purchasing power, they may decide to switch to more expensive products instead of consuming more of the former product. In such cases we say the income effect outweighs the substitution effect, and the product they abandon is called an inferior good.

This concept is formalized as the income elasticity of demand, defined as $(\partial Q/\partial I)(I/Q)$, where I is a measure of consumer income. Most products have an income elasticity between zero and one and are called *normal goods*. Those goods with income elasticity greater than one are called *superior goods*, while those with income elasticity less than zero are *inferior goods*.

Another measure of demand sensitivity that we will use later is the relationship between the price of one good and the quantity demanded of another. This measure is known as the *cross-price elasticity* of demand and is computed for product X as $(\partial Q_x/\partial P_y)(P_y/Q_x)$, where Y is the other good. If the cross-price elasticity is positive, then goods X and Y are substitutes; if it is negative, they are complements.

Price Discrimination.   In the foregoing analysis we were looking for the best *single* price that maximizes the seller's profits. If consumers are homogeneous, and only a single price can be charged, then that is the best the firm can do. But if consumers differ in their willingness to pay, then the profit-maximizing firm can increase its profits by charging a variety of prices, that is, by *price discriminating*. In what follows, we will explore some of the mechanisms for price discrimination and try to understand how and why they work.

To see this, suppose there are four equal-sized segments of consumers in the market, each characterized by a different willingness to pay for the product. Segment A is willing to pay up to $40 for a unit of the product, segment B up to $30, segment C up to $20, and segment D up to $10. Assume that no consumer will buy more than 1 unit of the product and will buy only if his *consumer surplus* (i.e., his reservation price minus the price he is asked to pay) is nonnegative. Suppose that the firm's unit variable costs are $5 and that there are no fixed costs. To determine the best single price to charge, note that there is no point in charging a price less than $10—everyone is willing to pay at least $10, so profits are increasing in price up to that price. Similarly, there is no point in charging a price in between the various reservation prices. So let us begin our analysis with $10. At this price, all segments will buy, so the profits will be $4N(\$10 - 5) = \$20N$, where N is the number of consumers in each segment. If the firm charged $20, then it would serve segments A, B, and C and the profits would be $3N(\$20 - 5) = \$45N$; if it charged $30, then it would serve segments A and B and the profits would be $2N(\$30 - 5) = \$50N$; and if it charged $40, then it would only serve segment A and the profits would be $N(\$40 - 5) = \$35N$. So the best single price is $30 yielding $50N in profits. Our calculations have done nothing but implement the marginal revenue equal to marginal cost rule in a discrete setting.

Now suppose the firm can charge four different prices to the four segments. Then it could charge $40 to segment A, $30 to segment B, $20 to segment C, and $10 to segment D. The firm's profits would be

$$N(\$40 - 5) + N(\$30 - 5) + N(\$20 - 5) + N(\$10 - 5) = \$80N$$

Note the following features of this price-discrimination scheme:

1. Every consumer's surplus is completely *extracted* by the firm. ("No money is left on the table.")

2. Every consumer who is willing to pay at least as much as it costs the firm to serve him (in this case $5), is served. Adams and Yellen (1976) call this criterion *inclusion*. Direct price discrimination based on the consumer's reservation price always has this feature, and it is a desirable feature. It is one reason why price discrimination is so appealing to non-profit and public sector enterprises as well.

3. No consumer whose willingness to pay is less than what it costs the firm to serve him is served. Adams and Yellen (1976) call this criterion *exclusion*. To see that direct price discrimination always has this feature, suppose the firm's variable cost are $15, not $5. Then direct price discrimination will call for a price of $40 to A, $30 to B, and $20 to C, but segment D would be excluded.

4. Direct price discrimination is *efficient*. That is, no other pricing scheme can be found that will simultaneously improve the welfare of consumers and increase the profits of the seller. In the realm of single price policies only a price equal to marginal cost is efficient. (This is the sense in which perfect competition is efficient.) Thus, whereas the optimal single price for a monopolist is inefficient, the optimal price discrimination policy is efficient.

Direct price discrimination, seems like an excellent idea for the firm, but implementing it in practice involves several difficulties:

1. Identifying consumers' reservation prices is difficult. It is unlikely that observable characteristics of consumers will be closely correlated with their reservation prices and asking them how much they will pay often gives inaccurate information (Morrison, 1979).

2. Targeting a particular price to a particular segment is difficult. Most consumer goods, for example, are sold with posted prices and thus are available to everyone on an equal basis. In certain situations, however, targeting is possible, such as when price is set via a bargaining mechanism, as for cars (Chapter 3).

3. It is difficult to prevent arbitrage. Consumers with low reservation prices may buy up a lot of the product and supply it to high reservation consumers at a price lower than their high reservation price.

4. Charging different prices to different segments may be illegal on various grounds, for example, sex and race discrimination, the Robinson-Patman Act governing discrimination among channel intermediaries, and so on.

5. Customers may view price discrimination as "unfair." Customers paying the higher price for the same item may resent the price breaks given to others unless that price break can be positioned positively, perhaps as charity (senior citizen discounts, student discounts). In many other situations, the seller may "throw in" other items in the package—free service, beneficial financing, free software, and so on—that make the price discrimination less obvious and, seemingly, more tolerable.

Despite these difficulties, direct price discrimination schemes do exist. For example, local telephone companies price discriminate between residential and business users. Senior citizen and student discounts are other forms of price discrimination. And many of the business products and services, whose terms and conditions of sale are customized (Chapter 3), satisfy the conditions for price discrimination as well. Services lend themselves particularly well to direct price discrimination. The seller (e.g., lawyer) deals with the customer one on one and services are difficult to resell. In all these cases, the identification, targeting, arbitrage prevention, and legality requirements are satisfied.

Much price discrimination in practice is not as direct as these examples, however. In fact, the need for indirectness in the price discrimination scheme is one source of the considerable variety in the pricing schemes we see today. The key challenge is to locate a correlation between the reservation prices of different segments and their preferences for some attribute of the product. If such a correlation is discovered, then the firm can tie its different prices to the different levels of the attribute and allow consumers to choose freely the level of the attribute they want to buy.

An example of this idea is pricing in the airline industry. Airlines offer a variety of fares with various restrictions (and some with no restriction). The higher fares are associated with no advance purchase requirements, no Saturday-stay-at-destination requirement, no cancelation penalties, and so on. The lower fares, for example, Supersaver fares, have many of these restrictions. The effect is to create a product line differentiated on the "restrictions attribute" with different products in the line appealing to different segments. The business traveler finds the restrictions costly and opts for the higher unrestricted fares; the vacation traveler, however, finds the lower fares appealing and doesn't mind the restrictions. Note that essentially the same results emerge even if business travelers differ in how costly they find the restrictions (Gerstner and Holthausen, 1986).

Let us now examine some common manifestations of indirect price discrimination.

Quantity Discounts. A common form of price discrimination is in the form of quantity discounts, where high-volume buyers get lower prices than small-volume buyers. The correlation being exploited here is between purchase quantity and reservation price. People who avail themselves of the discounts have higher reservation prices for the later units (of a large order) than those who don't. There are various ways of implementing quantity discounts that differ in how finely they discriminate among consumers, including two-part-tariffs and block tariffs (Monroe, 1990).

Two-part tariff. In a two-part tariff (Oi, 1971; Schmalensee, 1982), there is a fixed, upfront payment F and then a per unit charge p. For example, video clubs commonly charge a "membership fee" and also a per movie charge. The pricing of a durable good such as a camera and the nondurable supplies that go with it can also be thought of as a two-part tariff. Here the price of the durable good is the "fixed fee," the unit price of supplies is the "per unit charge" of using the durable good. Other examples include the pricing of razors and blades, copying machines and copier paper and the like.

A two-part tariff is similar to a simple linear price in that the marginal price charged is constant in quantity. Everyone who buys pays the same marginal price regardless of quantity. A two-part tariff is a quantity discount scheme only because the "average price" paid—$(F/Q) + p$—decreases with quantity purchased. In a linear pricing scheme, on the other hand, both marginal and average prices are constant in quantity purchased. The presence of a fixed fee in a two-part tariff allows it to extract more consumer surplus than a simple linear pricing scheme.

To see this, reconsider Exhibit 4.2, which can be thought of as representing a homogeneous market where every consumer has the same demand curve. One way to increase the seller's profits over the optimal linear price solution considered earlier is to employ the two-part tariff (F^*, p^*), where p^* is the optimal linear price and F^* is the residual consumer surplus under the optimal linear pricing scheme. (F^* is the area between the demand curve and the price p^*.) But the seller can do even better than this. The optimal two-part tariff is (F_c, C), where C is the seller's (constant) marginal cost and F_c is the area between the demand curve and marginal cost C. By lowering the unit price to C, the seller increases the quantity purchased, and thus the consumer surplus, which he then extracts with a higher fixed fee. The fixed fee becomes the sole source of profits.

Besides providing a way to extract the consumer surplus of those who purchase, a two-part tariff can also be used to price discriminate. There are two ways for price discrimination to happen. First, the fixed fee can be set so high that some, but not all, consumers don't purchase the product. These consumers' surplus, at the quantity they would purchase if they did buy, is less than the fixed fee. For example, in Exhibit 4.3, the customer with demand curve A would not purchase the product at all if the fixed fee is set equal to the consumer surplus of the "large" customer B.

The second way that a two-part tariff price discriminates is by charging different average prices to different customers. For example, in Exhibit 4.3, if there were a sufficiently large number of small customers of type A, then Oi (1971) has shown that the optimal two-part tariff is to charge a unit price greater than marginal cost and a fixed fee equal to the consumer surplus of the small customer. In this case, no one is being excluded from the market, but the average price paid by the larger customer is lower than the average price paid by the smaller customer.

Block tariffs.   Block tariffs are the most widely used form of quantity discounts. A block tariff has at least two marginal prices; it may or may not have a fixed fee. For example, local telephone company tariffs typically have a fixed "subscription fee" as well as several price breaks built into the schedule. In Exhibit 4.4 we show a three-block pricing scheme with no fixed fee. The customer pays p_1 per unit if he purchases Q_1 or less; he pays p_1 for each of the first Q_1 units and p_2 ($< p_1$) for each unit between Q_1 and Q_2 if he purchases between Q_1 and Q_2 units; and for purchase quantities greater than Q_2, he pays p_1 per unit for the first Q_1 units, p_2 per unit for the next $(Q_2 - Q_1)$ units, and p_3 per unit ($p_3 < p_2$) for any units beyond Q_2. The more the number

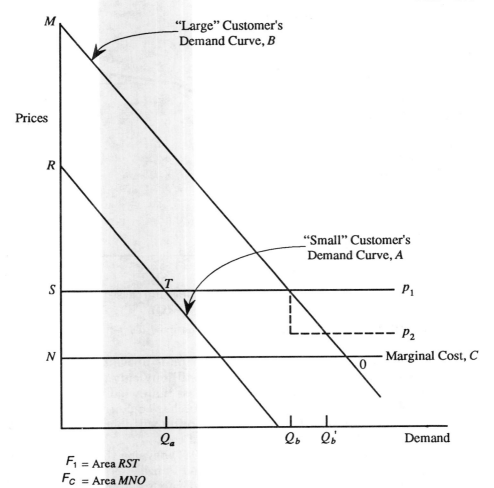

F_1 = Area *RST*
F_C = Area *MNO*

EXHIBIT 4.3   The optimal two-part tariff is either (F_1, p_1) or (F_c, C). If (F_1, p_1) is the optimal two-part tariff, then the two-block scheme (p_1, Q_b, p_2) with fixed-payment F_1 yields even greater profits.

of price blocks, the finer the price discrimination possible, but, also, the greater the difficulty of administering and explaining the tariff to consumers. A quantity discount schedule, where each unit is priced differently, and a simple linear schedule, where each unit is priced the same, represent opposite sides of this spectrum.

To see how block pricing can improve two-part tariffs, we return to Exhibit 4.3 with consumers A and B. Suppose (F_1, p_1) represents the optimal two-part tariff. Now consider the following two-block pricing scheme. The customer pays a fixed fee F_1 and, in addition, a price per unit of p_1 for the first

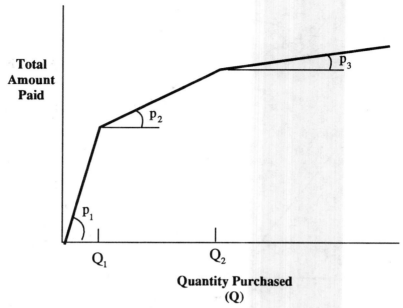

EXHIBIT 4.4   A three-block tariff with no fixed fee.

Q_b units and a price per unit of p_2 for units above that. Given this quantity discount scheme, consumer A would still buy only Q_a units because his reservation price for units beyond Q_a is less than what he is being asked to pay. But consumer B would increase his purchase quantity from Q_b to $Q_{b'}$, paying p_2 for units beyond Q_b. The seller's profits will increase because these additional sales are priced above marginal cost.

Goldman, Leland, and Sibley (1984) develop the theory of general nonlinear pricing schedules. Faulhaber and Panzar (1977) show that a block tariff can be implemented by offering consumers a choice among several two-part tariffs. The number of two-part tariffs will be equal to the number of blocks in the original block tariff. One practical application of Faulhaber and Panzar's idea is in the rental policies for copiers. Typically the higher-throughput machines have a higher monthly rental charge and a lower per copy charge. Willig (1978) shows that given any linear pricing scheme, one can develop a two-part tariff such that if consumers are offered a choice between the linear pricing scheme and the two-part tariff, then everyone—consumers as well as the seller—is better off. This result has obvious implications for regulatory policy regarding public utilities. Dolan (1987) lists a number of other applications of quantity discounts.

Note that price discrimination can lead to quantity *premiums*, not just quantity discounts. Gerstner and Hess (1987) present data demonstrating that, for grocery store items that come in a variety of package sizes, the larger size is sometimes sold at a premium. They explain this phenomenon by noting that some high consumption households (which should prefer larger package sizes) also have high storage costs and several small packages may take up more space than a single large package. Or, alternatively, the large package may be easier (less costly) to transport than the several, comparable, small packages.

A Product Line of Partial Substitutes.   Almost every product comes in a variety of models, the models distinguished by the attribute levels provided. For example, Honda makes several model lines—Acura, Accord, and Civic—and within each of these model lines there are several "trim levels." Having a variety of models with different combinations of attributes allows the manufacturer to price discriminate among various segments while allowing free customer choice. For example, the consumer who values luxury and performance chooses the Acura line; the more economy-minded consumer who wants basic transportation opts for the Civic line.

A potential difficulty in pricing a product line of substitutes is the possibility of cannibalization. This happens if the positive correlation between reservation prices and preference for the differentiating attributes is too high. To see this, consider Exhibit 4.5, where two reservation price maps are depicted. In each map, there are two segments that differ in their intensity of preference for an attribute. In Exhibit 4.5(a), the reservation price lines cross, so it is possible to sell product y at segment A's reservation price for it, r_y^A, and sell product x at segment B's reservation price for it, r_x^B, and neither product would cannibalize the other. On the other hand, in Exhibit 4.5(b), the reservation price lines do not cross. Now it is not possible to offer the pricing scheme just mentioned without segment A switching to product x. In other words, if x and y are priced at the reservation prices of segments B and A, respectively, then product x would cannibalize product y. The way to avoid cannibalization is to reduce the price of y from r_y^A to below $r_y^A - (r_x^A - r_x^B)$. That way segment A gets a higher surplus from y rather than x.

If the cannibalization problem is especially serious, that is, the reduction in price of Y is too large, then the seller may profit from eliminating the cannibalizing product. For example, if N_A and N_B are the number of consumers in segments A and B and $N_B r_x^B + N_A(r_y^A - r_x^A + r_x^B) < N_A r_y^A$, then it is more profitable to sell to A alone with y priced at r_y^A. This suggests that it may be optimal to reduce product variety for purely demand reasons.

Mussa and Rosen (1978) and Moorthy (1984) develop the theory of product line design and pricing when all the elements in the product line have to be introduced simultaneously. Moorthy and P'ng (1991) consider the possibility of postponing the introduction of some elements of the line as a means of reducing cannibalization further. (Obviously, this is possible only for durable products.)

All these results have to be tempered in the case of competition. If com-

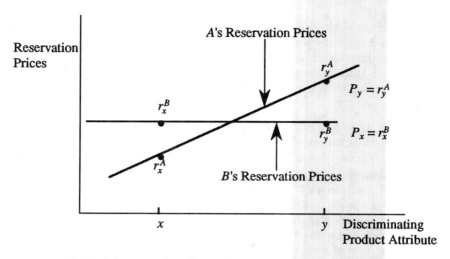

(a) Pricing a product line with no cannibalization: Here the optimal prices equal consumer reservation prices, leaving no consumer surplus.

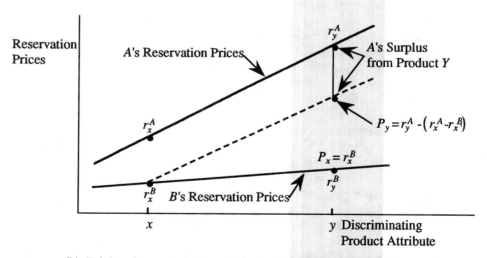

(b) Pricing the product line with potential cannibalization: Here product y must be priced below A's reservation price to prevent cannibalization.

EXHIBIT 4.5   Pricing a product line of partial substitutes: x and y are the two products in the line.

petition is already serving the low-reservation price segments with distinctive products—or is expected to do so soon—then it may be better for the firm to do so as well. Otherwise, the firm loses margins on its existing products *and* loses the low reservation price segments altogether. Similarly, a sequential product introduction strategy may not be optimal if competition is expected to preempt the segments that the firm doesn't currently serve.

EXAMPLE _____

Monroe (1990, p. 308).
When Chevrolet introduced its Corvair in the early 1960s, the car was priced close to the regular sized models to encourage the sale of those regular models. Ford, however, priced the Falcon to differentiate it from larger models, as we discuss here. Thus Falcon outsold the Corvair, but the larger and more profitable Chevrolet models outsold the larger Ford models, illustrating the complexity of product line pricing considerations when facing competition.

EXAMPLE _____

The Dobson and Kalish (1988) Model.
Dobson and Kalish develop an operational, heuristic procedure to position and price a line of related, substitute products, based on theoretical models of Mussa and Rosen (1978) and Moorthy (1984).

As Reibstein and Gatignon (1984) point out, ignoring interactions and interdependencies among a firm's line of products can lead to some significant inefficiencies in setting optimal prices. Dobson and Kalish deal with both the product positioning issue and the pricing issue in an operational framework. As we will see, as they move toward an operational framework, their model must make some important simplifying assumptions.

Their model requires information on market composition (what do the different customers want) and cost data on what it costs to produce each type of product.

Specifically, they make the following assumptions:

1. The market is composed of different segments of various sizes, each of which is homogeneous.

2. The market can be represented by a sample of customers, each representing a market segment and from whom population preferences can be inferred.

3. Customers choose one brand only, the one that provides the best value for the money.

4. Quantity purchased is not a function of price; price serves to determine the brand selected, not the quantity. (This assumption is most relevant for consumer durables and for consumption-inelastic consumables like perfume and cigarettes.)

5. The firm has fixed and variable production and marketing costs for each product, which the firm knows or can obtain.

6. The firm is a monopolist or competitors do not respond to the firm's moves.

They formulate the product line decision/pricing problem as

$$\text{Find } \{p_j\}\{y_j\}\{x_{ij}\}$$

to

$$\max \sum_{i=0}^{m} \sum_{j=0}^{n} q_i(p_j - c_j) x_{ij} - \sum_{j=1}^{n} f_j y_j \qquad \textbf{(4.8a)}$$

Subject to

$$\sum_{j=0}^{n} x_{ij} = 1, \qquad \text{for all } i \qquad \textbf{(4.8b)}$$

$$x_{ij} \leq y_j \qquad \textbf{(4.8c)}$$

$$\sum_{k=1}^{n} (u_{ck} - p_k) x_{ik} \geq (u_{ij} - p_j) y_j \qquad \textbf{(4.8d)}$$

$$p_0 = 0 \qquad \textbf{(4.8e)}$$

$$x_{ik}, y_k = 0 \text{ or } 1, \qquad \text{for all } i \text{ and } k \qquad \textbf{(4.8f)}$$

where

u_{ij} = reservation price of the ith segment for the jth product, $i = 1, \ldots, m$ segments; $j = 1, \ldots, n$ products

q_i = number of individuals represented by segment i

c_j = unit production cost of product j

f_j = fixed cost incurred if product j is produced at all

$y_j = \begin{cases} 1, & \text{if product } j \text{ is offered} \\ 0, & \text{otherwise} \end{cases}$

$$x_{ij} = \begin{cases} 1, & \text{if segment } i \text{ is assigned to product } j \\ 0, & \text{otherwise} \end{cases}$$

(Note: x_{ij} is an intermediate variable used by the solution procedure to assure that assignments are consistent with customers' self-selected products.)

p_j = price of product j

If a segment is not assigned to a product, it is assigned to product 0, with $c_0 = 0$, $u_{i0} = 0$ for all i.

Taking the components of (4.8) in turn,

(4.8a) is the firm's objective, to maximize the contribution across all introduced products ($y_j > 0$), where the product contributions are weighted by the segment sizes (q_i).

(4.8b) guarantees that each segment is assigned to only one product.

(4.8c) requires that the fixed cost be "paid" for every product the company carries in its line.

(4.8d) enforces the requirement that every segment chooses its consumer surplus maximizing product. (That is, if segment i chooses product k, then $x_{ij} = 1$ and thus $u_{ik} - p_k \geq u_{ij} - p_j$ for any other available product, i.e., when $y_j = 1$).

Conditions (4.8e) and (4.8f) are accounting constraints, needed to ensure that a realistic solution emerges.

The authors develop a heuristic (nonoptimal, but efficient) solution procedure for the problem that (1) assigns segments to products and (2) finds prices that are consistent with that segment. While their heuristic procedure does not guarantee optimality, they provide numerical experiments that show quite good results and suggest, therefore, that the procedure can be applied to realistic-sized problems.

The authors recommend developing the critical consumer measurements, the u_{ij}, by estimating the value of the product *without price*, as a dollar-metric or willingness-to-pay measure. (See Kalish and Nelson, 1991, for a discussion of this approach.) However, they point out that if price is included as an additive term in a standard conjoint measurement procedure (and the resulting utilities are suitably re-scaled), then the result of such a measurement procedure can be used as well.

The Dobson and Kalish model has a number of special features. Unlike models like Urban (1969), Monroe and Della Bitta (1978), Reibstein and Gatignon (1984), Monroe and Zoltners (1979), Saghafi (1988), Oren, Smith, and

Wilson (1984), and others, this model deals with measurements at the individual consumer level. As such, it doesn't require the specification of an aggregate demand curve and the possible associated specification errors. In addition, the math programming structure should allow easy introduction of other, situation-specific constraints (some prices are fixed, some segments must be assigned to certain products, and the like). And, as an operational procedure, the model is directly amenable for use in a decision support tool framework. Green and Kreiger (1991) describe a decision support system to determine the optimal price for a single product in a competitive environment, while Kohli and Mahajan (1991) use the reservation price concept to determine optimal prices when measurement errors are explicitly accounted for.

Bundling Schemes.   Often manufacturers will bundle two or more products and sell them as a package. Sometimes this is the only way these products are sold (pure bundling) but at other times the products are sold bundled and unbundled (mixed bundling). The advantage of bundling comes from the fact that if consumers' preferences for the products in the bundle are negatively correlated, that is, if the people who like product X dislike product Y and vice versa, then selling the products unbundled either leads to too low a price for the products or leads to exclusion of some segments from some products. Bundling reduces the variation in reservation prices in these circumstances and a single bundle price can be found that neither leaves too much money on the table nor excludes anyone.

EXAMPLE _____

Suppose a firm sells a razor (R) and blades (B) to two equal sized consumer groups, X and Y, whose reservation prices for the two products are ($12, $4) and ($4, $12), respectively. Suppose the variable cost per unit for each product is less than $4. If R and B are sold individually, then R would be sold at $12 and B at $12. Customer types X would not buy blades and customer types Y would not buy razors even though these consumers are willing to pay more for these products than what it costs the manufacturer to supply them. On the other hand, because both types of consumers have the same reservation price for the bundle, $16, the bundle can be priced at $16 and sold to both of them. Now the revenues are $32 and all customers buy all products.

_____

The efficacy of bundling in this example illustrates the principle that heterogeneity among consumers is good for the seller only if he can take advantage of it by charging different prices to the different segments. If he cannot price discriminate, then heterogeneity can be a handicap, and ways of reducing heterogeneity may be useful. In the last example, the seller was unable to take advantage of the heterogeneity in consumers' preference for X and Y, individually, because he could charge only one price for each product. By bundling, he converted a heterogeneous market to a homogeneous one and then the single bundle price was able to extract the entire consumer surplus.

Bundling is thus useful when there is a negative correlation between consumers' reservation prices for two or more products. But bundling also has a weakness. It can force the seller to sell a product to customers whose reservation price for the product is *less* than the seller's marginal cost. For example, suppose in the previous example that the variable cost was actually $6 for each product. If the products were sold unbundled, once again A would be excluded from Y and B from X. The profits would be $12. But if the products are sold bundled, then the optimal bundle price of $16 would permit A to buy Y and B to buy X. The profits would then be $8. In this case, because bundling violates the exclusion principle, unbundling is better.

Mixed bundling combines the advantages of pure bundling and pure unbundling. The products are sold both as a package and unbundled, that is, as razors, blades, and the combination. This allows the seller to exclude people from buying a product for which their reservation price is less than marginal cost and at the same time include people with a negative correlation between their reservation prices for the various products.

For more detailed discussions of bundling schemes, see Stigler (1963), Adams and Yellen (1976), Schmalensee (1984), Drumwright and Dolan (1989), and Hanson and Martin (1990).

Temporal Price Discrimination.   The idea behind temporal price discrimination is to introduce a new product at a high price initially, intending to sell it to high-reservation-price consumers and then lower it gradually to sell to lower and lower reservation-price consumers. For example, books are introduced in hardcover at a high price and after about a year or so the paperback version is introduced at a lower price. One condition necessary for such skimming strategies to work is that the product be a durable good; otherwise, the early purchasers will return to the market when the price is lowered. The other condition is that the high reservation price customers be at least as anxious to consume the product as the low reservation price customers. For example, the hardcover buyers who have a high reservation price for the book must be at least as desirous to read the book early as the paperback buyers.

Stokey (1979, 1981), Narasimhan (1989), Bulow (1982), Besanko and Winston (1990), Moorthy (1988), and Moorthy and P'ng (1991) have analyzed temporal price discrimination possibilities when consumers expect the price to decline in the future. Intuitively, if the price were to come down too fast, then some of the more patient customers may choose to wait for the lower price. Thus, temporal price discrimination possibilities may be substantially reduced when consumers anticipate the seller's future pricing strategy. From the seller's point of view, given consumers' expectations, it might be better to *commit* to a pricing strategy—for now and for the future—rather than price each period.

Again let us assume there are four segments A, B, C, and D, each of size N with reservation prices \$40, \$30, \$20, and \$10, respectively. Suppose each segment discounts next period consumer surplus at the rate of δ; suppose the seller also discounts next period profits at the rate of δ. (Thus \$1 in the next period is worth $\$1\delta$ now to either the seller or the consumers.) The seller's marginal cost is \$5/unit. Assume the seller's pricing flexibility is limited to two periods; that is, he can charge a price p_1 in the first period, a (possibly) different price p_2 in the second, but then he has to keep his price constant at p_2. What is the seller's optimal pricing strategy?

If consumers were myopic, that is, if they only look at current prices and don't consider future prices, then the seller's optimal strategy is to set $p_1 = \$30$, $p_2 = \$20$. Segments A and B will buy in the first period—even though clearly segment B would gain by waiting to buy in the second period—and segment C will buy in the second period. The firm's present value of profits will be $N(50 + 15\delta)$. Obviously, in this case, it is better not to commit, because commitment will inform otherwise myopic consumers about future prices.

If consumers had foresight, however, this strategy would not be good for the seller. Segment B would clearly shift its purchase to the second period and segment A might also do that if $\delta > 0.5$. So if, for example, $\delta = 0.6$, then the seller's profits will be $N(45\delta)$, not $N(50 + 15\delta)$. So what is the best pricing strategy when consumers have foresight? The best pricing strategy when the seller doesn't make any commitments is $p_1 = 30 - 10\delta$, and $p_2 = \$20$, yielding $N(50 - 5\delta)$ in profits. Note that $p_1 > p_2$. That is, there is price discrimination. Segments A and B buy in the first period, and segment C buys in the second period. The seller can do better than this strategy, however, by committing to a price of \$30 for both periods, that is, by announcing a price of \$30 for the first period and committing to not reducing it in period 2. All the sales will then take place in period 1—only segments A and B will buy—and profits will be \$50. This strategy is not feasible without commitment because consumers will anticipate that once the seller has sold to segments A and B in the first period, he will then lower the price to \$20 in the second period.

How can a seller commit to future prices credibly? One way is by building a reputation for sticking to commitments. Clearly, there is value to building such a reputation. Another way is by forcing oneself to incur additional costs if commitments are not kept. For example, the seller can announce a marketing policy of passing on future "sale prices" to earlier "regular price" customers. Such a policy—which could be contractually binding on the seller— would make it uneconomical to reduce price in the future.

Price Promotions.   Various forms of price promotions are price discrimination devices. For example, coupons price discriminate between high- and low-reservation-price consumers by exploiting the correlation between reservation price and transaction costs to redeem the coupon (Narasimhan, 1984). Randomly timed store sales do the same thing by taking advantage of the correlation between reservation price and "knowledge of sales" (Varian, 1980; Jeuland and Narasimhan, 1985). Periodic, predictable, price discounts for durable goods (e.g., "white sales" for sheets and towels and annual rebates for cars) rely on the correlation between reservation price and "impatience to consume" as well as the arrival of new cohorts of customers (Conlisk, Gerstner, and Sobel, 1984). (See Chapter 7.)

DEVELOPING DEMAND AND COST INFORMATION FOR PRICING DECISIONS

In order to implement pricing schemes of the kind we just discussed, the firm needs cost and demand information. In measuring costs it is wise to keep in mind that the relevant costs are those that change depending on the price chosen. Most fixed costs (overhead, for example) don't change with pricing, and therefore they are irrelevant for the pricing decision. (But most fixed costs are relevant for the decision to produce or not produce the product.) The determination of whether a fixed cost is truly fixed or whether it changes with price must be made on a case-by-case basis. Airplanes, for example, are different from shampoos in this respect. Johnston (1984) describes econometric techniques for estimating demand functions from existing data.

In measuring the demand function for pricing purposes, one important thing to remember is that the pricing analyst needs *disaggregate* information. Only from disaggregate information can the analyst build up the segments among whom he will price discriminate. Also, the demand function must be estimated with the other marketing-mix variables set at levels comparable to those planned for the market plan. This is because the other marketing-mix variables—product, advertising, distribution, and so on—strongly affect the demand function. For example, Eskin and Baron (1977) have shown that price sensitivity for grocery store products increases with the advertising budget. Similarly, the presence or absence of the brand's name can affect consumer's willingness to pay for it.

Several techniques are available to estimate disaggregate demand functions including econometric methods (Appendix D), conjoint analysis (Chapter

5), and value-in-use analysis. This last technique is particularly useful for industrial products. Typically, these products will lower the cost of doing something. In this case, the reservation price of a product is simply the cost savings generated by using the product in preference to an existing product (Forbis and Mehta, 1979 and Monroe, 1990, Ch. 5).

EXAMPLE

Suppose a chemical plant uses 200 o-rings per year to seal valves carrying corrosive materials. Those o-rings cost $5 each and must be changed during regular maintenance every two months. A new product has twice the corrosive resisting power of the incumbent. Equating costs between the incumbent and the new product yields the value-in-use (V):

Solution 1.

$$\text{Annual cost of incumbent} = 200 \text{ o-rings/year} \times \$5/\text{ring}$$

$$\times 6 \text{ changes/year}$$

$$= \$6,000$$

$$= 200 \text{ (o-rings)} \times \$V/\text{ring}$$

$$\times 3 \text{ changes/year}$$

or

$$V = \$10$$

Solution 2. Suppose that the new product will allow a longer time between shutdowns (to replace the rings)—four months versus two months—and the cost of a shutdown is $5,000. Then we get

$$(200 \times 6 \times 5) + (5000 \times 6) = (200 \times 3 \times V) + (5000 \times 3)$$

| Equipment Cost | Shutdown Cost | Equipment Cost | Shutdown Cost |

$$\underbrace{\text{Incumbent}} \qquad \underbrace{\text{New}}$$

or

$$V = \$35$$

Note the dramatic difference between the two calculations of V: it is critical to incorporate all the customer's costs in the calculation, both those that are tangible and those that are intangible. Aside from the initial cost and operating costs suggested, the value-in-use model should consider the buyer's planning horizon, cost of capital, switching costs (retraining, product reformulation, likely start up inefficiencies), maintenance costs differences, performance differences, and any difference in flexibility. In addition, the uncertainty of the new versus the certainty of the incumbent means that the value-in-use must be adjusted for performance risk that the buyer will be expected to bear (see Appendix B).

In order to apply value-based pricing on a large scale, the selling firm normally performs in-depth engineering studies at a sample of key customer locations to get a distribution of customer values for the product. The seller then can select between a skimming strategy (setting a high price that is attractive to a small segment of the market) and a penetration strategy (setting a low price that makes the product attractive to a range of market segments).

MODEL EXTENSIONS

The foregoing models have made several key assumptions that limit their applicability, including the following:

> The firm's objective in setting prices is to maximize short or long run profits.
>
> The only parties to consider in setting the price are the firm's immediate customers.
>
> Competition, if any, is assumed to be passive.
>
> Price can be set independent of the levels set for the other marketing variables.
>
> Buyers tend to react to price changes similarly.
>
> Demand does not change over time.
>
> Costs do not change over time.
>
> Competition remains passive over time.
>
> Pricing is a static phenomenon.
>
> Prices do not signal product benefits.
>
> Absolute prices (not relative prices) are what matter to customers.

We consider these limitations in turn.

Objectives. Organizational objectives affect pricing. A firm seeking to maximize market share would probably price lower than would one that wants to maximize current profits. A nonprofit firm seeking to break even must price differently than a profit-maximizing firm. A regulated public utility required to obtain a specific rate of return would price differently than a profit-maximizing utility.

The differences in optimal pricing strategies between a profit-maximizing firm on the one hand and a nonprofit or public sector firm on the other are mainly in the *level* of the prices charged, rather than the form. Indirect price discrimination of the kinds just discussed is a useful pricing strategy for nonprofit as well as public sector organizations (Brown and Sibley, 1986). For example, many theaters offer plays or shows bundled in the form of subscriptions and unbundled in the form of tickets for individual events. Product line pricing is practiced on various attributes: times of shows (Saturday night tickets are generally more expensive than midweek tickets), guaranteed seating at regular prices versus no-guarantee lower priced tickets 10 minutes before the show, the location of the seats (close-to-the-stage seats are more expensive than back-of-the-hall seats), and so on. Similarly, the U.S. Postal Service, whose prices are set by the Postal Service Commission, practices price discrimination of various kinds. Just like the for-profit Federal Express, it offers a varied menu of products distinguished on attributes such as speed of delivery, assurance of delivery, and so on.

Intermediate Customers. The firm must think through its pricing not only for its ultimate customers but for its intermediate customers as well. In fact, most companies set a price for distributors and allow them to set whatever final price they wish. Alternatively, the manufacturer determines both the final price and the distributor's margin necessary to provide sufficient distributor incentive. These issues are developed at length in Chapter 9.

Competition. The results we developed for monopoly pricing also hold when competition is passive or nonreactive (nonstrategic). Nonstrategic competitors do not take into account the effect of other firms' prices on their own fortunes. These competitors will not respond when another competitor changes its price. So a firm facing such competition can make its pricing decision taking its competitors' fixed prices as given.

If competitors are strategic, however, things get more complicated. Every pricing move will elicit a response from competitors. What prices will ultimately prevail depends on how the competitors compete. One possibility is that each firm chooses its price without knowledge of its competitors' prices and the prices chosen are the Nash equilibrium prices (Appendix E). This would be the Bertrand equilibrium. If the firms' products are undifferentiated, then the Bertrand equilibrium will have each firm pricing at marginal cost. With product differentiation, however, price competition will be more muted and prices above marginal cost will prevail in equilibrium (Shaked and Sutton, 1982; Moorthy, 1988) (see Chapter 5).

Another possibility is that the firms compete on quantities, not prices. This would be the Cournot equilibrium. Unlike the Bertrand equilibrium, the Cournot equilibrium yields positive profits to each firm even with no product differentiation. Kreps and Scheinkman (1983) have provided one motivation for how a Cournot equilibrium can arise in practice even with firms competing on prices. They have shown that the one-stage Cournot equilibrium is also the equilibrium of a two-stage game where the firms choose capacities first and then compete on prices. In general, whether Cournot or Bertrand outcomes prevail depends on the nature of costs in the industry. If quantity adjustment is costly the Cournot model is a better model. Examples include perishable food products where the lead time between initiation of production and sales is considerable or situations where production capacity is a constraint. On the other hand, if supply quantities can be easily adjusted, the Bertrand model is better.

Besides the choice between Bertrand and Cournot, other ways of competing include price leadership and implicit collusion. (Explicit collusion of the kind where the competitors formally agree to set prices jointly is, of course, illegal per the Sherman Act.) With price leadership, one firm serves as a leader and commits to a price, anticipating the reaction of its competitors. In many cases, the reaction of the followers is simply to match the leader's price, and usually this price yields a healthy profit for everyone. The role of leadership, then, is to signal the leader's pricing intentions, and serve as a coordination device in the industry. In other words, price leadership is a way to collude implicitly. Such collusion is sustained by the implicit threat that "cheaters" will be "punished" by means of price wars. So, for example, if the followers try to undercut the leader's price, then the leader will also lower his price in future periods, and the resulting price war will hurt the cheaters more than their short-term gain from cheating. See Friedman (1971), Green and Porter (1984), Abreu, Pearce, and Stachetti (1985) for formalizations of this argument.

Whether the threat of a price war will actually deter cheaters in any particular case depends on a number of factors, including how easy it is to detect cheating, the size of the short-term gain from cheating, how credible the threat of punishment is, how long-term oriented every firm is, the possibility of "renegotiating" after cheating, and so on. Sultan (1975) describes how the turbine generator industry colluded implicitly in the 1960s through General Electric's price leadership and a book pricing policy. Bresnahan (1987) analyzes the U.S. automobile industry in the 1950s and provides evidence for how the implicit collusion was sustained by the threat of price wars. Brander and Zhang (1990) have recently examined the competition between United Airlines and American Airlines on common routes from Chicago and find evidence for the Cournot equilibrium (over Bertrand and implicit collusion).

The Problem of Marketing-Mix Interaction.   In determining the effect of price on sales, the classical pricing model assumes that other marketing variables are held at some constant level. This assumption is evident in the usual treatment of the demand function as a relationship only between quantity demanded (Q) and price (P). But this assumption begs the question of how advertising and selling effort affect price elasticity and similar interactions. These issues are dealt with throughout the volume.

Variation in Buyer Response.   Note that individual buyers vary in their response to price changes. An interesting perspective on this problem is reviewed by Krishnamurthi and Raj (1988, 1991) who demonstrate that brand-loyal customers are less price sensitive than nonbrand loyals (as expected) in the brand choice decision, but *more price sensitive* in the purchase quantity decision. This finding suggests that aggregate analysis of price sensitivities (which confound the choice and quantity decision) may provide misleading results.

Changes in Demand over Time.   The nature of demand for a product may change over time for a variety of reasons. When a product is new, not many people know what it offers, but over time they learn about the product from other users or from advertising. One way to capture this effect is to say that consumers' reservation prices for the product are uncertain in the beginning, but as they find out more about the product their reservation prices become certain. If consumers were risk-neutral and their initial beliefs about the product unbiased, then their initial willingness to pay will be their final willingness to pay and no change in pricing strategy is called for. In fact, even if the market consists of some (but not too many) risk-averse consumers, the firm may start and stay with the price that is optimal in the long term.

However, if the number of risk-averse consumers is large relative to the number of risk-neutral consumers—which is often the case—the optimal pricing strategy may be to start at a low price to facilitate trial by the risk-averse consumers and then gradually increase it as information about the product spreads. In this case it pays to be proactive and anticipate how current prices will affect future reservation prices and hence the prices charged in the future. In general, this means that a proactive firm will price lower than a reactive firm initially and raise its price faster (Robinson and Lakhani, 1975; Dolan and Jeuland, 1981; Kalish, 1983).

Optimal pricing in communication networks is a special case of this phenomenon. A potential customer's utility, and hence reservation price, for joining a communication network is an increasing function of how many other customers the network already has. (This is similar to the effect of word of mouth in spreading information and reducing risk about an experience good.) This leads to the "critical size" effect: if the network's size is below the critical size, then it will shrink and die even if the subscription price is zero; if the network size is above the critical size, then the network will grow even if the subscription price is positive. Another example of this network effect is VCRs, and video rental stores, where a critical mass of VCR owners is needed to support a store structure, yet consumers are reluctant, initially, to buy VCRs if a rental network is not available. To get to the critical size, the network operator must start at a low price, and then, once critical size has been reached, he can raise his price (Rohlfs, 1974). Dhebar and Oren (1985) extend these results to a dynamic framework where consumers have expectations about the future network size. Xie and Sirbu (1991) develop equilibrium pricing strategies for two networks competing with each other.

Many studies of the time-varying nature of demand have focused specifically on price elasticity. Tellis (1988) reports on a meta-analysis of those studies. His review covered 41 studies over 15 years involving 367 price elasticities for 220 different brands or makes. His conclusions are

1. The mean level of price elasticity is significantly negative and about eight times larger than that found in a similar study involving advertising elasticities by Assmus, Farley, and Lehmann (1984).

2. The omission of certain variables from the estimating equation leads to some consistent biases: when quality is omitted, price elasticities are biased upward; when distribution is omitted, price elasticities are biased downward.

3. The use of cross-sectional data and/or temporal aggregation can lead to an upward bias in the estimate.

4. Significant differences exist over the brand life cycle, across product categories, estimation methods and countries.

In Exhibit 4.6, we see results reported by Lilien and Yoon (1988) on price elasticity variation across the product life cycle. The results of research in this area have, so far, been inconclusive: Mickwitz (1959) speculated that price elasticity increases over the first three stages of the product life cycle and declines during the last state. Lambin (1970) and Kotler (1971) concurred with this argument. Liu and Hanssens (1981), using data for inexpensive gift goods, found that price elasticity increases slightly over time. Empirical research in the diffusion literature (Rogers, 1983) supports this argument.

Parsons (1975) contended that price elasticity exhibits a nonlinear decline over time up to the mature stage of the product life cycle. Using consumer products data, Wildt (1976b) observed that promotional elasticity declines over time. Simon (1979), focusing on the price elasticity of consumer products over the "brand" life cycle, reported that price elasticity decreases to a minimum at the maturity stage and then increases (Shoemaker, 1986, suggests that Simon's results may be a result of his selection of functional

Reference	Product	Stage of Product Life Cycle			
		Intro ➤	Growth ➤	Maturity ➤	Decline
Mickwitz* (1959)		Increase	Increase	Increase	Decrease
Parsons* (1975)		Decrease	Decrease	Decrease	
Wildt (1976)	Consumer products	(Promotion elasticity decreases over time)			
Simon† (1979)	Pharmaceuticals, detergents	Decrease Decrease	Decrease Decrease	Stable Increase	
Liu and Hanssens (1981)	Inexpensive gift items	(Increases over time)			
Lilien and Yoon	Industrial chemicals	Stable	Decrease/ Stable	Stable/ Decrease	

* No empirical support was provided for these propositions.

† Simon's (1979) study was on the brand life cycle rather than product life cycle.

Source: Lilien and Yoon (1988), p. 25.

EXHIBIT 4.6   Research on the dynamic behavior of price elasticity

form however). Lilien and Yoon's (1988) results show price elasticity as stable in the early part of the life cycle and then either stable or decreasing in the latter phases.

The implications of this work are that, while we should expect significant variations in elasticity over the product life cycle, the direction and magnitude of those variations have not yet been definitively determined by research to date.

Cost Changes over Time.   Costs can go down over time due to experience curve effects (Chapter 11). Again, it pays to be proactive in pricing. Anticipating the effect of current sales on future costs, a proactive firm would price more aggressively than a reactive firm—its prices will be lower and they will come down faster. See Dolan and Jeuland (1981) and Kalish (1983) (reviewed later) for the monopoly analysis and Spence (1981) for the oligopolistic case. Lieberman (1984) provides empirical evidence from the chemical processing industry.

Changes in Competition over Time. As competition increases over the product life cycle, prices will have to come down (Eliashberg and Jeuland, 1986). But the firm may be able to deter the entry of new competitors by its current pricing actions. The idea—due to Bain (1956)—is that by pricing lower than what the firm would have priced at if it knew there was going to be no new competition, the firm may be able to convince future entrants that profit margins would be low in the industry and it is better to avoid the fixed costs of entry. For a rigorous analysis of this argument, see Milgrom and Roberts (1982). For a recent review of limit pricing, see Ordover and Saloner (1989).

Integrating Dynamics into Pricing Models. To illustrate how market dynamics have been addressed in pricing models we develop two examples.

EXAMPLE _____

Kalish (1983)
In his 1983 paper (extended in Kalish, 1988), Kalish develops a framework for studying dynamic pricing in a monopoly.

He makes an important distinction between two types of dynamic effects: those that are the result of what has happened previously and those that are not. An unforeseen or unaffectable event (change in consumer tastes, for example) is an example of the latter type of effect, where the optimal price will change over time, but in each period the firm will maximize immediate profits.

However, if changes are temporally linked, then the price in one period may affect demand or cost in another period. Thus, the price in any single period may not maximize that particular period's profit.

It is useful to distinguish here between demand-related and cost-related effects.

Demand-related effects that are not intertemporally linked include changes in income, economic conditions, taste, seasonality, the legal environment, and so on. The critical factor with these *exogenous* elements is that pricing actions in a given period will not affect the future pricing rule.

Of more interest are *endogenous* changes in demand, where future demand is directly affected by decisions taken in the past. Positive influences in demand (which Kalish calls "demand learning effects") include (1) information effects, where risk-averse customers see a product's expected utility increase as market penetration increases (and, therefore, product performance uncertainty decreases); (2) network effects, where the value of the product is related to how many other people have the product (electronic mail, for example); and (3) other positive phenomena, such as brand loyalty, reputation, and so on.

Some carryover effects are negative; Kalish cites two: (1) saturation effects, especially for durable goods, where every customer who makes a purchase is out of the market for a substantial period of time, and (2) social snob effects, especially for fashion items, where the value of a good decreases as it is no longer new or too readily available to be fashionable. (These phenomena are developed in Chapter 10.)

Cost-oriented effects are critical here as well. External environmental factors may affect costs. However, of more concern to us here are endogenous cost changes due to experience effects, primarily (see Hax and Majluf, 1982, or Chapter 11). Note that it is important to distinguish between experience curve effects and economies of scale. Although the latter provides production cost declines over time due to volume increases; there is no effect under economy-of-scale situations of increasing production in one period affecting future costs directly.

Kalish introduces the following notation, common in dealing with dynamic models:

$$
\begin{aligned}
x(t) \quad &= \text{cumulative sales volume sold by } t \\
s(t) \quad &= \text{sales rate at } t = dx(t)/dt = \dot{x}(t) \\
p(t) \quad &= \text{product's price at } t \\
E(t) \quad &= \text{exogenous factors at } t \\
c(x(t)) &= \text{cost at } t \text{ (specifically related to cumulative production)} \\
r \quad &= \text{discount rate} \\
\varepsilon \quad &= \text{price elasticity of demand (as a positive number)}
\end{aligned}
$$

We also adopt the convention that a partial derivative is denoted by a variable subscript; for example $\partial c / \partial X = c_X$.

The problem the monopolist faces is to maximize profits over some planning horizon 0 to T:

$$
\text{Maximize } Z = \int_0^T e^{-rt}(p - c)s \, dt
$$

where $\dot{x} = s = f((x(t), p(t))$, and $x(0) = x_0$, the initial output level.

Using optimal control methods (see Kamien and Schwartz, 1981), he derives the following results, but with the time subscript suppressed:

$$
p^* = \left(\frac{\varepsilon}{1 - \varepsilon} \right)(c - \lambda) \tag{4.9}
$$

where λ is the current value of one additional unit produced in the objective function.

We see from equation (4.9) that price is related to marginal cost with that cost adjusted to incorporate the effects of current additional product on future profits through λ. If λ is positive, the price is below the myopic level (i.e., when $\lambda = 0$)and vice versa. Following Dolan and Jeuland (1981), pricing above the myopic price is "penetration pricing"; below the myopic price is "skimming." Thus, the time path of λ determines the optimal price relative to the myopic price. $\lambda(t)$ can be determined from

$$\lambda(t) = \int_t^T \left(-c_X f - \frac{f_X p}{\varepsilon} \right) e^{-r(\tau - t)} \, d\tau \tag{4.10}$$

The first term in (4.10) is positive, since sales are positive ($f > 0$) and we are assuming that costs decline with learning ($c_X < 0$). Thus, the second term, f_X, in (4.10) determines the behavior of $\lambda(t)$ over time since $\varepsilon > 0$ and $p > 0$. If $f_X > 0$ (that is, the positive, demand learning effects outweigh the demand-negative/saturation effects), then $\lambda < 0$ and a penetration strategy would be called for. Conversely, if $f_X < 0$, then a skimming strategy is most appropriate.

But the penetration or skimming is defined relative to the myopic price which may take any shape itself. The critical question is what happens to price over time? Costs, demand effects, and investments in the future (captured through λ) determine the result here. Kalish shows that the sign of $\dot{p}$ (the direction of the slope of $p(t)$) at any point in time, designated as sign ($\dot{p}$) is

$$\text{sign}\,(\dot{p}) = \text{sign} \left[-r\lambda - 2\frac{f_X f}{f_p} + \frac{f_{XP} f^2}{f_p^2} + c_t + p \frac{\partial}{\partial t}\left(\frac{1}{\varepsilon}\right) \right] \tag{4.11a}$$

The five terms in (4.11a) determine the direction of the price trend. The first term handles future investment through λ and the discount rate. If λ is positive (through the learning curve and/or demand learning), then the higher the discount rate, the faster prices will decline. The second term is the effect of experience on demand and, if it is positive ($f_X > 0$), creates a pressure to price lower now, but increase over time to reap future benefits. The third term is the second-order effect of price change on demand and will generally not affect the first-order effect found in the second term. The fourth and fifth terms capture the (exogenous) effect of time on cost and elasticity, respectively: increasing costs or decreasing elasticity ($1/\varepsilon$ increasing) leads to increasing prices.

Exhibit 4.7 summarizes the qualitative effects for a variety of special cases. Note that in some circumstances the result is undetermined because the magnitude of the effects (and not just the signs) must be know to determine the result.

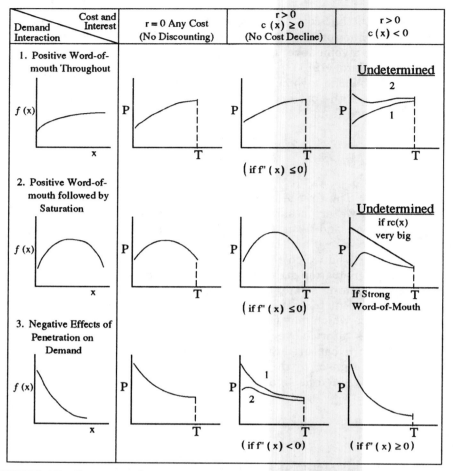

EXHIBIT 4.7 Summary of pricing over time: Separable demand function under different cost-demand experience interactions.

Two special cases for which the results are clear are for learning only (static demand) and for durable goods with a zero discount rate. In the former case (static demand), (4.11a) reduces to

$$\text{sign} \, (\dot{p}) = \text{sign} \, (-r\lambda + c_t) \qquad \textbf{(4.11b)}$$

and $\lambda > 0$ (from equation 4.10, since $c_X < 0$). Thus, aside from any exogenous effects introduced by c_t, price will decline over time and the rate of that decline will be governed by the discount rate r.

For the durable good, zero discount rate case ($r = 0$), the sign of f_X largely determines the sign of $\dot{p}$. Thus, early in the life cycle when

$f_X > 0$ (in **Bass's** 1969a framework, the innovation effect is overshadowing the imitation effect) prices will increase over time. Similarly, as the market is reaching saturation later in the life cycle, $f_X < 0$, and prices will decrease over time.

EXAMPLE

Dockner and Jorgensen (1988a)

Dockner and Jorgensen develop a model that is essentially the same as Kalish's (1983) model but which incorporates a *fixed* number of competitors. It, therefore, does not deal with the problem of competitive entry (or exit) from the market, but does deal with price competition.

Using an open-loop Nash equilibrium concept (where each firm is assumed to optimize its price time path, given knowledge of what all other firms are doing), the multifirm analogy to result (4.9) is

$$p_i^* = \frac{\varepsilon_{ii}}{\varepsilon_{ii} - 1} \, (c_i - \lambda_{ii}) + \frac{\displaystyle\sum_{j \neq i} \lambda_{ji} \varepsilon_{ji}}{\varepsilon_{ii} - 1} \tag{4.12}$$

where

$$\varepsilon_{ii} = \text{(minus) own brand price elasticity}$$
$$\varepsilon_{ji} = \left(\frac{\partial f_j}{\partial p_i}\right)\left(\frac{p_i}{f_j}\right)$$
$$\quad = \text{change in competitor } j\text{'s sales relative to } i\text{'s sales as a result of a price change by } i$$

Note that the first term on the right of (4.12) is the same as the result of (4.9); that is, the difference from the myopic pricing rule is through the shadow price term. λ_{ii}—thus, as earlier, if more output today has a positive impact on future profit ($\lambda_{ii} > 0$) then prices today should be lower than if one considers current profits only.

The second term in (4.12) adjusts this result by measuring the effect of i's price on competitor j's sales, which in turn affects i's profit in the future through λ_{ji}. Note that $\varepsilon_{ji} > 0$ and that $\varepsilon_{ii} - 1 > 0$; thus λ_{ji} determines the sign of that second term.

In most cases the λ_{ji}'s will be expected to be negative, leading to results that are consistent with the monopoly case except that the prices will be lower. Here, the additional lowering of price acts as a wedge to prevent competitors from gaining experience through learning. In circumstances where saturation effects dominate the story, λ_{ji} will be positive and the oligopolist will use a discrimination policy, pricing higher than the monopolist.

In terms of the price path over time, Dockner and Jorgensen analyze several cases similar to Kalish and show

1. For the static demand case with learning, price declines over time for $r > 0$ (and is constant for $r = 0$).

2. If demand has only self learning effects and can be "separated" as

$$\dot{x}_i = k(x_i)q_i(p_1, \ldots, p_n)$$

and $r = 0$ (zero discount rate), then

a. prices increase over time if $\partial k_i/\partial X_i > 0$ for all i

b. prices decrease over time if $\partial k_i/\partial X_i < 0$ for all i.

Note that this also generalizes the monopoly result: case (1) is typical for a repeat purchase good, where prices increase from introduction until they reach steady state. Case (2) results for the mature stage of the life cycle for a durable good (after market learning effects are no longer important) where prices are decreasing.

The latter paper generalizes several previous papers including Dockner (1985) and Thompson and Teng (1984). For other, closely related work, see Wernerfelt (1985, 1986), Rao and Bass (1985), and Narasimhan (1989).

None of the models discussed addresses the future entry problem. This problem has been modeled in two ways: (1) with future entry as exogenous, that is, independent of the action of the current firm(s), and (2) with future entry endogenous, with the entrant (and competitors) consciously dealing with one another as part of the competitive environment. Some example of the exogenous entry type include the work of Spence (1981) (who considers the learning curve shown); Bass and Rao (1983); Fudenberg and Tirole (1983b); Eliashberg and Jeuland (1986); and Dolan, Jeuland and Muller (1986). The last paper provides a nice summary of the important issues associated with the dynamics of market entry. Rao (1988), has considered endogenous entry and Kalish (1988) provides a brief review of the relevant work in this area as do Hanssens, Parsons, and Schultz (1990, pp. 280–293).

The Relationship Between Price and Quality. Under classical economic theory, price's main role is to indicate the cost of acquiring a good or service. If perfect information is assumed in the marketplace, price in itself has no informational content. Thus, except for several recognized irregularities, economic theory prescribes a downward-sloping demand curve, indicating increasing quantities demanded at lower prices.

Seminal work by Scitovsky (1944–45), Stoetzel (1954), Adam (1958), and Gabor and Granger (1966) has modified this view of demand, suggesting that because consumers do not have perfect information about products, price may be taken as a quality signal to reduce the perceived risk of purchase. Indeed in many product categories like cosmetics, objective information on product quality is difficult or impossible to obtain. In these categories price can serve as an indicator of quality and price discounts are not effective. In such product categories, marketers often find it more effective to build image through high levels of advertising than to offer price deals.

In the work of Gabor and Granger (1966) and Sowter, Gabor, and Granger (1971), the relationship between price and quality is specified via a "limit concept." A consumer intent on purchasing a product in a particular class has two price limits in mind: an upper limit above which purchase will not be made because the good or service is too expensive and a lower limit below which purchase will not be made because the quality of the item is suspect. Within the range created by these limits, price does not act as an absolute barrier to purchase, as it does outside the range.

Monroe (1971b) developed a model expressing a log-normal buy-response function and was able to estimate upper and lower price thresholds. Rao and Shakun (1972) extended the model to a multibrand environment and to different consumer segments.

Srinivasan (1982) argues that price should be included as an attribute in utility function estimation because its inclusion provides additional cues about product quality and other attributes. In other words, price plays a dual role: disutility associated with potential economic sacrifice and a surrogate for product quality when other product attribute information is not available. Several models have been developed that attempt to incorporate this dual role that price takes (see, for example, Dodds and Monroe, 1985; Zeithaml, 1986; and Monroe and Chapman, 1987). Note that Hauser and Shugan (1983) and others incorporate price via an "attribute-price" ratio (Chapter 5).

Recent research suggests that price may not always serve as an effective indicator of quality. Devinney (1988b) shows that there must be severe penalties (in terms of loss of long-term goodwill to the firm for example) for firms *not* to take advantage of the price-indicating quality phenomenon and charge prices higher than those that would be optimal with perfect information. Empirical work by Tellis and Wernerfelt (1987), Tellis (1987), and Curry and Riesz (1988) generally support Devinney's argument: in general, stronger relationships exist between price and (objectively measured) quality in markets with a high level of consumer information.

Reference Prices.   A reference price is an internal price that consumers use to compare to actual prices. Winer (1988) presents a fine review of the concept; he indicates that David Ricardo mentioned something called a "just price"—that is, something a good ought to cost. Thus, if reference prices are important in determining reaction to price, then the reference price, P^r as well as the actual price P^o must be considered in making pricing decisions.

EXAMPLE _____

Consider a linear demand function and profit function:

$$\pi = PQ - cQ \tag{4.13}$$

where

c = unit (constant) production cost.

If $Q = a - bP$, then P^*, the profit-maximizing price, is $(a + bc)/2b$. However, if the demand function is linearly related to the reference price,

$$Q = a - b(P - P^r)$$

then P^* can be shown to be $(bP^r + bc + a)/2b$. For this demand function then, the optimal price, P^*, moves up or down with the reference price, regardless of the level of the market response parameters (a, b, and c).

_____

What this example illustrates is that, if a reference price exists, optimal pricing levels should incorporate that information.

There have been a variety of explanations for this phenomenon, leading to different demand functions:

- *the Weber-Fechner law*, which states that individuals respond to relative or proportional change in a stimulus (Monroe, 1971a)
- *the adaptation-level theory*, which states that individuals respond to a stimulus relative to the preceding stimulus (Helson, 1964)
- *the assimilation contrast theory*, which states that there is a range of acceptable levels for a stimulus, and individuals respond significantly to response outside that range of acceptable levels (Sherif and Hovland, 1961)
- *prospect theory*, in which individuals react differently to gains and losses relative to a specific "frame" (the reference price here)

While other explanations exist, these can be cast in demand equation form (see Exhibit 4.8).

Two of the equations in Exhibit 4.8 (the alternative Weber-Fechner model and the prospect theory model) require knowledge of the reference price. Oliver

Theory	Model
Standard Demand Model	$Q_t = a + b\, p_t^o + cX_t + \varepsilon_t$
Weber-Fechner Models	$Q_t = (a - bd) + b\,(p_t^o - f \ln p_t^o) + cX_t + \varepsilon_t$
	$Q_t = a + b \ln \left[\dfrac{(p_t^o - p_t^r)}{p_t^r} \right] + cX_t + \varepsilon_t$
	for all $(p_t^o - p_t^r) > 0$
Adaptation-Level Theory	$Q_t = a + b\,(p_t^o - e^{d + f \ln p_{t-1}^o}) + cX_t + \varepsilon_t$
	$Q_t = (a - bd) + b\,(p_t^o - fp_{t-1}^o) + cX_t + \varepsilon_t$
Assimilation-Contrast Theory	$Q_t = (a - bd) + b\,(p_t^o - fp_t^o - gp_t^{o^2} - hp_t^{o^3}) + cX_t + \varepsilon_t$
Prospect Theory	$Q_t = a + b_1\,(p_t^o - p_t^r)\,d_1 + b_2\,(p_t^o - p_t^r)\,d_2 + cX_t + \varepsilon_t,$
	where $d_1 = 1$ if $(p_t^o - p_t^r) > 0,$ $= 0$ otherwise $d_2 = 1$ if $(p_t^o - p_t^r) < 0,$ $= 0$ otherwise

p_t^o = current observed price.
p_t^r = current reference price.
X_t = other marketing variables.
Q_t = demand.
$a, b, c, d, f, g, h,$ = parameters.

EXHIBIT 4.8 Demand models developed from psychological theories

and Winer (1987) review alternatives, and point out that it is most common to use an error-learning process:

$$p_t^r - p_t^{r-1} = (1 - k)(p_{t-1}^o - p_{t-1}^r) \qquad \textbf{(4.14)}$$

where k is a constant between 0 and 1. Successive substitutions for p_t^r, p_{t-1}^o, and so on yields a distributed lag form,

$$p_t^r = (1 - k)\, p_t^o + (1 - k)kp_{t-1}^o + (1 - k)k^2 p_{t-2}^o + \cdots \qquad \textbf{(4.15)}$$

which can be substituted into the appropriate demand equation, (usually truncating after two or three terms) adding only one parameter, k, to be estimated.

Winer (1988) points out that there appear to be at least five different concepts underlying what makes up a reference price:

1. *Fair and just price.* What the product ought to cost (Rao and Gautschi, 1982)

2. *Reservation price.* The upper threshold limit used by economists to describe the price just low enough to overcome a consumer's reluctance to purchase (Scherer, 1980)

3. *Lowest acceptable price.* That price, below which the product is perceived to be of inferior quality (Stoetzel, 1970)

4. *Expected price.* What consumers think will be charged for the product in the future (Winer, 1985)

5. *Perceived price.* A price that the consumer pays most frequently, paid last, or pays, on average, for goods in this category (Uhl, 1970; Olander, 1970; Tull, Boring, and Gonsior, 1964; Emery, 1970)

One or more of the concepts can be used in operationalizing or measuring reference price.

Winer (1988) reviews the empirical literature on the relationship between demand and reference price and concludes that while that literature is small, it generally provides support for the concept. He calls for more research in six areas: (1) concept validation: more empirical work supporting the concept; (2) multiple reference prices: using multidimensional reference-price constructs; (3) normative modeling: demonstrating the impact of the concept on optimal behavior; (4) size effects: how demand changes as price varies from one or another of the reference price concepts; (5) explicit versus implicit modeling of reference price: determining if it is better to infer the reference price or to ask people; and (6) choice of reference-price theory: deciding, as some of the theories and models conflict, which are better and when?

SETTING PRICE IN PRACTICE

With an area of such importance and with so much at stake, it might be assumed that a great deal of continuing research and planning would by now underlie the formulation of pricing strategy and the setting of prices. One might also expect that a well-developed body of theory would have resulted in principles to guide pricing decisions. But this does not appear to be the case:

> The significant variations in what managers are most concerned about signals limited attention to, interest in and use of the "general purpose" pricing prescriptions academics strive to establish. *(*Bonoma, Crittenden and Dolan, 1988, p. 337*)*

Pricing models and procedures used in practice generally emphasize either cost, demand, or competition, while neglecting the others. Nevertheless, they meet some of the more practical requirements for price determination in the presence of imperfect information and multiple parties. Now, we briefly examine cost-oriented, demand-oriented, and competition-oriented pricing.

Cost-Oriented Pricing. Many firms set their prices largely or even wholly on the basis of their costs (Hutt and Speh, 1989; Simon, 1989). Construction companies submit job bids by estimating total costs and adding a standard markup to those costs. General Motors prices its automobile to yield a 15–20% return on its investment (cost). Typically, firms count all costs, including a usually arbitrary allocation of overhead made on the basis of expected operating levels.

Does the use of a rigid, customary markup over cost make logical sense in the pricing of products? Generally, the answer is no. Any model that ignores current demand elasticity in setting prices is not likely to lead, except by chance, to the achievement of maximum profits, either in the long or the short run. As demand elasticity changes, the optimum markup should also change. If markup remains a rigid percentage of cost, then under ordinary conditions it would not lead to maximum profits. However, under special conditions a rigid markup at *the right level* may lead to optimum profits. Those conditions are that variable costs are fairly constant over time and quantity and that fixed costs are negligible.

EXAMPLE _____

In a similar development as in (4.3) we can show that marginal revenue is related to price,

$$MR = \left(1 - \frac{1}{\varepsilon}\right) P \tag{4.16}$$

where ε = price elasticity of demand, expressed as a positive number. Profits are maximized when marginal revenue is equated to marginal cost (MC). Therefore the optimality condition is

$$MC = \left(1 - \frac{1}{\varepsilon}\right) P \tag{4.17}$$

Suppose that average costs (AC) are constant in quantity. Then $AC = MC$, and the condition for optimality is

$$AC = \left(1 - \frac{1}{\varepsilon}\right) P \tag{4.18}$$

Equation (4.18) can be rearranged to yield a formula for the optimal markup:

$$\frac{P}{AC} = \frac{1}{[1 - (1/\varepsilon)]} = \frac{\varepsilon}{\varepsilon - 1} \tag{4.19}$$

Subtracting AC/AC from both sides and simplifying, we obtain

$$\frac{P - AC}{AC} = \frac{\varepsilon}{(\varepsilon - 1)} - 1 = \frac{1}{\varepsilon - 1} \tag{4.20}$$

or

$$\text{Optimal markup} = \frac{1}{\varepsilon - 1} \tag{4.21}$$

According to equation (4.21), the optimal markup is inversely related to price elasticity. If brand-price elasticity is high, say, 5.0, as it might be in the case of branded sugar, then the optimal markup is relatively low (25%). If brand elasticity is low, say, 2.0, as it might be in the case of branded frozen pastry, the optimal markup is relatively high (100%). Furthermore, if the price elasticity remains fairly constant over time, then a fairly rigid markup would be consistent with optimal pricing. But without considering price elasticity (the key term in equation 4.21) it is hard to know what that markup should be.

If prices can be changed continuously and costs vary over time and with cumulative demand, the dynamic extension of (4.21) is as derived by Kalish (1983), discussed earlier.

Demand-Oriented Pricing.   Cost-oriented approaches rely on the idea of a standard markup over costs and/or a conventional level of profits. Demand-oriented approaches look instead at the intensity of demand. Most of the developments presented in this chapter have taken this demand-oriented approach. Such an approach requires a sound estimation of disaggregate demand curves, discussed earlier. Simon (1989) provides a number of practical examples of demand-oriented pricing and Wind and colleagues (1989) describe how the Marriott Corporation used a conjoint analysis-based approach to estimate customer demand and set prices for a new hotel chain (Chapter 5).

Competition-Oriented Pricing. When a company sets its prices chiefly on the basis of what its competitors are charging, rather than on the basis of cost or demand, its pricing policy can be described as competition oriented. The most common type of competition-oriented pricing occurs when a firm tries to keep its price at the average level charged by the industry. This type is called going-rate or imitative pricing.

Going-rate pricing is practiced primarily in homogeneous product markets, like steel, paper and fertilizer, although the market structure itself may vary from pure competition to pure oligopoly. The firm selling a homogeneous product in a purely competitive market actually has very little choice in setting its price. In a pure oligopoly, in which a few large firms dominate the industry, firms also tend to charge the same price as competition, although for different reasons. Because there are only a few firms, each firm is aware of the others' prices, and so are the buyers. Price differences are likely to favor the lower-priced firm, discouraging price increases by a single firm.

On the other hand, in markets characterized by product differentiation, the individual firm has more latitude in its price decision. Product differences, whether in styling, quality, or functional features, serve to desensitize the buyer to existing price differentials. Product and marketing programs are made compatible within a chosen pricing zone, and firms respond to competitive changes in price to maintain their pricing zone.

A common form of competition-oriented pricing occurs in competitive bidding, a common form of pricing in markets where the firm is in competition with an unknown number of suppliers and has no deterministic knowledge of their prices. Many manufacturers and service organizations selling to the Defense Department, municipal governments, original equipment producers, and so forth must bid against others for the work; the contract usually goes to the lowest bidder. Therefore, the seller must carefully think through two issues regarding each bidding opportunity: (1) should he bid at all (the decision to bid) and (2) if so, what bid should he make (the bid-size problem)?

If the supplier decides to make a bid on a particular job, he must search for a price that is somewhere above his costs but below competitors' bids. The higher the seller sets his price above his costs, the greater will be the conditional profit but the smaller will be the probability of getting the contract. These considerations can be formalized in a simple model in which bids are calculated to maximize the company's expected profits. The expected profit in a potential bid is the product of the probability of getting the contract and the estimated profit on the contract:

$$E(Z_p) = f(P)(P - C) \tag{4.23}$$

where

$E(Z_p)$ = expected profit with a bid of P
$f(P)$ = probability of winning contract with a bid of P
P = bid price
C = estimated cost of fulfilling contract

Each possible price, then, is associated with a certain probability of winning the contract. A company may logically choose the expected profit-maximizing price. The chief problem with this model is guessing the probabilities of winning the contract at various bidding levels. Where price is the buyer's only concern, this probability is the probability of submitting a lower bid than those of all the other competitors, and the probability of submitting the lowest bid is the joint probability that the company's bid is lower than each competitor's bid (assuming competitors' bids are independently formed):

$$f(P) = f_1(P)f_2(P) \cdots f_j(P) \cdots f_n(P) \tag{4.24}$$

where $f_j(P)$ is the probability that a bid of P is lower than competitor j's bid.

Competitors' bids are uncertain but may be derived from past bidding behavior, as follows. Assume that competitor j has bid on a number of past contracts and that those data are available. Then for each bid,

$$r_j = \frac{P_j}{C} \tag{4.25}$$

where

r_j = ratio of competitor j's bid to company cost
P_j = past bid by j
C = company's cost at time of bid

The ratios for several past bids of a competitor form a distribution $g_j(y)$, where y is competitor j's bid. (King and Mercer, 1991, discuss estimation methods and choice of distributions for g.)

We go from an absolute to a ratio scale in (4.25) because past bids have different magnitudes. If we assume that bidders use a "markup over cost" percentage as a bidding procedure, the bids from equation (4.25) should appear to come from the same distribution.

If for a given contract our cost is C, then we might guess that the probability of j's bid price being greater than ours is $\int_r^\infty g_j(y)dy$, where $r = P/C$. With k competitors, our likelihood of winning is

$$\prod_{j=1}^{K} \int_r^\infty g_j(y)dy \qquad (4.26)$$

If each competitor has the same bid distribution $g(\cdot)$, equation (4.26) reduces to

$$f(P) = \left[\int_r^\infty g(y)dy \right]^k \qquad (4.27)$$

and the expected profit of bid price P is

$$E[Z(P)] = (P - C)\left[\int_r^\infty g(y)dy \right]^k \qquad (4.28)$$

Given knowledge of g and C, equation (4.28) can be solved for an optimal value of P.

In the last step we knew that there would be exactly k bidders. If k is only known probabilistically, then equation (4.27) is modified as follows. Suppose a distribution $h(k)$ is found that describes well the past number of bidders (which may correlate with the size of the contract). Then the probability distribution for company bid of P winning is

$$f(P) = \sum_k h(k)\left[\int_r^\infty g(y)dy \right]^k \qquad (4.29)$$

and equation (4.29) is used in equation (4.28) to determine an optimal bid.

Like the pricing model of classical demand theory, the bidding model has a nice intuitive structure. But for practical use it clearly needs modification. Realistically, the company may be missing an adequate past history for certain competitors. In this case, for each potential competitor management will have to develop a subjective probability distribution for r, based on whatever information is available. Furthermore, the company may believe that competitors will depart from their past pattern of bidding, in which case management will again want to replace historical probability distributions with ones that more accurately reflect its subjective expectations.

The model may need further modifications to meet other special circumstances present in the competitive-bidding situation. For example, the company may expect a sequence of opportunities to open up, one at a time and with different values, and because of limited resources, it cannot afford to win all the contracts. Here the company must decide when to bid and how much. Clearly, the availability of further opportunities will influence the company's bid in a particular case. Another circumstance that would modify the bidding process occurs when the buyer is known to take other factors into consideration besides the bid, such as the bidder's reputation for reliability, service, quality, proximity, past relations with buyer, and so forth. In this situation a supplier with a good reputation may set a bid higher than his competitors by the amount of superior reputation he enjoys. In other circumstances, two or more bidders may be awarded a contract when the buyer wants to maintain multiple sources of supply (Seshadri, Chatterjee and Lilien, 1991).

Competitive-bidding models have generally been of two types. One is decision theoretic, as the one here, where the modeler assumes the actions of competitors can be determined probabilistically and independently of the decision makers action (Edelman, 1965). The other is game theory, which can be used when all competitors are assumed to have similar analytic capabilities and can jointly optimize against each other.

Recent bidding models have dealt with issues such as incorporating opportunity costs into bidding strategies, bidding over time and across contracts, biases, and uncertainties in cost estimates and the design of auctions. See Monroe (1990) for a discussion on how to operationalize competitive bidding procedures. Stark and Rothkopf (1979), Engelbrecht-Wiggans (1980), McAfee and McMillan (1987), Milgrom (1989), and Rothkopf (1991) provide extensive reviews of the literature on bidding and auctions and Keefer, Smith, and Back (1991) discuss how the lease-sale bidding system at Gulf Oil operated.

Pricing Strategies.   Tellis (1986) provides a useful taxonomy of pricing strategies, based on the objective of the firm and the characteristics of consumers (Exhibit 4.9). He provides a rationale for why these strategies are appropriate for these combinations of objectives and customer types. This rather compelling framework awaits empirical validation—what are pricing practitioners doing relative to the prescription of the theory that Tellis synthesizes?

SUMMARY

Nonprice factors continue to grow in importance in the modern marketing process, but price will continue to hold a central position.

Setting price requires knowledge of the organization's objectives, consumers' willingness to pay for the product, the costs of producing the product,

	Objective of Firm		
Characteristics of Consumers	Vary Prices Among Consumer Segments	Exploit Competitive Position	Balance Pricing over Product Line
Some have high search costs	Random discounting	Price signaling	Image pricing
Some have low reservation price	Periodic discounting	Penetration pricing Experience curve pricing	Price bundling Premium pricing
All have special transaction costs	Second market discounting	Geographic pricing	Complementary pricing

EXHIBIT 4.9   A taxonomy of pricing strategies

the reactions of competition, changes in these factors over time, and the interaction of price with other elements of the marketing mix.

Some powerful theoretical results have been developed to provide both insight and guidance about pricing decisions. These results suggest when two-part and block tariffs should be expected to be cost-beneficial; how to price product lines when products substitute for one another; when product-price bundling schemes should be effective; and how organizational objectives, competition, and variations in market conditions overtime affect some of these basic theoretical results.

Major challenges in the pricing area include the development of more complete theories to explain the wide variety of pricing mechanisms that exist in the marketplace and the development of operational models that integrate competitive interactions with market dynamics and measurement procedures to make these models operational.

PROBLEMS

4.1. A manufacturer sells its product in two distinct markets, A and B. The demand equation associated with each market, respectively, is

$$Q_A = 400 - 2P_A$$

$$Q_B = 150 - 0.5P_B$$

The firm's total cost equation is

$$C = 10,000 + 20(Q_A + Q_B)$$

The current selling price is $120 in both markets. Assuming that the conditions necessary for the successful practice of price discriminations hold true, could the company benefit by charging different prices in markets A and B? If so, what prices should be set in each market?

4.2. A television manufacturer wishes to determine the price for a new portable model that will maximize the company's current profits on the model. The marketing research department's estimate of demand for the new product is represented by the function $Q = 15,000 - 80P$, where Q is the quantity demanded and P is the price. In manufacturing the product, the company will incur fixed costs of $300,000 and variable costs of $20 per unit.

a. Find the optimum price and determine the level of demand, costs, and profit at this price.

b. The demand equation shown is a familiar one. What assumptions are implicit in such a demand equation that may greatly limit its usefulness?

4.3. A leading pharmaceutical company wants to model the revenue generated by a new hypertension pill. The company researchers believe that the revenue depends on the price per pill, the percentage of the population that is susceptible to hypertension, and the amount of research money spent. Data are available for 1982–1989 and are given as follows (dollar figures have been adjusted for inflation):

Year	Revenue ($ in millions)	Research (in $1,000s)	Price per Pill	Percentage Hypertension
1982	$5.0	$10	$0.50	0.25%
1983	5.1	30	0.48	0.25
1984	5.5	40	0.40	0.26
1985	5.6	50	0.50	0.26
1986	5.8	80	0.55	0.26
1987	6.5	90	0.55	0.27
1988	7.5	100	0.65	0.27
1989	8.2	110	0.60	0.28

At first, the model $y = a_0 + a_1 x_1 + a_2 x_2 + a_3 x_3 + \varepsilon$ was proposed. A company statistician warned that the assumption of homoscedasticity might be violated if that model was used. He proposed that the model

$$\ln y = a_0 + a_1 x_1 + a_2 x_2 + a_3 x_3 + \varepsilon$$

be used instead.

a. Fit both models to the data given and determine which is best. (Define "best.")

b. Is heteroscedasticity present in the simple linear model? How do you know?

4.4. What is price elasticity? Differentiate elasticity, inelasticity, unit elasticity, and cross-elasticity.

4.5. Differentiate among cost-oriented pricing, demand-oriented pricing, and competition-oriented pricing with regard to the company's goals, the degree of competition, and the stage of the product life cycle.

4.6. The marketing management of a firm has suggested a price increase of $0.74 on a product currently selling at $8.95. Current unit variable costs are $4.65, while the elasticity of demand is estimated to be -1.75. Would you recommend that the price increase be adopted?

4.7. The ABC Plumbing Company is invited to bid for a contract to install the plumbing system in a new apartment building. The company estimates that the cost of installation as specified in the contract will be \$10,000. From past experience the company has determined that the probability of winning the contract is

$$f(P) = e^{-P/10,000}$$

Should the company make a bid? At what price? What is the company's expected profit at this price?

4.8. a. A caterer is about to submit a sealed bid to run a restaurant concession at a municipal airport for the next five years. He must state the fixed rent that he is prepared to pay annually. He estimates that gross profits, before rent is paid, will be \$100,000 the first year and will increase by 10% per year. Past experience shows that if R is the annual rent offered by a winning bid and G is his own estimate of the total gross profit of a contract running n years, the ratio nR/G is normally distributed about 0.5 with a standard deviation of 0.07. What should be bid so as to maximize his expected net profit?

b. Suppose that in the preceding circumstance the caterer wishes to bid so that, on average, the money left on the table does not exceed 10% of his bid. What should the bid be? (The money left on the table is the difference between the winning and the second bid. When all bids are published, the winner does not wish to appear foolish for having bid way above his competitors. The average value is computed only over the cases in which the caterer wins the concession.)

4.9. Consider the problem of developing a two-product pricing strategy given a linear price interaction model:

$$Q_i = k_i - a_i P_i + b_i P_j$$
$$Q_j = k_j - a_j P_j + b_j P_i$$

where

Q = quantity demanded
P = price

and k, a, and b are positive constants. Assume a cost function of the form

$$C = F + c_i Q_i + c_j Q_j$$

a. Interpret the terms k, a, and b.
b. Form a total profit function.
c. Differentiate the profit function to determine optimal prices P_i and P_j.
d. Suggest some more realistic functions for Q and C.

4.10. How does Simon's (1979) model handle the issue of competitive pricing? Suggest an alternative.

4.11. In the early 1960s, the X Corporation faced the following pricing problem for its copying machines. (There was hardly any competition then.) There were two segments of potential users, the large users—whose copying needs were 20,000 copies per year—and the small users—whose copying needs were 2,000 copies per year. X found that a large user would be willing to pay as much as $25,800 for a machine, whereas a small user would be willing to pay only $6,700 maximum. These reservation prices accounted for the expected life of a machine (five years), its resale value at the end of that period ($0), and the cost of supplies (mainly copying paper from X—only X copying paper could be used in its machines in the early 1960s). In other words, a large user would be willing to pay $25,800 to buy an X machine provided supplies from X were free of charge over the life of the machine; similarly, a small user would be willing to buy an X machine for $6,700 provided X supplied free supplies. There were equal numbers of large and small users. X's marginal cost of producing each of these machines was estimated to be $1,900. Its marginal cost of paper was $0.03 per sheet. X uses a 10% discount rate when evaluating costs and revenues over time.

    a. What should be the selling price of these machines (bundled with paper)? (Only one price can be charged, that is, everyone who buys must pay the same price, and the buyer must pay immediately.)

    b. X wonders if it can make more money leasing the machines instead of selling them. The leasing policy will involve a yearly rental charge (payable at the end of each year) and a charge per copy made (monitored via the copy meter on the machines) accumulated over each year and payable at the end of the year. Only one leasing plan—that is, a single rental charge and a single per copy charge—is being contemplated. What should be X's leasing policy? (Assume that each user also uses a 10% discount rate.)

    c. Explain in a few words why the leasing plan does better than the selling option.

    d. Would the advantage of leasing over selling increase or decrease if the relative proportion of small to large users increased from $1:1$ to $2:1$? Why?

4.12. You have just been appointed a pricing analyst at KLM Communications on the basis of your having read this chapter. (KLM Communications is known for its reckless hiring practices.) Presently the company has the following linear structure of prices for long-distance calls between NuYork and Raachester: $2.00 for each minute of calls. Market research indicates that there are five types of consumers in the market, equal numbers of each type, demanding the following numbers of minutes per day at various prices per minute.

	$1	$2	$3	$4	$5
Type 1	5 min	4 min	3 min	2 min	1 min
Type 2	4 min	3 min	2 min	1 min	0 min
Type 3	3 min	2 min	1 min	0 min	0 min
Type 4	2 min	1 min	0 min	0 min	0 min
Type 5	1 min	0 min	0 min	0 min	0 min

Assume zero marginal and fixed costs.

    a. Compute the profit-maximizing linear pricing scheme. (In a linear pricing scheme, every minute is priced the same.)

    b. Compute the profit-maximizing quantity discount scheme.

    c. If the quantity discount yields higher profits than the linear scheme, why does it do so? If not, why not?

4.13. Photographic film companies face the problem of deciding whether to sell their slide film only bundled with development (a pure bundling strategy), or sell film and development separately (a pure components strategy), or offer both options (mixed bundling).

Suppose Company K's marketing research department has identified four broad categories of consumers interested in slide photography, segments A, B, C, and D, each of which comsumes one 36-slide roll per month. The four types differ in their relative preference for K film and K development. Segment A tends to value the film much more than the development; segment B values the development much more than the film; segment C values both about equally and low; and segment D values both high. The marketing research department is quite certain about its reservation price estimates for types A, B, and C, but is somewhat uncertain about its estimates for type D. And it is also uncertain about the sizes of these groups. As for costs, you have some estimates from the production department, but they are also somewhat uncertain.

Consider the following four alternative reservation price/market composition/cost scenarios. In each scenario, the relevant demand data are given as triples of numbers. The first number in each triple is the reservation price for a 36-slide roll of K film, the second number is the reservation price for K developing this roll of film, and the third number is the segment's size as a fraction of the picture-taking population. (Of course, for each type, the reservation price for K film and K development is the sum of the component reservation prices.) For example, in (a), A's willingness to pay for film is $3, A's willingness to pay for development is $1, and this segment constitutes 10% of the population.

Determine the profit-maximizing selling strategy in each environment given. (Note: It is technically possible to sell K film and K development separately if K chooses to do so. In other words, a customer can get his Fuji film developed at K; similarly, K film doesn't have to be developed by K.) Relate your answers to the criteria of extraction, inclusion and exclusion.

(1) A ($3, $1, 0.10); B ($1, $3, 0.10); C ($1, $1, 0.70); D ($3, $3, 0.10). Unit cost of film: $0.50; unit cost of development: $0.50.

(2) A ($3, $1, 0.25); B ($1, $3, 0.25); C ($1, $1, 0.25); D ($3, $3, 0.25). Same unit costs as above.

(3) A ($3, $1, 0.25); B ($1, $3, 0.25); C ($1, $1, 0.25); D ($2.50, $2.50, 0.25). Same unit costs as above.

(4) A ($3, $1, 0.25); B ($1, $3, 0.25); C ($1, $1, 0.25); D ($2.50, $2.50, 0.25). Unit cost of film: $1.50; unit cost of development: $1.50.

5 | PRODUCT

The (new) product decision is generally the most important marketing decision a manager can make because it is both extremely costly, requiring substantial investments in R&D, design, manufacturing, promotion, and distribution, and it is also very difficult to change. In this chapter, we will deal with the new product and product repositioning decisions from a theoretical perspective first; then we will describe some of the operational models and procedures that have been developed to support product decisions. In Chapter 10 we address the issue of new product dynamics, forecasting, and market diffusion.

THE PRODUCT: DEFINITIONS AND CLASSIFICATION

To begin, we ask, *What is a product?* We define a product as follows:

> A *product* is anything that can be offered to a market for attention, acquisition, use, or consumption that might satisfy a want or need.

Most products we think of are *physical products*. But products also include *services*, such as haircuts, concerts, and vacations. A *place* like Hawaii can be marketed, in the sense of either buying some land in Hawaii or taking a vacation there. An *organization* like the American Red Cross can be marketed, in the sense that we feel positive toward it and will support it.

In developing a product, one needs to think about it on three levels. The most fundamental level is the *core product,* which answers the question: What is the buyer really buying? Every product is really the packaging of a want-satisfying service. A woman buying lipstick is not simply buying lip color. Charles Revson of Revlon, Inc., recognized this early: "In the factory, we make cosmetics; in the store, we sell hope." The marketer's job is to uncover the needs hiding under every product and to sell *benefits,* not *features.*

The product planner has to turn the core product into a *tangible product.* Lipsticks, computers, education seminars, and political candidates are all tangible products. Tangible products may have a *quality level, features, styling, a brand name,* and *packaging.*

Finally, additional services and benefits such as installation, delivery, credit, warranty and after-sale service make up an *augmented product.*

Marketers have traditionally classified products into different types on the basis of different product characteristics. Each product type has a distinctive marketing-mix strategy. Exhibit 5.1 presents the major classifications of consumer and industrial goods and their marketing strategy implications.

THE THEORY OF PRODUCT STRATEGY

The product decision interacts intimately with other marketing-mix decisions. For example, the price charged for a product is a function of how much people are willing to pay for it, and that depends on how closely the product meets consumers' preferences. The greater the distance between the product and consumers' ideal products, the lower the price at which the product will sell. On the other hand, if the product is close to what consumers want, then the price can be higher. Product choice also affects the way it is promoted. What is said in an advertising campaign depends both on what customers want and on what the product offers. What advertising media are used depends on which segments are being targeted and that is a function of product design as well. Product choices determine distribution channel choices because, again, different channels cater to different market segments. Finally, these other marketing-mix variables may help "position" the product for the consumer. For example, to convey the high quality and exclusiveness of a line of clothing, a manufacturer may charge a high price for it, advertise only in high-fashion magazines, and distribute only through upscale department stores.

We focus here on the interaction between product and pricing decisions. First, we consider industries where the manufacturer is a monopolist. While true monopolies are rare (except for limited periods of time after a new product class has been introduced), this analysis is nevertheless useful because it

Products can be classified in a number of ways

...by durability/tangibility:

Non-durable goods—Goods that (1) are made from materials other than metals, hard plastics, and wood; (2) are rather quickly consumed or worn out or (3) become dated, unfashionable, or in some other way no longer popular. An awkward term that includes a highly varied set of goods and is useful primarily as a contrast with durable goods.

Durable goods—consumer goods that are used over an extended rather than a brief period of time. Usually, but not necessarily, of more substantial manufacture. Examples are automobiles and furniture.

Services—products, such as a bank loan or home security, that are intangible, or at least substantially so. If totally intangible, they are exchanged directly from producer to user, cannot be transported or stored, and are almost instantly perishable. Service products are often difficult to identify, since they come into existence at the same time they are bought and consumed. They are comprised of intangible elements that are inseparable, they usually involve customer participation in some important way, they cannot be sold in the sense of ownership transfer, and, they have no title.

...by consumer/industrial:

Consumer products are produced for and purchased by households for their use. They include

Convenience products—consumer goods and services (such as soap, candy bars, and shoe shines) that are bought frequently, often on impulse, with little time and effort spent on the buying process. They usually are low priced and are widely available.

Shopping products—products such as better dresses and hair treatments, for which the consumer is willing to spend considerable time and effort in gathering information on price, quality, and other attributes. Several retail outlets are customarily visited. Comparison of product attributes and complex decision processes are common.

Specialty products—products that have unique attributes or other characteristics which make them singularly important to the buyer. Multiple store searching, reliance on brand, and absence of extensive product comparisons are the rule. Cigarettes, deodorants, and specialized insurance policies are examples.

EXHIBIT 5.1 Product classifications

Industrial products are destined to be sold primarily for use in producing other goods or rendering services, as contrasted with consumer products. They include

Accessory equipment—portable factory equipment and tools that are used in the production process and do not become part of the finished product. They are generally inexpensive, shortlived, and relatively standardized. Examples are hand tools, lift trucks, and office equipment (typewriters, desks).

Business services—intangible products (services), such as banking and maintenance, that are purchased by organizations who produce other products.

Installations—nonportable industrial goods such as furnaces and assembly lines that are major and that are bought, installed, and used to produce other goods or services. Often grouped with accessory equipment to comprise capital goods. Also called heavy equipment.

Parts—manufactured products such as bicycle sprockets and lenses that are bought as components of other goods being produced. Parts are often sold simultaneously in industrial (original equipment) channels and in consumer channels for replacement purposes.

Raw Materials—(1) Products such as lumber and minerals that are bought for use in the production of other products, either as part of the finished item or in the industrial process; (2) natural products (coal, iron, crude oil, fish) and farm products (wheat, cotton, fruits) that are sold in their natural state. They are processed only to the level required for economical handling and transport.

Semimanufactured goods—industrial goods that are at least one stage past being raw materials and are sold for use as components of other products. They are comprised of parts and processed materials.

Supplies—industrial goods that are consumed in the process of producing other products. They facilitate the production process and do not go into the product itself. Frequently referred to as MRO (maintenance, repair, and operating supplies).

EXHIBIT 5.1 Product classifications (continued)

focuses attention on two of the forces involved in product strategy: consumer preferences and costs. Then we bring in the third force, competition, as we move to product and pricing strategy in oligopolistic industries.

Definitions and Preliminaries.   A product can be described by its performance on multiple attributes as we discussed in Chapter 2. Suppose n attributes characterize a class of products. Then a brand r can be represented as $(r_1, \ldots, r_n)$. Consumers' preferences for a brand can be captured in a utility function $u(r_1, \ldots, r_n)$, which we will assume to be additively separable: $u(r_1, \ldots, r_n) = u_1(r_1) + \cdots + u_n(r_n)$. If we express the consumer's utility function, in dollars, as a *reservation price function*, then we can model the consumer's brand choice problem as maximizing *consumer surplus*, $u_1(r_1) + \cdots + u_n(r_n) - p_r$, where p_r is the price of a unit of brand r.

The multiple attributes of a product generally fall into two classes, *monotone* attributes and *nonmonotone* attributes. Monotone attributes are attributes like gas-mileage, workmanship, and quality, on which all consumers agree in their preference ranking of the various attribute levels. For example, holding the other attributes at certain levels, everyone will agree that a car giving 40 mpg is better than a car giving 20 mpg. Similarly, in evaluating various brands of mail delivery services, consumers will prefer a service with a delivery time of one day to one with a delivery time of three days, everything else being the same. A monotone attribute can be ordered so that consumers' reservation prices are increasing in the level of the attribute. If all attributes of a product were monotone and if all available brands of the product were priced the same, then every consumer would choose the same brand—the brand with the highest level of each attribute.

But different brands are not priced the same, and those price differences lead to trade-offs between price and other attributes. Also, in most situations a brand that does best on every attribute is not available. For example, the only car choices available to a consumer may be a 40-mpg car that takes 15 seconds to accelerate from 0 to 60 mph and a 20-mpg car that takes only 9 seconds to accelerate from 0 to 60 mph. In such situations, even if two brands are priced the same, there is a trade-off, and depending on the consumer's *intensity* of preference for each attribute, the trade-off may be resolved differently by different consumers. This leads to the notion of an *efficient frontier*. No consumer will pick a brand that doesn't lie on the efficient frontier. But along the efficient frontier, different consumers may pick different brands depending on how they tradeoff one attribute against another (Exhibit 5.2). Hauser and Shugan (1983) develop such a model, and we discuss it in detail later in this chapter.

Nonmonotone attributes, in contrast, are attributes on which people have different preference orderings. For example, people disagree on their favorite colors for cars: some prefer white, others silver, others black. A nonmonotone

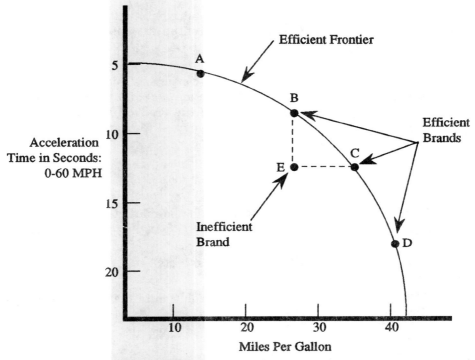

EXHIBIT 5.2   Five cars, equal on all other dimensions (including price), that vary
in acceleration and mileage. Acceleration-oriented people will choose
models *A* or *B*; mileage-conscious people will choose *C* or *D*. No one
will choose *E* (because mileage-oriented people will prefer *C* and acceleration-oriented people will prefer *B*).

attribute cannot be ordered so that *all* consumers' utility functions are increasing in the level of the attribute.

Product Strategy for a Monopolist

Suppose a manufacturer is trying to decide how he should configure his new
brand in a durable good product class. Every consumer will buy one unit of
the product or none at all. Also, assume that the manufacturer's product decision is limited to choosing the level of one attribute, *s*. That is, the product
has already been configured on all but one attribute, and the manufacturer
is now deciding on the level of the remaining attribute.

In making his product decision, the manufacturer must consider consumer preferences and costs. If all consumers had the same ideal point on the
attribute and this level of the attribute were the cheapest to produce, then
the solution would be very simple: offer the ideal level of the attribute and
charge a price equal to the maximum these consumers are willing to pay for

it. But what if the ideal level of the attribute were to cost more to produce than some other, less than ideal level of the attribute? Then the manufacturer has to tradeoff revenues and costs.

A Homogeneous Market.   Suppose consumers' reservation price for a unit of product s is described by the function $u(s)$ and the seller's unit costs (assumed to be constant across units of the product) are described by $c(s)$. The manufacturer's optimal pricing strategy is to charge the consumers' reservation price for the product. So

$$p^* = u(s) \tag{5.1}$$

If there are a total of N consumers in the market, then the manufacturer's profits are

$$N(u(s) - c(s)) \tag{5.2}$$

The s that maximizes profits is the solution to the first-order condition

$$N[u'(s) - c'(s)] = 0 \tag{5.3}$$

assuming that the profit function is strictly quasi-concave (see Appendix A). Call this solution s^*. Thus the optimal strategy for a monopolist manufacturer is to produce the product s^* and sell it at the consumers' reservation price, $u(s^*)$.

Note that $N(u(s) - c(s))$, besides being the seller's profits when he sells s at the consumers' reservation price, is also the aggregate consumer surplus when s is sold at cost, $c(s)$. Define the *efficient product* as the product that maximizes consumer surplus when all feasible products are sold at cost. We have shown that the manufacturer's profit-maximizing product is the efficient product.

Also note that this result extends easily to the multiattribute case. We simply interpret s as the vector $(s_1, ..., s_n)$. So if $s^e = (s_1^e, ..., s_n^e)$ is the efficient product that maximizes $N(u(s_1, ..., s_n) - c(s_1, ..., s_n))$, then the manufacturer's optimal strategy is to offer s^e at $u(s^e)$.

EXAMPLE

Suppose $u(s) = ks$, $c(s) = \alpha s^2$, and $N = 100$, where α and k are constants. What is the profit-maximizing product design and price?

Here, customer valuation for the product is linear in the performance dimension, s, for all consumers and cost goes up quadratically with performance. The profit-maximizing price for a product design, s, is ks. Thus

$$\text{Profit} = 100(ks - \alpha s^2) \tag{5.4}$$

and, using the first-order condition from equation (5.3) we get

$$100(k - 2\alpha s) = 0 \Rightarrow s^* = \frac{k}{2\alpha} \tag{5.5}$$

Thus, the profit-maximizing strategy for the seller is to offer the product of performance level $s^* = k/2\alpha$ at price $k^2/2\alpha$ with profits of $25k^2/\alpha$. The optimal performance level, price and profit decrease as α increases because both total and marginal costs increase as α increases.

EXAMPLE

Suppose the manufacturer is dealing with two attributes, s_1 and s_2 with $u(s_1, s_2) = k_1 s_1 + k_2 s_2$, $c(s_1, s_2) = \alpha s_1^2 s_2^2$, and $N = 100$. What are the profit-maximizing product and price?

As before, the profit-maximizing price for any product (s_1, s_2) is the reservation price $k_1 s_1 + k_2 s_2$.

Now, however, we need two first-order conditions to determine the optimal attribute levels:

$$100(k_1 - 2\alpha s_1 s_2^2) = 0 \tag{5.6}$$

$$100(k_2 - 2\alpha s_1^2 s_2) = 0 \tag{5.7}$$

Solving (5.6) and (5.7) yields

$$s_1^* = \left(\frac{k_2^2}{2\alpha k_1}\right)^{1/3} \; ; \quad s_2^* = \left(\frac{k_1^2}{2\alpha k_2}\right)^{1/3} \tag{5.8}$$

and the profit-maximizing price is

$$\text{Price} = 2\left(\frac{k_1^2 k_2^2}{2\alpha}\right)^{1/3} \tag{5.9}$$

A Heterogeneous Market. When the market is not homogeneous but the seller can offer only one product, then the analysis changes slightly. Suppose there are T segments in the market and segment $t(t = 1, ..., T)$ is of size N_t. Suppose also that the segments differ in their reservation prices for various levels of the attribute. Let segment t value product s at $u_t(s)$. Assume that the segments can be ordered so that $u_1(s) < u_2(s), < ..., < u_T(s)$ for any s. Note that we are not assuming that the product attributes are all monotone.

Because the market is not homogeneous now, the seller could price certain segments out of the market. For example, if the price charged for s is greater than $u_2(s)$, then segments 1 and 2 will not buy the products. Given our assumed ordering of the segments, if segment t is priced out, then segments 1, ..., $t - 1$ are also priced out because their reservation prices are even lower. So we can describe the market served by the *marginal* segment served; given our assumptions, this is the lowest-indexed segment served. If t is the marginal segment served, then the optimal price will be $u_t(s)$, and the manufacturer should design his product to maximize

$$\left(\sum_{i=t}^{T} N_i \right)(u_t(s) - c(s)) \qquad (5.10)$$

The solution to this is given by the first-order condition

$$\left(\sum_{i=t}^{T} N_i \right)(u'_t(s) - c'(s)) = 0 \qquad (5.11)$$

Once these solutions, s_i^*, have been determined for each $t = 1, ..., T$, all that remains is to compare the T profits

$$\left(\sum_{i=1}^{T} N_i \right)(u_1(s_1^*) - c(s_1^*)), ..., \left(\sum_{i=T}^{T} N_i \right)(u_T(s_T^*) - c(s_T^*))$$

and choose the maximum. If t^* is the optimal marginal segment, that is, $(\sum_{i=t^*}^{T} N_i)(u_{t^*}(s_{t^*}^*) - c(s_{t^*}^*))$ is the largest of the T quantities, then the profit-maximizing product is $s_{t^*}^*$ and the profit-maximizing price is $u_{t^*}(s_{t^*}^*)$.

Note that, unlike the homogeneous market case, the profit-maximizing product isn't efficient for every consumer served. If $t^* < T$, then segments $t^* + 1, ..., T$ do not get their efficient product. This is just a reflection of the fact that if consumers' preferences differ, it is impossible to satisfy everyone's preferences with just one product.

Note also that in a heterogeneous market, it may be optimal not to serve every consumer. If $t^* > 1$, then segments 1, ..., $t^* - 1$ are not being served. The reason is that the segments with the smaller reservation prices are a mixed blessing for the manufacturer. On the one hand, they represent revenue opportunities. But on the other hand, they force the manufacturer to

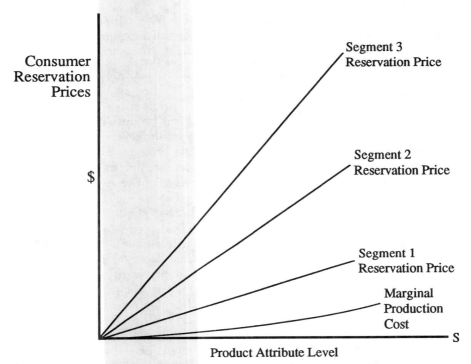

EXHIBIT 5.3 Consumer reservation prices and marginal costs for a heterogeneous market.

offer the same low price that he charges them to other segments who are willing to pay more. If the low-reservation-price segments are small relative to those with higher reservation prices and the discrepancy in reservation prices between the low and the high segments is large, then the seller may well decide that he is better off not serving the low segments. The following example illustrates these points.

EXAMPLE _____

Suppose that $T = 3$, $u_t(s) = ts$ for $t = 1, \ldots, 3$, $N_1 = 30$, $N_2 = 50$, and $N_3 = 20$, and $c(s) = \alpha s^2$. What is the optimal product design?

Consumer reservation prices and the manufacturer's costs are shown in Exhibit 5.3. If the seller chooses to serve only segment t, where $t = 1, 2,$ or 3, then ts is the optimal price and the optimal product solves the first-order condition

$$(N_t + \cdots + N_3)(t - 2\alpha s) = 0 \qquad (5.12)$$

Solving (5.12) for s yields $s_t^* = t/2\alpha$ for $t = 1, 2,$ and 3 with associated profits (from equation 5.10) of $(30 + 50 + 20)/4\alpha$, $(50 + 20)(1/\alpha)$, and $20(9/4\alpha)$. Thus segment 2 should be the marginal segment and the product should be designed as $s_2^* = 2/2\alpha = 1/\alpha$, priced at $2/\alpha$ with associated profits (from equation 5.10) of $70/\alpha$.

Selecting a Product Line. If product preferences are heterogeneous, the marketing concept would seem to call for a product line rather than a single product. By offering a product line, the manufacturer can tailor his products to consumers' preferences; with a single product, he cannot. We show now that this also makes sense from a profit standpoint as long as new product development costs and product line management costs are not too high (Mussa and Rosen, 1978, and Moorthy 1984).

Suppose in the preceding example that the seller could offer three different products to the three segments. What products should he offer? At first glance it seems that he should offer each segment its efficient product and charge each segment its corresponding reservation price, that is, offer $s_1 = 1/2\alpha$, $s_2 = 2/2\alpha$, and $s_3 = 3/2\alpha$ at prices $p_1 = 1/2\alpha$, $p_2 = 4/2\alpha$, and $p_3 = 9/2\alpha$, respectively. But this strategy is not implementable in an open market, because certain segments will prefer products other than the ones meant for them. Segments 2 and 3 would both prefer $s_1 = 1/2\alpha$ at $p_1 = 1/2\alpha$ to the offerings meant for them because they get a positive consumer surplus from s_1, whereas their own efficient products give them zero surplus. In other words, the product meant for segment 1 will cannibalize the products meant for the other two segments, and the seller will see less profit than what he thought he was going to get.

So what should the seller do? Suppose s_1, s_2, and s_3 are the products meant for segments 1, 2, and 3, respectively, and p_1, p_2, and p_3 are the corresponding prices. We first determine the profit-maximizing prices assuming that the product designs have been fixed. Fix the price for s_1 at segment 1's reservation price for it, that is,

$$p_1 = s_1 \tag{5.13}$$

Now note that segments 2's surplus would be $2s_1 - p_1$, if it were to buy s_1 at p_1. Therefore, the maximum that can be charged for s_2 is $2s_2 - (2s_1 - p_1)$ since if $p_2 > 2s_2 - (2s_1 - p_1)$, then $2s_2 - p_2 < 2s_1 - p_1$, and segment 2 would rather buy s_1 at p_1. So

$$p_2 = 2s_2 - (2s_1 - p_1) = 2s_2 - s_1 \tag{5.14}$$

Similarly,

$$p_3 = 3s_3 - (3s_2 - p_2) = 3s_3 - s_2 - s_1 \tag{5.15}$$

Now we focus on the optimal product designs given these prices. The manufacturer's total profits are

$$30(s_1 - \alpha s_1^2) + 50(2s_2 - s_1 - \alpha s_2^2) + 20(3s_3 - s_2 - s_1 - \alpha s_3^2)$$

Therefore, the first-order conditions determining s_1^*, s_2^*, s_3^* are

$$30(1 - 2\alpha s_1) - 50 - 20 = 0 \tag{5.16}$$

$$50(2 - 2\alpha s_2) - 20 = 0 \tag{5.17}$$

$$20(3 - 2\,\alpha s_3) = 0 \tag{5.18}$$

The first of these equations yields a solution for s_1 that is less than zero. Hence the profit-maximizing value for s_1 is really zero, that is, the seller should not serve segment 1. The other two conditions give us feasible solutions. Equation (5.17) implies that $s_2^* = 4/5\alpha$ and equation (5.18) implies $s_3^* = 3/2\alpha$. So the optimal product line strategy for the seller is to offer products $s_2 = 4/5\alpha$ and $s_3 = 3/2\alpha$ at prices $8/5\alpha$ and $37/10\alpha$, respectively.

Note that the optimal product line strategy is more profitable than the optimal single-product strategy. Also, note that the manufacturer's optimal product line strategy leaves some consumers unsatisfied just as the optimal single-product strategy did: serving segment 1 is too costly for the manufacturer because any product that he designs for it cannibalizes the demand for the other products. This shows that even when there are no production reasons for limiting product variety, a manufacturer may nevertheless limit variety in order to manage cannibalization.

Finally, observe that while the manufacturer's optimal strategy induces segment 3 to buy its efficient product, segment 2 gets *less* than its efficient product. Once again, the reason is cannibalization. If segment 2 were also to be offered its efficient product, then the two products in the product line would be too close to each other and the price reduction called for in segment 3's product would be excessive. By spreading the two products apart, the seller is able to limit cannibalization.

Cannibalization is not always a problem in choosing product lines. If consumers are sufficiently heterogeneous, then it may be possible to sell each segment its efficient product at its reservation price. To see this, consider Exhibit 5.4, where the two segments cannot be ordered on the basis of their reservation prices because the reservation price lines cross. The segments' efficient products are such that even if they are priced at their respective reservation prices, there is no cannibalization.

Product Strategy with Competition

The monopolist's product strategy, as we just saw, essentially amounts to trading off consumer preferences and costs. This result also applies to a manufacturer

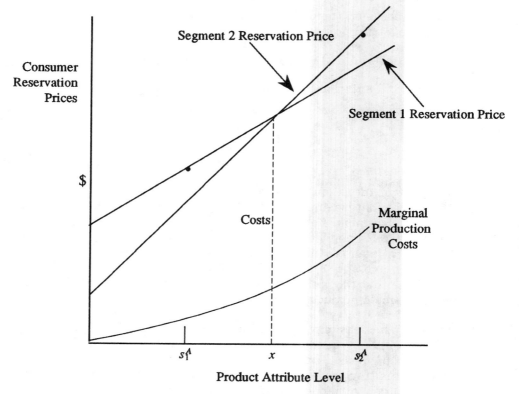

s_i^A = Segment i's efficient product, $i = 1$ or 2.

EXHIBIT 5.4 Optimal product designs in a two-segment market with preference functions that cross. Here there is no cannibalization because s_1^A and s_2^A are on opposite sides of the crossover point, x.

facing passive competition from other firms, that is, firms that keep their products and prices fixed, even though their strategy may not be optimal with respect to the other firms' strategies. Given passive competition, a manufacturer can choose his product and pricing strategy just as a pure monopolist would. The only difference is that the manufacturer must take account of the opportunities available to consumers from the other firms.

More interesting aspects of competition arise when competitors are *strategic,* not passive. Strategic competitors recognize the effect of their strategies on their competitors, and expect them to react. Oligopolistic industries where there are few competitors, each with a significant share of the market, exhibit this kind of competition. For example, in the worldwide photographic film market, Kodak, Fuji, and Agfa compete strategically.

We begin by looking at a simple competitive situation, that of two identical firms competing on a single nonmonotone attribute. Assume that all levels of this attribute cost the same to produce, say, c. This is not unrealistic for nonmonotone attributes because they tend to reflect individual "tastes." Hotelling's (1929) model of two stores competing for households located uniformly along a road is the pioneering model of this situation. In Hotelling's model, the stores first decide where to locate, and once located, they decide their prices. In our terminology, store location is the product attribute, and it is nonmonotone because every household would like the store to be located right where its house is.

The choice of product first, and then prices parallels the way we analyzed the monopoly case, but now it is a substantive assumption. It means that when choosing prices, the two firms have already committed to their product configurations. This is reasonable because products are harder to change than prices. In terms of our analysis, it means that each firm, when choosing its product design, must anticipate the effect its product will have on *both* firms' prices. Another change from the monopoly analysis is that now our solution concept will be a Nash equilibrium, in particular a subgame-perfect Nash equilibrium (see Appendix E). In other words,

> **1.** *For each possible choice of product by the two firms, we will be looking for prices with the property that neither firm would want to change its price unilaterally.*
>
> **2.** *The product choices will be such that neither firm would want to deviate from its product choice unilaterally, while anticipating the price equilibrium in the first step.*

Assume that consumers' ideal points on the single attribute are distributed uniformly in the interval $[a, b]$. Consumers whose ideal point is t evaluate a product s by using the utility function $u(t, s) = R - (t - s)^2$. Their consumer surplus if the product is priced at p is, therefore, $R - (t - s)^2 - p$. A consumer's ideal product (assuming price is not an issue) is t.

Suppose that the two manufacturers' products are s_1 and s_2, with $s_1 < s_2$ and that their prices are p_1 and p_2. Firm 1 will sell to those segments for whom the consumer surplus is higher with firm 1's offering than with firm 2's offering. Now a segment t will prefer product 1 to product 2 if

$$[R - (t - s_1)^2 - p_1] \geq [R - (t - s_2)^2 - p_2] \tag{5.19}$$

Equation (5.19) implies, after some rearranging of terms, that segment t will prefer s_1 to s_2 if

$$t < \frac{(p_2 - p_1)}{2(s_2 - s_1)} + \left(\frac{s_1 + s_2}{2}\right) \tag{5.20}$$

and vice versa. Denote this critical value of t (i.e., the value of t that makes equation (5.20) an equality) by t^i; t^i is the ideal point of the segment that is indifferent between the two products. Note that if $p_1 = p_2$, then $t^i = (s_1 + s_2)/2$; that is, when both products are priced the same, then anyone whose ideal product is to the left of the midpoint between the two products will go with product 1. Also, $t^i < a$ implies that no consumer prefers product 1 to product 2 and $t^i > b$ implies that no consumer prefers product 2 to product 1. Assuming t^i is in the interval $[a, b]$, product 1's market share is $(t^i - a)/(b - a)$, product 2's market share is $(b - t^i)/(b - a)$, and the two firms' profits are given by

$$\text{Firm 1 profits: } \Pi_1 = \left(\frac{t^i - a}{b - a}\right)(p_1 - c) \tag{5.21}$$

$$\text{Firm 2 profits: } \Pi_2 = \left(\frac{b - t^i}{b - a}\right)(p_2 - c) \tag{5.22}$$

Differentiating equations (5.21) and (5.22) with respect to p_1 and p_2, respectively, and simplifying, we get the following first-order conditions:

$$(p_2 - c) - 2(p_1 - c) + (s_2^2 - s_1^2) - 2a(s_2 - s_1) = 0 \tag{5.23}$$

$$-2(p_2 - c) + (p_1 - c) - (s_2^2 - s_1^2) + 2b(s_2 - s_1) = 0 \tag{5.24}$$

From (5.23), we see that the larger p_2 is, the higher the price p_1 that firm 1 will choose; similarly, (5.24) implies that firm 2 responds to a price increase by firm 1 by increasing its own price. Solving (5.23) and (5.24) for p_1 and p_2, we get

$$p_1^* - c = \frac{2(s_2 - s_1)}{3}\left(b - 2a + \frac{s_2 + s_1}{2}\right) \tag{5.25}$$

$$p_2^* - c = \frac{2(s_2 - s_1)}{3}\left(2b - a + \frac{s_2 + s_1}{2}\right) \tag{5.26}$$

The market shares for the two firms at these equilibrium prices are

$$m_1^* = \frac{1}{3(b - a)}\left(b - 2a + \frac{s_2 + s_1}{2}\right) \tag{5.27}$$

$$m_2^* = \frac{1}{3(b - a)}\left(2b - a + \frac{s_2 + s_1}{2}\right) \tag{5.28}$$

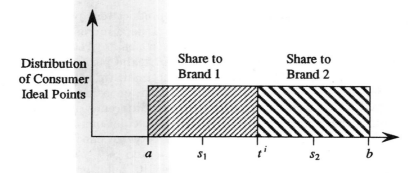

a = lowest ideal point in the market
b = highest ideal point in the market
s_1 = position of Brand 1
s_2 = position of Brand 2
t^i = ideal point of a consumer who is indifferent
     between the two brands

EXHIBIT 5.5   The Hotelling competitive positioning model.

Now we come to the product choices. We substitute (5.25)–(5.28) in the two firms' profit functions (5.21) and (5.22) and get

$$\Pi_1 = \frac{2(s_2 - s_1)}{9(b - a)} \left(b - 2a + \frac{s_2 + s_1}{2} \right)^2 \tag{5.29}$$

$$\Pi_2 = \frac{2(s_2 - s_1)}{9(b - a)} \left(2b - a + \frac{s_2 + s_1}{2} \right)^2 \tag{5.30}$$

The first-order conditions governing the choice of s_1 and s_2 yield the following "best response functions":

$$s_1 = \frac{s_2 - 2(b - 2a)}{3} \tag{5.31}$$

$$s_2 = \frac{s_1 - 2(2b - a)}{3} \tag{5.32}$$

Equations (5.31) and (5.32) tell us that the larger s_2 is, the larger s_1 should be, and vice versa. The larger s_2 is, the more room there is to the left of s_2, so firm 1 moves its product design, s_1 to the right to enlarge the market it controls. Similarly, the smaller s_1 is, the more room there is to the right of s_1, so firm 2 moves its product design s_2 to the left to enlarge the market it controls (Exhibit 5.5).

But what if one firm moves its product to a point where it "squeezes" the other firm? For example, if firm 1 kept increasing s_1 and firm 2 kept responding by raising s_2, soon there won't be any room left for firm 2. In this situation, firm 2 will "jump" over firm 1 and position itself to the left of s_1. To see when this "jumping" will be optimal, we calculate the value of s_1 at which firm 2 will be indifferent between choosing an optimal response on either side of firm 1. Intuitively, this indifference point is $(b + a)/2$, for example, the midpoint of the market. Calculations confirm this. If s_1 is at $(b + a)/2$, then firm 2 is indifferent between choosing $[s_1 + 2(2b - 1)]/3$, which is the optimal response above s_2, and $[s_1 - 2(2b - 1)]/3$, which is the optimal response below s_1. Similar results hold for firm 2. Thus, each firm has the reaction function depicted in Exhibit 5.6. Solving (5.31) and (5.32), we get the product position equilibrium:

$$s_1^* = \frac{5a - b}{4} \tag{5.33}$$

$$s_2^* = \frac{5b - a}{4} \tag{5.34}$$

Because $s_1^* < a$ and $s_2^* > b$, these products are on opposite sides of $(b + a)/2$, so there will be no jumping if the two firms offer these products. Hence (s_1^*, s_2^*) is a product equilibrium. Substituting these product positions into (5.25) and (5.26), we get the equilibrium margins

$$p_1^* - c = \frac{3(b - a)^2}{2} = p_2^* - c \tag{5.35}$$

and each firm's equilibrium profit is

$$\Pi_1^* = \frac{3(b - a)^2}{4} = \Pi_2^* \tag{5.36}$$

Note that $s_1^* < a$ and $s_2^* > b$; that is, neither of the products offered in equilibrium is the ideal product for *any* consumer. This contrasts with our intuitive notion of product strategy as "filling holes in the market." One reason for this is that if the firms were to offer products that were ideal for some consumer, then the price competition between them would actually reduce their profits. A second reason is developed below.

We have implicitly assumed in our calculations that the alternative to buying either of the two firms' products is not to buy in the product class at all. This alternative gives zero surplus to the consumers, so our equilibrium is valid if it doesn't give negative surplus to consumers. To see if it does,

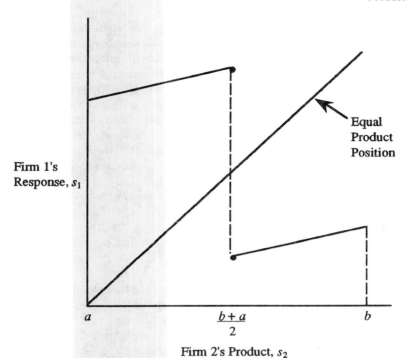

Firm 1's
Response, s_1

Equal
Product
Position

a

$\dfrac{b+a}{2}$

b

Firm 2's Product, s_2

EXHIBIT 5.6   Firm 1's product reaction to firm 2's product position. Note the jump
point at $(b + a)/2$.

consider the segment that gets the *least* consumer surplus in equilibrium: the
segment with $t = (b + a)/2$, in the middle of the market. (The equilibrium
products are farthest from this segment's ideal product). This segment's consumer   surplus   from   either   firm's   equilibrium   offering   is
$R - c - [33(b - a)^2/16]$, which is nonnegative if $R \geq c + [33(b - a)^2/16]$.
So the results are valid provided R is in this range. If $R < c + [33(b - a)^2/16]$,
then the firm will lose segments in the middle of the market. This effect will
temporize their desire to move "far apart."

Finally, consider how competitive strategy differs from a monopolist's
strategy. If a monopolist were to introduce one product, he would place it at
$(b + a)/2$ and price it at $R - (b - a)^2/4$ if he wanted to serve everyone in
the market. With two products, the products will be positioned at $(3a + b)/4$
and $(3b + a)/4$ and priced at $R - (b - a)^2/16$; each product would serve half
the market. Compared to the duopoly, the monopolist's two products are closer
to each other, and each product fills the "hole" in the market left by the other.

Moorthy (1988) has analyzed product and price competition for the case
of a monotone attribute with manufacturing costs increasing in the level of
the attribute. Because marginal costs are increasing in the level of the at-

the attribute. Because marginal costs are increasing in the level of the attribute, each segment has a distinct efficient product. Moorthy also finds that price competition induces the two firms to move their products farther apart than a monopolist would. Hauser (1988) studies product and price competition in a two-monotone-attributes model with an efficient frontier. Each consumer segment has a distinct ideal location on this frontier under equal pricing of all products. The equilibrium in this case involves maximum separation among the competitors' products. Shaked and Sutton (1982) analyze the monotone-attribute case assuming equal costs for all attribute levels. In this case, one firm chooses the maximum feasible attribute level and the other firm chooses a level below that.

The main insight arising from these analyses is that competitive product strategy is a reconciliation of two forces. One force, price competition, moves the competitors apart. The other force, the desire to get close to the location that best trades off consumer preferences and costs, brings them closer to each other.

Sequential Entry and Defensive Product Strategy. In the foregoing analysis we assumed that firms choose their products simultaneously. In many situations, firms choose their products sequentially. Often one firm enters an industry first with a product, then another firm enters with another product, and so on. Among the questions this raises are: Does the first-mover have an advantage by virtue of seizing the most attractive product location? How does the industry's equilibrium product configuration compare with that of an industry without a first-mover? How will a first-mover's strategy differ between when he anticipates a second entrant and makes defensive preparations, and when he doesn't?

We can address these questions in the framework of our model. Suppose the two firms choose their prices simultaneously after both have chosen their products.

Recalling our earlier results, if the first entrant introduces a product to the left of $(b + a)/2$, then the second entrant will introduce a product to the right of $(b + a)/2$, and vice versa. Suppose the first entrant introduces a product $s_1 \leq (b + a)/2$. Then the second entrant's optimal response is $[s_1 + 2(2b - a)]/3$. Anticipating this response, the first entrant's profit function is

$$\Pi_1 = \frac{2[s_1 + 2(2b - a) - 3s_1]}{27(b - a)} \left(b - 2a + \frac{2s_1 + 2b - a}{3} \right)^2 \qquad (5.37)$$

Maximizing Π_1 with respect to s_1, we get

$$s_1^* = \frac{b + a}{2} \qquad (5.38)$$

If the first firm positions its product at $(b + a)/2$, then the second firm is actually indifferent between being below firm 1 and being above firm 1, as the profits at those positions are identical. That is, while the first entrant chooses $(b + a)/2$, the second entrant chooses

$$s_2^* = \frac{3b - a}{2} \quad \text{or} \quad \frac{3a - b}{2} \tag{5.39}$$

The equilibrium margins, market shares, and profits are

$$p_1^* - c = \frac{4(b - a)^2}{3} \tag{5.40}$$

$$p_2^* - c = \frac{2(b - a)^2}{3} \tag{5.41}$$

$$m_1^* = \frac{2}{3} \tag{5.42}$$

$$m_2^* = \frac{1}{3} \tag{5.43}$$

$$\Pi_1^* = \frac{8(b - a)^2}{9} \tag{5.44}$$

$$\Pi_2^* = \frac{2(b - a)^2}{9} \tag{5.45}$$

The first entrant's profits are greater than either firm's profits in the simultaneous-moves equilibrium. This shows that there is a first-mover advantage (of $2:1$ in share and $4:1$ in profit in our model) that comes from being able to preempt a product location.

By virtue of moving first, the first-entrant chooses the most desirable product location in the market and forces the second entrant to choose between two relatively less desirable product positions. The first-entrant ends up controlling more than half the market due to the better placement of its product and that location is the same as that of a monopolist choosing a single product. Thus, in this model, the first-mover's product is the same whether or not he foresees the second firm's entry, so no special defensive strategies are called for. This is not true in general, however. In Moorthy's (1988) model, a monopolist who doesn't foresee new competition will choose a different product than one who does.

DECISION MODELS FOR PRODUCT DESIGN

The theoretical results developed in the previous section assumed that brands could be described as vectors of attributes and that consumers had preference or utility functions defined over those attributes. We now try to operationalize some of these concepts. Perceptual mapping procedures attempt to identify the key product dimensions, while preference and choice models relate those product positions to consumer actions.

Perceptual Mapping.   A group of procedures called perceptual mapping aid in understanding how consumers think about products in existing markets. In perceptual maps, products are represented (mapped) by locations in a space of several dimensions (such as "value for the money," "gentleness," and "effectiveness" for pain relievers) that distinguish among the products.

Perceptual theory suggests that although consumers can be questioned about literally hundreds of different product attributes, they generally use a small number (two to four) when they think about a particular product or product class. Thus an objective of perceptual-mapping procedures is to identify the relevant dimensions and to locate the positions of existing and potential new products along these dimensions.

Although a number of approaches have been suggested for the perceptual-mapping task, most fall into one of two categories: attribute-based procedures (factor analysis) and similarity-based procedures (multidimensional scaling). Chapter 2 reviews and compares these techniques; later on in this chapter we show how the perceptual map can be used as part of the new-product-design-and-positioning process in several model-based methodologies.

Preference-Choice Models.   Urban and Hauser (1980) suggest that while early work in most product categories may concentrate on the mapping of existing product spaces to identify potential opportunities, later work should concentrate on estimating how products with given physical features are likely to perform in the marketplace. This estimation is done with preference models. Most product-design approaches use preference data because of the loss of information when one is considering only choice (Shocker and Srinivasan, 1979): when preference is used as a criterion variable, the entire preference ranking is available as data input.

In this section we discuss three widely used preference models: expectancy value, preference regression, and conjoint analysis. In each case the product design can be considered a vector of attributes $\{y_k^*$, where $k = 1, \ldots, K$, the number of attributes. We also consider Y_{ijk} as individual i's perception of product j along dimension k.

Expectancy-Value Models. Wilkie and Pessemier (1973) review the development and use of expectancy-value models in marketing. These models are based on a compositional or buildup principal, where an object's total utility is the weighted sum of its perceived attribute level and the associated value ratings as judged explicitly by the respondent:

$$p_{ij} = \sum_{k=1}^{K} w_{ik} Y_{ijk}, \quad i = 1, \ldots, I, \quad j = 1, \ldots, J \tag{5.46}$$

where

p_{ij} = (inferred) value or utility of product j for individual i

w_{ik} = importance placed by individual i on attribute k

Generally, there will be a number of attributes and associated product and importance ratings. Other measurements of attribute importance can be used as input; in particular, collecting paired comparison data on attributes eliminates having all attributes rated very or extremely important.

For predicting use of a new product or concept, the expectancy-value approach is low in cost and easy both to administer and to evaluate. Furthermore, it gives a quick early guide to the likely success of the product.

However, it has several disadvantages. First, it is not as accurate as other methods in predicting preference. Second, it deals with the attributes themselves rather than the underlying perceptual dimensions. Third, it is subject to halo effects (Beckwith and Lehmann, 1975), in which an individual rates his most preferred product high on all scales, biasing the results. In addition, the model is a linear additive form and therefore is appropriate only for use as a guide in early design work, especially in those categories, such as frequently purchased products, where the consumer choice process is relatively simple. Another possible, significant problem is that of scale redundancy. If two scales are, in fact, measuring the same underlying attribute, this model double-counts the weight. And because the weights are specified by the respondent, their reliability and validity are questionable.

Preference Regression. On the surface, preference regression looks a lot like an expectancy-value model. However, there are several important differences: (1) overall preferences for alternative products are measured directly and are used as dependent variables, (2) importance weights are inferred from consumer-preference ratings, (3) importance weights are assumed homogeneous across a response group, and (4) perceptual or evaluation dimensions (resulting from, say, a factor analysis) are used rather than the attribute items in the analysis.

The linear model for preference regression is

$$p_{ij} = \sum_{k=1}^{K^*} w_k x_{ijk} + \text{error} \tag{5.47}$$

where

w_k = (inferred) importance weight

x_{ijk} = individual i's rating of product j along evaluation dimension k, for $k = 1, \ldots, K^*$ (note that $K^* \leq K$, the number of original attributes)

p_{ij} = (rank-order) preference judgments for product j by individual i

Several algorithms are available for determining the model weights. In general, the $\{p_{ij}\}$ are rank orders, and a number of techniques have been developed to find the $\{w_k\}$ that best reproduce the original preference ranks. These include monanova (Green and Wind, 1973) and monotone regression (Johnson, 1975).

However, empirical results by Green (1975), Hauser and Urban (1977), and others have demonstrated that in most cases it is sufficient to use simple regression analysis with the preference rank as the dependent variable.

In the preference-regression process, original attribute ratings are usually factor analyzed to develop evaluation dimensions. The individuals' evaluations of each product (the factor scores) are regressed against the rank order of preferences. The regression is usually run across a group of individuals believed to be homogeneous in the importance they place on evaluation dimensions. The estimated $\{w_k\}$ are associated with the more important dimensions for affecting consumer choice.

Note that

$$\frac{\partial p_{ij}}{\partial x_{ijk}} = w_k \tag{5.48}$$

that is, $\{w_k\}$ represents the sensitivity of preference to a change in attribute k for individual i. If the $\{x_{ijk}\}$ are standardized, then the larger values of $\{w_k\}$ are associated with the more important dimensions for affecting consumer choice.

Advantages of the preference-regression approach are the (1) it is easy to use because it uses regression, (2) it is more accurate than the expectancy-value approach, and (3) the derived importance weights $\{w_k\}$ can be used to guide both product-design modifications and advertising copy development.

Disadvantages of preference regression are that (1) a linear model form is usually used, so nonlinear threshold saturation effects are not handled well;

(2) it should not be used with the basic attributes because of intercorrelations; and (3) importance weights are average weights and do not reflect differences at the individual level.

Conjoint Analysis. Conjoint analysis is a set of methods designed to measure consumer preferences for a multiattribute product. It is the most widely applied and studied method for assessing buyers' multiattribute utility functions (Green and Srinivasan, 1990, and Green and Kreiger, 1989). The respondent is traditionally asked to react to a total product profile, and then the resulting total preference score is decomposed into a set of utilities for each of the attributes. The procedure treats combinations of attributes set at discrete levels (i.e., it is a decompositional method).

EXAMPLE _____

This study (Green and Tull, 1975, p. 641 ff.) used conjoint analysis to evaluate consumers' utilities for various types of retail discount cards that differ in (1) size of discount, (2) number of cooperating stores in the respondent's trading area, and (3) annual cost of the card. Each card was described with a three-component profile, and each component had three levels:

1. Size of discount: 5%, 10%, and 15% off regular retail prices

2. Number of cooperating stores in the subject's shopping area: 10, 20, and 30 stores

3. Annual cost of the card: $10, $15, and $25 annual cost

This design, known as a complete 3^3 factorial design, produces 27 separate combinations, which were presented to subjects in random order. Each subject sorted the cards into four groups, ordered the cards within a group, and then was asked to make certain the poorest of a better group was better than the best of a poorer group. This procedure resulted in a strict rank order of the 27 cards from "poorest" to "best buy for the money."

Monanova was applied to each respondent's data to obtain individual utility functions for each level of each attribute that best reproduced the original rank order. Exhibit 5.7 shows one individual's part worths (individual attribute-level utilities). Note that the major contributions to total utility are size of discount and annual cost, with number of cooperating stores essentially flat over the relevant range. These part-worths are interval scaled with a common unit, allowing for comparison of utility ranges across the factors making up the product profiles.

As seen in the example, individual utility functions are not considered

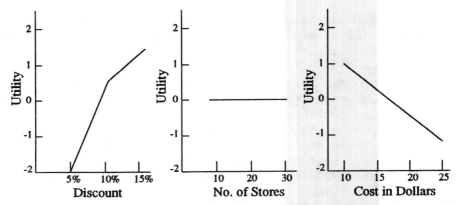

EXHIBIT 5.7 Part-worth functions: conjoint-analysis study. (*Source:* Greene and Tull, 1975, p. 644.)

linear. Generally, in this form of conjoint analysis, indicator variables are used to represent each level of each feature:

$$d_{mkp} = \begin{cases} 1, & \text{if product } m \text{ has feature } k \text{ at level } p \\ 0, & \text{otherwise} \end{cases}$$

Then the utility function of feature k for product m is

$$u_{ik} = \sum_{p=1}^{P} \lambda_{ikp} d_{mkp} \tag{5.49}$$

where i refers to the individual respondents and P is the number of possible levels of the feature. Note that because $d_{mkp} = 1$ for only one level, equation (5.49) sets u_{ik} equal to product m's utility at that level of feature k.

With all K attributes, then the conjoint-analysis estimating equation is

$$R_{im} = \sum_{k=1}^{K} \sum_{\ell=1}^{L} \lambda_{ik\ell} d_{mk\ell} + \text{error} \tag{5.50}$$

where R_{im} is the rank-order preference given by individual i for product m ($m - 1, \ldots, 27$ in the example). Note that although the utilities in equation (5.50) are additive, interactions of any order can be included by defining a set of $\{d_{mkpk'p'}\}$, where this indicator would be one only when feature k was at level p and k' was at level p'. In practice, degrees of freedom for estimation usually prevent inclusion of many interaction items, and the linear additive form is used most frequently.

In equation (5.50) the $\lambda_{ik\ell}$'s, called part-worths, can be estimated with monanova, regression, or linear programming.

An extension of conjoint analysis uses constant-sum paired comparisons instead of rank orders for preference measures. In this approach a consumer is given, say, 100 chips to allocate between two alternatives in a way that reflects his overall relative preference. Hauser and Shugan (1980) develop the associated theoretical basis for using the resulting (ratio-scaled) data. Under appropriate conditions the preference model is

$$p_{ij} = \mu_{i1}(x_{ij1})\mu_{i2}(x_{ij2}) \ldots \mu_{ik}(x_{ijk}) \tag{5.51}$$

If, say, 100 chips are allocated between two products m and n, such that a_m equals the number of chips allocated to product m, then if we use a similar dummy-variable convention to that just developed, we get

$$\log \frac{a_m}{100 - a_m} = \sum_k \sum_\ell (d_{mk\ell} - d_{nk\ell}) \log \lambda_{k\ell} \tag{5.52}$$

Again, the consumer is given a complete (or fractional factorial) set of design pairs, and regression can be used to estimate the log $\lambda_{k\ell}$'s from equation (5.52).

One difficulty with conjoint analysis is that it becomes unwieldy if the number of attributes and/or levels is high, because the consumer must then rank a large number of combinations. For example, four attributes at four levels would lead to $4^4 = 256$ combinations! Green and Srinivasan (1990) describe three approaches to the problem of a large number of attributes:

The self-explicated approach. Here respondents are first asked to evaluate the levels of each attribute on a 0–10 desirability scale and then allocate 100 points, say, across the attributes in a way that reflects their relative desirability, very similar to the expectancy-value method described earlier (Green, Goldberg, and Montemayor, 1981; Srinivasan, 1988; Leigh, MacKay and Summers, 1984).

Hybrid models. The hybrid approach uses self-explicated data to get a preliminary set of individual part-worths for individuals. These are then used to construct homogeneous market segments; each member of the segment gets a subset of a full profile, and individual as well as segment-level parameters are combined in an individual's utility function (Green, Goldberg, and Montemayor, 1981; Green, 1984; Moore and Semenik, 1988).

Adaptive conjoint analysis. Adaptive conjoint analysis collects preference data in a computer-interactive model, where the individual gives a rough ordering of attribute importance and then is asked to refine the trade-offs between more important attributes in a real-time, interactive setting dealing with both individual products and product lines (Johnson, 1987, 1991; Agarwal, 1988; Agarwal and Green, 1991; Finkbeiner and Plantz, 1986; Kohli and Sukumar, 1990; Green, Krieger, and Agarwal, 1991).

Green and Srinivasan (1990) review the advantages and disadvantages

Properties	Expectancy Values	Preference Regression	Conjoint Analysis
Underlying theory	Psychology	Statistics	Mathematical psychology
Functional form	Linear	Linear and non-linear	Additive, with interactions
Level of aggregation stimuli presented to respondent	Individual attribute scales	Group actual alternatives or concepts	Individual profiles of attributes
Measures taken	Attribute importances	Attribute ratings and preference	Rank-order preference
Estimation Method	Direct Consumer input	Regression	Monotonic analysis of variances or linear programming
Use in new product design	Early Indications	Core-benefit proposition	Selection of product features

EXHIBIT 5.8 Summary of the preference-analysis methods as they are used in a new product design. *Source:* Urban and Hauser, 1980, p. 256.

of the various approaches: they recommend the full profile approach if the number of attributes is six or fewer and one of the methods just noted (since studies of the relative performance of the methods have provided mixed results) if the number of attributes is higher. (See Wind et al., 1989, for an application of hybrid conjoint to the design of the Courtyard by Marriott Hotel chain—a task that involved over 160 levels of 50 attributes!)

Evaluation of Approaches. Exhibit 5.8 summarizes the properties of the three techniques used or product-design/preference analysis. Urban and Hauser (1980) summarize their evaluation of these techniques as follows:

> Each of these models plays an effective role in new product design. If cost is a constraint, expectancy value models offer an inexpensive way to get a rough idea of the linear effects of product attributes in forming preferences. In defining the positioning of a new product for the core benefit proposition [a short statement describing the key physical and psychological benefits the product provides], preference regression excels in analyzing the importance of psychological dimensions used to define perceptual maps. Conjoint analysis is best when physical features of products are the focus of the design problem. *(p. 255).*

Model-Based Procedures for Product Design.

In this section we review three widely referenced methods for product and design and positioning: (1) Urban's (1975b) PERCEPTOR model, (2) Shocker and Srinivasan's (1974) LINMAP-based approach, and (3) Hauser and Shugan's (1983) DEFENDER model. Because PERCEPTOR focuses on perceptual dimensions and the trial-repeat process, it is most appropriate for frequently purchased packaged goods, while LINMAP, based on conjoint analysis, is more appropriate for consumer durables or other products where attributes are actionable. DEFENDER attempts to operationalize some of the issues of product repositioning and response we developed earlier.

Urban's (1975b) PERCEPTOR Model.   The PERCEPTOR model and measurement methodology was developed for the design and positioning of new, frequently purchased consumer products. The main idea is to model the distance from an ideal brand to brand trial and repeat purchase estimates for a new product in an existing market. As such, the structure provides a basis for evaluating, refining, and selecting among alternative product concepts.

  Long-run-share model.   Urban postulates a trial-repeat framework similar to that of Parfitt and Collins (1968) (see Chapter 10):

$$m = ts \tag{5.53}$$

where

  m = long-run market share
  t = fraction of target market that ever tries the new brand
  s = long-run share of purchases among those who have ever tried the
        brand

  Trial model.   Ultimate trial is modeled as

$$t = qwv \tag{5.54}$$

where

  q = ultimate probability of trial given awareness and availability
  w = long-run awareness of the brand
  v = long-run availability (volume-weighted percentage of stores carrying the brand)

Note that at the design stage w and v are managerial inputs: brand management is expected to have some feel for their probable levels. In general, w will be higher with heavier advertising, and v will be higher with more dealer promotions.

Share among those who tried. Urban models long-run share as the equilibrium of a two-state Markov process:

		Purchase at $t + 1$	
		New Brand	Other Brands
Purchase at t	New Brand	p_{11}	$1 - p_{11}$
	Other Brands	p_{21}	$1 - p_{21}$

The steady-state share in the process is

$$s = \frac{p_{21}}{1 + p_{21} - p_{11}}$$
(5.55)

Probability of purchase (trial). The basic probability-of-purchase model is

$$q = \alpha_0 + \alpha_1 d_B^2$$
(5.56)

where

q = as defined in equation (5.54)

d_B^2 = squared distance of the new brand on the perceptual map to the average ideal brand for those who are aware of but who have not yet tried the brand

α_0, α_1 = parameters to be estimated

Specifically, assume that a reduced perceptual space has K dimensions and that the new brand is perceived to occupy position $\{X_k\}$ and an ideal brand is perceived to occupy position $\{I_k\}$ in that space. Essentially, d_B^2 is modeled as

$$d_B^2 = \sum_k h_k (X_k - I_k)^2$$
(5.57)

where h_k is the relative importance of dimension k.

Probability of repeat. Following use of a product, consumers' perceptions of it may change. Denote $\{X_k^*\}$ as the perceptions among those who have tried the brand. Then

$$p_{11} = \tilde{\alpha}_0 + \tilde{\alpha}_1 d_B^2 \qquad (5.58)$$

where

$$\tilde{d}_B^2 = \sum_k h_k (X_k^* - I_k)^2 \qquad (5.59)$$

that is, distance from the ideal after use. Urban stated that p_{21}, the probability of repeat purchase if the new product is not chosen, is determined empirically for each case.

Source of new brand share. Urban postulates that new brand share is obtained from the other brands, proportional to their appearance in consumer evoked sets and inversely proportional to their (squared) distance from the new brand,

$$V_b = \frac{m(e_b / D_{bB}{}^2)}{\displaystyle\sum_{j=1}^{B-1} \frac{e_j}{D_{jB}{}^2}} \qquad (5.60)$$

where

$\quad V_b \quad$ = estimated loss in share by existing brand b, $b = 1, \ldots, B - 1$
$\quad m \quad$ = estimated share of new brand
$\quad e_b \quad$ = fraction of people having brand b in their evolved set
$\quad D_{bB}^2 \quad$ = squared distance from brand b to new brand B in the perceptual map

Measurements and estimation. After exploratory work to determine market boundaries and relevant dimensions (usually conducted by personal interviews at a central location), a survey is conducted to elicit individuals' (1) evoked set of brands, (2) similarity judgments (if multidimensional scaling is to be used), (3) ratings of brands on perceptual scales, (4) brand preferences, and (5) brand choice, which is obtained by giving the respondent a small sum of money and asking him to select a desired brand. In each case one or more new brand concepts or prototypes are included along with the descriptions of other recognizable brands. If the brand looks reasonable, a group of people is given the product to try for a while, and postuse measurements are taken, much as has been done here. For those who did not want to rebuy the brand after use, a 5-point, intent-to-repeat scale is used to estimate p_{21}.

	R^2	α_0	α_t	t^*	$df^\dagger$
Beer	0.87	12.5	-13.3	6.9	6
Skin care product	0.68	21.0	-16.9	6.25	11
Over-the-counter medicinal	0.94	36.3	-15.8	9.63	5
Pain-reliever product	0.84	28.7	-16.1	5.71	6

* **t-statistic.**

† **degrees of freedom.**

EXHIBIT 5.9 PERCEPTOR-distance-function fits. *Source:* Urban (1975b), p. 867.

Regression analysis is used to estimate the parameters. The dependent variable for each product in the class is the percentage who choose the product at the end of the survey (divided by the percentage who evoke the brand), and the independent variable is the standardized distance to the ideal point. Exhibit 5.9 gives the estimates reported for four new product cases, all of which fit quite well.

Evaluation. Several empirical tests of the individual elements, as well as of the overall model structure, are presented by Urban with the following results: the average absolute deviation for observed versus predicted trial rates across 8 products was 0.07 and for repeat rates the average absolute deviation for 5 products was 0.067. Of these 13 cases only one difference was statistically significant at the 0.10 level. In a macrotest of the market-structure equations (5.53)–(5.55), test-market data were used for 6 products, and the average absolute difference between actual and predicted shares was less than 1%. Other tests of the cumulative trial structure and of the source of new brand share were similarly satisfactory.

The model has a number of apparent uses including (1) identification of potential new product opportunities, (2) evaluation of a number of new product concepts, and (3) diagnosis of needs for product redesign/repositioning for frequently purchased consumer packaged goods. Urban reports several applications, including (1) diagnosing and correcting differences between product claims and performance for a personal care product, which led to a projected share increase of between 1% and 3%, and (2) identifying a new product opportunity in the medicinal care field.

PERCEPTOR is an intuitively appealing model that is easy to use. However, it has several problems that limit its value. First, the concept of relating share and draw to squared distance from an ideal point is not without its critics. The approach is also limited by the fact that it is deterministic, does not consider competitive reactions and analysis is performed at the market level. Finally, the estimation of the long-run repeat rate with short-run switching probabilities, while innovative, ignores changes in those probabilities over time (Kalwani and Silk, 1980).

Shocker and Srinivasan's LINMAP Procedure. Shocker and Srinivasan (1974) propose a four-stage procedure to identify new product alternatives that address specific firm objectives. At the heart of the procedure are a consumer-choice model, relating product choice to distance to the individual's ideal brand, LINMAP, a linear programming procedure that jointly derives individual ideal points and attribute-importance weights, and a firm's objective function, which guides the search for new product opportunities. The four stages of the procedure are (1) identify the market, (2) represent products in attribute space, (3) estimate utility functions and likely product choices, and (4) identify the best new opportunity.

Identification of the relevant market.   The authors note that the first stage of their procedure is to identify the relevant market as determined by interproduct competition *perceived by users* rather than by manufacturers. Brand-similarity ratings and/or analysis of brand-switching behavior in the marketplace can be used.

Representation of brands in attribute space.   The authors stress that whatever the procedure used to derive an attribute space, the dimensions must be "actionable." Thus the attributes must be important to consumers, and movements along those dimensions must clearly specify actions to be taken by the manufacturer in developing the product as a physical and psychological entity. In this model, the authors assume that each individual shares the same product perceptions while differing in preferences and, hence, in importance weights and ideal points.

Estimation of consumer response to new product ideas.   In developing a consumer-response model at the *individual level,* the authors assume the following:

1. A set of attributes exist that are known and relevant to brand preferences.

2. Each brand j can be characterized by its position in multiattribute space as $\{y_{jp}\}$ for $p = 1, ..., T$.

3. For each individual there is a set of ordered pairs of brands $\Omega = \{(j, k)\}$ where, in each pair (j, k), j is preferred to k on a forced-choice/paired-comparison basis.

4. Each individual has an idiosyncratic ideal brand, as well as attribute saliencies, representing the importance of each attribute dimension. We define $\{w_p\}$ as the importance of dimension p ($w_p > 0$) and $\{X_p\}$ as the ideal brand positions along dimension p.

5. Likelihood of consumer choice of a brand is a function of its distance to the ideal brand, with the individual preferring the product nearer his ideal.

The authors define a distance function:

$$s_j = \sum_p (y_{jp} - X_p)^2 w_p, \qquad j = 1, ..., J \text{ (number of brands)} \qquad \textbf{(5.61)}$$

where s_j is the importance-weighted squared distance between brand j and the ideal brand. In equation (5.61) there are two quantities that are unknown, the $\{X_p\}$ and the $\{w_p\}$. If those quantities were known, then ideally, following assumptions 3 and 5:

$$s_k \geq s_j, \quad \text{for all} \quad (j, k) \text{ in } \Omega \tag{5.62}$$

The authors suggest the use of LINMAP (Srinivasan and Shocker, 1973) for calculating the unknowns. In essence, a set of $\{X_p\}$ and $\{w_p\}$ is sought such that equation (5.62) most nearly holds for all pairs of brands. Formally, the problem is to find $\{X_p\}$ and $\{w_p\}$ that

$$\text{Minimize} \sum_{(j,k)\in\Omega} z_{jk} \tag{5.63a}$$

(i.e., minimize discrepancies from equation (5.62)) subject to

$$s_k - s_j + z_{jk} \geq 0 \tag{5.63b}$$

(equations defining discrepancies) for all (j, k) in Ω, and

$$\sum_{(j,k)\in\Omega} (s_k - s_j) = 1 \quad \text{(scaling factor)} \tag{5.63c}$$

In the foregoing formulation, model (5.63c) serves to eliminate the acceptability of the otherwise feasible solution $w_p = 0$ for all p. Although the formulation is perhaps best understood as detailed in model (5.63a), a number of transformations and additional constraints are needed to put the problem into the linear programming form used by LINMAP.

Once values of $\{w_p\}$ and $\{X_p\}$ have been determined, the relationship between distance and choice must be specified. The authors suggest the form

$$\pi_j = \frac{a}{s_j^b}, \quad a > 0, b \geq 0 \tag{5.64}$$

where π_i is the probability of choosing brand j and a is a normalization constant such that $\Sigma_j \pi_j = 1$ (i.e., an individual must choose some brand). The parameter b can be estimated by using historical data from a number of users in the product class. Pessemier and colleagues (1971) show that b is more a function of the product market and less one of individual characteristics and suggest an estimation procedure.

Search for new product ideas. The firm may have one of a number of different objectives; the authors suggest considering total incremental revenue for all products in the specific market. From equation (5.64) π_j is known for every brand j for every individual. If we index individuals by i, then

$$\pi_{ij} = \frac{a_i}{s_{ij}^b} \tag{5.65}$$

where j ranges over brands available to individual i. Then, if we denote the new brand as r and ψ as the set of the firm's brands, q_i, the likelihood that individual i buys some brand from the firm is

$$q_1 = \frac{\pi_{ir} + \sum\limits_{j \in \psi} \pi_{ij}}{\pi_{ir} + \sum\limits_{j} \pi_{ij}} \tag{5.66}$$

That is, the numerator of equation (5.66) is all the company's brands, while the denominator reflects all the brands in the market. (Equation 5.66 is equivalent to recalculating a in equation (5.64)). If we let $\Sigma_{j \in \psi}\, \pi_{ij} = h_i$, then h_i represents the share of individual i's purchases that the firm received before the new brand introduction. The incremental revenue associated with the new product then is

$$\text{Incremental revenue} = \sum_i (q_i - h_i)V_i \tag{5.67}$$

where V_i represents the purchasing power of individual i.

Finally, if variable costs can be associated with $\{y_{rp}\}$, the new brand position, then a profit equation can be constructed:

$$Z = \sum_i (q_i - h_i)Q_i[P - c(y_{r1}, \ldots, y_{rt})] \tag{5.68}$$

where

Q_i = annual volume (in units) associated with individual i
P = unit price
c = incremental manufacturing costs per unit associated with product design $\{y_{rp}\}$

The authors suggest nonlinear programming or grid-search methods to find the product design $\{y_{rp}\}$ (or set of designs) that maximizes equation (5.68) or another appropriate objective.

Assessment.   LINMAP has a number of advantages. First, analysis is at the individual level, and therefore multiple-product designs appealing to different market segments can easily be generated. Second, the procedure specifically incorporates the firm's objectives (profit, revenue, etc.) and considers the total impact on the firm of the new product decision, including cannibalization and other factors. In addition, this work helped serve to introduce linear programming as a procedure for calibrating utility functions in conjoint analysis. The approach has had some popularity: it has been used in health care, communications services, razor blades, and other product categories. (See Braun and Srinivasan, 1975, Hauser and Shugan, 1980, Parker and Srinivasan, 1976, and Pekelman and Sen, 1979, for examples.)

This approach has several drawbacks as well. First, the model is static, and the market is assumed nonreactive. There is no trial-repeat structure like PERCEPTOR, and competitive response is not considered, making the revenue and/or profit calculation suspect. In addition, the model of choice behavior, although intuitively attractive, is not without criticism. And, finally, because of the structure of solutions to linear programming problems, in general, there will be only as many nonnegative $\{x_p, w_p\}$ as there are preference pairs calibrated for an individual. Thus the ideal points and/or importance weights will be determined by the number of paired comparisons generated, an undesirable property. Indeed, Horsky and Rao (1984) extend the procedure to include comparisons of pairs of pairs, improving results in some simulation studies and several applications.

The DEFENDER Model (Hauser and Shugan, 1983).   The DEFENDER model was developed to study how a brand should adjust its marketing efforts, pricing, and positioning in a competitive environment. The model incorporates the following assumptions:

1. Existing brands can be positioned in a multi-attribute space, where brand positions are ratio scaled (i.e., the dimensions are defined on a "per dollar" basis).

2. Consumers choose their utility-maximizing brands.

3. Consumers' utility functions are linear or linearizable (via a monotone transformation of the attributes).

4. Awareness and distribution are concave functions of advertising and distribution spending, respectively.

Exhibit 5.10 illustrates the perceptual map idea and shows the (taste-distribution) regions in which consumers prefer each of the existing (efficient) brands.

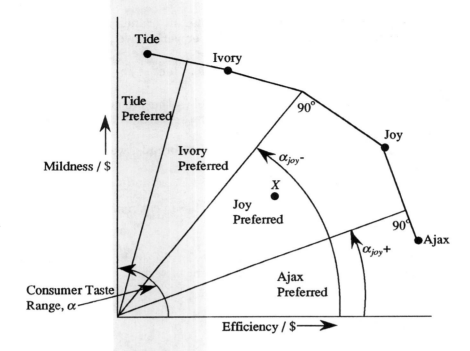

α = $tan^{-1}(w_1/w_2)$, the taste trade-offs for individual preference weights w_1 and w_2.

$\alpha_{joy}+$, $\alpha_{joy}-$ = angle that defines the upper (+) and the lower (-) limits of the taste region where Joy is the preferred brand.

X = an inefficient brand (i.e., X maximizes no consumer's taste distribution), postulated to have 0 market share when consumers have 100% awareness.

EXHIBIT 5.10   A pictorial representation of the DEFENDER production/taste distribution space with four brands and two attributes.

The model requires the following notation:

p_j = price of brand j

x_{ij} = position of brand j on attribute i, $i = 1, 2$

w_{ik} = individual k's importance weight for attribute i

μ_{jk} = $w_{1k}x_{1k} + w_{2k}x_{2k}$ = utility of brand j to individual k

α_k = $tan^{-1}(w_{2k}/w_{1k})$, the "preference angle" for individual k (in Exhibit 5.10, α_k is the angle through the origin orthogonal to individual k's indifference curve)

$f(\alpha)$ = distribution of the taste function, α, across the population

m_j = market share for brand j

Assuming that all consumers evoke all brands and that all consumers purchase the same number of brands per period, we get

$$m_j = P_r(\bar{\mu}_j > \bar{\mu}_i, \quad \text{for } i \neq j) \tag{5.69}$$

Note that m_j here is a random variable—the probability that a randomly chosen customer selects brand j. Thus m_j represents the distribution of μ_{jk} as k varies over the population ($\{\mu_{jk}\}$).

Since all consumers do not evoke all brands, we define

A_ℓ = a subset of all brands, A, $\ell = 1, ..., L$ and

s_ℓ = probability that a randomly chosen customer selects from choice set A_ℓ

Taking the choice set and the linearity of the utility functions into consideration yields, after some rearrangement of terms:

$$m_{j|\ell} = Pr\left[\frac{X_{1j}}{p_j} - \frac{X_{1i}}{p_i} > \left(\frac{\bar{w}_2}{\bar{w}_1}\right)\left(\frac{X_{2i}}{p_i} - \frac{X_{2j}}{p_j}\right)\right], \quad \text{for all } i \neq j \text{ in } A_\ell \tag{5.70}$$

where

$m_{j|\ell}$ = market share of brand j among customers with evoked set ℓ

Note in equation (5.70) that, as with $\bar{\mu}_j$, we get $\bar{w}_1, \bar{w}_2$, representing the taste distribution ($\{w_{1k}, w_{2k}\}$) in the model.

In an interesting geometric analysis, the authors show that equation (5.70) is equivalent to

$$m_{j|\ell} = Pr(\alpha_{jj-} < \bar{\alpha} < \alpha_{jj+}), \quad \text{where } \alpha_{jj-}, \alpha_{jj+} \text{ are defined by } A_\ell \tag{5.71}$$

Following equation (5.71), we get

$$m_{j|\ell} = \int_{\alpha_{jj-}}^{\alpha_{jj+}} f(\alpha)\, d\alpha \tag{5.72}$$

and

$$m_j = \sum_{\ell=1}^{L} m_{j|\ell} s_\ell \tag{5.73}$$

The authors develop 14 theorems concerning defensive marketing and repositioning following a competitive entry. Their analysis can be illustrated by considering the pricing response of a brand to competitive entry. (Note that a price response implies a repositioning because of the way the attributes are measured.)

A new brand can enter the market in several ways in the DEFENDER model: (1) if it is inefficient (i.e., within the "shell" of brands—like brand X in Exhibit 5.10), (2) if it exactly matches a competitor, (3) if it is not adjacent to the brand under study (Ivory and Ajax are adjacent to Joy in Exhibit 5.10; Tide is not), or (4) an adjacent attack (brand N in Exhibit 5.11 for example). In case 3, it will not affect our brand's (Joy's) sales. An adjacent attack (an efficient brand between Ivory and Ajax) will affect Joy's sales. Assuming that the attack comes between Joy and Ivory, then the profit for our brand after attack becomes

$$\Pi_a(p) = (p - c)N_a \int_{a_{jj-}}^{a_{jn}} f(\alpha)\, d\alpha \qquad (5.74)$$

where n refers to the new brand and N_a is market volume after the attack. By studying the behavior of $d\Pi_a(p)/d_p$, Hauser and Shugan show that, if $f(\alpha)$ is uniformly distributed (and the brands in the market meet a technical condition called "regularity"), then $d\Pi_a(p)/dp < 0$, and a price decrease is the optimal response to the entry (Exhibit 5.11). Furthermore, profits have to come down.

Intuitively, these results are reasonable. With the entry of the new brand, the market has become more competitive. So prices and profits have to come down. Somewhat counterintuitive, however, are the results for awareness advertising and distribution. In Hauser and Shugan's model, both have to come down after the new entry, whereas one normally expects new competition to provoke an increase in advertising and distribution spending. To see why this occurs, consider Hauser and Shugan's profit function:

$$\text{Profit} = (p - c)N_a M_a AD - k_a - k_d$$

Here A is the amount of awareness advertising, D is the amount of distribution, k_a and k_d are the associated fixed costs, and M_a is the firm's market share. Note that advertising and distribution are mathematically identical in the profit function. So whatever applies to advertising will apply to distribution as well, and vice-versa. Note, also, that competitors' advertising and distribution have no effect on the firm's profits. Thus, there is no possibility of an advertising or distribution "war" here. The marginal revenue from advertising or distribution is proportional to $(p - c)N_a M_a$. This quantity goes down after the new entry because (as argued above) the profit margin goes down. Hence advertising and distribution have to be lowered.

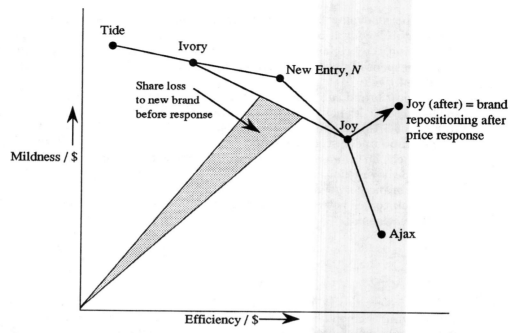

EXHIBIT 5.11 The optimal price response, according to DEFENDER, of Joy to Brand N's entry is to lower price, repositioning Joy in the noted direction.

Assessment. Hauser and Gaskin (1984) test the DEFENDER consumer model, using data collected for the ASSESSOR model (Silk and Urban, 1978; see Chapter 11), with generally encouraging results, suggesting that the model has practical value for estimating the market-share effects of different positioning strategies. (Indeed, all the models reviewed here are commercially available). DEFENDER has been criticized because it is not an equilibrium analysis, that is, it does not consider the responses of all incumbents and assumes the new product does not respond in turn. Hauser (1988) extends the model to a full equilibrium analysis, but without a new entrant. In addition, DEFENDER considers one product per firm and does not study how the multi-product firm should respond. See Lane (1980) for a similar model and Hauser and Wernerfelt (1988), Carpenter (1989), Choi, Desarbo, and Harker (1990), and Kumar and Sudharshan (1988) for further, closely related developments and Horsky and Nelson (1989) for a model using automobile attribute data showing price response by incumbents to a new market entry. Further issues, like entry deterrence, the dynamics of response and the extension to more dimensions seem fruitful areas for research.

Other Approaches. DEFENDER, PERCEPTOR, and LINMAP are but three of a number of model-based procedures for product strategy. In Shocker and

Srinivasan's (1979) review of the literature, they find, on the positive side, that methodologies are being developed that fulfill the promise of the marketing concept—integration of consumer wants and desires into the product-design process. On the negative side, they report that "the frameworks reviewed represent unfulfilled promises. . . . Will managements use them?" (p. 178). Clearly, the use of such procedures calls for changes in organizational decision-making styles. As with any innovation, the greater the change required for implementation, the greater will be the benefits that must be promised for diffusion. These procedures need more compelling demonstrations of their comparative advantage over alternative procedures for wider use. (Sudharshan, May, and Shocker, 1987, compare four "optional" product positioning algorithms in a simulation study).

Product design and positioning models have seen some clear uses. Stefflre (1971) reports having fully developed six products. Wind (1973), Myers (1976), Johnson (1974), Pessemier (1976), and Hustad, Mayer, and Wipple (1975) all hint that clients have used their approaches successfully. Urban (1975b) reports use for eight new products, while Parker and Srinivasan (1976) report a successful application in the design of rural health care facilities. Furthermore, Hauser and Urban (1977) report good results for design of a health maintenance organization, of financial service packages, and of several new, frequently purchased consumer goods. Urban and Hauser (1980) also report a number of applications, and Choffray and Lilien (1982) report that their procedure for industrial products has been applied in several cases. Wittink and Cattin (1989) report about 400 commercial applications of conjoint analysis per year.

All the noted approaches are proactive—using consumer input in active evaluation of new product or optimal response opportunities. Furthermore, they all assume that the new product enters an existing market; a new product that creates a new market or a new market dimension is not addressed. Truly novel products generally do not come from consumer ideas; consumers tend to be interpolators (within existing markets) rather than extrapolators.

The methods also assume that a product can be decomposed and analyzed as a vector of attributes. Most methods assume a single use and/or use situation; they do not allow for variety seeking and/or the maintenance of a portfolio of products (breakfast cereals, beers, soft drinks, etc.). Customer decision models need more work: the material in Chapter 2 suggests that a single-choice model is unlikely to be applicable to all decision situations or even to all consumers for a given product category. The structure, dynamics, and competitive nature of the marketplace need to be addressed more completely.

However, to keep these procedures in perspective, we must view them not as complete answers to product-design questions but rather as decision support of the design process and product strategy. As such, they suggest the advisability of multiple methods of data collection and analysis, and they provide a structure to explore and learn about market opportunities and the sensitivity of the marketplace to errors in analysis and marketing. As we develop better theories to go along with the improved procedures, product strategy decision should become more scientific and more efficient.

SUMMARY

In the past several decades, we have seen exciting developments of theories, techniques, and models to support product-strategy decisions. The theoretical approaches we described helped to develop insight about strategic product decisions. These theoretical results have their operational counterparts, so that theory and practice can advance together.

A number of techniques exist to support product-design decisions. We separate perceptual-mapping techniques (factor analysis and multidimensional scaling) from preference-choice models (expectancy-value models, preference regression, and conjoint analysis), where the former methods structure perceptual space, suggesting product opportunities, while the latter techniques are most useful for evaluating opportunities in those perceptual spaces.

We reviewed three model-based procedures for product design and strategy: PERCEPTOR, useful for frequently purchased goods; LINMAP, most useful for durables; and DEFENDER, which considers response to new competition. While the procedures have seen application, they are only part of an evolution in the development of product-strategy models.

Thus we have both developing theory and a number of valuable aids for supporting product-strategy decisions. These procedures give incomplete answers to complex questions and therefore must be applied with care and wisdom to be of most use.

PROBLEMS

5.1. A study of consumers' perceptions of coffee revealed that they could be described in terms of two dimensions, X_1 and X_2, which were described as flavor and aroma. The location of the three bands in the market are shown in the table, as is the location of four consumer segments, described in terms of their ideal points.

	Product			Segment (Ideal Point)			
	1	2	3	A	B	C	D
X_1, flavor	2	−1	−3	1	−2	−2	2
X_2, aroma	1	2	−3	2	1	−1	−2
Segment share				40%	30%	20%	10%

Assume that the probability of purchase of a brand is given by $p = a/d^2$, where d is the distance of the ideal point to the brand and a is a normalizing constant.

a. Estimate the expected market shares for each brand in each segment.

b. Suggest a marketing strategy for product 3.

5.2. In a large sample, people were asked to rate how much they liked each of five beverages: milk, coffee, tea, fruit juice, and soda pop. Through factor analysis the following table of factor loadings was obtained. What might each of the three factors be?

		Factors	
Beverage	*I*	*II*	*III*
Milk	0.504	−0.213	−0.217
Coffee	−0.209	0.373	−0.328
Tea	−0.137	0.682	0.307
Fruit juice	0.475	−0.107	0.110
Soda pop	−0.368	−0.645	0.534

5.3. In a segment of the coffee market two main dimensions have been identified: flavor $[F]$ and richness $[R]$. Three brands share this market, with market shares and positions as follows (including a rating for an ideal brand):

	Position		
Brand	*F*	*R*	*Market Share*
A	1	−2	15%
B	2	1	45%
C	1	2	40%
Ideal	3	3	

a. Use this information to estimate α_0 and α_1 in equation (5.56). What assumptions are you making?

b. A new brand, positioned at $F = 1$, $R = 1$, is considering market entry. Assuming that $w = 100\%$ in equation (5.54), that $\tilde{\alpha}_0 = \alpha_0$ and $\tilde{\alpha}_1 = \alpha_1$, and that $p_{12} = p_{21}$, use the PERCEPTOR model to estimate this brand's long-run market share. What is the source of that share?

5.4. Compare the conjoint-analysis approach with the feasibility submodel of the Choffray-Lilien methodology in Chapter 3 for designing a new industrial durable product. What are the strengths and the weaknesses of the two approaches?

5.5. A new product X is being evaluated for entry into the detergent market. A laboratory test was performed on a sample of housewives, who were clustered on the basis of a battery of attitude and life-style variables, as follows:

Group	Group Description	Percentage of Housewives	Percentage of Product Class Used
1	Old-fashioned	45	50
2	Swingers, like new things	20	5
3	Cleaning, like clothes/house spotless	35	45

Blind product tests for X and the remaining three brands yielded the following results, where each brand was rated on a scale from 1 to 10:

Group	Brand X	Other Brands
1	8.5	8.0, 7.5, 7.0
2	6.0	6.5, 7.5, 8.0
3	6.5	6.0, 6.5, 8.0

When the groups were shown advertising for the product, and where all the other brands were made known, brand X's share of expected net purchases was 10% in group 1, 14% in group 2, and 22% in group 3. Assume that $r_i/\Sigma r_j$ is a measure of product preference, where r_i is the rating of brand i.

a. How does the blind preference for brand X vary across segments?

b. How does this preference compare to expected-purchase share?

c. What are the implications for redesigning/repositioning product X for market entry?

5.6. The Crawford Corporation is considering introducing a retail discount card similar to the one described in the chapter. However, they have refined the annual price levels to two, $10 and $20, with the other two attributes as follows:

Discount level: 5%, 10%, or 15% off regular retail price
Number of local cooperating merchants: 10, 20, or 30

One consumer provided the following preference ranking for the $3 \times 3 \times 2$ possible product combinations:

Preference Order	Discount	Number of Cooperating Stores	Price
18 (Best)	15	30	$10
17	15	20	10
16	15	10	10
15	10	30	10
14	10	20	10
13	10	10	10
12	15	30	20
11	15	20	20
10	15	10	20
9	10	30	20
8	10	20	20
7	10	10	20
6	5	30	10
5	5	20	10
4	5	10	10
3	5	30	20
2	5	20	20
1 (Worst)	5	10	20

  a. Using a regression-based method, estimate the part worths for this individual. How well does this model reproduce (predict) this individual's preference ordering?

  b. Assume that this is an average customer and that the firm is considering two plans (each with 30 stores): (i) 10% discount per $15 or (ii) 12% discount per $18. Which should the firm select? Why?

  c. What price will make this individual indifferent between the 10% discount at $15 and a card with a 12% discount?

5.7. Use the Defender model, as in Exhibit 5.10, in a market segment that only evokes Ivory, Joy, and Ajax. Assume the perceptual positions of the brands are

	Mildness/$	*Efficacy/$*
Ivory	1.1	3.9
Joy	3.0	3.0
Ajax	3.9	1.1

  a. If these brands split this segment of the market equally between them, that is, all market shares = 1/3, graph the taste distribution, $f(a)$.

  b. Suppose the shares are as follows:

Ivory	30%
Joy	50%
Ajax	20%

  What does $f(a)$ look like in this case?

  c. Suppose Ajax's price is $1 per box. Assuming that Joy and Ivory do not respond, what would Ajax's share be if it cut the price to $0.90? What is Joy's share at this price? At what price does Joy's share = 0?

5.8. What is the equilibrium product configuration in a Hotelling model with two firms competing for market share, not profits? Assume that each firm's variable costs are c per unit and neither firm's price can be below c. Relate this to the competition between the Democratic and Republican parties in presidential elections.

5.9. Consider the following "quality choice" model of Moorthy (1988). Each consumer chooses the quality level to purchase by maximizing his consumer surplus, $ts - p$, where t is the consumer's "importance weight" for quality, s is product quality, and p is the price of the product with quality level s. Assume t is distributed uniformly on $[a, b]$ $(0 < a < b)$, and let each firm's variable cost of manufacturing s be $as^2/2$.

  a. Compute the optimum product qualities for a profit-maximizing monopolist when he serves everyone in the market.

  b. Compute the product and price equilibrium between two firms when they jointly serve everyone in the market.

    c. Compute the product and price equilibrium when one of the two firms in part (b) chooses its product before the other (while anticipating the latter's entry). What is the first-mover's profit advantage?

    d. Compare the results in this problem with the solutions for the Hotelling model discussed in the text.

6 | ADVERTISING

One of the most important and bewildering promotional tools of modern marketing management is advertising. No one doubts that it is effective in presenting information to potential buyers. There is also widespread agreement that it can be persuasive to some extent and can reinforce buyer preference for a company's product. These potential values of advertising are attested to by the fact that in 1988 the top 100 U.S. advertisers increased their advertising spending by 6.7% over the previous year to an estimated $32 billion. Each of the top four advertisers exceed $1 billion in advertising, with Philip Morris accounting, for over $2 billion (*Advertising Age*, September 27, 1989, p. 1).

Advertising is bewildering because, among other reasons, its effects typically play out over time, may be nonlinear, and interact with other elements in the marketing mix in creating sales. Currently, no one knows what advertising really does in the marketplace. However, what advertising is supposed to do is fairly clear: advertising is undertaken to increase company sales and/or profits over what they otherwise would be. However, it is rarely able to create sales by itself. Whether the customer buys also depends on the product, price, packaging, personal selling, services, financing, and other aspects of the marketing process.

More specifically, the purpose of advertising is to enhance potential buyers' responses to the organization and its offerings by providing information, by channeling desires, and by supplying reasons for preferring a particular organization's offer.

For advertising, even more than for other elements of the marketing mix, it is important to keep in mind that advertising decisions and their effectiveness are influenced to a great extent by their interaction with marketing objectives, with product characteristics, and with other elements of the marketing mix. Consider these examples:

Personal Selling. When personal selling is an important element in the marketing mix (in industrial markets, for example), the role of advertising is diminished. Personal selling is a far more effective (but expensive) communication method than advertising. But because of its extra expense, it can be used more effectively when the expected level of sales to a single prospect is large (generally, sales to industrial customers, wholesalers, and retailers).

Branding. If a company produces several variations of its product under a family or company name (Kellogg's, Campbell Soup), advertising is appropriated to the entire line, with special-brand attention given from time to time. When different brand names exist (Tide at Procter & Gamble, for example), each brand and the advertising budget and copy and media decisions associated with it can be addressed independently.

Pricing. The copy or message of the advertising should reinforce and be consistent with the brand's price position. A premium-priced brand should emphasize differentiating qualities, while a low-priced brand should stress the price differential.

Distribution. The length of the distribution channel and the overall marketing strategy dictate different targets for advertising messages. If wholesalers or retailers are involved, two different strategies are generally available: push versus pull. A push strategy is aimed at salespeople or the trade, and the objective is to push the product through channels; a pull strategy is aimed at the ultimate consumer, and its objective is to have consumer interest pull the merchandise through the distribution channels.

The differences among product characteristics, marketing-program objectives, and marketing strategies explain to an extent the differences in advertising-spending levels of products. The median advertising-spending level for a large sample of industrial products was found to be 0.7% of sales (Lilien, 1979), while *Advertising Age* annually reports rates of around 2% of sales for industries like automobiles, tires, oil, and appliances and over 7% for soaps, cleansers, drugs, and cosmetics. These wide variations reflect differences in the relative importance and efficiency of advertising (Balasubramanian and Kumar, 1990) and our understanding of the relative magnitude of its effectiveness (Broadbent, 1989a, b; Tellis, 1989).

In developing an advertising program, marketing managers must address five closely related decisions:

1. What are the objectives of the program? (communications objectives/ sales objectives)

2. How much should be spent on the program?

3. What message should be sent? (copy development, evaluation, and execution)

4. What media should be used? (reach, frequency, impact, media type, message timing)

5. How should the results be evaluated? (communications/sales impact)

Points 1 and 5 are two sides of the same issue—setting objectives and evaluating program results against those objectives. We address points 2–4 in detail separately here, but all decisions are closely interrelated: advertising objectives drive copy decisions, and copy effects, varying by response group, affect media decisions. In addition, time is an issue for all three decision areas. For budgeting, dollars must be spent over time, and pulsing versus more continuous spending patterns must be evaluated. Furthermore, advertising copy varies in its effectiveness over time, eventually wearing out. Thus the creation of new copy must be phased in. Finally, media decisions are closely connected with the timing and scheduling of messages, as well as with the selection of media.

To guide our discussion, we first review what is known about the effects of advertising—that is, what does advertising seem to do? This review aids the discussion and evaluation of advertising models for the three decision areas given in the following sections.

THE EFFECTS OF ADVERTISING

Response Phenomena.   Little (1979b) identifies three sets of controversies for aggregate (as opposed to individual) advertising response models:

Shape.   This notion refers to the long-term level of sales expected at each different level of advertising. Is the relationship linear? S-shaped? What are sales when advertising is zero? Is there a supersaturation point, where large amounts of advertising depress sales?

Dynamics.   This notion refers to the speed of sales increase when advertising is increased and the rate of decay when advertising is decreased. Another question is whether hysteresis exists—that is, whether advertising can move sales to a new level at which it will stay without further advertising input.

Interaction.   Two main questions exist here. The first is: what type of market (strong or weak-market-share markets) is a more appropriate target for advertising? The second is: what is the appropriate structure of the interaction of advertising with other elements in the marketing mix?

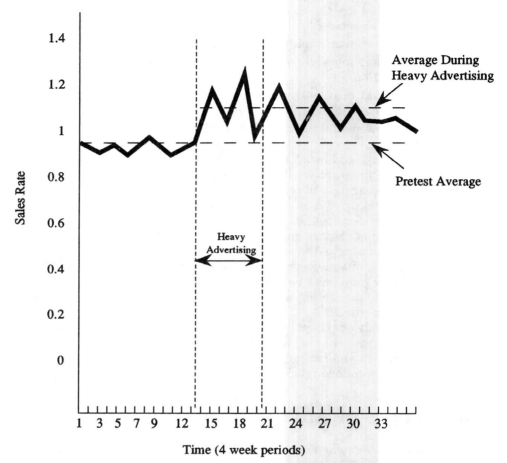

EXHIBIT 6.1   Sales rate of a packaged good rose quickly under increased advertising
but declined slowly after it was removed. The vertical axis shows the
ratio of sales in test areas to sales in control areas not receiving the
heavy advertising. (*Source:* Little, 1979b, p. 637.)

Little (1979b) also reviews many empirical examples in an all-too-infre-
quent attempt to unify and generalize what we have observed. Exhibit 6.1
illustrates several of the observed phenomena. First, we note that advertising
increases sales here: there are considerable increases in sales after the introduction of substantial new advertising dollars. We also note that the sales
rate increases within a month or so, substantially faster than many managers
purport to be the case. Bloom, Jay, and Twyman (1977) and Pekelman and
Tse (1976) report similar results with a change in copy, indicating that dollar
spending may not be the same as effective spending. Krishnamurthi,

Narayan, and Raj (1986) report that the buildup effect is almost immediate, typically of the order of a purchase cycle.

The exhibit also shows sales leveling off under the new spending regime: apparently, the total effect of the advertising was seen before spending stopped. Little (1979b) in other studies and the Bloom, Jay, and Twyman (1977) article show these effects as well. Haley (1978) refines this observation by demonstrating that the magnitude of the sales increase actually decreases over time. Thus the increased advertising may lead a group of nonusers to buy the product for a change, and then some of these customers continue to purchase.

Finally, Exhibit 6.1 shows the beginning of decay following the lowering of advertising. Furthermore, this sales decay seems to take place more slowly than sales growth. Hence two separate phenomena are involved: the rise is related to advertising communications, while the decline is related to product experience, a different phenomenon, and should be expected to occur at a different rate.

Exhibit 6.2 shows the sales of a line of products that have never been advertised. Supermarkets and department stores are literally stocked with house brands, price brands, and others that see quite healthy sales in the absence of advertising. Therefore an advertising-response model should admit the possibility of sales with zero advertising.

Perhaps the most interesting set of controversies surrounds the shape of the response function (Stewart, 1989). Logic demands that a linear or everywhere-convex response is unreasonable: a product with linear response would have an optimal advertising rate at either 0 or infinity; a convex response curve would lead to (optimal) infinite spending with sales becoming arbitrarily large. The most commonly discussed advertising response curve shapes, then, are concave and S-shapes. Exhibit 6.3 shows two products that exhibit concavity in response, with Exhibit 6.3(b) suggesting an S-shape.

While a good deal of discussion and modelling concerns S-shaped response, most of the empirical evidence supports concavity. Reviews by Simon and Arndt (1980) and Aaker and Carman (1982) indicate diminishing returns; Lambin (1976) reports that there is no S-curve, based on his analyses of 107 brands in 16 product classes in 8 Western European countries.

The work of Rao and Miller (1975) and that of Eastlack and Rao (1986) is consistent with an S-shaped response as is Wittink's (1977) analysis, reporting larger advertising-sales slopes at higher advertising rates, implying a region of increasing returns as dictated by the S-shaped hypothesis. Broadbent (1984) concludes that data uncertainty and methodological questions make either proving or disproving the S-shaped hypothesis problematical, a point consistent with the analysis of Schultz and Block (1986).

In terms of advertising dynamics, two critical questions concern the accumulation of advertising effects and the advertising wear-out phenomena. Little (1979b) shows the results of a series of tests of the impulse response of advertising—the response over time to a short but heavy increase in adver-

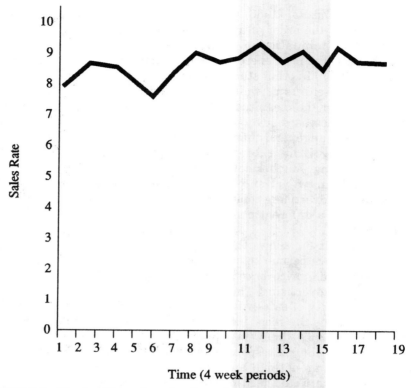

EXHIBIT 6.2 The healthy sales of a line of unadvertised food products show that advertising is not always required in order to sell something. (*Source:* Little, 1979b.)

tising spending—which is reproduced in Exhibit 6.4. These data (as well as similar results from Bass and Clarke, 1972) show that advertising response is fairly quick (within one to two months) and that there is negative sales reaction about four months after the pulse. This effect, common in consumer promotions, reflects the borrowing of future sales. (See Clarke, 1976, for a more complete evaluation of this phenomenon.) Econometric studies of the cumulative effects of advertising run into the "interval bias" problem, where researchers find different advertising durations for different data intervals. (See Hanssens, Parsons, and Schultz, 1990, p. 221, for a fuller discussion of this issue.)

Another phenomenon that Little (1979b) reviews is difference in rise and decay rates when advertising is increased and decreased. This phenomenon is known as "wear-out." The ADPULS model of Simon (1982) reviewed later treats this specific phenomenon. Another related phenomenon is that of hysteresis, where response falls off even as advertising remains constant.

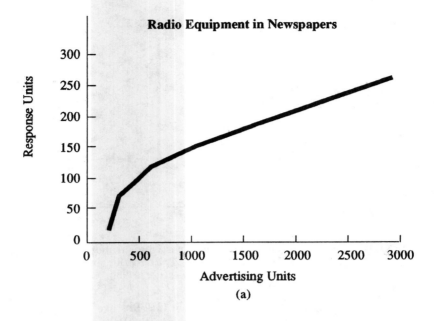

Radio Equipment in Newspapers

(a)

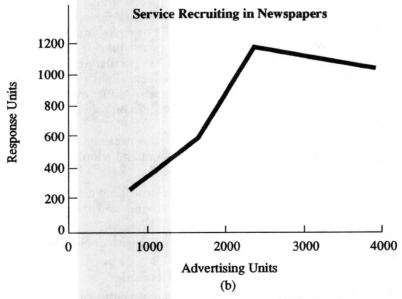

Service Recruiting in Newspapers

(b)

EXHIBIT 6.3 Two examples of nonlinear response exhibit the phenomenon of diminishing returns at high advertising rates. (*Source:* Little, 1979b.)

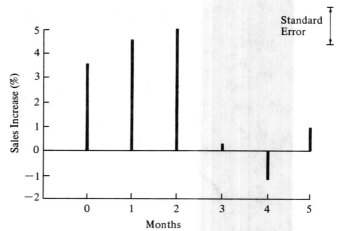

EXHIBIT 6.4 A large impulse of advertising in month 0 yields substantial sales increases in months 0, 1, and 2 for an infrequently purchased consumer durable. (*Source:* Little, 1979b.)

Other effects reviewed by Little (1979b) are the (relatively rapid) sales response for infrequently purchased goods (those people react who are in the market), the market-depletion phenomena for such goods, and competitive effects. Where the evidence is weak or nonexistent is on the question of where to advertise (in strong markets? in weak markets?) and on the structure of interactions. The issue of interactions is particularly difficult, and such effects are harder to measure than main effects (Eskin and Baron 1977; Swinyard and Ray 1977; Wildt, 1977). Effects also differ over the product's life cycle, from market to market and are dependent on other elements of the marketing mix (Winer and Moore, 1989).

Finally, Little summarizes his observations with a list of five phenomena that a good advertising response model should admit:

1. Sales respond dynamically upward and downward, respectively, to increases and decreases of advertising and frequently do so at different rates.

2. Steady-state response can be concave or S-shaped and will often have positive sales at zero advertising.

3. Competitive advertising affects sales.

4. The dollar effectiveness of advertising can change over time as the result of changes in media, copy, and other factors.

5. Products sometimes respond to increased advertising with a sales increase that falls off even as advertising is held constant (Little, 1979b, p. 644).

Copy Research.   Part of the interest in copy research involves its impact on sales relative to advertising weight. For example Aaker and Carman (1982) reviewed 48 AdTel advertising experiments and reported that 30% showed significant weight results while 47% involving ad copy showed significant results. Similarly, Fulgoni (1987) reported on over 400 BehaviorScan tests, with from 40 to 55% showing response to weight (depending on the year) while 75% showed a significant response to copy. Carroll and colleagues (1985) reported no effect of weight in an experiment involving an enlistment program for the Navy, but did report statistically significant results for copy tailored to the local area. Eastlack and Rao (1989), reviewing 19 advertising experiments at Campbell Soup, concur, reporting that "good copy in the right media will produce sales increases without increases in budget" (p. 70). Using data on 92 British TV advertising tests, Stewart (1990) reported 48% of the tests showed a significant increase in sales for new copy and 31% of the tests showed a significant sales increase for a "heavy-up" test for established brands.

Given the importance of ad copy, there is good reason for interest in what makes a good ad. Copy research involves investigations of myriad phenomena from how the physical and mechanical aspects of ads relate to recognition, recall, and other measures (Hendon, 1973) to the humor and seriousness of TV commercials (Wells, Leavitt, and McConnell, 1971). In his review of a large number of copy-testing studies, Ramond (1976) provides the following principles, where the term "principle" implies a basic finding with implications for future practice. These principles, like the preceding observations, hold in many circumstances, all other things being equal.

> The bigger the print ad, the more people will recognize it later (Starch 1966; Trodahl and Jones, 1965; Twedt, 1952; Yamanaka, 1962), possibly as a function of the square root of the size increase.
>
> Color ads are recognized by more people than are black-and-white ads (Gardner and Cohen, 1966; Twedt, 1952).
>
> The shorter its headline, the greater the recognition of an ad (Leo Burnett bulletin, unpublished).
>
> Because TV commercials vary in more ways than print ads and have been studied for a shorter time, less is known about their copy tests (McGuire, 1976). Shorter TV commercials are recalled as well as longer ones. Product class has a significant effect on recognition or recall of both TV and print ads.
>
> Sex, humor, and fear have no consistent effect in what advertising communicates. Awareness and attitude changes are sensitive to differences in TV commercial execution and can predict changes in brand choice (Assael and Day, 1968; Axelrod, 1968).
>
> Ads need not be believed to be remembered (Leavitt, 1962; Maloney, 1963).

These observations have not been sufficiently understood or generalized to justify the term "theory"; however, they have led to the development of some "contingency theories" of copy and message effects—that is, what messages to use in what circumstances. Rossiter and Percy's (1987) contingency theory of advertising tactics and the simpler FCB grid address the contingency nature of advertising tactics (Rossiter and Donovan, 1991). Research in this area continues. For example, Hanssens and Weitz (1980) reported that industrial ad recall and readership scores were strongly related to a variety of characteristics, such as size and position in magazines. Sewall and Sarel (1986) performed a similar analysis for radio commercials. Goodwin and Etgar (1980) have reported on relationships between communication effects and the type of advertising appeals, and Rossiter (1981) reports on regression analyses that reproduce Starch readership scores. For a good treatment of what seems to drive effective TV ads, see Stewart and Farse's (1986) study of 1000 commercials.

Frequency Phenomena.   For media planning and scheduling, knowledge of the effect of advertising exposures over time is critical. In an important effort at consolidating the literature, Naples (1979) summarizes theoretical and empirical research related to effective advertising frequency.

The theoretical foundations of the effects of frequency are based on laboratory research in psychology and can be traced to the work of Ebbinghaus (1902) in which he showed that the forgetting rate is made slower by repeated learning of the same lessons. Later work by Zielski (1959) applied Ebbinghaus's findings to ads for grocery products.

The work of Appel (1971) and Grass (1968) shows that response to a simple stimulus first increases, then passes through a maximum, and finally declines, as shown in Exhibit 6.5. From studies for a number of Dupont products, Grass concludes that attention increases and maximizes at two exposures, while the amount of learned information increases and maximizes at two or three exposures. Krugman (1972), on the basis of his brainwave and eye-movement studies, has been an advocate of the idea that the third and subsequent exposures are reinforcement of the effects of the second exposure.

In a paper on the results of a unique data collection exercise, McDonald (1971) reports on the effects of frequency. In this study, purchasing records and newspaper, magazine, and media exposure records for 50 product fields were kept for 255 housewives over a 13-week period. The main result was that over 9 product fields studied in depth, housewives were, on average, 5% more likely to switch into, rather than out of, a particular brand if, between the two purchases, they saw two or more ads for that brand than if they saw zero or one ad. Exhibit 6.6 reproduces the main results, showing that the added value of more than two ads is marginal. McDonald also found that the effect is stronger for advertising seen within four days of the last purchase.

In a study conducted for four advertisers, Ogilvy and Mather (1965), us-

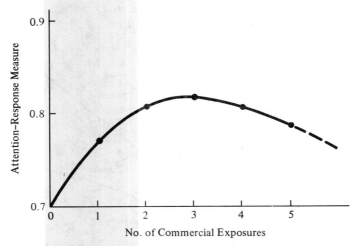

EXHIBIT 6.5   Attention paid to TV commercials versus exposure frequency. (*Source:* Grass, 1968.)

ing television viewing diaries, tracked brand preference and related it to number of exposures. The results of their study showed (1) no more than minimal effects for one exposure in an 8-week period, (2) major differences by time of day, and (3) major differences by brand. (See Exhibit 6.7.) In another study using diary recorded purchasing within a split-cable television market, the results were pretty much consistent with the suggestion of at least two exposures for maximum effectiveness (Naples, 1979). An interesting additional finding was that the brands that showed the greatest response were those with the highest share of advertising in their categories. On the basis of these

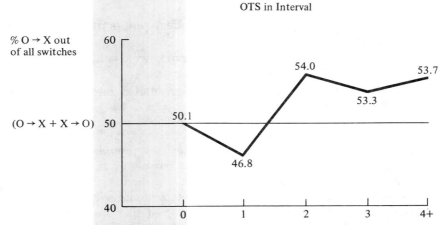

EXHIBIT 6.6   The effect of advertising exposure (opportunity to see or OTS) on brand switching. (*Source:* McDonald, 1971.)

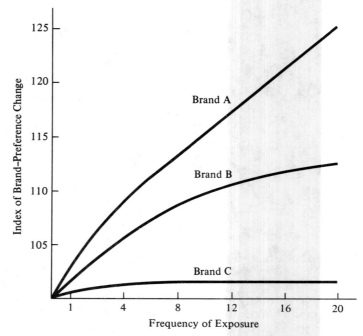

EXHIBIT 6.7 Brand-preference change induced by frequency of exposure to daytime television (food products). (*Source:* Ogilvy and Mather, 1965.)

studies and a review of others, Naples (1979, pp. 63–81) offers the following conclusions:

1. Optimal exposure frequency appears to be at least three exposures within a purchase cycle.

2. Beyond three ad exposures, effectiveness increases but at a decreasing ratio.

3. Frequency by itself does not cause wear-out, although it can advance the decline of an effective campaign.

4. Response to advertising appears smaller for the brand with dominant market share.

Cannon (1987) provides 27 propositions (like "Proposition 25, Vivid images will require low frequency since they provide unique and memorable experiences," p. 41) that suggest that frequency is an individual, copy, and situation-specific phenomenon and that a media schedule can, at best, segment the market appropriately and select media vehicles and a schedule that works best for each of those segments. (See also Cannon and Goldring, 1986, and Wenzel and Speetzen, 1987, and, for industrial ads, Cort, Lambert, and Garret, 1982.)

In summary, although our knowledge about advertising response, effective frequency, and effective copy is limited, some principles clearly exist. These principles must be validated in specific situations and product areas prior to making advertising decisions.

OBJECTIVE SETTING AND BUDGETING

Practice and Models

Objectives.   The first step in developing an advertising program is to set the advertising objectives. These objectives must flow from prior decisions on the target market, market positioning, and marketing mix. The market-positioning and marketing-mix strategies define the job that advertising must do in the total marketing program.

Advertising objectives can be classified as to whether their aim is to inform, persuade, or remind.

Informative advertising figures heavily in the pioneering stage of a product category, where the objective is to build *primary demand*. Thus the yogurt industry initially had to inform consumers of yogurt's nutritional benefits and many uses.

Persuasive advertising becomes important in the competitive stage, where a company's objective is to build *selective demand* for a particular brand. For example, Chivas Regal attempts to persuade consumers that it delivers status as no other brand of Scotch does. Some persuasive advertising has moved into the category of *comparison advertising*, which seeks to establish the superiority of one brand through specific comparison with one or more other brands in the product class. Comparison advertising had been used in such product categories as deodorants, fast-food hamburgers, toothpastes, tires, and automobiles.

Reminder advertising is highly important in the mature stage of the life cycle to keep the consumer thinking about the product. Expensive four-color Coca-Cola ads in magazines have the purpose not of informing or persuading but of reminding people to purchase Coca-Cola. A related form of advertising is *reinforcement advertising*, which seeks to assure current purchasers that they have made the right choice. Automobile ads will often depict satisfied customers enjoying some special feature of their new car.

The choice of the advertising objective should not be arbitrary but should be based on a thorough analysis of the current marketing situation. For example, if the product class is mature, and the company is the market leader, and if brand usage is low, the proper objective may be to stimulate more brand usage. On the other hand, if the product class is new, and the company is not the market leader, but its brand is superior to the leader, then the proper objective is to advertise the brand's superiority over the market leader.

Thus setting objectives for advertising requires an understanding of the advertising process and the role advertising plays in a products marketing program. We first discuss the influence of the single advertisement on a potential buyer and then review the influence of a whole advertising campaign.

The Influence of a Single Ad.   Consider a single ad inserted in a particular medium. The difficulty of estimating the resulting exposure varies for the different media. In the case of TV the exposure value of the ad is related to audience size, which can be measured, albeit with some error, by various TV-media-rating services. (BehaviorScan and similar commercial "single-source" data organizations—integrating purchase diaries with TV and other media consumption—can provide accurate exposure measures for frequently purchased items.) We will ignore for the present the desirability of weighting the exposures differently for the buying power of the persons exposed, a refinement that will be taken up later in the media-decision section.

Then only a fraction of the number of persons who are exposed to the media vehicle carrying the advertisement will actually see the advertisement, where seeing the advertisement is measured by finding out whether the person recognizes or can recall it. Let this fraction be f_1. Furthermore, only a fraction of those who see the advertisement registers or comprehends the message. Let this fraction be f_2. Although the advertisement has some value if it is only seen (in creating or maintaining brand identification), it has more value if the person can recall the appeals. Finally, some fraction of those who register the advertisement will be moved by the appeals (which will be related to the quality of the advertisement). Let this fraction be f_3. It is this effect that finally enters into the effective value of the advertising insertion, $V(E_A)$. In summary, the actual effective value of a single advertisement is given by

$$V(E_A) = f_1 f_2 f_3 E_A \tag{6.1}$$

where

$$
\begin{aligned}
V(E_A) \;=\;& \text{effective value of single advertising insertion}\\
f_1 \;=\;& \text{percentage of persons exposed to medium who have seen advertisement (exposure value)}\\
f_2 \;=\;& \text{percentage of persons seeing advertisement who registered message}\\
f_3 \;=\;& \text{percentage of persons registering message who were favorably impressed}\\
E_A \;=\;& \text{average number of persons exposed to medium carrying advertisement}
\end{aligned}
$$

Thus the effective value of a single advertising insertion is not given by its exposure value but is possibly by much less, depending on the values of the various downward adjustments for audience shrinkage. Advertising-readership-measurement services tend to supply management with some measure of f_1 and f_2 based on controlled-sampling techniques. The fraction f_3 is harder to define and measure, although field surveys aim to provide this information as well. Note that estimates of f_2 and f_3 can be obtained from advertising pretests.

The Influence of an Ad Campaign. As noted earlier, the timing of ads and their spacing within a purchase cycle may influence the buyer: there may be too few repetitions for an ad to rise above a threshold, and too many ads may be counterproductive. Thus a central objective of advertising decision makers is to determine the minimum exposure frequency per period that will accomplish the advertising objectives of the advertiser. (See Naples, 1979, and Rossiter and Percy, 1987, for full discussions on "minimum effective frequency.")

Setting Goals. To the extent that the advertiser has realistically appraised the manner in which advertising might influence the sales of his brand, he is able to decide on goals for the advertising program. As an example, consider a company that is preparing to set advertising objectives for two of its brands, A and B, with equal sales. For each brand the company has conducted marketing research to determine the number of persons in the market and the percentage distribution of these persons in three classes: awareness, brand trial, and satisfaction. Brand A, with low awareness, low trial, but highly satisfied customers (among triers), should have an ad campaign stressing awareness and trial. Brand B, with high awareness, high trial, and low satisfaction, has had an effective ad campaign but is not delivering to the consumer what the ad is promising.

The company's advertising goals for a brand are suggested by this type of analysis; the company can identify the type of advertising job it must do and the cost of doing it.

Setting the Advertising Budget. Each year the firm must decide how much to spend on advertising. Four of the more common methods for making this decision are described shortly. Patti and Blasko (1981) and Blasko and Patti (1984) provide some statistics on the prevalence of these methods for consumer marketers and industrial marketers, respectively. (In the discussion that follows, we use C to refer to the consumer percentage of firms that report using the method and I to refer to the industrial percentage.)

Affordable Method ($I = 20\%$, $C = 33\%$). Many companies set the advertising budget on the basis of what they think the company can afford. As explained by one advertising executive,

> Why it's simple. First, I go upstairs to the controller and ask how much they

can afford to give us this year. He says a million and a half. Later, the boss comes to me and asks how much we should spend, and I say, "Oh, about a million and a half." Then we have an advertising appropriation. *(Seligman, 1956, p. 123)*

Setting budgets in this manner is tantamount to saying that the relationship between advertising expenditure and sales results is at best tenuous: whatever funds the company has available, it should spend on advertising as a form of insurance. The basic weakness of this approach is that it leads to a fluctuating advertising budget that makes it difficult to plan for long-range market development.

Percentage-of-Sales Method (Anticipated: I = 16%, C = 53%; Past year's: I = 23%, C = 20%). Many companies set their advertising expenditures at a specified percentage of sales (either current or anticipated) or of the sales price. For example, a railroad company executive once said,

> We set our appropriation for each year on December 1 of the preceding year. On that date we add our passenger revenue for the next month, and then take 2 percent of the total for our advertising appropriation for the new year. *(Frey, 1955, p. 65)*

Furthermore, automobile companies typically budget a fixed percentage for advertising based on the planned price of each car, and oil companies tend to set the appropriation as some fraction of a cent for each gallon of gasoline sold under their own label.

A number of advantages are claimed for this method. First, advertising expenditures are likely to vary with what the company can afford. Second, it encourages management to think in terms of the relationship between advertising cost, selling price, and profit per unit. Third, to the extent that competing firms spend approximately the same percentage of their sales on advertising, it encourages competitive stability.

In spite of these advantages, the percentage-of-sales method has little to justify it. It uses circular reasoning in viewing sales as the cause of advertising rather than as the result, and it leads to an appropriation set by the availability of funds rather than by the opportunities. Furthermore, the method does not provide a logical basis for the choice of a specific percentage, except what has been done in the past, what competitors are doing, or what the costs will be. Finally, it does not encourage the constructive development of advertising appropriations on a product-by-product and territory-by-territory basis but instead suggests that all allocations be made at the same percentage of sales.

Competitive-Parity Method (I = 21%, C = 24%). Some companies set their advertising budgets specifically to match competitors' outlays—that is, to maintain competitive parity. This thinking is illustrated by the executive who asked a trade source, "Do you have any figures that other companies in the builders' specialties field have used that would indicate what proportion of gross sales should be given over to advertising?" (Frey, 1955, p. 49).

Two arguments are advanced for this method. One is that competitors' expenditures represent the collective wisdom of the industry. The other is that maintaining a competitive parity helps to prevent advertising wars. But neither of these arguments is valid. There are no a priori grounds for believing that the competition is using more logical methods for determining outlays. Advertising reputations, resources, opportunities, and objectives are likely to differ so much among companies that their budgets are hardly a guide for another firm to follow. Furthermore, there is no evidence that appropriations based on the pursuit of competitive parity do, in fact, stabilize industry advertising expenditures.

Knowing what the competition is spending on advertising is undoubtedly useful information. But it is one thing to have this information and another to follow it blindly.

Objective-and-Task Method (I = 74%, C = 63%). The objective-and-task method calls upon advertisers to develop their budget by (1) defining their advertising objectives as specifically as possible, (2) determining the tasks that must be performed to achieve these objectives, and (3) estimating the costs of performing these tasks. The sum of these costs is the proposed advertising budget (Colley, 1975; Wolfe, Brown, and Thompson, 1962).

Advertising goals should be formulated as specifically as possible in order to guide the copy development, the media selection, and the measurement of results. The stated goal "to create brand preference" is much weaker than "to establish 30% preference for brand X among Y million housewives by next year." Colley listed as many as 52 specific communication goals, including the following:

> Announce a special reason for buying now (price premium, etc.).
> Build familiarity and easy recognition of the package or trademark.
> Place advertiser in a position to select preferred distributors and dealers.
> Persuade the prospect to visit a showroom and ask for a demonstration.
> Build morale of the company's sales force.
> Correct false impressions, misinformation, and other obstacles to sales.

This method has strong appeal and popularity among advertisers. Its major limitation is that it does not indicate how the objectives themselves should be chosen and whether they are worth the cost of attaining them. Indeed, Patti and Blasko (1981) report that 51% of major consumer advertisers use quantitative methods to set their budgets, although the figure for industrial advertisers is a disappointing 3% (Blasko and Patti, 1984).

Model-Based Approaches. In recent years there has been significant research in the development of decision models for setting advertising budgets. The related articles in this area have focused on the size and allocation of the advertising budget. While the research efforts differ widely on their purpose, methodology, and so on, most can be viewed being closely related to the following general form:

Find $A_i(t)$ to

$$\text{maximize } Z = \underbrace{\sum_i \sum_j \sum_t S_i(t|\{A_i(t)\}, \{C_{ij}(t)\}) \cdot m_j}_{\text{gross profit}} - \underbrace{\sum_i \sum_t A_i(t)}_{\text{advertising spending}} \qquad (6.2)$$

Subject to

$$\sum_i \sum_t A_i(t) \le B, \text{ budget constraint}$$

$$L_i \le \Sigma A_i(t) \le U_i, \text{ regional constraint}$$

where

$S_i(t|\{A_i(t)\}, \{C_{ij}(t)\})$	=	sales in area i at time t as function of current and historical brand and competitive advertising
$C_{ij}(t)$	=	competitive advertising for competitor j in area i
$A_i(t)$	=	advertising level in area i at time t
m_i	=	margin per unit sales in area i
$\{A_i(t)\}$	=	entire advertising program
U_i, L_i	=	upper, lower regional constraints
B	=	budget constraint

The quantitative models reviewed here differ most importantly in their specifications of the form of $S_i(t)$.

As the review in the last section indicated, there is a set of major advertising phenomena that a response model should exhibit. But approaches have varied in form and to the extent that these phenomena are incorporated. Some researchers have developed a priori models (Little, 1979b) designed to postulate a general structure. Examples of this approach are the models of Vidale and Wolfe (1957), Nerlove and Arrow (1962), Little (1966, 1975), Simon (1982), Basu and Batra (1988), Zufryden (1989), and Mahajan and Muller (1986a). Another approach is essentially econometric and starts with a specific data base, usually a time series of sales and advertising. These models include those by Bass (1969b), Bass and Clarke (1972), Montgomery and Silk (1972), Lambin (1976), Rao and Miller (1975), and Eastlack and Rao (1986). We review several of these model forms next.

A Priori Models.   In Appendix A we develop the Vidale-Wolfe (1957) model. When compared with Little's catalog of desirable phenomena, we find that (1) it has different rise and decay times, in accordance with his first phenomenon; (2) the response cannot be S-shaped and the model has zero sales at zero advertising, contrary to his second phenomenon; (3) the model has no provision for competitive advertising, contrary to his third phenomenon; (4) changes in copy or media effectiveness are not included, contrary to his fourth phenomenon; and (5) temporary sales increases do not decay with constant advertising, contrary to his fifth phenomenon. Similarly, Little (1979b) shows that the Nerlove-Arrow model fails on all five phenomena and that his BRANDAID model, reviewed in detail in Chapter 11, handles the first, second, and fourth phenomena; treats the third phenomenon (competition) in a special way, external to the advertising model; but provides no mechanism for the temporary sales increases of his fifth phenomenon.

Timing/Pulsing Models.   The issue of advertising scheduling, specifically, on whether advertising programs should be steady or turned on and off (or *pulsed*) has captured the recent attention of marketing scientists. Two interesting models have been proposed by Simon (1982) and by Mahajan and Muller (1986a).

EXAMPLE _____

Simon's (1982) ADPULS model was designed to deal with the issue that advertising wears out over time (Haley, 1978; Little, 1979b), while few models are able to address this phenomenon, characterized in Exhibit 6.8.

In order to deal with this phenomena, Simon proposes the following model:

$$q_t = f(A_t, \bar{A}_t, q_{t-1}) + \max[0, g(\Delta A_t)] \qquad (6.3)$$

where

q_t = sales (or market share) at t.
A_t = advertising effort in period t.
$\bar{A}_t$ = competitive advertising at t.
ΔA_t = $A_t - A_{t-1}$ or $(A_t - A_{t-1})/A_{t-1}$
$g(\cdot)$ = a positive transformation of the difference between A_t and the anchor value, A_{t-1}.

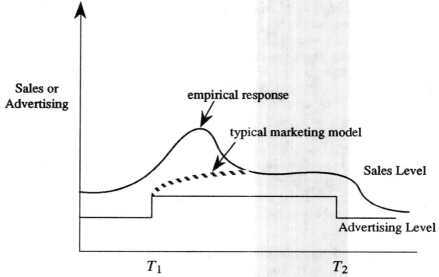

EXHIBIT 6.8 Typical marketing models deal with downward adjustment in sales after a drop in advertising spending $(t > T_2)$ but do not handle an increase in ad spending properly $(T_1 < t < T_2)$.

max($\cdot$) = used to represent the asymmetry between upward and downward response as indicated in Exhibit 6.8.

In an empirical application, Simon uses the following form:

$$q_t = a + \lambda q_{t-1} + b \ln A_t + c \max(0, \Delta A_t) \qquad \textbf{(6.4)}$$

and

$$\Delta A_t = (A_t - A_{t-1})/A_{t-1}$$

(In one case he uses the form $[A_{t-5}(A_{t-1} + A_{t-2})]/5(A_{t-1} - A_{t-2})$, arguing that it fits the empirical data better.)

The model gives decreasing marginal returns to advertising (through $\ln A_t$) and is interpreted as a partial adjustments model, with λq_{t-1} representing customer holdover and not lagged advertising (see Saunders, 1987, for a discussion of the differences here). Note that the model excludes competitive effects due to lack of availability of the data. Using generalized least squares (to account for autocorrelated errors), Simon reports adjusted R^2 values of between 0.91 and 0.99 and excellent visual tracking of the data.

He formulates an objective function as the net present value of accumulated contribution margins:

$$\pi_t = \sum_{\tau=0}^{T} (dq_{t+\tau} - A_{t+\tau})\, z^{\tau} \tag{6.5}$$

where

π_t = net present value of profit stream, beginning at time t
d = contribution margin (assumed constant)
z = $1/(1 + r)$, the discount factor, when r = discount rate

Simon introduces the term m as:

$$m = \frac{d}{(1 - \lambda z)} \tag{6.6}$$

that is,

$$m = \lim_{T \to \infty} d \sum_{t=0}^{T} \lambda^t z^t$$

(i.e., m is the marketing multiplier, the total cumulative marginal effect of advertising in present value terms relative to its short-term effect, d).

He then shows that his model admits three possible policies:

Policy 1: No pulse (constant advertising)
Policy 2: Alternating pulse (pulse—no pulse—pulse—etc.)
Policy 3: Repeat pulse (pulse—pulse—no pulse—pulse—pulse—etc.)

Exhibit 6.9 gives the optimal ad budgets for each of these three policies. Note that, relative to the constant budget, mb, the pulse budget (policy 2) is higher in the pulse period and lower in the base period. (A similar result holds for policy 3.)

A driving force behind the intensity of the pulse is the parameter, c. Recall that the parameter c measures the intensity of difference between upward and downward response to advertising; thus as c increases the difference between the pulse and nonpulse budgets widens.

Using data for one of the products he studies, Simon shows that alternating pulsation does best, followed by repeat pulsation which in turn is better than the constant spending policy. Indeed, his figures show

	Policy 1 (No Pulse)	Policy 2 (Alternative Pulse)	Policy 3 (Repeat Pulse)
Base	bm	$\dfrac{mb}{(1 + mcz)}$	$\dfrac{mb}{(1 + mcz)}$
Pulse 1	—	$\dfrac{mb}{(1 - mc)}$	$\dfrac{mb}{(1 - mc\,(1 - z))}$
Pulse 2	—	—	$\dfrac{mb}{(1 - mc)}$

EXHIBIT 6.9   Optimal pulse and nonpulse advertising spending levels for ADPULS model.

a present value more than three times greater for alternating pulsation versus repeat pulsation.

Simon's model is an important contribution, as it yields an optimal policy when response is not S-shaped. The pulsing policy is a straightforward result of the asymmetry of response: if, by increasing the level of advertising, the firm gains, but by decreasing it does not lose, then the firm should pulse as often as possible. In addition, the model does not include any consideration of the production scheduling and inventory costs brought about by the pulsing policy, which may render a pulsing strategy nonoperational. It raises questions about how long the pulse/nonpulse periods should be, how competitive advertising (ignored in the specific model analyzed) might affect the results, how copy effectiveness relates to these results, whether pulsing periods should be constant over time and the like.

EXAMPLE

Mahajan and Muller (1986a) deal with pulsing policies, focusing on awareness generation for new products. They assume an S-shaped, steady-state advertising effectiveness function as shown in Exhibit 6.10. Drawing an argument from Sasieni (1971) and Lodish (1971b), they note that a firm will not advertise in the convex part of the curve $(\alpha\bar{u})$, since the effectiveness of this policy, $f(\alpha\bar{u})$, is less than what could be achieved by doing what they call "chattering" between the $u = \bar{u}$ and $u = 0$, and thus yield a response on the tangent line, $\alpha f(\bar{u})$.

They introduce a model to address the question of whether a pulsed advertising schedule is superior to an even policy and, if so, what should be the timing of those pulses be.

They define five policies for investigation:

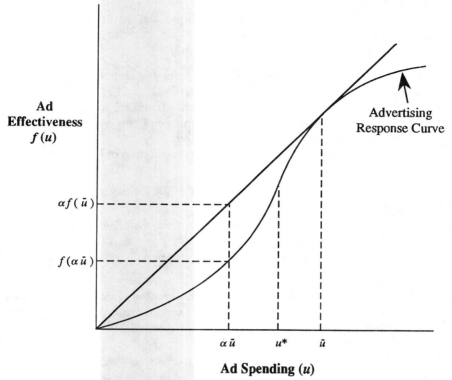

EXHIBIT 6.10   Mahajan and Muller's S-shaped ad effectiveness function. Here, u^* is the point of inflection and $\bar{u}$, the tangent point of line through the origin and the advertising effectiveness curve. The spending level $\alpha \bar{u}$ is in the convex portion of the curve.

Blitz	a one-pulse policy, where the firm concentrates all spending in some initial period.
Pulsing	in which the firm alternates between high and zero levels of advertising. (What other authors call "flighting.")
Chattering	where the firm (theoretically) alternates an infinite number of times between high and zero advertising levels. (A theoretical limit of a pulsing policy when the time between pulses gets arbitrarily small.)
Even	in which the budget is spent at a constant level over the planning period.
Pulse/maintenance	in which any of the policies above is combined with

a nonzero level of advertising during the "off" periods.

Exhibit 6.11 shows these policies (except for chattering, which cannot easily be graphed).

Note that in each case, the firm advertises an amount $\bar{u}\alpha T$ during the time period T. (Note also, that the nature of the S-shaped response precludes spending greater than $\bar{u}$ in any period.

The model they formulate defines pulsing using the following notation:

α = $B/\bar{u}T$, proportion of time (out of time T) that the firm advertises at level $\bar{u}$

k = number of times the firm switches from advertising at $\bar{u}$ to zero

B = ad budget

Note that for the even policy, the level of spending is $\alpha\bar{u}$; for the pulsing policies, either $\bar{u}$ or 0 is spent. For the Blitz policy, $k = 1$ and $u = \bar{u}$ for $0 \le t < \alpha T$, and 0 for $t \ge \alpha T$. In general, in a k-pulsing policy

$$u = \begin{cases} \bar{u} \text{ for } iT/k \le t < (i + \alpha)T/k; 0 \le i \le k - 1 \\ 0 \text{ for } (i + \alpha)T/k \le t \le (i + 1)T/k \\ \text{and for } t = T; 0 \le i \le (k - 1) \end{cases} \tag{6.7}$$

To link advertising pulsing to awareness they use the following functional form:

$$dA/dt = \underbrace{f(u)(1 - A)}_{\substack{\text{Learning} \\ \text{Effect}}} - \underbrace{bA}_{\substack{\text{Forgetting} \\ \text{Effect}}} \tag{6.8}$$

where

A = fraction of market aware of the product at any point in time

b = decay or forgetting parameter

The authors show that using any pulsing policy, awareness is

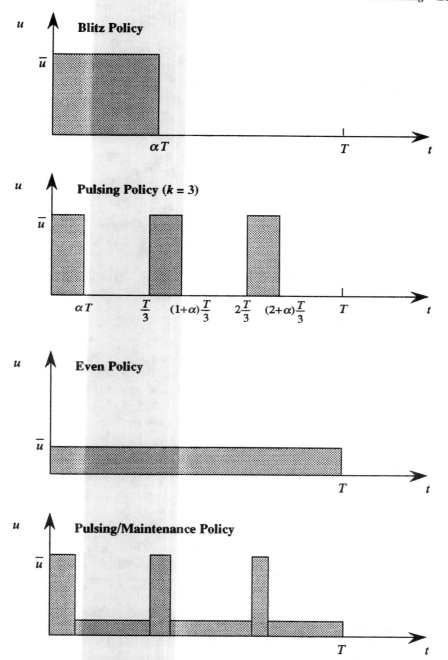

EXHIBIT 6.11 Four categories of advertising policies. (*Source:* Mahajan and Muller, 1986a, p. 92.)

$$A(t) = \begin{cases} A(iT/k)\, e^{(x+b)(iT/k-t)} + \dfrac{x}{x+b}\,[1 - e^{(x+b)(iT/k-t)}], & \text{when advertising} \\[2mm] A[(i+\alpha)T/k]\, e^{b[(i+\alpha)T/k-t]} & \text{when not advertising} \end{cases}$$

$$(6.9)$$

where

$$x = f(\bar{u})$$

Assuming that no advertising after T occurs, the authors evaluate alternative advertising policies on the basis of the "total awareness" they generate:

$$R = \int_0^{\infty} A(t)\, dt \qquad\qquad (6.10)$$

Indexing R by the number of pulses yields R_1 = blitz, R_k = response with k pulses and R_{∞} = chattering.

The authors compare the quantities in Exhibit 6.12 to derive a series of propositions that can generally be summarized as follows:

If the advertising response function is S-shaped:

- Chattering is better than pulsing, which is better than blitz.
- Chattering is better than even.
- Blitz is better than even if $y = f(\alpha\bar{u})$ is "small" (i.e., the more convex the lower part of the curve is, the better blitz is).
- Pulsing/maintenance is dominated by pulsing (i.e., the optimal maintenance level is 0).

Alternatively, for a concave response function, an even spending policy is optimal. The authors do some empirical testing and some simulations to demonstrate the applicability of their results.

Mahajan and Muller take a careful look at pulsing policies under an S-shaped response assumption. Their results show how much results degrade from the chattering ideal when a small number of pulses (or an even policy) is applied. Their calculation assumes that a fixed, known S-shaped response function exists however and, as Little (1986) points out in a comment, their results highlight the need for more empirical research on the extent to which S-shaped responses exist (see Simon and

Policy	Total Awareness, R
Blitz $(k = 1)$	$$\frac{\alpha x T}{(x + b)} + \frac{x^2\left[1 - e^{-\alpha(x+b)T}\right]}{b\,(x + b)^2}$$
Pulsing, any k	$$\alpha x T\,(x + b) + \frac{B\,L\,x^2}{b\,(x + b)^2} \quad \text{where}$$ $$B = \frac{1 - e^{(-\alpha(x+b)\frac{T}{k})}}{1 - e^{-((\alpha x + b)T/k)}} \qquad \text{and}$$ $$L = B\left[1 - e^{-(\alpha x + b)\,T}\right]e^{-(1-\alpha)bT/k} + k\left[1 - e^{-(1-\alpha)\,bT/k}\right]$$
Chattering, $k \Rightarrow \infty$	$$\frac{\alpha x T}{(\alpha x + b)} + \frac{(\alpha x)^2\left[1 - e^{-(\alpha x + b)T}\right]}{b\,(\alpha x + b)^2}$$
Even	$$y T\,(y + b) + \frac{y^2\left[1 - e^{-(y+b)T}\right]}{b\,(y + b)^2}$$

where $x = f(\bar{u})$ and $y = f(\alpha\bar{u})$

EXHIBIT 6.12   Total Impact of Advertising Policies Using Mahajan and Muller's Model

Arndt, 1980, Zielski, 1986, and Mahajan and Muller, 1986b, for further discussion of this latter point and the remaining controversies).

Neither Simon's model nor that of Mahajan and Muller attempt to deal with all of Little's response phenomena; Simon's model can include all but phenomenon 3 (competitive advertising).

EXAMPLE _____

A controversial but clever model that combines data from multiple markets over time is that of *Rao and Miller (1975)*. The main idea behind their approach is that many national advertising campaigns provide a quasi-experimental set of conditions due to natural market-to-market variations in exposure rates and other characteristics. The idea is to derive an advertising-response coefficient from each of a number of sales districts and then to combine those coefficients in a way that produces a general sales-response function.

The authors assume that advertising has an immediate and a lagged effect and that the lagged effect decays exponentially. Although they show how to handle price offers and other trade promotions, we concentrate here only on the aspects of the model that relate to advertising. Their individual market model is

$$S_t = c_0 + c_1 A_t + c_1 \lambda A_{t-1} + c_1 \lambda^2 A_{t-2} + \cdots + \mu_t \qquad (6.11)$$

where

$$
\begin{aligned}
S_t &= \text{market share at } t \\
A_t &= \text{advertising spending at } t \\
c_0, c_1, \lambda &= \text{constants } (\lambda < 1) \\
\mu_t &= \text{random disturbance}
\end{aligned}
$$

This equation means that an incremental expenditure of one unit of advertising in a given period will yield c_1 share points that period, $c_1 \lambda$ in the following period, $c_1 \lambda^2$ the period after that, and so on.

The distributed lag form in equation (6.11) can be simplified by multiplying λ times S_{t-1},

$$\lambda S_{t-1} = \lambda c_0 + \lambda c_1 A_{t-1} + \lambda^2 c_1 A_{t-2} + \cdots + \lambda \mu_{t-1} \qquad (6.12)$$

and subtracting equation (6.12) from equation (6.11):

$$S_t = c_0(1 - \lambda) + \lambda S_{t-1} + c_1 A_t + \mu_t - \lambda \mu_{t-1} \qquad (6.13)$$

Note that the short-run effect of advertising here is

$$\frac{dS_t}{dA_t} = c_1 \qquad (6.14)$$

while the long-run effect is c_1 in the first period, then $\lambda c_1 + \lambda^2 c_1 + \ldots$ in subsequent periods, or

$$c_1 + \lambda c_1 + \lambda^2 c_1 + \cdots + = \frac{c_1}{1 - \lambda} \qquad (6.15)$$

Now if

I = industry sales per year in district
P = district population
AV = average rate of advertising during period

then with k periods per year, by equation (6.15), a \$1,000 increase in advertising produces a share increase of $c_1/(1 - \lambda)$. Thus the sales increase of an additional \$1,000 in advertising is

$$y_i = \Delta\text{sales}_i = \left(\frac{c_1}{1 - \lambda}\right)\frac{I}{k} \quad (\text{in market } i) \qquad \textbf{(6.16)}$$

at a per capita advertising rate of $AV_i/P = x_i$. In other words, equation (6.16) can be interpreted as the derivative of a general response curve at the per capita spending rate AV/P.

This procedure gives a set of values (y_i, x_i) for each market i, where the $\{y_i\}$ are the derivatives of a more general response function $g(x)$, so $y = dg/dx$. Assuming that $g(x)$ is S-shaped, the authors propose using a polynomial in x to approximate it; specifically, they assume that $g(x)$ can be modeled as a cubic function in x, while $y(x)$ is a quadratic function in x:

$$y = k_1 + k_2 x - k_3 x^2 + k_4 z \qquad \textbf{(6.17)}$$

where

z = percentage share of premium brands (an empirical adjustment factor that accounted for variability in marginal response)

$k_1, \ldots, k_4$ = parameters to be estimated

Given a set of $\{y_i\}$ and $\{x_i\}$ (as well as $\{z_i\}$), the coefficients in equation (6.17) can be estimated using standard econometric methods. The total advertising-response function can be obtained simply by integrating equation (6.17). Note that after integration we obtain

$$g(x) = k_0 + k_1 x + \frac{k_2}{2}x^2 - \frac{k_3}{3}x^3 + k_4 z \qquad \textbf{(6.18)}$$

with k_0 unspecified. The authors assume $k_0 = 0$ (zero advertising equals zero sales), but this model can clearly accommodate a nonzero sales level at zero advertising, in line with Little's second phenomenon. Then equation (6.18) can be used in equation (6.2) to allocate an advertising budget over districts and over time.

The basic procedure is illustrated with applications to five brands. The average value of the coefficients of determination (R^2) for the within-market models, equation (6.13), was 0.69, and the average R^2 for the response curves, equation (6.17), was 0.60. Thus the fits appear adequate. Exhibit 6.13(a) graphs the relationship between marginal sales due to advertising and average expenditure levels for one of the five brands reported (brand B), while Exhibit 6.13(b) reproduces the associated advertising-response function. The authors show how this model can be used to evaluate alternative advertising policies, making a case for pulsing when response is S-shaped.

The method appears to have been widely applied, incorporating dealing and price effects as well (Rao, 1978, and Eastlack and Rao 1986, 1989). Some products show S-shaped responses, while others show concave responses. On the other hand, this modeling approach, like most other econometric models, has a variety of weaknesses. Of Little's desirable phenomena, only the second, a possible S-shaped response, is included. However, the model could be extended to include competitive effects (phenomenon 3), and copy/media effectiveness could be included as an effectiveness factor in the x's. Equation (6.13) does not readily admit differing rise and decay times. As with all econometric-based models, the data quality and its variability determine the acceptability of the model fit. In addition, while the authors report S-shaped response, Hanssens, Parsons, and Schultz (1990) criticize their methodology.

In conclusion, this approach is both interesting and useful. It uses econometric methods to estimate local conditions of a (postulated) global response curve. Furthermore, it blends well with the type of data typically collected for frequently purchased packaged goods. Although it has theoretical problems and reports of its use are incomplete, it appears to have considerable applicability.

Other Approaches

Little (1979b) reviews a number of other a priori models and finds that most lack flexibility in rise and decay rates and have constant, concave steady-state responses. Many of the more recent approaches have either considered advertising within the framework of new product situations (e.g., Dockner and Jorgensen, 1988b; Horsky and Simon, 1983; Monahan, 1984; Kalish, 1985; Simon and Sebastian, 1987) or have specifically dealt with advertising in a competitive situation (e.g., Horsky and Mate, 1988, and Erickson, 1985). These issues will be addressed in Chapters 10 and 11.

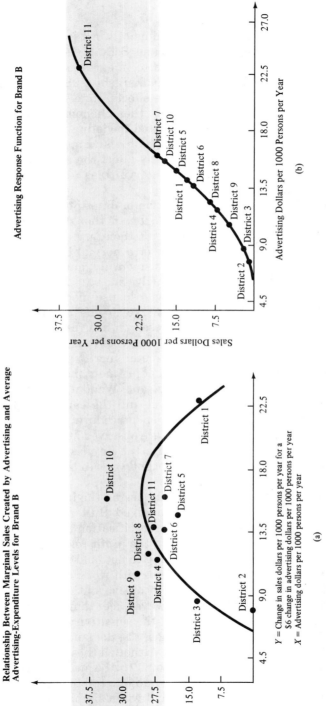

EXHIBIT 6.13 Rao and Miller's econometric model for advertising decisions. (*Source:* Rao and Miller, 1975, p. 13.)

In the econometric area, the volume of work is large and a fine review can be found in Hanssens, Parsons, and Schultz (1990). While historically econometric studies have been limited to linear and log-linear forms, Hanssens and colleagues and Cooper and Nakanishi (1988) report on and review scores of studies including competitive effects, time-varying response parameters, market-brand asymmetries and other phenomena. The availability of better data as well as more sophisticated modeling and estimation methods have made these models much more flexible and more widely used.

Two important issues that crucially affect the applicability of all econometric advertising models are data interval bias and the robustness of the "optimal" ad budget.

Clarke (1976) introduced the notion of data interval bias in a review of the advertising response literature: the idea is that statistically sound results may be "wrong" if the data that support them are aggregated over too long a "data interval." Accounting practice or a normal business convention may result in data being collected biweekly, monthly, quarterly, or the like; however, those intervals are not necessarily the best for inferring market response. Clarke found that advertising response models estimated using annual sales data implied advertising carryover effects 20 to 50 times as long as those using monthly sales. Much research has resulted here. Some empirical work (e.g., Bass and Leone, 1983) suggests that as the data interval gets longer, the short-term response parameter increases and the carryover parameter decreases for Koyck or partial adjustment models. On the other hand, simulation work by Weiss, Weinberg, and Wendal (1983) did not reveal a relationship between aggregation level and the carryover parameter. Vanhonacker (1990) suggests an estimation procedure for situations where the independent and dependent variables are observed at different time intervals. Srinivasan and Weir (1988) summarize the key issues here; however, their work is similar to much of the more recent work in that it relies on simulated rather than real marketing data.

In an interesting set of articles discussing the impact of misspecification of the lag structure the results are also mixed. Bultez and Naert (1979, 1988a) argue that the situations in which misspecification of the response curve are most likely to occur are those in which the profit response curve is relatively flat, that is, large changes in advertising to not lend to major change in profit. In a different context, this is consistent with work reported by Tull and colleagues (1986), where they consider alternative static response curves. Magat, McCann, and Morey (1986, 1988), however, feel that Bultez and Naert's conclusions are a bit too general and that the sensitivity of a firm's profit relates to the specific lag form(s) being studied, the demand function, the cost function, and the discount rate of the firm. Although these sets of discussions have not resolved themselves, they also point to the need for generalizations so that marketing scientists will be better able to tell how sensitive their results are to the specification of the model and when simple methods are sufficient.

Work like that of Assmus, Farley, and Lehmann (1984), using meta-analysis to synthesize what we have learned from econometric studies of the advertising-sales relationship, is particularly important in building marketing generalizations.

An interesting issue that is just beginning to see some research in the advertising budgeting area concerns incorporation of uncertainty and risk preferences in the optimal advertising decision rule. For example, Aykac, Corstjens, Gautschi, and Horowitz (1989) show that if the level of advertising that minimizes the variance in profits (A_v) occurs at other than the expected profit-maximizing spending (A'), then the risk averse manager should spend somewhere between A_v and A'. They point out, therefore, that if applied model aids are to be useful, they must incorporate real-world characteristics (risk preference and uncertainty in responses function estimates).

Perhaps, because of the lack of understanding about the effectiveness of advertising response, industry-norm models are quite widely used. The basic premise is that, on average, market factors will drive competitors to advertise at efficient levels and that careful study of those norms can be used to guide budget-setting practice. Lilien and Weinstein (1984) and Farris and Buzzell (1979) provide examples of this model-based approach, which is particularly appropriate for industrial markets.

In conclusion, then, advertising is rich with phenomena, many of which occur regularly in reported empirical studies. But more needs to be known about the dynamics of the effects and their estimation.

Advances in measurement, particularly from the point-of-sale equipment in retail stores, are refining our understanding of advertising phenomena, leading to further refinements of advertising models and better advertising decisions.

MESSAGE AND COPY DECISIONS

Much of the effect of an advertising exposure depends on the creative quality of the ad itself. But rating the quality of the ad is extremely difficult, and much controversy surrounds the area of copy testing. An advertisement may have very good aesthetic properties and win awards, and yet it may not do much for sales. Another advertisement may seem crude and offensive, and yet it may be a major force behind sales. Such properties in advertisements as humor, believability, informativeness, simplicity, and memorability have not shown consistent relationships with sales generation. In this section we discuss three issues: copy testing and the measurement of copy effectiveness, the rating of the creative quality of ads, and the proper number of ads to screen.

Copy Testing and Measures of Copy Effectiveness

Copy strategy is based on advertising objectives. For a new brand, copy is oriented toward building broad awareness and inducing trial, while for established brands it focuses on reminding individuals to use the brand, increasing the rate of use, and distinguishing the brand from other brands. Thus the ad-creation process involves finding the facts and ideas that match a brand's message with its copy objectives.

The basis of copy testing is to determine if an ad is likely to work. There are two elements involved in copy testing: the dependent-variable measure and the measurement setting. The possible measures of response include the following:

1. Attention and impression—the ability of the ad to attract attention and be memorable

2. Communication/understanding—the ability of the ad to convey the message clearly and unambiguously to the target market

3. Persuasion—the ability of the ad to modify attitudes and beliefs about the product on certain key attributes or to change overall purchase intentions

4. Purchase—the ability of the ad to generate a positive impact on purchasing behavior

The last two measures, while most appropriate, are also the most difficult to measure.

Copy tests can also be classified by whether they use a laboratory setting, a simulated natural environment, or a totally natural environment (i.e., market tests). Laboratory and simulated-natural-environment methods include focus group interviews as well as a variety of physiological recording devices, including eye cameras (measuring eye movement), polygraphs and related devices (measuring emotional/psychological responses), pupilometers (measuring pupil dilation, which occurs when something interesting is seen), and the like.

In simulated natural environments, subjects are usually brought to a theater, and measures of interest, liking, and often likelihood of purchase before and after exposure are obtained from them. Some procedures provide on-line measurements during exposure. For example, Schwerin shows ads in a program environment and measures changes in liking arising from the ad.

Market tests are provided by a number of companies. Usually, the campaign is limited to a small region, and various measures of recall and preference are asked of those exposed/not exposed to the ad. Burke's Ad Tel and IRI's BehaviorScan can use split-cable techniques and personal interviews, plus a mail panel, to measure the effects of ads.

These methods provide some measures that may (or may not) be related to product sales. In an interesting cross-cultural comparison of attitudes toward copy testing, Boyd and Ray (1971) found that emphasis is placed on predictive validity, explanatory power, and reliability and that sales should not be used as a criterion because of measurement problems.

EXAMPLE

Developing AT&T's Cost of Visit Campaign. Kuritsky and colleagues (1982) report on the development and testing of a new ad copy program for AT&T Long Lines—the "cost of visit" campaign. The research they report doing involved five years, cost over $1 million and had four "projects": (1) a segmentation study of the residential long-distance market, (2) tracking studies to test customer awareness of interstate phone rates, (3) qualitative research on customer attitudes to develop an ad concept, and (4) a large-scale, split-cable experiment that measured the effect of the program in the marketplace.

The first project established that there was a light user group that looked (demographically) just like the heavy user group, but which thought phoning was expensive: they had a "price barrier." The second phase showed that most people overestimated the cost of long-distance phoning by over 50%. The third phase established the "cost of visit" theme, involving four elements:

1. *Surprise* that the cost is so low.

2. *Appropriateness* of a 20-minute "visit" on the phone

3. *Maximum cost* ($3.33 or less)

4. *Taxes included* (no hidden costs)

The fourth phase of the study was the AdTel, split-cable experiment. In the AdTel system, two cables distribute programming to user. A geographic area is divided into small cells of 40–50 subscribers in a checkerboard pattern, each of which receives either signal "A" or signal "B." (On a checkerboard, the red squares would get program "A," the black squares program "B.")

The cost-of-visit campaign was tested against AT&T's very successful "Reach-Out" Campaign using a panel of 16,000 households. Because there is no (necessary) delay between the time an ad is shown and when someone can make a call, and because AT&T automatically records the transaction, response to advertising in this setting can be read much more clearly than in other field environments. (For example, the data interval bias discussed in the previous section disappears.)

The experiment lasted for over two years and had three phases:

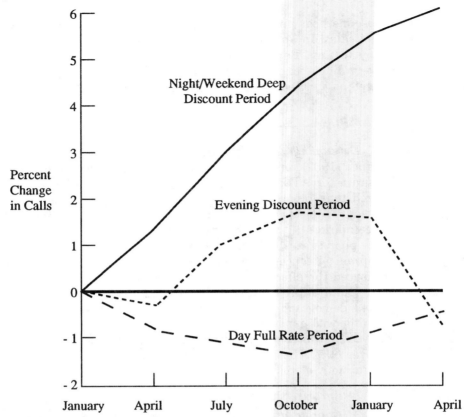

EXHIBIT 6.14 For all usage segments combined, the cumulative difference in calls per telephone number during the 15-month treatment period shows the greatest increase in calls during the night/weekend deep discount period. (*Source:* Kuritsky et al., 1982, p. 28.)

(1) preassessment (5 months), (2) treatment period (15 months), and (3) postassessment (6 months).

During the preassessment phase, records of all households were tracked to establish a norm for their calling behavior. In addition all respondents received a questionnaire to determine if their attitudes were the same as those in the 1975 study and whether the test and control groups were demographically balanced (they were).

During the treatment period the two ad campaigns were aired at a rate that gave each household about three exposures per week. The objective of the "cost-of-visit" campaign was to encourage all user groups, but particularly the light user group, to call during the 60%-off, deep discount period (nights and weekends). Exhibits 6.14 and 6.15 show the results. Overall, an average household made about half again more long

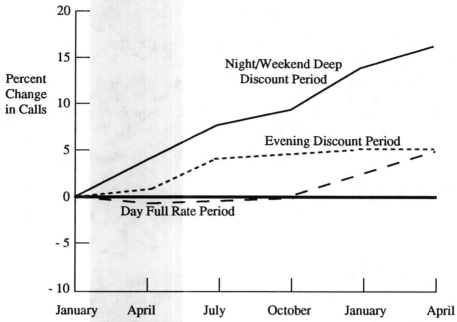

EXHIBIT 6.15 For the targeted light usage segment, the cumulative difference in calls per telephone number during the 15-month treatment period shows a migration from light to heavier use. (*Source:* Kuritsky et al., 1982, p. 29.)

distance call(s) during the deep discount period while the targeted light user group about one and a half more long-distance calls. (These results were significant at the 0.01 level.) In addition, there was an overall increase in revenue of about 1% overall and the targeted light user group yielded a 15% increase in revenue.

In order to make these assessments and to project them to the rational level they used the following definitions:

USDF = usage difference between test group (cost of visit) and control group (Reach-Out)

   = [average usage during treatment − average usage during preassessment for *test group*] *minus* [average usage during treatment − average usage during preassessment for *control group*]

UNOFF = dummy variable

   = $\begin{cases} 0 \text{ for pretest weeks} \\ 1 \text{ for test weeks} \end{cases}$

ε = disturbance

The regression equation

$$USDF = \alpha + \beta UNOFF + \varepsilon \qquad \textbf{(6.19)}$$

models the difference in usage/household/week as a preperiod constant (α) and a treatment constant ($\alpha + \beta$). So the statistical significance of β for any segment (light users in a deep discount period, for example), can be read from standard confidence limits resulting from linear regression analysis.

In order to project the results to the national level, they used the following model:

$$y = \sum_{i=1}^{I} \left(n_i \sum_{j=1}^{J} z_{ij} \, p_{ij} \right) \qquad \textbf{(6.20)}$$

where

y = projected usage in a given area, assuming a given level of advertising exposure

i = index of usage segment (light, regular, etc.), $i = 1, \ldots, I$

j = index of calling category (rate period), $j = 1, \ldots, J$

z_{ij} = usage measure per household in cell i for calling category j

n_i = number of households i of segment type c in the area

p_{ij} = fraction increase or decrease in cell i, category j for "cost of visit" versus "reach-out"

The national or any regional projection can be made by summing over the appropriate areas.

The results of the analysis showed that AT&T could expect to earn more than \$100 million more from the light user segment without any increase in capital expenditures by introducing this new ad copy.

This study is one of relatively few (Bloom, Jay, and Twyman, 1977; Rao, 1978; Rhodes, 1977) that has demonstrated a significant impact on purchase behavior in usage based on a variation in ad copy strategy. It demonstrates the effectiveness of a systematic approach for testing ad copy.

Other reports on the techniques, design, value, and limitations of copy-testing procedures include the work of Young (1972); Dunn and Ziff (1974); Roshwalb (1975); Silk (1977); Ostlund, Clancy, and Sapra (1980); and Hodock (1980).

Estimating the Creative Quality of Ads

Several studies have attempted to relate desirable characteristics of ads to quantifiable mechanical and message elements. Most of these studies have focused on readership or recall scores for print ads, the easiest types of ads and response variables to measure. An interesting early study of this type, performed by Twedt (1952), regressed readership scores of 151 advertisements in *The American Builder* against a large number of variables and found that the parameters of size of the advertisement, size of illustration, and number of colors account for over 50% of the variance in advertising readership. Interestingly, these mechanical variables explained advertising-readership variation better than many of the content variables that were also tried out in the regression.

A well-known regression study of the effect of advertising format variables on readership scores was performed by Diamond (1968). His data were 1,070 advertisements that appeared in *Life* between February 7 and July 31, 1964. For each advertisement he had six different Starch readership scores: noted, seen associated, and read most for both men and women readers. In addition to these six Starch scores, he measured 12 variables related to each ad: product class, past advertising expenditure, number of ads in issue, size, number of colors, bleed/no bleed, left or right page, position in magazine, layout, number of words, brand prominence, and headline prominence.

Diamond fitted several regression models and used the coefficients to draw conclusions about the effect of different variables on readership score. He found that the Starch score was higher the larger the advertisement, the greater the number of colors, and the fewer the number of advertisements in the issue; he found that right-hand-page advertisements gained more attention than did left-hand-page advertisements, that advertisements with photographs did better than advertisements with illustrations, and that both did better than nonpictorial advertisements.

In a study of the effectiveness of industrial print ads, Hanssens and Weitz (1980) related 24 ad characteristics to recall, readership, and inquiry generation for 1,160 industrial ads in *Electronic Design*. They used a model of the form

$$y_i = e^a \prod_{j=1}^{p_t} x_{ij}^{bj} \prod_{j'=p_{t+1}}^{p} (1 + x_{ij'})^{bj'} e^{\mu_i} \tag{6.21}$$

where

y_i = effectiveness measure for ith ad

x_{ij} = value of jth nonbinary characteristic of ith ad (page number, ad size), $j = 1, ..., p_t$

$$x_{ij}' = \text{value}(0 \text{ or } 1) \text{ of } j' \text{th binary characteristic of } i \text{th ad (bleed, color, etc.)} \quad j' = p_{t+1}, \ldots, p$$

e^a = scale factor

μ_i = error term

They segmented 15 product groups into three categories—routine purchase items, unique purchase items, and important purchase items—by factor analysis of purchasing-process similarity ratings obtained from readers of the magazine. Their results are similar to those of Twedt (1952) and Diamond (1968): advertising characteristics were found to account for more than 45% of the variance in the seen effectiveness measure, more than 30% of the read-most effectiveness measure, and between 19 and 36% of the variance in inquiry generation. Thus the variance explained by the seen measure is significantly greater than that explained by the read-most measure, which, in turn, is greater than that explained by the inquiry measure. These results are consistent across the three product categories. They are also in line with a hierarchy-of-effects model, which postulates that communication variables typically have a greater effect on lower-order responses (awareness) than on higher-order responses (behavior).

Both recall and readership were found to be strongly related to format and layout variables (ad size, colors, bleed, use of photographs/illustrations, etc.), while the effects were weaker for inquiry generation. The effects of some factors, such as ad size, were consistently related across product groups and effectiveness measures, while others, such as the use of attention-getting methods (woman in ad, size of headline, etc.), were specific to the product category and the effectiveness measure.

As noted earlier, the only reported similar study for broadcast ads was that of Sewall and Sarel (1986). Much of the research cited here and in the previous section uses some recall measure(s) as dependent variable(s) (rather than an action measure) and neglects the effect of timing of exposures; measures of advertising believability, validity and reliability assessment, and the like. (See Rossiter and Percy, 1987, Ch. 19, for a good discussion of the practical issues involved in ad testing.)

More research is needed on how individuals process the information in ads, how to measure ad effects, and how to link those effects to ad copy development. (See Finn, 1988, Bagozzi and Silk, 1983, and Gatignon, 1984, for discussion of some of the critical issues here.)

How Many Advertisements Should Be Created and Pretested?

When an advertising agency undertakes the development of a creative campaign for a client, the agency generally does not stop with the first idea it develops. The first creative idea may be the best, but typically it is not. Often, the client wants the agency to create and test a few alternative ideas before making a selection. The more advertisements (which we use here to mean advertising campaign themes) that the agency creates and pretests, the higher is the probability that it will find a really first-rate one. But the more time it spends trying to create alternative advertisements, the higher its costs are. Therefore, there must be some optimal number of alternative advertisements that an agency should try to create and test for the client.

If the agency were reimbursed by the client for the cost of creating and pretesting more advertisements, then the agency might create the optimal number of advertisements for pretesting. Under the normal commission system, in which the agency's income is mainly a 15% commission on media billings, the agency does not have an incentive to go through the expense of creating and pretesting many alternative advertisements. This question was studied in an ingenious way by Gross (1972), who concluded that agencies generally create too few advertisements for pretesting. This result means that the advertiser does not typically get the best ad for his money but only the best (it is hoped) of the few that have been created. Here we examine his reasoning.

EXAMPLE

Gross developed three models for (1) the creation of alternative advertisements, (2) the screening of advertisements, and (3) the determination of the optimal expenditures. In the first model he visualizes each of n creative men given the same data on a product and asked to create an advertisement independently. He assumes that each resulting advertisement has a certain level of effectiveness that must be measured by a pretest measure and that the individual effectivenesses of the n advertisements are normally distributed. An advertisement at the center of the distribution has an average effectiveness, and the other advertisements are better or worse than this one. Let E stand for the relative effectiveness of an advertisement—that is, its effectiveness relative to an average advertisement—which can be defined as the discounted present value of the increment in net profits over the profits from an average advertisement that would accrue with that advertisement. Therefore, the distribution of the relative effectiveness of all possible advertisements has a mean relative effectiveness of zero—that is, $\mu_E = 0$—and a standard deviation of relative effectiveness of σ_E.

Thus, creating n different advertisements independently is like making n independent draws from the relative effectiveness distribution. Presumably, the greater the number of advertisements generated, the better the best one will be. At the same time it is assumed that the average cost of creating an advertisement is c. Therefore the cost of creating n independent advertisements is

$$C_{cn} = cn \tag{6.22}$$

where

C_{cn} = cost of creating n advertisements at average cost of c
c = average cost of creating advertisements
n = number of advertisements created

The second model deals with the pretesting of the n advertisements to determine the best one. There are many different ways to pretest advertisements, and each may differ in its reliability and its validity. The observed pretest score of advertisement j on the ith replication of the pretest is given by

$$0_{ij} = \mu_0 + T_{ij} + t_{ij}, \qquad j = 1, 2, \ldots, n; \quad i = 1, 2, \ldots, r \tag{6.23}$$

where

0_{ij} = observed score of advertisement j on the ith replication of the pretest
μ_0 = mean pretest score for all advertisements generated by independent processes
T_{ij} = true deviation of jth advertisement's score from the mean of all scores
t_{ij} = deviation from true score of advertisement j introduced by random error in the ith replication of testing procedure

Thus the observed score of advertisement j of the ith replication of the pretest is equal to the sum of the mean score of all advertisements, the true deviation of this advertisement's quality from the average quality, and the error occurring on this replication. Replication error arises from differences between samples and the administration of the sampling procedure. It is assumed that this error is normally distributed with a mean of zero and a variance of σ_t^2.

The range of variation in the quality of advertisements can also be assumed to be normally distributed with a mean of zero and a variance of σ_T^2. If a number of advertising alternatives were independently generated and tested just once each with the pretest, the observed variance σ_0^2 would be

$$\sigma_0^2 = \sigma_T^2 + \sigma_t^2 \tag{6.24}$$

The relationship in equation (6.24) enables us to use the following measure of reliability for a particular pretest:

$$R = \left(1 - \frac{\sigma_t^2}{\sigma_0^2}\right) \tag{6.25}$$

This measure produces a number between zero and one. When there is no measurement variance—that is, $\sigma_t^2 = 0$—the reliability of the pretest is one, as it should be. When there is a considerable measurement variance in relation to true quality variance —that is, $\sigma_t^2 \rightarrow \sigma_0^2$—the reliability of the pretest approaches zero. This formula for reliability is quite operational, because σ_t^2 may be estimated empirically by testing the same advertisement several times and σ_T^2 may be estimated by observing the scores achieved by a number of alternative advertisements.

Gross defines the validity of the particular pretesting procedure to be the correlation ρ between the advertisement's true pretest score and its relative profit effectiveness. A correlation of $+1$ means that the pretest measure correlates perfectly with the advertisement's relative effectiveness, and a correlation of 0 means that the pretest measure is really of no use in identifying the better advertisements.

With these definitions of the reliability and validity of a particular pretesting procedure, Gross shows that the expected relative profitability of the advertisement that achieves the highest pretest score is

$$V_n = e_n \sigma_e \rho R \tag{6.26}$$

where

V_n = expected relative profitability of advertisement that achieves the highest score on the pretest when the sample size is n

e_n = expected value of the advertisement having the greatest relative effectiveness in a sample of size n from a standardized normal distribution of relative effectiveness

σ_e = standard deviation of the relative-effectiveness distribution

ρ = validity of the particular pretesting procedure, that is, the correlation between the true score on the pretest and the relative effectiveness of advertisement

R = reliability of the particular pretesting procedure, as defined earlier

According to equation (6.26), the expected relative profitability of the best scoring advertisement on the pretest is higher (1) the higher the expected value of the advertisement (which is a function of the number of advertisements independently drawn), (2) the higher the standard deviation in the quality of the possible advertisements, and (3) the higher the validity and reliability of the particular pretesting procedure. If the validity and reliability of the pretest were perfect, then the relative profitability of the advertisement would depend only on the number of advertisements drawn and the dispersion of advertising quality.

Each pretesting procedure will have its particular cost, which can be assumed to have the form

$$C_{sn} = C_F + c_s n, \qquad n \geq 2 \qquad \qquad (6.27)$$

where

C_{sn} = cost of screening n advertising alternatives over and above the cost of screening one advertisement

C_F = fixed costs of setting up for screening

c_s = marginal screening cost per alternative

n = number of alternatives to be screened

Gross is now able to bring together the two descriptive models into a decision model for determining the number of advertising alternatives to create and screen. The decision model must compare the increases in expected value and in costs from creating and testing more advertisements. At the point at which the incremental expected return is no longer sufficient to cover the incremental cost, the optimal point is reached. Analytically, we find that

$$P_1 = 0 \qquad \qquad (6.28)$$

$$P_n = V_n - g(n - 1) - C_{sn} \quad , \quad n \geq 2 \qquad \qquad (6.29)$$

where

P_n = expected contribution to profits of generating and screening n advertising alternatives instead of just generating one

g = cost of generating each ad alternative beyond the first one

The "best" number of ads to test, then, is that number, n, that maximizes P_n in equation (6.29). Using some "conservative" figures for the variables in that equation, Gross suggested that the optimal expenditure should be about 15% of the advertising budget, more than five times the "typical" value.

Although these specific results have been challenged (see Longman, 1968, for example), Gross's basic result yields important implications for pretesting procedures. He found that the value of pretesting depended more on the validity of the pretest than on its reliability. Furthermore, he found that the higher the validity of the pretest, the greater was the justification for a large sample size to increase reliability.

Although advertisers and agencies pay lip service to Gross's idea of creating more alternatives, Jones (1986, p. 268) comments that "the system is not really concerned with generating a wide range of creative alternatives. It is really concerned with finding an alternative; the elimination of the others becomes a tool for selling this selected one."

MEDIA SELECTION AND SCHEDULING

There are two major areas in which advertising agencies specialize: one is the creative decision, reviewed previously, and the other is the media decision. Media selection is the problem of finding the best way to deliver the desired number of exposures to the target audience and to schedule the delivery of those exposures over the planning period.

The concept of "desired number of exposures" needs elaboration. Presumably, the advertiser is seeking a response to its advertising from the target audience. Assume that the desired response is a certain level of product trial, which depends, among other things, on the level of audience brand awareness. Suppose the rate of product trial increases at a diminishing rate with the level of audience awareness, as shown in Exhibit 6.16(a). Then if the advertiser wants to achieve a product trial rate of, say, T^*, it must achieve a brand-awareness rate of A^*, and the task is to find out how many exposures E^* are needed to produce this awareness.

The effect of exposures on audience awareness depends on the exposures' reach, frequency, and impact. These factors are defined as follows:

Reach (R):   the number of different persons or households exposed to a particular media schedule at least once during a specified time period

Frequency (F):   the number of times within the specified time period that an average person or household is exposed to the message

Impact (I):   the qualitative value of an exposure through a given medium (thus a food ad would have a higher impact in *Good Housekeeping* than it would have in *Popular Mechanics*)

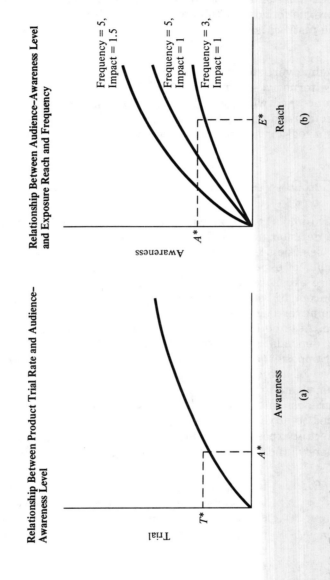

EXHIBIT 6.16 Relationship among trial, awareness, and the exposure function.

Exhibit 6.16(b) shows the relationship between audience awareness and reach. Audience awareness is greater the higher the exposures' reach, frequency, and impact. Furthermore, there are important trade-offs among reach, frequency, and impact. For example, suppose the media planner has an advertising budget of $1 million and the cost per thousand exposures of average quality is $5. Then he can buy 200 million exposures (equal to $1,000,000 $\times$ 1,000/$5). If he seeks an average exposure frequency of 10, then he can reach 20 million people (equal to 200,000,000/10) with the given budget. But if he wants higher-quality media, costing $10 per thousand exposures, he can reach only 10 million people, unless he is willing to lower the desired exposure frequency.

The relationship among reach, frequency, and impact is captured in the following concepts:

Total number of exposures (E) is the reach times the average frequency, that is, $E = R \cdot F$. It is also called gross rating points (GRP). If a given media schedule reaches 80% of the homes with an average exposure frequency of 3, the media schedule is said to have a GRP of 240 (equal to $80 \cdot 3$). If another media schedule has a GRP of 300, it can be said to have more weight, but we cannot tell how this weight breaks up into reach and frequency.

Weighted number of exposures (WE) is the reach times the average frequency times the average impact, that is,

$$WE = R \cdot F \cdot I \qquad (6.30)$$

The media-planning problem can now be viewed as follows. With a given budget, what is the most cost-effective combination of reach, frequency, and impact to buy?

In choosing a combination of media types, the media planner considers (1) target audience media habits, (2) the characteristics of the product, (3) the message, and (4) the relative cost. On the basis of media impacts and costs, the media planner chooses specific media within each media type (women's magazines, daytime TV, daily newspapers in 20 major markets) that deliver the desired response in the most cost-effective way. He or she then makes a final judgment on which specific vehicles will deliver the best communication of reach, frequency, and impact for the money.

Some agencies (and firms) use mathematical models to aid in making media plans. In more quantitative terms the media-decision problem can be stated as follows:

Given a media budget, an advertising message and copy, a set of media alternatives, and data describing the audiences and costs of the media alternatives, decide on (1) the media alternatives to use, (2) the number of insertions in each and their timing, and (3) the type of advertising units (e.g., the size and color for print ads of the media options in each case) in such a way that these decisions maximize the effect (measured in some way) of the media budget.

The output of the media-decision process is called the media schedule.

The Choice of an Objective Function. The most desirable measure of the effect of alternative media schedules is the impact on company profits. Because the media budget is assumed to be fixed, the profit-maximizing schedule is the same as the sales-maximizing schedule. However, most media models do not presume a knowledge of the current or long-run sales that will be generated by advertisements placed in different media. (MEDIAC, reviewed shortly, is an exception.) Various communication surrogates are commonly used to measure the effectiveness of advertising when sales would be difficult or impossible to measure. In media models the surrogate that is used most often is the number of exposures to relevant members in the target audience—that is, the weighted number of exposures, defined earlier.

To determine the total weighted-exposure value of a media schedule, we must know two things: (1) the net cumulative audience of each media vehicle as a function of the number of exposures and (2) the level of audience duplication across all pairs of vehicles. In the case of two media alternatives we would typically have an equation for net coverage as follows:

$$R = r_1(X_1) + r_2(X_2) - r_{12}(X_{12}) \tag{6.31}$$

where

R = reach of media schedule (i.e., total weighted-exposure value with replication and duplication removed)

$r_i(X_i)$ = number of persons in audience of media i

$r_{12}(X_{12})$ = number of persons in audience of both media vehicles

(The $r_i(X_i)$ are typically concave; an old study of the *Saturday Evening Post* showed only 55% more families are reached with 13 issues than with 1 issue.) With three media alternatives their reach would be

$$R = r_1(X_1) + r_2(X_2) + r_3(X_3) - r_{12}(X_{12})$$
$$- r_{13}(X_{13}) - r_{23}(X_{23}) + r_{123}(X_{123}) \tag{6.32}$$

In this case net coverage is found by summing the separate reaches of the three vehicles with the triplicated group and subtracting all the duplicated audiences. This equation can be generalized to the case of n media alternatives.

Obtaining data on the size of audience overlap for different sets of media vehicles requires large and expensive samples. Agostini (1961) has developed a useful estimation formula based on data from a French study of media-audience overlap, showing that total reach for magazine insertions may be estimated by

$$R = \left[\frac{1}{K(D/A) + 1} \right] A \tag{6.33}$$

where

R = total reach

K = constant, estimated as 1.125

A = $\sum_{j=1}^{n} r_j(X_j)$

= total number of persons in audiences of media 1, 2, ..., n

D = $\sum_{j=1}^{n} \sum_{k=j+1}^{n} r_{jk}(X_{jk})$

= total of all pairwise duplicated audiences (if D_{ab} is the number of people simultaneously covered by a and b, then $D = D_{ab} + D_{ac} + \cdots + D_{an} + D_{bc} + \cdots + D_{bn} + \cdots$)

This relationship with parameter $K = 1.125$ has been shown to be a useful approximation for American and Canadian magazines as well (Bower, 1963). See Claycamp and McClelland (1968) for an analytical interpretation of the formula. For alternate approaches, see Metheringham (1964) and Craig and Ghosh (1985). In a review of reach models, Rust (1986) recommends using the Agostini model to estimate the reach of a single vehicle and recommends Hofmans's (1966) model for two or more vehicles. Rust also provides an excellent review of models that have been developed to estimate audience overlap and exposure frequency models. For some other methods for estimating both reach and frequency, see Rice (1988a, b); Rust, Zimmer, and Leone (1986); Lancaster and Martin (1988); and Danaher (1989, 1991).

Because either the GRPs or the weighted number of exposures is normally available for any campaign, equation (6.33) can be used in equation (6.31) to estimate the implied frequency of a schedule. Media-scheduling models have the option of working with a sales objective function, an effective-exposure value, or with reach and frequency separately. The more appropriate sales and effective-exposure measures are also more difficult to operationalize, calling for model-analytic trade-offs. We treat some of these trade-offs in the paragraphs that follow.

Modeling Approaches

There are usually three components in models for media decisions: (1) the objective function, which assigns a value (profit/effective exposures, etc.) to an insertion schedule, (2) the solution strategy (heuristic, optimization, etc.), and (3) the constraints (budget, other).

There are generally five principal components of the objective function:

1. The vehicle exposure measure—used to measure the net reach, schedule exposure, or GRPs.

2. Repetition effect—What is the relative impact of successive exposures on the same person? (The material reviewed earlier suggests this function should be S-shaped.)

3. The forgetting effect—What forgetting occurs between exposures and what is the nature of the decay?

4. The media-option source effect—What is the relative impact exposure from a given source?

5. The segmentation effect—Who is exposed and what is the fraction of the audience that represents target segments?

Media models can usefully be classified by their solution approach: optimizing models and nonoptimizing approaches. Under the optimizing-model category are several classes of mathematical programming models, and within the area of nonoptimizing approaches there are heuristic programming, stepwise or marginal-analysis procedures, and simulation models.

Much of the work on media models in the early and middle 1960s focused on linear programming approaches. The main constraints in the programs were the size of the advertising budget, the minimum and maximum uses of specific media vehicles and media categories, and the desirable, minimum exposure rates to different target buyers. Then the choice of a best plan requires the specification of an effectiveness criterion, which, in media selection, most frequently is the weighted number of exposures.

Linear programming applications to media-scheduling problems include the works of Miller and Starr (1960), Day (1963), Learner (1961), Engel and Warshaw (1964), and others. (See Stewart and Blackwell, 1980, for a more complete review.)

The linear programming approach has several important limitations (Kotler, 1965):

1. Linear programming assumes that each exposure has a constant effect.

2. It further assumes constant media costs (no discounts).

3. It cannot handle audience duplication and replication.

4. It fails to say anything about when the advertisements should be scheduled.

Some of these problems can be addressed by using more advanced programming techniques, such as goal programming (Charnes et al., 1968), separable programming (Brown and Warshaw, 1965), and dynamic programming (Little and Lodish, 1966; Maffai, 1960b). But this tack has not proven fruitful: attempts to use optimizing methods for the media selection decision have fallen far short of their intended mark. A clear trend away from optimization methods and toward nonoptimizing procedures has been evident for some time now (Stewart and Blackwell, 1980, p. 8).

Simple approaches to solving the media-scheduling problem, which are popular with advertising media planners but have attracted little enthusiasm from academic researchers, are the stepwise or marginal-analysis models. These procedures construct a media schedule in steps, at each step introducing the insertion that gives the greatest increase in "effectiveness" for the money (a so-called greedy algorithm). Although this approach handles many of the objections to the mathematical programming approaches, it suffers from the following difficulties (Gensch, 1973):

1. It does not guarantee an optimal or even a near-optimal solution.

2. It does not handle advertising timing.

3. The criterion function is limited.

4. Data demands are somewhat unrealistic.

5. It does not handle carryover effects.

Some of the reported simulation models are those of Gensch (1973), Simulamatics Corporation (1962), the University of London's DYNAMO (1972) system, and Intermarco's (1971) Planex model. The two most critical difficulties with all simulation models are validation, the relationship between the simulated sample and the real world, and optimization—that is, simulation models are designed to be used as evaluative tools, not optimization tools. As such, they complement rather than compete with optimization and stepwise procedures.

Dissatisfaction with the optimization approaches encouraged modelers in the late 1960s and the 1970s to relax the optimization criterion in an attempt to develop more realistic model structures. Now we discuss one of the best known models of this heuristic type, Little and Lodish's MEDIAC model.

EXAMPLE _____

MEDIAC (Little and Lodish, 1969) assumes an advertiser is seeking to buy media for a year with B dollars that will maximize his sales. He can identify S different segments of his market, and for each segment he can estimate its sales potential in time period t:

$$\bar{Q}_{it} = n_i q_{it} \tag{6.34}$$

where

$\bar{Q}_{it}$ = sales potential of market segment i in time period t (potential units per time period)

n_i = number of people in market segment i

q_{it} = sales potential of person in segment i in time period t (potential units per capita per time period)

The sales potential represents the maximum attainable sales in a segment in a given time period if advertising and other company marketing resources are used maximally. Actual sales are likely to be below potential sales and depend on the per capita advertising exposure level in the segment and time period. The more dollars spent on advertising in media reaching that segment, the higher the per capita exposure level and the higher the percentage-of-sales potential that will be realized. Thus the percentage-of-sales potential realized is a function of the per capita exposure level:

$$r_{it} = f(y_{it}) \tag{6.35}$$

where

r_{it} = percentage-of-sales potential of market segment i that is realized in time period t

y_{it} = exposure level of average individual in market segment i in time period t (exposure value per capita)

As an example of one possible sales function for equation (6.35), Little and Lodish suggest the modified exponential, which shows diminishing marginal returns to increased advertising exposure:

$$r = r_0 + a(1 - e^{-by}) \tag{6.36}$$

where r_0, a, and b are nonnegative constants specific to the product.

Returning to the more general function in equation (6.35), we find that the total sales for the year is given by

$$Q = \sum_{i=1}^{S} \sum_{t=1}^{T} n_i q_{it} f(y_{it}) \tag{6.37}$$

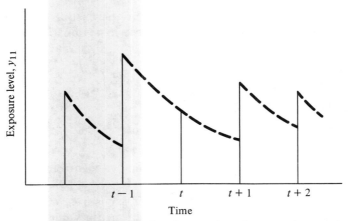

EXHIBIT 6.17 Per capita exposure level over time in a market segment. (*Source: Little and Lodish, 1969, p. 12.*)

that is, the realized sales potentials in each time period summed over all the market segments.

The next task is to indicate how y_{it}, the per capita exposure level in segment i in time period t, is determined. In the absence of new advertising reaching this segment in time period t, the per capita exposure level will be some fraction α of last period's exposure level:

$$y_{it} = \alpha y_{i,t-1} \tag{6.38}$$

The fraction α represents the percentage of the advertising that is remembered from one period to the next by an average person in the segment. If there is new advertising in time period t, then the exposure level this period will be given by the more general expression

$$y_{it} = \alpha y_{i,t-1} + \Delta E_{it} \tag{6.39}$$

where ΔE_{it} is the increase in per capita exposure level in market segment i in time period t due to new advertising reaching this segment.

The net effect of equation (6.39) is a pattern for per capita exposure level over time that resembles that shown in Exhibit 6.17. Between periods of new advertising, the exposure value falls at a diminishing rate because of forgetting. New advertising, on the other hand, increases the exposure value in the segment.

Now we must show the relationship of the increase in exposure value, ΔE_{it}, to purchases of specific media options. The advertiser must decide how many insertions he wants to buy in each available media vehicle in each time period. The increase in per capita exposure value is related to the number of these insertions in the following fashion:

$$\Delta E_{it} = \sum_{j=1}^{n} e_{ij} k_{ijt} x_{jt} \qquad (6.40)$$

where

e_{ij} = exposure value of one exposure in media vehicle j to person in market segment i

k_{ijt} = expected number of exposures produced in market segment i by one insertion in media vehicle j in time t (exposure efficiency)

x_{jt} = number of insertions in media vehicle j in time period t

Suppose that he decides to buy x_{jt} insertions. Each insertion in medium j will yield an exposure value $e_{ij,}$ where

e_{ij} = f(media class, editorial climate of media vehicle j, media option, market segment)

Different media classes have different potentials for demonstration, believability, color, and informativeness. Thus if a food product is involved and color is important, magazines may be given a higher-rated exposure value than newspapers or radio. Furthermore, the editorial climate recognizes that readers have images of particular vehicles that may add or subtract from the believability of the advertisement. In addition, advertising impact increases with the size and use of color in ads and should be reflected in the exposure value. This impact is reflected in the "media-option" factor. Thus the exposure value of an insertion may be assumed to rise with the size of the ad. Finally, the exposure value of an insertion can vary by market segment.

The exposure value of any particular insertion in medium j is a number showing how good this insertion is in relation to a reference insertion in some medium. Suppose that the highest exposure value is arbitrarily called one and is achieved for a particular segment by a two-page, four-color ad in *Time*. Then every other possible media option that might reach this segment is assigned a value relative to this ideal value.

The exposure value of a particular insertion in medium j is further modified by the exposure efficiency k_{ijt} in the particular market segment in the particular time period (see equation 6.39). The exposure efficiency depends on the following factors:

$$k_{ijt} = h_j g_{ij} n_i s_{jt} \tag{6.41}$$

where

h_j = probability of exposure to advertisement in vehicle, given that person is in audience of vehicle j

g_{ij} = fraction of people in market segment i who are in audience of vehicle j (average value over year)

n_i = number of people in market segment i

s_{jt} = seasonal index of audience size for vehicle j in period t (average value = 1.00)

Thus exposure effectiveness reflects the size of the media vehicle's audience at that time of the year, modified by the percentage that are likely to be exposed to the advertisement if they are in the audience of the vehicle.

The description of the MEDIAC model just given must now be embodied in a mathematical programming statement designed to find the best media plan. The problem can be stated as one of trying to find the x_{jt}, for all j and t, that will maximize

$$\sum_{i=1}^{S} \sum_{t=1}^{T} n_i q_{it} f(y_{it}) \tag{6.42}$$

subject to current exposure-value constraints

$$y_{it} = \alpha y_{i,t-1} + \sum_{j=1}^{N} k_{ijt} e_{ij} x_{jt} \tag{6.43}$$

lower and upper media-use-rate constraints

$$l_{jt} \le x_{jt} \le u_{jt} \tag{6.44}$$

a budget constraint

$$\sum_{j=1}^{N} \sum_{t=1}^{T} c_{jt} x_{jt} \le B \tag{6.45}$$

and nonnegativity constraints

$$x_{jt}, y_{it} \geq 0 \qquad \qquad \textbf{(6.46)}$$

In this form the problem has a nonlinear but separable objective function that is subject to linear constraints. If the nonlinear objective function is assumed concave, the problem can be solved by piecewise linear approximation techniques. If it is assumed to be S-shaped and the problem is of modest size, Little and Lodish show that it can be solved by dynamic programming. If the problem is not of modest size, the authors show that satisfactory, though not necessarily optimal, solutions can be obtained through the use of heuristic methods.

The model was extended by Lodish (1971a) to consider the effect of competitors' schedules. This extension is the only reported attempt to incorporate the effect of competition into a media-decision model.

The model formulation, while quite complete, has several weaknesses. It assumes a linear cost structure for media, while actual rates are considerably more complex and often subject to negotiation. Also, the exposure value depends on whether the exposure is the first, second, or nth exposure.

MEDIAC represents an important attempt to include the dimensions of market segments, sales potentials, diminishing marginal returns, forgetting, and timing into a media-planning model. However, its use has been limited by its sophistication: it seems to be too complex for most media planners.

Other heuristic procedures include those by Urban (1975a), Rust and Eechambadi (1989), the SOLEM model (Bimm and Millman, 1978), and Aaker's ADMOD (1975) model.

Since the surge of the 1960s there has been a marked decline in the development of media-decision models. The reason appears to be that satisfactory tools are available for practitioners and that the more complete models bring with them added complexity, which makes them difficult to understand and use (Simon and Thiel, 1980). For example, MEDIAC has not seen much reported use, and the academic literature reports little new in the way of media models. We reported on MEDIAC here because we believe that the increasing availability of "single-source data"—data including media/program consumption along with product purchases—combined with improved computer power will make this an area for further development (Eskin, 1985; Kamin, 1988). For an example of how to model consumer response to an advertising media schedule using split-cable panel data, see Zufryden (1987) and Pedrick and Zufryden (1991); for recent reviews of media decision models, see Rust (1986) and Leckenby and Ju (1989).

SUMMARY

Advertising is one of the most potent tools available to the modern marketer for informing and possibly persuading buyers of the virtues of his product. However, its actual communication effects and sales impact are hard to establish outside of an experimental situation in which everything extraneous is held constant. To guide their budgeting, advertisers need whatever theoretical assistance they can get on how advertising works and what its effect depends on.

A number of general effects of advertising phenomena that impact on advertising-spending policy development, media selection, and copy development strategies were reviewed. Advertising goals should be set with an understanding of the conditions under which an advertising exposure is likely to have an effect. The effect of advertising depends on several qualities of the ad (its creative quality, media class, media vehicle, media option, and time of appearance) and several qualities of the potential buyer (buyer class, buyer state, advertising attentiveness of buyer, and buyer's frequency of exposure to media j). The sales impact of an advertising campaign depends on the number of people in the market in such states as brand awareness, brand acceptability, and brand satisfaction and the power of the campaign to improve the ratios of triers to potential buyers and of users to triers.

Quite a few advertising-response models have been built over the last several years; they fall into two general classes: a priori models and econometric models. A priori models provide a more conceptually sound set of characteristics, while the econometric models are better related to available data. Better data collection, as well as improved and eclectic estimation methods, are leading to a synthesis of these different approaches.

Advertisers are concerned with measuring the quality of the message and the copy making up the advertisement. Various measures have been developed to evaluate the impact of an advertisement or advertising campaign on sales, comprehension, and awareness. The sales impact is the most desirable effect to measure, but most of the successful work has measured the market's awareness of the advertisement. In addition, statistical analyses of readership scores on various content and mechanical features of an ad have been able to show the contribution of different variables to the size of the readership score. An advertising agency usually prepares some alternative ads before testing and selecting one as the most effective. Gross developed a model based on the premise that the more ads an agency prepares, the better the best one will be. He came to the conclusion that advertising agencies tend to spend far too little in creating and screening ads in relation to the amount they spend on media purchases.

The media decision received much early attention from model builders. Most of the resulting models use the weighted number of exposures for judging the merit of a media plan. These media models have been built along the lines of optimizing and nonoptimizing methods. The availability of expert systems and single-source data promises to revitalize interest in this area.

PROBLEMS

6.1. In a given company, let

$$
\begin{aligned}
s &= \text{sales rate, dollars per year} \\
x &= \text{advertising rate, dollars per year} \\
p &= \text{profit rate, dollars per year} \\
c_0 &= \text{fixed-cost rate, dollars per year} \\
g &= \text{incremental profit (before advertising costs) as fraction of sales (assume } g \text{ is constant)}
\end{aligned}
$$

For each of the following sales-response functions;
a. Make a rough sketch of the function
b. Find the advertising rate for maximum profit rate.
c. Find the sales rate at maximum profit rate.

(1) $s = \alpha \ln \beta x$ **(4)** $s = \alpha + \beta(1 - e^{-\gamma x})$

(2) $s = \alpha + \beta \dfrac{(\gamma x)^{\varepsilon}}{1 + (\gamma x)^{\varepsilon}}$ **(5)** $s = \alpha + \beta \left(\dfrac{X}{\beta}\right)^{\gamma}, \quad \gamma < 1$

(3) $s = \alpha + \beta x$

6.2. In Problem 6.1 we expressed advertising in terms of dollar-spending rates, whereas exposure rate is more fundamental. Let

$$
\begin{aligned}
v &= \text{advertising-exposure rates, exposures per year} \\
k &= \text{media efficiency, exposures per dollar} \\
x &= \text{advertising-spending rates, dollars per year}
\end{aligned}
$$

Thus,

$$v = kx$$

Consider the sales-response curves (1), (2), and (4) in Problem 6.1 but with x replaced by v (e.g., $s = \alpha \ln \beta v$).
a. By inspection of Problem 6.1, write down the spending rates for maximum profit.
b. Suppose the advertising agency could make a more efficient media buy, thereby increasing k. Would this company's budget increase or decrease? (Discuss each curve.)

6.3. A model of advertising effects on sales is of the form

$$\frac{dQ}{dt} = \frac{rx(V - Q)}{V} - \lambda Q$$

where

$$
\begin{aligned}
Q &= \text{sales volume} \\
x &= \text{advertising spending} \\
V &= \text{market volume}
\end{aligned}
$$

r = sales-response rate

λ = sales-decay rate

a. Interpret the meaning of the terms in this model, $(V - Q)$, r, and λ, in particular.

b. Suppose that $Q(0) = Q_0$ and $x = 0$ for all future time. Solve for $Q(t)$.

c. Suppose that $Q(0) = 0$ and $x(t) = x$ (constant) for all future t. Solve for $Q(t)$.

6.4. The annual sales for widgets from 1973 to 1989 are given here, along with associated advertising spending. Company management had a major price decrease during the years 1980–1985 that was believed to shift sales upward.

a. Run a simple linear regression of advertising on sales.

b. Add a dummy variable for the years 1980–1985. Are the results significantly different?

c. Interpret the coefficients in your model.

Year	Advertising (in $10 millions)	Sales (in $100 millions)
1973	2.4	2.6
1974	2.8	3.0
1975	3.1	3.6
1976	3.4	3.7
1977	3.9	3.8
1978	4.0	4.1
1979	4.2	4.4
1980*	5.1	7.1
1981*	6.3	8.0
1982*	8.1	8.9
1983*	8.8	9.7
1984*	9.6	10.2
1985*	9.7	10.1
1986	9.6	7.9
1987	10.4	8.7
1988	12.0	9.1
1989	12.9	10.1

*Different pricing program.

6.5. A company's advertising expenditures average \$5,000 per month. Current sales are \$29,000, and the saturation sales level is estimated at \$42,000. The sales-response constant is \$2, and the sales-decay constant is 6% per month. Use the Vidale-Wolfe formula in Appendix C to estimate the probable sales increase next month.

6.6. A firm has determined that the actual effective value of a single advertising insertion for its brand A in a particular medium is 2160. It has also found that the percentage of people exposed to the medium who have seen the ad (f_1) is 0.9, the percentage seeing the ad who register the message (f_2) is 0.6, and the percentage registering the ad who are favorably impressed (f_3) is 0.4. Determine the following:

(1) The percentage of the people exposed to the medium who saw the ad, registered the message, but were not favorably impressed

(2) The percentage of those exposed who saw the ad but did not register the message

      (3) The average number of persons exposed to the medium

6.7. An advertising agency plans to create a number of advertisements for one of its clients and pretest them in order to select the best one. It wishes to know how many advertisements to create and test. The following information has been obtained:

      (1) The average cost of creating and screening one advertisement is about 2.5% of the media budget.

      (2) An outstanding advertisement is one that is at the 3σ level in probability, and in the long run it will return in profits an amount equal to the media expenditure.

      (3) The pretest's validity is 0.7.

      (4) The reliability of the pretest is 0.8.

Determine the optimal number of advertisements to be created and pretested, using the Gross formulation and the following table:

n	e_n	n	e_n
2	0.564	8	1.423
3	0.846	9	1.485
4	1.029	10	1.538
5	1.163	11	1.586
6	1.267	12	1.629
7	1.352		

6.8 A manufacturer wishes to determine the level of advertising that will maintain its current sales growth rate at 4%. Current sales are $50,000, and it is estimated that sales could reach a level of $150,000 at saturation. Sales response to advertising dollars is estimated at 1.1, and it has been determined that the company would lose 0.2 of its sales per period if no advertising expenditure were made.

    a. How much advertising is needed to maintain the desired growth?

    b. What rate of growth would be sustained if $20,000 was spent per period for advertising?

6.9 A company buys weekly television spots in the New York market. Each quarter the company reviews the ratings, drops spots that have a high cost per exposure, and adds any spots it can find with low cost per exposure in an effort to maximize profit. No budget restriction is set. Sales response is

$$s = \alpha + \beta(1 - e^{-\gamma v})$$

where v is total exposures per week in the market and s is sales per week in the market. Each spot can be characterized by Δv, its audience; Δx, its cost per week; and $k = \Delta x/\Delta v$, its cost per exposures.

    a. Find a procedure for rearranging the spot schedule so as to maximize profit rate. (Ignore the discrete nature of spots if you wish.)

    b. Express the decision rules of part a as a control curve, that is, a plot of maximum tolerable cost per exposure, k, versus accumulated exposures per week bought, v.

6.10. The reach of a media schedule is the fraction of the target population that receives at least one exposure. Consider a series of n advertising insertions in a certain publication. Let

p = probability that member of population receives exposure with one insertion

$f(p)$ = probability density function of p over target population (beta density)

$$= \frac{\Gamma(\alpha + \beta)}{\Gamma(\alpha)\Gamma(\beta)} p^{\alpha-1}(1-p)^{\beta-1}, \qquad 0 < p < 1; \quad \alpha, \beta > 0$$

a. Suppose that the exposures to the n successive insertions are independent events. Calculate the reach of the schedule.

b. Suppose that the fraction of the population receiving an exposure from one issue is 0.3 and the fraction receiving exposures from successive issues is 0.1. Assume the beta density and independence assumptions are correct. What will be the reach of four insertions? Note that

$$\Gamma(\alpha) = \int_0^\infty e^{-x} x^{\alpha-1}\, dx = (\alpha - 1)\Gamma(\alpha - 1)$$

If α is an integer, then

$$\Gamma(\alpha) = (\alpha - 1)!$$

7 | PROMOTION

In recent years, sales promotion has clearly moved out of the second-place shadow in many firms' A&SP (advertising and sales promotion) budgets. For example, according to Donnelley Marketing (1988), sales promotion as a percentage of the A&SP budgets grew from 58% in 1976 to 65% in 1987, and Bowman (1986) reports sales promotion expenditure growing by 12% per year over the past decade (versus 10% for advertising). Thus, sales promotion is a widely used and increasingly important element of the marketing mix.

In this chapter, we define categories of sales promotion and their reported effects. We then review some modeling approaches aimed at describing and explaining those effects. The last section assesses the field and discusses what can (and should) be accomplished in furthering our understanding of the effects of promotions.

SALES PROMOTION: TYPES AND EFFECTS

Sales promotion comprises a wide variety of tactical promotion tools of a short-term incentive nature designed to stimulate earlier and/or stronger target market response. Among the more popular forms are coupons, premiums, and

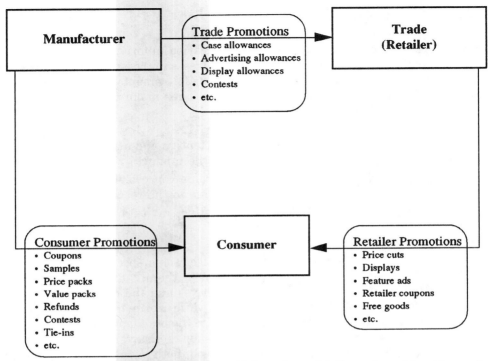

EXHIBIT 7.1   Promotion types vary widely and can be directed at either the trade
(retailer) or the consumer.

contests for consumer markets; buying allowances, cooperative-advertising
allowances, and free goods for distributors and dealers; discounts, gifts, and
extras for industrial users; and sales contests and special bonuses for members of the sales force.

A key factor associated with most types of promotions is that, properly
applied, they are *complementary* with other elements of the market mix and
therefore involve a coordinated effort among retailers, wholesalers, salespersons, advertising, and (often) manufacturing and distribution. This issue is
often overlooked in studies of manufacturer-based deals, which neglect temporary retailer specials and other activities by the retailer or distributor. Exhibit 7.1 shows the types and the flow of promotion and suggests the importance of understanding and modeling the individual and combined effects of
promotional activity at several levels.

Thus to model promotional effects, we must determine (1) the objectives
of the promotion, (2) characteristics of different promotion types and their
purported effects on the objectives, (3) the effectiveness of different promotions, and (4) the range of promotion decisions.

Objectives of Promotions

Because sales-promotion tools are so varied in form, no single purpose can be advanced for them. For example, a free sample stimulates consumer trial, while a free management advisory service cements a long-term relationship with a retailer. Sales-promotion techniques make three contributions to exchange relationships:

1. *Communication.* They gain attention and usually provide information that may lead the consumer to the product.

2. *Incentive.* They incorporate some concession, inducement, or contribution designed to represent value to the receiver.

3. *Invitation.* Most include a distinct invitation to engage in the transaction now.

Exhibit 7.2 gives a (partial) list of some specific marketing objectives and how promotions can be used to meet them.

Note the range of possible objectives and the multiplicity (and possible confounding) of effects. For example, while a primary purpose of a promotion may be to attract nonbrand purchasers to the brand, promotions are also adopted by sellers to reward brand-loyal users for their loyalty. Because both types of buyers buy during the promotion period, both purposes are served. The nonbrand purchasers are of two types: those who are loyal to other brands and those who are brand switchers. Incentive promotions primarily attract the brand switchers; the brand-loyal users of other brands do not always notice or act on the promotion. But because brand switchers are what they are, sales promotions are unlikely to turn them into loyal brand users. Therefore incentive promotions used in markets of high brand similarity produce a high sales response in the short run but little permanent gain. However, in markets of high brand dissimilarity, incentive promotions are more likely to alter market shares permanently.

Thus it is important to set objectives for the particular promotion, whether they relate to the level of retail inventory, to increased retail distribution, to coupon redemption rates, or to sales effects. A further complicating factor is that even for the same brand, objectives for promotional activity may vary over time. Occasionally, a promotion may be aimed at countering the advertising or promotions of a competitive brand, especially if the competitor is new to the market. Promotions that require an individual to save coupons or package labels aim at building a high degree of purchase loyalty among buyers. But, while many promotions are aimed at attracting consumers who are not regular users of the brand (obtaining trial), it is often difficult to evaluate how customers alter their subsequent purchasing behavior (and brand perceptions) on the basis of having bought a brand on a deal.

Objective	Promotional Type
Increase repeat buying	In-pack coupons, continuity programs (e.g., frequent flyer), "*N* for" retail promotions
Increase market share among brand switchers	FSI coupons, targeted coupons to other brand users, retail promotions
Increase retailer's promotion frequency	Trade deals, combination of consumer promotions and trade deals (big-bang theory)
Influence the product's image	Coop image advertising with image-oriented retailers
Increase category switching	Retail promotions, FSI coupons, large rebates
Target deal-sensitive consumers	Coupons, "*N* for" retail promotions
Increase category consumption	Retailer promotions, promotions tied to events (e.g., back to school)
Increase trial among nonusers	Cross-couponing, free samples, trial packs, direct-mail coupons
Liquidate short-term inventories	Trade deals, rebates, inventory financing
Increase distribution	FSI coupons, (increase demand), trade deals (increase DPP)

"*N* for" = multiple unit promotion (6 for 99 cents)
  FSI = freestanding insert
  DPP = dealer price promotion

EXHIBIT 7.2   A range of marketing objectives and promotions that can be used to meet them. (*Source:* Blattberg and Neslin (1990), p. 464.)

Characteristics of Promotions

Marketing managers choose promotions for their cost-effectiveness given the task at hand. Some of the key considerations vary with promotional type.

For *sampling*, implementation can be door to door, by mail, or free with the purchase of another product. Furthermore, the size of the sample can vary. (The promotion for the introduction of Gainesburgers by General Foods, which included, in a sample pack, *half* the recommended size of a dog's meal, had less than ideal results.) Because the number and type of households vary by area, different variables may be important for different situations. For example, the package size of the sample may target the product to one particular usage group and not another. In theory, marketers should target samples at prospects who hold the greatest potential (conversion rate, usage, or both) for future sales.

For a *manufacturer-price-off offer* the total quantity of the promotion must be determined, which, in turn, is affected by the amount the retailer will accept—too small a deal quantity may not motivate the retailer to feature the item. Furthermore, the price-off offer can cover one size, all sizes, or a selected set of sizes. Finally, the percentage of the price off must be carefully determined, as must the frequency. A too-frequent price-off offer may lead to expectations of continuation and to perceptions of regular price as an increase.

For *couponing*, the redemption rate is key, which, in turn, depends on the value of the coupon (Reibstein and Traver, 1982). As with sampling, the manufacturer has partial control of the type of household reached.

For *in-* and *on-pack premiums* the selection of premium type and duration is important. The premium should be consistent with the quality image of the brand and, if appropriate, should be in place long enough (as with glassware) so that a set can be obtained by a regular buyer.

In-store displays are recognized as effective means of moving merchandise, but display space is limited and the display must pay for itself by the retailer's standards. Many promotions of this type fail because the materials provided to retailers are not used.

In sum, each promotion type has some different dimension that makes it unique and that affects its cost and its impact on short- and long-term brand sales differently. When several promotions are introduced simultaneously, the situation is even more complicated. Furthermore, costs vary widely—door-to-door sampling is exceedingly expensive while mail-away premiums can be quite cheap. The execution and effectiveness of promotions also vary widely, differentially affecting sales as well as profitability. A sales-promotion program typically involves a number of management decisions, including the size of incentive, conditions for participation, distributor vehicle, duration, timing, and the overall promotion budget.

For the size of the incentive, the usual assumption is that for most products there are threshold and saturation effects: a certain minimum size is needed for response, and past a certain point higher incentives produce sales increases at a diminishing rate. This sales-response function varies with the type of product and delivery medium.

In addition, conditions for participation may vary. By carefully choosing these conditions, the seller can selectively discourage those who are unlikely to become regular users of the product.

Furthermore, distribution vehicles for the promotion vary in terms of cost and reach. Options include in or on the package, in the store, in the mail, and in the advertising media. In-package coupons reach current users, while mailed coupons can be directed at nonusers at a greater cost.

The duration of the promotion also plays an important part in its effect.

If the promotion is too short, many prospects will not have a chance to take advantage because they may not be repurchasing at the time. On the other hand, a promotion that lasts too long is perceived as a long-term price concession, and the deal loses its act-now character.

Closely tied to a promotion's duration is its timing and frequency. The timing of a promotion requires the coordination of production, sales force, and distribution personnel.

Finally, the size of the budget for promotions, as with that for advertising, is most frequently determined by a rule of thumb and not on the basis of cost effectiveness.

Evidence of Promotional Effects

There is lack of agreement among researchers about what promotions do and how they should be viewed, although there seems to be general agreement among many practitioners that, in contrast to advertising, promotions do not generally build up a long term consumer franchise. Blattberg and Neslin (1989 and 1990) have provided some useful summaries of the results of research in promotions. Those results can be classified as "intermediate effects" (I) and "longer-term effects" (L), where the latter category spans the period from a single repeat sale to the development of long-term loyalty.

1. *Sales promotions affect immediate sales.* Exhibit 7.3 shows the dramatic effect of a price cut for a brand of bathroom tissue at a major chain, accompanied by a special display and a feature ad.

The sales in promotional periods can be as much as ten times normal sales levels. These results are common for packaged goods (Schultz and Robinson, 1982; Totten and Block, 1987). Scanner data at the household level have been used extensively in recent years to demonstrate these types of significant effects (Guadagni and Little, 1983; Krishnamurthi and Raj, 1988; Gupta, 1988).

2. *Most of the immediate sales increase comes from brand switches.* Totten and Block (1987) and Gupta (1988) report that over 80% of all immediate promotion-related sales comes from brand switching (versus purchase acceleration or increased consumption).

3. *Promotional elasticities are asymmetric.* If promotional effects come from switching, then it is natural to ask if promotional elasticities are symmetric (does brand A's promotion affect brand B in the same way B's promotion affects A?). The indication appears to be that these elasticities are *not* symmetric (Blattberg and Wisniewski, 1989; Cooper, 1988), which suggests that the effects of promotional competition are likely to borne disproportionately by some brands relative to others.

4. *Promotional effects may be nonlinear and/or interact with one an-*

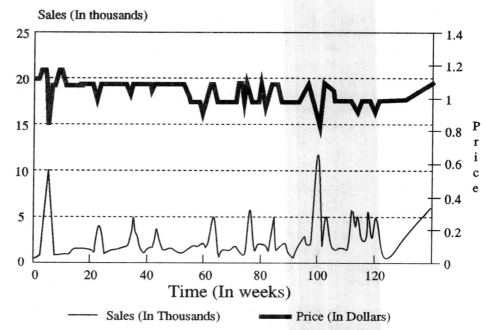

EXHIBIT 7.3   The sales of a brand of bathroom tissue showing frequent price promotions and the corresponding immediate increase in brand sales.
(*Source:* Blattberg and Neslin, 1989, p. 82.)

other. Promotional tools are often used together (a price cut, featured in a
newspaper ad combined with an end-aisle display, for example) making the
separate effects difficult to read. In addition, the effects may be nonlinear and
interact with one another (Woodside and Waddle, 1975; Moriarty, 1985;
Guadagni and Little, 1983).

Research on longer-term effects has focused on two main issues: the effect of promotions on repeat buying and their effect on purchase acceleration.

1. *Evidence on repeat buying effects is mixed.* Promotions have been posited to have at least two effects (that may conflict with one another) relative
to repeat sales. The first is *purchase reinforcement*, resulting from the "habit"
of buying the brand. The second is the *promotional usage effect*, resulting from
buying a brand that is being promoted. This results in the (often negative)
attribution to a brand that is promoted, the expectation of always buying on
deal or the (positive) reward associated with buying the brand. As Exhibit
7.4 demonstrates, research to date has not been able to disentangle these several, possible conflicting effects.

2. *Promotions seem to induce purchase acceleration for durables but the*

Type of Data	Article	Effect
Market Level	No Studies	
Market Level Choice Models	Jones and Zufryden (1981) Guadagni and Little (1983)	Negative Negative
Household Level Laboratory experiments	Scott (1976)† Scott and Yalch (1980)† Scott and Tybout (1979)† Tybout and Scott (1983)† Kahn and Louie (1988)	Negative and Positive Negative and Positive Negative and Positive Negative and Positive Negative and Positive
Household Level Panel Data	Dodson, Tybout and Sternthal (1978) Shoemaker and Shoaf (1977) Bawa and Shoemaker (1987) Currim and Schneider (1991)	Negative Negative Slightly Positive Mixed Effects

† These studies examine post-trial attitudes rather than actual repeat purchase rates.

EXHIBIT 7.4   The empirical research on the effect of promotions on repeat purchase shows mixed results. (*Source:* Blattberg and Neslin (1989), p. 87.)

results for nondurables are mixed. Promotions may induce consumers to buy more of the product or to alter the timing of their purchases. As Exhibit 7.5 shows, while there appears to be support for the acceleration effect among durables, the effect on nondurables is less clear. It may be that a promotion of some products (snack foods) leads naturally to increased consumption while for others (salad oil) increased consumption is unlikely. And it may also be that consumers decelerate their purchases in anticipation of a promotion, causing depressed sales before the promotion. This latter effect may account for the apparent effects that can be read at the household level (where the baseline is at the level of the individual) but not generally at the market level.

Some Speculations and Some Unknowns.   While the foregoing results point to a few areas (especially for immediate effects) where some generalizations are emerging, Blattberg and Neslin (1989, p. 924) point out the following important unknowns:

For immediate effects,

How do promotions affect category volume?
Why are promotional elasticities greater than price elasticities?
What effect do retail promotions have on store traffic?

For longer-term effects,

Type of Data	Article	Effect
Durables	Doyle and Saunders (1985)	Purchase deceleration
Market Level	Thompson and Noordewier (1988)	Timing acceleration
Household Level	Bayus (1988)	Timing acceleration
Non-Durables	Blattberg and Wisniewski (1988)	No Acceleration
Market Level	Leone (1987)	Timing acceleration
	Moriarity (1985)	Limited acceleration
	Neslin and Shoemaker (1983)	No Acceleration
	Wittink, et al. (1987)	No Acceleration
Household Level	Shoemaker (1979)	Quantity Acceleration
	Wilson, et al. (1979)	Quantity and Timing Acceleration
	Blattberg, et al. (1981)	Quantity and Timing Acceleration
	Neslin, et al. (1985)	Quantity and Timing Acceleration
	Gupta (1988)	Timing acceleration

EXHIBIT 7.5　The empirical research suggests that promotions may accelerate the purchase of durables but may have little effect on nondurables. (*Source:* Blattberg and Neslin (1989), p. 88.)

How and why do promotions affect repeat purchase behavior?

How and why do promotions affect purchase acceleration behavior?

What is the best way to measure promotional profitability?

How do promotions affect (positively and negatively) a brand's franchise?

Thus, while our knowledge of promotional effect is growing, much is still unknown about many aspects of the promotional puzzle.

The evidence cited leads to the following observations for modeling and evaluating promotional results:

Brand loyalty may (or may not) be affected.

New triers may (or may not) be attracted.

Promotions interact with other elements of the marketing mix (advertising, in particular).

Promotional results interact with production and distribution, affecting inventory levels in a rapid and dramatic manner.

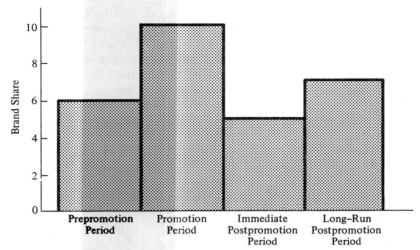

EXHIBIT 7.6   Ideal effect of a consumer deal on brand share.

Promotional frequency influences promotional effects and is linked to
the average length of the product's purchase cycle.

The type of promotion selected may have differential effects on brand
loyalty and promotional attractiveness.

Promotion size may have threshold and saturation effects, suggesting
an S-shaped sales-response relationship.

Finally, different promotions may be implemented with different degrees
of success, resulting in ambiguous measures of market response.

Historically, the most common consumer-promotion evaluation technique has been to compare sales or market share before, during, and after a
promotion. Increased sales then are attributed to the impact of the sales-promotion program, all other things being equal. Exhibit 7.6 shows an example
of results that manufacturers would like to see. In the promotion period the
company's brand share rose to 10%. This share gain of 4% is made up of (1)
deal-prone consumers, who switched to this brand to take advantage of the
deal, and (2) brand-loyal customers, who increased their purchases in response to the price incentive. Immediately after the promotion ended, the brand
share fell to 5% because consumers were overstocked and they were working
down their inventory. After this stock adjustment brand share went up to 7%,
showing a one-percentage-point increase in the number of loyal customers.
This pattern is likely to occur when the brand has good qualities that many
nonbrand users did not know about.

If we assume that the effects of a promotion are relatively shortlived
(ignoring the unknown effect on the franchise we noted), then the approach

seems sound. However, even with the increased availability and use of scanner data, the problem is quite challenging: in order to get accurate measures of incremental sales, we need accurate estimates of baseline sales—those sales for the brand that would have occurred if the promotion had not taken place. If nonpromotional period sales (as in Exhibit 7.6) are used as a base and if there are strong acceleration effects, then the baseline will be biased *downward*, and the effect and profitability of the promotion will be overstated: note that the immediate postpromotional sales rate is much lower than the long-run postpromotional sales rate.

In addition, to calculate the profitability of a trade promotion, it is necessary to evaluate how much of the promotional effect is passed on to the consumer and how much is simply forward buying by the retailer to stockpile for future use. As Blattberg and Levin (1987) (reviewed shortly) point out, forward buying is so extensive that it may be impossible to infer a baseline from wholesale sales data and, therefore, manufacturers need good models of both consumer response to retailer promotions and retailer response to trade promotions in order to evaluate the profitability of trade promotions.

PROMOTIONAL MODELS

A number of promotional models have been developed and proposed in the marketing literature. They generally fall into three categories: (1) theoretical models without empirical support, (2) regression-type models without theoretical justification, and (3) empirically supported models derived from or related to some behavioral hypotheses. Models in the first category are often untested and will be briefly reviewed later. The second types of models, while widely used by many firms, do not provide much general insight. Now we review four models of the third type: the Rao-Lilien (1972) model, the Little (1975) model, Narasimhan's (1984) model, and Blattberg and Levin's (1987) model.

EXAMPLE _____

Rao-Lilien Model.   We investigate the Rao-Lilien (1972) model for several reasons. First, the model was developed in a franchised-retail environment—gasoline in particular—and demonstrates model customization for this type of market. Second, the model demonstrates how a set of behavioral assumptions leads to a reasonable model form. And third, the model deals with multiple, simultaneous promotions and shows how joint effects of multiple promotions can be handled.

Problem setting.   The incentive for model development arose from the need to improve a sales-forecasting system for Mobil Corporation in the late 1960s. Two main types of promotions were leading to highly erratic retail sales patterns: competitive games and unsolicited credit card mailings (legal at the time). In addition, many markets showed rather drastic price fluctuations, and price variation was modeled as promotional activity as well.

Gasoline games were offered in many varieties in the late 1960s, but they all had certain common elements. A customer would obtain a game form with a number or other identification from the promoting brand, and, periodically, winners would be selected by random drawings. Initially, the objective was to draw customers from competitors' brands, who would then become regular customers. Later, however, the games took on a more defensive flavor and were instituted more to avoid a loss than to acquire new customers.

Credit cards were mailed to residents in certain neighborhoods who satisfied specific demographic and socioeconomic criteria. Again, a shift of customers to the mailing brand was the objective.

Note that in both these cases it was not expected that customers would buy more than their normal quantity; rather, sales gains were seen as coming only through acquisition of new customers.

Modeling approach.   Because of the lack of knowledge about customer heterogeneity, the authors chose an aggregate-modeling approach. In the given franchised-retail setting they hypothesized that incremental gains in sales from a promotion depend on three factors:

1. *Promotion potential, P.* The potential of a promotion is related to the fraction of individuals not currently participating in a promotion. If the promoting brand(s) has a joint market share of m, then $(1 - m)$ can be switched, and potential P, the likelihood of a randomly chosen customer being in the target market, is an increasing function of $(1 - m)$.

2. *Promotion reach, R.* The more outlets the promoting brand (or brands) has, the easier a willing individual will find it to participate. Thus if m is defined as above, then reach R, the likelihood that a randomly chosen customer can reach the promoting outlet, is an increasing function of m.

3. *Promotion strength, S.* The more interesting the promotion, the more likely an individual will be to take advantage of it. The strength S of the promotion is modeled as $K(x, t)$, where x represents the characteristics of the promotion and t is time. The analyst might hypothesize that K is S-shaped in x (as in a price promotion) and decreasing in t (as the novelty wears off).

From these assumptions we find that the probability that a randomly chosen customer will respond to the promotion is PRS, and the expected gain, V^* per customer in the market for a promotion is

$$V^* = PRSg \qquad (7.1)$$

where g is the average quantity purchased per customer during the promotional period. If there are C customers in the market, then

$$V = PRSG \qquad (7.2)$$

where V is the incremental sales gain to promoting brands and $G = Cg$.

Application to gasoline games.   The authors argue that reasonable forms for the terms in equation (7.2) are

$$P = 1 - m \qquad (7.3)$$

$$R = m^{\alpha} \qquad (7.4)$$

$$S = K \text{ (at least in the short term)} \qquad (7.5)$$

These separate functional forms and the way they fit together are illustrated in Exhibit 7.7. Exhibit 7.7(c) shows that for all promoting brands the percentage volume gain is small when the share of those involved is very small (reach is low) or where share is very large (potential is low). Plugging equations (7.3–7.5) into equation (7.2) yields

$$V_G = KG(1 - m)m^{\alpha} \qquad (7.6)$$

where V_G is the volume gained by all game-playing brands.

Similarly, consider a nonpromoting brand with share m_0. If we let V_L be the loss of that brand to promoted brands and assume loss is proportional to share, the loss is

$$V_L = KGm^{\alpha}(1 - m)\frac{m_0}{1 - m} \qquad (7.7)$$

$$= KGm^{\alpha}m_0 \qquad (7.8)$$

Because the expected sales volume with no promotions is m_0G, the promotional loss P_L is

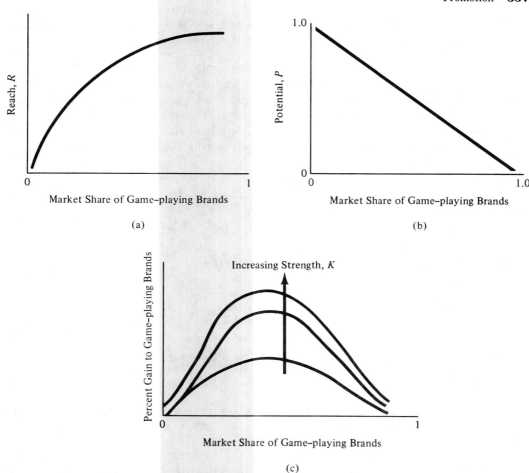

EXHIBIT 7.7   The structure of the Rao-Lilien game-promotion model.

$$P_L = \frac{V_L}{m_0 G} = Km^\alpha \tag{7.9}$$

Similarly, a **proportional gain** P_G to a game-playing brand is modeled as

$$P_G = KGm^\alpha(1 - m)\frac{m_0}{m}\frac{1}{m_0 G} \tag{7.10}$$

$$= Km^{\alpha-1}(1 - m) \tag{7.11}$$

Note that as $m \to 1$, $P_L \to K$; therefore K is the largest proportional loss that a company can incur by not participating in the promotion.

Other promotions. A similar development leads to a model for price changes and for credit card mailings. In gasoline markets in the 1960s, most price competition was between the group of majors (national brands) and the independents (local brands). From the standpoint of the majors, then, an increase in the price differential can be viewed as a promotion by the independents against the majors. The price model is similar to the game-promotion model:

$$P = 1 - m_I \tag{7.12}$$

$$R = m_I^\alpha \tag{7.13}$$

$$S = f(\delta) \tag{7.14}$$

where

m_I = market share of independents
δ = change in usual price difference between majors and independents

The approach for credit card mailings is analogous, although slightly more complicated.

Multiple promotions and interactions. Suppose that there were a game and a credit card mailing in a market at the same time. Then we need to calculate the joint effect of the promotion, $V_G \cup V_C$, which can be decomposed as

$$V_G \cup V_C = V_G + V_C - V_G \cap V_C \tag{7.15}$$

If the effects are not synergistic, the intersection $V_G \cap V_C$ can be bounded logically by min (V_G, V_C) from above (all people attracted by the game, say, would have been attracted by the mailing) and from below by $V_C V_G / G$ (assuming that the proportions of the population attracted to each type of promotion are independent). Because the populations are unlikely to be independent, this latter term should understate the interaction.

The authors suggest modeling the intersection as a convex combination of the bounds:

$$V_G \cap V_C = \lambda \min(V_G, V_C) + (1 - \lambda) \frac{V_G V_C}{G}, \qquad 0 < \lambda < 1 \quad \textbf{(7.16)}$$

Note that relaxing the restrictions of $\lambda < 1$ allows for positive synergy.

Estimation of parameters. The approach for estimating parameters of this model assumes that some past periods of no promotional activity exist for forecasting sales during the promotional period:

$$Y = \mu + \text{promotion effect} + \varepsilon \qquad \textbf{(7.17)}$$

where

Y = actual sales divided by forecast sales for the period
μ = $E(Y|\text{ no promotions}) = 1 + \text{promotional forecasting bias}$
ε = random error

The promotion model gives the promotion effect in each market as a function of $\{K_i\}$, α, λ, and so on. Historical experience with the forecasting procedure yielded estimates of μ. Parameters of the model were then estimated with a nonlinear estimation procedure from the equation

$$Y^* = Y - \mu = \text{promotion effect} + \varepsilon \qquad \textbf{(7.18)}$$

Implementation. The authors also report the results of introducing the model into the existing sales-forecasting system. Exhibit 7.8 compares the results of the time-series forecasts alone (the alternative system in use at the time) with the results after the addition of the promotion model in a market used for validation. The lag in pickup of the July–August 1967 sales spurt was attributed to an advertising campaign, not treated in the model structure. In a test of 19 markets the variance in error between 12 actual and predicted monthly sales figures was reduced by over 50% with the use of the model.

In updating the parameters, the authors found that the game-strength parameter K was approximately half its original value one year after games were introduced.

Furthermore, the strength of a credit card mailing was found to peak about four months after the original mailing and then gradually

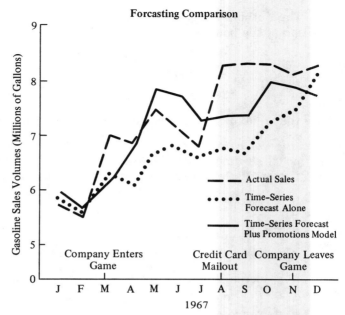

EXHIBIT 7.8   Rao-Lilien model's results. (*Source:* Rao and Lilien, 1972, p. 159.)

decline until, after one and one half years, its value was half that at its peak. Finally, the pricing-model parameters were reported to be the least stable, suggesting that the price-model structure might be too simplistic.

The authors report using this model as a simulation tool as well. In addition to providing improved sales forecasts, a real-time version of the model was available to marketing planners to experiment (on the model) with different promotional plans and competitive assumptions.

This modeling approach has the advantage of providing a modular structure that can be applied to many promotional types. Furthermore, it appears to be a logical model development and has been used.

However, it is not clear whether the modeling assumptions and approach are widely applicable outside a franchise-retailing environment with nondifferentiated products. But it is one of few promotional models that deals with competitive effects and with the joint effects of several promotions explicitly.

EXAMPLE ─────────────────────────────────

Little's 1975 BRANDAID Promotional Model.   BRANDAID contains a promotional submodel that is investigated separately here because of its unique approach. BRANDAID, as developed in Chapter 11,

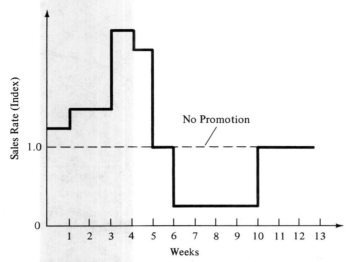

EXHIBIT 7.9   Time pattern of response to reference promotion (from an application). (*Source:* Little, 1975, p. 641.)

is an aggregate-marketing model, and Little's structure and model calibration are based on past observation rather than specific theory.

Background.   Little notes that for a typical promotion, stores stock up on the product, often reduce shelf price, and sell much more of the product than they normally do. He also notes that the period of high sales is often followed by a period of reduced sales or, at least, reduced factory shipments, caused by stocking up by retailers and, often, by consumers (Blattberg, Eppen, and Lieberman, 1981). Furthermore, when retailers discover that a promotion is coming, they may hold back on their orders, causing sales to be depressed in advance of the promotion. Finally, sales of promoted packs may reduce the sales of other packs via cannibalization.

Little's model incorporates these phenomena through two constructs: a promotional time pattern and a promotional response function. The promotional time pattern (Exhibit 7.9) is characteristic of the given type of promotion and may include a prepromotion period of depressed sales, a postpromotion depression of varying time and intensity, and so forth. The promotional response function acts as a scale factor for the basic or reference promotion. It depends on the promotional intensity and products a promotional-amplitude value of one for a reference promotional intensity of one. (See Exhibit 7.10.) The argument here is that at small values of a price-off, say, the promotion works poorly because of its lack of visibility or reluctance by retailers to accept it. Then after a certain level of intensity, the promotion reaches a peak because most

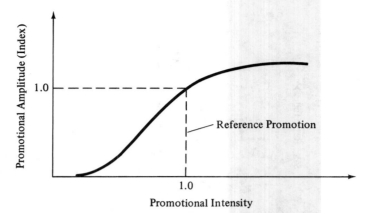

EXHIBIT 7.10 Sales response to promotional intensity, a scale factor on the amplitude of the time pattern (hypothetical curve). (*Source:* Little, 1975, p. 641.)

retailers have accepted the promotion and are doing as much with it as they possibly can.

Modeling Approach. Little proceeds as follows. Let

$q(\tau)$ = reference index per time pattern (as in Exhibit 7.9) for reference promotion in τth period after start

$a(t)$ = promotional intensity of promotion starting in t ($a = 1$ for reference promotion and $a = 0$ for no promotion)

$r(a)$ = sales response to promotional intensity, a scale factor of time pattern [$r(1) = 1$ and $r(0) = 0$]

Q_{np} = sales expected when there is no promotion

With the foregoing we can build up a promotional effect as follows:

Net sales gain from reference promotion at time

$$t_p = Q_{np}[q(t - t_p) - 1] \tag{7.19}$$

Net sales gain from promotion of intensity

$$a = Q_{np}[q(t - t_p) - 1] \, r[a(t_p)] \tag{7.20}$$

With no promotion for the full line, as well as cannibalization, we have

Sales gain at t from promoted portion of line

$$= Q_{np}\ell[q(t - t_p) - 1] \, r[a(t_p)] \tag{7.21}$$

and

Total sales of line under given promotion

$$= Q_{np}\{1 + \ell(1 - b)\,[q(t - t_p) - 1]\,r[a(t_p)]\} \qquad (7.22)$$

where

ℓ = fraction of line promoted
b = fraction of sales gain due to cannibalization (so $1 - b$ is true gain for total product line)

When a series of promotions, indexed by subscript p, occurs, we obtain

Total sales of line under promotion schedule p

$$= Q_{np}\left\{1 + \sum_p \ell_p[1 - b_p][q_p(t - t_p) - 1]r_p[a_p(t_p)]\right\} \qquad (7.23)$$

Equation (7.23) suggests that each promotion can have its own set of parameters, but, in practice, the same time pattern and response function will usually apply to all promotions of a given type.

To account for different levels of promotional intensity, Little suggests incorporating factors similar to those for copy or media efficiency:

$x(t)$ = promotional size at t (in dollars per sale unit)
$h(t)$ = coverage efficiency at t (function of customers reached by promotion)
$k(t)$ = consumer effectiveness at t (effect of point-of-display premium quality or other consumer-oriented enhancements of basic offer)

Using the subscript zero to denote the reference promotion, we get

$$a(t) = \frac{h(t)k(t)x(t)}{h_0 k_0 x_0} \qquad (7.24)$$

This equation allows for more detailed examination of promotional intensity by decomposing it into several components before applying it to equation (7.23).

Model calibration and use. The performance of the promotional submodel is not discussed separately but, rather, as an integrated part of the calibration and use of the BRANDAID model (Chapter 11). Calibration of this model includes an unspecified combination of historical, statistical analysis, and managerial judgment as first steps, followed by tracking and, if possible, field measurement and adaptive control. In a reported case study—GROOVY—the BRANDAID model as a whole tracked sales well both during the period of calibration and afterward. Because the promotional submodel was an important element in this market, we can infer that the promotional model performed adequately.

This promotional model has been used as part of the BRANDAID structure for brand promotional planning in a number of companies, reportedly with success, especially in diagnosis and tracking. There the brand-management team is concerned with understanding why an effect is taking place and with determining which of several alternative actions are best. The model appears well suited to this purpose.

Little's model is both modular and flexible. Its reliance on a template of past promotional patterns as a base to adjust from is innovative and quite realistic because promotional effects are bumpy. The weakness of the model is that it is not based on theory—a future promotion is assumed to be a modified form of a past promotion. In addition, because the calibration is part statistical and part judgmental, it is not clear how to determine if the model is adequate in a specific situation. Furthermore, this model would be difficult to adapt to situations other than consumer packaged goods.

EXAMPLE _____

Narasimhan's (1984) Model. Narasimhan develops and tests a theory of coupons as price discrimination devices, that is, as mechanisms that allow the firm to charge different prices to different customers for the same product. If consumers vary in terms of price sensitivity, then pricing theory suggests that price discrimination (where implementable) is profit maximizing for the firm. In Narasimhan's model, the idea is that consumers are required to allocate valuable time to using coupons, and the higher the wage rate of the consumer, the more costly (time consuming at a higher wage rate) the coupon is for the consumer. However, consumers with higher education are assumed to be more efficient at using coupons, so they require less time to use coupons.

Narasimhan's model assumes that the consumer's goal is to maximize utility, $U(\cdot)$, over two goods, X (the good being studied) and L (Leisure), subject to an income constraint, a time constraint and several other "reasonableness" assumptions.

Formally, his model is

$$\text{maximize } U(X, L) \tag{7.25a}$$

Subject to

$$\underbrace{\alpha W(H) + A}_{\text{income}} = \underbrace{P_1X - SX_1 + P_2L}_{\text{expenditures on } X \text{ and } L} \text{ (income constraint)} \tag{7.25b}$$

$$\underbrace{T}_{\text{total time}} = \underbrace{t_1X + t_2X_1 + L + H}_{\substack{\text{consumption time} + \\ \text{coupon usage time} + \\ \text{leisure time} + \\ \text{working time}}} \text{ (time constraint)} \tag{7.25c}$$

where

$X \geq X_1$ (coupon purchases are only a portion of total purchases) **(7.25d)**

$X_1 \geq 0$ (purchases are nonnegative) **(7.25e)**

where

U	=	utility
X	=	total amount of good purchased
L	=	leisure time
P_1	=	price of one unit of X
P_2	=	price of one unit of L
X_1	=	quantity of X bought with coupon
S	=	savings per unit bought with coupon
H	=	hours spent in labor market
t_1	=	time spent consuming X
t_2	=	time spent using the coupon
A	=	nonwage income
$W(H)$	=	effective number of hours worked (a mathematical convenience)
α	=	wage rate
T	=	total hours available

Based on this model (and some simple extensions to multiple brands and multiple sizes), Narasimhan's model implies that

1. Price elasticity increases with lower wages and lower opportunity cost of time.

2. Coupon usage increases with consumer price elasticity.

3. Coupon usage decreases with opportunity cost of time and wage rate.

4. Higher-priced brands should offer larger coupon savings.

5. Across sizes of a brand, savings per unit of product bought will be inversely related to size.

6. Heavier users of coupons will include
   a. Better educated consumers
   b. Nonworking consumers
   c. Lower-income groups.

Using data from a consumer diary panel, he tested his theoretical results using a demand elasticity model and a demographic model: The structure of Narasimhan's demand elasticity model is

$$\ln [QTY_C] = a_1 \ln [price_i] + a_2 \, \delta \ln [price_i] \qquad \textbf{(7.26)}$$

$$+ \text{ demand/taste controls} + \varepsilon$$

where

QTY_i = annual quantity purchased by household i

$price_i$ = average price paid by ith household

δ = dummy variable

$= \begin{cases} 1, & \text{if household uses coupons} \\ 0, & \text{otherwise} \end{cases}$

demand/taste controls = other variables (like income, family size, education, etc.) included in the model to control for their effect on purchase quantity.

Narasimhan's empirical results have 16 out of 20 values of a_2 significantly less than 0, supporting the hypothesis that coupon users are more price sensitive than nonusers (even while controlling for income, education, etc.).

His demographic model focuses on demographic differences between users and nonusers:

$$Cupunt = a_0 + a_1\,Income + a_2\,Income^2$$

$$+ a_3\,EDUFEM + a_4\,FEMEMP \tag{7.27}$$

$$+ a_5\,QTY + a_6\,QTY^2 + a_7\,DUMCHD$$

$$+ a_7\,OCCUP_1 + a_8\,OCCUP_2 + \varepsilon$$

where

$Cupunt$	=	quantity bought using coupons
$Income$	=	annual household income
$EDUFEM$	=	educational level of female head of household
$FEMEMP$	=	1 if wife employed; 0 otherwise
QTY	=	quantity purchased
$DUMCHD$	=	1 if household has children under 18; 0 otherwise
$OCCUP_1, OCCUP_2$	=	dummy variable for two sets of occupation—groups

The model was estimated separately for three groups: no male head of household; household, female not employed; and household, both employed. The results are

The income effect is nonlinear, an inverted U, with middle-income households the most deal-prone.

Female education and the presence of children were both associated with deal-prone users.

Female employment was not consistently negative as hypothesized.

Narasimhan also develops some models to test for couponing effects across brands and sizes and his evidence supports the following results:

Higher-priced brands generally offer greater savings per unit.

Larger package sizes offer lower savings per unit.

While Narasimhan's results are derived from a fairly simplistic model of consumer choice, it does provide some useful managerial results: (1) his model (and its empirical test) suggests that several demographic variables

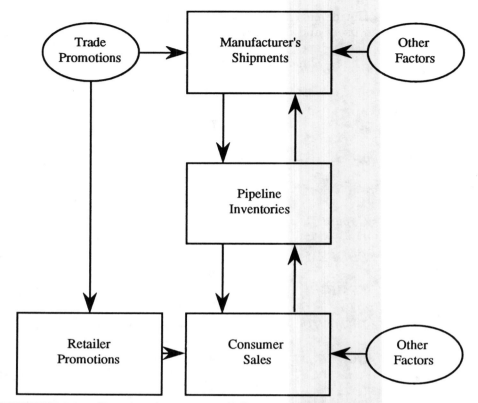

EXHIBIT 7.11   How a trade promotion influences shipments and sales. (*Source:* Blatt-berg and Levin, 1987, p. 127.)

(income, education, presence of children) can be used to identify coupon-prone consumers, and (2) his model identifies the price/size combinations that can benefit most from couponing.

However, his model does not incorporate couponing costs, redemption rates, product competition, interactions with other promotion or marketing mix elements, or the economic value of the promotional program, so it can best be viewed as a useful step in developing insight in this area.

EXAMPLE _____

Blattberg and Levin's (1987) Model   Blattberg and Levin developed a model to evaluate the effectiveness of trade promotions. Exhibit 7.11 gives the overall structure of the model. The important part of this model is that a trade deal has two effects: (1) The trade promotion en-

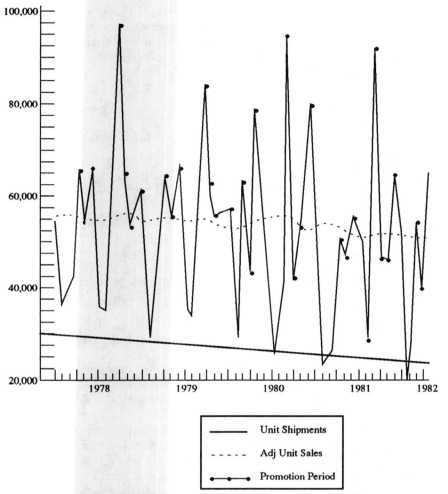

EXHIBIT 7.12   A plot of consumer sales and shipments shows major promotional peaks and troughs for shipments to the trade but less apparent effects at the consumer level. (*Source:* Blattberg and Levin, 1987, p. 128.)

courages the retailer to run a consumer promotion (the desired outcome by the manufacturer), and (2) the promotion also may encourage the retailer to buy more during the trade period (forward buying), resulting in increased shipments during the trade period and decreased shipments afterward.

Exhibit 7.12 shows the net effect of this activity: while consumer sales (ADJ UNIT SALES) show relatively little variability, there are generally large jumps in shipments (to retailers) during the promotional period, followed by troughs afterward. Thus, a complete understanding of the effectiveness of a trade promotion requires analysis of each of the stages of the process; indeed, the equations that follow correspond to Exhibit 7.11 in that each equation represents the flow in and out of a box in that exhibit:

Manufacturer's Shipment Model:

$$\text{Shipments}_t = f_1(\text{inventory}_{t-1}, \text{trade promotions}_t, \text{other factors}_t) \qquad \textbf{(7.28a)}$$

Retail Promotions Model:

$$\text{Retail promotions}_t = f_2(\text{trade promotions}_t,$$
$$\text{trade promotions}_{t-1}, \text{inventories}_{t-1}) \qquad \textbf{(7.28b)}$$

Consumer Sales Model:

$$\text{Consumer sales}_t = f_3(\text{retailer promotions}_t, \text{other factors}_t) \qquad \textbf{(7.28c)}$$

Inventory Model:

$$\text{Inventory}_t = f_4(\text{inventory}_{t-1}, \text{shipments}_t, \text{consumer sales}_t) \qquad \textbf{(7.28d)}$$

Note that equation 7.28d is simply an accounting equation, as

$$\text{Inventory}_t = \text{Inventory}_{t-1} + \text{Shipments}_t - \text{Consumer sales}_t \qquad \textbf{(7.28e)}$$

Thus, in general, there will be three equations to specify and estimate.

Assuming that consumer sales revert to their baseline level at some time after retail promotions cease, the profitability of the promotion can be assessed as the gross margin gain associated with incremental consumer sales less the gross margin loss associated with sales on promotion to the trade. Formally

$$\text{Promotion profitability} = I \cdot \text{MARGIN} - P \cdot \text{DISC} \qquad \textbf{(7.29)}$$

where

P	=	total sales to the trade during the promotional period
I	=	incremental sales to the consumer
DISC	=	average discount/unit given to the trade during the promotional period
MARGIN	=	gross margin per unit sold

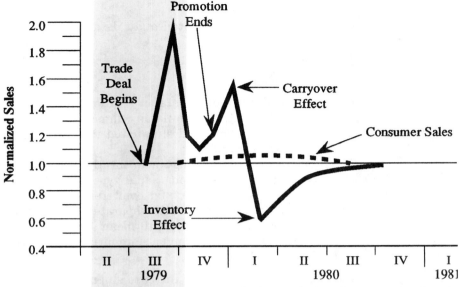

EXHIBIT 7.13 Consumer and trade sales during and after the promotional period. The area under the dashed line represents incremental consumer sales and is (generally) much less than the area under the solid line during the promotional period. (*Source:* Blattberg and Levin, 1987, p. 137.)

Exhibit 7.13 illustrates what is happening: since shipments during the trade period are partially "stolen" from future periods and sales during that period are at a discount, these stolen shipments represent a decrease in profitability of the promotion. In general, we have

$$F = P - N - I \qquad (7.30)$$

where

F = forward buying, and
N = "normal" (baseline) sales of the product

As F increases relative to I, the profitability of the promotion generally becomes lower.

Application. Blattberg and Levin report using this approach in an application with a manufacturer studying ten products in six markets. The data that they had were

Factory shipments

Nielson sales (bimonthly retail audit data)

Manufacturer's price

Trade promotions

Advertising expenditures

The manufacturer did not have data on retailer promotion activity (although such data are routinely available commercially), so the researchers dropped equation (7.28b) and eliminated the "retailer promotions" variable from equation (7.28c).

The remaining models (in log-linear form) incorporated "other factors" to account for different promotional types, for the difference between retail orders and shipments, for over trends, seasonality and the like. The researchers estimated sixty separate equations for the shipments and the consumer equation, with mean adjusted R^2's of 0.66 and 0.57, respectively. Their results can be summarized as follows (Blattberg and Levin, 1987, pp. 141–142):

1. Trade deals significantly increase shipments.

2. Forward buying is significant, leading to significant decreases in sales after the promotional period.

3. Consumer sales increase during the promotion, but to a significantly lower degree than shipments.

Blattberg and Levin also performed the type of profitability analysis just outlined and concluded that most deals lost money. They argue that this result may be due to several factors:

1. Trade deals probably do not directly pay out and are used defensively rather than to increase profits.

2. The models do not directly adjust for maintaining distribution through trade dealing.

3. They cannot easily adjust for competitive effects because data are rarely collected for trade promotions of other firms.

4. Sales will decline and profits increase if trade deals are reduced. Most managers appear to be afraid of market share declines.

The major limitations of the Blattberg and Levin approach as discussed by the authors as well as in some commentaries on this work (Kruger, 1987; Struse, 1987; Blattberg, 1987) are generally associated with data quality and robustness. The lack of data availability at the time this analysis was run is no longer such an important issue; scanner data and other associated higher-quality data sources eliminate many of the data problems in the approach. Questions about robustness of the results for forecasting can only be addressed after we have a good, historical collection of well-designed and well-reported studies. While the state of measurement in this area is still rather primitive, model-based approaches like this (and PROMOTER by Abraham and Lodish, 1987b) are beginning to provide such intelligence.

Other Promotional Models

Recent modeling in the promotional area has proceeded along two main dimensions: (1) theoretical models and (2) operational models. We review some key developments in the former area here and the following section addresses development in the latter area. (The reader should consult Blattberg and Neslin, 1990, for a more thorough review of promotional models.)

Theoretical Models.   A number of theoretical models have tried to explain the justification for and the effects of promotions. Following Blattberg and Neslin (1990, Ch. 4), we discuss these models along the dimensions of demand uncertainty, inventory cost-shifting, differential information, price brand loyalty, and competitive analysis.

Demand Uncertainty.   Using a fairly simple model, Lazear (1986) tries to explain why retailers often price high at the beginning of a season and reduce price at the end. If the seller does not know the buyers' valuation for the product, a high initial price should prove acceptable (and lead to sales) for those buyers with high valuation, while the lower price captures customers with lower valuations later. His conclusions from his model are

1. Flexible pricing increases profitability (relative to a single fixed price).

2. The smaller the number of potential buyers, the lower the price in the first period (relative to the still lower price in the second period).

3. Products that will become obsolete (e.g., toys around Christmas) should be priced lower than those that retain value over time.

Inventory Cost Shifting.   Researchers have dealt with two forms of inventory cost shifting: consumers can buy more of an item (consumable) when sold on deal, or they can accelerate their timing of purchase (for durables, as in an earlier replacement of a car).

Blattberg, Eppen, and Lieberman (1981) develop a model in which consumers minimize holding costs while retailers maximize profits subject to the consumer's behavior. Consumers are assumed to be of one of two types: high or low holding costs. Their model predicts

1. The higher the rate of consumption, the lower the degree and the higher the frequency of deals.

2. The higher the holding costs, the higher *both* the degree and frequency of deals.

3. The lower the percentage of low holding cost customers, the lower the degree and the higher the frequency of deals. Blattberg and colleagues offer some empirical tests of their model, providing evidence for consumer stockpiling as well as general support for the predictions noted earlier.

Using a different explanation (consumer search costs versus differentiated holding costs) Salop and Stiglitz (1982) demonstrate that a single low price (generated by some retailers offering a promotion) and a single high price are the equilibrium price distribution in a market.

Differential Information. In a different article, Salop and Stiglitz (1977) model a market with informed and uninformed customers, where the latter shop at random while the former shop only at the lower-priced stores. Their model again yields a two-price equilibrium. Varian (1980) argues that uninformed customers become informed by shopping behavior and suggests that, to maintain the two-price equilibrium (i.e., to keep uninformed customers that way), stores must randomly select the high- versus low-price portions in any period. The idea here is that promotions capture the informed customers, but are only temporary so they can get full price sometime from the informed customer.

Price Discrimination. Price discrimination (Chapter 4) is a mechanism that allows firms to charge different prices to customers with different demand curves. Narasimhan's (1984) analysis, reviewed earlier, studied coupons as a price discrimination mechanism. Jeuland and Narasimhan (1985) analyze a situation (similar to that of Blattberg, Eppen, and Lieberman, 1981, but with a different objective) where buyers are heterogeneous in demand and holding costs did derive the following results:

1. Dealing increases demand by attracting customers with lower reservation prices.
2. A trough will *not* occur after a promotion.
3. Regular buyers will not stockpile, while occasional buyers will.
4. Package size will not affect deal frequency.
5. Retailers will differ in their frequency of offering deals (addressing different demand segments).

Brand Loyalty. If a market consists of customers who are loyal to a brand and others who are "switchable," promotions can be used as bait for the switchers. Narasimhan (1988) developed a two-brand model and showed if one firm has more loyal customers than the other, its average price should be higher and it should run fewer promotions. In a similar vein, Raju, Srinivasan, and Lal (1990) show that strong brands (those with more loyal customers) should promote less frequently than weak brands.

Using a similar model, Rao (1991) tries to explain national brand (versus private-label) promotions, where buyers have higher reservation prices for national than private-label brands. He shows that it is optimal for the national brand to promote in a random manner to prevent the private-label brand from maintaining an optimal price differential and that it is optimal for the private label not to promote.

Lattin (1988) incorporates trade promotions into his model and shows that the manufacturers should offer trade deals occasionally to induce the retailer to promote who will, indeed, promote according to the arguments of Rao's (1991) model.

Lal (1988) argues that, when there are multiple brands in a price tier (i.e., two identical national brands and one private-label brand), it is optimal for the national brands to collude, that is, to alternate dealing periods *systematically*.

Competition.   A common explanation for promotions is the familiar "prisoner's dilemma" paradox: while it might be jointly optimal for two (or more) firms to collude to maintain uniformly higher prices, it is (individually) optimal for each to cut price (promote) if the other does not. Thus, both firms argue similarly and both end up promoting. Several studies (Axelrod, 1980a, b; Fader and Hauser, 1987) have shown that a form of a "tit-for-tat" strategy (A promotes if B promotes, A stops if B stops) appears to be effective in inducing cooperation.

Operational Models of Promotion.   The models by Rao and Lilien (1972), Little (1975), and Blattberg and Levin (1987) reviewed earlier, all report operational use. Several other operational models have been reported.

Abraham and Lodish (1987b) developed a methodology called PRO-MOTER, extended to PROMOTIONSCAN (Abraham and Lodish, 1989b), to provide a better baseline for planning promotions and evaluating their effectiveness than a simple before-and-after analysis. Their model incorporates trends, seasonality, exception indices (for special factors), as well as promotional types in a combined multiplicative-additive model and is reported to be in regular use.

Neslin and Shoemaker (1983) develop a decision calculus model aimed at planning coupon promotions. It is similar to BRANDAID, but focuses great detail on the element of coupon promotions. The authors report an application of the model for deciding between a freestanding insert and a direct-mail coupon.

Lodish (1982) describes a decision calculus model for planning a retail promotion, in which sales are decomposed into regular sales, price-event sales, and markdown sales, and reports that it has been used by a large national retailer. (See Chapter 12.)

Dhebar, Neslin, and Quelch (1987) describe a decision calculus model for planning an individual retailer promotion that was developed for an au-

tomobile retailer. The model addresses a complex set of issues including repeat sales, trade-ins (effect on used car inventory) service contracts, competitive response, and the like.

Blattberg and Neslin (1990) review and suggest a number of other models
and approaches that have been proposed or should be considered in dealing
with the operational issues associated with promotional decisions.

The Future of Promotional Models

The large amount of recent work in the promotional area has been stimulated
to a large extent by an enormous improvement in the quality of available
data. As pointed out by Blattberg and Neslin (1990) in the best integrative
treatment of the promotions area to date, the term "promotions" covers a heterogeneous set of objectives with potentially different impacts in different
markets and for different product classes. We are in the process of collecting
much empirical information about promotions, but a single, dominant theory
or model of promotional effectiveness has not emerged, nor is it likely to any
time soon. With our current state of knowledge, we must continue to try to
understand and model the wide range of phenomena outlined in the section
on "promotional effects." We then must try to match those effects with an
appropriate model in an appropriate situation.

Shoemaker, Hardy, and MacKenzie (1989) expand on the needs for research in the data, modeling, and the management of the promotions area:

Data and software. We need to learn how to handle and draw information from data sets that are hundreds of times larger than those we
have seen before. This will require cooperation between academics,
researchers, and data suppliers and business.

Modeling. As data improve, our ability (and our need) for modeling the
entire range of promotional effects—short term/long term, manufac-
turer/retailer/consumer, within-store/between store competition, and
the like—will improve.

Promotional management. There is research needed on how organizational design, reward, and incentive structures and overall organizational climate affect the effectiveness of promotional decisions.

At the moment, there is also a continuing need for a taxonomy to help
the marketer identify one or more reasonable modeling approaches for his or
her particular promotional problem (and promotional environment). The development of such a taxonomy will provide clear indication of areas that need

modeling attention, and provide an agenda for further, fruitful research in this area.

In the meantime, there have been a number of important practical (and theoretical) developments, that, with suitable customization, can provide valuable and useful support in making promotional decisions and in understanding promotional effects. And as the quantity grows and quality of promotional data continues to improve dramatically, we can expect to see enormous improvements in our understanding of promotional phenomena in years to come.

Finally, in an intriguing attempt to share their experience, Abraham and Lodish (1989a) provide some generalizations based on ten years of evaluating promotions:

- Promotions almost always have a measurable impact on sales. However the effect is usually purely short run.
- Roughly 16% of trade and 11% of consumer promotions are profitable.
- Many brands are overspending on marketing support (advertising and promotions).
- The current trend toward promotion spending is not saved from a marketing productivity stand point.

It would be valuable to evaluate these generalizations independently and to determine their causes.

SUMMARY

Promotions include a mixed set of marketing activities aimed both at end users and channel intermediaries whose effects are not that well understood. Included as promotions are a wide variety of short-term incentive tools such as coupons, premiums, contests, and buying allowances designed to stimulate earlier and/or stronger market response, either by consumers or by the trade.

Models of sales promotion evaluation have considered several different phenomena. One is the long-term profit effect from brand switchers. Another is the short-term phenomenon of adding to inventory (stocking up) by regular buyers. A third phenomenon is the capture of deal-prone users. Empirical evidence is beginning to emerge about the relative importance of these phenomena across a range of different market types.

Promotional models have aimed both at developing insight about the effects of promotions and at developing operational tools that can be used to support promotional decision making. Those modeling approaches have dealt with the full range of promotional phenomena, looking at short-term and long-term effects at the individual and at the aggregate level.

The widespread availability of scanner data and the associated computer hardware and software is providing much sharper measurement instruments for determining the effect of promotions at the individual consumer level. This new rich data source will provide a spark for the development of better operational models as well as the empirical insights to improve theoretical models in the next few years.

PROBLEMS

7.1. In 1967 Booth Appliances, Inc., sold the following numbers of units in relation to its promotional effort:

	Jan.	Feb.	Mar.	Apr.	May	June	July	Aug.	Sept.	Oct.	Nov.	Dec.
Sales (in 1000s)	105	100	145	117	155	138	177	136	157	167	168	123
Promotional effort (in 1000s)	30	20	60	35	70	57	100	50	80	85	95	40

   a. Suggest some forms of demand functions that could be used to represent the data.
   b. Effort in November was $10,000 more than in October, yet sales were almost the same. To what can this be attributed?
   c. Suppose the demand function $Q = \bar{Q}(1 - e^{-a_0 x})$ gives a good fit to the data. Assume the company has a linear cost function, $C = a_1 + bQ$. Derive a rule for determining the optimal level of marketing effort.
   d. What would be the effect on demand of an increase in the quality of promotional effort per dollar?

7.2. Joe Prince, marketing manager of XYZ Snack, is considering offering a case allowance to the trade. He expects sales to be 40,000 cases in the absence of promotion. The case price is $10 and the gross profit contribution is 40%. He is considering a $1 case allowance. He expects sales of 20,000 cases during the promotional period. The estimated cost of developing this promotion is $12,000.
   a. Will he make a profit on this promotion?
   b. What is the break-even sales increase that will justify this case allowance?

7.3. A manufacturer of men's dress shirts has a promotional budget of $80 (in thousands of dollars) and wishes to determine which allocation of this budget between its two territories will maximize profits. The demand functions for territories 1 and 2 are

$$Q_1 = 10X_1^{1/2}, \qquad Q_2 = 5X_2^{1/2}$$

where X_i is the amount of promotional dollars spent in territory i. The respective cost functions are

$$C_1 = 100 + 6Q_1 + X_1, \qquad C_2 = 30 + 4Q_2 + X_2$$

   a. Suppose $P_1 = \$7$ and $P_2 = \$8$. What is the optimal allocation of the budget between the two territories?

b. Could additional profits be made by increasing the budget?

c. What is the optimal budget?

7.4. An interesting situation develops between a manufacturer and an independent distributor over promotional effort to the final customer. Let

$$
\begin{aligned}
i &= \text{1 refer to manufacturer, 2 to distributor} \\
z_i &= \text{profit rate, dollars per year} \\
x_i &= \text{promotional effort, dollars per year} \\
g_i &= \text{incremental profit as fraction of retail sales} \\
c_{0i} &= \text{fixed-cost rate, dollars per year} \\
s &= \text{retail-sales rate, dollars per year} \\
s &= \alpha \ln \beta(x_1 + x_2)
\end{aligned}
$$

a. What will x_1 and x_2 be if the manufacturer and the distributor independently try to maximize profit? Are you sure?

b. What value of $x_1 + x_2$ will maximize total profit in the system?

7.5. Use the Rao-Lilien model:

a. At what market share of game-playing brands is the total volume gained by game-playing brands maximized? (Assume $\alpha = 0.2$)

b. Consider a gasoline market. You are the manager at Pepgas who is in charge of deciding whether or not to have a game. You have determined that the market is stable with respect to price, there will be no credit card mailouts in the near future, and total market gasoline-sales volume (G) is stable. Right now a share of the market, m, is involved in games. Determine under what circumstances to have a game if π = profit margin per sales unit and K, the cost of running the game, is fixed.

7.6. The drug industry has been subject to considerable public criticism. It faces some interesting promotional problems. Suppose that a group of N pharmaceutical firms selling indistinguishable products for the same price are competing with one another by promotion. The market is of fixed size and is insensitive to price. For sales response, assume the following:

$$
s_i = \frac{x_i}{\sum\limits_{j=1}^{N} x_j} M
$$

Let

$$
\begin{aligned}
x_i &= \text{promotional spending rate of company } i, \text{ dollars per year} \\
s_i &= \text{sales rate of company } i \\
M &= \text{total market for product, units per year} \\
p &= \text{selling price} \\
c_1 &= \text{incremental cost of producing unit, dollars per unit} \\
c_0 &= \text{fixed-cost rate for company, exclusive of promotion dollars per year}
\end{aligned}
$$

Each company manipulates its x_i to try to maximize its own profit.

a. What will be the spending, sales, and profit rates for each?

b. If each company raises its price until its profit is a fraction r of sales, what will the price be?

c. With the price as in part (b), what will be the fraction f of the customer's dollars that is being spent on promotion?

d. Suppose $r = 5\%$, $N = 4$, and $c_0 = 0.15c_1M/N$ for each company. What will f be?

7.7. The product manager for Flaky Fritters is planning a national sales promotion campaign. Historically, the time pattern of sales response for a four week promotion has looked like this:

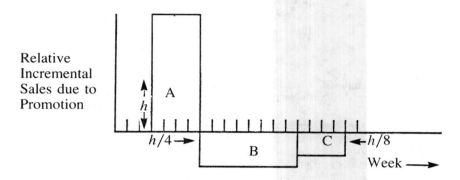

Relative Incremental Sales due to Promotion

A = promotional period (four weeks in length)
B = initial postpromotional period (eight weeks in length)
C = final postpromotional period (four weeks in length)

Note that for a reference promotion, if we call the sale rate increase in period A h, then the sales loss in B is $h/4$ and is $h/8$ in period C.

The sales rate increase, h, is a function of the promotional intensity, as follows:

$$h(x) = 5.3 \left(\frac{x^4}{x^4 + 64} \right)$$

(in millions of units/four week period) where x = promotional spending in $100,000s.

Assuming that the price to the trade for Flaky Fritters averages $1.10 per unit and that the cost per unit is $0.65, what level of promotional spending maximizes short-term promotional profitability? How could the model be extended?

8 | SALES FORCE

Every organization has one or more individuals who have direct responsibility for interacting with prospects and customers. This group of individuals is called the sales force. Their role in the marketing mix varies from firm to firm. Furthermore, anyone is a company salesperson when he is trying to win business for the company, including officers and service personnel, as well as salespersons who are hired to do full-time selling. We restrict the term "salesperson" here to those who earn their livelihood primarily through selling.

In this chapter we concentrate on field selling, which is found in almost every industry and involves a sales force that travels to actual and potential buyers. Salespersons may all work out of a central office, or they may be located in the different territories for which they have individual responsibility. Furthermore, they may report to district managers, who report to regional or general sales managers.

Sales management is involved in two main areas: administration and strategy. Administration includes recruiting, election, training, assigning, compensating, motivating, and controlling the sales force, while strategy deals with issues of force sizing, territory design, and call-planning procedures. We focus most of our attention on the strategy issue and deal with the one element of administration—sales force compensation—that has received much interest in recent years.

PERSONAL SELLING: TASKS, IMPORTANCE, AND MODELS

The Role of the Sales Force

Narrowly defined, the objective of the sales force is to sell. But the role of the salesperson has many dimensions. Selling is a communications process in which information is transmitted and persuasive messages applied. But it is a two-way process, and communications can be modified or adjusted during the process. As the link between the buying and the selling organization, the salesperson provides what Spekman (1979) refers to as boundary-spanning activities:

> *Represents and transacts.* The salesperson is the face of the organization but is charged with representing the needs of two organizations: his firm and the customer's organization.
>
> *Buffers.* The salesperson has to promote environmental stability, smoothing irregularities between production cycles in his organization and the sales-ordering cycle of the customer.
>
> *Processes information and monitors.* The salesperson provides a continual flow of information about market and environmental conditions that is vital to the activities of the producing firm.
>
> *Links and coordinates.* The salesperson guides informal coordination efforts between the producing and client firms or through middlemen to the client firm.

The salesperson must act as a problem solver, understanding the customer's problem and how it can be solved through the use of the firm's products. His role varies widely depending on the industry. In consumer goods companies, the salesperson calls on retail outlets, services the accounts, arranges for displays and shelf positions, and so on, while in many industrial product situations, the salesperson also has to identify and solve unique customer problems, a job requiring substantial independence and creativity.

Thus the salesperson performs a large number of functions, the impact and influences of which may be difficult to quantify, presenting a challenge for the quantitative model builder.

Sales Force Decision Problems

Exhibit 8.1 shows the four main phases of the management of the personal-selling function. First, the role of personal selling in the firm's marketing mix must be defined by establishing goals or criteria for use in sales force decision making. Second, a resource commitment to the effort must be established,

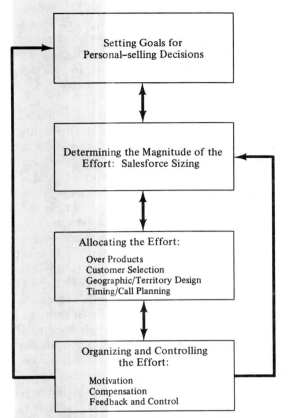

EXHIBIT 8.1   The structure of sales force decision problems. (*Source:* Montgomery and Urban, 1969, p. 244.)

which involves developing a sales force budget and determining the size of the sales force. Third, resources must be allocated to establish how effort is spread over the dimensions of customers, products, sales territories, and time (i.e., scheduling of calls). Finally, organization, motivation, and control of selling effort must be considered: the structure of the sales force and the levels of reporting responsibility must be set; motivation and compensation schemes must be established; training and assignment of salespersons must be considered; and the results of the selling effort—sales performance—must be monitored and fed back into these other decision areas to assist the firm in adapting to changing market conditions.

The two-directional flows in Exhibit 8.1 suggest that this process is cyclical rather than sequential. Sales force goals affect the magnitude of the effort, but the size of the effort limits possible goals as well. The size of the sales force affects its allocation, but at the allocation stage the firm may discover that sales response is greater (or less) than expected, and therefore profitability may be enhanced by allocating more (or fewer) resources in personal selling. The initial sales force size decision may also be updated in light of customer and territory allocations. Simultaneous determination of these management problems would be ideal, but, in practice, firms usually allocate resources sequentially across the dimensions.

The Importance of Sales Force Planning.   The sales force represents a large investment for most firms, especially in the industrial goods area. According to *Sales and Marketing Management,* the 1986 average cost of an industrial sales call was $230, with computer firms reporting higher costs ($453) per call and chemical firms reporting lower costs ($155).

Exclusive of the cost of sales management and overhead, the median cost of the sales force was 6.3% of sales for a sample of 125 U.S. industrial products and 9.9% for a sample of 80 European products (Lilien and Weinstein, 1984). In aggregate, sales force–related expenditures exceed those of other marketing functions; Lambert (1968) estimated that sales force spending is between 1.6 and 3.0 times the amount allocated to advertising.

In addition, as pointed out by Zoltners and Gardner (1980), these large expenditures are directed at a dynamic internal and external environment. They report that a leading consumer products firm increased a divisional sales force by 50% when it introduced a single new product. New products, in particular, are most often sold through the company's sales force; when these products mature, they are often removed from the sales force's portfolio and sold through distributors (Lilien, 1979).

The nature and structure of the sales force will change with changes in the internal environment. Zoltners and Gardner (1980) report that an industrial firm recently tripled its sales force for a particular division when the products of that division were classified as "stars" via the Boston Consulting Group classification (Chapter 11). Mergers of several firms often require a new territory alignment or reallocation of sales calls.

In addition, changes in the external environment of the firm affect sales force decisions in important ways. Changes in customers' purchasing organizations may necessitate sales force restructuring: a centralized purchasing facility can change with the location and the magnitude of the sale, requiring modification in sales call frequency, as well as potential reassignment of sales personnel.

Finally, sales force decisions, once made, are more difficult to change than decisions in other functional areas; people are affected by sales force decisions, and this human investment is not as easily changed as decisions in advertising, promotion, or pricing. Controlled experimentation and shifts in allocations are risky, expensive, and hard to justify. Shifts in sales force allocations may break old, favorable customer relationships. Furthermore, the long lead time involved in recruiting, hiring, and training new salespeople makes increases in sales resources a gradual process, and once a salesperson is a firm's employee, termination and replacement costs lobby against releasing the individuals during short-term economic downturns.

MODELING SALES FORCE PROBLEMS

There are a range of models aimed at salesforce decision problems. A review by Zoltners and Gardner (1980) covers over 60 articles in the field, Cravens (1979) reviews 22 models, Zoltners and Sinha (1980) produce 48 references for integer programming models of sales resource allocation alone, Zoltners and Sinha (1983) review numerous sales territory alignment models, and Coughlan and Sen (1989) review the models for sales force compensation.

On the surface, many problems that face sales management—sizing of the force, allocating the sales force, scheduling calls, structuring sales territories—appear well suited to many of the quantitative approaches that characterize the methodology of management science and operations research, such as integer programming, dynamic programming, assignment problems, and transportation problems. In fact, developments in the field are numerous, and both integrative models (Beswick and Cravens, 1977, for example) and empirical model tests (Fudge and Lodish, 1977) have been reported. Implementation rates, although not reported systematically, appear to be low, but models and computer applications in this area seem to be growing.

In the following sections we present model-based approaches for sales force sizing, sales resource allocation, territory design, and quota and compensation setting, as well as some integrative-modeling approaches to sales force problems.

Sales Force Sizing

The size of the sales force is one of the most important decisions facing executives in many industries. In practice, this decision is affected by other elements in the marketing mix and influences the overall marketing strategy. The specific options chosen—sales force size versus the use of wholesalers, distributors, agents, and so forth—depend on the relative costs and the selling tasks required and a range of methods are used.

Sales Force Sizing Heuristics.   To address the problem of sales force sizing, many firms use one of several relatively simple approaches: the breakdown, or percentage-of-sales, approach, the work load approach, or an industry guideline method.

In the *percentage-of-sales approach* a sales forecast is prepared, an historical (or otherwise justified) percentage of sales is applied against the forecast, and the average cost of a salesperson is divided into this figure to get the sales force size.

In the *breakdown method* the average revenue generated by a salesperson is divided into the sales forecast to get a sales force–sized figure. Neither the breakdown nor the percentage-of-sales variation have much to recommend it (besides simplicity) because each ignores the interaction between the number of salespersons and sales, as well as the factors that influence salespersons' productivity.

A number of firms are relying on new quantitative industry guidelines to support their selling (and communications) expenditure decisions. The basic idea is that budgeting expenditures are related to a number of product and market characteristics. Two efforts that have attempted to explain differences in marketing-spending levels by studying a cross section of business situations are the ADVISOR models (Lilien, 1979; Lilien and Weinstein, 1984) and the PIMS models (Buzzell and Farris, 1976). (See Chapter 11.)

While these sales force sizing heuristics have seen considerable use (see Fogg and Rokus, 1973, for example), they do not account for the impact that sales activity has on company sales and do not view sales force sizing as an investment.

Market-Response Methods.   To determine the most profitable sales force size, one must recognize that the sales force budget, the number of salespersons to employ, and the compensation scheme are intimately interconnected. The compensation scheme affects the quality of the people that can be attracted to a position, as well as the way they perform (i.e., the sales response to selling effort). With this simultaneity in mind, and with the recognition that all steps in Exhibit 8.1 may have to be performed iteratively, consider the following simplistic approach (from Montgomery and Urban, 1969).

Assume that the best level of sales force size is one that maximizes the profit rate. Then the sales force–sizing problem is to find X^*, the level of selling effort that maximizes Z, profit:

$$\text{Maximize } Z = PQ(X) - C_1(Q) - C_2(X) \tag{8.1}$$

where

$$
\begin{aligned}
Z \quad &= \text{profit} \\
P \quad &= \text{selling price} \\
Q(X) \quad &= \text{number of units sold as function of selling effort} \\
C_1(Q) \quad &= \text{total cost of producing and merchandising } Q \text{ units} \\
C_2(X) \quad &= \text{total cost of selling effort of level } X
\end{aligned}
$$

Equation (8.1) assumes all other elements in the marketing mix are fixed (price, advertising, etc.), no carryover or competitive effects exist, a single product is sold by the salesperson, a compensation scheme for the salesperson is well established, and so on. It also assumes that the salespersons have a given average quality that is linked to the (given) compensation scheme.

This equation is naive, yet it points out the key unknown variable: the elements P, $C_1(Q)$, and $C_2(X)$ are likely to be known (or at least readily estimable), but $Q(X)$, the sales response to selling effort, is not. Several approaches for estimating $Q(X)$ have been proposed, including analysis of historical data, field experimentation, judgmental calibration, and simulation. The first three of these are discussed in the paragraphs that follow. (Montgomery and Urban, 1969, pp. 253 ff., discuss the simulation approach in this context, but little use of that approach has been reported.)

Under the assumption that the future will in some way be like the past, historical sales records in many firms may form the basis to infer the relationship between selling effort and sales.

Lucas, Weinberg, and Clowes (1975) related sales level to territorial potential and work load. Using both linear and log-linear structures, the authors show that significant variation in sales can be explained by potential and work load. However, the relationships vary somewhat by region.

They suggest the following normative analysis for determining sales force size:

$$\text{Maximize } Z = mXf\left(\frac{P}{X}, \frac{W}{X}\right) - CX \qquad (8.2)$$

where

m = profit margin per unit sold
X = number of salespersons
C = cost per salesperson
P = corporate potential
W = corporate work load

They illustrate the optimization by specifying

$$f(P, W) = aP_i^{b_1} W_i^{b_2} \qquad (8.3)$$

and show that an optimal sales force size can be determined by

$$X = \left[\frac{maP^{b_1} W^{b_2}(1 - b_1 - b_2)}{C(b_1 + b_2)}\right] \qquad (8.4)$$

The limitations of this approach include the difficulty of evaluating equal-potential or equal-work-load markets. Furthermore, the controllable variables are not independent, all salespersons are not alike, and short-term variations in sales force size are limited. These problems suggest that the results should be used with caution:

> The impact of these limitations does not make the optimization procedure meaningless, but it does affect the way the solution should be used. Given the limitations, the results only provide directional information. For example, if the optimum size of the salesforce is substantially larger than the current size of the salesforce, then the implication is that the firm should reduce the average size of its territories and increase the number of salespersons it employs. Depending upon the specific problem this may imply that the firm should increase its capacity for training new salespersons or merely that the company should seek to reallocate its existing sales force. *(Lucas, Weinberg, and Clowes, 1975, p. 304)*

This approach uses historical analyses of the relationship between sales level and potential to develop normative implications for salesforce-sizing decisions. However, such aggregate relationships assume that the firm's current sales-effort-allocation program will remain unchanged. But sales revenues are also a function of how the sales effort is allocated across products markets, sales regions, and so forth, complications not included in the model. Lodish and colleagues (1988) describe a judgmental calibration approach, dealing with several of these issues.

Lodish and colleagues (1988) developed a series of subjectively calibrated models for Syntex Laboratories, a major pharmaceutical company, to decide how large its sales force should be. They constructed two models: one that looked at the allocation of salesforce effort to products (seven ethical drugs: Naprosyn, Anaprox, etc.) and one that considered allocation to physician specialty (nine specialties: general practice, internal medicine, etc.). Each model had the same form for a particular sales force size, S:

Find $\{X_i\}$ to

$$\text{Maximize } Z = 0.01 \sum_{i=1}^{I} r_i(X_i)\, S_i a_i \tag{8.5a}$$

$$\text{Subject to } \sum_{i=1}^{I} X_i e_i \leq S \tag{8.5b}$$

where

$\quad S_i \quad$ = strategic plan sales force allotment for product (or physician specialty) i

$\quad X_i \quad$ = index of effort to i, where $X_i = 100$ is the current effort level

$\quad r_i(X_i) \quad$ = sales response three years out to level of effort X_i (modeled as an ADBUDG function—see Appendix C)

$\quad a_i \quad$ = contribution margin per incremental dollar of sales for product i

e_i = strategic plan sales resource effort allocation to product i

Equation (8.5) gives an optimal allocation of sales effort for a given sales force size. If we call Z in equation (8.5), $Z(S)$, then we can structure the sales force sizing problem as

Find ΔS to

$$\text{Maximize } \Pi(S^*) = Z(S + \Delta S) - C(\Delta S) \qquad (8.6)$$

where

$C(\Delta S)$ = (annualized) cost of adding (subtracting) sales force level ΔS to the strategic plan level S

$\Pi(S^*)$ = profit associated with sales force level S^*

S^* = $S + \Delta S$

Equation (8.5) allocates sales force effort optimally, given a sales force size S. Equation (8.6), then, asks "if we add ΔS to S are we better off?" If the answer is yes, then $S^* = S + \Delta S$ becomes the new base point and problem (8.5) is repeated. In practice, (8.5) is solved to obtain $Z(S)$ for a range of values of S (or S^*); these are plugged into (8.6), and the highest value of Π gives the optimal salesforce size. (We sketch a procedure for solving equation (8.5)—a "loose knapsack procedure" —in the next section.)

Lodish and colleagues used a Delphi procedure (Appendix D) to calibrate the response functions $r_i(X_i)$. The calibration involved Syntex's senior vice president of sales and marketing, the vice president of sales, two representatives from the research department, two regional sales managers, and two salespeople. Each manager answered the following questions for each product and each physician specialty (p. 11):

> According to the strategic plan, if the current level of salesforce effort is maintained from 1982 to 1985, sales of Product A would be the planned level. What would happen to Product A's 1985 sales (compared with present [1982] levels) if during the same time period it received:
>
> 1. No sales effort?
> 2. One half the current effort?
> 3. 50 percent greater effort?
> 4. A saturation level of sales effort?

Each manager answered these questions privately first; the results were then summarized by a computer, fed back to the respondents, and discussed. A second round of completing the questions yielded consensus estimates.

Several important outcomes resulted from the modeling exercise. First, the current sales force level (433 reps) was significantly below what both the product and specialty models recommended (770–750 reps). Syntex management was quite sure that the optimum level would be below 550 reps. In addition, the model showed that most of the incremental effort should be applied to Naprosyn and to generalist physicians.

During the three years following the 1982 modeling exercise, the firm added approximately 200 sales representatives, the largest feasible number because of limitations on the firm's ability to train and deploy salespeople. In addition, Syntex generally deployed the salespeople consistent with the model recommendations. (In retrospect, Syntex management agreed that it allocated too much effort to oral contraceptives and not enough to Naprosyn and should have followed the model recommendations more closely.)

The model has a number of apparent weaknesses. First, it is static (looking at a three-year-out horizon only). Second, it does not deal with product-specialty interactions, because of lack of management time for calibration of such a model. Third, it is a judgmentally calibrated model and did not build in any intermediate checkpoints. As the authors stated, "the team felt that we should do the best we could with the people and data available" (p. 9).

How well did they do? A $30,000 investment in model building returned a verified $25,000,000 to Syntex, an 8% annual sales increase and the work was honored by the prestigious 1987 Edelman Prize in recognition of outstanding achievement in the practice of management science. This work was the first time (in 16 years of the Edelman Prize competition) that the prize had been awarded to a marketing application. (For more detail on the background of the study, see Clarke, 1987.)

Experimental Procedures.   The relationship between selling effort and sales can also be inferred by experimental procedures. In theory, this method is best, but practically, experimentation is a costly and time-consuming procedure. Furthermore, because changes in the size of the sales force for experimental purposes require changing the number and locations of people, it may be organizationally infeasible.

Nevertheless, several experimental studies have been reported. Brown, Hulswit, and Kettelle (1956) report on a study where salespersons were to allocate varying levels of effort to three groups of accounts, and response measures were inferred. The particular design allowed salespersons to choose which accounts would receive medium effort and which would receive low effort, while large accounts received the highest level of effort. This approach violates the random assignment assumption necessary for a good experimental design and contributes to an overstatement of market response to sales effort.

In another study Waid, Clark, and Ackoff (1956) report on experimental variations in the level of calling frequency. The results suggest that the company was operating in a saturation region of an (assumed) S-shaped sales-response curve. The Lamp Division of General Electric reduced the number of calls per customer and reported significant cost savings without increasing its sales force.

However, these examples of experimentation in sales force size are the exception. In general, experimentation is most likely to enter the sales force–sized decision indirectly, through the results of allocation studies or frequency-and-scheduling studies. Meidan (1982) provides an overview and evaluation of these and other methods for sales force sizing.

Allocation of Selling Effort

In the allocation of selling effort we address the following basic questions:

How can salespersons best utilize their time, allocating it between customers and prospects?

How should selling effort be allocated to products?

Here we assume that sales territories are fixed; we relax this assumption in the next section.

Time Allocation: Salesperson Call Planning (CALLPLAN).   In most markets all customers are not identical. Therefore three types of questions generally must be asked about a salesperson's call-selection procedure: (1) How much time should be spent with each prospect? (2) How much time should be spent with each current customer? (3) How should time be allocated between customers and prospects?

CALLPLAN (Lodish, 1971b, 1974) is an interactive salesperson's call-planning system. Its objective is to determine call-frequency norms for each client (current customer) and each prospect (account not currently buying from the salesperson). Call frequencies are the numbers of calls per effort period, which is the time period on which the allocations are based (usually one to three months).

The model is based on the assumption that the expected sales to each client and prospect over a response period (usually a year) is a function of the average number of calls per effort period during that response period. The response period is assumed to be long enough so that phenomena such as carryover in call effort from one period to the next are considered.

The CALLPLAN procedure has two phases:

1. The calibration stage, in which the expected profit associated with different call policies for each customer and prospect is determined

2. The optimization phase, in which optimal allocation of time to customers and prospects is established

Calibration phase.   Lodish suggests a decision-calculus approach, as in the Syntex problem, for calibrating the response function with each salesperson's own best estimate of customer response to changes in call frequency, as follows. For each customer i, let $r_i(X_i)$ be the expected sales to account i during the response period if X_i calls are made during the effort period.

In practice, Lodish recommends asking for discrete levels as discussed in the Syntex problem. Furthermore, he suggests an ADBUDG functional form to represent $r(X)$:

$$r_i(X_i) = r_0 + (r_\infty - r_0) \frac{X_i^{a_1}}{a_2 + X_i^{a_1}} \tag{8.7}$$

The values of a_1 and a_2 can be fit globally over the full range by nonlinear regression and the curve can either be concave or S-shaped.

The expected sales to a client or prospect are multiplied by an adjustment factor f_i, specific to the account, to obtain an adjusted number that reflects the contribution of sales to that customer.

The salesperson's territory is divided into J mutually exclusive geographic areas. A certain time per call is assumed that takes into consideration the average travel time to account i when in geographic area j. The number of trips to a geographic area is assumed to be the maximum number of times any one account is called upon during the effort period.

Optimization phase.   If we let

t_i = time spent with customer i (call length)
n_j = number of trips per effort period made to geographic area j
U_j = time it takes to get to geographic area j
C_j = out-of-pocket expenses involved in getting to geographic area j
e = number of effort periods per response period
T = selling plus travel time available per effort period
f_i = relative profit-adjustment factor for customer i

then

$t_i X_i$ = time spent with customer i during effort period
$n_j U_j$ = time getting to geographic area j during effort period

The problem is to

Find integer values $\{X_i\}$ to

$$\text{Maximize } Z = \sum_i f_i r_i(X_i) - e \sum_j n_j C_j \quad \text{(profit)} \tag{8.8}$$

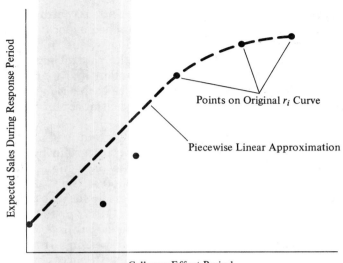

EXHIBIT 8.2 Sales-response levels and piecewise, linear, concave approximation that permits solution via incremental analysis.

Subject to

$$\sum_i X_i t_i + \sum_j n_j U_j \leq T \quad \text{(time constraint)}$$

$$n_j = \max_i (X_i \text{ in geographic area } j)$$

$$LB_i \leq X_i \leq UB_i \quad \text{(minimum and maximum bounds on calling frequency)}$$

Lodish (1971b) describes an intricate dynamic programming approach to solve system (8.8). However, when $r_i(X_i)$ is replaced by its linear concave envelope (see Exhibit 8.2), an incremental-analysis search procedure provides very efficient solutions. The CALLPLAN approach is usually interactive, with salesmen putting in input values, looking at the results, modifying the input values, and so on. Therefore, this fast, approximate approach is quite adequate.

Experimental test. A controlled experiment was run at United Airlines on the use of CALLPLAN (Fudge and Lodish, 1977). United Airlines has a sales force to promote passenger travel and another to promote airfreight operations. Account call frequency determines, to a large degree, the efficiency of their time allocation.

Twenty salespersons (16 passenger representatives and 4 cargo representatives) participated in the experiment; 10 pairs of salespersons (5 in New York and 5 in San Francisco) were matched by local management. Ten CALL-PLAN participants were chosen randomly, one from each pair. Then the remaining 10 salespersons comprised the control group. This group was told they were participating in an experiment and manually estimated call-frequency policies and anticipated sales for each account to compare with CALL-PLAN. Therefore, major sources of potential contamination were largely controlled for.

After six months the CALLPLAN group had an 11.9% increase in sales from the previous year, while the control group had only a 3.8% increase; thus the CALLPLAN users realized an 8.1% higher level of sales. This difference was significantly different from 0 at the 0.025 level. The actual sales improvement over that of the control group for just these 10 people was "well into seven figures" (Fudge and Lodish, 1977, p. 104).

The CALLPLAN model provides several important contributions. First, it is an operational procedure for salesperson's time allocation. Second, its value has been experimentally tested with success. And, third, it points out the value of modeling and computer analysis in this context. Because the judgments were made by the salespersons themselves, they could clearly be inaccurate or biased. Therefore the value of the approach is to provide the salesperson—the decision maker here—with a means of evaluating his decision by using the available information (his judgment); the computer and the model provide a systematic way of evaluating that information, identifying inconsistencies and allowing for sensitivity analysis.

The model appears to be best suited for repetitive selling situations with single (or at most a few) products. In these situations the amount of time with the client may well relate to the amount of sales generated. In addition, the model seems best suited for rather mature product lines where knowledge of the customer base and sales potential is greatest.

Allocation of Selling Resources Across Products (DETAILER).   Quite often a single sales force must handle a range of products. Under these circumstances selling time must be allocated across the products in a cost-effective manner. This decision is a difficult one. New products often need several years of selling before sales reach potential. During this time selling effort is an investment, and short-term measures of effectiveness, like sales volume or profitability, lobby against promoting them heavily. Yet effort on behalf of such products ties in closely with the long-term health of the firm. Thus the strategic direction of the firm—the longer-term commitment to a changing product and market mix—must be carefully considered in setting time allocations for certain products. The longer-term perspective may necessitate the sales force allocating a disproportionate amount of time to a certain set of products at the expense of short-term profits.

Management can take one of two main approaches to this allocation question. The first treats the problem directly while the second deals with the problem indirectly through the compensation system. Ideally, the salesperson's compensation should reward him for acting optimally for the firm. The compensation issue is explored in some depth later; we deal with a direct allocation model here.

DETAILER, by Montgomery, Silk, and Zaragoza (1971), is a decision-calculus model for the sales force allocation question that deals with the carryover effect of sales effort. Their approach assumes that the firm sells a group of products with a salesforce of fixed size and for which cross-elasticities of demand are minimal, and their objective function is the maximization of total company profits. Furthermore, they assume the salespersons are not compensated on commission, a normal practice in the ethical pharmaceuticals industry.

Model background. The model was developed for an ethical drug company, whose salespersons call mainly on doctors. Territories were designed so that there were approximately the same number of doctors (N) for each salesperson.

The authors assume that no more than three products can be effectively presented in a single sales visit. Then the key decision variables in planning time allocation are the number of times and the number of customers to whom a product should be promoted in a given period. Therefore the authors further assume that there are four discrete, alternative policies for coverage:

N calls per period (complete coverage)

$N/2$ calls per period (half coverage)

$N/4$ calls per period (quarter coverage)

0 calls per period (no coverage)

Because each salesperson contacts N customers and promotes three products on each call, there is a total effort of $3N$ product calls available.

Thus

$$3N = ND_c + \frac{N}{2}D_h + \frac{N}{4}D_q \tag{8.9}$$

where

D_c = number of products receiving complete coverage
D_h = number of products receiving half coverage
D_q = number of products receiving quarter coverage

Therefore as many as 12 products receiving quarter coverage or as few as 3 products receiving complete coverage could be promoted in any given period. The solution approach is similar to that of CALLPLAN in that it involves two stages: a response-function/calibration stage and an allocation/optimization stage.

Response-function development and calibration. To operationalize a response model, the authors define the *relative exposure value* R_t as an index of the relative effectiveness of alternative call policies in the current period. Specifically,

$$R_t\left(\frac{N}{2}\right) = 1$$

$$R_t(0) = 0$$

$$R_t\left(\frac{N}{4}\right) = q, \qquad 0 < q < 1 \tag{8.10}$$

$$R_t(N) = c, \qquad c > 1$$

This scaling of R_t eliminates effects such as seasonality and allows them to be added back separately. The scaling of $R_t(N/2) = 1$ implies that $N/2$ is equivalent to "saturation" detailing in the long term.

Then to accommodate forgetting and carryover effects, they define the *accumulated exposure level* A_t

$$A_t = f(R(X_t)) + (1 - \lambda)\, A_{t-1} \tag{8.11}$$

where

$\quad A_t \quad$ = exposure value in period t, resulting from current and past detailing

$\quad X_t \quad$ = current detailing level (equal to 0, $\dfrac{N}{4}$, $\dfrac{N}{2}$, or N)

$\quad f(\cdot) \quad$ = current effect of $R(\cdot)$

$\quad \lambda \quad$ = forgetting parameter

The specific form of $f\,(\cdot)$ used was $\lambda R(\cdot)$. Therefore,

$$A_t = \lambda R(X_t) + (1 - \lambda)\, A_{t-1} \tag{8.12}$$

For a value of sales in period t, a sales model is introduced

$$Q_t = P(t)I(A_t) \tag{8.13}$$

where

$Q(t)$ = unit sales in period t

$P(t)$ = sales potential in period t (saturation sales)

$I(\cdot)$ = sales index in t, fraction of sales potential that will be seen, a function of accumulated exposure value A_t

Then to specify the form of $I(A_t)$, certain constraints must be met. For instance, $I(0) = 0$, $I(\infty) \leq 1$, and $I(A)$ should generally be nondecreasing in A. In addition, as saturation is approached, there should be decreasing returns to additional effort, and the relationship should allow for increasing returns at low-exposure levels, suggesting threshold effects. A simple cubic function was proposed as a form that would handle these restrictions and also provide few parameters for judgmental calibration:

$$I_t = \begin{cases} a_0 + a_1 R_t^2 - a_2 R_t^3, & \text{if } a_0 + a_1 R_t^2 - a_2 R_t^3 \leq 1.0 \\ 1.0, & \text{otherwise} \end{cases} \tag{8.14}$$

The model is now complete, requiring the specifications of six parameters for each salesperson: c, q, λ, a_0, a_1, and a_2. For c and q, salespersons are asked to estimate the value of quarter and complete coverage relative to half coverage, and the value of λ is derived by asking them for a short-term sales forecast if no detailing effort is provided. To estimate a_0, a_1, and a_2, managers are asked to make forecasts of sales at different levels of (constant) detailing effort over an extended period of time. Other questions are asked of the managers to help check these values.

Allocation and optimization. The objective function suggested by the authors is to maximize total gross product-line profits over the planning horizon:

Find $\{X_{it}\}$ to

$$\text{Maximize } Z = \sum_{i=1}^{n} m_i \sum_{t=1}^{T} P(it) I(A_{it}) \tag{8.15}$$

Subject to

$$X_{it} = 0, N/4, N/2, \text{ or } N \text{ and equation (8.9)},$$

where

Z = total gross product line profits summed over planning horizon

m_i = gross margin for product i, $i = 1, \ldots, n$

n = number of products

T = planning horizon

This problem could be formulated as a dynamic program. However, as with

CALLPLAN, a fast, simple procedure that achieves good results is preferred to a computationally complex one, and the authors develop such a heuristic solution procedure.

DETAILER appears to be a conceptually sound, easy-to-use procedure for allocating selling effort across a line of products. As with CALLPLAN and all decision-calculus approaches, judgmental calibration plays a key role in deriving the results. A fixed number of salespersons is assumed, and no product line interdependencies are included. These simplifications are balanced by the models' parsimony and usability—it helps the salesperson and the sales manager develop a plan by allocating calls to products that result in substantially improved levels of sales. One division of a firm reported a one year profit improvement of $85,000 with the model; another application reported a profit improvement of over $1 million over a two year planning horizon.

Model Extensions and Related Work

The CALLPLAN model has been extended by Lodish in several ways. In one article (Lodish, 1975), he extends the concept to aid in designing sales force territories. A CALLPLAN analysis is used to find optimal-profit call frequencies for given territories. From this initial solution the marginal profit of an additional hour of sales effort is found. Sales territory boundaries are then restructured to equalize marginal profitability. Five firms have reportedly used this procedure successfully.

A further extension of CALLPLAN (Lodish, 1976) deals with assigning salespersons to accounts. In this extension the manager judges the effectiveness of each salesperson with each account and incorporates these judgments into the analysis of call frequency and territory alignment. The effectiveness of salesperson k on account i is called V_{ik}, and new variables $\{y_{ik}\}$ are set to one if salesperson k handles account i and to zero otherwise. This problem is now formulated as

Find $\{y_{ik}\}$ and $\{X_i\}$ to

$$\text{Maximize } Z = \sum_i f_i r_i(X_i) \sum_k y_{ik} V_{ik} \qquad (8.16)$$

Subject to

$$\sum_i y_{ik} X_i \leq T_k \qquad \text{(salesperson } k\text{'s time constraint, } k = 1, \ldots, K)$$

$$\sum_k y_{ik} \leq 1 \qquad \text{(assignment constraints)}$$

Lodish reports that this problem was solved with a piecewise linear approximation to the V_{ik} and a linear programming code. This model does not handle the y_{ij} as 0–1 variables as would seem appropriate in most applications. However, Lodish reports good results in an application involving a firm selling advertising to agencies, advertisers, and media-buying services in a single geographic area.

In a similar vein, Lodish (1980) developed a more integrated treatment dealing with sales force size, as well as the allocations of effort to the product and market segments. Furthermore, Zoltners, Sinha, and Chong (1979) have addressed a problem similar to CALLPLAN and propose an integer programming solution. Theirs is one of a number of models that address sales force allocation decisions. (See Zoltners and Sinha, 1980.)

A salesperson should visit the customers he or she wishes to contact in the most efficient manner—minimizing travel time, travel expense, and so on subject to constraints on plane schedules and limits on presentation time required by type of customer. Gensch (1979) developed an algorithm for metallographic specialists at U.S. Steel whose job was to visit specialty customers most efficiently and suggest various alloys to met changing technological needs.

This stream of research has been extending and generalizing basic models. Although some authors continue to develop and argue for more general model structures and improved solution algorithms, it appears as if the greatest short-term benefits could be achieved by studying two key problems:

1. Routes (and barriers) to implementation of sales force allocation models

2. The characterization of the determinants of sales force—sales-response functions

For the first research area, more reports like those of Fudge and Lodish (1977) and Lodish and colleagues (1988) are required. Detailed reports of successful implementation strategies (perhaps as case studies), as well as failures, would help enormously in bridging the theory-practice gap. Many good models are available, but too few are seeing use, and we need to understand why. (See LaForge et al., 1990, for discussion of how to improve decision calculus applications in this area.)

In terms of characterizing factors that should be considered in developing sales revenue functions, more research, such as that of Ryans and Weinberg (1979), is required. They developed a framework for specifying the major constructs that account for territory sales revenue, including the following:

1. Company marketing activities

2. Sales force policies and procedures

3. Field sales manager characteristics

4. Salesperson characteristics

5. Territory characteristics

6. Competition

They built a sales-response function, in multiplicative form, for each of three firms. Their results and their review of the related literature show the following:

1. Sales potential seems to be more important than measures such as work load in explaining variation in territory sales response.

2. Work load is difficult to operationalize and does not always yield consistent results.

3. The influence of the field sales manager, operationalized as span of control, was usually significant, with sales decreasing as span of control increased.

4. Competitive strength appeared to relate to territory sales response, suggesting the need for further work in this area.

Finally, their work shows that models of territory sales response can be developed and that results achieved in one setting can be replicated in others. Follow-up work (Ryans and Weinberg, 1987) also suggests that model parameters are stable over time. This result suggests that more work is needed to develop these findings further and integrate them into response-function estimation procedures.

Sales Territory Design

Most companies assign sales representatives to geographic entities called *territories*, which are aggregated into large groupings called *districts*, which, in turn, may be aggregated into major sales regions.

In designing a system of territories either for a new sales force or to update the territorial structure for an existing sales force, companies generally try to meet the following objectives:

The territories should be easy to administer.

Sales potential should be easy to estimate.

Total travel time should be kept under careful control.

Territories should provide a sufficient and equitable work load and sales potential for each salesperson.

These characteristics are achieved through decisions about the size and shape of territorial units.

In terms of territory size two main approaches are used: one forms territories of *equal sales potential* and the other forms territories of *equal work load*. Each principle has pluses and minuses.

The logic of creating territories of equal potential is to provide each sales representative with the same income opportunities and to permit the firm to evaluate performance more readily. Persistent differences in sales yield by territory are assumed to be due to differences in ability or effort. Thus this approach creates a competitive environment among salespersons.

But customer geographic density almost always varies, and so territories with equal potential can cover vastly different areas. For example, the potential for a large drill press is as large in Detroit as it is in a number of western states. A sales representative assigned to Detroit can cover that same potential with far less effort than the sales representative covering the several western states.

Alternatively, then, the firm can try to equalize work loads, which requires that territories be designed so that each representative can adequately cover his territory. In general, this approach leads to variations in sales potential. This latter approach may not present a problem when the sales force is on straight salary, but it is unfair to a commissioned sales force.

Operationally, any approach requires blending salary and commission structures and also trading off potential against work load. In practice, better territories are often assigned to better or more senior salespersons.

Territories are usually formed by combining smaller units, such as census tracts, or counties until they add up to a territory of a given potential or work load. They are put together with reference to the location of natural barriers, the compatibility of adjacent areas, adequacy of transportation, and so forth.

In recent years a number of automatic procedures generally based on linear or integer programing, have been developed. We review one next.

GEOLINE Model.   Hess and Samuels (1971) developed a model, called GEOLINE, based on the REDIST program used for legislative districting. Their procedure builds sales and service territories that satisfy three principles: (1) equal sales work load (or some other, single criterion); (2) contiguity, that is, each territory must consist of adjacent areas; and (3) compactness, that is, the territories should be as easy as possible to cover from a travel standpoint.

A measure of a territory's compactness is the *moment of inertia*, the sum of the squares of the distances from the home base to all customers weighted by the customers' volume of business, or

$$M = \sum_i V_i d_{hi}^2 \qquad (8.17)$$

where

$$M = \text{moment of inertial of territory}$$
$$V_i = \text{sales volume of customer } i$$
$$d_{hi} = \text{distance of customer } i \text{ from home base } h$$

The building up of sales territories starts with a large number of small areas, called standard geographic units (SGUs), usually census tracts or something of similar size. These units are considered as points, with the co-ordinates of each unit j being n_j (the north/south or y coordinate) and e_j (the east/west or x-coordinate), for $j = 1, ..., J$. Then for each of these SGUs there is an activity measure a_j. Initially, a number of territories and a starting set of area centroids, N_i and E_i, for $i = 1, ..., I$ (number of territories), must be established.

Hess and Samuels report that the homes or offices of existing salespersons provide excellent starting points. Alternatively, centroids of existing territories have been used.

Model formulation.   The problem (or sequence of problems) that they formulate is to

Find $\{X_{ij}\}$ to

$$\text{Minimize} \sum_j \sum_i c_{ij} X_{ij} a_j \qquad \text{(moments of inertia)} \qquad \textbf{(8.18)}$$

Subject to

$$\sum_j X_{ij} a_j = \frac{1}{I} \sum a_j \qquad \text{(equal-activity constraint)}$$

$$\sum_i X_{ij} = 1 \qquad \text{(assignment requirement)}$$

where

$$c_{ij} = (N_i - n_j)^2 + (E_i - e_j)^2 \qquad \begin{array}{l} \text{the cost (contribution to} \\ \text{moment of inertia) of} \\ \text{assigning the geographic} \\ \text{unit } i \text{ to territory } j) \text{ and} \end{array} \qquad \textbf{(8.19)}$$

X_{ij} = proportion of geographic unit j assigned to territory i

Equation (8.18) is a linear program that results in split territories—that is, some SGUs are assigned to more than one territory. In practice, this situation is handled by assigning the SGU to the territory for which its share of activity is the largest,

$$X_{ij} = \begin{cases} 1, & \text{if } X_{ij}^0 = \max_i [X_{ij}^0] \\ 0, & \text{otherwise} \end{cases} \qquad (8.20)$$

where the superscript in X_{ij}^0 indicates that it is the optimal solution to equation (8.18). As an example, suppose that $X_{14}^0 = 0.4$, $X_{54}^0 = 0.3$, $X_{84}^0 = 0.3$ and all other $X_{14}^0 = 0$. This procedure would modify the solution by setting $X_{14} = 1$ and all other $X_{14} = 0$.

The authors report that minor deviations from equality of work load result from recombinations of these split territories. In practice, about one geographic area is split per territory. Thus by making the number of SGUs large relative to the number of territories, these deviations will be small. With about 20 SGUs per territory, they report deviations of $\pm 10\%$ on average.

The solution algorithm is not finished after the solution of equation (8.18). The original centroids were set arbitrarily. Therefore the next stage of the solution procedure requires recalculation of territory centroids:

$$N_i = \frac{\sum_j X_{ij} a_j n_j}{\sum_j a_j X_{ij}} \qquad (8.21)$$

$$E_i = \frac{\sum_j X_{ij} a_j e_j}{\sum_j a_j X_{ij}} \qquad (8.22)$$

where the $\{X_{ij}\}$ used in equation (8.21) and (8.22) are the values from the previous linear programming solution rounded off to integers.

The calculation sequence then continues: centroids $\rightarrow$ linear programming allocations $\rightarrow$ integerize solution $\rightarrow$ new centroids, and so on. The calculation ends when successive linear programs give identical solutions or when a predetermined number of iterations have been performed. Careful examination of intermediate solutions is required to prevent looping, reported to occur in 10% of the cases. Managerial intervention is easy with this procedure, which allows special considerations, assignments, and adjustments to be made. Because the final solution is a local rather than a global solution, in practice, the procedure is restarted with other initial centers.

The GEOLINE model represents a practical, flexible, and useful tool. The model is not restricted to any specific activity measure; rather, the selection of this measure is up to sales management. In the seven applications reported by the authors, the activity measures used included customer count, calls, potential, and a weighted measure.

Although a useful procedure, this model is not without its limitations. The selection of an activity measure, while flexible, is ambiguous. The objective function is to minimize a weighted moment of inertia, but it is not clear how this measure relates to other, more objective criteria, such as cost and profit. Furthermore, SGUs may be split between territories, but the model does not consider accessibility or compatibility with geographic considerations, such as highways, mountains, and waterways. Finally, the model does not recognize the interaction between sales territory design, salespersons call planning, and sales force sizing.

Related Work.   A number of other models have been developed that deal with problems of territory design. Easingwood (1973) has developed a heuristic procedure that looks at average work load in an attempt to equalize that work load among regions or territories. Richardson (1979) presents a linear programming–based procedure that permits the balancing of up to five measures of sales potential. Zoltners (1979) presents an integer programming–based approach, allowing for single or multiple activity centers. Segal and Weinberger (1977) incorporate accessibility into their model but SGUs may still be split between territories. Zoltners and Sinha (1983) present a review and critique of sales territory alignment models and argue for math programming versus heuristic solutions. Segal and Weinberger (1977), satisfies the accessibility criteria, and does not split SGUs. In addition, in a reported application it produced more-balanced territorial alignments than the other two models.

Other models integrate territory design, along with other components of the salesforce decision. Lodish (1975) includes territory realignment along with call planning; Comer (1974) deals with call planning and territory design jointly. Beswick and Cravens (1977) and Glaze and Weinberg (1979) have both incorporated territory alignment in their models, allowing for the use of the Hess and Samuels procedure. Shanker, Turner, and Zoltners (1975) integrate territory design and salesperson call planning into one procedure that maximizes the total sales from all territories. Exhibit 8.3 gives the graphical output of the Shanker-Turner-Zoltner procedure.

In sum, there appear to be a number of sales-territory-design procedures that are user oriented, capture many real-life complexities, and are relatively easy to apply. In addition, there continue to be reports of the use of these procedures, especially those integrating models with graphics in an interactive PC-based computing environment. (See Collins, 1984, 1985, 1986, 1987; Layman, 1986; Locke, 1984; Martinott, 1987; *Sales and Marketing Management,* 1986, 1987; Steinberg and Plank, 1987; Taylor, 1987; and Young, 1987, for some examples of PC-based decision support tools for salespeople.)

Sales Territory Design

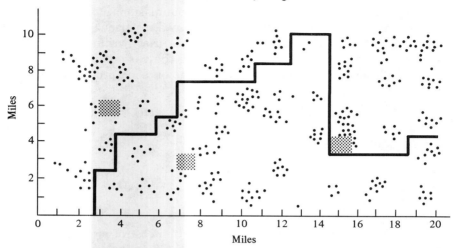

EXHIBIT 8.3 Optimal boundaries and resident locations for three sales territories. (*Source:* Shanker, Turner and Zoltners, 1975, p. 319.)

Setting Commissions and Quotas: Indirect Control of the Sales Force

While they consider the outcome—the desired allocation of time across customers, territories and the like—the models we have reviewed ignore how the optimal allocation will be implemented. In effect, these models assume the salesperson will do whatever he or she is asked to do. But a salesperson's incentives are often different from those of his or her employer. For example, if a salesperson is compensated on the basis of total sales, he may allocate all of his time to selling easy-to-sell products, even if they are low-margin items. He will also push for the firm to give price concessions; if a product has a 20% gross margin, then a 10% price reduction would cut the firm's profit in half but cut his commission by only 10%.

Therefore, much of the recent literature on sales force compensation addresses the following question: How can the firm motivate the salesperson to pursue the company's goals in his own self-interest? We discuss this literature here.

Deterministic Models with Observable Effort. Farley's 1964 article stimulated much research in this area. His formulation of the problem is as follows: Is there a commission scheme that will induce an income-maximizing salesperson to choose the same allocation of time as the profit-maximizing firm would like? The answer Farley gives is that if the commission scheme is based on sales, then this will not be possible in general, but if the commission scheme is based on gross margins, then *any* equal commission rate scheme will work. The reason is that with a sales-based commission scheme, only the firm takes into account margin differences among the various products; with a gross margin–based commission scheme, both the firm and the salesperson take into account margin differences among the various products.

However, if the margin percentage on each product (i or j) is the same, that is,

$$\frac{(p_i - c_i)}{p_i} = \frac{(p_j - c_j)}{p_j} \tag{8.23}$$

where

$$p_i = \text{price of product } i$$
$$c_i = \text{(constant) marginal production cost of product } i$$

for all $i \neq j$, then *any* equal commission rate scheme based on *sales* also aligns the firm's and salesperson's incentives. The time allocation that the salesperson chooses will be the same as he would choose if he also owned the company. In other words, the time allocation under an equal commission rate policy is the same as that in a "vertically integrated" firm where no commissions are used (because there are no incentive problems between the firm and the salesperson).

Note the flexibility in choosing the equal commission rate. This is because the commission rate divides only the firm's gross earnings between the firm's net earnings and the salesperson's income; it does not affect the time allocation among the various products and hence gross firm profits. The commission rate actually chosen will be a function of the bargaining power of the firm vis-à-vis the salesperson. If there is a large supply of qualified salespeople, then the salesperson's bargaining power will be low, and it is likely that the commission rate will pay the salesperson his approximate reservation wage—the wage he would get in his best alternative job.

We elaborate on the Davis and Farley (1971) extension of this model to give a flavor for the form of argument and analysis.

Davis and Farley (1971).   These authors extend and qualify Farley's original arguments. Consider a company that produces several products and pays its salespersons through commissions. Davis and Farley (1971) look at the profit-maximizing problem as it appears to the firm and the income-maximization problem as it appears to the salesperson and consider under what conditions these expressions can be jointly optimized. (For simplicity, we assume the firm has only one salesperson.)

Consider the salesperson first; his optimization problem is

Set (t_i) to

$$\text{Maximize } W = \sum_i r_i p_i S_i(t_i) \qquad \text{(commission income)} \qquad \textbf{(8.24)}$$

Subject to

$$\sum_i t_i \le T \qquad \text{(time constraint)}$$
$$t \ge 0 \qquad\qquad\qquad\qquad\qquad\qquad \textbf{(8.25)}$$

where

W	=	total commission earned by salesperson
r_i	=	commission rate paid on total sales of product i
p_i	=	price of product i
t_i	=	amount of time spent on product i by salesperson
$S_i(t_i)$	=	quantity sold of product i by salesperson
T	=	total time available to salesperson

Thus the salesperson's problem is to determine how much time to spend selling each product within the limits of his total time to maximize his commission (the commission rate times sales summed for all products).

The conditions for the salesperson to maximize his total commission can be found by combining equations (8.24) and (8.25) into the Lagrangian expression

$$L(W) = \sum_i r_i p_i S_i(t_i) + \lambda \left(T - \sum_i t_i \right) \qquad \textbf{(8.26)}$$

where λ is the Lagrange multiplier. A necessary condition for maximization of $L(W)$ is for the first derivative of equation (8.26) to equal zero:

$$\frac{dL(W)}{dt_i} = r_i p_i \frac{dS_i}{dt_i} - \lambda = 0 \qquad \textbf{(8.27)}$$

$$\text{or} \quad r_i p_i \frac{dS_i}{dt_i} = \lambda \qquad \textbf{(8.28)}$$

Condition (8.28) says that the marginal increase in commissions with an extra application of effort should equal the marginal cost of increasing the selling time.

The firm's optimization problem is

Find (r_i) to

$$\text{Maximize } Z = \sum_i \{(1 - r_i)p_i S_i(t_i) - C_i[S_i(t_i)]\} \qquad \text{(net revenue)} \qquad \textbf{(8.29)}$$

Subject to

$$\sum_i t_i \leq T$$

$$t_i \geq 0 \qquad\qquad\qquad \textbf{(8.30)}$$

where

$$C_i[S_i(t_i)] \ = \ \text{total cost to firm of producing product } i$$

Thus the firm's problem is to set commissions to motivate the salesperson to allocate his selling time to maximize the firm's profits. The firm's profits are shown in equation (8.29) as the difference between its total revenue after commissions and its total costs, which are some function (not necessarily linear) of its respective levels of output of the various products.

The condition for an optimal solution to this problem is given by combining equations (8.29) and (8.30) into the Lagrangian expression

$$L(Z) = \sum_i \{(1 - r_i)p_i S_i(t_i) - C_i[S_i(t_i)]\} + \gamma\left(T - \sum_i t_i\right) \qquad \textbf{(8.31)}$$

where γ is the Lagrange multiplier (not the same as λ). Again, a necessary condition for maximization is for the first derivative of equation (8.31) to equal zero:

$$\frac{dL(Z)}{dt_i} = (1 - r_i)p_i \frac{dS_i}{dt_i} - \frac{\partial C_i}{\partial S_i}\frac{dS_i}{dt_i} - \gamma = 0 \qquad \textbf{(8.32)}$$

or

$$\left[(1 - r_i)\,p_i - \frac{\partial C_i}{\partial S_i}\right] \frac{dS_i}{dt_i} = \gamma, \qquad \text{for all } i \qquad \textbf{(8.33)}$$

Equation (8.33) says that the company should encourage the salesperson to allocate his time among the company's products in such a way that, at the margin, the company's profit on each product is the same and equal to γ, the marginal return on additional selling time beyond $\Sigma_i t_i$ (γ = marginal cost of relaxing the time constraint, that is, increasing T).

Now under what circumstances will salespersons allocate their time among products to maximize their commissions and the company's profits at the same time? For this result to happen there must be some time allocation that satisfies both equations (8.28) and (8.33). This result is very unlikely to happen because two improbable conditions must exist. The first is that r_i in equation (8.28) must equal $(1 - r_i)$ in equation (8.33) for all i, and this could only happen if $r_i = 0.50$. But it is very unlikely that the commission rate of all products will be 0.50. The second condition is that the marginal cost of production must equal zero, that is, $\partial C_i / \partial S_i = 0$, which is also unlikely.

The implication of this analysis is that a system of commission rates paid on sales is unlikely to lead salespersons to allocate their time in a way that maximizes the firm's profits. The firm might attempt to set sales quotas for the various products for individual salespersons based on its profit-maximizing solution, but salespersons are not likely to heed these quotas if they prevent them from maximizing their commissions.

A system that may reconcile the conflicting interests of salespersons and the company calls for setting the commission rates on product gross margin instead of sales. The Lagrangian expression for the salesperson's optimization problem becomes

$$L(W) = \sum_i r_i\{p_i S_i(t_i) - C_i[S_i(t_i)]\} - \lambda\left(T - \sum_i t_i\right) \qquad \textbf{(8.34)}$$

And the Lagrangian expression for the company's optimization problem becomes

$$L(Z) = \sum_i ((1 - r_i)\{p_i S_i(t_i) - C_i[S_i(t_i)]\}) + \gamma\left(T - \sum_i t_i\right) \qquad \textbf{(8.35)}$$

The first expression is maximized when

$$r_i\left(p_i - \frac{\partial C_i}{\partial S_i}\right)\frac{dS_i}{dt_i} = \lambda \qquad \textbf{(8.36)}$$

and the second is maximized when

$$(1 - r_i)\left(p_i - \frac{\partial C_i}{\partial S_i}\right)\frac{dS_i}{dt_i} = \gamma \qquad \textbf{(8.37)}$$

Then the interest of the salesperson and the company are reconciled if there is some time allocation that can satisfy equations (8.36) and (8.37) simultaneously. Suppose that the marginal cost of producing each product is constant (though not necessarily identical) and known by the salesperson. The firm's problem then, is to determine a set of commission rates on the various products that will maximize its total profits, taking into account how its salesperson will respond to these rates.

In a firm with multiple salespeople, the problem of reconciling the interest of salespersons and the company is complicated if marginal costs are not constant. Under nonconstant marginal costs, the salesperson no longer knows the marginal cost of selling a product in his portfolio. The marginal cost will be determined by the product's output level, which will be determined by the separate decisions of all salespersons on how much time to spend in selling that product. Furthermore, the separate decisions of the salesperson will be influenced by the commission rates set by the company. If the company had full information about the individual salespersons' time-effectiveness functions, it could determine the profit-maximizing commission rates with equation (8.37). But the company usually does not have this information.

These difficulties have been a motivating force behind the search for decentralized solutions. Davis and Farley suggest that the firm determine alternate sets of commission rates on the various products on the basis of its knowledge of cost behavior (which it may not wish to reveal to the salesperson) and its price-setting capabilities. These sets of rates are transmitted to the salespersons, who transmit back desired quotas under each set of commissions. The company examines the discrepancies between what it would like to see sold of each product and what the salespersons indicate they would sell. The company then adjusts the commission rate to bring salesforce intentions into line with company intentions. Specifically, the commission rates are raised on products for which the planned sales levels are too low and are lowered on products for which the planned sales levels are too high. After several iterations, a final set of commission rates on gross marketing is found that brings planned sales into equilibrium with the company's desired rates.

Srinivasan (1981) extends Farley's analysis in several ways. First, he allows the salesperson to decide total time worked as well as the time allocation. This is meaningful only if the salesperson dislikes working hard. Therefore, Srinivasan changes the salesperson's utility function so that it is decreasing in total time worked. He also changes the way the problem is formulated. Instead of modeling the sales manager's problem as finding a commission scheme that will induce the salesperson to choose the same time allocation and total time worked as he (the sales manager) would like, he models the manager's problem as choosing a commission scheme that will maximize the firm's profits recognizing that the salesperson will respond by choosing total time worked and its allocation to maximize his utility. If a solution exists in Farley's formulation of the problem, then both formulations will pick the same solution, but when a solution doesn't exist in Farley's formulation, there may nevertheless be a solution in Srinivasan's formulation.

Srinivasan's main result is that in general it is not optimal to have equal gross margin–based commission rates across products when the salesperson sets total time worked to maximize his utility. This happens when the "gross margin response functions" of the various products do not have the same elasticity.

For example, let

$$s_i(t_i) = a_i t_i^{\beta_i} = \text{sales response of product } i \text{ to effort } t_i$$

then

$$(p_i - c_i) a_i t_i^{\beta_i} = \text{gross margin response function}$$

$$\{\beta_i\} = \text{gross margin response elasticities}$$

So, if $\beta_i \neq \beta_j$, then it is optimal to set unequal commission rates. In particular, the commission rate on the higher-elasticity product should be higher. This is what one would expect intuitively. The commission on a product is supposed to motivate the salesperson to devote time to selling it, but putting time on a product makes sense only if the product will respond to the increased time with increased gross margins.

Regardless of whether equal gross margin–based commission rates are optimal or not, once we allow the salesperson to set total time worked, the total time worked will be less than that in a salesperson-owned firm (a "first-best" outcome where the salesperson's and the firm's objectives are perfectly aligned). This is because, in a gross margin–based commission scheme, only the salesperson bears the cost of working hard. The firm's profits depend on total time worked only indirectly via the gross margins. This suggests that we can restore the first-best outcome as well as the optimality of an equal commission rate if we base the commission on *net* margin, that is, gross margin minus the opportunity cost of selling time.

For example, let

$$C(T) = \text{opportunity cost of total selling time for the salesperson}$$

$$g_i(t_i) = \text{gross margin for product } i$$

Then any commission rate, B, based on $\Sigma_i g_i(t_i) - C(T)$ aligns the salesperson's and the firm's interests completely:

The salesperson maximizes
$$B\left[\sum_i g_i(t_i) - C(T) \right] \qquad (8.38)$$

the firm maximizes
$$(1 - B)\left[\sum_i g_i(t_i) - C(T) \right] \qquad (8.39)$$

But there is a problem with this scheme as well: The firm must compute $C(T)$, and that requires knowledge of the salesperson's opportunity cost of time as well as knowledge of how hard the salesperson worked.

The only remaining solution, short of being satisfied with the "second-best" outcome achievable by using unequal commission rates, is for the current owners of the firm to "sell" the company to the sales force and let the sales force run the company. With ownership, the sales force would be directly responsible for its fortunes. Choosing the wrong allocation of time across products or not working hard at selling would only hurt the profits of the company and lower the sales force's income. The best time allocation and the best total time worked would both be achieved, and, everyone—the current owners as well as the sales force—would be better off.

Uncertain Sales Response to Selling Effort.   Farley and Srinivasan assume sales are a deterministic function of selling effort. As we argued, commissions are not necessary under this assumption because the firm could be sold to the salesperson and everyone would be better off. But we rarely see this happen, perhaps because sales are rarely certain and sales forces are rarely as risk-neutral as the firm. Sales are uncertain because selling effort is not the only force behind sales: other variables (competitors' actions, the state of the economy, and so on) influence sales, and the effect of these variables will not be known to the firm or the sales force. With uncertain sales, a risk-neutral firm, and a risk-averse sales force, selling the firm to the sales force will not work because, once the firm is sold, the sales force will be bearing all the risk and the firm none. It will be better for everyone concerned to spread the risk of uncertain sales between the firm and the sales force while motivating the sales force. A salary plus commissions compensation plan does that.

This is the main point of the "agency literature," on sales force compensation (Ross, 1973; Harris and Raviv, 1979; Holmstrom, 1979; Grossman and Hart, 1983; Basu et al., 1985). Consider the following model with only one product to be sold. Let

t = selling time or effort

$\tilde{S}(t)$ = sales response to selling effort t, a random variable with

$f(s; t)$ = probability density function of $\tilde{S}(t)$.

As t increases, $f(s; t)$ shifts to the right so that higher sales are more likely; that is $P\{\tilde{S}(t) \geq s\}$ is increasing in t. The sales manager can observe the salesperson's output, that is, sales $\tilde{S}(t)$, but cannot observe his input (t), nor can he infer the salesperson's effort from the output. The question is: Under these circumstances, what kind of compensation package should the manager use?

Let us begin by looking at the salesperson's problem. He has to decide how hard to work given his compensation package. Let $B(s)$ denote his income when he generates sales of s. If $B(s)$ is constant in s, then his income is all salary; if $B(0) = 0$, then his income is all commissions. The salesperson chooses t by maximizing his expected utility:

Find t to

$$\text{Maximize}_t \int_s U(B(s))f(s; t)\, ds - C(t) \tag{8.40}$$

where $U(\cdot)$ is the salesperson's utility function for monetary income and $C(t)$ is the salesperson's cost of effort. The first-order condition characterizing the choice of t is

$$\int_s U(B(s))f_t(s; t)ds - C'(t) = 0 \tag{8.41}$$

where

$$f_t(s, t) = \frac{\partial f(s; t)}{\partial t}$$

$$C'(t) = dC/dt$$

The sales manager wants to maximize the firm's expected profits

$$\text{Maximize}_{B(s)} \int_s [(p - c)s - B(s)]f(s; t)\, ds \tag{8.42}$$

Subject to

$$\int_s U(B(s))f(s; t)\, ds - C(t) \geq U_0 \tag{8.43}$$

$$\int_s U(B(s))f_t(s; t)\, ds - C'(t) = 0 \tag{8.44}$$

Constraint (8.43) ensures that the manager picks a compensation package that provides at least as much utility as the salesperson's best alternative job. Constraint (8.44) is simply the salesperson's first-order condition; it recognizes that the salesperson will react to the compensation package by choosing the effort level that is optimal for him. Using the Lagrangian technique for solving such optimization problems, Holmstrom (1979) shows that the solution to the manager's problem is characterized by the following equations:

$$\frac{1}{U'(B(s))} = \lambda + \mu \frac{f_t(s; t)}{f(s; t)} \tag{8.45}$$

$$\int_s U(B(s)) f(s; t)\, ds - C(t) = U_0 \tag{8.46}$$

$$\int_s U(B(s)) f_t(s; t)\, ds - C'(t) = 0 \tag{8.47}$$

$$\int_s [(p - c)s - B(s)] f_t(s; t)\, ds + \mu \left[\int_s U(B(s)) f_{tt}(s; t)\, ds - C''(t) \right] = 0 \tag{8.48}$$

Equation (8.46) says that the manager wouldn't want to pay the salesperson any more than what is necessary to keep him on the job. Equation (8.47) is the salesperson's first-order condition once again. Equation (8.45) is the main first-order condition characterizing the optimal compensation plan. It weighs the cost and benefits to the firm of increasing the salesperson's compensation for a given sales level s. At an optimal solution, these costs and benefits must be equal. To see this, rewrite (8.45) as

$$f = \lambda U' f + \mu U' f_t \tag{8.49}$$

Then, the left-hand side of (8.49) represents the marginal cost of increasing $B(s)$. The right-hand side represents the marginal benefit: $\lambda U' f$ is the marginal benefit from loosening constraint (8.43); $\mu U' f_t$ is the marginal benefit from loosening constraint (8.44). λ and μ are Lagrange multipliers for the (8.43) and (8.44) constraints, respectively: they represent the increase in the objective function—in this case, the firm's profits—from loosening the constraint by one unit. Finally, since an increase in $B(s)$ is designed to increase the salesperson's effort, t, equation (8.48) balances the costs and benefits of increasing t.

Holmstrom (1979) shows that the optimal solution involves $\mu \geq 0$. That is, if the manager would observe the salesperson's effort and pay him on the basis of his effort, then the salesperson would be working harder than he does in this solution. With observability of effort, a compensation system is solely concerned with reconciling the different risk preferences of the firm and the salesperson. Since the firm is risk-neutral and the salesperson risk-averse, such a system would place all the variation in income in the firm's hands and none in the salesperson's. The salesperson would be paid by salary alone. But such a scheme wouldn't work when the salesperson's work is unobservable. Paying by salary alone would make the salesperson shirk his selling responsibilities. So the optimal solution under unobservability sacrifices some risk sharing, that is, allows some variation in the salesperson's income depending on sales realized, in the interest of giving the salesperson the incentive to work hard.

Holmstrom (1979) notes that $|f_t|/f$ is the benefit-cost ratio for deviating from optimal risk sharing. The central role played by the density function of sales and its derivative with respect to salesperson effort suggests the "statistical inference" problem the manager faces in compensating his salesperson. Not knowing t, the manager must resort to using s as a signal of t. f_t/f is the derivative of the log of the likelihood function with respect to t; it measures how good a signal s is of whether or not the salesperson chose the "right" level of effort. When f_t/f is small—when s is not a good signal of t—then the manager cannot gain much from basing compensation on s, so he may as well not deviate much from the optimal risk-sharing arrangement; when f_t/f is large, then the manager can gain significantly by basing compensation on sales, so the optimal response is to deviate considerably from the optimal risk-sharing arrangement.

Equation (8.45) suggests that the optimal compensation scheme will be very responsive to changes in f and U. For example, if $f_t < 0$ in any region of sales, then the optimal compensation scheme in that region will be decreasing in sales, which is counterintuitive. Holmstrom and Tirole (1989) note that "The model can be made consistent with almost any shape of the sharing rule by altering the information technology suitably." In addition, the optimal compensation scheme depends on unobservable details of the salespersons utility function.

Basu and colleagues (1985) have computed the optimal compensation scheme for various distributions of sales. For $U(b) = b^\delta/\delta$ with $\delta < 1$, and f as the gamma density function, the optimal compensation contract is

$$B(s) = \left\{ \lambda + \frac{\mu g'(t)q}{g^2(t)} [s - g(t)] \right\}^{1/(1-\delta)} \tag{8.50}$$

where q and $g(t)$ are parameters of the gamma density function

$$f(s; t) = \frac{q}{\Gamma(q)g(t)} \left[\frac{qs}{g(t)} \right]^{q-1} e^{-qs/g(t)} \tag{8.51}$$

It is clear that $B(0) > 0$, that is, there is a salary component to compensation. Also, as Exhibit 8.4 shows, $B(s)$ is convex in s, that is, the commission rate is increasing with sales. But this is not a universal characteristic. If the salesperson's utility function were $\ln(b)$, then the optimal contract would be linear in sales, whereas if it were $-e^{-b}$, then it would be concave in sales. How the optimal compensation contract varies with other parameters of the compen-

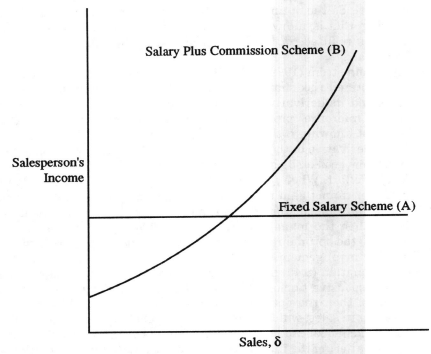

EXHIBIT 8.4 Optimal salesperson compensation schemes for the power utility function for $\delta = 1/2$. A: (Fixed) Salary with effort observable; B: Salary plus commission scheme when effort is not observable.

sation environment also depends on the utility function. For example, with the utility function above, when $\delta = 1/2$, Basu and colleagues find that the commission rate parameter is increasing in U_0, the minimum utility that needs to be guaranteed, but for $\delta = 1/3$, Basu and Gurumurthy (1989) report that it is decreasing. And for $U(b) = -e^{-b}$, Holmstrom and Milgrom (1987) show that the commission rate doesn't vary at all with $U(0)$.

The sensitivity of the optimal compensation contract with respect to the distribution of uncertainty and the salesperson's utility function does not explain the relative homogeneity of real-world compensation schemes. Holmstrom and Milgrom (1987) argue that real-world compensation schemes are usually linear precisely because the firm doesn't know the distribution of uncertainty or the salesperson's utility function. Given this lack of knowledge, any real-world compensation scheme must be robust to variations in distributions and utility functions and only the linear form is robust. Holmstrom and Milgrom (1987) formalize this argument for one particular kind of robustness. Unlike our static model where the salesperson chooses his actions as often as his performance is observed and is paid as often as his performance is observed, in the real-world salespeople are paid for performance over a given period of time, say, a quarter or a year. So the question arises, what kind of compensation scheme is optimal if it is going to be run on *aggregate* performance measures, not instantaneous performance measures? Holmstrom and Milgrom show, in a specific model, that only the linear contract allows aggregate performance measures.

The developments reviewed so far have focused on the design of compensation contracts on the basis of *absolute* performance. Holmstrom (1979) shows that if information is costless, then the optimal compensation contract must use all the signals that provide information about the salesperson's work and only those. This leads to the most robust prescription of principal-agent theory: compensation should be based on *relative* performance measures to the extent it is cost-effective. For example, if two salespeople work in the same industry and share some common sources of sales uncertainty, then how one salesperson does relative to the other is an optimal basis for compensation. In such a situation, a compensation contract based on a salesperson's absolute performance would be throwing away useful information as it would lead to too much risk-bearing by the salesperson for risks over which he has no control. This may explain the use of relative performance–based compensation arrangements such as promotions, sales contests, and so on. (See Nalebuff and Stiglitz, 1983.)

Current Developments and Trends

Coughlan and Sen (1989) review the sales force compensation literature and discuss extensions of Farley's basic model in the directions we have described and some others they consider:

Variation in the Firms' Objectives.   If the firm has different objectives (market share maximization, for example), then the problem remains the same, but with the commission rate set proportionally to the objective. If the firm has a different time horizon than the salesperson (and wants to launch a new product, say), then Dearden and Lilien (1990) show that (with uncertainty in sales response) the optimal compensation scheme has lower salary and higher commission rates for the newer than the older products.

The Sales Response Function.   In practice, a sales-response function can be affected by team selling (Smith and Watts, 1984); by other marketing mix elements, pricing in particular (Weinberg, 1975; Lal, 1986); and by variability in effort productivity across products, salespeople, and time (Lal, 1982; Sasieni, 1989; Lal and Srinivasan, 1988; Rao, 1990b).

Empirical Tests of Theoretical Results.   Recently there have been a number of tests of the principal-agent explanation of sales force compensation. One set of tests focus on the "information usage" predictions of the theory. Eisenhardt (1985) finds support for the prediction that output-based compensation schemes are more likely when the cost of monitoring inputs is high. In small retail stores, where presumably it is easier to monitor salespeople, she finds that input-based compensation schemes are more prevalent; in larger stores, where the cost of monitoring is high, output-based compensation schemes dominate. Antle and Smith (1986), in a slightly different context—the compensation of executives—find some evidence for the use of relative compensation contracts. Another set of studies test the comparative statics predictions of Basu and colleagues (1985): John and Weitz (1989); Oliver and Weitz (1989); and Lal, Outland, and Staelin (1990). Finally Basu and Kalyanaram (1990) show that for a range of reasonable parameter values, a simple linear compensation package approximates the Basu and colleagues (1985) "optimal" compensation plan quite closely.

It is important to note that the behavioral science literature on salesperson performance has identified a number of personal and job-related factors that are nonmonetary but nevertheless have an important effect on sales force actions. For example, a number of articles in a volume edited by Bagozzi (1979a) as well as an article by Ford, Walker, and Churchill (1981) deal with the issues in some detail. Churchill and colleagues (1985) perform a meta-analysis, summarizing the results of 116 articles related to a salesperson's performance.

In conclusion, the sales force compensation area is a rich one both for theoretical and for empirical work. Coughlan and Sen (1989) suggest that research opportunities exist here for more empirical research; for dealing with salesperson risk attitudes more explicitly (perhaps through prospect theory—Kahneman and Tversky, 1979); and for dealing more explicitly with the selling environment by explicit modeling of team selling, multiproduct selling, and incorporating richer specifications of the possible compensation plan, the sales response function, and the product itself.

Integrative Models for Sales Force Decisions

Most of the approaches we have analyzed thus far have focused on one problem element—sales force size, allocation, territory alignment, or commission rate. However, because these decisions are highly interrelated, it is unreasonable to expect that optimizing them separately will lead to an overall optimization of the system.

We earlier reviewed some integrative efforts: allocation strategy and territory alignment have been considered by Shanker, Turner, and Zoltners (1975), Lodish (1975), and Glaze and Weinberg (1979). Each of these models is broken into two stages and iteratively solves the allocation problem with fixed territory alignment and then the territory alignment problem with fixed allocation. Zoltners (1976, 1979) has shown how to incorporate these two decision problems into a single model. Lodish (1980) has also incorporated allocation strategy and sales force size into a single model. However, several more ambitious attempts at integrating strategy, size, and alignment elements have been developed. We review one now.

Beswick and Cravens (1977) view sales force decisions as a sequential, multistage optimization problem as presented in Exhibit 8.5. They see this process broken into five stages (assuming allocation of effort among products is external to the model.

Stage I: Developing market-response functions. The authors postulate that the way a control unit, the smallest unit of a market, responds to selling effort can be structured as

$$SR = f(E, W, P, X, Q) \qquad (8.52)$$

where

SR = sales response
E = selling effort
W = work load
P = potential
C = company effort
X = company experience
Q = salesperson quality

Following Beswick (1973), they suggest that a multiplicative form be used for equation (8.52).

$$SR = a_0 E^{a_1} W^{a_2} P^{a_3} C^{a_4} X^{a_5} Q^{a_6} \qquad (8.53)$$

Either managerial judgment or statistical analysis can be used to develop parameter estimates for equation (8.53).

Stage II: Allocating selling effort and salesforce sizing. Given the response functions in stage I, the allocation and sales force–sizing problem is formulated as follows:

Find $\{N, t_i\}$ to

$$\text{Maximize } Z = Sm - NV - F \qquad \text{(profit)} \qquad (8.54)$$

Subject to

$$NV \leq L_1 \qquad \text{(personal-selling budget)}$$

$$N = \sum_i t_i \qquad \text{(time constraint)}$$

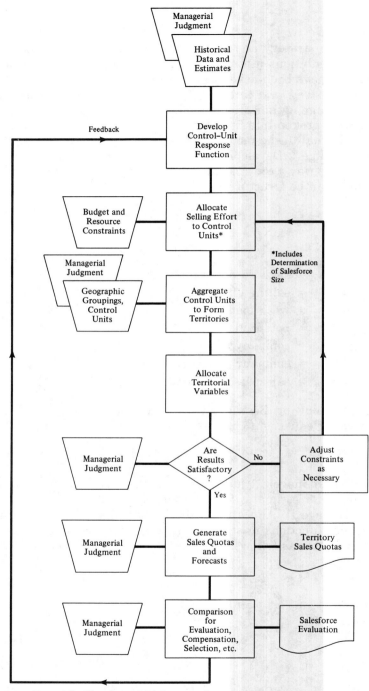

EXHIBIT 8.5 Beswick-Cravens model: a multistage decision model for sales force management. (*Source:* Beswick and Cravens, 1977, p. 136.)

$$S \leq L_2 \qquad \text{(capacity constraint)}$$

$$S = \sum_i SR_i \qquad \text{(sales-level equation)}$$

where

S = total sales dollars

m = margin

N = number of salespersons

V = variable cost associated with average salesperson

F = fixed cost, assumed constant (as long as L_2 is not exceeded)

t_i = time allocated to control unit i, roughly the same as E in equation (8.52)

For the response functions considered by the authors, equation (8.54) is very simple to solve (Beswick, 1977) assuming all variables except t_i are constant. The output of this stage is optimal or near-optimal sales force size and effort allocation for a given territory design.

Stage III: Territory design. Two approaches are suggested for realigning territories: one employs managerial judgment while the other uses the t_i from stage II as activity measures in the Hess-Samuels procedure, which then realigns the sales territories.

Stage IV: Allocation of territorial variables and comparison with objectives. Once stage III is completed, the variables that were held constant during stage II can be incorporated into the analysis. Territorial-level variables that changed during the territory-design process, such as salesperson ability and experience, are updated and computed to change equation (8.53). Other variables, such as advertising, can also be included in the model at this level. In addition, the output of previous stages needs careful review to see if the total system response (sales, profit, sales force size) and the proposed territory alignment are consistent with managerial objectives. Normally, several cycles through stages II, III, and IV are required.

Stage V: Forecasting, evaluation, and control. Equation (8.53) provides sales forecasts that can be used to set quotas and can also be used as controls. Furthermore, the results of stage II can be used for call planning. In essence, the model can be used at this stage as an outside benchmark for performance comparison. Large discrepancies between actual and forecast performance lead to model adjustments and/or performance feedback for the salesperson.

Application and evaluation. The authors report using the model for a manufacturer of a high-priced consumer food with a national salesforce of 100 salespersons, who call primarily on retailers. Groups of counties were used as control units; the test involved 38 sales territories and 232 control units.

The complete response-function form, equation (8.53), was calibrated with historical data; all but one term was significant at the 0.05 level, and 95% of variation in sales response was explained.

Applications of several stages of the model led to identification of two major alternatives:

1. By reallocation of the exiting sales force, the company can expect to see a $831,000 sales increase, an improved distribution of income and a $119,000 improvement in pretax profits associated with a commission rate decrease.

2. By expansion of the sales force from 38 to 42 salespersons, the firm can expect to see a total sales increase of $1,400,000.

This model is an understandable and managerially useful tool. Rather than treating sales force decisions part by part, it treats the problem globally (albeit in an iterative, hierarchical manner). Although it does not ensure global optimality, it gives a practical example of the value of incorporating interdependencies.

The flexibility of the modeling procedure is its weakness as well as its strength. How much customization this procedure needs in any specific application is not clear. How significant the role of management should be in model calibration and application is also unclear. Furthermore, the issues of sales force organization and allocation of effort across products are not considered either.

Other Multiple-Resource Models.   In addition to the aforementioned work of Shanker, Turner, and Zoltner (1975) and Lodish (1980), the most ambitious development is by Zoltners and Gardner (1980). Their model integrates sales force organization, size, and allocations over prospects, time and products, and sales territory design. Their approach, while exciting, has yet to see reported use and is currently in the proposal stage.

Rangaswamy, Sinha, and Zoltners (1990) develop an integrated model to deal with structuring and deploying a multiproduct sales force. The interested reader should also consult the December 1990 issue of the *International Journal for Research in Marketing*, dedicated to sales force management, for an overview of some other recent developments in the area.

SUMMARY

Most companies use a sales force to reach their intermediate and/or final customers. Salespersons perform a number of useful functions, including locating new prospects, communicating product information to customers, persuading customers to close a sale, learning of customers' changing needs, and bringing this and other market information back to the company. Many companies make a considerable investment in selecting, training, and motivating salespersons to perform these tasks effectively.

Marketing management faces a hierarchy of decision problems ranging from selling and sales force objectives to sales force sizing, effort allocation, territory design, and motivation and compensation. A number of model-based approaches have been developed that deal with each of these problems individually.

In recent years two streams of development have proven promising. The first deals with understanding differences in observed customer- or territory-response rates to selling effort. The response curve is at the heart of most operational models in this area. Recent developments have borrowed concepts from the behavioral literature on salesforce effectiveness to determine the elements in response models. The second development has been in integrative model structures. Without significantly altering the valuable individual sub-decison models, recent efforts have focused on piecing these models together in a logically consistent way. By recognizing the interdependencies among territory design, sales force time allocation, and sales force sizing, these models have added considerable credibility to the decision support structures available in the area.

Much recent work based on agency theory concepts has been focused on the sales force motivation and compensation area and the theory-practice gap in this area is slowly being bridged.

In sum, many concepts and tools in the sales force area are available and are being used by some. A challenge now is to integrate these concepts into the thinking and decision processes of more organizations and to further bridge the theory-practice gap.

PROBLEMS

8.1. The Carmine Company has been keeping detailed records on new salespeople under the premise that sales will increase with sales force experience. A sample of eight people produced the data shown:

Months on Job	Monthly Sales (in $1,000s)
2	2.4
5	7.2
9	12.3
12	14.7
1	0.8
6	3.9
10	13.2
4	6.7

   a. Fit a least-squares line to the data and calculate its parameters.
   b. Predict the sales that could be expected from persons who have been on the job for 3 months, 7 months, and 9 months.
   c. Is this a reasonable model? Why? (Why not?)

8.2. A hydraulic value manufacturer saw the following sales levels and personal-selling expenditures in four territories (in thousands of dollars):

Sales Level (S)	Personal-Selling Expenditures (P)
500	40
600	40
400	30
500	50

   a. Fit a regression line of P on S.
   b. Graph the data and the fitted line.
   c. Does this regression line show how personal selling affects sales?

8.3. An automobile parts manufacturer sells its product to three types of customers: (1) automobile manufacturers for use as original equipment (OE), (2) wholesale distributors who in turn distribute to parts retailers (WD), and (3) parts retailers, primarily jobbers and service stations (PR). From past experience the company has found it most efficient to have three salesmen selling in each territory, one for each type of customer. In a particular territory the sales manager asks each salesman what he expects to be able to sell to each type of customer. These estimates are shown in the following table:

| Salesman | Customer Type | | |
	OE	WD	PR
A	100,000	90,000	80,000
B	92,000	92,000	85,000
C	102,000	95,000	75,000

To which customer type should each salesman be assigned in order to maximize sales in the territory?

8.4. A salesman has four open calls in the next period that he would like to devote to one of three prospects. The probabilities that these prospects will be converted to customers after four calls are 0.6, 0.8, and 0.4, respectively (for prospects 1, 2, and 3). If converted to customers, the respective prospects will yield the following profits to the firm in the coming three years:

		Year	
Prospect	1	2	3
1	2,000	2,000	3,000
2	4,000	1,000	1,000
3	2,000	2,000	6,000

The cost of each call is $500. Compute the expected rate of return for each prospect. In which prospect should the salesman invest his four calls? (Assume a time discount of 5%.)

8.5. A salesman calculates that he will be able to make approximately 720 sales calls during the coming year and wants to know how he can best allocate these calls between current customers and prospects in his territory. He has estimated his customer holding rate in the absence of sales calls at 0.6 and for a very large number of calls at 0.9. Total sales in his territory last year were $200 (in thousands). The maximum possible sales to prospects in the territory for the coming year are estimated at $100 (in thousands). All 720 sales calls allocated to customers would be expected to yield $175; if they were allocated to prospects, they would be expected to yield $80. Determine the optimal allocation of calls between customers and prospects.

8.6. An industrial firm has analyzed its sales territories and obtained the data given. Its total market can be divided into 12 small geographic regions, with (x, y) coordinates as shown. Also shown is the number of calls

Unit j	x-Axis Coordinate, x_j	y-Axis Coordinate, y_j	No. of Calls	Territory Allocation I	II	III
1	48	35	56		1	
2	53	11	44	1		
3	20	56	48			1
4	34	64	51		1	
5	20	22	45			1
6	29	31	51			1
7	44	75	46		1	
8	25	71	43		1	
9	78	31	63	1		
10	30	8	58			1
11	15	18	69			1
12	80	26	71	1		

required by each unit and the existing allocation of units to each of three sales territories. Can you suggest a new set of sales territories? (Fitzroy, 1976)

8.7. Gerald is a salesman who currently plans to spend five days in Plains, Georgia, where he has three customers: firm A, B, and C. He has determined that his sales to each customer depend on the time spent with him, following the functions

$$S_A = 20,000 \log(x_A + 1)$$

where

$$S_A = \text{sales to firm A, dollars per month}$$
$$x_A = \text{time spent in firm A}$$

and, similarly,

$$S_B = 40{,}000 \log(x_B + 2)$$
$$S_C = 50{,}000 \log(x_C + 2)$$

a. Assume Gerald can go from one firm to another in no time. How should he allocate his time among the three firms so as to maximize his sales? What will be his sales then?

b. Gerald wonders whether he should spend less time (4 days) or more time (6 days) or spend 5 days as scheduled in Plains discussing with these firms. What would be his time allocations and sales in the case of 4 days? or 6 days?

c. Gerald works only 10 days a month as a salesman (assume that is an absolute constraint), which he allocates between Plains, Georgia, and Grand Rapids, Michigan. He has determined, by means similar to those employed in parts (a) and (b), that his sales in Grand Rapids would be as follows:
(1) For 4 days in Grand Rapids, sales of $131,000
(2) For 5 days in Grand Rapids, sales of $140,000
(3) For 6 days in Grand Rapids, sales of $149,000
How should Gerald allocate his monthly 10 days of work between Grand Rapids and Plains to maximize his sales?

d. Gerald thinks about spending one more day a month working as a salesman and one less day doing consulting (his other occupation). If Gerald were to work one more day as a salesman, how should he allocate his 11 working days between Grand Rapids and Plains?

e. Gerald is paid, as a salesman, 10% of the sales he makes. His consulting fee is $1000 per day. Should he keep his monthly salesman schedule to 10 days or increase it to 11 days?

8.8. Consider the Basu et al. (1985) model of sales force compensation. Show that
a. If the distribution of sales given salesperson effort is uniform on $[a(t), b(t)]$ (here t is the salesperson's effort and $a(t)$ and $b(t)$ are increasing in t), then the first-best solution can be achieved.
b. If the distribution of sales given salesperson effort is normal, the salesperson's utility function is $-\exp(-I)$ (where I is monetary income), then the optimal commission rate is independent of U_0, the salesperson's reservation utility.

9 | DISTRIBUTION

The distribution decision is the determination of the most profitable ways to reach the market. The seller may either distribute or sell his product directly or indirectly through middlemen. If he decides to sell directly, this action has implications for, among other things, the size and type of the sales force, the size of the advertising budget, and prices. If he decides to sell through middlemen, a different plan of sales force activity, advertising, and pricing is needed. Thus the distribution decision is an important input to the planning of other marketing efforts. For example, Perreault and Russ (1976), in a survey of industrial purchasing managers, found that physical distribution services were second only to product quality and more important than price in influencing industrial purchase decisions.

THE DISTRIBUTION PROBLEM

Distribution channels, like other elements of the marketing mix, are not necessarily fixed or permanent, and innovators in the marketplace often adopt more efficient ways of making goods available to buyers (e.g., automated 24-hour tellers). In addition, channels of distribution may not even be directed by manufacturers. The traditional distribution channel—manufacturer → wholesaler → retailer—is being preempted by alternative channels, such as the following:

Corporate channels, which are centrally owned and operated *vertical* marketing systems, characterized by a combination of successive stages of production and distribution under a single ownership

Administered channels, where coordination of successive stages of production and distribution are achieved not through common ownership but through the size and economic power of one of the parties in the system (e.g., manufacturers of dominant brands in certain markets are able to secure strong trade support and cooperation from retailers)

Contractual channels, which are a group of independent firms at different levels of the production or distribution system integrating their programs on a contractual basis to achieve more economies or impact than they could achieve alone (e.g., wholesaler-sponsored voluntary chains, retailer cooperatives and franchise organizations).

In general, distribution comprises those functions of the firm involved in getting products from the manufacturer to the customer, including the following:

Distribution planning with its related activities of production planning and materials procurement

Inventory management and related problems of receiving, inbound transportation, and order processing

Packaging

In-plant warehousing

Shipping

Outbound transportation

Field warehousing

Retail-outlet planning, operations, and control

For simplicity, we divide the distribution decision into three components. The first is *distribution strategy,* which is the determination of the method for selling products to designated end markets and the types of contracting arrangements to employ. The company has options ranging from direct selling, to the use of a variety of intermediaries (manufacturers' agents, brokers, jobbers, wholesalers, retailers, etc.) and also has wide latitude in the selection of appropriate contract forms. The second decision category is *distribution location,* which is the determination of the number and location of outlets that the seller wants to work through. Here the company considers how many outlets will maximize return and what their best locations are. The third is *distribution logistics*, which is the determination of the best way to supply products to intermediary sellers or final buyers. Here the company seeks to balance high service to customers with low inventory, warehousing, and transit costs.

We noted that there is nothing sacrosanct or permanent about the particular institutions that constitute a company's distribution system at a point in time. The important thing about a distribution channel is not the institutions that make it up but the functions they perform. These functions can be performed in different ways by different distribution channels operating at different levels of costs and generating different levels of sales. The major reason for a channel change is a discovery of more effective or efficient ways to accomplish the same work.

EXAMPLE _____

Consider the circumstances under which it would be cost-effective for producers to benefit by working through middlemen, and how many middlemen may arise in a given market.

Although simplistic, the following model and analysis (originally suggested by Balderston, 1958) illustrates how to calculate the equilibrium number of middlemen that will grow to serve a channel in the presence of full information, freedom of entry and exit, and a given set of costs. The equilibrium number of middlemen is that number that minimizes the average cost of distribution to the participating producers.

Assume a market in which there are m producers and n customers and where each producer separately contacts each of the n customers. Since there are m producers, there will be

mn contacts per period in the system in the absence of a middleman

If each contact costs b, then

bmn is the cost of contacts per period in the system with no middlemen

If costs are borne equally, for any one producer,

bn is the producers' cost of contact per period

in the absence of middlemen

Now assume a middleman is established and all producers sell through him. Then there will be

$m + n$ contacts in the system per period with one middleman

Exhibit 9.1 illustrates the reduction in the number of contacts in the system brought about by a middleman, where there are three producers

**Number of Contacts with Three Producers (*m*)
Selling Directly to Three Customers (*n*):
mn = 3 × 3 = 9**

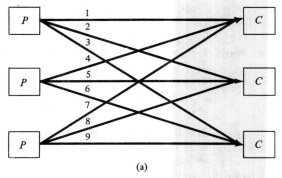

(a)

**Number of Contacts with Three Producers
Selling through One Wholesaler Who Sells to
Three Customers: *m* + *n* = 6**

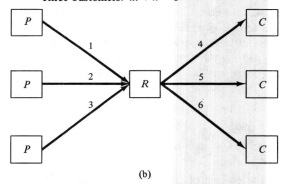

(b)

EXHIBIT 9.1 How a middleman reduces the number of required customer contacts
in a system.

and three customers. The middleman effects a reduction in the number
of required contacts from 9 to 6.

Suppose the cost of a contact between a producer and the middleman or the middleman and a customer is $\bar{b}$. Then,

$$\bar{b}(m + n) \text{ is the total cost of contacts in the system}$$

in the presence of one middleman

Then for any one producer, when the costs are borne equally,

$$\bar{b}(m + n)/m \text{ is a producer's cost of contacts}$$

per period with one middleman

Therefore, a producer would prefer to work through a middleman if

$$\frac{\bar{b}(m + n)}{m} < bn \tag{9.1}$$

If $b = \bar{b}$, equation (9.1) reduces to

$$m + n \leq mn \tag{9.2}$$

Inequality (9.2) is satisfied if $m > 2$ and $n \geq 2$ or if $m \geq 2$ and $n > 2$—that is, there must be more than two producers and/or two customers before a middleman is able to perform the customer-contact function at less cost than the producer can.

Now let w^* denote the equilibrium number of middlemen. Then the condition for a producer to prefer to work through middlemen is

$$w^*(m + n) = mn \tag{9.3}$$

or

$$w^* = \frac{mn}{m + n} \tag{9.4}$$

Equation (9.4) says that the equilibrium number of middlemen is equal to the ratio of total customer-contact cost without a middleman to that with middlemen.

If $b \neq \bar{b}$, then equation (9.4) becomes

$$w^* = \frac{bmn}{\bar{b}(m + n)} \tag{9.5}$$

However, this formulation is quite simplistic. It assumes that all producers sell to all customers (no segmentation), that contact costs are the same independent of customer or producer, that all contacts are equally effective, and that only one level of intermediary can be formed. (See Baligh and Richartz, 1967, for discussion and extensions.) For a real-world situation, it can be appropriately modified.

The importance of this illustration is to show that the use of middlemen and their equilibrium number are determined primarily by the extent to which they can perform the channel work more efficiently than producers can on their own.

The seller must select the channels of distribution with an eye not only on the economics but also on the control aspects of channels and their adaptability. A channel decision is a long-term commitment to a way of doing business, and it influences product development, marketing-communication strategy, sales force territories and plans, pricing, and so forth. The company must consider how much control it is likely to achieve through the desired channels.

As in the rest of this book we will focus on both theoretical models and decision support models here. There is also a large and vigorous literature on a channel's sociological behavior, focusing on the notions of power, conflict, and satisfaction. (See Gaski, 1984; Gaski and Nevin, 1985; Frazier, 1983; Frazier and Summers, 1984, and 1986; Lusch and Brown, 1982; Anderson and Narus, 1984; Eliashberg and Michie, 1984; McAlister, Bazerman, and Fader, 1986, for example.)

DISTRIBUTION STRATEGY

Hutt and Speh (1989) view the channel-design process as illustrated in Exhibit 9.2. Although specifically developed for industrial firms, the structure has more general applicability. The stages of their model are as follows:

1. *Channel objectives,* integrating the channel decision into the overall marketing plan and strategy

2. *Channel-design constraints,* recognizing that, practically, channel options may be severely limited by constraining factors, such as the availability of good middlemen, traditional channel patterns, product characteristics, company finances, competitive strategies, and customer dispersion (Stern and El-Ansary, 1977)

3. *Specification of channel tasks,* recognizing that a channel is a sequence of activities

4. *Evaluation of channel alternatives,* evaluating (a) the number of steps or levels to be included in the channel, (b) the number of intermediaries to employ, (c) the types of intermediaries to employ, and (d) the number of distinct channels to use

5. *Channel selection,* selecting the alternative that is "best," where best incorporates both short- and long-run aspects

There have been some theoretical and empirical studies of the channel

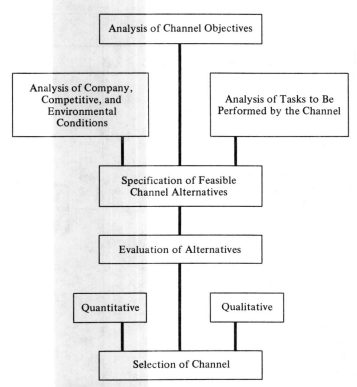

EXHIBIT 9.2   The channel-design process. (*Source:* Hutt and Speh, 1989, p. 393.)

evaluation and selection process for industrial products. Exhibit 9.3 depicts the six most common channels. Diamond's (1963) study of 167 industrial manufacturers, covering 220 product lines, found that these six basic channels accounted for all sales in his sample. Note that of the six basic channels, three represent captive or totally company-controlled channels (paths 2, 4, and 5) while the remaining three are independent or company-external channels.

To study the impact of product and market factors on the selection of internal versus external channels, Lilien (1979) ran a discriminant analysis with data from a sample of 125 industrial products. The most important variables that he found for classifying and predicting the channel of distributors are the following:

1. *Size of the firm.* Size is the most important variable for determining the directness of distribution. As firms grow larger, they are better able to support a company-owned distribution channel.

2. *Size of average order.* As the average order size increases, direct distribution becomes more economical.

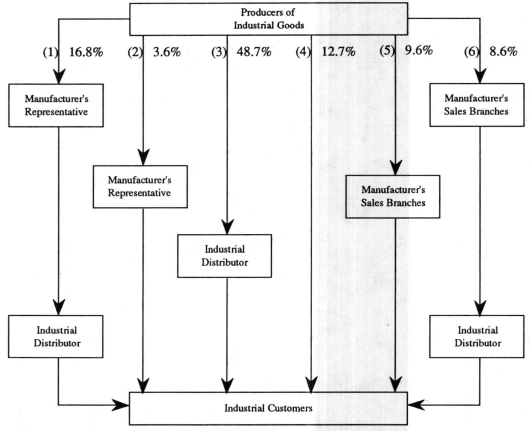

EXHIBIT 9.3 The six most common industrial channels. (*Source:* Haas, 1989, p. 239.)

3. *Technical-purchase complexity.* The greater the importance of technical service to the product's success and the more important the buyer views the purchase, the more likely is direct distribution.

4. *Stage in the product life cycle.* A new or growing product is more likely to use a captive form of distribution than a product whose sales have leveled off or are declining.

5. *Degree of standardization.* A product that is complex, unique, or made to order is more frequently sold directly.

6. *Purchase frequency.* Frequently purchased products require less selling effort to make a sale and are therefore less frequently sold directly.

In addition to the empirical work cited, researchers have focused considerable attention in recent years on theoretical modeling in the area of *dis-*

tribution strategy and *distribution management.* The main question addressed under distribution strategy is whether the manufacturer should use company-owned channels or independent channels, that is, should the manufacturer vertically integrate into distribution? The distribution management issues have been framed as contracting issues in independent channels: what kinds of contracts should the manufacturer offer the distributor (or should the distributor offer the manufacturer) that will maximize profits? Contracts here mean not only the price, but also the form of the price—linear or nonlinear (e.g., quantity discounts, two-part tariffs)—and vertical restraints such as resale price maintenance, minimum quantity requirements, exclusive territories, and so on.

The two issues are intimately related. We cannot answer the channel design question without addressing the contracting question. Different contracts will be optimal for different kinds of channels, so when designing a channel, a manufacturer must anticipate the associated contract. This type of analysis is quite similar to our analysis of product strategy, where the manufacturer had to anticipate its pricing strategy when designing a product. In what follows, we will first look at optimal channel contracts in given channel structures, and then consider the question of optimal channel structure. We will refer to the distributor as a "retailer," but what we say will apply equally well if the distributor is in fact a wholesaler.

Vertically Integrated Channels. The literature generally assumes that there are no contracting problems within a vertically integrated channel. In Exhibit 9.3, if the vertically integrated channel is implemented as a direct-from-factory-to-customer link—link 4— then the only contract required is between the manufacturer and the end users, so this assumption would seem to be true. One could, however, argue otherwise, noting that even in such a seemingly direct transaction, the manufacturer's salespeople will be involved and they need to be motivated through compensation contracts (as we discussed in Chapter 8). But other channel arrangements also involve salespeople. A manufacturer dealing with an independent retailer must contract with salespeople to deal with that retailer. And the retailer in turn must contract with its own salespeople to deal with final customers. Similarly, a manufacturer's sales branch (link 5 in Exhibit 9.3) is a collection of company salespeople selling to the end user, and comparable arguments follow with any other distribution arrangement. Since salesperson contracts are involved in *all* these channel designs, we will ignore such contracts in what follows.

What about the "contracts" between the manufacturer and the end user in vertically integrated channels? Assuming that the manufacturer's product design is fixed—which is usually the case when setting retail prices—then our earlier results on optimal pricing can be applied. If the manufacturer is a monopolist, or even if it faces competition as long as it is passive at the retail level, then the marginal revenue equal to marginal cost rule applies (see Chapter 4): the manufacturer should price so that at the quantity demanded, marginal revenue equals marginal cost. If other "retail services" besides price are needed—things like shelf-space, advertising, checkout clerks, and so on—then the optimal quantity of these services can also be found from the marginal revenue equal to marginal cost rule. (See Betancourt and Gautschi, 1988, 1990, and Ratchford and Stoops, 1991, for detailed models of the services provided by retailers.)

The vertically integrated manufacturer's profit function is

$$\pi_m = (p - m - r)D(p, A) - A \tag{9.6}$$

where

m = marginal cost of production (assumed constant)
r = marginal cost of retailing (also assumed constant)
A = fixed cost of retail services
$D(p, A)$ = demand level

and the marginal revenue equal to marginal cost rule can be expressed by the following first-order conditions:

$$(p - m - r)\frac{\partial D}{\partial p} + D(p, A) = 0 \tag{9.7a}$$

$$(p - m - r)\frac{\partial D}{\partial A} - 1 = 0 \tag{9.7b}$$

Denote the solution to equation (9.7) as (p^i, A^i) and the associated sales level by D^i. If p^i and A^i are both greater than zero and the profit function is strictly quasi-concave, then (p^i, A^i) solves the manufacturer's problem. (Note that our formulation views retail services as a fixed cost.)

If consumers are heterogeneous in their preferences for retail services, then by the arguments of Chapter 5, it may pay the manufacturer to offer a variety of service levels at different price levels. For example, one can imagine the manufacturer opening a discount store with minimal services and a "specialty-type" store with more salespeople, better service, and higher prices.

Interbrand Competition. If the manufacturer faces strategic competition from another vertically integrated manufacturer and the two firms offer similar products, then the Nash equilibrium pricing strategy for each manufacturer will be to price at marginal cost, that is, $(m + r)$. Given this result, the Nash equilibrium level of fixed-cost distribution services will be zero if these services cannot be differentiated: in equation (9.7b), when $(p - m - r)$ is zero, the first term is zero, so the left-hand side is negative. Thus, manufacturers offering identical products will compete on prices rather than on distribution services if these services cannot be differentiated. If the manufacturers can differentiate their retail services—because consumers are heterogeneous in their preferences for these services—then our discussion in Chapter 5 suggests that the two manufacturers will offer different retail service levels in order to reduce the price competition between them. In general, these service levels and the associated prices will not be the same as those a monopolist manufacturer would choose.

Now suppose the two vertically integrated manufacturers offer differentiated products. Each manufacturer will then have a pair of equations like (9.7), that must be solved simultaneously for the Nash equilibrium (assuming it to be positive in both price and retail services):

$$(p_1 - m - r) \frac{\partial D(p_1, A_1; p_2, A_2)}{\partial p_1} + D(p_1, A_1; p_2, A_2) = 0 \qquad \textbf{(9.8a)}$$

$$(p_1 - m - r) \frac{\partial D(p_1, A_1; p_2, A_2)}{\partial A_1} - 1 = 0 \qquad \textbf{(9.8b)}$$

$$(p_2 - m - r) \frac{\partial D(p_2, A_2; p_1, A_1)}{\partial p_2} + D(p_2, A_2; p_1, A_1) = 0 \qquad \textbf{(9.8c)}$$

$$(p_2 - m - r) \frac{\partial D(p_2, A_2; p_1, A_1)}{\partial A_2} - 1 = 0 \qquad \textbf{(9.8d)}$$

EXAMPLE _____

Suppose D is given by the linear demand function used by McGuire and Staelin (1983), modified to take into account retail services:

$$D_1(p_1, A_1; p_2, A_2) = \begin{cases} \dfrac{2A_1}{(A_1 + A_2)} - p_1 + \theta p_2, & \text{when } (A_1 + A_2) > 0 \\ 1 - p_1 + \theta p_2, & \text{otherwise} \end{cases}$$

$$\textbf{(9.9)}$$

where

D_1 = demand for product 1 given p_2 and A_2. D_2 is similar

θ = degree of substitutability between products 1 and 2, where $\theta = 0$ means not at all substitutable and $\theta = 1$ means perfectly substitutable ($0 \le \theta \le 1$)

The way we have specified the effect of retail services on demand, equal expenditures on these services by both firms yield the same demand regardless of what those expenditures are (including zero) and how they are spent. We require

$$(2 - \theta) > (1 - \theta)(1 + m + r) \tag{9.10}$$

to guarantee positive margins with equal services by both manufacturers. Solving for the equilibrium here gives us

$$p_1 = p_2 = \frac{1 + m + r}{2 - \theta} \tag{9.11a}$$

and

$$A_1 = A_2 = \frac{1 - (m + r)(1 - \theta)}{2(2 - \theta)} \tag{9.11b}$$

The "prisoners dilemma" effect on retail service competition should be clear as both manufacturers end up with the same level of demand they would have had if they had spent nothing on retail services. This is because of the way we have modeled the effect of retail services on demand. If the provision of retail services had expanded total retail demand or if the two manufacturers could differentiate their retail services, then our results would be different.

We next consider interbrand competition between a vertically integrated manufacturer and a manufacturer using an independent channel.

Independent Channels.   Consider a monopolist manufacturer dealing with an independent retailer under an exclusive territory arrangement, where the retailer is the only source of the manufacturer's product in the market under consideration. Suppose

w = the constant unit price charged by the manufacturer to the retailer

p = the price charged by the retailer to the end users

A = the level of retail services provided by the retailer

Then the manufacturer's profit function is

$$\pi^m = (w - m)D(p, A) \qquad (9.12)$$

and the retailer's profit function is

$$\pi^r = (p - w - r)D(p, A) - A \qquad (9.13)$$

Note that

$$\pi^m + \pi^r = (p - m - r)D(p, A) - A \qquad (9.14)$$

So, total channel profit (equation 9.14) is the same here as with the vertically integrated manufacturer (equation 9.6).

Assuming that the manufacturer offers a wholesale price on a take-it-or-leave-it basis (i.e., w is fixed), then the retailer's choice of p and A is given by the following first-order conditions:

$$(p - w - r)\frac{\partial D(p, A)}{\partial p} + D(p, A) = 0 \qquad (9.15a)$$

$$(p - w - r)\frac{\partial D(p, A)}{\partial A} - 1 = 0 \qquad (9.15b)$$

Note that the independent retailer's marginal revenues with respect to price and service, $p\partial D/\partial p + D(p, A)$ and $p\partial D/\partial A$ in equation (9.15a) and (9.15b), respectively, are the same as that of a vertically integrated manufacturer. What has changed are the independent retailer's marginal costs. Now they are $w + r$, instead of $m + r$. Clearly, w will be greater than m—otherwise the manufacturer could not make any money—so the optimal price of the independent retailer will be more than that for his vertically integrated counterpart and his optimal level of retail expenditures will be less than that of the vertically integrated retailer. This result, known as "double marginalization," was first noted by Spengler (1950). Accordingly, sales will be lower with an independent retailer than with a vertically integrated channel (see Exhibit 9.4). Channel profits will also be lower in the independent channel because p and A are being chosen to maximize the retailer's profits, not the total channel's profits as in the vertically integrated channel structure. So with a constant unit pricing contract between the manufacturer and the independent retailer, vertical integration is better for the manufacturer and the consumers. This sort of argument is the basis for ads that say: "Why pay the middleman; we would rather pass on the savings to you, the consumer."

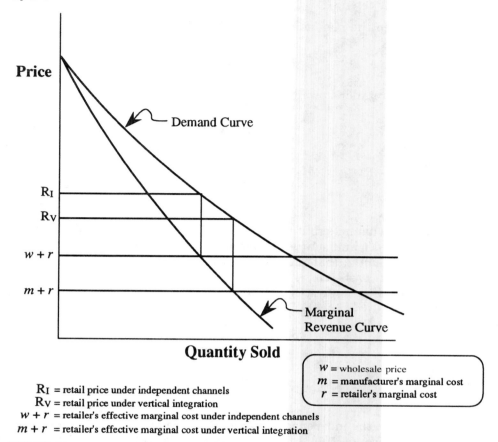

R_I = retail price under independent channels
R_V = retail price under vertical integration
$w + r$ = retailer's effective marginal cost under independent channels
$m + r$ = retailer's effective marginal cost under vertical integration

w = wholesale price
m = manufacturer's marginal cost
r = retailer's marginal cost

EXHIBIT 9.4   Prices are lower, sales are higher, and channel profits are higher for vertically integrated channels than for independent channels (assuming linear wholesale prices).

Can the vertical-integration price, retail service level, and channel profits be induced in an independent retailer channel? The answer is yes, but it involves more complicated contracts between the manufacturer and the retailer than the simple, linear contracts we have assumed so far. One way, as Jeuland and Shugan (1983) point out, is for the two parties to agree to a channel profit-sharing contract as opposed to charging the transfer price, w. Then monetary transactions between the manufacturer and the retailer will be through this profit-sharing arrangement. To see how this works, let f be the fraction of channel profits that will accrue to the manufacturer. Then the retailer's profit function becomes

$$(1 - f)[(p - m - r)D(p, A) - A] \qquad (9.16)$$

The first-order conditions with respect to p and A are

$$(1 - f)\left[(p - m - r) \frac{\partial D(p, A)}{\partial p} + D(p, A) \right] = 0 \qquad \textbf{(9.17a)}$$

$$(1 - f)\left[(p - m - r) \frac{\partial D(p, A)}{\partial A} - 1 \right] = 0 \qquad \textbf{(9.17b)}$$

Note that if we divide equations (9.17a) and (9.17b) by $(1 - f)$, that term drops out of the first-order conditions and we are left with conditions (9.7), those for the vertically integrated manufacturer. Thus, f determines the profit sharing between the two parties but not the price and service levels chosen by the retailer. This arrangement is like the gross margin–based commission schemes in the sales force compensation literature (Chapter 8), and the profit share the two parties agree to will be a function of their relative bargaining power. If the manufacturer has all the bargaining power, then f will be set so that the retailer's profits are just sufficient for him to stay in business. In this case, the manufacturer would be indifferent between vertical integration and dealing with an independent retailer. Lal (1990) suggests that such profit-sharing agreements may be particularly useful in situations where the manufacturer can take actions after the contract has been signed that will help or hurt the sales of the product. For example, by tying his income to how well the product does on the market, the manufacturer provides himself with the right incentives for maintaining product quality.

Other ways of inducing the same result, but based on nonlinear *pricing* schemes from the manufacturer to the retailer, are also available. Moorthy (1987) shows that these pricing schemes must make the retailer's effective marginal cost curve intersect the retailer's marginal revenue curve from below at the vertically integrated channel's optimum quantity, D^i. We have already noted that the independent retailer's marginal revenue curve is the same as the vertically integrated manufacturer's. So if the intersection between marginal cost and marginal revenue happens at the desired quantity, then the independent retailer's marginal cost will be $(m + r)$ at that point. There are several ways of achieving this desired intersection. One way is for the manufacturer to use a quantity-discount scheme where the marginal price paid by the retailer is greater than m for quantities below D^i but equal to m at D^i (Jeuland and Shugan, 1983). The discount scheme doesn't have to offer quantity discounts for all quantities—as Exhibit 9.5 shows, a variety of quantity discount schemes will do the job, even ones that have increasing prices for some quantity ranges. A simpler way of accomplishing the same thing is for the manufacturer to offer a two-part tariff (Chapter 4) where the unit price is equal to the manufacturer's marginal cost and the upfront "fixed fee" determines the manufacturer's profits. Once again, the retailer's effective marginal cost becomes $(m + r)$—the same as that of a vertically integrated manufacturer. Such a two-part tariff would be very much like "selling the company to the salesperson" in the sales force compensation literature.

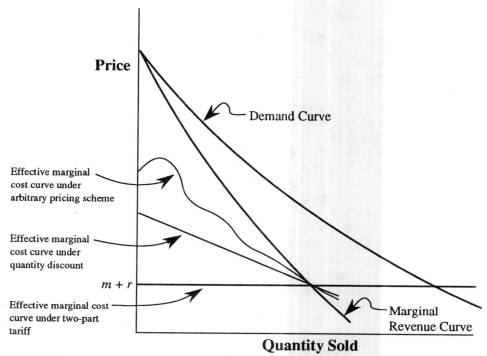

EXHIBIT 9.5   Various wholesale pricing schemes, all of which induce the same outcome in an independent channel as in a vertically integrated channel.

Rey and Tirole (1986a, 1986b) note that the two-part tariff solution works by making the independent retailer the residual claimant of the channel's profits. This is a general principle. Our formulation of the interaction between the manufacturer and the retailer makes controlling the retailer's actions —his choice of p and A—the main goal of the contract between the manufacturer and the retailer. The control problem arises either because the manufacturer cannot bind the independent retailer's actions through a legally, enforceable contract, or, because even though a legally enforceable contract is possible, the manufacturer is unable to monitor conformance to the contract in a cost-effective way. If legally enforceable binding contracts were possible and implementable in a cost-effective way, then both the manufacturer and the retailer would readily agree on (p^i, A^i) as the desired retailer price and service level. (Minimum buying quantity restrictions will accomplish the same thing. The manufacturer could require that the retailer buy at least D^i.) Some franchisor-franchisee contracts do satisfy these requirements (Stern and El-Ansary, 1988, p. 347), but most of these arise in "business-format" franchising, not in situations where the franchisee essentially resells the manufacturer's product. In the latter, more common case, contracts that bind the retailer's actions are likely to be found illegal under the Sherman Act unless they are structured as franchise contracts (Stern and El-Ansary, 1988). Therefore, the manufacturer must reconcile himself to the fact that the retailer will make price and service decisions in his own interest. The main task of contracting thus becomes one of framing the retailer's decision problem so that his interests will coincide with those of the manufacturer's. This coordination is achieved by making the retailer the residual claimant of the channel's profits.

These observations go through unchanged if the retailer faces passive competition from other retailers.

Proposition 1. A manufacturer using an independent retailer under an exclusive territory arrangement can achieve the same outcomes as in a vertically integrated channel if he uses a nonlinear wholesale pricing scheme such as a two-part tariff or quantity discounts. But if he uses a linear wholesale pricing scheme, then, compared to the vertically integrated channel, (1) channel profits will be lower, (2) retail price will be higher, and (3) retail service levels will be lower.

Trade Promotions versus Consumer Promotions. Gerstner and Hess (1990) have argued that direct coupon or rebate promotions from the manufacturer to the consumers may be more advantageous for the manufacturer than trade promotions. Consider a product being sold in a market with two types of consumers, H and L, with reservation prices V_H and V_L for a unit of the product, respectively. Suppose the need for a promotion arises because the composition of the market has changed from α_1 proportion of H-type consumers to α_2 proportion of H-type consumers, where $\alpha_2 < \alpha_1$. Currently the manufacturer sells the product to the retailer at V_H who then resells it at V_H, serving the H segment only. (We assume that the manufacturer's and retailer's costs are zero for simplicity.) With the change in the composition of the market, the manufacturer would like the retailer to serve segment L as well.

Consider these options available to the manufacturer:

1. Offer trade promotions only: reduce the wholesale price from V_H to p_w by offering a trade promotion worth $V_H - p_w$, but no consumer promotions.

2. Offer consumer promotions only: keep the wholesale price at V_H and offer a coupon or a rebate which will induce segment L to buy. We assume that segment H consumers (and only segment H consumers) incur a transaction cost of T to redeem this promotion.

3. Offer both consumer and trade promotions.

Offer trade promotions only. What wholesale price will induce the retailer to charge V_L at retail? The retailer's profits if he maintains his retail price at V_H—pocketing the trade promotion—will be $\alpha_2(V_H - p_w)$. But if he passes through the trade promotion by lowering the retail price to V_L, then his profits will be $V_L - p_w$. The latter is greater than the former if and only if $p_w \leq (V_L - \alpha_2 V_H)/(1 - \alpha_2)$. Thus the manufacturer's maximum profits under this strategy is $(V_L - \alpha_2 V_H)/(1 - \alpha_2)$. Note that the trade promotion gets larger—and the manufacturer's profits get smaller—the closer $\alpha_2 V_H$ is to V_L.

With consumer promotions only. What will be the size of the rebate R required to induce the retailer to serve the L segment while paying a wholesale price V_H? With the rebate, the retailer can charge $V_L + R$ at retail and still serve both segments. And both segments will be redeeming the rebate if $T < R$. In this case, the retailer's profits will be $V_L + R - V_H$. But the other possibility is that he raises his retail price to $V_H + R - T$ and serves only the H segment. Then his profits will be $\alpha_2(V_H + R - T - V_H)$, that is, $\alpha_2(R - T)$. For the former to be greater than the latter, the rebate has to be at least $(V_H - V_L - \alpha_2 T)/(1 - \alpha_2)$. So the manufacturer's maximum profits in this strategy are $[V_H - (V_H - V_L - \alpha_2 T)/(1 - \alpha_2)]$.

Comparing the maximum profits with the two options, note that consumer promotions are better. This is because the cost of getting the retailer to serve the L segment is lower when rebates are offered since the retailer sees a more homogeneous market in the presence of rebates. The H segment's reservation price is $V_H + R - T$ and the L segment's reservation price is $V_L + R$. The range of reservation prices is $V_H - V_L - T$ with rebates whereas it is $V_H - V_L$ without rebates.

With consumer and trade promotions. If the manufacturer offers a trade promotion as well as consumer promotions, then he can get the retailer to price discriminate between the H and L segments. The H segment will buy the product at the retail price, which will be just slightly less than $V_L + T$. They will not redeem the rebate which will be just less than T. The L segment will also buy at the retail price, but they will redeem the rebate. In order for the retailer to go along with this arrangement—and not raise his price to V_H—the wholesale price must not be more than $(V_L + T - \alpha_2 V_H)/(1 - \alpha_2)$. Hence the manufacturer's profits under this arrangement are $[(V_L + T - \alpha_2 V_H)/(1 - \alpha_2)] - (1 - \alpha_2)T$. Note that this is greater than the profits from consumer promotions alone.

Proposition 2. Consumer rebate (coupon) promotions are better than trade promotions and the combination of the two is better than either alone.

Interbrand Competition at the Retail Level. If the retailer actively competes with other retailers selling the same product, then his price to end users will be bid down to his marginal cost unless he can differentiate his services. Assume first that there can be no services differentiation at the retail level. Then, given zero margins, no retailer would want to spend any money on fixed-cost retail services even if they increase demand. Given no retail services, the best retail price from a channel point of view is the price p^{i0} that solves

$$(p - m - r)D_p(p, 0) + D(p, 0) = 0$$

The manufacturer can induce p^{i0} by selling his product to the retailers at the linear price $p^{i0} - r$. [Then the retailer's marginal cost will be $(p^{i0} - r) + r$, that is, p^{i0}.] If retail services can be differentiated, then the retailers will compete on prices as well as retail services. As discussed in Chapter 5, the Nash equilibrium will involve each retailer offering a different level of service and a different price above marginal cost. But it is unlikely that the retailers can be induced to offer the same service and price levels as a vertically integrated manufacturer would unless more complicated two-part tariffs with fixed payments dependent on the retail prices of *all* retailers are used (Bolton and Bonanno, 1988). In other words, encouraging competition among his retailers is good for the manufacturer if he is only concerned about retail price, but not if he is also concerned about retail services.

Proposition 3. When a manufacturer sells through multiple competing independent retailers, then, in general, it is impossible to induce the same retail price, service levels, and channel profits as in a vertically integrated channel.

Comparing this proposition with the corresponding one for exclusive territories, we can see why giving exclusive territories to retailers might be in the manufacturer's interest. By offering exclusive territories, the manufacturer effectively makes the retailer a monopolist in his territory. As we discussed, this makes it possible for the manufacturer to design nonlinear pricing contracts which induce the retailer to charge the right price and offer the right amount and variety of services.

Proposition 4. Giving exclusive territories to independent retailers allows the manufacturer to induce the same retail price, service levels, and channel profits as in a vertically integrated channel.

Interbrand Competition Through Exclusive Retailers. Suppose two competing manufacturers sell their products through exclusive retailers. McGuire and Staelin (1983) have analyzed this situation for the demand function (9.9) without the retail services component.

Let

w_i = wholesale price for manufacturer i, $i = 1, 2$

p_i = retail price for retailer i, $i = 1, 2$

Assume that the manufacturers first set their wholesale prices and, then, the retailers react to these prices by setting their retail prices. Given this Stackelberg formulation of the game, we start by looking at the second-stage equilibrium. Each retailer maximizes a profit function of the form

$$(p_i - w_i - r)(1 - p_i + \theta p_{3-i}), \qquad i = 1, 2 \tag{9.18}$$

Differentiating these profit functions with respect to p_i, and solving for the resulting first-order conditions we get the following price equilibrium

$$p_i - r = \frac{1}{2 - \theta} + \frac{2}{(2 + \theta)(2 - \theta)} \, w_i + \frac{\theta}{(2 + \theta)(2 - \theta)} \, w_{3-i}, \qquad i = 1, 2 \tag{9.19}$$

Note that each retailer increases his price when his wholesale price increases as well as when the other retailer's wholesale price increases.

Each manufacturer's profit function is of the form

$$(w_i - m)[1 - p_i(w_i, w_{3-i}) + \theta p_{3-i}(w_{3-i}, w_i)], \qquad i = 1, 2 \tag{9.20}$$

where the $p_i(w_i, w_{3-i})$ are the equilibrium prices from equation (9.19). Differentiating these profit functions with respect to w_i and solving the resulting first-order condition equation, we get the wholesale price equilibrium:

$$w_i - m = \left(\frac{2 + \theta}{4 - \theta - 2\theta^2} \right) [1 - r(1 - \theta)(2 - \theta) - m(1 - \theta)], \qquad i = 1, 2 \tag{9.21}$$

Now the equilibrium profits of each firm can be calculated by substituting these equilibrium prices in the respective profit functions. We do not write these equilibrium profit expressions here because of their algebraic complexity. (See McGuire and Staelin, 1983, for the case where $m = r = 0$.)

The intermediate case where one manufacturer uses an independent exclusive retailer while the other manufacturer is vertically integrated can be analyzed similarly. The equilibrium retail prices are still given by equation (9.19) if we substitute the marginal manufacturing cost, m, for the vertically integrated manufacturer's wholesale price. Assuming that manufacturer 1 is the one with the independent channel, the equilibrium retail prices are

$$p_1 - r = \frac{1}{2 - \theta} + \frac{2}{(2 + \theta)(2 - \theta)} \, w_1 + \frac{\theta}{(2 + \theta)(2 - \theta)} \, m \tag{9.22a}$$

$$p_2 - r = \frac{1}{2 - \theta} + \frac{2}{(2 + \theta)(2 - \theta)} \, m + \frac{\theta}{(2 + \theta)(2 - \theta)} \, w_1 \tag{9.22b}$$

The optimal wholesale price for the manufacturer with the independent retailer is given by

$$w_i - m = \left(\frac{2 + \theta}{4 - 2\theta^2}\right)[1 - r(1 - \theta)(2 - \theta) - m(1 - \theta)] \qquad \textbf{(9.23)}$$

This wholesale price is less than the equilibrium wholesale price when both manufacturers used independent channels because now the "other" manufacturer's wholesale price is marginal cost. Once again, by substituting this wholesale price in the manufacturers' profit functions, we can compute the equilibrium profits (McGuire and Staelin, 1983).

How do the equilibrium channel profits compare with what we found earlier for two vertically integrated manufacturers competing with each other? McGuire and Staelin (1983) show that *total channel profits* with an independent retailer are higher than that with a vertically integrated manufacturer if and only if $\theta \geq 0.43$ in this model. Moreover, *each manufacturer's profit* is higher when both use independent channels than when both are vertically integrated if and only if $\theta \geq 0.71$. Looking at the Nash equilibrium in channel structures, both manufacturers choosing vertical integration is a Nash equilibrium strategy on either profit criterion for all values of θ. In addition, each manufacturer choosing an independent channel is also a Nash equilibrium on the channel profits criterion for $\theta \geq 0.77$ and on the manufacturer-profits criterion for $\theta \geq 0.93$.

Note that it is easier to justify independent channels on the channel-profits criterion than on the manufacturer-profits criterion—the values of θ for which independent channels beats vertical integration are higher when comparing manufacturer profits than when comparing channel profits. This is because manufacturer profits are a fraction of channel profits when using independent channels, but they are equal to channel profits under vertical integration. So, in order to comprehend McGuire and Staelin's results, it is important to understand how channel profits with independent channels can be higher than channel profits under vertical integration.

Moorthy (1988) has shown that when a manufacturer switches from vertical integration to an independent channel, he raises his own equilibrium retail price due to the "double-marginalization" effect discussed earlier, and also raises the other manufacturer's equilibrium retail price. The first effect has negative consequences for channel profits, but the second has positive consequences when the products are demand substitutes. The raising of the other manufacturer's equilibrium retail price when one manufacturer switches to an independent channel is not always the case nor is it always desirable. This happens only if there is strategic complementarity between the two manufacturers at the manufacturing or retail levels: when one firm raises its price, the other must find it optimal to do so as well. For example, if there are economies of scale in retailing costs, then the two firms may be strategic substitutes at the retail level and switching to an independent channel may actually induce the other manufacturer's retailer to lower price. That will decrease channel profits if the two products are demand substitutes (i.e., if $\theta > 0$) and increase channel profits if the two products are demand complements (i.e., if $\theta < 0$).

Bonanno and Vickers (1988) and Coughlan and Wernerfelt (1989) have considered the effect of allowing two-part tariffs between the manufacturer and the independent retailer in interbrand competition. The two-part tariff can be interpreted as a franchise-fee system—the fixed payment is the franchise fee; in other words, these papers consider the case where each manufacturer can use a "franchised system." With two-part tariffs, manufacturers can count on the fixed payments for their profits, so they can even choose wholesale prices below their marginal manufacturing cost. This means that, regardless of the strategic relationship between them—strategic complementarity or strategic substitutability—each manufacturer, when it switches to an independent channel, can always move the other manufacturer's retail price in the "desirable" direction by choosing a wholesale price above or below his marginal manufacturing cost. So choosing an independent channel is always better—regardless of θ. Taken in conjunction with our earlier results for the monopoly case, this suggests that if two-part tariffs can be used, then independent channels perform at least as well as vertically integrated channels.

Proposition 5.   When manufacturers with differentiated products compete with each other, then they will prefer to have independent exclusive retailers paying franchise fees over vertical integration.

When Demand Is Uncertain.   Some of our conclusions are sensitive to our assumption that there is no uncertainty in demand. (Note that cost uncertainty is also relevant in channel contexts, but less so than demand uncertainty. See Rey and Tirole, 1986a, 1986b, for an analysis of cost uncertainty.) If uncertainty is allowed, then the symmetry of information between the manufacturer and the retailer at the contracting stage, the timing of resolution of uncertainty, and the risk attitudes of the protagonists become important. Indeed, consider the following sequence of events, in a channel arrangement:

Event 1: Contracting
Event 2: Manufacturer's marketing actions
Event 3: Retailer's marketing actions
Event 4: Sales (revenues) revealed/received

Then, the manufacturer and retailer may be equally well informed (or not) around the time of contracting. Uncertainty about demand can be resolved for either the manufacturer or the retailer anytime between event 2 and event 4, so we have the following cases:

Symmetric information, uncertainty resolved after retailer actions, manufacturer and retailers both risk-neutral.   All of our results go through in this case. For example, in the case of a single manufacturer dealing with a single retailer, a two-part tariff with unit price equal to the manufacturer's marginal manufacturing cost will bring about the vertical integration outcomes, as would any of the other nonlinear schemes discussed earlier. Similarly, our results with interbrand competition go through.

Symmetric information, uncertainty resolved after retailer actions, only the retailer risk-averse.   Now, with no competition, the equivalence between vertical integration and independent channels doesn't hold. Every contract must pay additional risk premiums to the independent retailer, which reduces the manufacturer's profits. A two-part tariff will not work because it puts all the risk on the retailer and none on the manufacturer. Any profit-sharing arrangement that allocates only a share of the channel profits to the retailer will induce the retailer to choose prices and service levels different from those of a vertically integrated channel. Moreover, these prices and service levels will vary depending on the retailer's profit share. So, with uncertainty and different risk attitudes between the manufacturer and the independent retailer, not only do the manufacturer's profits go down with an independent retailer, but the expected channel profits go down as well.

Symmetric information, uncertainty resolved before retailer actions, both manufacturer and retailer risk-neutral.   Now, with no interbrand competition, the equivalence of the various types of nonlinear contacts in inducing the vertically integrated vanishes (Rey and Tirole, 1986a, 1986b). At the contracting stage, both the manufacturer and the retailer(s) are equally uncertain about demand, but once the contract has been signed, and before the retailer chooses his price and service level, he knows what the demand is, while the manufacturer doesn't. So, while a two-part tariff with exclusive territories will induce the same outcomes in an independent channel as in a vertically integrated channel, resale price-maintenance or minimum quantity requirements will not work. The reason is that if demand is fluctuating but known at the time of decision making, then retail prices and service levels *should* respond to this fluctuation in order to increase expected channel profits. Resale price maintenance or minimum quantity requirements explicitly prohibit such responsiveness.

Asymmetric information, uncertainty resolved after contracting, symmetric or asymmetric risk-attitudes.   If the uncertainty is of the kind where either the manufacturer or the retailer comes to the contracting stage with superior information about demand (the retailer likely about local demand factors, the manufacturer likely about market-wide demand factors), then the contract proposed by the manufacturer or the retailer can serve a signaling or screening function as well as being a source of income. For example, if the manufacturer has superior information about product quality, then he can propose a wholesale price greater than his marginal manufacturing cost (and have the retailer return unsold quantities) as a signal of his willingness to make his income a function of how well his product does on the market. Alternatively, he can use the size of his advertising budget or his willingness to set up company stores (in addition to independent stores) as a signal of his product quality. The retailer can use "slotting allowances" as a screening device to separate "high-quality" manufacturers from "low-quality" manufacturers (Chu, 1990).

From Theory to Practice.   The results we have derived include many simplifying assumptions. We have assumed throughout that manufacturing costs and retailing costs, m, r, and A, are the same with an independent channel structure as with a vertically integrated channel structure. This is a standard assumption in the literature, but it is nevertheless a simplifying assumption. On the one hand, one can defend it by arguing that regardless of who does it, the tasks of distribution are the same. ("You can eliminate the middleman, but you cannot eliminate the services of a middleman.") For example, we noted earlier that selling costs to end users are likely to be borne by the manufacturer in a vertically integrated channel and borne by the retailer in an independent channel. Other distribution costs such as shelf space and point-of-purchase displays are also likely to be the same in the two kinds of channels. On the other hand, the independent retailer's distribution costs to end users can be higher or lower than those of a vertically integrated manufacturer depending on (1) the relative importance of retailing expertise and local market knowledge versus product knowledge in selling the product—the independent retailer is likely to have more of the former, the manufacturer more of the latter, (2) the importance of offering a full line of one-stop shopping products—the independent retailer can do this more readily than a vertically integrated manufacturer, and so on. Williamson (1975, 1986) has discussed these asymmetries in distribution costs in great detail. See McGuire and Staelin (1986) for an explicit analysis of the implications of differences in distribution efficiency between different types of channels.

The great diversity in channel structures in the real world—greater than what our theoretical results predict—could be due to these other factors. For example, many manufacturers use dual distribution channels, going direct to some consumer segments, going through independent channels for others (Moriarty and Moran, 1990). A specific example is Goodyear, which sells its tires through its own stores as well as through independent full-line retailers. A reason for this could be that some consumers are more brand loyal to Goodyear than others. Another reason could be that the company stores serve to curb the independent retailers' bargaining power. Yet another reason may be that Goodyear wants to assure its independent retailers that it will keep up its quality and advertising support. This multiplicity of reasons only reminds us of how complex distribution decisions are and of the value of theoretical modeling in sorting through these complexities.

DISTRIBUTION LOCATION

Let us return to operational aspects of channels issues. Assume that a firm has decided on vertical integration. It then faces a sequence of decisions:

1. Of all the potentially promising areas in the country or the world for locating one or more new outlets, which areas should be selected (market-selection decision)?

2. How many new outlets should be located in each selected area (number-of-outlets decision)?

3. In which particular sites should the new outlets be located (site-selection decision)?

4. What size and characteristics should each particular outlet have (store-size and characteristics decision)?

This sequence of decisions is illustrated in Exhibit 9.6

Market-Selection Decision

A company planning to develop n new outlets must determine in which market areas to place them. A market area is a city, country, state, or region in which company outlets can be opened. This problem can be called the macroproblem, in contrast to site location, which is a microproblem. Some of the outlets may be placed in market areas in which the company is already established and wants to increase its market share; the others can be placed in new market areas deemed promising by the company. In both cases the company is guided by the profit potential. The task, then, is one of developing a good measure of market-area profit potential. We propose an area profit measure that involves the following three concepts:

S_i = company sales potential of market area i

Z_i = company profit potential of market area i

$V(Z_i)$ = present value of company profit potential in market area i

The basic approach is to estimate the company's sales potential in market area i and then to subtract estimated selling costs to find the company profit potential in the area. The profit potential is assumed to grow or decline at a certain rate over a given number of years, which yields a projected earnings stream for n years that is then discounted at the company's target rate

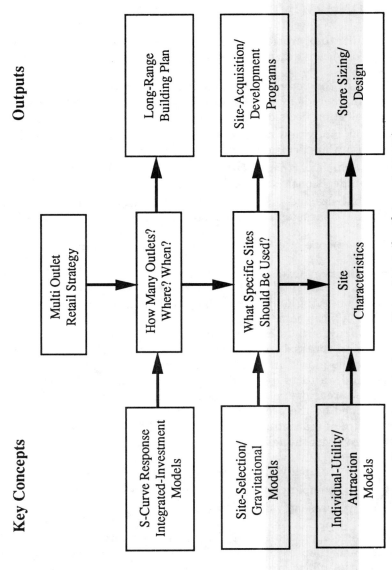

Key Concepts

Outputs

EXHIBIT 9.6 Structuring some key problems in retail outlet management.

of return to find the present value of the company profit potential in market area i. These steps are described in the paragraphs that follow.

Estimating Company Sales Potential in Market Area i.   The first step is to estimate the probable sales that a new or additional company store of average size and average location is likely to realize in this market area. Suppose the company examines the statistics on its other stores and calculates the average annual household expenditures spent by each income class at a typical company outlet. This average provides a starting point for estimating the expected sales of a new outlet in this market area. Suppose that the market area has a known frequency distribution of households by income class. Then the company can estimate that unadjusted sales of a new company store in this market area would be S_i dollars:

$$S_i = \sum_{j=1}^{n} s_j p_{ij} N_i \tag{9.24}$$

where

S_i = estimated annual sales of new company outlet in market area i (unadjusted)

s_j = average annual household expenditures of income class j at company outlet

p_{ij} = percentage of total households of market area i in income class j

N_i = number of households in market area i

At this point the company introduces certain adjustments in the sales estimate to compensate for the oversimplifications. Because this figure was based on the spending patterns of different income classes at any average company store now existing in the system, it should be adjusted for any factors present in the market area that are likely to increase or decrease this (average) level of expenditure. The most important factor to adjust in this figure is the amount of competition that exists in this market area relative to that in an average market area. Let I represent an index of competitiveness that normally stands at 1.00. Then adjusted, estimated company sales potential in market area i for a new store of average size is given by

$$S_i' = I_i S_i \tag{9.25}$$

This figure should be similarly adjusted for any additional factors that could cause sales to be different from those in an average company store.

Estimating Company Profit Potential in Market Area i.   The company now estimates its expenses of doing business in this market area. A good way to proceed is to express each major category of expense as a percentage of sales. Several expenses are likely to be in the same relation to sales in all market areas, such as depreciation, heat, light, and salaries. These items can be lumped together as a single percentage of sales. However, at least three other expenses may vary considerably from the normal percentage and should be stated separately—transportation costs, advertising and promotion costs, and real estate expenditures.

The profit potential of market area i can now be expressed as

$$Z_i = S_i' - (n_i + t_i + a_i + f_i)S_i' \qquad \textbf{(9.26)}$$

where

Z_i = profit potential in market area i

S_i' = adjusted company sales potential in market area i

n_i = estimated normal expenses of selling in market area i as percentage of sales (excluding transportation, advertising, and real estate)

t_i = transportation expense of selling in market area i as percentage of sales

a_i = advertising expense of selling in market area i as percentage of sales

f_i = real estate expense of selling in market area i as percentage of sales

Estimating the Present Value of Company Profit Potential in Market Area i.
The final step calls for an estimate of the expected trend in profit in market area i over the planning horizon. An area that is growing rapidly in population and income may mean healthy and growing profits for a number of years; a more stable area may mean profits will continue at their first-year level. The estimation of future profits can be made in some detail through separate estimates of sales growth and the growth of each cost item. Or, alternatively, a constant growth rate can be assumed. In either case, the firm must assess a discount rate and estimate $V(Z_i)$—the net present value of future profit potential in the area.

Armed with these net present value estimates, the company can rank the market areas in order of attractiveness.

Number-of-Outlets Decision

Among the key assumptions underlying the market-area evaluation is that share of market equals share of outlets.

But empirical studies have shown the relationship between outlet share

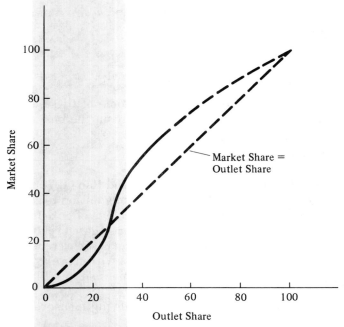

EXHIBIT 9.7 Typical outlet-share/market-share relationship.

and market share to be nonlinear and generally S-shaped (Hartung and Fisher, 1965; Lilien and Rao, 1976). Small outlet shares produce smaller market shares; as outlet share grows, market share grows at a faster rate until it exceeds outlet share. Then as outlet share continues to increase, the rate of market-share growth decreases. Few cases of very high outlet shares have been observed, but the lower part of the curve (below an outlet share of 50%) is well documented. But because market share must equal one when outlet share equals one, the shape of the upper part of the curve can be hypothesized with confidence. Exhibit 9.7 graphically illustrates the S-shaped curve, with the hypothesized portion shown by the dashed curve.

A number of hypotheses concerning consumer and/or corporate behavior have been offered to justify the S-shaped relationship. However, the explanation is still the subject of debate. Nonetheless, this empirically verified relationship is an important finding for decision makers.

The first attempt to operationalize this concept in the form of a planning model was reported by Hartung and Fisher (1965). They model the sequence of purchases by a customer as a two-state Markov chain. The states are "purchase company brand" and "purchase some other brand." The probability that a customer will buy the company's brand on the tth occasion, given that he bought it at $t - 1$, is assumed to be $k_1 s$, where s is outlet share, and the probability that the customer buys the brand at t, given that he bought some other brand at $t - 1$, is k_2s, where k_1 and k_2 are constants. This model implies that market share m is

$$m = \frac{k_2s}{(1 - s) + (1 + k_2 - k_1)s} \qquad (9.27)$$

Naert and Bultez (1975) relax some of these assumptions and develop more robust results. But they still rely on the basic Markovian assumption.

EXAMPLE

Lilien-Rao Model.   Lilien and Rao (1976) rely on a different set of assumptions. They assume that in addition to share of outlets, the share of market is closely related to the age of outlets relative to competition. New outlets are likely to be better situated relative to population centers and traffic patterns. In addition, most firms tend to support markets that have a large share of new outlets with more aggressive advertising and promotional policies. And customers simply like to try out and shop at new outlets.

The authors define the following measure of building activity and call it aggressiveness a:

$$a = \frac{\text{(number of recently built company outlets)} \div \text{(total company outlets)}}{\text{(number of recently built industry outlets)} \div \text{(total industry outlets)}}$$

$$(9.28)$$

They relate market share to outlet share and aggressiveness as $g = (a, s)$. Exhibit 9.8 is an example estimated from Mobil Corporation data.

The authors then incorporate this market-share/outlet-share model into an allocation procedure. The objective is to maximize the total net present value (NPV) of a Y-year building program, subject to restrictions on the total number of outlets that can be built (1) within a market, (2) across all markets in a given year, and (3) during the Y years:

$$\text{NPV} = \sum_{j=1}^{J} \sum_{t=1}^{Y} \frac{CF_{tj}}{(1 + r)^{t-1}} \qquad (9.29)$$

where

CF_{tj} = cash flow associated with market area j in year t

r = discount rate

J = number of market areas considered in plan

S = planning horizon ($S > y$)

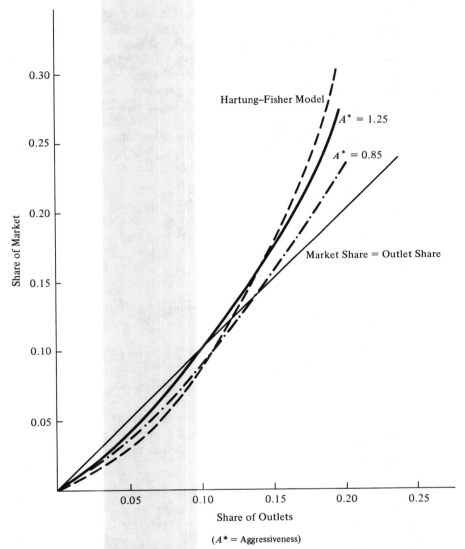

EXHIBIT 9.8   Market share as a function of outlet share and aggressiveness (A^*) estimated from Mobil Corporation data. (*Source:* Lilien and Rao, 1976, p. 6.)

The maximization procedure first selects the group of outlets in the market with the highest average NPV per outlet and then the next highest NPV group and so on until all allowable outlets have been allocated.

   To calculate cash flows and, hence, associated NPVs, the authors suggest that knowledge is required of the firm's building/investment plan, current market share, market-growth rate, discount rate, margins, competitive-building/investment plans, current age distribution of firm and industry outlets, and other financial information, such as land costs, improvement and equipment costs, depreciation methods, and working capital needs. Furthermore, before one can proceed, two additional assumptions are required: (1) "new" outlets are four years old or newer and (2) after Y years the firm will build enough outlets to maintain its ending market share. Assumption (1) is arbitrarily set at four years and could easily be changed; assumption (2) is an approach for handling end-off problems.

The problem, then, is to find $\{X_{it}\}$, the number of outlets to be built in market i at time t to

$$\text{Maximize } Z = \sum_{i=1}^{M} \sum_{t=1}^{Y} \sum_{j=1}^{X_{it}} V_{ijt} \quad \text{(NPV of profit)} \quad \textbf{(9.30)}$$

Subject to

$$\sum_{k=1}^{t} \sum_{i=1}^{M} X_{ik} \leq T_t \quad \text{(cumulative building constraints)}$$

$$0 \leq X_{it} \leq n_{it} \quad \text{(annual building constraints)}$$

where V_{ijt} is the incremental net present value of the ith outlet in market j given that it is opened at time t.

The algorithm and approach was used as an aid to outlet-building planning at Mobil from 1969–1972 (a peak outlet-building period) and became an integral part of the planning process.

In a similar vein, Mahajan, Sharma, and Kerin (1988) developed a market-selection model for a retailing operation with over 800 units in 130 geographic markets. They focused not only on adding and deleting units but also on how to extract untapped sales from existing units.

Site-Selection Decision

Once the commitment to locate in a market area or city has been made, a second key problem faced by the multioutlet business is new outlet placement. Approaches to this problem vary. Applebaum (1968) reports that 10% of a sample of 170 large retail chains performed no systematic analysis for location of retail outlets. The same study showed that research expenditures varied widely; the average research expenditure per new location was about 1% of the site-investment cost.

A variety of different methods have been suggested to assist in the evaluation and measurement of site potential. Some of these have been published and are briefly reviewed here. (Green and Applebaum, 1975, review quantitative approaches to this problem.) Many other approaches are commercially available, but their details are usually closely guarded and unavailable for critical review and publication. Most of the models appear to be ad hoc in nature. They consider neither the synergistic influences of other outlets (the company's or a competitor's) nor any well-developed theory of consumer motivation or behavior.

The problem of site selection is actually two problems: one of site search and one of site evaluation. Site search is the procedure used by the company to discover potentially good sites for its outlets. Large companies usually work through real estate agents or through a company real estate department to search out good sites. This process usually produces a number of new real estate opportunities each period. However, some of these sites will fail immediate tests, and the others will have to be evaluated more thoroughly.

Three methods that have been used include the *checklist method*, where analysts visit a site, observe the various factors likely to affect sales and costs, and integrates them into an over all evaluation (Nelson, 1958); the *analog method*, where zones are developed around the proposed site, and the sales that the proposed store is likely to attract from each zone are estimated on the basis of the drawing power rates of similar stores in the company's chain (Applebaum, 1966); and the *gravitational method*. We describe the last method next.

Gravitational Models of Site Selection.   This approach was pioneered by Huff (1962, 1963, 1964) and is based on the theory of individual, discrete choice originally developed by Luce (1959).

In most forms the model is defined as

$$p_{ij} = \frac{V_{ij}}{\sum_{n \in N_i} V_{in}} \tag{9.31}$$

where

p_{ij} = probability that individual i chooses jth alternative on next choice alternative

V_{ij} = individual i's utility for jth alternative

N_i = choice set of individual i

Huff's specification of this general concept held that the attraction (utility) exercised on any consumer in small area i by a retail center at location j is directly proportional to the size of the retail center and inversely proportional to the customer's distance from the center.

The reasoning is as follows. Suppose stores or shopping centers are pretty much alike, except for size and distance. A larger center means a larger product assortment and hence a greater utility for the consumer. On the other hand, distance represents a cost or disutility to the consumer. On the assumption that the consumer wants to be an efficient shopper, he will be attracted to any particular center in proportion to the ratio of utility to disutility. Huff expressed the consumer's attraction in the following form:

$$p_{ij} = \frac{S_j/D_{ij}^{\lambda}}{\displaystyle\sum_{n \in N_i} (S_n/D_{in}^{\lambda})} \tag{9.32}$$

where

p_{ij} = probability of consumer in area i shopping at a particular location j

S_j = size of retail center in location j

D_{ij} = distance between i and j

λ = estimated sensitivity parameter relating kinds of shopping trips and distance

N_i = choice set of retail locations from area i

To estimate the key parameter λ, we develop the following quantity,

$$E_{ij} = p_{ij}(\lambda)C_i \tag{9.33}$$

where

E_{ij} = expected number of consumers originating at i and terminating at j

C_i = total number of consumers at i

Estimates of parameters of this type of model are discussed in Cooper and Nakanishi (1988). Huff's approach and its extensions (Gautschi, 1981; Gautschi and Corstjens, 1979; Stanley and Sewall, 1976) are most applicable for shopping centers.

A more general structure for these models, applicable to a wider range of outlets, can be summarized as follows:

Site potential = Local sales component + transient sales component **(9.34)**

Equation (9.34) says that sales potential at a particular site has two separate components: sales to people who live nearby and sales to people who are driving through (i.e., who do not live in the area). The nature and importance of these two components vary considerably by product class, but the basic structure serves as a starting point for model development.

EXAMPLE

Reinitz Model.   Reinitz (1968) proposed an assessment procedure that has been used for a number of years to assess site potential for gasoline stations. In his model the local sales component is a simplified version of the Huff procedure, extended to incorporate attributes other than distance and size. Then the estimation of local potential for site i, f_i, has four steps:

1. Choose a local-area radius, usually 1 mile. (Model results are generally not sensitive to the size of this radius as long as it is not too small.) Obtain car population, gasoline use, and other descriptive information of the area.

2. Obtain a census of existing outlets, and rate them by a number of predetermined attributes. Let

$$r_{ij} = \text{rating of outlet } i \text{ in trading area, along attribute } j \text{ (e.g.,}$$
$$j \text{ may be ease of accessibility)}$$

One key attribute to include here is brand image or market presence, linking this model with the S-curve model reviewed in the previous section.

3. Obtain importance weights for these attributes from consumers. Let

$$w_i = \text{average importance weight of attribute } j$$

4. Now estimate local potential f_i:

$$f_i = \frac{\displaystyle\sum_j w_j r_{ij}}{\displaystyle\sum_i \sum_j w_i r_{ij}} GL \tag{9.35}$$

where

$$
\begin{aligned}
G &= \text{annual product (gasoline) consumption in area} \\
L &= \text{fraction of sales average customer buys locally} \\
i &= \text{index covering all outlets in local area}
\end{aligned}
$$

Functional forms other than equation (9.35) have been used with different normative results (Gautschi, 1981), but none has shown significant improvements in predictive power.

Next, the transient sales potential is estimated. Transient trading routes are composed of portions of roads passing the key site and along which the transient traffic flows. The potential customer may or may not stop. Two questions need to be addressed: (1) how many potential transient customers are there? and (2) what fraction will stop?

Identify all routes past the site and index those roads by k. (Note that at an intersection with two-way traffic in each direction, there are 16 possible routes through the intersection, so k would range from 1 to 16.) Define

$$
\begin{aligned}
L &= \text{road length, as a standard of measure (L usually equals a} \\
&\quad\ \text{few miles)} \\
\{R\} &= \text{set of road legs among transient trading routes (index k} \\
&\quad\ \text{identifies specific elements in $\{R\}$)} \\
L_0 &= \text{average distance between refuelings} \\
q &= \text{average gasoline consumption rate (units of product per mile} \\
&\quad\ \text{per customer)}
\end{aligned}
$$

Assuming that the amount of gasoline left in the tank is a random variable, we would expect that for a randomly selected customer,

$$
p(\text{needing fuel}) = \frac{L}{L_0} \tag{9.36}
$$

and the average quantity purchased is

$$
Q = L_0 q \tag{9.37}
$$

If traffic flow along route k is T_k cars per day, then the expected amount purchased per day is

$$
G_k = T_k Q p(\text{needing fuel}) \tag{9.38}
$$

Along each leg (route) this site should see the share of this potential relative to its attractiveness, so

$$g_{ik} = \frac{\sum\limits_{j} w_j r_{ij}}{\sum\limits_{i \in R_k} \sum\limits_{j} w_j r_{ij}} T_k L_0 q \qquad \textbf{(9.39)}$$

where

g_{ik} = potential along leg k

R_k = set of indices of stations along route k

Finally,

$$g_i = \sum_{k} g_{ik} \qquad \textbf{(9.40)}$$

where

g_i = total transient potential for site i

k = ranges over all transient routes that are associated with outlet i

Thus site potential = $f_i + g_i$, where f_i is determined from equation (9.35) and equation (9.40) determines g_i.

A number of judgments and measurements are needed to calibrate and use this model, such as the boundaries of local trading areas, the length of transient trading routes, area population measures, transient traffic flows, the fraction of sales bought locally, and strength and importance weights for the proposed and existing sites.

This model was in regular use for national and international site evaluations at Mobil for a period of about a decade. It serves as a structure for defining the data gathering needs, as well as the evaluation steps, required to support site-location decisions.

Stanley and Sewall (1976) replace the size variable in Huff's model with an image variable obtained through multidimensional scaling. Hlavac and Little (1970), in a study of auto dealership selection, use an approach that considers the distance customers travel, as well as the attractiveness (image) of the automobiles offered for sale. As Gautschi (1981) points out, these approaches are extensions of the multiplicative competitive-interaction (MCI) model of Nakanishi and Cooper (1974), and all may suffer to some extent by omitted attributes and heterogeneity of individual choice sets. Ghosh and McLafferty (1982) also use an MCI model to estimate store choice but address the problem of competitive uncertainty using multicriteria decision concepts.

The transient model of Reinitz is an important addition to the basic MCI structure, especially in such product classes as gasoline and fast foods. There, a great deal of brand-to-brand substitution is possible, and the purchase trip is often a secondary part of another journey.

In terms of predictive validity (Do any of the models predict site sales accurately?), two issues have clouded reports to date: lack of controlled evaluation and prediction of sales potential.

Model validation has usually been done by checking how well the model fits data from outlets used in its development or from a small holdout sample. Since many of the models have been implemented, these tests must have produced acceptable results. For example, Reinitz's model was subjected to extensive testing of this type; had the model's predictions been used, most of the unprofitable outlets and only a few of the profitable ones would have been eliminated.

The more rigorous type of testing—predicting the sales of unconstructed outlets and comparing these predictions with actual sales—has rarely been conducted in practice because sales potential is a long-range concept. Outlets may approach their potential in only six months or reach it over a period of several years.

In work by Kinberg and Rao (1978), data for checking and savings accounts for branch banks were analyzed to identify when a steady-state level of business was reached. It was found that the time required to reach the steady-state level varied from two years to over seven years, depending on such area characteristics as population turnover rate. Because of such large time lags, substantial changes occur in traffic patterns and neighborhood characteristics, which invalidate many original model assumptions and, thus, the forecasts of sales potential. Therefore evaluation of a model's predicative power is a long-range task, requiring the kind of effort and dedication to validation that many commercial organizations are unwilling to undertake.

All of the models predict sales potential. Actual sales achieved by a site depend critically on the management of the outlet. Once an outlet earns a reputation for poor service, it is almost impossible for it to reach a target sales level that approaches the predicted potential. Conversely, sites with good management consistently exceed their potential. Therefore because there is no method for estimating the ex ante quality of an individual manager, there is a large uncontrollable source of error intrinsic to every forecast. Site-selection models will remain incomplete and inaccurate unless they incorporate management quality into the model specifications.

In addition, as we saw earlier, interactions and synergies exist between outlets, suggesting that a portfolio approach might be appropriate (Achabal, Gorr, and Mahajan, 1982, and Mahajan, Sharma, and Srinivas, 1985).

A behavioral approach to the modeling of site potential is needed to balance more mechanistic approaches. Some interesting work reported by Ackoff (1962) relates the probability of a consumer stopping at a particular outlet to the perceived time it will take to obtain service, and it relates perceived time to actual time in a nonlinear fashion. This cognitive-distance approach has been explored by McKay, Olshavsky, and Sentell (1975); for a critical review of this and other research in a retailing setting, see Hirschman (1981).

Store-Size and Characteristic Decisions

Closely related to the analysis of site potential are the store characteristics that influence its attractiveness. In the analysis of a location opportunity, management considers not so much the effect of an average company store in that location but that of a store of a particular size, layout, product assortment, decor, parking capacity, and so forth. Management seeks those levels of these factors that have a maximum impact on profits.

Of all the outlet characteristics, store size is traditionally singled out as most important. The larger the store is, the greater its product assortment and neighborhood conspicuousness will be, and therefore the larger its store size in a proportional manner. To build stores of the right size, management needs some measure of the relationship between store size and store sales. If small stores yielded higher returns of investment than large stores, the company may be better off building several small stores, instead of a few large ones, with a given budget.

Baumol and Ide (1956) developed a model in which store size had both positive and negative effects on store sales as size increased. Instead of using store size directly, they focused on a correlated variable, the number of different items N that the retailer carried. They argued that the greater the number of different items there are, the more likely it is that the shopper will be attracted because he would have greater confidence in finding the items he wanted. On the other hand, the greater the number of different items there are, the more will be the time required by the shopper to get to the spot in the store where the items he wants are kept. Their particular formulation of the two effects of the number of items is as follows:

$$f(N, D) = k_1 p(N) - k_2(c_d D + c_n \sqrt{N} + c_i) \qquad \textbf{(9.41)}$$

where

$f(N, D)$ = measure of consumer's expected net benefit from shopping at store with N different items and distance D

$p(N)$ = probability that consumer will find some set of items in store that will make his trip successful

c_d, c_n, c_i = cost parameters

k_1, k_2 = respective weights for benefit and cost of shopping, $0 \le k_1 \le 1$ and $k_1 + k_2 = 1$

Their formulation permits a number of conclusions to be drawn. First, the expected net benefit of shopping in a store with very few items may be negative. Second, the expected net benefit of shopping in a store with a tremendous number of items may also be negative because the first term in equation (9.41) can never exceed k_1 while $k_2 c_n \sqrt{N}$ grows indefinitely large. Third, sales are likely to increase with store size at an increasing and then a diminishing rate, which eventually becomes negative. The exact shape depends on the parameters in the equation.

Fixing the size of the outlet, the amount of display space to allocate to different items is a critical retailer decision that affects both manufacturer and retailer profit.

Corstjens and Doyle (1981) provide a review of the literature on shelf space allocation and, in spite of a proliferation of commercially available procedures to aid in the shelf-space decision (see Bultez and Naert, 1988b, for a review), they argue that few theoretically sound procedures exist. They propose a formulation in which they optimize the space allocation across product categories to maximize total store profit, where product demand is modeled as a multiplicative power function. Bultez and Naert (1988b) simplify and operationalize their model.

EXAMPLE _____

The S.H.A.R.P. Model. Bultez and Naert (1988b) formulate the shelf space allocation model as

Find $\{s_i\}$ to

$$\text{Maximize} \sum_i g_i q_i(s_1, \dots, s_n) - \sum_i C_i \qquad (9.42)$$

$$\text{Subject to} \sum_i s_i \le S$$

$$s_i \ge 0, \qquad \text{for all } i$$

where

s_i = total shelf space available for the product assortment
s_i = shelf space available for item i, $i = 1, ..., n$
q_i = items i's sales volume as a function of $\{s_i\}$
g_i = gross profit/markup for item i
C_i = replenishment cost of carrying item i in the assortment

The authors show that

$$\sigma_i = \frac{s_i}{S} = (\gamma_i c_i + \bar{\eta}_{\cdot i})/(\bar{G} + \bar{N}) \qquad \textbf{(9.43)}$$

where

σ_i = proportion of shelf space allocated to product i
γ_i = percentage decrease in product i's handling cost resulting from a unit percentage increase in space allocated to it (handling cost/shelf space elasticity).
c_i = C_i/Π = relative importance of product i's replenishment cost compared to total line profitability, Π
$\bar{\eta}_{\cdot i}$ = $\Sigma_j r_j \eta_{ji}$ = weighted mean of all elasticities with respect to product i's shelf space
η_{ji} = cross-elasticity of item j's sales
r_i = π_i/Π = relative profitability of item i
$\bar{N}$ = $\Sigma_j \bar{\eta}_{\cdot i}$
$\bar{G}$ = $\Sigma_k \gamma_k c_k$

Note that equation (9.43) implies that priority should be given to products whose display contributes most to boosting sales of the most profitable product (and to reducing handling costs).

The authors outline an estimation procedure and a heuristic solution approach and report that four tests of the procedure in Belgian supermarket chains lead to increases in profitability ranging from 6.9% to 33.8% (without affecting handling and replenishment operations).

As scanner data becomes more widely available, procedures like S.H.A.R.P. will become more commonly applied to support shelf space allocation decisions at retailers worldwide. For a related system dealing with the development of retail promotional strategy based on customer inputs, see Green and colleagues (1984).

DISTRIBUTION LOGISTICS

In addition to establishing locations for its outlets, a company must also design an efficient physical-distribution system for getting goods to its outlets and customers. This system consists of decisions on warehouse location, inventory levels, packaging and handling procedures, and transportation carriers. These decisions have both cost and demand aspects. The cost aspect of physical distribution has received the most attention, and many successful operations research models have been developed in this area. However, the demand aspect has come to the foreground more recently and deserves the serious attention of designers of physical-distribution systems.

Of course, marketing executives are particularly interested in the demand aspect of physical distribution. Each component decision can affect company sales. Warehouse locations are a promotional tool in that they give confidence to local buyers of better availability and faster service. Inventory-level policies affect availability and hence sales. Packaging and handling procedures, insofar as they affect the damaged-goods rate, affect the number of customers. Transportation modes, insofar as they can mean faster or slower arrival of goods, affect buyer satisfaction and sales.

In Exhibit 9.9 a comprehensive distribution-planning system is outlined. According to Geoffrion (1975, pp. 18–19), such a system should satisfy the following primary questions:

1. How many warehouses should there be?

2. Where should they be located (given a list of current and plausible candidate locations)?

3. What size should each warehouse be (including selection among specific expansion and contraction projects under consideration)?

4. Which warehouse should service which customer?

5. How should each plant's output be allocated among warehouses and customers for each product?

6. What should the transportation flows be on an annual basis throughout the entire distribution system?

7. What is the breakdown of cost savings and customer-service implications associated with the best distribution-system design compared with a projection of the current system to the target period?

He does not include inventory control, order processing, packaging materials handling, vehicle routing, and other operational problems in the model. For planning it is sufficient to assume that these tactical functions are performed as economically as possible and are consistent with desired levels of customer service. Their cost consequences should be woven into the individual cost elements of the planning model.

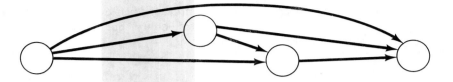

Sources   Existing and Candidate   Customers
                           Distribution Centers

List of Commodities   Eligible Commodities for   Customer Demands
                           Each Candidate DC

                                                           Split-Delivery Policy
Supply Limits
(for Multisource Commodities)   Minimum and Maximum Allowable Annual
                           Throughput Volume for Each
Supply Costs   Candidate DC
(for Multisource Commodities)
                           Distribution Center Costs,
                           Fixed, Variable

            Freight Rates: Inbound, Direct, Interwarehouse Transfer, Outbound

MAIN FUNCTION OF THE SOLVER

Determine
  How Many DCs, Where, and What Size
  DC Territories
  All Transportation Flows
  Source Loadings

                    So as to Minimize Total Costs
                       Supply (e.g., Manufacturing)
                       Transportation
                       Warehousing
                       Inventory
                       System Reconfiguration

                                Subject to All Appropriate Constraints
                                   Supply Capacity
                                   DC Throughput Capacity
                                   Demands to Be Met
                                   Single Sourcing of Customers
                                   Customer Service

EXHIBIT 9.9   Sketch of a comprehensive distribution-planning system. (*Source:* Geoffrion and Powers, 1980, p. 24.)

Furthermore, because they all interact with one another, the questions just posed should be resolved simultaneously, not piecemeal. The cost elements of the mode include the following:

1. Transportation costs between plants, warehouses, and customers
2. All warehouse and inventory costs
3. Costs and savings of expanding, opening, and closing warehouses
4. Production costs by product at the plants

When these questions have a significant influence on demand, revenues from sales must be incorporated into the mode (as negative costs). The sum of all these costs must then be minimized subject to all necessary restrictions, including the following:

1. The stipulated production capacities of each plant must not be exceeded.
2. The size of each open warehouse must be between prescribed lower and upper limits.
3. Each customer must (often) be served by a single warehouse for certain products.
4. A warehouse is eligible to serve a customer only if it is sufficiently close that the transit times under economical delivery modes are in accord with the desired level of customer service.
5. All forecast customer demands must be satisfied (any undesirable demands would be eliminated from the forecast).
6. Any other desired constraints on configuration, such as lower and upper limits on the number of open warehouses, subsets of warehouses, among which at least one or at most one should be open, more complex constraints on warehouse capacity, and desired levels of customer service.

A solution strategy for this problem has been formulated by Geoffrion and Graves (1974) who state the problem as follows:

$$\text{Find } \{X_{ijkl}\} \{Y_{kl}\} \{Z_k\} \text{ to}$$

$$\text{Minimize} \underbrace{\sum_l \sum_k \sum_j \sum_i c_{ijkl} X_{ijkl}}_{\substack{\text{Production and} \\ \text{shipping costs}}} + \sum_k \left[\underbrace{f_k Z_k}_{\substack{\text{Fixed} \\ \text{charge}}} + \underbrace{V_k \sum_i \sum_l D_{il} Y_{kl}}_{\substack{\text{Variable cost} \\ \text{(inventory and} \\ \text{holding)}}} \right] \qquad (9.44)$$

Subject to

$$\sum_l \sum_k X_{ijkl} \leq S_{ij} \qquad \text{(supply constraints)} \qquad \textbf{(9.45)}$$

$$\sum_j X_{ijkl} = D_{ik}Y_{kl} \qquad \text{(demand constraints)} \qquad \textbf{(9.46)}$$

$$\sum_k Y_{kl} = 1 \qquad \begin{array}{l}\text{(each customer zone}\\\text{must be served by a}\\\text{warehouse or distribution}\\\text{center, DC)}\end{array} \qquad \textbf{(9.47)}$$

$$V_k Z_k \leq \sum_i \sum_l D_{il}Y_{kl} \leq \bar{V}_k Z_k \qquad \begin{array}{l}\text{(upper and lower}\\\text{throughput constraints}\\\text{for open DC's)}\end{array} \qquad \textbf{(9.48)}$$

plus other configurational constraints on (Y_{kl}) and/or (Z_k). $\qquad$ **(9.49)**

In this model no customer zone is serviced by more than one distribution center (DC). Constraint (9.49) allows incorporation of the idiosyncrasies of most real applications, such as upper/lower bounds on the number of DCs open, precedence relations among the DCs (not A unless B), mandatory service constraints (if DC A is open, it must serve customer zone B), and so on.

The actual details of the optimization are beyond the scope of this book. The point is that optimization of full problems as formulated in equation (9.44) is currently possible by using an approach like that of Geoffrion and Graves. But because true optimization has been difficult until recently, most problems of this type have been solved by nonoptimizing heuristics. Geoffrion and VanRoy (1979) discuss the risks of using heuristics in distribution planning.

Analytical support for the design and operation of distribution systems using computer simulators is also well developed. The distribution-system simulator (Aggarwal, 1973; Connors et al., 1972; Hax, 1975), LREPS (Bowersox et al., 1972), and several other simulation packages have been designed specifically for distribution. In addition, many firms have programmed their own simulation studies by using specialized simulation languages, such as GPSS and SIMSCRIPT.

With simulation a fully specified system is modeled in great detail, and therefore simulation is a logical complement to the optimization approach (albeit, optimization at a more macrolevel) specified above. In this context inventory-control and waiting-line problems can be studied in detail. Practical applications of simulation-based studies have included supermarket sizing, bank office design, and airline ticket offices.

Another key element of physical distribution is inventory management. Although the marketer does not usually have control over inventory policy, he is inclined to seek a strong voice in setting that policy. The marketer's chief concern is in providing a high level of customer service, and inventory policy is a tool in the demand-creation-and-satisfaction process. But while marketers would like all their customers' orders to be filled immediately, such an inventory level is often very costly. Inventory-control decisions balance ordering and storage costs against the cost and likelihood of run-out and, hence, potential lost sales. Heskett (1977) points out that many companies have higher inventory-carrying costs than necessary because they try to offer their customers the same service standard on all their goods. But customers expect to wait longer for nonstandard items than for faster-moving ones. Therefore, savings are available (at no loss in overall customer satisfaction) by developing different inventory policies for products with different demand profiles. For a review of inventory control and a guide to the related literature, see Wagner (1980), for example.

An emerging trend in this area involves the development of integrated models that include logistics but span multiple functions. Klingman and colleagues (1986) and Klingman and colleagues (1987) provide fine illustrations, where an integrated approach centered on logistics management saved Citgo approximately $70 million dollars per year. In a similar vein, Rangan, Zoltners, and Becker (1986) developed and applied a model in an industrial packaging firm and increased firm profits by 10%. For a comprehensive discussion centering on the increase of flexibility in the distribution network—"just-in-time" and its relatives—see Stock and Lambert (1987), Johnson and Wood (1986), and Ansari (1986). Also see Eliashberg and Steinberg (1987) for a model that integrates the distributor's inventory and pricing strategy with the manufacturer's production and inventory plans.

SUMMARY

A company's channels of distribution represent a foundation for its other marketing policies. For this reason management will want to exercise great care in its decision on distribution strategy, location, and logistics. The first of these, distribution strategy, is the determination of the best way in which the company reaches its consumers. The strategic questions that need to be answered include should the manufacturer vertically integrate into distribution or not? If not, how many layers of independent middlemen should be used? Should the retailers be given exclusive territories via franchising? and so on. The answers to these questions depend on the product itself, particularly, on how important the middleman's selling effort is to the success of the product, on the degree of uncertainty about consumer demands, on the degree of competition at the manufacturer level, and on the kinds of contracts the manufacturer is able to negotiate with his middleman. Theoretical modeling has shed considerable light on these issues, but much more work needs to be done in understanding the way uncertainty interacts with the other channel factors.

The second decision area, distribution location, is concerned with four interrelated decisions: market selection, number of outlets, site location, and the size and other characteristics of the store. The first task is to determine the most attractive market areas in the country in which to locate new outlets. A good procedure is to estimate discounted cumulative profits on a new average-sized outlet that might be opened in each area and then to rank the locations from the most to the least profitable. The company should then turn to the question of the optimal number of outlets per market area. Quantitative approaches to this question incorporate an S-shaped, market-share/outlet-share relationship. As for site location, current techniques range from primitive checklists to the analog method to gravitational models. Also, store size was shown to be an important factor in affecting the level of sales. Other characteristics of the outlet, such as its decor, caliber of management, product assortment, and so forth, also affect demand.

Distribution logistics, the third area of distribution decision making, is concerned with determining the best way to supply company outlets with product. This decision involves four major variables: the number of warehouses, inventory levels, packaging and handling procedures, and transportation carriers. For an optimal physical-distribution system, an appropriate cost function must be formulated, which includes the cost of lost sales. Once this cost is included with the other physical-distribution costs, the task is to minimize the distribution cost function subject to certain constraints.

New theoretical results are providing more insight into this subtle area and more comprehensive models are showing the potential to provide significant operational benefits as well.

PROBLEMS

9.1. Find an optimal outlet decision by using the algorithm of the Lilien-Rao model for the situation given by following data:

Number of Outlets	Cumulative NPVs		
	Market 1	Market 2	Market 3
1	5	4	6
2	8	9	7
3	12	16	13
4	15	21	14

9.2. The ABC Corporation currently sells one of its products directly to retailers through its own sales force. Present sales are 100,000 units per year, and the company's profit margin is $2 per unit. Management estimates that the cost of maintaining the sales force is $1 per unit. The company is considering the use of wholesalers rather than selling directly to retailers. The wholesaler's commission would be $0.75 per unit, but sales force costs per unit sold would be cut by one-half.

a. The initial cost of converting to the wholesaler distribution system is $18,000. How many additional units would the company have to sell to cover its transition costs in one year?

b. Management's estimates of the pessimistic, most likely, and optimistic levels of sales for the coming year under the wholesaler strategy are 100,000, 110,000, and 120,000, respectively. Should the company change its distribution channels?

9.3. A large fish-and-chips restaurant franchiser is considering opening a new outlet in a large metropolitan area. There are presently 200 fish-and-chips outlets in the area, of which 20 hold his company's franchise. Each outlet in the area has average monthly sales of $10,000

a. using the Hartung-Fisher model, determine the amount of additional sales that would be created by opening up a new outlet in this area (assume $k_1 = 4.44$ and $k_2 = 0.64$).

b. What would be the amount of additional sales if 30 of the 200 stores in the area were company franchises?

9.4 A men's shoe manufacturer plans to establish a new outlet in one of its two major market areas, A_1 or A_2. The company and its competitors currently sell a total of 100,000 pairs of shoes in each area. There are 250 outlets in A_1 (of which 25 are company outlets) and 200 outlets in A_2 (40 of which are company outlets). In a recent study the company found that it was able to retain about 30% of its customers in A_1 and about 40% in A_2 from purchase to purchase. It was also found that the company was able to persuade 10% of its competitor's customers in A_1 (8% in A_2) to switch to its own brand. Should the new outlet be established in A_1 or A_2?

9.5. A company is considering the development of one of two new market areas. Estimates of potential sales, expenses, and growth rates for each area are presented in the following table:

	Area 1	Area 2
Adjusted annual sales potential, S_t	$500,000	$750,000
Transportation expenses (percentage of sales), d_t	0.20	0.15
Advertising expenses (percentage of sales), a_t	0.25	0.30
Real estate expenses (percentage of sales), l_t	0.10	0.12
Other expenses (percentage of sales), n_t	0.29	0.35
Expected growth rate of profit potential	0.04	0.06

It is estimated that it would cost the same amount to develop either area ($150,000). Suppose the company's cost of capital is 10%. Which area offers the more attractive rate of return over a three year planning horizon?

9.6. Huff's gravitational model assumes that the consumer's marginal utility with respect to distance varies according to the value of the exponent λ. For instance, $\lambda = 2$ indicates that the consumer experiences diminishing marginal utility with respect to increases in distance. The model, however, assumes that the consumer experiences constant marginal utility with respect to increases in store size.

Suppose that the consumer actually experiences diminishing marginal utility with respect to increases in store size. Using an exponent as the parameter that accounts for the consumer's marginal utility of store size, modify Huff's formulation to accommodate this diminishing marginal utility.

9.7. You manufacture mattresses. The amount of mattresses you sell at the retail level is a function of all the elements in the marketing mix, including the commission you give to retailers. Currently, all manufacturers give a commission of 4%. You are thinking about changing your commission rate. Your (constant) profit per mattress sold is 10% of the mattress retail price, before the commission is deducted from your profits.

Your current (stable) market share is 5%. You assume your market share, with a different commission, would be

$$5\% \times \frac{\text{your commission}}{\text{other brands' commissions}}$$

  a. What happens if you decrease your commission (e.g., to 2%) and other manufacturers do not? What will be your market share and profit?
  b. What happens if you increase your commission (e.g., to 6%) and other manufacturers do not?
  c. What happens if you increase your commission (e.g., to 6%) and other manufacturers follow your move?
  d. You assume that competitors will follow your move if you increase your commission but will not if you decrease it. Graph a curve of your share against possible commission levels between 0 and 8%. Graph a curve of your profit against possible commission levels.
  e. What should you do?

9.8. Retail sales of a product are given by

$$s = \alpha \ln \beta x$$

where s is the sales rate and x is the advertising rate. Let

  g_1 = retailer's incremental profit as fraction of *retail* sales
  g_2 = manufacturer's incremental profit as fraction of *retail* sales

The manufacturer has made contracts with its retailers for cooperative advertising. Under the contract the retailer advertises the manufacturer's product in local media and the manufacturer pays part of the cost. Consider the following case: (1) The retailer decides the amount of advertising. (2) The retailer pays a fraction w of the cost. (3) The manufacturer pays a fraction $(1 - w)$ of the cost. (4) The manufacturer sets w. Suppose that the retailer spends to maximize his profit and the manufacturer picks w to maximize his, knowing how the retailer is going to act. What will w be?

9.9. Suppose you are a manufacturer facing a market that has changed in its composition since the last time you set prices. There are two market segments H and L with reservation prices $20 and $10, respectively, for a unit of your product. The purchase frequency is one unit every quarter. Your variable costs are $2 per unit. You sell through a large retailer whose fixed costs of doing business with you are $2,500 per quarter.

Until last month your market consisted of 5,000 people with the $20 reservation price and 5,000 people with the $10 reservation price, and your price to the retailer was $19.50. But now you realize that there are only 2,000 potential consumers with the $20 reservation price; the other 8,000 have a $10 reservation price. There are three possible options you can pursue at this point: (1) offer a trade discount to the retailer; (2) don't change the wholesale price, but offer a coupon to consumers as a freestanding insert in the local newspaper (the coupon value is to be determined; the coupon will only be valid for a short time and it will cost segment H—and only segment H—$4 to redeem); (3) offer a coupon to consumers and offer a trade promotion to the retailer (both the coupon value and the trade deal will have to be determined). Which option should you pursue?

10 | NEW PRODUCT PLANNING

Most companies recognize that a continuing stream of new product developments is essential to ensure long-term organizational health. But they also recognize that innovation is accompanied by high costs and risks. These risks can be controlled through a well-conceived and professionally managed program of new product development. The key ingredients of such a program are (1) effective organizational arrangements for new product research and development, (2) professional staffing, (3) adequate expenditures for marketing research, and (4) the use of sound explicit models for planning and forecasting new product sales.

This chapter will focus on the last ingredient: building on the product design models in Chapter 5, we address new product planning and forecasting models here. A number of new product decision models have been developed recently, varying in the number and type of variables considered, the level of aggregation, and the method of solution. All these models attempt to explain and/or control the level of sales of a new product over time.

The first section of this chapter establishes some basic distinctions of new product problems, based on the product's newness and its likely frequency of purchase. The second section focuses on the theory of the consumer-adoption process and the underlying behavioral phenomena driving the sales of new products. The third section examines first-purchase models—that is, models designed to predict the cumulative number of new product triers over time. These models are used to forecast sales of durable goods and novelty items. The fourth section examines repeat-purchase models—that is, models designed to predict the repeat-purchase rate of buyers of frequently purchased goods. Predicting the sales of a frequently purchased new product requires combining an appropriate first-purchase model with a repeat-purchase model. That section deals primarily with test-market models and pretest-market models, both of which attempt to forecast product sales prior to national introduction.

TYPES OF NEW PRODUCT SITUATIONS

Presumably, a new product is introduced by a company when a favorable estimate has been made of its future sales, profits, and other impacts on the firm's objectives. A new product's sales are shaped by many factors, including the size of the potential market, the nature of competition, and the company's marketing plan and resources. The appropriate sales-forecasting model varies with the type of new product situation. These situations are distinguished by the degree of newness of the product and the degree of product repurchasability.

Product Newness. We do not rigorously attempt to define a new product but instead distinguish among three categories.

The first category, *new product innovation,* is composed of products that are new both to the market and to the company. These are the really new products that establish new product classes to compete against other product classes.

The second category is the *new brand*, consisting of products that are new to the company but not very new to the market. The new brand represents the effort of a company to add its own entry into an established product class. Consumers recognize the brand as part of the established product class, and less learning has to take place compared with the case of innovations.

The third type of new product is the *new model*, style, or package size. Here the company's product is only superficially new to the company and to the market and is immediately recognized and understood as an extension or deepening of the company's product line.

Frequency of Purchase. In addition to distinguishing degrees of product newness, it is also helpful to distinguish among products that buyers are likely to purchase only once, until it needs to be replaced like a camera (durable); those they are likely to purchase occasionally, like automobile tires; and those they are likely to purchase frequently.

In a population of a given size, once all the potential buyers have bought a product in the first category, there are no more sales. The expected sales over time for a new product are illustrated in Exhibit 10.1(a). The number

Sales Volume, Noncumulative

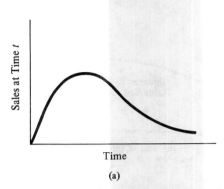

Sales Volume, Cumulative

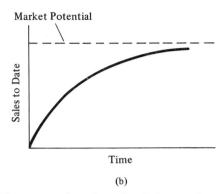

(a)

(b)

EXHIBIT 10.1   Sales life cycle for a durable new product in a fixed-size market.

sold in each period rises at the beginning and later falls, until no potential buyers are left. If the curve is recast in terms of cumulative sales of the product, it would resemble the curve in Exhibit 10.1(b). In this form the curve illustrates the rate of market penetration, which is shown approaching a limiting value representing total possible sales—that is, market potential. If the number of potential buyers is not fixed, then the market potential line in Exhibit 10.1(b) is no longer horizontal and the curves are modified accordingly.

Products that are purchased occasionally are exemplified by many durable goods, such as automobiles, toasters, industrial equipment, and certain clothing items. These goods exhibit replacement cycles, dictated either by their physical wearing out or their psychological obsolescence from changing styles and tastes. Most sales forecasting for these products consists of separately estimating sales to first-time buyers and replacement sales. Replacement sales are usually estimated from data on the age distribution of existing goods and product mortality data. Exhibit 10.2 shows the sales life cycle of an infrequently purchased product made up of new sales and replacement sales.

New products that are likely to be repurchased frequently, such as consumer nondurables, have a different-looking sales life cycle, as shown in Exhibit 10.3. The number of persons buying the product for the first time increases and then decreases over time, since each period there remains fewer persons left who have not tried it (assuming a fixed population). Superimposed on the first-purchase sales volume is the repeat-purchase sales volume, assuming that the product satisfies some fraction of triers, who then became steady customers. The sales curve eventually falls to a plateau, a level of steady repeat-purchase volume; by this time the product is no longer in the class of new products.

The reason for the characteristic early peak and then decline to a (steady-state) sales or share position is not necessarily due to any inherent product

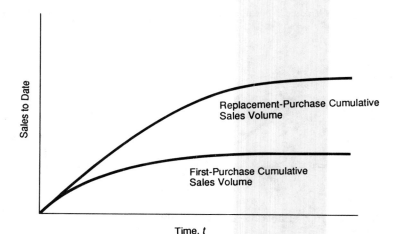

EXHIBIT 10.2   Sales life cycle for an infrequently purchased product, involving replacement sales.

weakness; it simply reflects that any new product will only be able to satisfy and convert from other brands a fraction of those who try. The long-term share is made up of satisfied triers.

Because all new products, whether they are purchased once, occasionally, or frequently, must be adopted by a purchasing population who initially do not know about them, we next review some basic concepts of the consumer-adoption process.

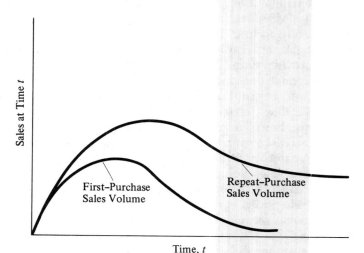

EXHIBIT 10.3   Sales life cycle for a repurchasable new product.

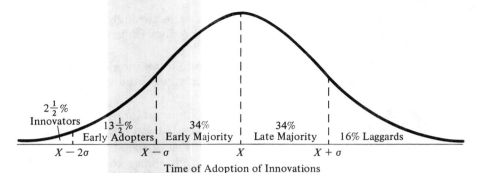

EXHIBIT 10.4   Adoption categorization on the basis of relative time of adoption of innovations. (*Source:* Rogers, 1983, p. 24.)

THE ADOPTION PROCESS
FOR NEW PRODUCTS

The theory of the *diffusion of innovations* addresses how a new idea, a good, or a service is assimilated into a social system over time. This topic has been studied in depth by scientists from different disciplines, including sociologists, economists, and marketers.

The *diffusion process* is the spread of an idea or the penetration of a market by a new product from its source of creation to its ultimate users or adopters, while the *adoption process* is the steps an individual goes through from the time he hears about an innovation until final adoption, the decision to use an innovation regularly. The difference among individuals in their response to new ideas is called their innovativeness; it represents the degree to which an individual is relatively early or late in adopting a new product or idea (Midgley and Dowling, 1978). Individuals are often classified into different adopter categories on the basis of their innovativeness, as illustrated in Exhibit 10.4. (See Mahajan, Muller, and Srivastava, 1990, for an alternative classification procedure based on diffusion models.)

Individuals can also be classified by their influence on others with respect to innovation. *Opinion leaders* are those individuals from whom others seek information and advice and who therefore influence the action of later adopters. These concepts have important implications for modeling the adoption process. In the early stage of the process, innovators alone are involved in purchase decisions. Later, word of mouth from innovators (if they are also opinion leaders) increases the likelihood of trial. However, as more try, there are fewer left who have not tried, and the rate of trial decreases. Bass's (1969a) model operationalized these concepts in a marketing framework.

There have been many studies on how individuals react to new ideas and products. Rogers (1983) attempts to synthesize over 3,000 studies of the diffusion process and reaches the following conclusions.

First, he proposes that consumers go through a sequence of five stages when accepting and adopting a new product (Rogers, 1983, p. 164):

1. *Knowledge* occurs when an individual (or other decision-making unit) is exposed to the innovation's existence and gains some understanding of how it functions.

2. *Persuasion* occurs when an individual (or other decision-making unit) forms a favorable or unfavorable attitude toward the innovation.

3. *Decision* occurs when an individual (or other decision-making unit) engages in activities that lead to a choice to adopt or reject the innovation.

4. *Implementation* occurs when an individual (or other decision-making unit) puts an innovation into use.

5. *Confirmation* occurs when an individual (or other decision-making unit) seeks reinforcement of an innovation decision already made, but he or she may reverse this previous decision if exposed to conflicting messages about the innovation.

Second, he reports that the rate of adoption of an innovation can be modeled as a function of that innovation's attributes. For example, other things being equal, an innovation will diffuse more quickly through a population if it

Has a strong *relative advantage*—a greater perceived value in terms of higher return on investment, reliability, ease of operation or whatever the relevant dimensions compared to the current product or products. (relative advantage)

Has a high degree of *compatibility*—that is, it is consistent with the existing attitudes, values and operations of the individuals in the social system. (compatibility)

Is not *complex*. (complexity)

Can be *tried on a limited* basis. (trialability)

Is *observable*—that is, the results or benefits of the innovation are easily visible to others. (observability)

In addition to the perceived attributes of the innovation, other variables that affect the adoption rate include

The *type of innovation decision*. The fewer people involved and the less structured the decision process (in an organization), the more rapid the diffusion.

The *communications channels used*. Mass media are effective for simple

innovations but interpersonal (sales force) contacts may be essential
for more complex innovations.

The *nature of the social system*. A highly interconnected social system
(e.g., linked by an effective trade association) will see more rapid diffusion than a less connected system.

The *effect of change agent's promotional efforts*. Enthusiastic and highly
visible early adopters will speed the diffusion process.

Third, Rogers suggests that individuals differ markedly in their likelihood of trying new products. As Exhibit 10.4 suggests, the continuum of innovativeness can be partitioned into a number of adoption categories. He
characterizes innovators as "venturesome," early adopters as "respectable,"
early majority as "deliberate," late majority as "skeptical," and laggards as
"traditional." Early adopters appear to differ from later adopters in terms of
socioeconomic characteristics, personality variables and communication behavior:

Socioeconomic characteristics. Education, income literacy and social status are positively related to early adoption, but no consistent relationship with age has been found.

Personality variables. Early adopters have greater empathy (ability to
project into the role of another), are less dogmatic in their beliefs, are
better able to deal with abstraction, are more rational, have greater
intelligence, have a more favorable attitude toward change, are better
able to cope with risk, are more favorably disposed toward education
and science, are less fatalistic, and have both higher levels of aspiration and achievement than later adopters.

Communication behavior. Early adopters tend to rate more highly on
range of communication-related dimensions such as social participation, exposure to mass media, contact with change agents, knowledge
of innovations, and degree of belonging to interconnected communications systems than later adopters.

Finally, Rogers stresses the importance of and role of interpersonal influence, or opinion leadership, in activating diffusion networks. Innovators
and early adopters communicate their experiences to others; later adopters
look to these persons for opinion leadership, which either encourages or discourages them from adopting the product. The role of personal influence varies across individuals and decision situations, and it is more important in the
evaluation stage of the decision process than in other stages, for late adopters
than for early adopters, and in risky situations than in safe situations. In
general, the traits of opinion leaders have been difficult to identify. Some
opinion leaders are innovators while others are not. Furthermore, opinion

leadership appears to be product-area specific and is a relative phenomenon, because leaders have more information than followers.

These generalizations have been extended to apply to organizational adoption. In addition to individual variables, studies of organizational adoption have considered internal characteristics of the organization (such as centralization of decision-making authority, organizational slack—the level of uncommitted organization resources, organizational size, and the like) as well as external characteristics (such as the degree of market competitiveness, the length of the life cycle for new products in the industry, and the like).

AGGREGATE DIFFUSION MODELS: MODELS OF FIRST PURCHASE

The task of a diffusion model is to produce a life-cycle sales curve based on (usually) a small number of parameters, which may or may not have behavioral content. The presupposition is that these parameters may be estimated either by analogy to the histories of similar new products introduced in the past, by consumer pretests, or by early sales returns as the new product enters the market. In the past three decades a great deal of work on diffusion modeling has been done, initially based on the earlier, well-developed theory of contagious diseases or the spread of epidemics.

Prior to 1969 most diffusion models in marketing could be classified as pure innovative or pure imitative. A pure innovative model assumes that only innovative or external influences are operative in the diffusion process while a pure imitative model assumes that the only effects on the process are driven by imitation or word of mouth. We give an example of each in the paragraphs that follow.

A Pure Innovative Model: Fourt and Woodlock (1960).   One of the earliest market-penetration models was the exponential one proposed by Fourt and Woodlock (1960), which was tested against several new products. Their retrospective observation of many market-penetration curves showed that (1) the cumulative curve approaches a limiting penetration level of less than 100% of all households and frequently far less and (2) the successive increments of gain declined. They found that an adequate approximation to these observations was provided by a curve of the following form:

$$Q_t = r\bar{Q}(1 - r)^{t-1} \tag{10.1}$$

where

Q_t = increment in cumulative sales (i.e., sales at time t) as fraction of potential sales

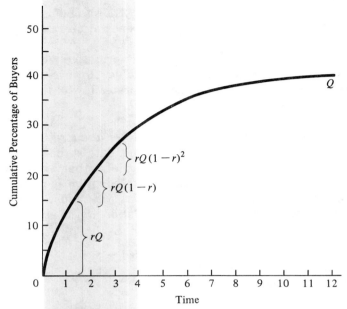

EXHIBIT 10.5 Increments of new buyer penetration. (*Source:* Fourt and Woodlock, 1960, pp. 33–34.)

r = rate of penetration of untapped potential (a constant)

$\bar{Q}$ = total potential sales as fraction of all buyers

t = time period

The formula is completely specified by the two parameters r and $\bar{Q}$.

As an illustration of how it works, we assume that a new product is about to be introduced. Assume that 40% of all households will eventually try the new product ($\bar{Q} = 0.4$) and that in each period 30% of the remaining new buyer potential buys ($r = 0.3$). Therefore, the first-period increment in new buyer penetration of this market is

$$Q_1 = r\bar{Q}(1 - r)^{1-1} = r\bar{Q} = 0.3(0.4) = 0.12 \qquad \textbf{(10.2)}$$

And the second-period increment in new-buyer penetration of this market is

$$Q_2 = r\bar{Q}(1 - r)^{2-1} = r\bar{Q}(1 - r) = r(\bar{Q} - r\bar{Q}) \qquad \textbf{(10.3)}$$
$$= 0.3[0.4 - 0.3(0.4)] = 0.084$$

Note that equation (10.1) produces an (exponentially) declining curve of new-buyer sales over time. Exhibit 10.5 displays the shape of this curve. To use the model, we need an estimate of $\bar{Q}$, the ultimate penetration, usually derived from market research studies. The second parameter r can be derived from the cumulative decline in the penetration rate observed in several periods of sales data.

In theory, the model can be used normatively by setting $r = r(x)$, where x is some controllable marketing variable. However, in this form, diffusion is purely a function of time and incorporates few of the adoption-process characteristics just outlined.

A Pure Imitative Diffusion Model: Fisher and Pry (1971). A model that has been widely applied to industrial product data is that of Fisher and Pry (1971). The underlying hypotheses of their model is that when a new product or process replaces an older one, the rate of adoption is proportional to the interaction of the fraction of the older one still in use and the current level of penetration. Mathematically, this relationship is expressed as follows:

$$\frac{df}{dt} = b(1 - f)f \tag{10.4}$$

where

f = fraction of market having adopted new product, $Q/\bar{Q}$

b = constant characterizing growth to potential associated with particular technology

Integrating equation (10.4) yields a logistic curve:

$$f = \frac{1}{1 + e^{-b(t - t_0)}} \tag{10.5}$$

where

t_0 = time when adoption of new product has penetrated half the market

t = time since introduction

Equation (10.5) can be conveniently rewritten:

$$\left(\frac{f}{1 - f}\right) = e^{b(t - t_0)} = e^{b_0 + bt} \tag{10.6}$$

Exhibit 10.6 demonstrates how the (log-linear) form of equation (10.6) fits the data for a number of products and processes. The Fisher-Pry model has been demonstrated to work quite well retrospectively with data from a new tech-

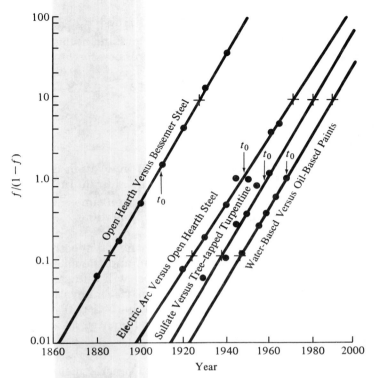

EXHIBIT 10.6 Substitution data and their fit to the model for a number of products and processes. (*Source:* Fisher and Pry, 1971, pp. 75–88.)

nology that completely replaced an older one. As a predictive tool, when little data are available and when it is unclear that one technology completely substitutes for another, its value is more questionable.

The work of Blackman, Seligman, and Solgliero (1973) and Blackman (1974), building on the work of Mansfield (1961, 1968), provides a means of making projections for substitution in the *absence* of an adequate, historical data base. The Mansfield-Blackman model, written in the same form as equation (10.6), is as follows:

$$\left(\frac{f}{L - f}\right) = e^{b_0 + bt} \tag{10.7}$$

where L is the upper limit in the market share that the new innovation can capture in the long run.

Mansfield's important contribution was the decomposition of the constant b. He argued that b should be higher when (1) the relative profitability associated with the new product is high and (2) the initial investment is low.

Note that this is in line with Rogers's (1983) propositions as well. In studies of diffusion in disparate industrial sectors, including railroads, coal, steel, and breweries, he found an empirical expression for b:

$$b = Z + 0.53\pi - 0.27S \tag{10.8}$$

where

Z = industry-specific constant

π = estimated rate of return of innovation divided by minimum rate of return for investment (i.e., hurdle rate)

S = initial investment in innovation times 100 divided by total assets of average firm adopting innovation

This equation is consistent with Mansfield's hypothesis: the more profitable the innovation is to the adopting firm and the smaller the (relative) cost of adoption, the more quickly the product will diffuse.

A critical term is still Z, the industrial innovation coefficient in equation (10.8). Blackman, Seligman, and Solgliero (1973) related this coefficient to more general industry coefficients and created an *industry coefficient* index (I), which is derived as follows:

1. They create a matrix of eight general measures of industry innovativeness—such as current and planned R&D expenditures, new product sales as a percentage of total sales, value added—for each of a dozen industrial sectors.

2. They factor analyze this matrix to obtain a set of factor scores for each industry.

3. They regress the score for the first factor (I) against the value of Z to obtain

$$Z = 0.222I - 0.316 \tag{10.9}$$

They get a t-statistic for the coefficient of I of 3.38, and the coefficient of determination (r^2) is 0.85. Thus, in general, the fit appears quite good. They found that I was 2.29 for aircraft and missiles and -0.76 for rubber products, for example.

To use this model for prediction, we must know the current level of market penetration (i.e., the initial conditions), the ultimate level of penetration, and the economic consequences of adopting the innovation. The initial conditions will specify b_0 and b. The coefficient of the time-dependent term in equation (10.7) is developed from economic calculations involving equation (10.8) plus an industry innovation factor derived from Blackman, Seligman, and Solgliero (1973) and used in equation (10.9). Note that π, S, and I may all vary with time over the life of the innovation.

Choffray and Lilien (1986) extended the approach, relating the variables b_0 and b to a wide range of variables including relative price, order of entry, sales force pressure, competition entry, level of customer satisfaction, and the like. They report values of r^2 of 0.85 for b_0 and 0.77 for b using data from 112 industrial products introduced in France.

Bass's (1969a) Model.   Fourt and Woodlock model a process of pure innovation. The Fisher-Pry/Mansfield-Blackman efforts represent pure imitation models. In an important integrative effort in the marketing field, Bass (1969a) combined the innovative and imitative components (in discrete-time form):

$$Q_t = \underbrace{p(\bar{Q} - N_t)}_{\substack{\text{innovation} \\ \text{effect} \\ \text{or} \\ \text{external} \\ \text{influence}}} + \underbrace{r\left(\frac{N_t}{\bar{Q}}\right)(\bar{Q} - N_t)}_{\substack{\text{imitation} \\ \text{effect} \\ \text{or} \\ \text{internal} \\ \text{influence}}} = \left(p + r\frac{N_t}{\bar{Q}}\right)(\bar{Q} - N_t)$$

(10.10)

where

Q_t = number of adopters at time t

$\bar{Q}$ = ultimate numbers of adopters

N_t = cumulative number of adopters to date

r = effect of each adopter on each nonadopter (coefficient of internal influence)

p = individual conversion ratio in the absence of adopters' influence (coefficient of external influence)

One traditional interpretation of this model has both innovators and imitators buying the product. The innovators are not influenced in their purchase timing by the number of persons who have already bought, but they may be influenced by promotions. As the process continues, the relative number of innovators diminishes monotonically with time. Imitators are influenced by the number of previous buyers and increase relative to the number of innovators as the process continues. Another, more recent interpretation has "internal" and "external" influence going on simultaneously, even within the same individuals (Tanny and Derzko, 1988). Also see Chatterjee and Eliashberg (1990) for a micro-level interpretation of the parameters.

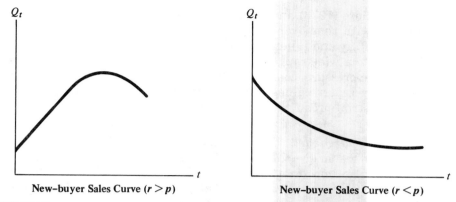

Q_t Q_t

New–buyer Sales Curve ($r > p$)   **New–buyer Sales Curve ($r < p$)**

EXHIBIT 10.7   New buyer sales curve, Bass's model. (*Source:* Bass, 1969a, pp. 217–218.)

The combined rate of first purchasing by innovators and imitators is given by the term $p + rN_t/\bar{Q}$ and increases through time because N_t increases through time. In fact, the rate of first purchasing is a linear function of the cumulative number of previous first purchases. But the number of remaining nonadopters, given by $\bar{Q} - N_t$, decreases through time. The shape of the resulting sales curve of new adopters depends on the relative rates of these two opposite tendencies. In the case of a successful new product, when the coefficient of imitation is likely to exceed the coefficient of innovation—that is, $r > p$—the sales curve will first rise and then fall. When $r < p$ the sales curve will fall continuously. Exhibit 10.7 illustrates both cases.

Bass applied his model to the sales time series of 11 major appliance innovations, including room air conditioners, electric refrigerators, home freezers, black-and-white televisions, power lawn mowers, and so forth. In each case he used annual sales data from the year of the new product's introduction to the year when replacement sales began to be important. He estimated the equation by least-squares regression after equation (10.10) was rewritten as follows:

$$Q_t = p\bar{Q} + (r - p)N_t - \frac{r}{\bar{Q}}N_t^2 \tag{10.11}$$

This equation is simply a second-degree polynomial in N_t, the cumulative sales to time T. Thus,

$$Q_t = a + bN_t + cN_t^2 \tag{10.12}$$

where

$$a = p\bar{Q} \tag{10.13}$$

$$b = r - p$$

$$c = -\frac{r}{\bar{Q}}$$

This procedure is what Mahajan, Muller, and Bass (1990) refer to as a *"time-invariant" data-based approach*—that is, parameter estimates are made using hard data and those estimates are assumed not to vary over time. While conceptually simple, Mahajan, Mason, and Srinivasan (1986) have shown that the foregoing procedure is subject to multicollinearity and biased estimates and that both maximum-likelihood approaches and nonlinear estimation procedures produce superior estimates.

However, for a model like this to be of value requires that estimates be available *prior* to the generation of much data, or even before product launch. Indeed, most reported applications have estimated market potential exogenously and have then used either managerial judgment (Mahajan and Sharma, 1986), historical analogues (Srivastava, Mahajan, Ramaswami, and Cherian, 1985; Gatignon, Eliashberg, and Robertson, 1989; Sultan, Farley, and Lehmann, 1990; Montgomery and Srinivasan, 1989) or Bayesian/feedback filter approaches (Lilien, Rao, and Kalish, 1981; Lenk and Rao, 1990; Sultan, Farley, and Lehmann, 1990; and Bretschneider and Mahajan 1980). The idea behind the latter approaches is generally to use analogies or judgments as "priors" for parameter estimates and then to update the parameters.

Exhibit 10.8 gives the results of Bass's calibration for room air conditioners. Two useful bits of information from this model are the time to peak sales (t^*) and the magnitude of the sales peak (Q^*):

$$t^* = \frac{1}{p + r} \ln \frac{r}{p} \tag{10.14}$$

$$Q^* = \frac{\bar{Q}(p + r)^2}{4r} \tag{10.15}$$

Bass's model is one of the most frequently referred to marketing models. It is a simple, elegant model that makes a number of important assumptions. Much research in the past 15 to 20 years has focused on relaxing several of these assumptions (following Mahajan, Muller, and Bass, 1990):

Market potential remains constant over time. A number of researchers have questioned this assumption: Kalish (1985), relates market potential to product price and to the reduction of uncertainty in product performance that goes along with increased adoption. Other effects on market potential that have been studied include growth in population (Mahajan and Peterson, 1978; Sharif and Ramanathan, 1981); product profitability (Lackman, 1978); growth in retail outlets carrying the product (Jones and Ritz, 1987), and income dis-

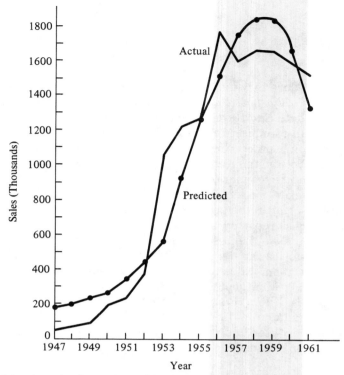

EXHIBIT 10.8 Actual sales and predicted sales for room air conditioners (Bass model). (*Source:* Bass, 1969a, p. 219).

tribution, price, and product uncertainty (Horsky, 1990). Other models involving price include those of Chow (1967); Kamakura and Balasubramanian (1988); and Jain and Rao (1989).

Diffusion of an innovation is independent of all other innovations. Other innovations exist in the market place and may have a (positive or negative) influence on the diffusion of an innovation. Building on work by Peterson and Mahajan (1978), Bayus (1987) models compact disc (*CD*) software adopters as dependent on adoption of *CD* hardware: in this application, market potential is the (time-varying) number of *CD* hardware adopters. Norton and Bass (1987) demonstrate that, in addition to creating its own demand, each generation of a high-technology product cannibalizes the diffusion of its predecessors, dynamically affecting market potential.

The geographical boundaries of the system in which diffusion takes place do not vary over time. Most marketing applications of diffusion models have ignored the spatial nature of that diffusion. One exception is the model of Mahajan and Peterson (1979). Reinterpreting the Peterson and Mahajan (1978) model as dealing with multiple markets, Eliashberg and Helsen (1988) have addressed the problem of how diffusion in a leading country affects product diffusion in a lagging country.

Innovation is a two-stage process (not adopt → adopt). Bass's model does not match up well with our notion of adoption as involving a number of stages from unaware to aware to interest to adopting, and so on. Although data limitations have often precluded calibration, models by Midgley (1976); Dodson and Muller (1978); Sharif and Ramanathan (1981); Mahajan, Muller, and Kerin (1984); and Kalish (1985) have tried to add stages in which (positive or negative) product knowledge is spread.

Marketing actions do not affect the diffusion process. Much recent research has centered on mechanisms for incorporating elements of the marketing mix in diffusion models. Kalish and Sen (1986) provide a review, focusing in the two most frequently studied variables: price and advertising. Models incorporating price include those of Robinson and Lakhani (1975), Bass (1980), Dolan and Jeuland (1981), Bass and Bultez (1982), and Kalish (1983), while those involving advertising include Horsky and Simon (1983) and Simon and Sebastian (1987), both of which offer empirical validation. Other marketing mix elements considered have included detailing effort (Lilien, Rao, and Kalish, 1981, and product quality, Srivastava et al., 1985, and Kalish and Lilien, 1986a).

There are no supply restrictions. The Bass model is a demand model, but that demand may not be satisfied if production or distribution difficulties prevent that demand from being satisfied. Excess current demand can lead to a queue of potential customers (Simon and Sebastian, 1987; Jain, Mahajan, and Muller, 1989).

Adopting units adopt a single product. Either repeat sales or replacement sales are significant in many markets. Models by Lilien, Rao, and Kalish (1981) and Mahajan, Wind, and Sharma (1983) include repeat purchases, while models by Olson and Choi (1985), Kamakura and Balasubramanian (1987), and Kalish and Lilien (1986b) report on replacement sales.

Adoption is an individual decision. The Bass model is an aggregate market model; a number of researchers (Hiebert, 1974; Stoneman, 1981; Feder and O'Mara, 1982; Oren and Schwartz, 1988; Chatterjee and Eliashberg, 1990; and Lattin and Roberts, 1989), have developed diffusion models by aggregating adoption decisions across individuals. Most of these models assume that an individual's utility for an innovation is based on his (uncertain) perceptions of that innovation's relative value or benefits. Those perceptions change over time based on information from external sources (like advertising) or internal sources (like price), and individuals adopt when their utility for the innovation exceeds that of the status quo. Lattin and Roberts (1988) provide empirical data for their model, suggesting that it fits historical data better than the Bass model, although unlike Chatterjee and Eliashberg (1990), their model does not predict sale prior to launch.

Innovation diffusion is a deterministic process. Most aggregate diffusion models are deterministic. As Eliashberg and Chatterjee (1986) point out there are a number of stochastic elements that should be modeled in a diffusion environment. These include uncertainties about the real performance of the product by consumers, uncertainties about the impact of marketing programs, uncertainty about competitive effects, and environmental uncertainty. These issues are developed in models incorporating structural stochasticity (modeling the process probabilistically) and parameter stochasticity (a process whose stochastic elements are in parameter values). See Eliashberg, Tapiero, and Wind, 1987, for an example of the stochastic coefficients approach: their results show that the deterministic Bass model is robust with respect to parametric stochasticity.

As the discussion shows, there have been scores of extensions of the basic Bass model. Review articles by Mahajan and Peterson (1979), Mahajan and Wind (1988), and Mahajan, Muller, and Bass (1990) as well as a book edited by Mahajan and Wind (1986) will provide efficient access to the literature. Next, we briefly summarize some frequently referred to models that illustrate some of the ways the Bass model has been extended.

EXAMPLE _____

Horsky-Simon (1983) Model. Horsky and Simon (1983) essentially use the original Bass model but explicitly incorporate the effect of advertising in Bass' innovation coefficient . Specifically, they assume

$$p = a_1 + a_2 \ln A(t) \tag{10.16}$$

where

$A(t)$ = level of advertising at time t

a_2 = coefficient reflecting effectiveness of advertising

a_1 = coefficient reflecting part of information conveyed to innovators by alternative means such as samples, displays, publicity

Thus equation (10.10) becomes

$$Q_t = [a_1 + a_2 \ln A(t)](\bar{Q} - N_t) + r\frac{N_t}{\bar{Q}}(\bar{Q} - N_t) \tag{10.17}$$

Note that equation (10.17) incorporates both diminishing returns to advertising (through the logarithm function) and the lagged and carryover effects of advertising through the innovation term. The authors point out that in industries within the capital goods sector, the level of selling effort would probably be used in place of advertising as the conveyor of information.

The authors tested their model with data on the diffusion of a telephone banking service, introduced independently by five banks. Each of the banks was isolated geographically from the others and essentially did not face competition from rival products during the period under test. Furthermore, none of the banks changed other elements of their marketing mix during the period analyzed. The parameters of the models were estimated for the five banks in much the same way as described by Bass, with the result that the effect of advertising (the coefficient a_2) was found to have the correct logical sign in each case and to be statistically significant in three out of five cases.

The authors also show how to incorporate this model in a procedure for a deterministic optimal advertising policy. They show that the advertising rate should decrease over time, which is consistent with intuition. This result shows that the heaviest spending is required when the product needs to become known.

This model is a straightforward extension of the basic Bass model. By incorporating an advertising term, it transforms the descriptive Bass model into a normative framework. However, in its current form it allows unbounded values for innovation for large $A(t)$ and, thus, provides a local rather than a global evaluation for marketing policies.

EXAMPLE _____

Kalish (1985) Model.   In an integrating effort, Kalish considers how price, advertising, and uncertainty affect diffusion. He assumes a two-stage model, where the rate of adoption is determined by (1) awareness (information) diffusion, controlled by advertising and word of mouth, and by (2) adoption within a (growing) potential adopter population, whose size depends on awareness, price, and uncertainty concerning product performance.

Awareness diffusion.   Kalish assumes that information about the product is spread by advertising, by those who are aware but who have not adopted and by those who have adopted the innovation:

$$\frac{dI(t)}{dt} = (1 - I)\{f(A(t)) + b[I - X/N_0] + b''[X/N_0]\} \qquad (10.18)$$

where

I = proportion of potential population aware at t

X = number of adopters at t

N_0 = potential population

$A(t)$ = advertising spending rate

$f(\cdot)$ = impact of advertising on unaware population

b = impact (contact rate) of those aware but who have not adopted on the unaware population

b'' = impact of those who have already adopted on the unaware population

Market potential.   Kalish assumes that individuals value products differently and that a customer will buy if the price of the product is less than its value to him (i.e., less than its reservation price). He also assumes that individuals are risk-averse, and that, therefore, the more experience the market has with a product, the less uncertain the valuation of the product is to the population and hence, the greater the market potential.

He specifies that relationship as

$$\text{Market potential} = N\left(\frac{P}{\mu(X/N_0)}\right) \tag{10.19}$$

where

P = price at t and

μ = discount factor due to performance uncertainty:

$$\mu(1) = 1 \text{ and } d\mu/dx > 0$$

Equation (10.19) specifies that (generally) potential goes up as customer value goes up, where customer value is directly related to discounted price. Value is higher when price is lower and when μ (and, hence, X) is higher.

Dynamics of adoption.   Multiplying equation (10.18) by (10.19) gives the number of members of the potential population who are aware of the product. Kalish assumes that a constant proportion of the aware population that has not adopted the product will, indeed adopt each period:

$$\frac{dX}{dt} = k\left\{N\left[\frac{P}{\mu(X/N_0)}\right]I - X\right\} \tag{10.20}$$

where

k = rate of adoption (which could, in turn, be a function of advertising, distribution, product quality and the like)

Kalish tests this model against several competing models and reports good results both in terms of fit and prediction. He also derives several propositions from this model.

Advertising. Under full information (where there is no discounting for uncertainty) and where there are decreasing returns to scale for advertising, the optimal advertising policy is monotonically decreasing over time. (This generalizes the result from Horsky and Simon, 1983.)

Pricing. For durable goods, price should decrease over time unless adopters are very effective in generating awareness (i.e., b'' is much larger than b) or early adopters are very effective in reducing uncertainty (i.e., $d\mu/dX$ is much greater than zero). In these latter cases, prices should increase initially, but should generally decline later. For repeat purchase goods, where advertising is decreasing as suggested, the introductory price should be below the long-term, steady-state price and increase to that level over time.

Kalish's model extends Bass's model in several important ways, including reasonable assumptions about the impact of price, advertising, and uncertainty. As a two-stage model, it clearly separates information diffusion from adoption, consistent with the behavioral literature on adoption. As with any model in analytical form, it has a variety of limitations, including that it focuses on potential as a function of price only, that awareness is homogeneously distributed throughout the population, that all individuals have the same attitude toward risk, and that consumers act myopically, that is, do not form expectations about future price fluctuations. In addition, it is a monopoly model, ignoring competitive activities. On net however, it is an important addition to the literature, both synthesizing past research and providing a framework for future developments.

EXAMPLE

Gatignon, Eliashberg, and Robertson (1989). Gatignon and colleagues (1989) try to use a system of Bass-like equations to explain differences in diffusion rates across countries. In particular, they specify the following:

$$X_i(t) - X_i(t-1) = [p_i + q_i X_i(t-1)][1 - X_i(t-1)] \quad \textbf{(10.21)}$$

where

$X_i(t)$ = cumulative proportion of the potential adopting population having adopted at time t in country i

p_i = propensity to innovate in country i

q_i = propensity to imitate in country i

and where

$$p_i = \alpha_0 + \sum_j \alpha_j Z_{ji} \qquad \textbf{(10.22)}$$

$$q_i = \beta_0 + \sum_j \beta_j Z_{ji} \qquad \textbf{(10.23)}$$

and

Z_{ji} = set of country characteristics
α_j = impact of country characteristics on propensity to innovate
β_j = impact of country characteristics on propensity to imitate

Note that for simplicity we have dropped error/disturbance terms in these equations and have assumed that market potential has been exogenously estimated for each country.

A generalized least squares procedure was developed to estimate the coefficients in equations (10.22) and (10.23) for six consumer durables in 14 European countries. In general, the results show that

—higher cosmopolitanism is related to higher propensity to innovate and a lower propensity to imitate

—higher mobility is generally but not conclusively related to higher propensity to imitate

—higher female work force participation gave mixed results, where the effect appears innovation specific and depends on the female's role in the purchase decision for that product

The model fit the data well, with 39 of the 42 coefficients statistically significant at the 0.01 level.

While only a basic diffusion model was used here, the results suggest a systematic procedure for explaining how and why diffusion rates differ across cultures. Thus, this model incorporates geographical diversity and, in much the same vein as the Mansfield/Blackman work described earlier and the Choffray/Lilien (1986) analysis, suggests how product and market characteristics can be used to explain (and predict) differences in rates of new product diffusion.

EXAMPLE _____

Easingwood, Mahajan, and Muller (1983). The Easingwood and colleagues nonuniform influence (NUI) model was developed to allow for either a symmetrical or asymmetrical diffusion curve and to permit the word of mouth to vary over time. Using the same notation as equation (10.10) the model becomes

$$Q_t = \left[p + r\left(\frac{N_t}{\bar{Q}}\right)^d \right](\bar{Q} - N_t) \qquad (10.24)$$

where d is the nonuniform influence coefficient. By varying the value of d, the model can have an increasing, decreasing, or constant coefficient of imitation; can be symmetric or asymmetric; and can have its turning point (point of inflection) anywhere.

The authors test the fit of the model using data from five consumer durables. They compared the model to some competing models, and it both fit and predicted much better than the Bass model. Most important, the coefficient, d, was generally statistically significantly different from 1, suggesting that the word-of-mouth effect varies, generally declining in impact over time.

The importance of this model (and other so-called "flexible diffusion models"—see Mahajan, Muller, and Bass, 1990, for a review) is that it removes some of the restrictiveness of the basic Bass formulation in a systematic way. Coefficients of these models should be expected to vary dynamically, and this model is one that provides for such a structure.

_____

A main limitation of this model is that, unlike that of Gatignon and colleagues, for example, there is no causal or behavioral theory to help predict what the value for the extra coefficient should be.

Model Extensions and Refinements. Even from this brief review, it is clear that models of the diffusion of innovations have been extended to incorporate marketing-mix variables, product and market characteristics, different diffusion shapes, stochastic components, time and spatial considerations, multiple stages of adoption, individual and aggregate characteristics, across-product linkage (across generations of products and complementary or contingency products like hardware and software), and the like. Some work has attempted to extend these models to competitive situations (see Dolan, Jeuland, and Muller, 1986, for a review) although from an operational standpoint, we prefer to use a diffusion model as a product-category model and combine it with a (dynamic, perhaps) market share model to deal with the issue of competition (see Kalish and Lilien, 1986b). In addition, more work is needed to calibrate diffusion models for durables *before* they have been launched, when the forecasting problem is most critical. (See Urban, Hauser, and Roberts, (1990), and Chatterjee and Eliashberg (1990) for two recent examples).

On balance, there have been many important developments in the diffusion model area. However, as Mahajan, Muller, and Bass (1990, p. 10) show, most of the models that have actually seen reported use still rely on the basic Bass formulation (although Mahajan, Sharma, and Bettes, 1988, show that other, alternative formulations are logically consistent with S-shaped diffusion patterns and that some do not include an imitation component). Also, Herbig (1991) suggests catastrophe theory models as alternatives to the traditional S-shaped model structure. More reports of successful use of more sophisticated models and more sharing and cross-comparison of results will allow the more recently developed and more general models to see wider use.

REPEAT-PURCHASE MODELS
FOR NEW PRODUCTS

Many new products are of the repurchasable kind. These include virtually all the nondurables consumed by the household and the factory. The sellers of these products are even more interested in the repurchase rate than in the trial rate. A low trial rate could be attributable to poor distribution, promotion, or packaging, all of which are correctable. Trial of a new product can be stimulated by distributing free samples, introductory pricing, and so on. But a low repurchase rate may suggest a product that does not meet the consumer's expectations, which is harder to correct. Unfortunately, early aggregate sales figures do not distinguish between the two rates. A rising sales curve could mean a high trying rate with a low rebuying rate (a bad situation) or a low trying rate with a high rebuying rate (a correctable situation).

Exhibit 10.9 outlines most of the phenomena that are modeled in the efforts reviewed in this section. From the exhibit we see that individual consumers, facing a new, frequently purchased product

1. *must be made aware* (advertising, promotion and sampling are the main tools the marketer has control of here)
2. *must be induced to try* (advertising, promotion, and samples are useful here; distribution and product price may also affect likelihood of trial)
3. *must be induced to repeat once* (product quality, relative price, and distribution affect repeat likelihood)
4. *must be induced to repeat regularly (become a loyal customer)* (product quality, relative price, and distribution affect this likelihood as well)

As noted earlier, the costs and risks of introducing a new, frequently

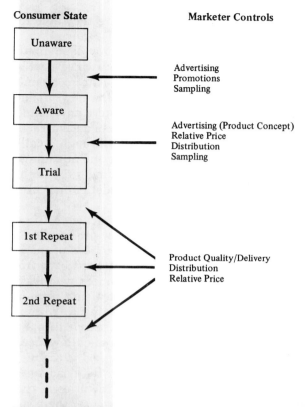

Consumer State

Marketer Controls

Unaware

Advertising
Promotions
Sampling

Aware

Advertising (Product Concept)
Relative Price
Distribution
Sampling

Trial

1st Repeat

Product Quality/Delivery
Distribution
Relative Price

2nd Repeat

EXHIBIT 10.9 The structure of repeat purchasing and marketer controls.

purchased consumer product are high. Indeed, Urban, Hauser, and Dholakia (1987), report a cost range of $6.3 million to $28 million in the U.S., covering about two-thirds of all consumer products. To help reduce those costs, consumer goods manufacturers have instituted a series of methods for investigating how the market is likely to react to the new-product offering. The major methods of market testing are, from least to most costly (Tauber, 1977), (1) sales-wave research, (2) pretest markets or purchase labs, (3) controlled test marketing, and (4) test markets.

Sales-wave research is an extension of home-use testing in which consumers who initially try the product are given an opportunity to obtain more of the product or any competitor's product at reduced prices. They may be offered the product as many as three to five times (sales waves), while each time the company notes how many consumers selected its product. Sales waves permit some estimates of repeat-purchase rates under marketer-controlled conditions and the testing of different advertising copy programs under conditions secure from competitive scrutiny. However, they do not simulate the actual shopping situations well, nor are they able to reproduce the effects of advertising media other than print.

Pretest markets (purchase labs) provide a simulated shopping situation, usually involving intercept interviews with several hundred shoppers and inviting them to participate in the test. After some measurements the shopper is exposed to a series of ads (one for the new product) and then given some money to keep or use in a simulated store environment where the advertised brands are available for purchase. These measures give an indication of product trial. Repeat is usually measured through a callback and an offer to buy more of the product. This method has the advantage of giving quick results (especially for trial) at a cost usually under 5% of that for a full test market. We review below the ASSESSOR model, which uses pretest-market–generated data to project market results.

Controlled test marketing (minimarket testing) involves several panels of stores that have agreed to carry new products for a certain fee. After specification of the number, types, and locations of the stores, a test is set up for the new product. Sales results are audited both from shelf movements and from consumer diaries kept by consumers who frequent the stores, and the company can also do small-scale advertising tests in local newspapers. This approach has the advantage of providing a true in-store environment. The procedure is usually handled by a research firm, so the manufacturer does not have to use its sales force, give trade allowances, or develop distribution and many such procedures are now linked to scanner data, providing greater accuracy and control than previously. Its disadvantage is that the minitests may not adequately represent the difficulties of the marketplace, including problems of distribution, and, furthermore, these minimarkets are carefully monitored by competitors.

Test markets provide the ultimate forum for testing a new consumer product short of national introduction. A number of representative markets are chosen, and the company's sales force tries to sell the trade on carrying the product and giving it good shelf exposure. The company also puts on full advertising and promotional campaigns in the test markets, similar to those anticipated to accompany national introduction. The primary motive for test marketing is usually to obtain a reliable forecast of future sales. A second motive is to pretest alternative marketing plans. Firms often use multiple test-market sites to test different positioning strategies or entire marketing-mix alternatives. Test marketing calls for several key decisions, including the number and location of test cities, the level of the test, the type of information to collect, and the action to take. Generally, actions following test marketing can be categorized as described in Exhibit 10.10.

In spite of their advantages, test markets have some problems, including (1) finding representative markets, (2) quantifying the impact of competitive and/or extraneous and uncontrolled factors, and (3) the problem of competitive scrutiny (Achenbaum, 1964). Because of these problems and the $1–6

Test-Market Result		Marketer Actions
Trial Rate	Repurchase Rate	
High	High	Commercialize the product
High	Low	Redesign/drop product
Low	High	Redesign/increase advertising, use sales promotion, sampling
Low	Low	Drop the product

EXHIBIT 10.10   Test-market results and marketer actions

million reported average cost (Urban, Hauser, and Dholakia, 1987), some companies are skipping test marketing, preferring to go national after earlier pretest marketing. Such a decision often appears reasonable: the expected savings associated with test marketing a product that has been successfully pretest marketed is about equal to the expected cost (Urban and Hauser, 1980, pp. 56–57; Urban and Katz, 1983).

Given the large costs that are associated with new consumer product introduction and testing, it is not surprising that a number of models have been developed that are of considerable help in evaluating and interpreting test-market and pretest-market results. We now focus on three of these models in some detail: the Parfitt-Collins (1968) model and the Tracker model (Blattberg and Golanty, 1978), both used for test-market evaluation, and ASSESSOR (Silk and Urban, 1978), used for pretest-market evaluation. We then review other approaches and developments in the field.

EXAMPLE _____

Parfitt-Collins (1968) Model.   The Parfitt-Collins (1968) model is reviewed here primarily because its development exerted influence on the structure and development of later models. The objective of their effort was to develop a simple method for obtaining an early prediction of ultimate market share with panel data.

Parfitt and Collins see ultimate brand share as the product of three factors:

$$s = prb \tag{10.25}$$

where

s = ultimate brand share

p = ultimate penetration rate of brand (percentage of new buyers of this product class who *try* this brand)

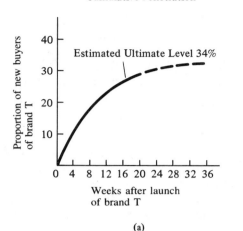

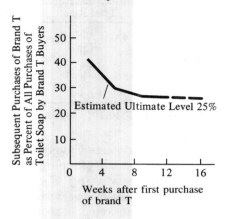

EXHIBIT 10.11   Cumulative penetration and repeat-purchasing rate for brand T (*Parfitt-Collins model*). (*Source:* Parfitt and Collins, 1968, pp. 132–133.)

r = ultimate repeat-purchase rate of brand (percentage of repurchases of this brand to all purchases by persons who once purchased this brand)

b = buying rate index of repeat purchase of this brand (average buyer = 1.00)

The definitions of these variables and the working of this model can be conveyed by an example. Assume that a company launches a new brand in an established product field.

Trial rate. Its share of new buyers in this product field will rise from zero to some ultimate percentage as weeks pass. Exhibit 10.11(a) illustrates this situation with the cumulative penetration of a new brand in the toilet soap field.

The penetration rate increases at a decreasing rate beginning at time zero. A curve can be fit to these data after a few weeks; the authors recommend

$$p(t) = p(1 - e^{-at}) \qquad (10.26)$$

where

$p(t)$ = cumulative trial by t

p = ultimate (long-run) trial in equation (10.25)

a = growth-rate parameter

Alternatively, a freehand extrapolation can be performed to yield the ultimate penetration rate p—the rate that would apply between 12 and 18 months after the product is launched.

Repeat rate. The repeat rate for this brand will also be monitored as data come in. This rate shows the percentage of repurchases of this brand relative to purchases of all brands by those who have tried the brand. Exhibit 10.11(b) shows the repeat-purchase rate for the new brand of toilet soap, which is approximately 40% in the first four weeks after purchase—that is, four out of ten purchases of toilet soap by triers of brand T were again brand T. The exhibit shows this rate as falling with the passage of time toward an asymptote of 25%; the earlier triers of a new product tend to like it more than later triers.

Use rate. If purchasers of the new brand buy at the average volume of purchasers of all brands in this product class, then $b = 1.00$.

We are now ready to predict the ultimate brand share. According to equation (10.25)

$$s = 0.34(0.25)(1.00) = 0.085$$

That is, if 34% of new buyers in this market ultimately try this brand, if 25% of their subsequent repurchases go to this brand, and if those buying the brand buy an average quantity, the brand share should settle at an equilibrium level of 8.5%. If this brand attracts heavier than average buyers, say, with an index of 1.20, then the share prediction would be 10.2% ($0.34 \times 0.25 \times 1.20$).

The nice feature of this model is that ultimate-share prediction can be made as soon as the penetration curve and the repeat-purchase curve tend toward clear asymptotic values, which usually occurs before a stable brand share is achieved.

Parfitt and Collins report on the accuracy of their market-share forecasts for 24 products that were successfully introduced. From six four-week reporting periods one year after introduction, the predicted market share in all but two cases was within the range of market shares observed during this period. The actual level of market share was, of course, far from stable.

The Parfitt-Collins model assumes that market conditions do not change during or after the test period and that the new product has entered an existing and well-defined product category; clearly, trial and repeat rates are category dependent.

Its other limitations include (1) lack of consideration of an aware state prior to trial; (2) no effects of advertising, promotion, or distribution; and (3) no consideration of different repeat rates for different repeat classes (first repeat, second repeat, etc.). A correlate of the latter limitation is an assumed lack of development of loyalty with different levels of repeat purchase. In addition, the estimation method for the repeat purchase rate is clearly ad hoc.

In summary, the Parfitt-Collins model is a simple, useful starting point for modeling in this area. Later models have extended this basic structure.

EXAMPLE _____

The Tracker Model (1978). The Tracker (Blattberg and Golanty, 1978) model uses survey data to predict year-end, test-market sales. The model is relatively inexpensive to implement, with the cost reported at $15,000. Potential users are tracked through an awareness stage to trial and, finally, to various repeat levels. The method requires three waves of questionnaires of 500–1,000 respondents, launched once every four weeks, to support estimation of parameters in the awareness, trial, and repeat submodels.

Awareness Model.   Total brand awareness is developed as

$$A_t = \frac{UR + AR}{N} \tag{10.27}$$

where

A_t = awareness at t
UR = unaided recall of new brand
AR = aided recall of new brand given lack of unaided recall
N = sample size

The model relates the change in awareness at t to advertising spending as

$$\ln\left(\frac{1 - A_t}{1 - A_{t-1}}\right) = a - b(GRP_t) \tag{10.28}$$

where

GRP_t = gross-rating points of advertising at t
a, b = parameters

Note that equation (10.28) shows diminishing returns to advertising spending and that, without advertising, awareness may be stable ($a = 0$), it may grow ($a < 0$), or it may decline ($a > 0$). The parameter b is a measure of the awareness response to advertising: the greater b, the greater the advertising effectiveness is.

Forgetting is not explicitly included in this formulation. The authors estimate A_0, the initial awareness level, and a and b by regressing previous introductions in the same product class against advertising spending. A problem may be that a and b should not be constant over a period of time; in particular, the authors recommend that b be adjusted downward after a period of time.

Trial model. In this model, trial rates are estimated with two separate populations; the newly aware and those aware for more than one period. In particular, the authors specify trial rates as

$$T_t - T_{t-1} = \underbrace{c(A_t - A_{t-1})}_{\text{newly aware}} + \underbrace{d(A_{t-1} - T_{t-1})}_{\substack{\text{past aware but} \\ \text{not yet trying}}}, \quad \text{for} \quad 0 < d < c < 1$$

$$(10.29)$$

where

T_t = cumulative percentage of triers by period t

A_t = percent aware in period t

c = probability of trial by consumers who became aware this period

d = probability of trial by consumers aware last period or earlier but who have not yet tried

Here the model postulates a greater conversion rate among the newly aware.

The trial rate in equation (10.29) is adjusted for relative price:

$$(T_t - T_{t-1})^* = (T_t - T_{t-1})RP_t^\gamma \qquad (10.30)$$

where

RP_t = relative price at t

γ = price-elasticity parameter

The authors add an error term to equation (10.29) for estimation: it is both autocorrelated and heteroscedastic (where the heteroscedasticity is related to relative price). Parameters of the model are assumed constant in a product class and are estimated by a nonlinear procedure, pooling data for a number of products in the class.

Repeat model and projection model. The projection model for market share or sales is based on tracing the percentage of triers who become first-time users, second-time users, and so on. Triers or repeat users who discontinue use are classified as nonusers. Triers are assumed to have a constant, average purchase rate TU, and repeaters are assumed to have a different use rate RU. Total sales per potential trier is then given as

$$TS_t = (T_t - T_{t-1})TU + \sum_{i=1}^{t-1} UC_{it}RU \qquad (10.31)$$

where

$$
\begin{aligned}
TS_t &= \text{total sales per potential trier in period } t \\
T_t &= \text{cumulative triers by period } t \\
TU &= \text{trial-use rate} \\
RU &= \text{repeat-use rate} \\
UC_{it} &= \text{percentage of new triers in period } i \text{ who are still users during period } t
\end{aligned}
$$

To model UC_{it}, the authors use a **depth-of-repeat** model. For simplicity they assume that

$$UC_{t-1,t} = r(T_t - T_{t-1}) \qquad (10.32)$$

that is, that the percentage (r) of triers who repeat at least once is independent of time. The rest of the structure of UC_{it} develops as follows:

$$UC_{t,t+i+1} = k_i(UC_{t,t+1}) \qquad (10.33)$$

where k_i is the percentage of triers in period t who continued to purchase after period $t + i$. Note that the $\{k_i\}$ are also assumed independent of time.

According to the authors, r and RU are estimated with telephone surveys, while the $\{k_i\}$ are estimated subjectively with product-satisfaction data from the questionnaires; the trial rate TU is set equal to one by definition. The reason for the subjective estimates of the $\{k_i\}$ is that no quantitative, long-term, depth-of-repeat information is available; this problem exists in all cases where a short purchase history is used to project future sales.

If sampling is instituted during the test market, the model must be replicated for the sampled and nonsampled potential customers.

The authors report 11 new product introductions evaluated with Tracker. The predications appear reasonable, being within 10–15% of actual in 8 of the cases. In 2 of the other cases the model predicted an early failure.

The model provides a relatively complete, practical structure that is apparently being applied with success in evaluating test markets. Its weaknesses are that numerous parameters (the $\{k_i\}$, for example) are subjectively estimated and based on little data. In addition, the estimation procedures are somewhat ad hoc; for example, the awareness model often will not discriminate between company and brand identification. Furthermore, parameters are often estimated partially from related products; this feature limits the model's use in cases where a product is relatively unique. Finally, the model assumes that the repeat rate is independent of time of first purchase, contrary to the evidence seen in Parfitt and Collins (1968) and elsewhere.

EXAMPLE _____

ASSESSOR (Silk and Urban, 1978). ASSESSOR is a pretest market model designed to give a market-share projection for the new brand and the source of the new brand's share. In addition, it produces diagnostic information about the new brand's positioning and permits low-cost screening of various marketing-mix elements (copy, price, package, etc.).

One of the innovative features of ASSESSOR is its *convergent approach* to modeling. For greater confidence in the results, it uses a trial-repeat structure and a parallel preference model. The disadvantage of the convergent measurement is its increased cost. However, this disadvantage may not prove serious, because input for more than one model can be obtained from the same consumer measures. Exhibit 10.12 shows the overall structure of the ASSESSOR system. The measurements for both models are obtained from a research design with laboratory and use tests.

Research design and measurements. Exhibit 10.13 outlines the basic steps of the research design and identifies the main types of data required at each stage. The idea is to parallel the basic stages of consumer response to a new product from awareness, through trial and to repeat. For simulation of awareness, a sample of consumers (usually recruited through an interview conducted in the immediate vicinity of a shopping center) is exposed to advertising for the new product and a small set of competing products already established in the marketplace. Following this step, for simulation of trial, the consumers enter a simulated shopping facility where they have an opportunity to purchase quantities of the new and/or established products. Those who do not try (purchase) are given a sample of the product to simulate product sampling. Repeat is assessed by one or more follow-up interviews with the

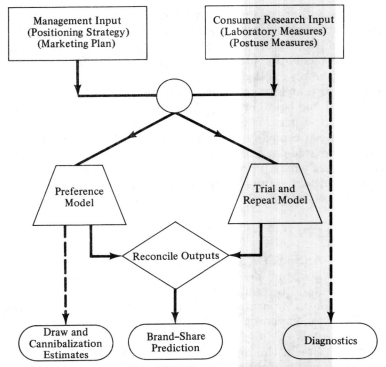

EXHIBIT 10.12   Structure of ASSESSOR system. (*Source:* Silk and Urban, 1978, p. 173.)

same respondents conducted after enough time has passed for them to consume a sufficient quantity of the new product at home.

Trial-repeat model. Awareness for the ASSESSOR model is developed as a managerial input. Long-run market share is calculated with the basic trial-repeat model from Parfitt and Collins (1968), without the use-rate term:

$$s = pr \tag{10.34}$$

where

s = ultimate market share

p = ultimate penetration rate (long-run trial)

Design†	Procedure	Measurement
O_1	Respondent screening and recruitment (personal interview)	Criteria for target-group identification (e.g., product-class use)
O_2	Premeasurement for established brands (self-administered questionnaire)	Composition of relevant set of established brands, attribute weights and ratings and preferences
X_1	Exposure to advertising for established brands and new brand	
$[O_3]$	Measurement of reactions to the advertising materials (self-administered questionnaire)	Optional (e.g., likability and believability ratings of advertising materials)
X_2	Simulated shopping trip and exposure to display of new and established brands	
O_4	Purchase opportunity (choice recorded by research personnel)	Brand(s) purchased
X_3	Home use/consumption of new brand	
O_5	Postuse measurement (telephone interview)	New brand use rate, satisfaction ratings and repeat-purchase propensity: attribute ratings and preferences for relevant set of established brands plus the new brand

† O = measurement; X = advertising or product exposure

EXHIBIT 10.13   ASSESSOR research design and measurement (*Source:* Silk and Urban, 1978, p. 174.)

r = ultimate repeat rate among triers

The ASSESSOR model decomposes these quantities:

$$p = \underbrace{FKD}_{\substack{\text{those} \\ \text{who} \\ \text{try}}} + \underbrace{CU}_{\substack{\text{those} \\ \text{sampled}}} - \underbrace{(FKD)(CU)}_{\substack{\text{adjustment} \\ \text{for double} \\ \text{counting}}} \qquad \textbf{(10.35)}$$

where

F = long-run probability of trial given unlimited distribution and awareness

K = long-run probability of awareness

D = long-run probability of availability in consumer's retail outlet (weighted average of retail outlets carrying brand)

C = probability of consumer receiving sample

U = probability that a consumer who receives sample uses it

The first item in equation (10.35), FKD, represents those consumers who will be aware of the brand, have it available, and then try it. The second term, CU, represents those who will try a sample. The third term, $(FKD)(CU)$, represents the intersection of these first two populations and is subtracted to eliminate double counting in the trial estimate. The parameter F is measured as the proportion of laboratory shoppers who buy the brand, while the rest of the parameters are estimated on the basis of past experience with similar products and by managerial judgment.

The repeat rate r is modeled as the equilibrium share of a two-state Markov process (see Urban, 1975b):

$$r = \frac{q(k, z)}{1 + q(k, z) - q(z, z)} \qquad \textbf{(10.36)}$$

where

$q(k, z)$ = probability that consumer who last purchased some established product k will switch to new brand z on next purchase occasion

$q(z, z)$ = probability that consumer who last purchased new brand will repurchase it on next buying occasion

These transition probabilities are estimated from the postuse survey. If those sampled display a different repeat rate from those who made a purchase in the laboratory, separate repeat rates are calculated and applied to the trial model.

Preference model. Following Luce (1959) and an adaptation and operationalization by Pessemier and colleagues (1971), ASSESSOR assumes that brand preferences obtained in a laboratory situation can be used to predict consumer purchase behavior. The preference model is a variation of the logit model discussed in Chapter 2, which is derived from a constant-sum, paired-comparison task in which consumers allocate a fixed number of chips between each pair of brands in their evoked set. A scaling technique developed by Torgerson (1958) transforms these constant-sum measures into a ratio-scaled preference V_{ij}, indicating consumer i's preference for brand j. These preferences are linked to purchase probabilities:

$$L_{ij} = \frac{(V_{ij})^b}{\sum_{\ell \in m_i} (V_{i\ell})^b} \qquad (10.37)$$

where

L_{ij} = probability of choice by consumer i of product j
V_{ij} = preference measure
m_i = brands in consumers i's evoked set
b = parameter to be estimated

In practice, the b coefficient, reported in the range of 1.5 and 3.0 for most applications, increases the relative distance between the more and less preferred products relative to the simple Luce model (where $b = 1$).

Two main assumptions are required for the use of this model. The first is that the set of brands be true competitors: if choices are first made between groups of products within a class and then between products within groups, the choice process is hierarchical and the model is inappropriate. The second required assumption is that the market has stabilized; if it has not stabilized, preferences will be changing.

ASSESSOR assumes that the b coefficient does not change with the introduction of the new product. This assumption is equivalent to assuming that the product is entering an existing product category. The coefficient can be estimated by a maximum-likelihood procedure using paired-comparison data for existing brands, with the brand last bought or bought most often as the dependent variable.

The model for choice after trial of the new brand (z) is given by

$$L_{iz} = \frac{(V_{iz})^b}{(V_{iz})^b + \sum_{\ell \in m_i} (V_{i\ell})^b}$$ (10.38)

where

L_{iz} = probability that consumer i chooses brand z after having tried it

m_i = brands in i's evoked set

$V_{iz}, \{V_{i\ell}\}$ = preference scores after trying new brand

Thus equation (10.37) is used *before* trial to calibrate coefficient b, and equation (10.38) is used *after* the new product is tried to estimate purchase probabilities.

The market-share calculation takes into account that not all consumers have the new product in their relevant or evoked set of choices,

$$s = \frac{E_z \sum_{i=1}^{N} L_{iz}}{N}$$ (10.39)

where

s = estimated market share

E_z = proportion of consumers who evoke new brand

N = number of consumers measured

When significant variation in use rates exist, each L_{iz} is weighted by a use-level index. Similarly, the L_{iz} are weighted differently if they are not representative of the market demographically or in other ways.

Silk and Urban (1978) develop a relationship between E_z, the fraction of consumers who eventually evoke the new brand and include it in their relevant set of brands, and both the unaided-brand-awareness and the advertising-recall measures, which are collected on the premeasurement questionnaires.

Draw and cannibalization estimates. It is important for the multibrand manufacturer to develop an estimate of cannibalization and draw— the effect of the new brand on the market shares of their own and other manufacturers' brands, respectively. After the new product is introduced, the market consists of two subpopulations: those who include the new brand in their relevant set of brands and those who do not. Let these population proportions be E_z and $1 - E_z$, respectively. Under a suitable set of assumptions, the effect of the new brand on any other brand j can be estimated:

$$
L_{ij} = \begin{cases} \dfrac{(V_{ij})^b}{\displaystyle\sum_{\ell \in m_i} (V_{k\ell})^b} & \text{if } z \text{ is not included in evoked set} \\[4ex] \dfrac{(V_{ij})^b}{(V_{iz})^b + \displaystyle\sum_{\ell \in m_i} (V_{i\ell})^b} & \text{if } z \text{ is included in evoked set} \end{cases} \tag{10.40}
$$

Now consider two populations: the brand z evokers (of which there are n^*) and the nonevokers (n^{**}), where $n^* + n^{**} = N$. Suppose we order the consumers so that the brand z evokers come first. Then for $i = 1$, ..., n^*, individual i evokes the brand; for $i = n^* + 1$, ..., N the individual does not evoke the brand. The market shares for these two populations are (assuming independence of evoking and draw):

$$
S_j^* = \sum_{i=1}^{n^*} \frac{L_{ij}}{n^*} \tag{10.41}
$$

$$
S_j^{**} = \sum_{i=n^*+1}^{N} \frac{L_{ij}}{N - n^*} \tag{10.42}
$$

where the appropriate value of L_{ij} in equations (10.41) and (10.42) is taken from equation (10.40). Now the evoking proportion E_z is a controllable quantity that depends on advertising, and the total share of brand j after introduction of the new brand is

$$
S_j = E_z S_j^* + (1 - E_z)S_j^{**} \tag{10.43}
$$

while the draw from brand j for z is

$$
\text{draw}_j = S_j^{**} - S_j \tag{10.44}
$$

Note that the draw_j in equation (10.44), when summed over all competitors' brands, equals the share estimate for the new brand.

The ASSESSOR model makes two contributions. The first is a proposal for a convergent methodology, providing for increased diagnostics and checks of consistency for the pretest-market procedure. The second is the development of theoretical support for a modeling system for pretest-market evaluation.

In a follow-up study of the accuracy of prediction and value of the procedure, Urban and Katz (1983) report on 44 products that had used the procedure and had also gone to test market. After adjusting the model outputs for realized (as opposed to forecast) awareness, distribution, and sampling, the average test market share was 7.16%, and the average predicted by ASSESSOR was 7.15% with a standard deviation of 1.12%. The authors develop a Bayesian decision model and report that over a 6:1 benefit-cost ratio is realized on average, assuming a $50,000 investment in ASSESSOR.

The procedure, while providing key benefits, has several significant weaknesses. Although trial is probably adequately measured, it is questionable whether repeat rates can be adequately measured by telephone questioning and/or purchasing. In addition, the repeat model, equation (10.36), only considers first repeat and does not consider any depth-of-repeat information. Also, the selection of a distribution index (d) is somewhat arbitrary and may serve more as a tuning factor than a control variable. A well-defined and relatively homogeneous market class and choice set are clearly required here, or the draw and cannibalization estimates will be inappropriate. Furthermore, extension of the procedure beyond grocery products is questionable.

The model also does not explicitly include positioning information, marketing-mix diagnostics, or competitive effects, although model adjustments are possible. However, on net, the procedure is quite complete, is fundamentally sound, and has been widely used.

Other Models. A number of repeat-purchase models for new products are available; they differ in assumptions, structure, and reported applicability.

Mahajan and Wind (1988) provide a comprehensive overview of a range of test market models and include a review of key review papers (Exhibit 10.14). They also provide a number of suggestions for research and implementation in this area, including

> **1.** *Compare the models.* Many models appear to be in regular use. They should be compared both analytically and empirically, following the lead of Mahajan, Muller, and Sharma (1984).
>
> **2.** *Validate the models.* Following Urban and Katz (1983), we should see more reports on "what happened in the market."
>
> **3.** *Combine models and forecasts.* The early suggestion of Silk and Urban (1978) to use two independent models is in line with current thinking (Armstrong, 1986) that suggests combining of forecasts to improve forecast accuracy.

4. *Develop models for the breakthrough products.* Models work best for new product entries into well-established markets. But Booz, Allen and Hamilton (1982) report that the 30% of new product entries that were truly innovative accounted for more than half the sample of "most successful" products.

5. *Developing models from new data bases.* Scanner data and people meters are providing great impetus for new modeling developments throughout the packaged goods market including the new product area.

6. *Develop strategic, competitive models.* Defensive as well as offensive marketing strategies (Hauser and Shugan, 1983), pre-announcing behavior (Eliashberg and Robertson, 1988), and market pioneering and entry timing (Urban et al., 1986; Lilien and Yoon, 1990) all have a major impact on new product sales and share and these issues should be incorporated in operational new product models. Indeed, we need models that address how new product entries affect the structure and total demand of the market (Mason, 1990).

7. *Consider expert systems.* Expert or rule-based systems are being developed in many areas of marketing, as either substitutes for or complements to the types of models reviewed here (see Chapter 12).

8. *Develop global market models.* As markets become more global, we will see needs for models that forecast and suggest strategies for global market entry. Ohmae (1985) suggests that, with short life cycles, products should be introduced simultaneously (sprinkle strategy) versus sequentially (waterfall strategy), with consequent model needs.

In sum, many new product models have been developed and used and a sound theoretical basis appears to exist for many of these developments. More and better reporting of model validation and performance is required and there are clearly some promising directions for further model development.

SUMMARY

Decision making is most hazardous in new product development and introduction. Companies must introduce new products to survive and yet do so with the knowledge that a substantial number will fail. The costs involved are considerable, and alert management is taking whatever steps will help reduce the risks in the way of organization, professional staffing, marketing research, and model construction.

The variety of current models for new product forecasting and planning reflects to a large extent the variety of new product situations in which companies engage. New product situations can be distinguished by the degree of newness of the product and the degree of product repurchasability. Product

Type of models reviewed	Review article	Criteria used	Specific models included	Remarks
Pretest market models	Robinson (1981)	37 varieties related to the following 12 aggregate characteristics are used: (1) Scope of test product configuration, (2) Scope of test marketing plan, (3) Scope of test environmental conditions, (4) Measurement of buyer purchase behavior, (5) Conditions of exposure environment, (6) Competitive context, (7) Conditions of measurement, (8) Sampling procedure, (9) Projectability of results, (10) Assumptions used, (11) Model specification, (12) Operational characteristics	PURCHASE ACTION (ASI Marketing Research Inc.), ASSESSOR (Silk and Urban 1978), COMP (Burger, Gundee and Lavidge 1981), LTM (Yankelovich, Skelly and White 1981), SPEEDMARK (Robinson Associates), MICRO-MARKET (Tele-Research)	The article does not include several new simulated test market services currently offered in the marketplace such as LITMUS (Blackburn and Clancy 1983) and BASES (Burke Marketing Services 1984). The comparison, although very comprehensive, is highly subjective. Clustering analysis results suggest that conventional test markets and limited rollouts are more closely related to each other than to any of the simulated test market procedures. SPEEDMARK is identified as the procedure which approaches this pairing proximity. No indication of the forecasting efficiency of these approaches is provided. Levine (1981) has argued that these approaches need to be validated before they will be accepted by industry.
Pretest market models	Shocker and Hall (1986)	14 varieties are used for comparisons: (1) Type of model, (2) Data sources, (3) Product categories, (4) Forecast by time period, (5) Marketing plan inputs, (6) Cannibalization effects, (7) Competitive reactions, (8) Respondent screening, (9) Output, (10) Diagnostics, (11) Sensitivity/optimization, (12) Average sample size, (13) Time to complete, (14) Approximate cost	BASES II (Burke Marketing Services 1984) ASSESSOR-FT (Information Resources 1985) LITMUS-II (Blackburn and Clancy 1983) NEWS/PLANNER (Pringle, Wilson and Brody 1982)	The article provides an overview of pretest marketing models including their historical development, and strengths and weaknesses. A descriptive comparison of four pretest market models on selected dimensions is also included. No best model is identified.

EXHIBIT 10.14 A Summary of the Focus and Key Results of Major Review Articles on Pretest and Test-Market Modes. *Source:* Mahajan and Wind (1988), pp. 344–346.

Type of models reviewed	Review article	Criteria used	Specific models included	Remarks
Pretest and test market models	Larréché and Montgomery (1977)	(1) Structure, a) Adaptability, b) Completeness, c) Ease of testing, d) Ease of understanding, e) Robustness (2) Expected value, (3) Initial cost, (4) Usage characteristics, (5) Usage context, (6) Validation history	DEMON (Learner 1965), Hendry (Butler and Butler 1971) STEAM (Massy 1969), NEWS (Pringle, Wilson and Brody 1982, NW Ayer (Claycamp and Liddy 1969), SPRINTER (Urban 1970)	The models are evaluated as part of a larger Delphi study on the evaluation of marketing models. NEWS and NW Ayer's model scored highest (4) on a 5-point scale of likelihood of acceptance.
Pretest and test market models (repeat purchase diffusion models)	Mahajan and Muller (1982)	(1) Model formulation (deterministic vs. stochastic), (2) Use of integrated adoption/diffusion framework, (3) Model distinguishes between: a) Unaware potential, b) Types of information, c) Depth of repeat, (4) Model includes: a) a-word-of-mouth, b) impulse purchase, c) decay, d) recycle	Fourt and Woodlock (1960), Parfitt and Collins (1968), NW Ayer (Claycamp and Liddy 1969), Nakanishi 1973), STEAM (Massy 1969), NEWPROD (Assmus 1975), SPRINTER (Urban 1970), Midgley (1976), TRACKER (Blattberg and Golanty 1978), Dodson and Muller (1978), Lilien, Rao, and Kalish (1981)	The comparison is limited to the adoption/diffusion structure of the models. The article ignores all other important considerations related to the implementation of the models. Although the article does not identify the best model, the comparison suggests that SPRINTER scores highest on most of the selected dimensions.
Pretest and test market models (awareness models only)	Mahajan, Muller and Sharma (1984)	(1) Features of models (marketing mix variables considered, word-of-mouth, forgetting, initial awareness, maximum level of awareness), (2) Forecasting accuracy	TRACKER (Blattberg and Golanty 1978), NEWS (Pringle, Wilson and Brody 1982), LITMUS (Blackburn and Clancy 1983), Dodson and Muller (1978), NW Ayer (Claycamp and Liddy 1969)	Using actual data, this article provides an empirical comparison of awareness models included in five new product introduction models. Analytical similarities among the models are derived. All the models are shown to perform equally well with TRACKER marginally leading the compared models.
Test market models	Narasimhan and Sen (1983)	(1) Model objective, (2) Stages modeled, (3) Consideration of marketing, (4) Level of model complexity, (5) Type of sales data required, (6) Diagnostics, (7) Number of applications reported at time of publication, (8) Degree of commercial acceptance	Fourt and Woodlock (1960), Parfitt and Collins (1968), STEAM (Massy 1969), SPRINTER (Urban 1970), Eskin (1973) Nakanishi (1973), NEWS (Pringle, Wilson and Brody 1982), NEWPROD (Assmus 1975), TRACKER (Blattberg and Golanty 1978)	The comparison, although very comprehensive, is subjective. It identifies TRACKER and NEWS as the best test market models on the selected dimensions.

EXHIBIT 10.14 (continued)

newness ranges from the truly new product innovation to the new brand to the new model, style, or package size of an existing brand. Product repurchasability ranges from those that are bought only once to those that are bought occasionally to those that are bought frequently.

This last distinction enables us to separate the analyses of the first-time purchase from the repeat purchases, under the assumption that different factors are involved. The occurrence of first-time purchases can be analyzed as a diffusion process. Such a process uses a few macroparameters to locate a curve that describes the spread of the innovation through a population over time.

A number of different models have been developed that treat the diffusion as an imitative process, a purely innovative process, or a combination of processes. Recently, control variables that influence the rate of diffusion have been incorporated into these models. In addition, important work is continuing on ways of predicting the parameters of these models so that product success and sales forecasts can be developed earlier and more accurately.

Frequently purchased products require that attention be paid to the repeat-purchase phenomenon. The modeling and estimation of repeat rates is a key feature in the models that were developed for analyzing test-market and pretest-market laboratory simulation results. More recent models incorporate and operationalize the concept of depth of repeat, because the probability of repeat purchase appears to vary with the number of past purchases.

Both for frequently and for infrequently purchased products, a number of clearly useful models are available. The major needs in the area are better reporting and consolidation of results for improved comparative analysis and attention to market situations in which the product is clearly new.

PROBLEMS

10.1. Growth models in biology usually take on a form characterized by several assumptions. Assume that a population has size N at time zero and the growth of that population is a constant fraction of its current size.
   a. Formulate this problem as a differential equation.
   b. Solve the equation.

   Assume that the total growth rate in the population is a sum of two factors: the natural growth rate (above) plus modification due to the environment. Assume that an incoming member must compete with existing members of the population for resources. If A represents the number of individuals in the population at time t, there are $A(A - 1)/2$ possible pairs in conflict. Assume that this competition restricts the growth by an amount proportional to $A(A - 1)/2$.
   c. Incorporate this information in a differential equation.
   d. Solve the equation.
   e. Can you think of any uses for such a model in marketing?

10.2. A wholesale dealer is considering the introduction of a new product throughout the eastern region of the United States. We will assume the following:

1. If the product is introduced, it will cost $150,000 to introduce it.
2. The result of introducing the product would be great success, mild success, or failure.
3. It is possible to conduct a test-marketing project to be able to predict the degree of success of the new product. This test will cost $20,000 and will indicate the results as being RI (good chances of success), RII (less favorable), and RIII (unfavorable). The following probabilities have been assigned by the company specialist:

$$P(\text{great success}|\text{RI}) = 0.4 \qquad P(\text{mild success}|\text{RI}) \ = 0.3$$
$$P(\text{great success}|\text{RII}) = 0.1 \qquad P(\text{mild success}|\text{RII}) \ = 0.4$$
$$P(\text{great success}|\text{RIII}) = 0.0 \qquad P(\text{mild success}|\text{RIII}) = 0.3$$
$$P(\text{RI}) = 0.2 \quad P(\text{RII}) = 0.3 \qquad P(\text{RIII}) = 0.5$$

4. If the product turns out to be a great success, the dealer will get a $900,000 bonus from the manufacturing company; he will receive only $300,000 if it is a mild success.

   Assume that the decision maker wants to maximize his expected profit:
   a. Draw the decision tree for the problem and show all the possibilities and outcomes.
   b. What is the probability of the product being a success (either great or mild)?
   c. The manager would like to know the best possible strategy to use. What is it?
   d. What is the expected value of the test-marketing project?
   e. What should the manager be willing to pay to get perfect information about the success of the product?
   f. Calculate $P(\text{RII}|\text{mild success})$ and $P(\text{RI}|\text{great success})$.

10.3. A brand manager expects his new product sales to grow continuously so that he will sell $100 + 4t$ units of the product per day, t days after introduction. [That is, on the initial day ($t = 0$) he will sell 100 units, on the next day ($t = 1$) he will sell 104 units, etc.] Set up the appropriate equations and solve for the day that the 10,000th unit will be sold.

10.4. Using the Fourt-Woodlock market-penetration model, compute the increments in penetration for the first five periods for a company whose rate of penetration of untapped potential is 0.4 and whose potential sales as a percent of all buyers is 0.6. Verify mathematically that the sum of the individual increments approaches 0.6 as t goes to infinity.

10.5. For a particular product, the coefficient of innovation p (for the Bass model) is 0.05 and the coefficient of imitation r is 0.2. The total number of potential buyers is 100,000.
   a. Determine the time when sales will reach its peak.
   b. Calculate the magnitude of peak sales.
   c. Suppose that the Bass model is fitted to empirical data, resulting in the following expression:

   $$Q_t = 410 + 0.39N_t - 10^{-6}N_t^2$$

   From this equation, determine the total number of potential adopters $\bar{Q}$.

10.6. A group of consumers is asked to rate five different brands of coffee on two characteristics: strength and body. Each brand is rated on a scale of 1 to 7 for each characteristic. Each consumer is also asked to rate an ideal coffee. The average brand ratings are as follows:

Brand	Strength	Body
A	3	4
B	6	2
C	6	3
D	2	3
E	1	1
Ideal	5	5

a. Represent these perceptions in Euclidean two-dimensional space and order the brands according to their probable market share if product characteristics were the only factor that counted.

b. Suppose that a regression analysis found the following relationship to be true:

$$M_i = \frac{K}{d_{iS}^2} + \frac{3K}{d_{iB}^2}$$

where

M_i = market share of brand i
K = constant
d_{iS} = distance for brand i from ideal on strength
d_{iB} = distance for brand i from ideal on body

i. Find K. (Hint: What does ΣM_i equal?)
ii. Calculate the shares of brands A through E from the model.

c. Suppose a new brand F was found to be rated as

Strength = 3;   Body = 3

What would the estimate of its market share be? How would it draw that share from other brands? (Hint: Remember that market shares *must* sum to 1)

10.7. The ABC Company recently introduced a new product. The product has been on the market for seven weeks, and the sales manager wishes to determine the product's long-run share of the market. The research department has provided data on the cumulative-penetration and repeat-purchase rates for the product to date. These data are presented in the following table:

Week	1	2	3	4	5	6	7
Cumulative penetration	0.13	0.20	0.26	0.30	0.33	0.35	0.36
Repurchase rate		0.48	0.42	0.37	0.33	0.30	0.28

A test-market survey has estimated that product awareness in the market is 73% and that 92% of the outlets are carrying the brand. Company customers tend to be somewhat lighter users than average product-class users (index = 0.92, where 1.0 is average).

a. Provide a long-term market-share projection for the product
  i. Assuming test-market conditions are duplicated nationally.
  ii. Assuming national awareness is 62% and only 80% of the outlets are carrying the brand.

b. Suppose that management has found that

$$\text{Awareness} = 0.4 \ln (\text{advertising dollars})$$

where advertising dollars are measured in millions. Assume 90% distribution, $10,000,000 in sales per market-share point, and gross margin, before advertising, is 15% of sales. How much should be spent on advertising to maximize profit? [*Hint*:

$$\text{Profit} = \text{Market size} \cdot \text{share} \cdot \text{margin} - \text{advertising dollars}$$
$$\text{Share} = \text{Awareness (advertising dollars)} \cdot \text{other factors}]$$

10.8. After a number of weeks in the test market, a consumer product has reached a penetration level of 42% with repeat purchases of 32%. For the product field in question, total annual sales are estimated to be 186,000 units in the test-market area, and the test area contains 12.3% of all households. What is the predicted national sales of the product if it is further estimated that while it is in the national market, distribution efficiency will be at a level of 82% of that reached during test? On what assumptions is your estimate based? (Fitz-roy, 1976, p. 308)

10.9. The government wishes to stimulate the growth of photovoltaics (solar cells) in order to reduce dependence on fossil fuels. We assume that PV (photovoltaic) sales will increase according to a diffusion-of-innovation process with the following characteristics.

(1) The potential market is determined by the value in use of PV products, expressed as the cost per kilowatt-hour of the best competitive fuel minus the cost per kilowatt-hour of PV. (The latter is an imputed cost since the sun is free and the expense is largely a fixed investment.)

(2) The sales of PV will follow a growth curve in which sales rate will be proportional to the following: (a) the number of units already installed, (b) the visibility (publicity and advertising) given to the installed units, (c) a function of the cost-per-kilowatt-hour difference between PV and the best competitive fuel, and (d) the amount of the potential PV market not yet converted.

(3) The cost, and therefore, the price, of PV will follow a learning curve, that is, will decrease as a function of total units produced, rapidly at first and then slowly.
To model the process, let

$$y = \text{cumulative amount of PV capacity installed at time } t, \text{ in megawatts}$$
$$m = \text{maximum potential demand for PV, in megawatts}$$

a. As a sample first model, suppose

$$\frac{dy}{dt} = ay\left(1 - \frac{y}{m}\right)$$

Find $y(t)$ for this model. Starting from an initial installation of y_0 megawatts, sketch $y(t)$. Note

$$\int \frac{dx}{x(ax^n + c)} = \frac{1}{cn} \log \frac{x^n}{ax^n + c}$$

b. For a second model we go to discrete time and include more phenomena. Consider a particular PV application (e.g., irrigation). Let

$$\begin{aligned}
y_t &= \text{cumulative installed capacity at } t, \text{ in megawatts} \\
p_t &= \text{installed price of PV, dollars per kilowatt-hour} \\
c_t &= \text{delivered price of best competitive fuel, dollars per kilowatt-hour} \\
u_t &= c_t - p_t \text{ price advantage of PV at } t \\
g(u) &= \text{attractiveness function for buying PV} \\
m &= \text{total market potential of application} \\
p(y) &= \text{unit price after } y \text{ units have been built and installed}
\end{aligned}$$

i. Sketch what $g(u)$ and $p(y)$ might look like. To take specific analytic forms, suppose that the attractiveness function for buying PV is exponential, with relative price

$$g(u) = e^{u/a}$$

Take $a = \$0.10$ per kilowatt-hour. For a learning curve, assume

$$p_t = p_0 e^{-y_{t-1}/b}$$

Currently, a peak kilowatt (i.e., a photovoltaic cell that generates a kilowatt with the sun shining on it) costs $50,000. Suppose that after 10,000 MW of PVs has been produced, the price will be $500 per kilowatt. Assuming the current amount of installed PV is 1 MW, find p_0 and b.

ii. Suppose the process follows the following growth model:

$$y_t = y_{t-1} + \alpha y_{t-1} g(u_t)\left(1 - \frac{y_{t-1}}{m}\right)$$

where

$$\begin{aligned}
m &= \text{total potential sales, MW} \\
&= 20{,}000 \\
\alpha &= \text{proportionality constant determining basic growth rate of process; represents new PV sales as a fraction of cumulated sales to date under conditions of price parity (fraction per year)} \\
&= 0.5
\end{aligned}$$

Starting with $y_0 = 1$ MW, follow the process for two years, determining y. Assume $c_t = \$0.05$ per kilowatt-hour for all t.

c. The government proposes to intervene and buy the initial production up to y such that $u = 0$ and give it away or otherwise see that it is installed.

   i. How much will it cost to buy that production?
   ii. Starting with y_0 at the production found in part i, run the process five years.
   iii. Suppose the government also conducts a publicity program that increases α by 50%. Run the process for three years.

d. What improvements would you suggest in the model?

10.10. Consider the following market situations, characterized by a discrete-time version of the Horsky-Simon model:

$$Q_{t+1} = [a + b \ln A(t + 1)](N - N_t) + r \frac{Q_t}{N}(N - N_t)$$

where

Q_{t+1}	=	sales in next period
$A(t + 1)$	=	advertising in that period
N	=	market potential
N_T	=	cumulative sales to time t
a, b, r	=	parameters

Suppose that $a = 0.01$, $b = 0.005$, $r = 0.4$, and $N = 70,000$ units. Suppose further that the profit margin for the product is $\$0.50$/unit. The product has an effective life of ten two-month periods and the firm buys advertising in blocks of five two-month periods (i.e., the advertising rate for the first five periods must be the same; however, it can be a different level for the second five periods.

a. Find the optimal time path of advertising (i.e., the monthly level in the first five periods and the monthly level in the second five periods).

b. Find the optimal steady level of advertising.

c. Which result, (a) or (b), more closely corresponds to Horsky and Simon's theoretical result?

11 | STRATEGY

In previous chapters we have discussed and compared developments in marketing modeling, focusing mostly on marketing-specific issues. In this chapter we broaden the scope to model-building approaches for more integrative efforts addressing broader business planning issues. We first develop a framework for analyzing strategic marketing and planning problems. Next we define market planning and relate it to the more general business planning function. Then we review phenomena that underlie most of the analytic approaches used in this area. Finally we review a series of approaches, varying in objectives and analytic style, for integrating these concepts into procedures to support business planning decisions.

MARKETING PLANNING AND STRATEGY DECISIONS

In this chapter we assume that we deal with a large organization with several business divisions and several product lines within each division. Marketing plays a role at each level. At the organizational level, marketing contributes perspectives and estimates to help top management decide on the corporation's mission, opportunities, growth strategy, and product portfolio. Corporate policies then provide the context for strategy formulation in each of the business divisions by the divisional managers. Finally, the managers of each product and/or market within each division develop their marketing strategy within the context of the policies and constraints developed at the divisional and corporate levels.

The term *strategic management process* is often used to describe the steps taken at the corporate and divisional levels to develop long-run strategies for organizational survival and growth, while the parallel *strategic marketing process* refers to the steps taken at the product and/or market level to develop viable marketing positions and programs. The strategic marketing process takes place within the larger strategic management process of the corporation.

Wind and Robertson (1983) present a useful framework to capture marketing concepts and models within a marketing framework (Exhibit 11.1).

The model breaks into three main, interrelated sections:

Section I: A traditional assessment of market opportunities and business strengths, including

    a.   analysis of opportunities and threats

    b.   analysis of business strengths and weaknesses

Section II: The marketing strategy core

    c.   segmentation by positioning analysis (linking market segments with the benefits they seek)

    d.   opportunity analysis (linking the segments/positionings to market opportunities and business strengths/weaknesses)

    e.   synergy analysis (the positive negative synergies in advertising, distribution, manufacturing, and so on, among products, segments, and marketing-mix components)

    f.   functional requirements (specification of what each segment/positioning requires in terms of success and the company's ability to satisfy those requirements)

    g.   portfolio analysis, the analytical core of the process (providing an integrated view of the strategic process both for existing and new business)

Section III: The generation and evaluation of objective and strategies, including

    h.   generation of objectives and strategies

    i.   evaluation of objectives and strategies

    j.   implementation, monitoring and control of the program

The authors claim that this framework helps to overcome seven key limitations of analysis in the marketing profession. We address these limitations in the framework of this chapter as follows:

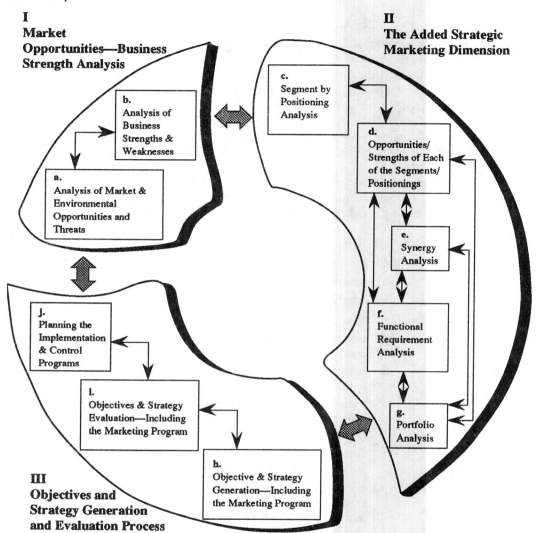

EXHIBIT 11.1 A marketing-oriented approach to strategy formulation and evaluation. (*Source: Wind and Robertson, 1983, p. 16.*)

Limitation (Wind and Robertson, 1983)	Approach (This chapter)
1. Improper analytic focus	Market definition
2. Functional isolation	Integration (especially manufacturing cost dynamics)
3. Ignoring synergy	Marketing-mix/product-line analysis

4. Short-run analysis	Dynamics, especially product life-cycle analysis
5. Ignoring competition	Competitive analysis
6. Ignoring interactions	Proper market definition (point 1)
7. Lack of integrated view	Integrated models

In previous sections of the book, we have introduced and addressed many of these issues. In this chapter we draw together and integrate much of that material.

We proceed as follows. First, we deal with underlying concepts: market definition (points 1 and 6), dynamics/product life cycle (point 4), and functional interactions (point 2). We then address synergy, competition, and strategic integration (points 3, 5, and 7) in the final three sections.

Market Definition and Market Structure

We have assumed throughout that a market is well defined or understood. But what is a market? And how is it structured?

Key strategic issues, such as the basic business definition, opportunity assessment, threat analysis, and the like, are closely tied to the breadth or the narrowness of the market. When attainment of market share represents a desirable objective, market boundaries must be defined to determine the extent to which the objective is met.

The traditional approach for describing markets has been by generic title and then by physical properties. For example, in the auto market (generic title), the size of the car (subcompact, compact, midsize, full size) has been used. The main idea behind the traditional approach is that there is relatively more (actual or perceived) competition within markets than across markets. In fact, most economists and marketing analysts argue that the definition of a market should depend on how consumers view it.

Day, Shocker, and Srivastava (1979) define a product market as follows:

> The *set of products* judged to be substitutes within those usage segments in which similar patterns of benefits are sought and the customers for whom such usages are relevant. *(p. 10)*

That is, a product market is a group of physical products perceived to be substitutes by a particular group of customers for specific occasions.

Day, Shocker, and Srivastava classify methods for identifying product markets by whether they rely on behavioral or judgmental data (Exhibit 11.2). Their classifications are reviewed next.

Cross-elasticity of Demand. This approach is considered by most economists to be the standard one against which other approaches should be judged. Mathematically, the cross-elasticity of demand is $(\partial Q_i/\partial X_j)(X_j/Q_i)$, where X_j

A: Purchase or Use-Behavior Approaches		B: Customer-Perceptions/ Judgmental Approaches	
A1.	Cross-elasticity of demand	B1.	Decision-sequence analysis
A2.	Similarities in behavior	B2.	Perceptual mapping
A3.	Brand switching	B3.	Technology-substitution analysis
		B4.	Customer judgments of substitutability

EXHIBIT 11.2 Analytic methods for defining product markets. (*Source:* Day, Shocker and Srivastava, 1979, p. 11.)

represents some marketing activity (price generally) associated with brand j and Q_i is the volume of brand i. In essence, if this term is large, i and j are said to be in the same market. This approach, despite its seeming logic, is frequently criticized and rarely used because (1) it assumes no response by one firm to price variations of another, (2) it is static and cannot accommodate changing product market composition, and (3) it is difficult to estimate in relatively stable markets, where there is frequently insufficient data variation.

Similarities in Use Behavior.   A study by Cocks and Virts (1975) addressed the question of substitutability of drugs with different chemical makeup but of similar therapeutic value. The data required information on the need for the drug (the diagnosis) as well as the drug prescribed to treat the problem, and a panel of 3000 physicians produced these data. As yet, few consumer panels have tracked use occasions for products, limiting the applicability of this approach.

Brand Switching.   This approach suffers from some of the same limitations as the cross-elasticity method—the measures can be used only *after* a set of competitive products has been established. In general, the approach breaks down a matrix of brand-switching probabilities or proportions into competitive markets (Chapter 2).

Brand-switching data as potential measures of market boundaries are flawed because of their limitations to markets with high repeat rates, the need to assume stable switching behavior, and their inability to handle multiple-use occasions, multiple users, and multiple, simultaneous purchases.

Furthermore, all the approaches that use behavioral data suffer from analyzing what was rather than focusing on what might be. For instance, problems, such as lack of availability, may prevent substitution of one brand for another when they might otherwise be substitutes. Unless data are collected in a laboratory-based setting, these approaches, at best, provide a partial solution to the problem of market definition. To complement them, consumer perceptions and judgments are useful.

Decision-Sequence Analysis.   Decision-sequence analysis considers protocols of the consumer decision-making process that indicate the sequence in which decision criteria are used for final product choice (Bettman, 1971). For example, a potential customer might be asked, when choosing a margarine, whether he chose a form first (stick versus tub), a raw material first (corn oil, safflower oil, etc.), or a brand first. Because respondents are not used to this type of introspection, the approach has several empirical problems. There is also a problem of declaring two decision processes similar.

Perceptual Mapping.   As discussed in Chapter 2, perceptual mapping is a set of approaches used to represent the position of brands in geometric space. Those brands close together are considered to form a market and be substitutes. The approach is flexible and has seen wide use in market-definition studies.

Technology Substitution.   Technology substitution is an approach for determining how products (industrial products, generally) are likely to compete. The rate at which one material substitutes for another (e.g., polyvinyl for glass in bottles) is related to its relative utility in each situation (Stein, Ayers, and Shapeneso, 1975). The result is a quantitative measure of relative utility that can be used to estimate substitutability among competing products or technologies in certain situations.

Consumer Judgments of Substitutability.   There are a variety of ways to gather information on substitutability from consumers, ranging from simply asking consumers to methods with more diagnostic power. (See Day, Shocker, and Srivastava, 1979, for a critical review of these methods.)

Shocker, Zahorik, and Stewart (1984) suggest that a procedure for market structure analysis should produce:

1. A means for specifying the appropriate set of products for analysis (i.e., the procedure should generally be robust to the addition/deletion of products)

2. A means for dealing with diverse requirements of different usage segments and contexts (i.e., the procedure should consider the use occasion)

3. A means for dealing with different degrees of appropriateness in use for the same product (i.e., some products are better suited for some uses than others—for example, dishwashing liquid can be used to clean clothes, but laundry detergent is more appropriate)

4. Evidence that the structure obtained is reliable and valid (i.e., the structure should be consistently obtainable through independent measures and should correspond to measurable outcomes, like purchase activity and switching).

Few existing procedures provide complete answers to these challenges. Indeed Shocker, Zalronk, and Stewart (1984) criticize Fraser and Bradford's (1983) procedure specifically, and most others in general, for failing to address many of these problems (see Fraser and Bradford, 1984, for a reply).

Some recent approaches to this challenging problem area include those of Urban, Johnson, and Hauser's (1984) PRODEGY model, which permits idiosyncratic market structures (i.e., assigns consumer-use occasions applications to different structures) and develops methods for testing for the adequacy of such structures; Srivastava, Alpert, and Shocker (1984), who show that, when products have multiple uses, overlapping market structures may be most appropriate; Holbrook and Holloway (1984), who argue that by looking separately at aggregate preferences, at segment-specific preferences and at "differential preferences" (those preference differences specific to a segmentation basis) one can develop strategy insights for undifferentiated marketing, differentiated marketing, and product-oriented selling, respectively; and Grover and Srinivasan's (1987) approach, which simultaneously addresses the issue of segmentation and market structure in a brand-switching framework.

In an interesting development, Kannan and Wright (1991) use a nested logit approach that recognizes that different individuals have different choice trees. They also show how brands compete within these structures by incorporating marketing mix variables.

The integration of some of the empirical approaches for understanding market structure (like those outlined here) with some of the theoretical work defining product spaces (see Chapter 5) will continue to be a challenge in the years to come. We have yet to solve Day, Shocker, and Srivastava's (1979, p. 18) concern: "the most persistent problem is the lack of defensible criteria for recognizing [market] boundaries." Perhaps, however, we need to recognize and model the fuzzy regions where markets blend together.

The Product Life Cycle

An important concept underlying most business planning models is the product life cycle. Because sales position and profitability can be expected to change over time, a product's strategy needs periodic revision. The concept of the life cycle is an attempt to recognize distinct phases in the sales history of the product and to develop strategies appropriate to those stages.

Most discussions of the product life cycle (PLC) portray the sales history of a typical product as following an S-shaped sales curve, as illustrated in Exhibit 11.3. This curve is typically divided into four stages known as introduction, growth, maturity, and decline. *Introduction* is a period of slow growth as the product is introduced in the market. The profit curve in Exhibit 11.3 shows profits as low or negative in this stage because of the heavy expenses of product introduction. *Growth* is a period of rapid market acceptance and

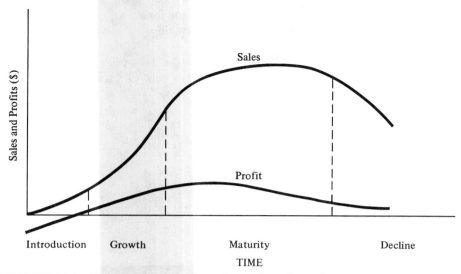

EXHIBIT 11.3 Typical stages in the sales and profit cycles.

substantial profit improvement. *Maturity* is a slowing-down period of sales growth because the product has achieved acceptance by most of the potential buyers. Profits peak in this period and start to decline because of increased marketing outlays needed to sustain the product's position against competition.

Finally, *decline* is the period when sales continue a strong downward drift and profits erode toward zero.

We can understand this phenomenon as follows. Assume that a human need (calculating power) exists and that a product (a calculator) satisfies those needs. Exhibit 11.4(a) shows how different technologies can successively substitute for one another (leading to a sequence of technology cycles within an overall demand cycle). Exhibit 11.4(b) breaks things down further, showing how successive product forms can replace one another within the context of a single technology cycle.

The empirical evidence of the existence and pervasiveness of the product-life-cycle concept is quite uneven. In a literature review Rink and Swan (1979) were able to identify 12 types of product life-cycle patterns. For example, Cox (1967) studied the life cycles of 754 ethical drug products and found the most typical form was a cycle-recycle pattern, shown in Exhibit 11.5(a). He explains that the second hump in sales is caused by a promotional push during the decline phase. In another study Buzzell (1966) reports a scalloped life-cycle pattern, shown in Exhibit 11.5(b), representing a succession of life cycles based on the discovery of new product characteristics, new uses, or new markets.

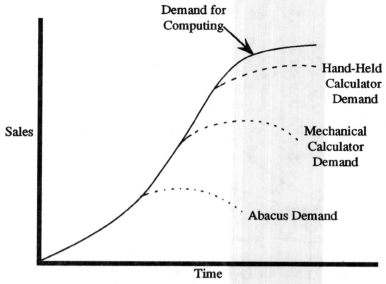

EXHIBIT 11.4(a) The demand for computing is satisfied over time by different technologies that substitute for one another.

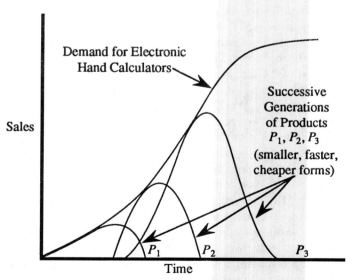

EXHIBIT 11.4(b) The demand for a product class is driven by the replacement of one generation (product form) by another.

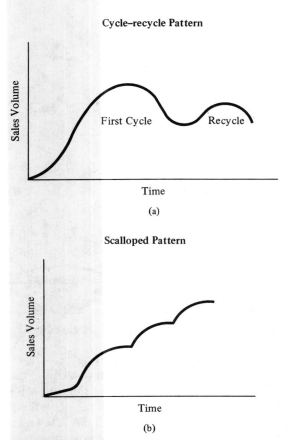

EXHIBIT 11.5 Some anomalous product life-cycle patterns.

Studies by Harrell and Taylor (1981) and by Thorelli and Burnett (1981) conclude that growth rates are only one aspect of the product life cycle: elements such as market innovation, market concentration, competitive structure, economic cycles, and supply constraints, as well as the influence of replacement sales, affect the structure of the life cycle as well.

In fact, research is further confused by differences in the level of product aggregation and by difficulties with the definition of a new product. Typically, there are three possible levels of aggregation: product class (cigarettes), product form (plain filter cigarettes), and brand (Philip Morris, regular or nonfilter). (See Exhibit 11.6.) The PLC concept is applied differently in these three cases. Product classes have the longest life histories, longer than particular product forms, and certainly longer than most brands. The sales of many product classes can be expected to continue in the mature stage for an indefinite duration because they are highly related to population (cars, perfume, refrig-

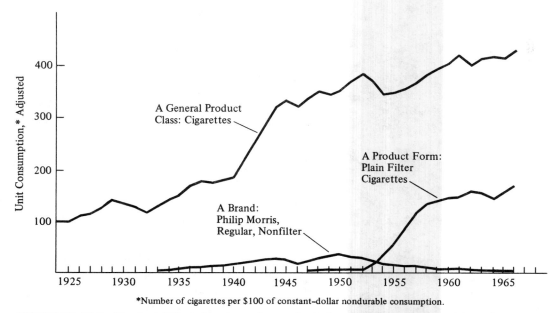

Unit Consumption,* Adjusted

A General Product
Class: Cigarettes

A Product Form:
Plain Filter
Cigarettes

A Brand:
Philip Morris,
Regular, Nonfilter

1925   1930   1935   1940   1945   1950   1955   1960   1965

*Number of cigarettes per $100 of constant-dollar nondurable consumption.

EXHIBIT 11.6   Product life-cycle curves for product class, product form, and brand. (*Source:* Polli and Cook, 1969, p. 389.)

erators, and steel). Product forms tend to exhibit the standard PLC histories more faithfully. Product forms, such as the dial telephone and cream deodorants, seem to pass through a regular history of introduction, rapid growth, maturity, and decline. On the other hand, a brand's sales history can be erratic because changing competitive strategies and tactics can produce substantial ups and downs in sales and market shares, even to the extent of causing a mature brand to suddenly exhibit another period of rapid growth.

Another difficulty in life-cycle studies is the definition of a new product. How "new" must a product be to be considered a new product? Furthermore, is a variation in an established product a new product? This difficulty is more than semantic and has not been resolved.

Two problems frequently tackled by life-cycle researchers are the forecasts of stage transitions and phase duration. Chapter 10 reviews a number of new product growth models useful for the early stage of the life cycle. Lambkin and Day (1989) explicitly develop such a model to describe and explain the product life cycle. Wilson (1969) suggests using a series of leading indicators for the timing of the maturity and decline phases, such as declining industry profits or overcapacity in the industry, while Cooke and Edmundson (1963) recommend using a time-series–based analysis developed on early data points.

Although some success has been claimed for these methods, they typically use data from one phase to forecast the timing and length of the next stage. Accurate long-range forecasting is quite difficult and therefore little is known about the length and sequence of life-cycle phases (Day 1981). The problems of forecasting phase change and phase length are made more difficult by the widely held belief that life cycles are becoming shorter; Qualls, Olshavsky, and Michaels (1981) provide empirical support of this notion.

What, then, is the value or use of the product life-cycle concept in planning and strategy formulation? Clearly, a single life cycle does not exist; neither does a single life-cycle strategy. A realistic view is that life-cycle analysis is only one important element in the overall analysis of marketing opportunities. The life cycle acts as a classification device and suggests conditions under which market growth, for example, may occur. During market growth, competitors are better able to enter the market, and new opportunities for product offerings are available in selected market segments. Price and advertising elasticities are believed to change over the product life cycle as well (Chapter 4). However, other writers feel that the product life-cycle concept is a dependent variable, determined largely by marketer action, rather than an independent variable to which firms should adapt their marketing programs (Wind and Claycamp, 1976; Dhalla and Yuspeh, 1976).

In sum, while there continues to be much discussion concerning definition and measurement, the product life cycle is clearly critical in determining appropriate marketing strategies (Thietart and Vivas, 1984).

Cost Dynamics: Scale and Experience Effects

Another phenomenon affecting marketing strategy is cost dynamics. One of the most widely discussed findings of the profit impact of marketing strategy (PIMS) program (reviewed later in this chapter) is that market share is a primary determinant of business profitability: the PIMS results show that, on average, a difference of market share between competitors of 10% translates into a 5% difference in pretax return on investment. One reason for this increase in profitability is that firms with larger market shares have lower costs, due partly to *economies of scale*—where very large plants cost less per unit of production to build and run—and partly to the *experience effect*—where the marginal cost of many products declines 10–30% in real terms each time the company's experience in producing and selling them doubles.

Although it has long been observed that manufacturing costs seem to fall with cumulative experience, and not just with scale of production, it is only recently that this phenomenon has been studied carefully and quantified (Yelle, 1979). Initially, it was believed that only the labor portion of manufacturing costs decreased with cumulative production. The commander of the Wright-Patterson Air Force Base noted in the 1920s that the number of hours required to assemble a plane decreased as the total number of aircraft increased. The relationship between cumulative production and labor costs became known as the *learning curve*.

In the 1960s evidence began mounting that the phenomenon was broader. The Boston Consulting Group (1970), in particular, showed that each time cumulative volume of production of a product doubled, marginal value-added costs—including sales, administration, and so on—fell by a constant percentage. This relationship between marginal costs and cumulative production became known as the *experience curve*.

The simplest form of the learning or experience curve is the log-linear model:

$$C_q = C_n \left(\frac{q}{n}\right)^{-b} \tag{11.1}$$

where

$$
\begin{aligned}
q &= \text{cumulative production to date} \\
n &= \text{cumulative production at particular, earlier time} \\
C_n &= \text{marginal cost of } n\text{th unit (in constant dollars)} \\
C_q &= \text{marginal cost of } q\text{th unit (in constant dollars)} \\
b &= \text{learning constant}
\end{aligned}
$$

In practice, experience curves are characterized by their *learning rate*. Suppose that each time experience doubles, cost per unit drops to 80% of the original level. Then the 80% is known as the *learning rate*. The learning rate is related to the *learning constant* as follows:

$$r = 2^{-b} \cdot 100 \tag{11.2}$$

or

$$b = \frac{\ln 100 - \ln r}{\ln 2} \tag{11.3}$$

where

$$
\begin{aligned}
r &= \text{learning rate (percentage)} \\
b &= \text{learning constant}
\end{aligned}
$$

Exhibit 11.7 shows how costs fall with experience for various learning rates and levels of experience.

Many alternative models of the experience curve have been proposed

Ratio of Old Experience (n) to New Experience (q)	Learning Rate (r)					
	70%	75%	80%	85%	90%	95%
1.1	5	4	3	2	1	1
1.25	11	9	7	5	4	2
1.5	19	15	12	9	6	3
1.75	25	21	16	12	8	4
2.0	30	25	20	15	10	5
2.5	38	32	26	19	13	7
3.0	43	37	30	23	15	8
4.0	51	44	36	28	19	10
6.0	60	52	44	34	24	12
8.0	66	58	49	39	27	14
16.0	76	68	59	48	34	19

EXHIBIT 11.7 Cost reductions following from equations (11.1) and (11.2). (*Source:* Abell and Hammond, 1979, p. 109.)

(see Carlson, 1961, 1973, for discussion), including the plateau model, the Stanford-B model, the DeJong model, and the S model (Exhibit 11.8).

Alberts (1989) contends that the causes of most cost declines are confounded, sharing some characteristics of economies of scale and some with experience as follows:

Innovation-based causes of cost reductions:

1. Operator innovations—where workers figure out how to procure, manufacture and distribute goods more efficiently with current technology

2. Management innovations—where supervisors and managers figure out how to improve operations with existing technologies

3. Process innovations—where new procurement, assembly and distribution technologies lead to increased efficiency

Scale-based causes of cost reductions:

1. Reduction of excess capacity—which reduces the ratio of fixed costs per unit of production

2. Scale dependent substitutions—where larger assembly, procurement and distribution systems are more cost-effective on a per unit basis

3. Procurement power—where increases in procurement volume lead to better deals and lower unit prices

Exhibit 11.9 outlines Alberts's (1989) view of the experience "hypothe-

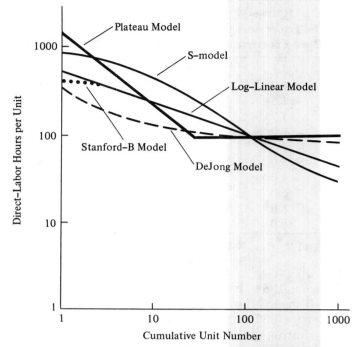

EXHIBIT 11.8 Various learning curve models all having the same direct-labor input at 100 units. (*Source:* Yelle, 1979, p. 304.)

sis," although he contends that neither repetition nor growth "cause" process innovations—rather they arise through R&D investments that may or may not be linked to volume or experience.

These observations suggest that experience by itself does not cause cost declines but, rather, provides the opportunity for such declines. Many of the foregoing effects (work specialization, for example) may become possible because of the size of the operation and therefore are part of a scale effect. In fact, growth in experience usually occurs at the same time the size of an operation grows, although scale effects can be used to bypass experience (as the Japanese did in the steel industry). And it is clear that process innovations will not just happen—they must result from an R&D program targeted at such cost reductions.

While the experience concept is rather simple, its application in a model requires ingenuity. It is important to (1) adjust prices for inflation; (2) plot cost versus experience (not time); (3) consider cost components separately, because each may have different learning rates; (4) correct for *shared experience*, where two or more products share a common resource or activity; (5) adjust for different experience rates between competitors (firm A, a late entry, may benefit from B's experience, may be able to exploit shared experience

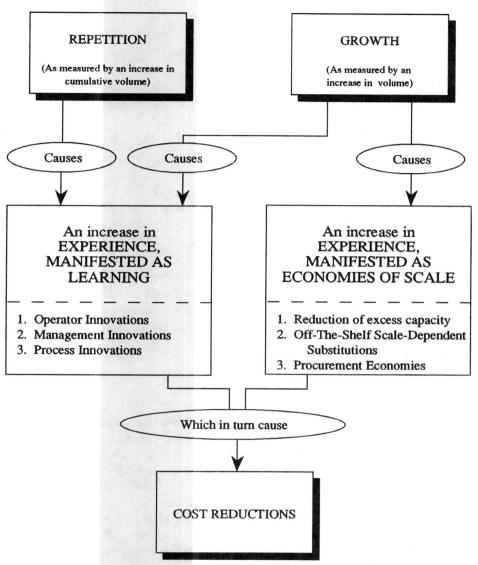

EXHIBIT 11.9 The classical view of production cost reductions: they arise from both learning and scale economics. (*Source:* Alberts, 1989, p. 40.)

that B cannot, may have a different proportion of value added than B, etc.); (6) begin at the right starting point choosing n and C_n in equation (11.1); (7) measure costs properly over a reasonably long-term time frame; (8) define properly the unit of analysis (a firm may have a large share of a small market yet have less experience than a competitor with a small share in a much

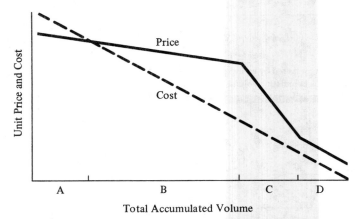

EXHIBIT 11.10   A typical price-cost relationship. (*Source:* The Boston Consulting Group, Inc., 1970, p. 21.)

larger market!); and (9) treat process innovation effects as separately budgeted effects. These and other practical considerations in developing and using the experience curve are discussed by Abell and Hammond (1979), Boston Consulting Group (1970), Hax and Majluf (1982), Day (1986), Day and Montgomery (1983), and Alberts (1989).

The experience curve concept is of strategic importance in business planning for many industries. In stable industries, where profit margins remain at a constant percentage of cost, the experience curve allows for long-range cost, price, and profit projections. Many situations are similar to the one illustrated in Exhibit 11.10. In phase A, costs exceed prices, as is often the case in a *start-up* situation. In phase B the market leader maintains a *price umbrella* over higher-cost producers entering the market, trading future market share for current profit. In phase C, the *shakeout period,* one producer begins lowering prices faster than costs, perhaps because of overcapacity. In phase D *stability* occurs when profit margins return to normal levels, following industry costs again. This illustration suggests the importance (as well as the risks) associated with a market-dominance strategy. While being the market leader and operating at a low-cost position are desirable, a shakeout period (phase C) can be precipitated in a market by aggressively pursuing market share.

In Chapter 4 we discussed the use of the experience curve in developing an optimal *monopoly*-pricing strategy. The more difficult question raised here suggests that informed strategic decisions in the face of experience curve cost declines require information about market growth, competitive costs, and likely competitive reaction. However, many of these considerations have yet to find their way into operational strategic marketing/planning models.

In conclusion, the experience curve cost declines, where they can be carefully *modeled* and *forecast,* provide an essential piece of information for informed business planning.

Marketing-Mix Analysis and Models

Throughout this book so far, we have dealt with individual elements of the marketing mix and have tried to show how contemporary developments have begun to deal with synergies. We deal with one form of synergy here: synergies within the marketing mix (marketing mix models); we have addressed synergies across products previously, in Chapter 5, and will revisit the issue later here as well.

In previous chapters we have dealt in detail with a number of marketing-mix interactions. Several key phenomena appear to pervade the marketing literature that should be considered in building marketing mix models:

1. *Marketing-mix elements interact in general.* Specifically, many models, either in multiplicative form or ones that explicitly include interactions, outperform those without interactions, in general. (See Weiss, 1968; Sexton, 1970; Wildt, 1974.)

2. *Advertising and price interact.* Depending on whether advertising is aimed at differentiating a product or in making consumers aware of the better deal associated with a similar product at a lower price, advertising may either increase or decrease price elasticity. (See Eskin and Baron, 1977; Prasad and Ring, 1976; Wittink, 1977; Sasieni, 1981; Farris and Albion, 1980; and, Krishnamurthi and Raj, 1988.)

3. *Responses vary over segments, purchase situations, and time.* Models dealing with response that varies by purchase situation (store, for example), by market segment and over time tend to outperform more aggregate models. (See Best and Hozier, 1980; Carpenter and Lehmann, 1985; Rao and Lilien, 1972; McCann, 1974; Moriarty, 1975.)

4. *Advertising and selling interact.* Advertising and selling are alternative communication mechanisms, with some overlapping functions— either can be used to inform or help generate awareness and to help move customers at least part-way to purchase.

This discussion suggests that a good marketing-mix model (one that incorporates the most important phenomena) should have the following properties: it should

1. Allow for interactions among marketing-mix elements in general
2. Permit advertising to increase or decrease price sensitivity
3. Permit price to increase or decrease advertising effectiveness

4. Permit positive or negative interactions among promotional vehicles

5. Permit varying effectiveness over time and across market segments

6. Incorporate advertising/selling interactions that are positive and that include order effects

7. Incorporate advertising and promotional effectiveness explicitly

These seemingly reasonable properties are not trivial for an operational marketing-mix model, as we will see. In addition, we add the following property:

8. A good marketing-mix model should incorporate competitive effects.

Descriptive Models of the (Industrial) Marketing Mix.   Our focus in this book has been primarily on normative or decision-making models. However, in the absence of clear analytical guidance or a good normative framework, decisions still get made, and we can learn a great deal from how they are made. When faced with developing an operating rule in a dynamic situation, managers often rely on guidelines, rules of thumb, and coefficients of industry behavior. There are at least two arguments to support this approach.

The first argument deals with the concept of shared experience. Managers dealing with similar problems over a period of time may develop some equilibrium behavior that appears to be reasonable. Bowman (1963) suggests that through experience managers learn what the critical variables are that affect their decisions and acquire reasonable implicit models of these problems. However, in a specific decision situation they may respond selectively to particular information clues and organizational pressures. Thus Bowman argues that experienced managers make good decisions on the average but may display considerable variance in behavior. Therefore managers' decisions could be improved by making them more consistent.

A second, related argument takes a Darwinian view of management practice: by and large, those products in place have survived, and therefore they are successfully managed. With this motivation we consider quantitative descriptions of marketing practice, specifically in the industrial marketing area. Two separate efforts have attempted to explain differences in marketing spending levels by studying a cross section of business situations: the ADVISOR models (Lilien, 1979, and Lilien and Weinstein, 1984) and PIMS-based models (Buzzell and Farris, 1976).

EXAMPLE _____

The ADVISOR Models (Lilien and Weinstein, 1984).   The ADVISOR studies were developed to identify and quantify those factors that determined the levels of spending for elements of the industrial marketing communications mix. An earlier study (ADVISOR 1, Lilien, 1978) established that such models should

1. Incorporate the effect of interactions between product characteristics

2. Allow product characteristics to reflect proportional changes in the marketing level

3. Check the form of the relationship between marketing spending and sales (Are marketing/sales or advertising/sales ratios constant?)

The level of advertising (or marketing) spending is dictated primarily by the size of the product (as measured by last year's sales) and by the number of customers the marketing effort must reach. That spending is then modified by such factors as stage in the life cycle of the product, customer concentration, and technical complexity of the product. Following these arguments, the models used to describe advertising and marketing spending both have the following log-linear structure:

$$B_t = \beta_0 \, S_{t-1}^{\beta_1} \, U_{t-1}^{\beta_2} \left(\prod_i C_{\mathrm{var}i}^{\beta_i} \right) \left(\prod_j \beta_j^{D_{\mathrm{var}j}} \right) \qquad \textbf{(11.4)}$$

where

B	=	marketing or advertising spending budget
S	=	sales dollars (prior year's values are included because they provided a somewhat better fit than contemporaneous values)
U	=	number of individuals the marketing program must reach
$C_{\mathrm{var}i}$	=	continuous, independent variable i, transformed to be greater than 1
$D_{\mathrm{var}j}$	=	$0-1$ indicator for discrete, independent variable j

Two things should be noted about this postulated log-linear form. First, the coefficient of sales (β_1) allows a test for constant returns to scale. Second, the model allows for interactions between the variables. Then a multiplicative error term of log-normal form permits the use of ordinary least squares on the logarithm of Equation (11.4).

Lilien (1979) provides justification and complete definitions for the variables included in the models. The Lilien and Weinstein (1984) study pools data from U.S. and European companies and finds that separate models are remarkably similar, justifying the pooling of data leading to the results in Exhibit 11.11.

In the sales row of this exhibit, we see that both advertising spending and marketing spending are strongly and positively related to sales. In addition, both coefficients are significantly less than one (both standard errors are in the 0.05 to 0.07 range). This means that both spending models exhibit decreasing returns to spending-level scale.

Independent Variable	Marketing Budget		Advertising Budget	
	Regression Coefficient	(*t* value)	Regression Coefficient	(*t* value)
Constant	-0.043	—	-0.111	—
Sales	0.706	(10.12)	0.553	(10.08)
Number of users	0.079	(3.58)	0.104	(3.45)
Customer concentration	-1.329	(3.43)	-1.871	(3.53)
Fraction of sales made to order	-0.792	(2.57)	-1.704	(3.65)
Prospect-customer attitude difference	-0.120	(0.84)	—	—
Proportion of direct sales	0.149	(0.55)	—	—
Stage in life cycle	-0.327	(2.19)	-0.845	(4.21)
Product plans	0.693	(4.37)	1.197	(4.24)
Product complexity	0.633	(4.14)	—	—
D (constant)*	—	—	-0.019	(2.83)
D (number of users)*	—	—	0.114	(1.92)
D (fraction of sales made to order)*	0.648	(1.68)	1.890	(2.81)
D (Product plans)*	—	—	-0.702	(1.66)
Adjusted R²	**0.72**		**0.53**	
Sample size	**187**		**184**	

* Variables are adjustments to individual coefficients in the pooled equation when the product is "European."

EXHIBIT 11.11   The results of the ADVISOR model for a pooled U.S./European sample. (*Source:* Lilien and Weinstein, 1984, p. 51.)

In the second row we see that with more users, more money is spent in marketing and advertising. The interpretation of the other coefficients is similar. Note that there are more significant, Europe-specific coefficients for advertising than for marketing spending in total, perhaps due to different communication consumption habits or different levels of availability in the two environments.

The models seem to fit well and give results that are readily interpretable. (See Lilien, 1979, 1983, for models of the advertising-to-marketing ratio, media selection, trade show use, distribution channel choice, and the dynamics of spending pattern changes.)

EXAMPLE

The PIMS/Buzzell-Farris Models.   Buzzell and Farris (1976) analyzed 386 businesses in the PIMS data base that were primarily industrial. They used four ratio measures of marketing expenditures as dependent variables: advertising and sales promotions to sales, advertising to sales, sales force to sales, and total marketing to sales. They divided their analysis into three broad product categories: capital goods, supplies, and raw materials and components. The models in the 1976 study used a linear regression equation to explain the ratios A/M, A/S, and so on. In later work, using better model forms and improved justification for their structure, Farris and Buzzell (1979) analyze a sample of 791 industrial businesses and use the logarithm of the ratio of advertising and promotion to sales as the dependent variable. Their results are shown in Exhibit 11.12.

In evaluating their results, the authors conclude that "In spite of some evidence for instability of a few regression coefficients, . . . the overall pattern seems to be one of consistent relationships across a wide variety of industrial business" (pp. 119–120).

How do these two studies with similar objectives compare? In evaluating these models, Galper (1979) reports:

> The descriptive analyses of total marketing communications expenditures that have recently been completed on the PIMS data base and under the ADVISOR project represent major contributions to the field. These studies have demonstrated that there are discernible underlying product, market, behavioral, and strategic characteristics that are related to the communications spending decisions of industrial marketers. Furthermore, the results of these two studies reinforce each other. Four of the eight significant variables determined in the ADVISOR model were found to be significant in the Buzzell and Farris models. More importantly, five out of six signs were also determined to be the same. In addition, the development of "guideline" models that permit marketing practitioners to calibrate their current spending practices is a valuable operational tool.   *(p. 9)*

A discussion of the differences and similarities between these two studies appears in a series of notes (Farris and Buzzell, 1980; Lilien, 1980).

These two models are different in their user orientation from most of the other models discussed in this book. While they can be used to generate a guideline ("general industry judgment") for spending levels for products not studied, they do not provide causal relationships. Marketing managers wish to know what they should spend, which may (or may not) be what others in similar situations spent in the past.

Two Consumer Models.   We now turn to two marketing mix models that are appropriate for consumer packaged goods: Little's (1975) BRANDAID model and Carpenter and Lehman's (1985) model.

Independent Variables	Regression Coefficients	Estimated Standard Deviations[*]
Produced to order (dummy variable) (x 10)[†]	- 3.59	(0.71)
Number of end users (scale) (x 100)	6.54	(3.07)
Purchase frequency (reverse scale) (x 10)	1.72	(0.26)
Purchase amount (scale) (x 10)	- 1.75	(0.26)
Importance of auxiliary services (scale) (x 10)	1.66	(0.46)
Percentage of sales direct to end users[‡] (x 1000)	- 5.15	(0.93)
Market share[‡] (x 1000)	- 7.26	(1.84)
Relative price[‡] (x 100)	1.47	(0.46)
Contribution margin on sales[‡] (x 100)	2.34	(0.27)
Percentage capacity utilized[‡] (x 1000)	- 7.12	(1.95)
Percentage sales from new products (x 1000)	7.19	(1.69)
Constant	- 1.77	(0.56)

$$R^2 = 0.416$$
$$N = 791$$
$$F = 50.44[§]$$

[*]All coefficients significant at the 0.05 level.

[†]For ease of reading the tables, coefficients have been multiplied by the noted numbers: either 10, 100, or 1000.

[‡]4-yr average.

[§]Significant at the 0.01 level.

EXHIBIT 11.12   Farris-Buzzell advertising-model results: regression analyses of cross-sectional variations in the logarithm of A and P/S ratios. (*Source:* Farris and Buzzell, 1979, p. 119.)

EXAMPLE

BRANDAID (Little, 1975) is a flexible marketing-mix model not linked to a specific data base. The model is different from other published efforts in that (1) its structure is generally inclusive (at the expense of

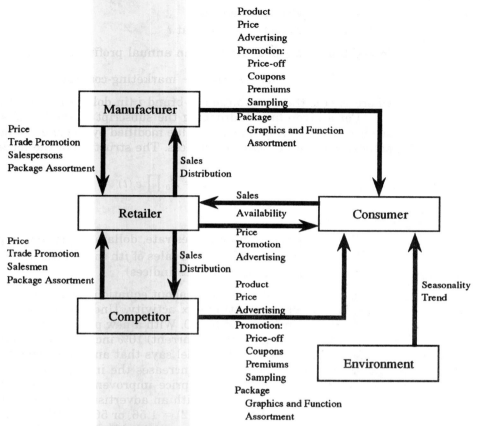

EXHIBIT 11.13   The BRANDAID view of the marketing system to be modeled. (*Source:* Little, 1975.)

leaving many parts of the model calibration to the manager) and (2) it is modular and flexible, providing specific, customized submodels that can be used or not used as desired.

Exhibit 11.13 shows the marketing system to be modeled. The elements are a manufacturer, competitive manufacturers, retailers, consumers, and the general environment. The model is clearly addressed at consumer packaged goods.

Model structure.   The model structure is based on the concept of a product class and sales rate:

$$m_i(t) = \frac{s_i(t)}{S(t)} = \text{market share of } i \text{ at } t \tag{11.5}$$

where

$$s_i(t) = \text{sales of brand } i \text{ at } t$$
$$S(t) = \text{product-class sales at } t$$

In addition, the model develops an annual profit rate, $z_i(t)$:

$$z_i(t) = g_i(t)s_i(t) - \text{marketing-cost rate} \qquad \textbf{(11.6)}$$

where $g_i(t)$ is the contribution of brand i (in dollars per sales unit).

For a given brand (dropping the subscript i), the brand sales rate $s(t)$ is expressed as a reference value modified by the effect of marketing activities and other sales influences. The structure of the model is

$$S(t) = S_0 \prod_{i=1}^{I} e_i(t) \qquad \textbf{(11.7)}$$

where

S_0 = reference-brand sales rate, dollars per customer per year

$e_i(t)$ = effect index in brand sales of jth sales influence, $i = 1, ..., I$
(I = number of sales indices)

Two points should be made about equation (11.7). First, each e_i refers to a different marketing-mix activity. Under reference conditions, the advertising index would be 1.0. With a new program that index might be changed to 1.1, indicating a (current) 10% increase due to advertising. Second, the structure of the model says that an improvement in the effect of one marketing variable increases the improvement that can be obtained from another. Thus a price improvement of 30% (relative to reference conditions) together with an advertising improvement of 20% yields an improvement of $(1.3)(1.2) = 1.56$, or 56%. Little points out that other degrees of interaction can be provided by adding effect indices that depend on more than one marketing activity. However, that would likely reduce the model's applicability and ease of use somewhat. The model can also be adjusted for geographic or other forms of market segmentation by providing different parameters and control variables for each segment.

The specific submodels are described next, in turn. In each case we drop the subscript i in $e_i(t)$ for the particular promotional activity because it will be clear from the context.

Advertising submodel. The advertising submodel starts with the brand's sales at a reference value and assumes that there exists some advertising rate that will maintain sales at that level. This rate is called the maintenance or reference advertising rate. When advertising is above reference, sales are assumed to increase; below reference, they decrease. Exhibit 11.14 shows the idea graphically. Steady-state sales at each advertising rate defines a curve of long-run sales response to advertising. Exhibit 11.15 plots $r(a)$, the set of asymptotes from Exhibit 11.14.

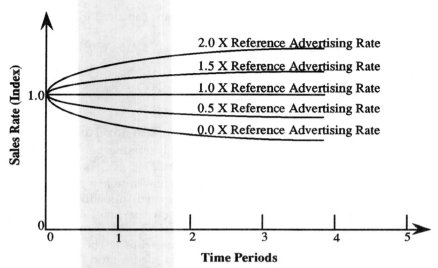

EXHIBIT 11.14   Sales response over time to different advertising rates (curves adapted from an application). (*Source:* Little, 1975).

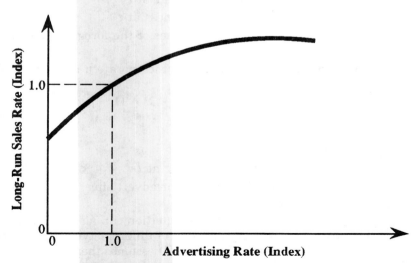

EXHIBIT 11.15   Long-run sales respond to advertising corresponding to Exhibit 11.14. (*Source:* Little, 1975.)

The dynamics of the process are captured in the following equation:

$$e(t) = \alpha[e(t - 1)] + (1 - \alpha)r(a(t)) \tag{11.8}$$

where

$e(t)$ = advertising-effect index
$r(a)$ = long-run sales response to advertising (index)
α = carryover effect of advertising per period

The value of α determines how quickly a long-run sales rate is reached; if $\alpha = 0$, this rate is reached immediately, but if $\alpha = 1$, it is never reached. When α depends on the level of advertising, it can be viewed as $\alpha(a)$.

Operationally, the advertising rate is the rate of messages delivered to individuals by exposure in media paid for in dollars. Thus,

$$a(t) = \frac{h(t)k(t)X(t)}{h_0 k_0 X_0} \tag{11.9}$$

where

$X(t)$ = advertising spending rate
$h(t)$ = media efficiency at t
$k(t)$ = copy effectiveness at t
X_0, h_0, k_0 = reference values of the foregoing quantities

The model can be customized to incorporate a memory effect,

$$\hat{a}(t) = \beta \hat{a}(t - 1) + (1 - \beta)a(t) \tag{11.10}$$

where

$\hat{a}(t)$ = effective advertising at t
β = memory constant for advertising (fraction per period)

The effective advertising equation can also be customized by making advertising a weighted sum of different types of advertising.

Price submodel.   BRANDAID assumes there will be an overall price effect, plus perhaps an effect due to price ending (where a jump from

\$0.97 per pound to \$0.99 per pound produces a smaller loss than the jump from \$0.99 to \$1.01). The price index submodel has the form

$$e(t) = r[a(t)]\psi[X(t)] \tag{11.11}$$

where

$$a(t) = \frac{X(t)}{X_0} = \text{relative price}$$

$X(t)$ $\quad= \text{manufacturer's brand price}$

$r(a)$ $\quad= \text{response function}$

$\psi(X)$ $\quad= \text{price-ending effect}$

Note that the price model includes a response function $r(a)$.

Sales force submodel. The sales force submodel is also structured in the form of a response function. Salesperson effort is defined as

$$a(t) = \frac{h(t)k(t)X(t)}{h_0 k_0 X_0} \tag{11.12}$$

where

$X(t)$ $= \text{salesperson-effort rate, dollars per customer per year}$

$h(t)$ $= \text{coverage efficiency, calls per dollar}$

$k(t)$ $= \text{effectiveness in store, effectiveness per call}$

$a(t)$ $= \text{index of normalized salesperson effort rate}$

To account for memory and carryover effects, we use $\hat{a}(t)$:

$$\hat{a}(t) = \beta\hat{a}(t-1) + (1-\beta)a(t) \tag{11.13}$$

where

$\hat{a}(t)$ $= \text{effective effort at } t$

β $\quad= \text{carryover constant (fraction per period)}$

Finally, the salesperson effect index includes a carryover (loyalty) constant α, as well as a response function:

$$e(t) = \alpha e(t-1) + (1-\alpha)r(\hat{a}(t)) \tag{11.14}$$

Other influences. Other influences, such as seasonality, trends, package changes, and the like, can be handled by direct indices. For example, trend can be treated as a growth rate. In this case a trend would be modeled as

$$e(t) = e_0 \prod_{\tau=1}^{t} [1 + r(\tau)] \qquad (11.15)$$

where $r(\tau)$ is growth rate in period τ. The promotion submodel was presented in Chapter 7.

Competition.   In BRANDAID, competition is handled in the same way as direct sales effects; each effect (competitive advertising, competitive pricing, etc.) goes into the model either as an index or as an additional submodel, depending on the level of detail available. Individual brands generate unadjusted incremental sales, while competitive interactions produce adjusted sales. Consider a brand b and a single sales influence (price, for example) for which

$$S'_b = S_{0b} \, e'_b \qquad (11.16)$$

where

$$\begin{aligned} S'_b &= \text{unadjusted sales} \\ S_{0b} &= \text{reference sales} \\ e'_b &= \text{unadjusted effect index} \end{aligned}$$

Let

γ_{bc} = fraction of brand c's unadjusted incremental sales that comes from b

Because brand c's unadjusted sales relative to reference are $S'_c - S_{0c}$, adjusted sales for b become

$$S_b = S'_b - \sum_{c \neq b} \gamma_{bc}(S'_c - S_{0b}) \qquad (11.17)$$

By dividing equation (11.17) through by S_{0b}, we get

$$e_b = e'_b - \sum_{c \neq b} \frac{S_{0c}}{S_{0b}} \gamma_{bc}(e'_c - 1) \qquad (11.18)$$

which can be used in the general multiplicative form (equation 11.18). Equation (11.18) can be generalized to conclude arbitrary sales influences, allowing a separate index for each influence. Without knowledge of market structure, a useful assumption is that a brand draws sales from competing brands in proportion to their sales. Thus,

$$\gamma_{bc} = \frac{S_{0b}(1 - \gamma_{cc})}{\displaystyle\sum_{c \neq b} S_{0c}} \tag{11.19}$$

where

$$\gamma_{cc} = 1 - \sum_{b \neq c} \gamma_{bc} \tag{11.20}$$

= fraction of unadjusted incremental sales of brand c coming from product-class sales gain

Use. "A model is not productive until people use it and take different actions because of it" (Little, 1975, p. 656). The implementation of BRANDAID can be viewed as the development of a decision support system for aiding brand management decisions. (See Chapter 12.) Little recommends a team approach to implementation; the ideal team involves an internal sponsor, a marketing manager, a models person on location, and a top-management umbrella. Implementation is viewed as passing through an introductory, then an ongoing period, following the guidelines in Chapter 12.

Calibration of the model involves two types of data: state date (reference values of sales, share, product-class sales, etc.) and response information. The former are easy to obtain; the latter require a creative blending of judgment, historical analysis, tracking (running the model on past data and getting managers to review the results and, if necessary, refine parameters), field experimentation, and adaptive control (the formal processes of using marketing activities to refine parameter estimates through an ongoing measurement process).

Little describes a case, called GROOVY, for a well-established brand of packaged goods sold through grocery stores. The model tracked sales well over a five-year period and has proved useful for advertising, pricing, and promotional planning. For example, by tracking months 72 to 78, analysis made it clear that year-to-date sales were good. However, since most of the year's advertising was spent, most of the promotional activity was over, and price had been increased, the prospects for the rest of the year were bleak. The brand manager used this analysis to support a request for additional promotional funds, a proposal accepted by management. This action is one that "almost certainly would not have been taken without the tracking and forecasting of the model."

BRANDAID provides a sound and usable approach to support marketing-mix decisions for frequently purchased packaged goods. The richness of its model structure calls for an eclectic blend of calibration procedures and, because of its blend of models, data bases, and software, should be viewed in the larger sense as a decision support system.

Nevertheless, because of the model's richness, it can be "overcalibrated"; in other words, different calibrations may provide equally good fits with different policy implications. Furthermore, it is a complicated structure that requires heavy involvement from the user, a potential barrier to implementation. In addition, it does not consider competitors as "active." Also, as with any marketing-mix model, it assumes that the firm's decision-making structure corresponds to the model structure. To the extent that pricing is a product-line decision and different model components are managed at different levels of the firm, the model will be of less use.

EXAMPLE

Carpenter and Lehmann (1985) develop what we have referred to as a "measurement" model of brand switching that incorporates marketing-mix variables (price and advertising), product features, and their interactions. The model considers aggregate brand switching as the movement of buyers from one product to another based on relative prices, advertising, and utility-yielding features of each alternative (brand, type, and form, for example).

They consider segment i (composed of persons who bought product i on the last purchase) facing a set of M out of N products and assume that for segment i, product j (in set M) yields utility u_{ij}, where utility is composed of a deterministic component (v_{ij}) and a random component (e_{ij}) so that

$$u_{ij} = v_{ij} + e_{ij} \qquad (11.21)$$

If e_{ij} is assumed to be distributed double exponential, the probability of switching between elements of M is given by

$$\pi_{ij} = \frac{e^{v_{ij}}}{\displaystyle\sum_{k \neq l \in M} e^{v_{kl}}} \qquad (11.22)$$

The deterministic component of the utility is given by

$$v_{ij} = \sum_{k \in C} \alpha_{ik} X_{ijk} + \sum_{l \in F} \beta_{il} W_{ijl} + \sum_{m \in C} \sum_{n \in F} \gamma_{imn}(X_{ijm} W_{ijn}) \qquad \textbf{(11.23)}$$

where

C	=	set of marketing mix or control variables
F	=	set of product features
X_{ijk}	=	value of alternative j relative to i on control variable k
W_{ijk}	=	value of j relative to i on product feature k
a_{ij}, β_{ik}, and γ_{ik_l}	=	weights for the kth control variable, product feature, and interaction, respectively

The authors use UPC scanner data to estimate two forms of the model: a restricted form where the effectiveness parameters (α_i, β_i, and γ_i) are assumed equal across brands and an unrestricted form where no restrictions are placed on the v_i's, which means N equations need to be estimated. They summarize their empirical results as follows (Carpenter and Lehmann, 1985, p. 326):

> Taken as a whole, the results for the unrestricted model suggest patterns of competition defined principally by product types, forms, and to a lesser extent brand names. Within each product type, stronger brand names restrict interbrand competition through increased intrabrand competition. Buyers are drawn to weaker brand names by price reductions. Patterns of competition for both product types are largely unaffected by advertising, though some significant effects are evident.

In building any marketing-mix model, especially one that includes competition, it is important to identify your competitors, the variables on which you compete, and the variables on which you can make your best response. Estimation of a model like this one can help here. The coefficients of the product-feature variables reveal groups of competing products. The marketing-mix coefficients describe the effectiveness of products' marketing policies in retaining or switching buyers, whereas marketing-mix/product-feature interactions reveal how marketing mix actions affect patterns of competition within and across groups of competitors. Note, however, that the model is a stimulus response model; your competitors are assumed not to respond to any activity on your part (although the levels of their marketing-mix variables will affect the efficacy of your policy). In addition, it is a measurement/descriptive model and needs an objective function to develop policy implications. Finally, it has been explored with only one data set and should be tested in other contexts and compared with other models.

Other marketing-mix models include those that are mainly decision support systems (Lambin, 1972a; Dutta and King, 1980; and Rao and Sabavala, 1981, for example), optimization models (Bensoussan, Bultez, and Naert, 1978, and Balachandran and Gensch, 1974, for example) and theoretical and measurement models aimed at understanding (Monahan, 1987, Moorthy, 1988, and Carpenter, 1987). Earlier chapters developed a number of marketing-mix-element models, some of which have incorporated competition, as well.

Competition

Substitutes exist for most products, and it is naive to assume that an investigation of marketing strategy can be performed without regard to competition. Until recently, marketing scientists have focused most of their attention on consumer response to marketing actions, with little regard to competitive response. Dolan (1981) presents an overview of approaches to competition from microeconomics and marketing, as well as empirical evidence about the type of competition from various industry studies.

Microeconomic Approaches.   In the monopoly and perfect-competition cases, microeconomic theory provides unambiguous results for optimal marketing-mix decisions. But for oligopoly, the problem of specifying competitors' behavior makes it difficult to determine what the optimal marketing mix should be. Singer (1968) points out that the models of oligopoly provide no single solution or strategy for a firm to follow.

The actual difficulty is that different assumptions about competition lead to different normative results. Chamberlain (1957) shows that, depending on the behavioral assumptions underlying a model of duopoly, price competition between two firms may lead to a price anywhere between the monopoly price and the perfectly competitive price. Or the price may perpetually oscillate.

Baumol (1972) agrees that consideration of the entire sequence of moves and countermoves by competitors is a problem that is hopelessly complex. Instead, he proposes one of two approaches: (1) ignore the interdependence or (2) assume each competitor is a rational economic agent and then determine, as a likely set of actions, those that will allow him to maximize this expected utility.

These two approaches are akin to the early work on *reaction-functions,* proposed by Cournot in 1838, and to *game-theory models.* The classical reaction-function hypothesis is that each seller assumes the output (action) of rival firms to be fixed and then sets price to determine profit-maximizing output. This approach leads to unrealistic results that are apparently nonoptimal (Mansfield, 1979; Scherer, 1980), although Green and Krieger (1991) claim this approach closely approximates actual market behavior.

Dolan (1981) points out that many in marketing seem to feel that game-theory models would solve many competitive issues if only some critical mathematical hurdles could be overcome. This is unlikely to be the case: game theory has "insuperable problems as a prescriptive theory of rational decisions in conflict situations (and) the prescriptive aspect of game theory ought to be written off" (Rapoport, 1966, pp. 202–203). A main problem is that game theoretical results are critically dependent on assumptions about the objectives, level of information, and analytical capabilities of *all* competitors, factors unlikely to be known by the decision-making firm. However, the models are quite important for gaining insight into market structure and operation as we have seen throughout this book (see especially Chapters 4–6). For recent assessments of the uses and limitations of game theory, see Aumann (1987) and Rubinstein (1991).

Empirical Evidence. One focus of research in the area of industrial organization is the nature of the structural variables that influence competitive behavior. The type and intensity of competition are attributed to eight major factors (Porter, 1980):

1. Number and size distribution of competitors
2. Industry growth rate
3. Cost structure and storage costs
4. Extent of product differentiation
5. Divisibility of capacity additions
6. Diversity of competitors
7. Importance of the market to firms
8. Heights of exit barriers

Dolan (1981) has examined a number of industry studies to determine the extent to which these structural variables determined the mode of competition. He summarizes his results in a set of four lessons:

1. High fixed costs promote competitive responses to share gain attempts.
2. Low storage costs reduce competitive reactions.
3. Growing primary demand reduces competitive reactions.
4. Large firms avoid price competition.

Exhibit 11.16 gives the details of the studies he compared. His observations suggest that structural dimensions of the market affect the likelihood of market response as well as the form of that response. These observations also suggest the major factors affecting response and show the need to incorporate the measurement and use of those factors in marketing models of competitive response. (See Carpenter, 1987; Gatignon, Anderson, and Helson, 1989;

Major Lesson	Interacting Factors	Industries Studied
High fixed costs promote competitive response to share gain attempts	Cost structure Number of firms Size distribution of firms	Steel Aluminum Coal
Low storage costs reduce competitive reactions	Cost structure Storage costs	Aluminum Rayon Airline
Growing primary demand reduces competitive reaction	Industry growth Product differentiation Number of firms	Cigarette Motorcycle
Large firms avoid price competition	Size distribution of firms Diversity in cost positions	Farm machinery Electrical equipment

EXHIBIT 11.16 Four comparisons of industry behavior. (*Source:* Dolan, 1981, p. 231.)

Gatignon and Robertson, 1989; Robinson, 1988b; and Karakaya and Stahl, 1989, for some empirical studies of entry barriers and competitive response.)

Marketing-Model Approaches. In Appendix C we suggest that the best way to model product sales is by decomposing a sales model (Q) into market demand (V) times market share (S). The best marketing models that incorporate competitive effects separate these two components of demand. Marketers have handled competitive behavior in three ways: (1) by ignoring it, (2) through the judgmental-model approach, and (3) through the reaction-matrix approach.

The *judgmental* approach to calibrating response functions is developed in Appendix D; its use for developing competitive-response estimates is less widely reported. Little (1975), as discussed earlier, uses this approach, and a case by Buzzell (1964), based on a model at Dupont, employs a probabilistic model of competitive response to find an optimal pricing strategy. In addition, the General Electric Company (1980) uses a pricing model based on deterministic judgments of the timing of a competitive response to a GE price move and the degree to which the competition follows the GE price move (degree is defined as percentage change in competitive price divided by percentage change in GE price). On the basis of these inputs, the model simulates marketing activity to determine the effect of price changes. Although not aimed at optimal decision making, the procedure provides a tool to answer "what if" questions about GE's pricing behavior.

The judgmental approach, while used in many firms, has not been sub-

Firm 2

$$P_2 \qquad A_2$$

	P_2	A_2
P_1	$\eta_{P_1 P_2}$	$\eta_{P_1 A_2}$
A_1	$\eta_{A_1 P_2}{}^\dagger$	$\eta_{A_1 A_2}$

Firm 1

$^\dagger \eta_{A_1 P_2}$ = percentage change in A_1 with a 1% change in P_2 .

EXHIBIT 11.17(a)   Reaction matrix: two firms, two marketing variables.

ject to rigorous empirical or theoretical testing in general. Most applications have been in the competitive-bidding area, characterized by price competition only and by little data analysis to infer the nature of competitive activity. (See Engelbrecht-Wiggans, 1980.)

An econometric approach to modeling competition uses *reaction matrices*. The reaction-matrix idea can be best understood with an example. Assume there are two competitors in the market, competing on price (P) and advertising (A). Their reaction matrix is shown in Exhibit 11.17. Under the assumption that these elasticities are constant and stable over time and that a multiplicative function is a reasonable representation of the structure of interaction, equations, such as (11.24a) and (11.24b), can be used to estimate the η in Exhibit 11.17(a).

$$\log P_1(t) = a_1 + b_1 \log P_2(t) + b_2 \log A_2(t) \tag{11.24a}$$

$$\log A_1(t) = a_2 + b_3 \log P_2(t) + b_4 \log A_2(t) \tag{11.24b}$$

Then b_1 is an estimate of η_{p_1, p_2}, b_2 is an estimate of $\eta_{A_1 P_2}$, and so on. A portion of the reaction matrix for the application reported in Lambin, Naert, and Bultez (1975) is reproduced in Exhibit 11.17(b). That exhibit shows that all di-

Firm 2

		Price	Advertising (Lagged)
Firm 1	Price	$0.664^\dagger$ (0.030)	$1.898^\dagger$ (0.825)
	Advertising	0.008 (0.005)	$0.273^\dagger$ (0.123)

$\dagger$ Significant at the 0.05 level

EXHIBIT 11.17(b)   Partial reaction-function example. (*Source:* Lambin, Naert, and Bultez, 1975, p. 119.)

agonal elements are significantly different from zero, signifying that firm 2 reacts directly to any change in the marketing mix of firm 1 (it changes price in response to a price change, for example). In addition, the lagged advertising-price elasticity is also significant, showing that indirect responses are important as well. This example shows that reaction behavior is complex, involving multiple responses and potential lags in time; therefore tracking direct responses could lead to mistaken inferences.

This approach has been used by Bensoussan, Bultez, and Naert (1978) to optimize marketing-mix decisions in a competitive environment. Lambin (1976) and Hanssens, Parsons, and Schultz (1990) report additional applications of the approach for assessing competitive behavior. Hanssens (1980) extends the basic model to explicitly represent multiple competitors and to develop interrelationships among the marketing elements within a particular firm, and Carpenter and colleagues (1988) show how to address markets where competitive effects are differentially and asymmetrically distributed.

Proponents of the reaction-matrix approach stress the need for incorporating managerial judgment here as well:

> The econometric measures should be regarded as reference values rather than as constants, given the instability of competitive behavior in most cases. The relevant reaction elasticities should then be obtained by subjective adjustment of the econometric estimates. *(Lambin, Naert, and Bultez, 1975, p. 127)*

Hanssens (1980) concurs, calling for the integration of three types of information: judgment, marketing and economic theory, and statistical procedures. One of the main contributions of the approach is the development of a tool to decompose sales elasticity:

$$\text{Sales elasticity} = \text{share effect} + \text{size effect} \qquad \textbf{(11.25a)}$$

$$\text{Share effect} = \text{direct effect} + \text{competitive-response effect} \qquad \textbf{(11.25b)}$$

$$\text{Size effect} = \text{direct effect} + \text{competitive-response effect} \qquad \textbf{(11.25c)}$$

This decomposition permits a more careful assessment of the firm's marketing-mix options as well as their direct and indirect effects.

An alternative method based on a conjoint analysis approach for estimating self- and cross-price elasticities within a conditional logit framework and based on conjoint analysis is called ELASTICON (Mahajan, Green, and Goldberg, 1982). This approach has seen some commercial popularity.

Modeling Pioneering Advantages.   We have introduced and developed many models of competition in previous chapters—price competition (Chapter 4), product positioning competition (Chapter 5), advertising competition (Chapter 6), and competition in distribution channels (Chapter 9). For additional reviews of competition in marketing models, see Eliashberg and Chatterjee (1985) or Rao (1990a).

An important, additional topic, critical for marketing strategy development, is the idea of market entry timing and the issues associated with market pioneering or first-mover advantages. Lieberman and Montgomery (1988) provide a fine, integrative review of the area, suggesting that first-mover advantages arise from three sources:

1. *Technological leadership,* either through experience curve effects via being further down the learning curve than competitors or via success in R&D or patent cases

2. *Preemption of scarce assets,* such as scarce raw materials, channels of distribution, superior product "positioning," shelf space, and the like

3. *Switching costs and buyer choice under uncertainty,* where late entrants have to invest more (provide lower prices or more value) to overcome the costs buyers see when switching or to overcome product performance uncertainty among (risk averse) buyers

Lilien and Yoon (1990) review the entry time literature and summarize its results in 11 propositions (Exhibit 11.18). Three papers that report on the empirical value of order of entry effects on market share are Robinson and Fornell (1985), Urban et al. (1986) and Parry and Bass (1990). Robinson and Fornell use the PIMS data base to show that pioneers, on average, had higher market shares than early followers. The early followers, in turn had higher market shares than late followers. They explain these effects by noting that early entry affects four factors: product quality, breadth of product line, product price, and product cost. After controlling for the pioneering advantage impact on those factors, they find *no* significant direct effect on market share.

Urban et al. (1986), in a study of 129 consumer packaged goods, found that entry order did have a significant effect on market share. However, their model did not include explanatory variables such as production cost and price advantages (although it did incorporate product positioning, advertising and time-log variables).

Parry and Bass (1990) use PIMS data to calibrate an econometric model, focusing on the issue of concentration as a surrogate for entry barriers. Their model shows significant effects due to pioneering, with the magnitude of the effects differing by industry type and end-user purchase amount.

EXAMPLE _____

Fershtman, Mahajan, and Muller (1990) Model. Fershtman, Mahajan, and Muller (1990) have attempted to study this problem with the following analytical model:

Qualitative Decisions: Pioneering or Following
[Advantages and Disadvantages of Pioneering]

PROPOSITION 1. *The pioneer sees the advantages of building reputation and capitalizing cost dynamics, but also sees the disadvantages of absorbing the risks and costs associated with product and market development* (Bain 1956; Abell and Hammond 1979; Lane and Wiggins 1981; Schmalensee 1982; Porter 1985; Robinson 1988a).

[Pioneering or Following and Market Performance]

PROPOSITION 2. *If a new product performs well, the pioneer is likely to see a larger market share than the followers who enter the market later* (Biggadike 1976; Bond and Lean 1977; Dillon et al. 1979; Whitten 1979; Urban et al. 1986).

PROPOSITION 3. *Followers are most successful when they develop superior products and support them with strong promotional spending and aggressive pricing* (Bond and Lean 1977; Whitten 1979; Urban et al. 1986).

Quantitative Decisions: When to Enter the Market?

1. Entry Time of the Pioneer

   [R&D Competition]

   PROPOSITION 4. *If a pioneer's market entry creates a new product class, entry too early may push an underdeveloped product into the marketplace; however, if entry is delayed too long, the firm may sacrifice the benefits of being first with a new product or technology* (Kamien and Schwartz 1972; Deshmukh and Chickte 1977).

   [Demand Potential]

   PROPOSITION 5. *Success or failure of the pioneer depends on the level of demand potential at the time of entry, a quantity that is not easily predicted correctly at an early stage of the product development* (Abell 1978; Bucknell 1982; Jones 1985).

2. Entry Time of a Follower

   [Entry Competition]

   PROPOSITION 6. *The earlier the entry of a follower, the better the performance of that product* (Yoon and Lilien 1985; Urban et al. 1986).

   PROPOSITION 7. *The entry-time decision of a follower is driven by how quickly and effectively the follower can overcome entry barriers* (Bain 1968; Porter 1985).

   [Market Evolution]

   PROPOSITION 8. *Early followers that enter the market in the introductory or growth stages are likely to obtain greater market performance than later entrants* (Biggadike 1976; Shaw and Shaw 1986).

   PROPOSITION 9. *Later entrants require special circumstances (e.g., rapid technological evolution) and resources (e.g., heavy marketing investments) to gain a jump on competition against earlier entrants* (Levitt 1965; Capon 1978; Schnaars 1986).

   [R&D and Product Competition]

   PROPOSITION 10. *If the quality of a follower's new product can be easily improved relative to that of existing products, then a delay of market entry may lead to a better market performance* (Cooper 1979; Kalish and Lilien 1986a; Meyer and Roberts 1986a; Lilien and Yoon 1989).

   [Marketing Competition]

   PROPOSITION 11. *The marketing effort required to introduce a new product into the marketplace depends on the stage of the life cycle at the time of market entry as well as the degree of familiarity customers have with the technology and the level of competitive responses* (Goldish 1982; More 1984; Robinson 1988b; Gatignon et al. 1989).

EXHIBIT 11.18   Propositions on market entry timing and competitive advantage. (*Source:* Lilien and Yoon, 1990, p. 574.)

Assume a two-firm market, with

$x(t)$, $y(t)$ = accumulated goodwill of firms 1 and 2, respectively

$\mu_i(t)$ = effective advertising level of firm i, $i = 1, 2$

$D_i(\mu_i)$ = cost of advertising effectiveness level μ_i

δ_i = goodwill depreciation rate of firm i

They posit that goodwill accumulates (via the Nerlove-Arrow, 1962, relationship) as

$$dx/dt = \mu_1(t) - \delta_1 x(t) \tag{11.26a}$$

$$dy/dt = \mu_2(t) - \delta_2 y(t) \tag{11.26b}$$

In equations (11.26) goodwill goes up with (effective) advertising and deteriorates at a firm-specific rate.

The sales of a firm are governed by a long-term component (goodwill) and a short-term component (price) as

$$S_1 = x^{d_1} y^{-\beta_1} b_1(p_1, p_2) \tag{11.27a}$$

$$S_2 = y^{d_2} x^{-\beta_2} b_2(p_1, p_2) \tag{11.27b}$$

where

b_i = short-term effect of brand 1 and 2 prices on the sales of brand i

p_i = price of brand i

The market share of brand i is $S_i/(S_1 + S_2)$. If $b_1 = b_2 = b$ and $\alpha_1 = \alpha_2 = \alpha$, $\beta_1 = \beta_2 = \beta$ (i.e., the brands are symmetric), then

$$\frac{S_1}{(S_1 + S_2)} = \frac{x^{\alpha+\beta}}{x^{\alpha+\beta} + y^{\alpha+\beta}} \tag{11.28}$$

or market share is the (weighted) goodwill share.

The (instantaneous) profit for each firm is

$$\Pi_i(p_1, p_2, x_1, y) = (p_i - c_i) S_i \tag{11.29}$$

where

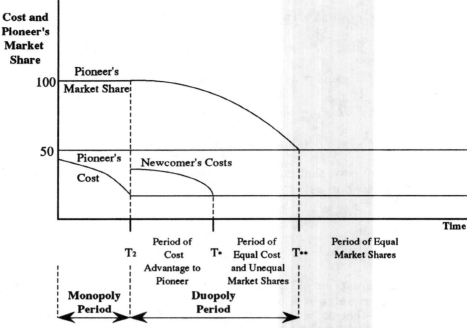

EXHIBIT 11.19 Several regimes of cost and market share in Fershtman, Mahajan, and Muller, 1990. (*Source:* Fershtman, Mahajan, and Muller, 1990, p. 905.)

c_i = production cost of firm i (which may change over time, but which is not linked formally to production experience)

Finally, each firm is assumed to maximize its payoff—its discounted net profits:

$$J_i = \int_0^\infty e^{-rt}\{\Pi_c(p_1, p_2, x, y) - D_i(\mu_i)\}\, dt \qquad \textbf{(11.30)}$$

where

r = discount rate

Exhibit 11.19 displays the (up to) four possible regimes that can be studied with the model: (1) the monopoly period, (2) the duopoly period when the pioneer has a cost advantage, (3) the duopoly period with unequal market shares but with no cost advantage, and (4) the period of equal market shares.

The authors show that, according to their model, none of the short-term advantages (due to advertising or production cost advantages) persist in the long run. In addition, price-elasticity differences or the length of the periods (regimes) in Exhibit 11.19 do not affect this result. The authors also study the forces that affect the speed of convergence to this equal-market-share equilibrium and show that it is stationary (does not vary with time) and unique under fairly general conditions.

However, if the market is finite (potential $= N$), equation (11.26a) might be replaced by

$$dx/dt = \mu_1(t)[N - x(t) - y(t)] \qquad \textbf{(11.31)}$$

In this case, long-term market shares depend on the amount of firm i's capitalization, the level of $x(t)$ when firm 2 enters.

The authors also show that a monopolist who does not anticipate entry tends to overcapitalize (in terms of advertising investment) relative to a firm that correctly anticipates entry. (This result is similar to one that Eliashberg and Jeuland (1986) derive for a pricing game.)

The interesting result of this paper is that it highlights what the sources of and the determinants of the persistence of a pioneering advantage might be under their model-based conditions. They also suggest that firms that do not properly understand these sources and their persistence properly may overinvest in R&D and advertising.

While their results do not hold in markets of fixed size, when there is technological evolution occurring or when goodwill is not homogeneous (i.e., when purchase gives more of a goodwill boost than advertising, say, or when there are multiple market segments), the paper does provide a valuable framework for studying the continuing problem of pioneering advantage. (See Urban and Kalyanaram, 1990, for an indication of the empirical importance of this nonhomogeneity and Lawless and Fisher, 1990, for a discussion of an alternative framework for studying competitive advantage.)

Analytical Approaches to Market-Strategy Development

A wide variety of tools are used in practice to support market strategy decisions. These approaches can roughly be classified as follows:

1. Shared-experience models (the PIMS approach)
2. Product-portfolio models
   a. Standardized
   b. Customized
   c. Financial
3. Normative-resource-allocation models

All these approaches, explicitly or implicitly, incorporate life-cycle analysis, experience curve effects, competition, and market-definition and market-structure effects. Each approach is discussed in turn in the paragraphs that follow.

The Shared-Experience Approach: PIMS.   The PIMS (profit impact of marketing strategy) project began in 1960 at General Electric as an intrafirm analysis of the relative profitability of its businesses. It is based on the concept that the pooled experiences from a diversity of successful and unsuccessful businesses will provide useful insights and guidance about the determinants of business profitability. The term "business" refers to a strategic business unit, which is an operating unit selling a distinct set of products to an identifiable group of customers in competition with a well-defined set of competitors. By the mid-1980s the data base of about 100 data items per business included about 3,000 businesses from about 450 participating firms.

Perhaps the most publicized use of the PIMS data is in the form of the PAR regression model, which relates return on investment (ROI = pretax income/average investment over four years of data) to a set of independent variables (Buzzell and Gale, 1987). Exhibit 11.20 presents that model for the entire PIMS data base.

The most widely cited (and frequently challenged) results of the PIMS studies are associated with market selection and strategic characteristics associated with profitability: Exhibit 11.21 summarizes some of those findings.

Firms participating in the PIMS program receive PAR reports for their business, which provides a comparison of the actual return on investment (ROI and ROS) of their business and the ROI and ROS (= pretax income/average sales over four years of data) that PIMS predicts for that business (based on its market and strategic characteristics). This type of analysis, showing the deviation of actual ROI from PAR ROI, yields insights into how well and why the business has met its strategic potential. Because PIMS has been the most widely publicized and widely supported source of cross-sectional information about business strategy, the results emerging from the program have undergone considerable scrutiny. These criticisms fall into three main categories: specification problems, measurement error, and interpretation. Most of these criticisms are summarized in Anderson and Paine (1978), Lubatkin and Pitts (1983, 1985), Chussil (1984), and Ramanujam and Venkatraman (1984).

In terms of *specification,* questions have been raised about the structure of the regression model—whether additive effects, multiplicative effects, interactions, multicollinearity, or heteroscedasticity exist. Furthermore, the use of ROI forces a short-term focus on strategy questions, and there is misspecification resulting from the presence of an investment term (investment intensity) among the independent variables, leading to a significant relationship with the dependent variable. In addition, the omission of business goals

Multiple Regression Equation for ROI and ROS
(Entire PIMS Database)

Profit Influences	Impact on:	
	ROI	ROS
Real market growth rate	0.18	0.04
Rate of price inflation	0.22	0.08
Purchase concentration	0.02**	N.S.
Unionization, %	-0.07	-0.03
Low purchase amount:		
Low importance	6.06	1.63
High importance	5.42	2.10
High purchase amount		
Low importance	-6.96	-2.58
High importance	-3.84	-1.11**
Exports-imports, %	0.06**	0.05
Customized products	-2.44	-1.77
Market share	0.34	0.14
Relative quality	0.11	0.05
New products, %	-0.12	-0.05
Marketing, % of sales	-0.52	-0.32
R&D, % of sales	-0.36	-0.22
Inventory, % of sales	-0.49	-2.09
Fixed capital intensity	-0.55	-2.10
Plant newness	0.07	0.05
Capacity utilization, %	0.31	0.10
Employee productivity	0.13	0.06
Vertical integration	0.26	0.18
FIFO inventory valuation	1.30*	0.62
R^2	.39	.31
F	58.3	45.1
Number of cases	2,314	2,314

Note: All coefficients, except those starred, are significant ($p < .01$).   ROI = Return on investment

   *Significance level between .01 and .05.   ROS = Return on sales

   **Significance level between .05 and .10.

EXHIBIT 11.20 The PIMS profitability equation (*Source:* Buzzell and Gale, 1987, p. 274.)

**Some market characteristics associated
with higher profitability**

- Market growth
- Early life cycle
- Higher inflation
- Few suppliers
- Small purchase levels
- Low unionization
- High exports/low imports

**Some strategic factors associated with
higher profitability**

- High market share
- Low relative costs
- High perceived quality
- Low capital intensity
- Intermediate level of vertical integration

EXHIBIT 11.21   Some general PIMS principles relating market selection, strategic
planning, and profitability. (*Source:* Buzzell and Gale, 1987.)

and the structure of the organization may be a problem, and the disguising
of sales data and other units only allows the modeling of operating ratios.
For some analyses this feature may lead to spurious relationships (See Lilien,
1979; Jacobson, 1990a, b; Buzzell, 1990; Boulding, 1990.)

In terms of *measurement error,* it is inevitable that different firms, with
different accounting methods, interpretations, and levels of understanding of
the data requirements, will provide noisy data. The potential significance of
this problem was underscored by Rurnelt and Wensley (1980), who report
little stability in market-share estimates when different measures were correlated over different time periods. These types of problems are inherent in
shared data; users of the results need to be made aware of the extent of the
possible problem.

Potentially the most serious problem is in the *interpretation.* The PIMS
results are norms; therefore the equations do not have a causal interpretation. High market share and high profit occur together. Although it is tempt-
ing to predict the consequences on profitability of changes in the independent
variables of the PAR model, it is not reasonable to do so. Lack of information
about goals and the extent to which certain strategies, exercised over time,
were able to achieve those goals make the problem more severe.

In conclusion, the PIMS models and data base provide an important empirical base and structure for asking intelligent questions about strategy. The results should be carefully considered but they should not be used as a substitute for informed judgment and analysis of specific situations.

Product-Portfolio Classification and Analysis Models. In the past two decades several product-portfolio models have come into common use. Following Wind (1981a), we classify these models as standardized models, customized models, and financial models. Some of the key dimensions of the major portfolio approaches are shown schematically in Exhibit 11.22. Wind, Mahajan, and Swire (1983), Aaker (1988), and Kerin, Mahajan, and Varadarajan (1990) provide detailed discussions of these models. We now discuss one from each category.

Standardized Models (Boston Consulting Group). Common to all standardized product-portfolio models is the recognition that the value of market position or market share depends on the structure of competition and the stage of the product life cycle. This recognition is consistent with our discussion of the importance of the product life cycle, the experience curve, and market structure in providing input into strategic decisions.

The earliest and most widely implemented standard approach is the growth-share matrix developed by the Boston Consulting Group (BCG). In this approach the company classifies all of its strategic business units (SBUs) in the business-portfolio matrix (also called the growth/share matrix), shown in Exhibit 11.23. There are several things to notice:

1. The vertical axis, the market-growth rate, shows the annualized rate at which the various markets in which each business unit is located are growing. Market growth is arbitrarily divided into high and low growth by a 10% growth line.

2. The horizontal axis, relative market share, shows the market share for each SBU relative to the share of the industry's largest competitor. Thus a relative market share of 0.4 means that the company's SBU stands at 40% of the leaders' share, and a relative market share of 2.0 means that the company's SBU is the leader and has twice the share of the next strongest company in the market. Relative market share gives more information about competitive standing than absolute market share; an absolute market share of 15% may or may not mean market leadership until we know the leader's share. The more SBUs with a relative market share greater than 1.5 that a company has, the more markets it is a leader in. The relative market share is drawn on a logarithmic scale.

3. The circles depict the growth-share standings of the company's various SBUs. The areas of the circles are proportional to the SBU's dollar sales.

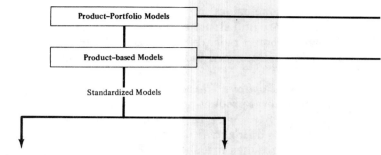

| Product–Portfolio Models |
| Product–based Models |

Standardized Models

Univariate Dimensions:

Boston Consulting Group's Growth–Share Matrix

		Relative M/S	
		H ◄——— L	
		H	L
Market Growth	H	"Star"	Problem child
	L	Cash cow	Dog

Composite Dimensions:

The McKinsey/GE Business–Assessment Array

		Industry Attractiveness		
		High	Medium	Low
Business Strengths	High	Investment and Growth (C)	Selective Growth (G)	Selectivity (Y)
	Medium	Selective Growth (G)	Selectivity (Y)	Harvest (R)
	Low	Selectivity (Y)	Harvest (R)	Harvest (R)

A.D. Little's Business–Profile Matrix

	Stage of Industry Maturity			
	Embryonic	Growth	Mature	Aging
Dominant				
Strong				
Competitive Position — Favorable				
Tentative				
Weak				

Shell International's Directional–Policy Matrix

		Prospects for Sector Profitability		
		Unattractive	Average	Attractive
Company's Competitive Capabilities	Weak	Disinvest	Phased Withdrawal / Custodial	Double or Quit
	Average	Phased Withdrawal	Growth	Try Harder
	Strong	Cash Generation	Growth / Leader	Leader

EXHIBIT 11.22 A classification of portfolio models. (*Source:* Wind , 1981a, pp. 220–221.)

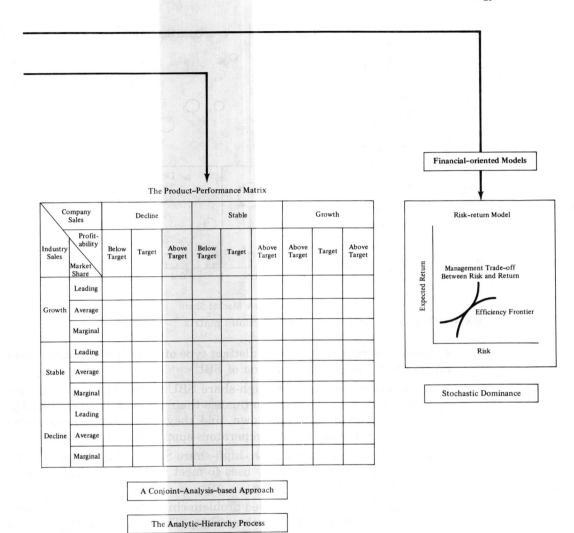

The Product–Performance Matrix

Company Sales		Decline			Stable			Growth		
Industry Sales	Profitability / Market Share	Below Target	Target	Above Target	Below Target	Target	Above Target	Above Target	Target	Above Target
Growth	Leading									
	Average									
	Marginal									
Stable	Leading									
	Average									
	Marginal									
Decline	Leading									
	Average									
	Marginal									

Financial–oriented Models

Risk-return Model

Management Trade-off Between Risk and Return

Efficiency Frontier

Expected Return

Risk

Stochastic Dominance

A Conjoint–Analysis–based Approach

The Analytic–Hierarchy Process

EXHIBIT 11.22   Continued

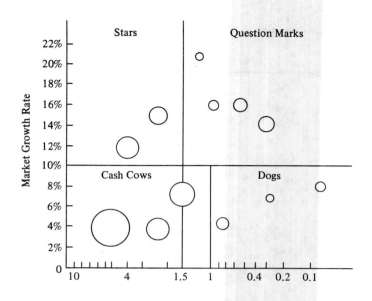

EXHIBIT 11.23   The BCG business-portfolio matrix.

4. Each quadrant represents a distinct type of cash flow situation, leading to the following classification of SBUs:

   a. *Stars* are high-growth, high-share SBUs. They often use cash because cash is necessary to finance their rapid growth. Eventually, their growth will slow down, and they will turn into cash cows and become major cash generators supporting other SBUs.

   b. *Cash cows* are low-growth, high-share SBUs. They throw off a lot of cash that the company uses to meet its bills and support other SBUs that are cash using.

   c. *Question marks* (also called problem children or wildcats) are low-share SBUs in high-growth markets. They require a lot of cash to maintain and increase their share. Management has to think hard about whether to spend more to build these question marks into leaders; if not, the question marks will have to be phased down or out.

   d. *Dogs* (also called cash traps) are low-grade, low-share SBUs. They may generate enough cash to maintain themselves but do not promise to be a large source of cash.

5. The higher an SBU's market share, the higher its cash-generating ability because higher market shares are accompanied by higher levels of profitability. On the other hand, the higher the market-growth rate,

the higher are the SBUs cash-using requirements for it to grow and maintain its share.

6. The distribution of the SBUs in the four quadrants of the business-portfolio matrix suggests the company's current state of health and desirable future strategic directions.

7. As time passes, SBUs will change their positions in the business-portfolio matrix. Many SBUs start out as question marks, move into the star category if they succeed, later become cash cows as market growth falls, and, finally, turn into dogs toward the end of their life cycle.

8. Management's job is to project a future matrix showing where each SBU is likely to be, assuming no change in its strategy. By comparing the current and future matrices, management can identify the major strategic issues facing the firm. The task of strategic planning is then to determine what role should be assigned to each SBU in the interest of efficient resource allocation. Four basic strategies are usually evaluated:

    a. *build*—improve market position and forgo short-term earnings to achieve this goal

    b. *hold*—preserve the market position

    c. *harvest*—get a short-term increase in cash flow regardless of the long-term effect

    d. *divest*—sell or liquidate the business because resources can be used better elsewhere.

The main concept behind the BCG approach is that of *cash balance*—that the long-run health of the corporation depends on some product generating cash (and profits) and others using the cash to support growth. Unless a company has an unusually favorable cash flow, it cannot afford to sponsor too many products with large cash appetites. On the other hand, if resources are spread too thin, the company may end up with a number of marginal businesses and reduced capacity to finance promising future opportunities.

In spite of their popularity, the BCG and other standardized approaches are limited by their attempt to boil down business strategy to the interplay of a small number of standardized dimensions, potentially ignoring important problems. The BCG approach gives market share (relative experience) and market growth (stage in the life cycle) fundamental positions in the development of strategy. But market division and market structure are difficult and often ill-defined quantities. Furthermore, the approach assumes that all competitors have the same overhead structures and experience curves and that position on the experience curve corresponds to market position. Also, the firm may have a number of other objectives besides cash flow balancing.

Wind, Mahajan and Swire (1983) studied the matrix positioning of 15 SBUs for a *Fortune* 500 firm and found that the same business could be classified as a dog, a cash cow, a star, or a question mark depending on the specific operational definition of the matrix dimension. Only 3 of the 15 businesses stayed in the same quadrant when alternative operational definitions of those dimensions were employed.

Thus, while standardized approaches are of value in helping to think about the problem, the use of only two or three dimensions, the lack of rules for portfolio formation, the lack of dimension weighting, and the lack of consideration of risk raise serious questions about the appropriateness of these approaches for more operational decisions. (See Wensley, 1982, for an interesting comparison of PIMS and BCG.)

Customized Approaches. In contrast to the standardized portfolio approaches, there are a series of customized approaches that do not prespecify dimensions or objectives.

The *product-performance-matrix* approach (Wind and Claycamp, 1976) allows management to choose specific dimensions. International Harvester used four: industry sales, product sales, market share, and profitability. In allocating resources, this approach follows that of BCG but is based on projected results in response to alternative marketing strategies.

Conjoint analysis (see Chapter 5) lets management select dimensions and their relative importance, combined in a utility function. On the basis of these functions together with product-performance data, any portfolio can be combined with another in terms of its overall performance. The approach has seen little application to date, perhaps because it is time consuming in application.

The *analytic-hierarchy process (AHP)* is another methodology for assessing and allocating resources in a portfolio. With the AHP, the analyst structures a problem hierarchically and then, through an associated measurement-and-decomposition process, determines the relative priorities consistent with overall objectives of all entities at the lowest level of the hierarchy. These priorities can then be used as guidelines in allocating resources among these entities.

The basic idea behind the AHP is that pairwise comparisons can be used to recover the relative weights (importance) of items or objects at any level of a hierarchy. Suppose that we have n objects, labeled $A_1, \ldots, A_n$ and that we know the vector of corresponding weights $w = (w_1, \ldots, w_n)$. We can then form a matrix of pairwise comparisons of weights:

$$A = \begin{matrix} & A_1 & \cdots & A_n \\ A_1 & \\ \vdots \\ A_n \end{matrix} \begin{bmatrix} \dfrac{w_1}{w_1} & \cdots & \dfrac{w_1}{w_n} \\ \dfrac{w_n}{w_1} & \cdots & \dfrac{w_n}{w_n} \end{bmatrix} \qquad (11.32)$$

We can recover the scale of weights $w_1, ..., w_n$ by multiplying A on the right by w and solving the eigenvalue problem:

$$Aw = \lambda w \tag{11.33}$$

Equation (11.33) has a nontrivial solution because $l = n$ is the largest eigenvalue of A. This result follows because A has unit rank and, therefore, one and only one nonzero eigenvalue:

$$\sum_{i=1}^{n} \lambda_i = \text{trace}(A) = n, \qquad \lambda_{\max} = n \tag{11.34}$$

In application, w_i/w_j are not known but must be estimated. Saaty and Vargas (1982) suggest comparing objects via a 9-point scale, where 1 signifies two activities that contribute equally to the attainment of an objective and 9 represents one activity having the highest possible priority over another. The reciprocal of the rating is then entered in the transpose position of A. The solution to equation (11.33), where $\lambda = \lambda_{\max}$, now gives an estimate of the weights.

EXAMPLE

This example is adapted from Wind and Saaty (1980, pp. 649–652). The AHP approach was used at the Colonial Penn Insurance Company to investigate whether the company should continue to focus its efforts only on insurance products or should diversify into other products and markets. Furthermore, given the firm's historical strength in a direct-mail operation, should they focus their operation on product and markets that can be reached effectively by mail or should they consider developing new distribution vehicles such as telephone, stores, and agents?

The AHP was used to help guide the selection of the desired target portfolio of products/markets and distribution outlets and direct the allocation of resources among the portfolio's components. A hierarchy was developed jointly with the company president and is presented (in a disguised form) in Exhibit 11.24. This hierarchy is based on three major levels:

1. Environmental scenarios are summarized as follows:

   a. an optimistic environment (low-risk and potentially high-return environment conditions)

   b. continuation of the status quo

   c. a pessimistic scenario (high-risk and potentially low-return environmental conditions)

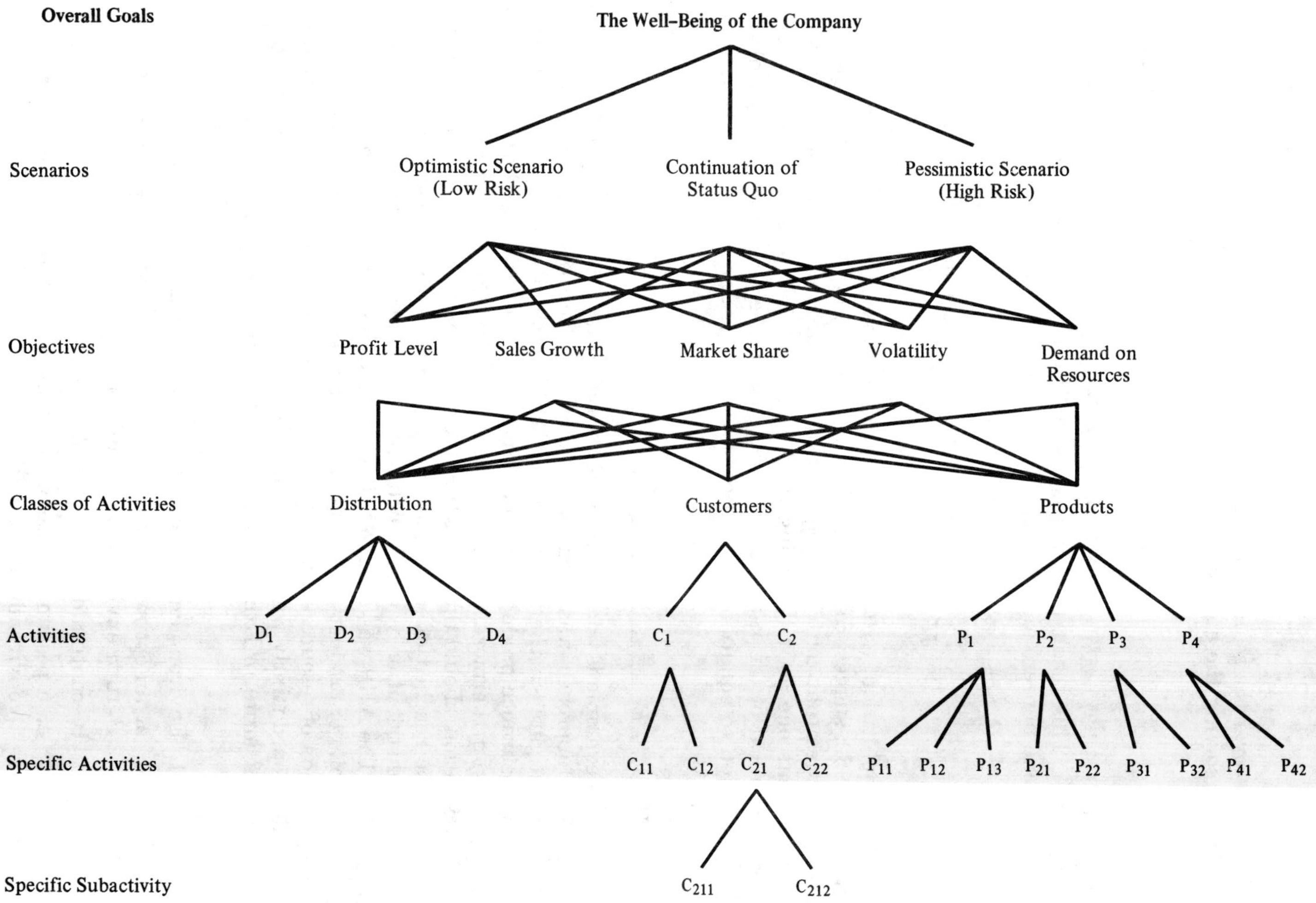

EXHIBIT 11.24 A disguised analytical hierarchy for the selection of a target product-market-distribution portfolio for Colonial Penn Insurance Company. (*Source:* Wind and Saaty, 1980, p. 650.)

	Products	Customers	Distribution
Products	1	$\frac{1}{3}$	$\frac{1}{5}$
Customers	3	1	$\frac{1}{4}$
Distribution	5	4	1

EXHIBIT 11.25   Pairwise-importance matrix example for profit objective

2. Corporate objectives are the criteria for the evaluation of the various courses of action. Five objectives are identified:

   a. profit level
   b. sales growth
   c. market share
   d. volatility
   e. demand on resources

3. The courses of activities include the three sets of products, markets, and distribution outlets that branch into a great number of specific potential activities, including various new distribution outlets not currently used by the firm, new market segments, and specific new product activities.

Having selected the hierarchical structure outlined in Exhibit 11.24, the president evaluated all pairwise comparisons by using the 9-point scale discussed earlier. These evaluations resulted in reciprocal matrices of the components of each level against the items in the level above. For example, consider the evaluation of the three major sets of activities against the objectives. This evaluation involved five matrices, one for each objective. (Exhibit 11.25 gives the matrix for the profit-level objective.)

In this case the president judged distribution to be of strong importance (5) over products in leading to the achievement of the firm's target profit level, but somewhat less important when compared to customers (4). Furthermore, he judged customers to be of weaker importance over products (3). The reciprocals of the three judgments were added, and the president continued with the pairwise-comparison tasks of other matrices. These tasks included the evaluation of the following:

scenarios against the overall objectives of the firm

objectives against each scenario

the classes of activities and subactivities against each of the objectives

the cross-impact evaluation of the likely occurrence and impact of

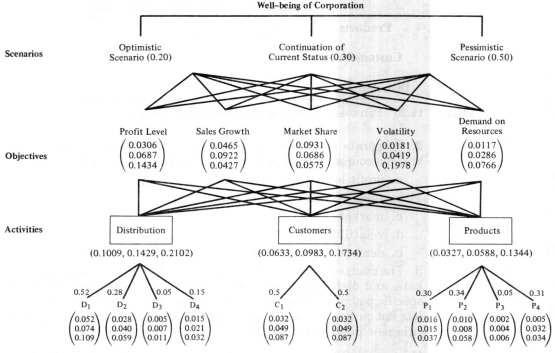

EXHIBIT 11.26 An analytical hierarchy of the products-customers-distribution portfolio at Colonial Penn Insurance. (*Source:* Wind and Saaty, 1980, p. 651.)

each component given each of the other components at the same level of the hierarchy.

These data provided the input to the eigenvalue analysis (Saaty and Vargas, 1982), and a resulting partial hierarchy is presented in Exhibit 11.26.

An examination of this exhibit reveals rules for allocating the firm's resources in developing products, markets, and distribution vehicles under three alternative scenarios. In the example presented in Exhibit 11.26, the president has a strong preference for the development of distribution outlets. In fact, the allocation of the developmental resources of the firm under this example should be 0.45 to (current and new) distribution outlets, 0.33 to (current and new) market segments, and 0.22 to (current and new) products. This rule suggests allocating resources in proportion to the priorities. (Other resource-allocation rules, such as the ratio of priorities or benefits to costs, can also be used.)

As this illustration shows, the AHP can be of aid in structuring and analyzing hierarchical problems in general and portfolio analysis problems in particular. It does not, however, provide either a sound rationale for or a reasonable alternative to allocating resources proportionally to their relative importance.

Financial Models. Financial portfolio analysis deals with investments in holdings of securities generally traced through financial markets. It typically takes as its objective the creation of an efficient (productive) portfolio—one that maximizes return for a given level of risk or minimizes risk for a specified level of return (see Van Horne, 1980, for example). In the model as applied to business portfolios, we assume management is able to assess the expected rate of return and the variance of that return, as well as the covariance between return for any pair of business.

Let

$$r_i \qquad = \text{(actual) annual return of product } i$$
$$E(r_i) \quad = \text{expected annual return of business } i$$
$$V(r_i) \quad = \text{variance of return for business } i$$
$$\qquad\quad = E[r_i - E(r_i)]^2$$
$$V(r_i r_j) = \text{covariance of return between product } i \text{ and product } j$$
$$\qquad\quad = E\{[r_i - E(r_i)][r_j - E(r_j)]\}$$

The fundamental theorem of portfolio analysis is that it is possible to select an investment subset that will yield a given return at less risk (variance) than the lowest risk of a single investment yielding that return.

To see this result, we consider n potential businesses to invest in and a vector of expected returns,

$$E(r_1), \ldots, E(r_n) \tag{11.35}$$

a vector of their relative shares of the total investment,

$$a_1, \ldots, a_n, \quad \text{where} \quad \Sigma a_i = 1 \tag{11.36}$$

a vector of the return variances,

$$V(r_1), \ldots, V(r_n) \tag{11.37}$$

and the matrix of covariances between the returns from all pairs of businesses,

$$\{V(r_i r_j)\}, \qquad i, j = 1, \ldots, n \tag{11.38}$$

With this information, the expected return and variance of any subset of m

businesses can be estimated, where $m < n$. The expected return from any portfolio is

$$E\left(\sum_{i=1}^{m} a_i r_i\right) = \sum_{i=1}^{m} a_i E(r_i) \tag{11.39}$$

and the variance (risk) associated with the portfolio is

$$V\left(\sum_{i=1}^{m} a_i r_i\right) = \sum_{i=1}^{m} a_i^2 V(r_i) + \sum_{i=1}^{m} \sum_{\substack{j=1 \\ i \neq j}}^{m} a_i a_j V(r_i r_j) \tag{11.40}$$

Equation (11.40) gives the key to the fundamental result found earlier, which we can see with the following example.

Consider two businesses with equal returns and equal risks but with returns not perfectly correlated, that is, $V(r_i r_j) < V(r_j)$. Then by equation (11.40),

$$V(a_1 r_1 + a_2 r_2) = a_1^2 V(r_1) + a_2^2 V(r_2) + 2a_1 a_2 V(r_1 r_2) \tag{11.41}$$

But we have assumed that $V(r_1) = V(r_2)$, so

$$V(a_1 r_1 + a_2 r_2) = (a_1^2 + a_2^2)V(r_1) + 2a_1 a_2 V(r_1 r_2) \tag{11.42}$$

We have also assumed $V(r_1 r_2) < V(r_1)$, so

$$(a_1^2 + a_2^2)V(r_1) + 2a_1 a_2 V(r_1 r_2) < (a_1^2 + a_2^2)V(r_1) + 2a_1 a_2 V(r_1) \tag{11.43}$$

The right side of equation (11.43) is $(a_1 + a_2)^2 V(r_1) = V(r_1)$ because $a_1 + a_2 = 1$. Thus,

$$V(a_1 r_1 + a_2 r_2) < V(r_1) = V(r_2) \tag{11.44}$$

This argument easily extends to n businesses.

Now assume the firm can find the minimum-risk portfolio for any specified return level. This can be done as follows:

Where $m = 3$, equations (11.40) and (11.41) imply that the isomean (constant-return) curves are a system of straight lines and the isovariance curves are a system of concentric ellipses of which the minimum variance corresponds to the center (Exhibit 11.27). For the specific return E_1, the least-risk portfolio corresponds to the point of tangency (A) with the lowest-value isovariance ellipse. This value defines the proportions of businesses 1 and 2 directly (i.e., a_1 and a_2), and through $\Sigma_{i=1}^{3} a_i = 1$, it defines the proportions of product 3. This portfolio has minimum risk corresponding to ellipse V_1.

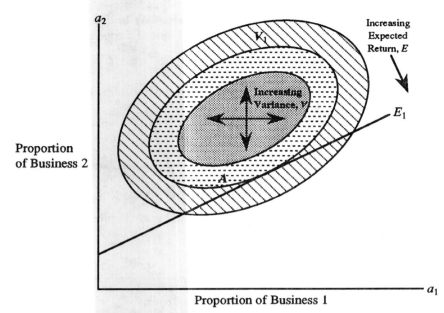

EXHIBIT 11.27 Isovariance return curves and the selection of the optimum two-business portfolio.

The set of all minimum-risk portfolios is called the *efficient set*. The shape of the efficient set is illustrated on the risk-return chart in Exhibit 11.28. It shows that higher-return portfolios are accompanied by proportionally higher risk.

The final question is which portfolio of products is the best one for the company to select? To answer this question, a company must determine its risk-return utility function and construct an indifference curve. The risk-return portfolio that maximizes management's utility is the one at the point of tangency of the efficient set and the risk-return indifference curve.

This procedure can be used when the expected-return variances and co-variances can be estimated, when they are stable over the planning horizon, and when the company's objectives can be reduced to a risk-return utility function.

This approach, while theoretically appealing, is somewhat inflexible and is apparently difficult to operationalize. (See Anderson, 1979, 1981, and Cardozo and Smith, 1983, for further development and discussion.) Cardozo and Wind (1980) show how the approach was used for one company. Recently, a more general approach has been proposed for product-portfolio analysis: the stochastic dominance approach. This approach provides greater flexibility than the mean-variance approach by not requiring specific information about the business's utility function and by considering the entire distribution of re-

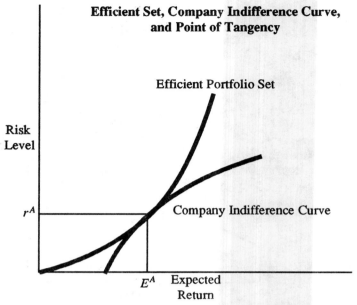

EXHIBIT 11.28   Efficient set of portfolios and company indifference curve for financial portfolio model.

turns. Mahajan, Wind, and Bradford (1982) and Mahajan and Wind (1985) discuss the approach and its potential application to business-portfolio analysis.

Normative Models.   There have been relatively few attempts to integrate business synergies, cost economies, marketing investment and financial considerations into an operational model. Larréché and Srinivasan's (1981, 1982) STRATPORT model is an exception. Its modules include

- An objective function, to maximize the sum of business-unit profits
- A set of business-unit-specific marketing-effort and experience curve cost relationships
- Investments in production capacity, working capital, and other costs
- A series of cash-flow balance equations to be sure the portfolio provides enough cash for the firm during the planning period. (These equations deal with discounting and tax rates as well.)

Given a specific portfolio strategy, the model can evaluate its profit implications and cash flow needs. In addition, STRATPORT has an optimization module to determine the allocation of resources among business units with the maximum net present value over the time horizon, subject to market-share and cash flow constraints. The cash flow constraint can be evaluated over ranges of borrowing activity, if desired. For details of the solution algorithm and an illustrative run of the model, see Larréché and Srinivasan (1981, 1982).

In the decade since it was first introduced, the STRATPORT approach has not seen reported applications. It may be that the model is simply too complex, requiring too much data and too much subjective model-calibration to show value. It is a rigorous attempt to deal with many product planning issues in a single model structure. However, it ignores competitive response and manufacturing synergies, two areas that are of increasing concern to business strategists.

Two other efforts that provide normative guidance for looking at the product-portfolio problem are those of Corstjens and Weinstein (1982) and of Choffray (1981). The Corstjens and Weinstein approach uses the risk-return concept and incorporates learning curve cost economies and a BCG-type matrix, center-of-gravity constraint to structure a portfolio. However, the model is static in nature and does not consider the dynamic complexities of marketing strategy addressed by STRATPORT. It has reportedly been used to evaluate portfolio strategies for a firm with ten strategic business units. Choffray's approach, based on risk decomposition, has been used to handle divestment as well as acquisition decisions.

Other Developments.   The general area of strategy, both from a theoretical and empirical perspective, has drawn considerable attention recently.

An area that is receiving increasing attention is what one might call "performance control"—how can we understand why our businesses are performing as they are and what actions can we take to get those businesses on target? Sharma and Achabal (1982) propose such a model and suggest that it be made an integral part of a firm's marketing information system.

Some other analytical approaches to general marketing strategy problems include those of McBride and Zufryden (1988), who suggest an integer programming approach for product line planning; Zoltners and Dodson (1983), who develop a market selection model for products seeing multiple end-use markets; and Coats (1983), who operationalizes the concept of differential advantage and builds the concept into a competitive strategy model.

On the empirical side, research like that of Capon, Farley, and Hoenig (1990) is beginning to derive some generalizations about the factors that drive financial performance. They used meta-analysis to synthesize the results from 320 studies and have found consistent findings for variables such as growth, market share, and capacity utilization affecting firm financial performance, but they were not able to develop generalizations about variables such as firm size and diversifications. They also note that company/organizational characteristics have been understudied.

For a contemporary view of strategy issues under current study, see the

October 1990 special issue on Strategy Research of *Management Science,* edited by Day, Farley, and Wind.

SUMMARY

An understanding of several basic phenomena in market planning strategy is developing, which is leading to important models in this area. Marketing planning loosely covers resource allocation among businesses under a firm's control. The objectives of the firm, the nature of the environment, and the development, evaluation, selection, and implementation of portfolios are the interrelated phases of the planning process.

Market strategy depends on the definition of a market and on the analysis of its structure. Markets should be defined via the set of products that are substitutes in use segments in which similar benefits are sought. A number of methods are available to define markets with either historical (use patterns or cross-elasticity data) or perceived similarity (judgmental) data.

The product life cycle is a key concept underlying strategy. Because of changes in a product's sales position and profitability over time and because of associated changes in price and advertising elasticity, the concept can be used in the selection of marketing actions and in planning. Although difficult to define and operationalize, the product life cycle provides a useful framework for organizing thinking about strategic alternatives.

The dynamics of cost—economies of scale and experience curve cost declines—are at the heart of modern business strategy. These concepts explain how declines in cost can be planned for, opening up important strategic opportunities and providing rationale for the relatively high profitability of high-market-share companies.

Marketing strategy requires an understanding of synergies, the interaction of marketing-mix elements for a single business, and the interactions across products or businesses.

And as more markets become saturated, strategy becomes almost synonymous with an understanding of the nature of competition, a field that will be at the forefront of developments in the marketing models area in years to come.

There are three classes of operational approaches to marketing-strategy development: the shared-experience approach, typified by the PIMS program; product-portfolio models, including standardized, customized, and financial approaches; and a few normative resource-allocation approaches. All these approaches make use of the life cycle, cost dynamics, and market-structure analysis and deal explicitly or implicitly with competition.

PROBLEMS

11.1. The manufacturer of a line of inexpensive watches determines that the demand for one of its products is represented by the following equation:

$$Q = 30,000P^{-2}A^{1/6}D^{1/3}$$

Unit cost for the product is estimated at \$8. What are the firm's optimal price, distribution, and advertising levels for this product?

11.2. A seller of inexpensive men's suits is currently selling one of the products in his line for \$70 while spending \$10,000 in advertising for this particular product. The sales and cost functions for this product can be expressed as

$$Q = 10,000 - 100P + 5A^{0.5}$$
$$C = 180,000 + 10Q + A$$

a. What are the seller's current sales and profits?

b. Are the current price and advertising-expenditure levels optimum? If not, what are the optimum levels?

11.3. The Chemco Corporation currently sells a commercial lubricant product at \$1.00 per quart and enjoys a current market share of approximately 30%. The company's major competitor sells a similar product of somewhat lower quality for \$0.90 per quart and holds a market share of approximately 65%. Chemco management is considering reducing the price of its product to \$0.90 in order to increase its market share. Without such a price change the company's market share is expected to remain unchanged in the coming period. If the price reduction is implemented, the competitor is expected to react in one of two ways: (1) it will maintain its price at \$0.90 with probability of 0.4, or (2) it will lower its price to \$0.81 with probability 0.6. If the competitor maintains its price at \$0.90, Chemco's market share will either increase to 40% with probability of 0.7 or to 50% with probability of 0.3. If the competitor reduces its price to \$0.81, Chemco's market share is expected to remain unchanged with probability of 0.8 or to decrease to 25% with probability of 0.2. Use decision-tree analysis to determine if Chemco management should implement the price reduction.

11.4. Draw the risk-return relationship for a product portfolio with the following characteristics. Product 1 has an expected return of 7.5 with a standard deviation of 3. Product 2 has an expected return of 15.7 with a standard deviation of 5, and there is a correlation of −0.7 between the two returns.

11.5. In analyzing its product mix, a firm has collected the following data. In the firm the sales effort is the only important marketing expense, and contribution is defined as the product contribution to selling expenses, overheads, and profit. (Fitzroy, 1976).

Product	Annual Sales (\$1,000s)	Market Share (%)	Sales Growth per Year (%)	Market Growth (%)	Product Contribution (\$1,000s)	Selling Effort (\$1,000s)	Assets Employed (\$1,000s)	Incremental Sales per \$1,000 Increase in Selling Effort (\$1,000)
1	37	45	24	25	6.7	5.5	168	10.1
2	75	32	3	−1	15.8	6.1	310	9.5
3	148	12	8	7	56.2	7.5	393	18.6
4	18	53	28	26	2.9	3.1	60	12.6
5	195	19	7	8	74.1	8.9	537	21.3

a. If the firm wanted to reduce its product line, which product would you eliminate and why?

b. Write an overall evaluation of the current product mix. Specify any additional data that may be required.

c. Assume that the firm has available an extra $6,000 of selling effort, which can be applied to any product. For any product, however, the minimum increment in selling effort is $2,000. How would you allocate this $6,000 across the product mix? On what assumptions is your recommendation based?

11.6. The experience-curve concept suggests that total costs decline with experience. The usual experience-curve form is exponential decline. Suggest behavioral assumptions and derive this result from those assumptions.

11.7. Consider a firm marketing a particular product. Let

$$
\begin{aligned}
\pi &= \text{profit rate, dollars per year} \\
p &= \text{price, dollars per unit} \\
c &= \text{incremental cost, dollars per unit} \\
x &= \text{advertising rate, dollars per year} \\
s &= s(p, x) = \text{sales rate, units per year} \\
c_0 &= \text{fixed-cost rate, dollars per year}
\end{aligned}
$$

a. State conditions on the derivatives of $s(p, x)$ such that it will be profitable to increase advertising. Do the same for price.

b. Let

$$
y = y(p, x) = -\frac{p}{s}\frac{ds}{dp} = \text{price elasticity of demand}
$$

What is the implication of $y < 1$?

c. Let

$$
\mu = \mu(p, x) = p\frac{ds}{dx} = \text{marginal revenue product of advertising}
$$

Show that under some circumstances the firm maximizes profit when it chooses p and x so that

$$
\mu = y
$$

What are those circumstances?

11.8. A large-appliance manufacturer, dissatisfied with its current market share, decides to increase its marketing effort substantially. As a result, the marketing budget is increased by 20% over a two-year period. What assumptions could be drawn under the following conditions?
  a. After a sufficient length of time, the company had increased its sales volume but not its market share.
  b. After a sufficient length of time, the company's market share had increased, but its sales volume was unchanged. In which of these cases does the increase in marketing effort appear to have had the greatest effect?
  c. Interpret the results in parts (a) and (b) in terms of the effects used in the reaction-matrix approach.

11.9. An experiment was performed by a local retailer in which the price of an item varied between 30¢ and 40¢ during eight weekly periods. During some of these periods an advertisement was also run. The sales of the product in each period are tabulated as follows:

Week	1	2	3	4	5	6	7	8
Price	30	40	30	40	30	40	30	40
Ad	Yes	No	Yes	No	No	Yes	No	Yes
Sales	7	7	9	5	1	13	3	11

What can you conclude about the sales response to the different prices?

11.10. An industrial-equipment manufacturer is trying to decide between making additional investments in advertising for its product or using this investment to improve product quality. At present it is spending about $4 (in units of $10,000) on advertising and nothing on the improvement of product quality. The relationship between profits and advertising has been determined as

$$Z(A) = 0.3 + 0.4A - 0.06A^2$$

where

$Z(A)$ = profits, units of $10,000 per period
A = advertising expenditures, units of $10,000 per period

Similarly, the effect of improvements in product quality is expressed as

$$Z(R) = 0.3R - 0.1R^2$$

where

R = expenditures on improvement in quality, units of $10,000 per period

The joint effect of these two variables is estimated as

$$Z(A, R) = Z(A) + Z(R) + 0.06AR$$

  a. Determine the amount the manufacturer should be spending on advertising and product-quality improvement, respectively, to obtain maximum profits.
  b. If the manufacturer can increase its total marketing budget to $7 (in units of $10,000), how should it be split between advertising and quality improvement?
  c. Determine the marginal profit on increasing the budget of $7 (in units of $10,000) by $1.

11.11. On the basis of an analysis of past data, a firm has developed the following market-share model:

$$\ln m_t = b_0 + b_1 \ln p_t + b_2 \ln a_t + b_3 \ln m_{t-1}$$

with $b_1 = -2.85$; $b_2 = 0.356$, and where

m_t = level of market share at time t
p_t = price level at time t
a_t = advertising share at time t

a. If total industry demand and total industry advertising can be assumed constant, show that

$$\frac{\partial m}{\partial a} = b_2 \frac{m}{a}$$

b. Sales of the firm have averaged 156,000 units per year at an average selling price of $8.95, and its current market share is 15%. The firm's average advertising expenditures have been $426,000 per year, with total industry advertising of $2,130,000. Past analysis has indicated an advertising retention rate of 0.6. The cost of capital for the firm is 12%. Investigate the short-term and long-term profitability of advertising.

11.12. The Delicious Donut Store faces the following planning problem: it would like to be able to tell its individual franchise dealers how its sales are related to pricing variation. Products are denoted by i, where $i = 1$ might be donuts, $i = 2$ might be coffee, $i = 3$ might be minidonuts, and so on. Assume the following, for a product i:

Product effect. Sales of i are affected by the difference between the price of i at t [$P_i(t)$] and the expected price at t [$\tilde{P}_i(t)$], perhaps as projected from past history. If $P_i(t) = \tilde{P}_i(t)$, sales are as projected by a linear trend. Sales go up when $P_i(t) < \tilde{P}_i(t)$, and vice versa. Sales have upper and lower bounds.

Cross-line effect. Sales of i are affected by the difference between the prices of products other than i and the expected price of those products. (A volume-weighted average of prices for products other than i may be relevant here.) If the price of products other than i increases, sales decrease. Again, sales are bounded above and below.

Competitive effect. Sales of product i are affected by changes in the difference between Delicious' price for the product and the (volume) weighted, average market price for the product, $Q_i(t)$. As the difference $P_i(t) - Q_i(t)$ increases from its normal amount, sales decrease, and vice versa. Sales again are bounded above and below.

a. Formulate a mathematical model relating sales to each of the foregoing effects for a particular product. Try to use no more than three parameters per effect. Graph the expected form, given the function you used.

b. Put the models together in an additive form and in a multiplicative form for the joint effects.

c. From part (b) for each of, say, three products (coffee, donuts, other), what parameters of the model need to be estimated? Suggest a method of estimation.

d. Assuming the parameters of your model are known, as is whatever competitive information you need, use your model to develop an expression for outlet profit per period. Solve the model for optimal product prices. What assumptions have you made? What additional data did you need to assume was available?

11.13. We hear much from industrial advertising practitioners about their rules of thumb for budgeting advertising. It is of interest to find some situations under which it is optimal to budget a constant percentage of sales for advertising. Consider a monopoly model. Let profit Z be

$$Z = PQ(A, P) - C[Q(A, P)] - AT$$

where

$$
\begin{aligned}
Q &= \text{quantity sold, a function of } A \text{ and } P \\
A &= \text{number of advertising messages bought by firm} \\
P &= \text{prevailing price of product} \\
C &= \text{total production cost} \\
T &= \text{cost per ad message}
\end{aligned}
$$

a. Set the first derivative of Z with respect to A equal to 0.
b. Let a be the elasticity of demand with respect to advertising, and

$$a = \frac{\partial Q / \partial A}{Q / A}$$

Substitute this equation into the result from part (a) and solve for AT/PQ (the advertising-to-sales ratio). Interpret the result.
c. Refer to part (a). Differentiate the relationship with respect to P, set the derivative equal to 0 and obtain the condition for monopoly pricing,

$$\frac{P - \partial C / \partial Q}{P} = ?$$

letting $e = -(\partial Q / \partial P)(Q / P) = $ price elasticity of demand.
d. Substitute the result in part (c) into the result you got from part (b). What does it say about the ratio of dollar advertising to dollar sales if a and e are constant? What if the price of ad message changes?

11.14. Generalize Problem 11.13 a little. Let $Q = Q(A, \bar{A}, P)$, where

$$\bar{A} = \text{number of messages purchased by competitors}$$

Then

$$Z = PQ(A, \bar{A}, P) - C[Q(A, \bar{A}, P)] - AT$$

a. Set the derivative of Z with respect to A equal to 0 and solve for T. What does the relationship say?
b. Let

a = elasticity of Q with respect to A

$\bar{a}$ = elasticity of Q with respect to $\bar{A}$

η = elasticity of $\bar{A}$ with respect to A

Resolve part (a) for AT/PQ. What conditions must hold now for the optimal ratio of dollar sales to dollar advertising to be constant?

c. Under what conditions will profit as a percentage of sales (Z/PQ) rise with P?

12 | DECISION SUPPORT AND IMPLEMENTATION

The main purpose of this book has been to organize and synthesize the theory and associated models relevant for marketing decision making. In this chapter we focus on the introduction and use of those developments in an organizational setting. First, we trace some of the data, software, and hardware trends that have been revolutionizing the way marketers interact with their environment. Then we review some of the more recent findings and guidelines for successful implementation of marketing models.

THE EVOLUTION OF BUSINESS SYSTEMS

If the 1980s will be remembered as the age of information availability, the 1990s will be remembered as the age of information explosion. Roughly speaking, the evolution of business systems can be traced through five stages: transaction-based systems (TBS), data-based systems (DBS, or data-based management systems, DBMS), management information systems (MIS), decision support systems (DSS), and intelligent marketing systems (IMS). Of these five system types, four are application systems that directly relate to business functions, while the other, DBS, is designed to support and improve the performance of application systems by providing better storage, maintenance, and access to data.

Transaction-Based Systems. Dating from the late 1950s and early 1960s, transaction-based systems represent the earliest use of computers in business applications. Their functions are to collect and report data generated by business transactions in standard business functions, such as accounting, finance, and marketing. TBSs, such as accounting and reporting programs, production-control programs, sales-reporting programs, and the like, emphasize essentially clerical activities and are aimed toward automating the storage and retrieval of regularly generated data. The focus is on reducing costs, improving accuracy, and allowing quicker access to data concerning day-to-day operations. The output of these systems is usually a set of standard reports produced on a periodic basis. The systems are usually expensive to design and must be extensively redesigned when there are major changes in transaction patterns.

Management Information Systems. After the introduction of DBSs for coordinating disparate files of transaction data, MISs were developed to facilitate management use of the diverse sets of data. Their purpose is to process data into information for more complete use of multiple data sources within the same firm. MISs represent an evolution from TBS, more because of the way data from diverse sources can be processed than because of the way reporting occurs. Examples of MISs include financial-control systems, material-requirements planning systems, and the like. As with TBSs, the system must be extensively redesigned if the DBS changes or if management's information needs change.

DECISION SUPPORT SYSTEMS

DSSs emphasize ad hoc use and flexibility in facilitating line-management, planning, and staff functions. In contrast to TBSs, which activate and facilitate data storage, DSSs aim to improve and expedite the processes by which people make and communicate decisions. Thus the emphasis in DSSs is on increasing individual and organizational effectiveness rather than improving data processing effectiveness. As the "state-of-the-art" systems of the 1980s, we elaborate on them here.

Little (1979a) calls a marketing decision support system (MDSS)

> a coordinated collection of data, systems, tools and techniques with supporting software and hardware by which an organization gathers and interprets relevant information from business and environment and turns it into a basis for marketing action. *(p. 11)*

In his view a manager uses an MDSS to learn about the business environment and to take action with respect to it. Little's artistic view of the inanimate part of this process is reproduced in Exhibit 12.1. This process has

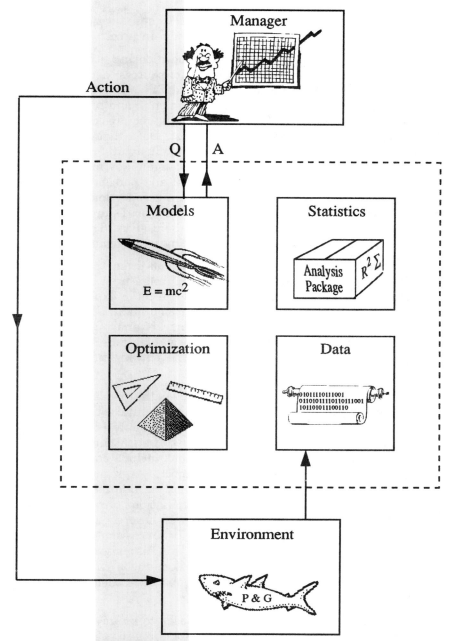

EXHIBIT 12.1   A manager uses a marketing decision support system to learn about the business environment and take action with respect to it. (*Source:* Little, 1979a, p. 10).

five components: data, models, statistics, optimization, and Q/A (communication with the system). We review them in turn.

Data. Organizations face an often bewildering stream of data and information, which arises from a number of sources: personal contacts, business publications, and marketing research data, as well as the multitude of business transactions, such as orders, shipments, and records of internal actions (advertising expenditures). Decision making requires certain information, which either may or may not currently exist. Data that already exist are called *secondary* data, while data that the firm must gather are called *primary* data. An MDSS must capture and make accessible key marketing variables, such as sales, price, advertising, promotion, and perceptual/attitudinal information, in sufficient detail and in readily accessible form. Few companies do an adequate data-collection-and-maintenance job. Data are often costly to collect and maintain and are worthless by themselves. The other elements of the MDSS and the interface with marketing management create the value.

Models. The main focus of this book has been the second element of the MDSS, the set of models. Models can range from a way of looking at and structuring data (implicit models) to the more explicit models discussed in this book. Models aid in planning, decision making, and a range of less publicized supporting tasks required for market analysis and understanding. We believe that explicit models are more valuable because of their direct relationship with data, statistics, and the optimization/policy-evaluation elements in the MDSS.

Statistics. Statistics is the process of relating models to data. Statistical operations range from the simple (addition, subtraction, etc.) to the most sophisticated multivariate techniques (factor analysis, nonlinear parameter estimation, etc.). In the DSS the simpler statistical functions are frequently the most useful. Simple statistical functions include adding (making significant figures from many smaller, trivial numbers), segregating numbers into groups, taking ratios, making comparisons, plotting relationships, identifying exceptional cases, and the like. These manipulations provide the basic information needed for many of the models reviewed here, as well as for the production of standard managerial models, such as forecasting and budgeting, pro forma profit and loss and balance sheets. This discussion should not be taken to minimize the importance of statistical methods but rather to point out the importance of the accessibility of simple, more basic statistical operations in the normal course of decision making.

Optimization. The decision maker seeks to improve the operation of his organization. The model-based method for doing so is loosely called optimization or policy evaluation. The most frequently used approach to optimization is case analysis, in which different numbers are calculated and compared. As the problem becomes more complicated, ranking a series of numbers may be required. Finally, as discussed in Appendix A, there are many cases where the more formal analytical-optimization and mathematical programming techniques of management science become appropriate.

Q/A. The last and in many ways the most critical element in the DSS is the user interface. The manager and his staff must communicate with the system. The right software (programs), interfaces (terminals or PC's), data files, and other information can be used in ways that are highly effective. The increasing speed and decreasing cost of computation are pushing the frontier of DSS application. Hardware costs are plummeting, and a revolution in software is making MDSSs accessible to an increasingly wide range of users.

EXAMPLE

The Marketing Manager, The Management Scientist, and the MBA (Little, 1979a, pp. 11–12).   Once upon a time (1973), an MBA student took a summer job with a large food manufacturer. He reported to a management scientist in the principal division of the company and was assigned to enter key marketing information, basically store audit data, on a time-shared computer. The goal was an easy-to-use retrieval system, essentially the DATA box of Exhibit 12.1.

OK. He did this.

By the end of the summer, word of the system had reached the marketing manager of the division's major product, who asked for a demonstration, and so the three met. The student and the management scientist showed the marketing manager how simple, conversational commands could retrieve data items, such as sales, share, price, distribution level, and so on, by brand, package size, and month.

The marketing manager was impressed. "You must be fantastically smart," he told the MBA. "The people downstairs in MIS have been trying to do this for years, and they haven't gotten anywhere. You did it in a summer."

It was hard for the MBA to reject this assessment out of hand, but he did acknowledge, and this is a key point, that the software world had changed. There are now high-level analytic languages available on time-sharing that facilitate data retrieval and processing.

The MBA and the management scientist, flushed with success, now said to the marketing manager, "OK. Ask us anything!" (Famous last words.) The marketing manager thought a minute and said, "I'd like to know how much the competition's introduction of a 40-oz package in Los Angeles cut into the sales of our 16-oz package."

The MBA and the management scientist looked at each other in dismay. What they realized right away is that there isn't going to be any number in the machine for sales that didn't occur. This isn't a retrieval question at all, it's an analysis question.

Here then is another point. The marketing manager had no idea the number would not be in the machine. To him, it was just a fact no different from other facts about the market. Notice also that the question is a reasonable one. One can visualize a whole string of managerial decisions that might be triggered by the answer, possibly even culminating in the introduction of a new package by the company.

What is needed to answer the question is a model—probably a rather simple model. For example, one might extrapolate previous share and use it to estimate the sales that would have happened without the competitor's introduction. Then subtraction of actual sales would give the loss.

The three discussed possible assumptions for a few minutes and agreed on how to approach the problem. Then the management scientist typed in one line of high-level commands. Out came the result, expressed in dollars, cases, and share points.

The marketing manager thought the answer was fine, a good demonstration. The MBA student and the management scientist thought it was a miracle! They had responded to the question with speed and accuracy unthinkable a few months earlier.

The story is simple, but it contains several important lessons. The same points come up again and again in various organizations, although not always so neatly and concisely:

Managers ask for analysis, not retrieval. Sometimes retrieval questions come up, of course, but most often the answers to important questions require nontrivial manipulation of stored data. Knowing this tells us much about the kind of software required for an MDSS. For example, a data-based management system is not enough.

Good data are vital. If you haven't done your homework and put key data on the system, you are nowhere. Thus a powerful analytical language alone is not enough.

You need models. These are often simple, but not always. Some can be prepackaged. Many are ad hoc.

The management scientist is an intermediary. He connects the manager to the MDSS. The manager does not use the system directly. The management scientist interprets questions and formulates problems in cooperation with the manager and then creates models and uses them to answer the questions and analyze issues.

Speed is important. If you can answer people's questions right away, you will affect their thinking. If you cannot, they will make their decisions without you and go on to something else.

Muscular software cuts out programmers. New high-level languages on time-sharing permit a management scientist or recently trained MBA to bring up systems and do analyses single-handedly for efficient problem solving. Furthermore, the problem solver identifies and deals

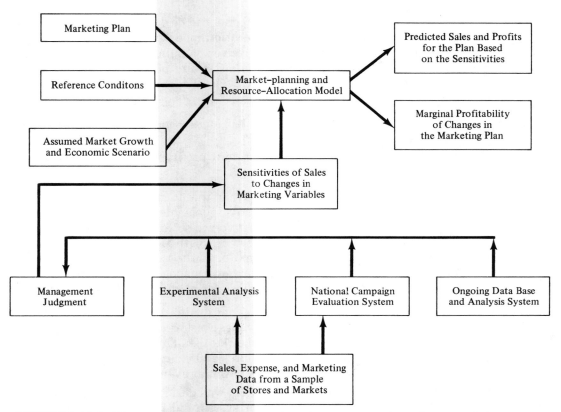

EXHIBIT 12.2 The retailing decision support system: an overview. (*Source:* Lodish, 1981, p. 171.)

directly with **marketing** management so that his understanding and motivation are high. Time-sharing costs more than batch processing, but an army of **programmers** is eliminated, and, far more importantly, problems get solved on time.

EXAMPLE

A Retailing Decision Support System. Lodish (1981) describes a decision-support system designed and developed over a period of a year to help the manager of a large mass retailer improve its marketing planning activities. Exhibit 12.2 outlines the structure of the decision support system.

The evolution of the system provides insight into successful MDSS development. The first system component to be developed was the yearly market-planning and resource-allocation model, which inputs reference conditions, marketing-plan alternatives, assumed market-growth and economic scenarios, and managerial estimates of the sensitivity of sales to changes in marketing variables. The system provides two types of output:

1. Sales and profits anticipated for the marketing plan based on the system inputs

2. An evaluation of the marginal profitability of changes in the marketing plan

It was designed to run modularly so that it could produce analyses for a department or group of departments independently or in the aggregate or for different subgroups of stores involved separately or together.

As management gained experience with the system, it found that it was not as confident of its estimates of the response elasticities as it would have liked to have been. Therefore, management added three other components to the system as methods for evaluating these elasticities:

1. A national campaign and event evaluation system was designed to estimate the sales effectiveness of large national campaigns or events seen periodically by the retailer. This system takes internal sales data from a sample of stores and examines the promoted items before, during, and after the national event.

2. A market experiment system was designed to be used when the national campaign and event system did not provide high-quality estimates of sensitivities. Typically, the sample of stores used here is specific to the design of the particular experiment being conducted.

3. An interactive data base and analysis system was developed to provide managers with a continuous picture of how well the marketing activities were doing. The data base is a nationally representative sample of stores, used to track the effectiveness of past decisions, providing rapid response to ad hoc managerial questions and acting as a general working system for identifying problems early.

The system has proved to be an important tool for assessing and improving company profitability. The result of one experiment provided an estimate of incremental sales per $1,000 of TV expenditures as $11,700 versus $4,200 for magazines (the current, most heavily used medium). The item, following the shift to TV, became one of the most successful in the history of the store.

According to Lodish, the decision model has caused managers of many departments to become much more rational in their market planning procedures. The firm's top management called for development of a longer-term version of the model so that strategic planning scenarios could be evaluated over a five-year planning horizon.

A critical ingredient in the success of this system was the interface person who related managers' needs to the MDSS and translated the output into the manager's terminology. The real-time, interactive system made this interface person as effective as possible, allowing rapid response to critical questions. Subjective data were often used to parameterize models where empirical data were not available.

Lodish notes that this (and other examples he cites) did not have "optimization or statistical parity as a primary goal. The goal of all was helping managers to consider and evaluate more alternatives than they had prior to the model" (p. 82).

INTELLIGENT MARKETING SYSTEMS

While DSSs have provided a quantum jump in our technical ability to process market information, they generally do not incorporate "intelligence." We use the term intelligence here broadly, but intuitively: a DSS can be a very powerful analytic device, but used inappropriately, it can provide results that are either worthless or, possibly, foolish. How can a DSS be made to give intelligent answers? One way is by having such systems run only by "experts," those who fully understand the data, the models and the relevant market phenomena. But such experts are rare in any field, and few can keep up with the explosive growth both in data and in market phenomena. An evolving alternative is what we refer to as an IMS (Choffray, 1990). The following two examples illustrate:

EXAMPLE _____

Rule-Based Forecasting In Collopy and Armstrong's "rule-based" forecasting system (1989a, b), a review of published literature on empirical forecasting research along with knowledge from five leading forecasters forms the "expert base." In addition, the system allows the user to input information about the situation (existence of thresholds, constraints, discontinuities, etc.).

Their forecasting system is organized as a series of "if-then" statements, categorized as rules for cleaning/adjusting historical data, rules to estimate several models (each of which has a current level, a trend factor and a "damping" level), and rules for blending the models.

In two tests of the system, involving 54 annual series, the proce-

THE LABORATORY MARKET

- Small to medium-sized city

- Scanners in all supermarkets

- Voluntary panel of 3000 households

- Identification of panelists in stores

- Controllable TV ads to households

- Observation of in-store conditions

- Store and panel data
  Purchases
  Price
  Promotion
  Advertising
  Coupons
  Displays

EXHIBIT 12.3   Laboratory markets are ideal for testing new products, TV advertising, and other marketing activities. (*Source:* Little, 1990.)

dure provided significantly lower mean absolute error, and less bias in forecast than did a formal combination of forecasts. The formal combining of forecasts was previously regarded as the best method.

The Collopy and Armstrong system contains a form of what previous DSS's do not—"intelligence" or "expertise." It attempts to include a knowledge base of how to use the system (how to clean the data, select a model, etc.) within the system itself.

EXAMPLE _____

The Data Glut and What to Do About It   John Little (1990, pp. 11–14) provides a bit of history about the proliferation of (*Universal Product Code*) (*UPC*) data in supermarkets and what it has done.

> Optical scanning of bar codes on grocery packages started in 1974 with the goal of saving labor by speeding up checkouts. Implementation of the *Universal Product Code (UPC)* represented a remarkable achievement of cooperation among manufacturers and retailers. However, growth of installations was slow, and, as late as 1980, less than 15% of national grocery sales were being scanned. Although there was much talk about using scanning information for "soft savings," that is, marketing purposes, nothing much happened because there were too few scanning stores. But in 1979 a pair of entrepreneurs in Chicago decided not to wait any longer. They simply bought and installed scanners themselves. The company, Information Resources, Inc. (IRI), developed what it calls BehaviorScan and may generically be called *laboratory markets*. Exhibit 12.3 describes the

idea. IRI initially put scanners in all the supermarkets in two small cities, Pittsfield, Massachusetts, and Marion, Indiana. This gave them sales and price data as a direct spinoff from the scanners. In addition, they started recording all the newspaper ads and all the special displays in the stores. In each market they recruited a panel of 3,000 to 4,000 households whose members identify themselves at checkouts so that their purchase records could be set aside in the store computer and accumulated. The two markets were chosen for high cable television usage and the panelists on the cable had specially modified television sets so that different groups of people could be sent different commercials in test and control fashion. Thus, was introduced a powerful testing laboratory for new products, television advertising and other marketing activities. The whole system was extremely successful and grew rapidly until now there are about eight such markets.

In instrumenting the markets IRI made a look-ahead move. It extracted the data directly from the stores electronically, polling the stores at night by telephone from Chicago. Although more expensive than sending tapes by UPS, it is obviously faster and is also more reliable. (UPS doesn't lose the tape, but the stores may lose data if it sits around too long). As happens so often in information technology, there are unexpected fringe benefits from the electronic delivery.

Here is an example of one such benefit. In late 1985 it became apparent that a drought in Brazil would very likely ruin the coffee crop and send world coffee prices skyward. A major food company contacted IRI and said, "How fast can you give us coffee prices and sales movement at retail?" The answer was nine days after the close of the store week for the IRI laboratory markets. This compared to an average age of four to eight weeks for top-line reports from more conventional syndicated sources. The data arrived by diskette to run under flexible DSS software on a personal computer.

The drought did indeed devastate the coffee crop, and, starting in late December, a coffee task force of senior managers in the food company met weekly to review the latest data on what the consumers and retailers were doing in the market. Out of these meetings came the company's pricing policy.

This is just part of the story:

A new generation of tracking and status reporting services has been created. Scanner stores now represent most of the sales volume through supermarkets, and it is therefore possible to design a valid national sample of 2,000–3,000 scanner stores and develop a data service based on them. The two major players are Information Resources and Nielsen Marketing Research. Their services provide coverage of individual major markets as well as the total U.S. Both companies include, besides basic sales and price data, specially collected information on store displays, newspaper advertising in the market, and coupon drops, all classified and broken out in a great variety of ways.

All this sounds wonderful. But there is a hitch. The amount of data is overwhelming. Consider the new detail now available: *weeks* instead of four-weeks or bimonths (this increases data by a factor of 4 to 8), *UPCs* instead of aggregate brands (a factor of 3 to 5), *top 40 markets* instead of broad geographic regions (a factor of 4 to 5), *new tracking measures* (a factor of 2 to 3), and *chain breakouts* (a factor of 1 to 3).

Multiplying out these factors reveals that roughly 100 to 1,000 times as much data are at hand than previously. Furthermore, any analysis that requires going to individual stores or to panel households brings in new, equally large data bases. Let's take 100 as a conservative multiplicative factor for the data that many companies are now bringing in-house for everyday use.

This kind of change is not easy to comprehend. In terms of a report, it means that, if a report took an hour to look through before, the corresponding document with all the possible new breakouts would take 100 hours to look through. In other words, the new detail won't be looked at.

Little describes three things to be done about this data explosion:

Stage 1   *Gain access:* which is well underway. Manufacturers have developed systems to allow them to deal with these data.

Stage 2   *Automate the analysis:* Here Little sees more systems like that described by Abraham and Lodish (1987a), that include procedures to draw a "sensible" baseline and to determine the difference between actual and baseline. He calls systems like these, market response analysis systems. They use expert system ideas (for cleaning the data in particular), derived from extensive market analysis experience, to process large volumes of data efficiently and sensibly.

Stage 3   *Find the news:* Here Little suggests that a computer should summarize what has happened, what the key points are that are buried in the tables that can be produced in stage 2. His idea is that the computer should write the managerial cover memo. At least one such system is currently available, called CoverStory (Schmitz, Armstrong, and Little, 1990). Exhibit 12.4 gives an example of the first page of a cover story memo.

Note that Little is describing the same type of system that Armstrong and Collopy are describing—much of the intelligence is programmed to be inside the system—is a prototype of the system of the 1990s, as we will see shortly.

IMS and Expert Systems.   We chose not to use the popular term "expert system" here, as we see an expert system as a (possible) component of an IMS. While definitions are a bit fuzzy at the moment, expert systems are most appropriately used in the following circumstances (Rangaswamy et al., 1987):

1. *The key relationships are logical rather than arithmetical.* New idea generation would seem more appropriate for an expert system while ad

To: Sizzle Brand Manager
From: CoverStory
Date: 07/05/89
Subject: Sizzle Brand Summary for Twelve Weeks Ending May 21, 1989

Sizzle's share of type in Total United States was 8.3 in the C&B Juice/Drink category for the twelve weeks ending 5/21/89. This is an increase of 0.2 points from a year earlier, but down .3 from last period. This reflects volume sales of 8.2 million gallons. Category volume (currently 99.9 million gallons) declined 1.3% from a year earlier.

Sizzle's share of type is 8.3 — up 0.2 from the same period last year.

Display activity and unsupported price cuts rose over the past year — unsupported price cuts from 38 points to 46. Featuring and price remained at about the same level as a year earlier.

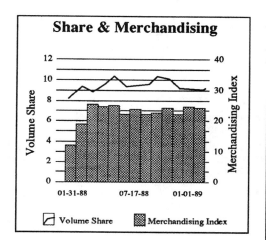

Components of Sizzle Share

Among components of Sizzle, the principal gainer is:

> Sizzle 64oz: up 0.5 points from last year to 3.7

and losers:

> Sizzle 48oz: down 0.2 to 1.9
> Sizzle 32oz: down 0.1 to 0.7

Sizzle 64oz's share of type increase is partly due to 11.3 points rise in % ACV with Display vs. year ago.

Competitor Summary

Among Sizzle's major competitors, the principal gainers are:

> Shakey: up 2.5 points from last year to 32.6
> Private Label: +.5 to 19.9 (but down .3 since last period)

and loser:

> Generic Seltzer: -.7 to 3.5

Shakey's share of type increase is...

EXHIBIT 12.4   The first page of a CoverStory memorandum. (*Source:* Schmitz, Armstrong, and Little, 1990, p. 38.)

budget allocation across media is most appropriately done outside the expert system domain.

2. *The problem is semistructured rather than structured or unstructured.* For structured problems, a traditional algorithm approach will do; for unstructured problems there may not be sufficient knowledge in the knowledge base to provide satisfactory results.

3. *The knowledge in the domain is incomplete.* Expert systems are most applicable in domains of incomplete knowledge.

4. *Problem solving in the domain requires a direct interface between the manager and the computer system.* Situations of decision urgency and on-line decision support are most appropriate for expert system use.

The major components of an expert system are (1) a user interface, (2) a knowledge base, and (3) an inference engine. (See Forsyth, 1984, Hayes-Roth, Waterman and Lenat, 1983, and Harman and King, 1985, for technical details.)

The *knowledge base* includes the definitions of the objects and variables in the system, including data, assumptions, production rules (if-then statements), heuristics and models.

The *inference engine* manipulates the elements in the knowledge base and combines it with information from the user to solve a particular problem. The two most common mechanisms that drive an inference engine are called "forward chaining" (where the process starts with the given facts to produce possible solutions) and "backward chaining" (where necessary conditions that lead to a hypothesized solution are determined).

Descriptions of expert system projects have begun to make their way into the marketing literature. The Marketing Workbench project at Duke (McCann, 1986; McCann and Galagher, 1990) represents what Rangaswamy et al. (1987) call a hybrid system (roughly our IMS): a combination of DSS and expert system capabilities. Keon and Bayer (1986) have developed a system for recommending consumer promotions. Rangaswamy et al. (1987) describe two expert systems developed at Wharton, one for suggesting commercial and communications approaches (ADCAD) and one for providing suggestions for international marketing negotiations (NEGOTEX) (Rangaswamy et al., 1989, and Rangaswamy, Harlam and Lodish, 1991, report on a system that automatically analyzes scanner data).

Rangaswamy et al. (1987) cite new product design (see Ram and Ram, 1989), product launch, positioning, advertising and promotional planning, retail site selection, pricing, and country selection as marketing problem areas that could be readily amenable to future expert system application. Wierenga (1990) provides a review of "marketing expert systems," pointing out that formal modeling is appropriate where marketing experts perform worse than analytical models, but the expert systems approach can be used when experts outperform formal models and have a "reasoning mechanism that can be captured."

In Wierenga's review, he uncovers 21 expert systems in marketing, but only 9 are complete, operational systems and of those, only 3 mention a formal comparison test as a means of system validation. (See Exhibit 12.5.)

The first 1991 issue of the *International Journal of Research in Marketing* (Vol. 8, no. 1) is dedicated to expert systems in marketing. It is interesting to note that four of the research papers in that issue (Alpar, 1991; Bayer and Harlter, 1991; Rangaswamy, Harlam, and Lodish, 1991; and McCann, Lahti, and Hill, 1991) deal with analysis of scanner data; the other (Burke, 1991) deals with consumer response to advertising. The other paper in that issue (Mitchell, Russo, and Wittink, 1991) positions the expert system as human "collaborator" rather than as a replacement for human decision making.

IMS/MDSS Design: Some Guidelines.   An IMS/MDSS should be designed so that it can be used. It will be used if it provides users with flexible decision-making leverage at moderate cost (in time and dollars). A number of authors have provided extensive guidelines for system design (Barbosa and Hirko, 1980; Huber, 1981; Keen, 1981; Keen and Scott Morton, 1978; Lucas, 1978; Schonberger, 1980; Sprague, 1980). We briefly synthesize these views, following Keen and Scott Morton (1978), into a three-step design process: the predesign stage, the design stage, and the postdesign stage.

Predesign Stage.   The purposes of the predesign stage are to make certain that the right problem is worked on (decision analysis) and to involve users in a contract for action (entry). The decision analysis clearly establishes how the current decision process takes place and how it can be supported, while entry builds the commitment and rapport that sets the stage for later implementation.

Generally, in the predesign phase several designs for evaluation should be developed. Analysis at this stage may suggest that only a small subset of the decisions being made in the area justify the use of a system, and a value analysis may suggest that no payoff exists for support of those decisions. In general, while the steps leading to a final design are often judgmental, the issues to be considered revolve around risk and payoff (Keen and Scott Morton, 1978, p. 176):

> Which alternative(s) offer the most improvement to the existing decision process? What are the likely economic payoffs? What is the cost of the organizational or behavioral gains?
>
> How difficult will it be to implement this degree of change? Are we ready to commit the dollars, time, prestige, and support necessary?
>
> What are the downside risks—if the system falls behind schedule or meets

	System	Purpose	Comments
1.	Abraham and Lodish (1987b) [PROMOTER]	To evaluate sales promotions, notably to determine the "baseline" (what sales would have been without promotion), using rule of thumb	• Three applications to frequently purchased consumer goods (FPCGs) are discussed. • Results compared with actual baseline • Knowledge base from authors' experience in industry
2.	Bayer and Harter (1991) [SCANEXPERT]	Tracing significant changes in m.s. (market sales) and finding the causes: trade support, retail distribution, competition	• Reported used for three FPCGs • No validation reported • Knowledge base from interviews with industry experts
3.	Bayer, Lawrence, and Keon (1988)	To find the right sales promotion type given the market position of the brand and the management objectives	• System is reported "operational" for FPCGs; no applications reported • Validated against "three cases in literature" • Knowledge base from expert-survey and analysis of scanner data
4.	Burke, Rangaswamy, Wind, and Eliashberg (1990) [ADCAD]	To make recommendations for advertisement development on different aspects, given marketing goals and characteristics of the situation	• System is complete/operational for FPCGs; no applications mentioned • Validation is informal, via comments by experts • Knowledge base from published material and agency creative personnel
5.	Collopy and Armstrong (1989a, and b) [rule-based forecasting]	To make forecasts on the basis of the time-series data	• System is operational; no applications reported • Validation against other models in "open forecasting competition" • Knowledge base via professional survey, protocols, direct assessment
6.	Little (1988) [COVERSTORY]	To find the news in a huge amount of data; select the major events and their causes	• Applications discussed for FPCG's • No validation discussed • Knowledge base from prior analytic experience
7.	Ram and Ram (1988) [INNOVATOR]	To screen new product ideas in the financial service industry, based on attributes of products, brand, and companies	• Systems operational for financial services; no applications reported • Validation is ad hoc comparison with "expert" • Knowledge base via professional survey, protocols, direct assessment
8.	Rangaswamy, Eliashberg, Burke, and Wind (1989) [NEGOTEX]	To prepare for a negotiating strategy in terms of preparation, team composition, communication approach, and behavioral response on the basis of characteristics of the situation	• Complete system; no applications reported • Validation via student and practitioner reactions • Knowledge base is published literature
9.	Schumann, Gongla, Lee, and Sakamoto (1987) [BUSINESS STRATEGY ADVISOR]	To make strategic recommendations on the basis of the position of a business in the BCG-matrix and in a technology portfolio matrix	• Operational system with no reported applications • No validation discussed • Knowledge base is published literature

EXHIBIT 12.5 Operational marketing expert systems. (*Source:* Adapted from Wierenga, 1990.)

resistance, what are the costs (financial, behavioral, political, etc.)? Does the system permit a phased evolutionary development?

Design Stage.   A system cannot be designed by a cookbook recipe, but it can be outlined with flow diagrams (Exhibit 12.6), which can be used as a checklist. When the predesign cycle is complete, the design specification is a statement of intention, focusing on what the system should do, not what it should look like. Answers to a number of key questions guide the design:

> What should the system accomplish? Design must be based on use. What can users reasonably expect to do with the system?
>
> What should the user see? This feature is the interface, the software, the means through which the user communicates with the system. A good software interface must be truly conversational, robust (bombproof and reliable), and easy to control (a user's system, not an analyst's system).

Postdesign Stage.   A distinguishing aspect of an IMS or a DSS is its evolutionary design. Competent managers learn from using the system and extend their analyses, requiring additional levels of support. The evolution of the DSS design is also one of change in a manager's decision process. But for a DSS to affect management action, evaluation must be incorporated as part of the design strategy.

In summary, by the very nature of its adaptability, an IMS or DSS must be designed to meet the evolving needs of a particular application. As such, the typical development process follows the steps of analysis (predesign), design and construction, and implementation (including evolutionary redesign). The design focus must be on system use and usability, and system design and implementation must be recognized as being inseparable.

IMS/MDSS: A BRIDGE TO SUCCESSFUL IMPLEMENTATION FOR MARKETING MODELS

A purpose of this book is to provide a model-building approach for making marketing decisions. The IMS or MDSS makes the model-building approach accessible. Furthermore, implementation, system design, and good marketing modeling are inseparable.

Implementation (whether of a DSS, a marketing model, or any new management technique) constitutes a change in the organization's work environment. Thus, implementation is a process of organizational change, and the process of planning for and introducing that change can critically affect its ultimate chance of acceptance.

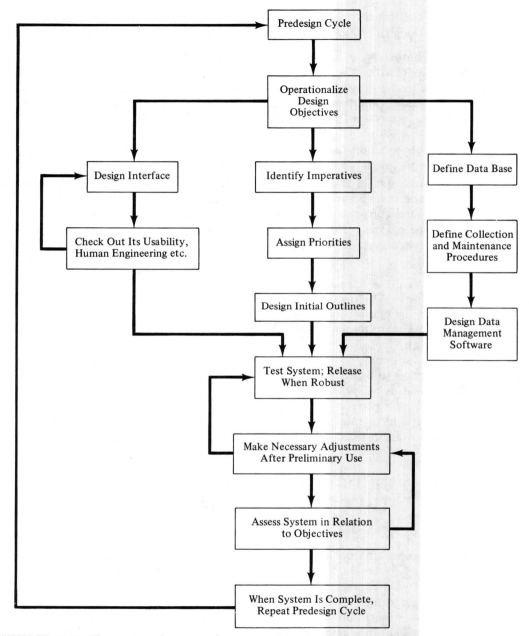

EXHIBIT 12.6 The system design cycle. (*Source:* Keen and Scott Morton, 1978.)

The value of models in marketing, as in any area of application, should be measured by their impact on organizational effectiveness. According to Schultz and Slevin (1979), implementation is the bridging of the gap between theory and practice and the improvement of organizational effectiveness through organizational change. Schultz and Henry (1981) distinguish between implementation and successful implementation. They contend that implementation means changed decision making. A *successful model,* on the other hand, is one that adequately represents the modeled phenomena and is used for the purpose for which it was designed. However, it may or may not result in successful implementation. Consider the development of a product-design model. Its goal is to optimize the design of product features. If it does so and is used for this purpose, it is successful. However, the process of model building and calibration might identify a new market segment, leading to a reassessment of marketing strategy. This is implementation success. Thus for a marketing science project to be successful in the broad sense (implementation success), it need not be associated with the success of a specific model (model success).

Schultz and Henry (1981) posit three stages of management science activity: (1) *intervention,* when management-science activity takes place (a model gets built); (2) *implementation,* when decision making is changed as a result of intervention; and (3) *improvement,* when a positive change results from the decision making. These three stages correspond roughly to the different views of implementation held by analysts, managers, and implementation researchers. Many management scientists view implementation as getting the results of their work into the hands of managers. Managers seek technical assistance in problem solving, so the specific problem must be successfully solved. Implementation researchers focus on the broader dimension of organizational change.

While the DSS or IMS may be the vehicle for implementation of marketing models, a number of factors affect whether that implementation will be successful. But what do we mean by successful implementation?

Successful Implementation. Schultz, Ginzberg, and Lucas (1984) and Lucas, Ginzberg, and Schultz (1989) identify several main factors associated with a number of the main dimensions of implementation success: management support, user involvement, personal stake, implementation strategy, and model/system factors.

Management Support. An old Chinese proverb goes, "Tell me and I'll forget, show me and I may remember, involve me and I'll understand." So it seems to be with management support for marketing models. Management support is required before, during and after a system has been invoked. As Hanssens, Parsons, and Schultz (1990, p. 324) point out, "The evidence for the need for management support is so strong that any attempt to implement a system without it or without the related conditions of commitment and authority to implement will probably result in failure." Several other factors related to management support are belief in the concept (Schultz, Ginzberg, and Lucas, 1984), authority (Schultz and Slevin, 1983), and power (Marcus, 1983, and Robey, 1984), where the last two concepts refer to gaining that support from the proper managers in the right way.

User Involvement. Much research seems to support the notion that greater user involvement leads to greater implementation success rates (Schultz and Slevin, 1983; Lucas, Ginzberg, and Schultz, 1989), although Ives and Olson (1984), in a review of this literature, point out that much of the supporting research is methodologically flawed.

Personal Stake. Closely akin to the notion of a new product champion as a critical success factor for a new product is the notion of personal stake. Personal stake measures the extent to which a system user's future job performance depends on the effectiveness of a system and its use. If an MDSS can help a manager make better decisions and those better decisions lead directly to rewards for the manager, then the system is more likely to be implemented. A number of individual variables are related to implementation success as well (Lucas, Ginzberg, and Schultz, 1990).

Implementation Strategy. Implementation must be planned for—it is a process of organizational change that takes place in stages over time. Some key factors associated with a successful implementation strategy relate to how well the implementation is staged or planned for (from simple to more complex models or systems, with sufficient time allocated to achieve satisfactory results) and whether sufficient resources in terms of funds and high-quality resources have been allocated or budgeted (Schultz, 1984). In addition, changes in the industry, in the environment and in technology all affect the likelihood of successful implementation.

Model/System-Related Dimensions of Implementation Success

As this book is on marketing models, we develop our discussion of a fifth implementation-success dimension rather more than the four just discussed. Little (1970) suggests that decision models should be simple, robust, easy to communicate with, adaptive, and complete on important issues. These characteristics are seemingly in conflict: simple models are rarely complete, and vice versa. Urban's (1974) view of evolutionary model building, along with Little's concept of a model's being adaptive, provides clues for resolving this conflict: "simple" and "complete" are understood to be relative concepts.

Little's most controversial dimension is that of ease of control. This feature means that the model is constructed in such a way that it can behave as a manager wants it to. But combined with subjective-calibration procedures, the easy-to-control model can potentially be self-serving, bearing out the manager's prejudices rather than performing well.

Naert and Leeflang (1978) downplay this concern:

> The manager has to keep control over the model, otherwise it is unlikely that he will ever use it. This view might be dangerous in the sense that the model can be manipulated at will by the manager. This, however, does not usually represent a real problem. After all, the manager is looking for help and not a fancy toy to play with. The manager who manipulates the model and its parameters thoughtlessly is only fooling himself.   *(p. 548).*

However, this view may be wishful thinking. Parsons and Schultz (1976) question the view and argue for extending it by adding an additional dimension to the set of model criteria: validity.

> We would extend the idea of decision calculus by imposing another requirement on models, namely that they be evaluated in terms of the *representativeness* of the mechanism describing market behavior. This additional requirement guarantees that at least the sales response component of the decision model faces a rigorous test of its validity as a theory of market response. We would argue that a test of a theory is its validity, while a test of a model is its utility and so it is possible for a model to be useful even though it is based on an inadequate theory of sales response. But it is better to have both a valid and useful model.   *(p. 33).*

We concur and append the notion of validity to the requirements for a successful model.

In line with the argument at the beginning of this section, we also add the notion of *potential cost-effectiveness.* Formal marketing models rarely become implemented in small organizations because they have a certain fixed-cost component in terms of managerial and analyst time, as well as expenditure. If the problem (and the organization) is too small, the model-building exercise will not be a valuable investment. The small-firm manager who says he "doesn't have the time for models" is probably right insofar as the size of his problems and the potential for improvement will not justify the cost of analysis. (The microcomputer and cheaper data are changing his mind, however.)

Model Validity.   Four main criteria for *validation* relevant for marketing models are measure reliability and validity, face validity, statistical validity, and use validity (Naert and Leeflang, 1978, Ch. 12).

Measure validity is the extent to which an instrument measures what it is supposed to measure. A measure with little validity has little value. However, even if a measure is valid, it may not be possible to measure it without error. *Measure reliability* is the extent to which a measure is error-free.

Measure validity has two parts: convergent and discriminant validity. *Convergent validity* is the extent to which an instrument correlates highly with other measures of the variable of interest; *discriminant validity* is the extent to which an instrument shows low correlation with other instruments supposedly measuring other variables.

Face validity is the *reductio ad absurdum* principle in mathematics, which shows the falsity of an assumption by deriving from it a manifest absurdity. The idea is to question whether the model's structure and its output are believable. Face validity is based on theory, common sense, and known empirical facts (experience). Massy (1971) describes four areas for face validity: model structure, estimation, information contribution, and interpretation of results.

The validity of the *model structure* means that the model should do sensible things. Sales should be nonnegative and have a finite upper bound. Market shares should sum to one. Sales response to advertising spending might account for decreasing returns or first increasing and then decreasing returns to scale. If it is easy to make a model do things that are not consistent with managerial experience or intuition, the model is unlikely to be used.

The choice of *estimation method* is another essential aspect of face validity. For example, if a reasonable set of assumptions about the process generating the data (or previous studies) suggests that residuals are autocorrelated, then the use of ordinary least squares is inappropriate and generalized least squares may be the appropriate and valid estimation procedure.

The *amount of information contributed* by the model also dictates its value as well as its validity. For example, Kuehn and Rohloff (1967) suggest calibrating promotional-response models before and after the promotional period to assess their impact. If model parameter changes are insignificant, the model is of limited value in assessing promotional impact, and different measures may be required.

Finally, the *level and interpretation of results* impact model implementability and validity in much the same way as model structure does. If the price or advertising elasticity of demand has the wrong logical sign, the model loses validity and hence implementability.

Another criterion for validing marketing models is *statistical validity,* the criterion employed to evaluate the quality of a relationship estimated by econometric methods. The important issues in a marketing context usually relate to goodness of fit and the reliability of the estimated coefficients, multicollinearity, and assumptions about the disturbance term (homoscedasticity and autocorrelation).

Validation also relates to the *intended use* of the model. Validity for descriptive models places heavy requirements on face validity and goodness of fit. For a normative model the reliability of a model's response coefficients, those that enter into policy calculations, would seem most critical. For predictive validity a goodness-of-fit measure, such as R^2 or mean-squared deviation, is often used on a holdout or validation sample. The use of such a sample makes the validation task predictive, while measuring goodness of fit on the estimation data gives information useful only for descriptive validity.

Most econometric studies include two sets of validity tests. The first set deals with checking the model's assumptions for problems, such as multicollinearity, autocorrelation, nonnormality, and the like. This task is called *specification-error analysis*. If no violations are identified, the model as a whole can be tested and, most important, *discrimination tests* between alternative models can be performed (Parsons and Schultz, 1976, Ch. 5).

Model Costs-Benefits.   By and large, modeling in marketing must be viewed as an investment. The ability of that investment to provide its value can frequently be estimated.

A thoughtful treatment of cost-benefit considerations in relationship to marketing models is found in Naert and Leeflang (1978, Ch. 14). We draw heavily on their discussion here.

Model development costs, in time and dollars, are generally of three types: development costs, maintenance costs, and costs inherent to use.

Development costs are usually fixed costs, incurred once when the project is undertaken. If these development costs alone are greater than the expected benefits (as may be the case for a small firm), the modeling task cannot be justified. One way to control development costs is to use an existing model, usually on a rental basis from a consulting firm.

Maintenance costs are those costs incurred in keeping a model up to date. For large-scale accounting systems, maintenance costs are often many times greater than development costs. For marketing models the level of maintenance costs is usually determined by two factors: the level/frequency of model use and the rate of structural change in the marketplace. Infrequently used models in relatively stable markets generally have low maintenance costs.

The *costs of use* have two main components: computer time and managerial time. Computer time is usually well accounted for, while managerial time is often perplexingly difficult to allocate.

These cost issues need to be assessed on a case-by-case basis. We recommend the following approach. Start off by making a worst case analysis for costs (as well as benefits). If the model shows value when burdened most heavily with allocated costs, its use is clearly justified. If it is only marginally profitable, a more refined analysis may be required. This worst case approach may greatly reduce the effort required to perform the cost-benefit analysis.

In general, model *benefits* are of two types: tangible and intangible. Models in some areas have almost all their benefits in the intangible category: many planning models—and, in fact, the entire planning function—in many firms have this characteristic. *Intangible* benefits often accrue from having the model ask the right questions.

Benefits are often tricky to pin down: an offshoot of the model development process may be an overall improvement in the understanding of marketing phenomena that benefits *all* firms in the industry. However, the benefit to the developing firm may not justify the investment (this is known as the "free-rider" problem in economics). These are situations in which multicompany-sponsored modeling activities (PIMS and ADVISOR, for example) are appropriate. A similar problem arises from the internal-external model development question. A model developed in-house may have lower operating costs than a consultant's model, but the fixed cost must be spread over a sufficiently large number of applications to justify its construction.

There are a series of experience-based and quality-based arguments that may be made either for or against in-house model development. In general, the greater the level and frequency of model use, the more beneficial in-house development is and the greater the justifiable sophistication in model development (the fixed-cost component) is.

The physical nature of the system will affect its cost-benefit ratio and its likelihood of success as well. Key system characteristics are format and organizational support. By format, we mean friendliness or the ease with which the system can be understood and used. By organizational support, we mean access to the organizational infrastructure: data, computer access, software, maintenance, and budget to keep the system operating and current over time (Ein-Dor and Segev, 1981).

Implementation Rules of Thumb

In addition to these guidelines, it is useful to highlight a few "don't's" along with the "do's":

Don't make unnecessary changes. If a manager has been receiving a report in a given format, continue to give him the same format he is used to even if the information is being generated by a new model. By changing as little as possible in a short time frame, barriers to implementation will be lowered.

Beware of false accuracy. A wise manager we know sends back any computer-generated results with more than two significant digits. Multidigit precision ("our market share in this market will be 12.372% if we introduce the new ad campaign according to plan") gives a false sense of security and discourages asking hard questions of the model.

Don't use models for advocacy. Models should be used to *explore* options for the future. Unfortunately, they are often misused to justify a favored set of actions, a practice we consider unethical as well as unwise.

Don't be afraid to modify. After the model is built, programmed, and documented, there is a tendency to treat it as an icon. The model should be continuously subjected to tests, should be updated, and should be treated as an *evolving* entity.

Don't skip steps: Build the simplest model/system first without worrying about its completeness. See where it works, and where it doesn't make sure everyone (model-builder, users and stakeholders) agrees on what needs to be added to make it more realistic. *Then* go to version 2, and so on.

A LOOK AHEAD

Rangaswamy and Wind (1991) provide a cogent discussion of the current status of information technology in marketing. Many opportunities exist and the future looks bright. What will the 1990s bring for the use of marketing models and IMS/MDSS's? A much higher level of successful use of marketing models than ever before for a number of reasons:

1. *Improved software and hardware.* Expert systems software, better MDSSs, better data retrieval capabilities, and large-scale networking and communication are all making more data more usable. Marketing models are central to the effective utilization of these resources.

2. *More and better data.* The UPC/scanner/single-source data explosion is just beginning. Better models and associated systems are required to make sense out of this data explosion.

3. *Diffusion of workstations/networks.* The marketing manager of today has the mainframe of yesterday on his desk linked to other computers and vast data resources. Modeling capabilities and better support systems will add tremendous value to these capabilities.

4. *Model/computer literate MBAs.* The MBAs being trained today take computers, modeling, and easy data access for granted. They will demand (or build their own) marketing models and associated support system.

5. *Knowledge and theory accumulation.* The explosive growth in marketing theories, combined with the useful combinations of meta-analyses are providing insight not only into what models are appropriate for what situations, but what likely values for the parameters of those models might be. In addition, as we continue to catalog success stories and thereby learn what works and what doesn't, we lower the risk of failure, and model and system implementation will accelerate.

To conclude, it is important to note that technology in general and the theory and practice of marketing in particular, are changing faster now than ever before. Many future changes will be driven by more and better data, by faster and friendlier access to expertise and information, by intelligent marketing systems, and by a receptive cohort of managers, trained to use the available tools and information to help make better decisions.

PROBLEMS

12.1. Some marketers view the emergence of computer models in marketing with hostility. They will make the following statements: (a) we don't use computer models; (b) computer models are typically unrealistic; (c) anyone can build a computer model; (d) a computer model is of no help unless you can get the data. How would you answer these objections considering the basic structure of an MDSS?

12.2. Distinguish among measure validity, face validity, statistical validity, and use validity.

12.3. "The diffusion and use of marketing models is inevitable; a creative analyst can only accelerate or forestall inevitable trends." Comment.

12.4. What differences would you suggest between implementation strategies for marketing models for (a) a large packaged foods manufacturer, (b) a small industrial component parts manufacturer, and (c) a public sector agency interested in marketing an issue? How would you evaluate costs/benefits?

12.5. Top management in a large manufacturing company felt that the marketing department could benefit greatly from the implementation of management science (MS) methods in the marketing operation. A group of experts from the firm's centralized MS group was assigned to study marketing problems and activities. After a number of months of independent work, the MS group came up with a lengthy report, which included recommendations for a comprehensive restructuring of the marketing operation and the implementation of a number of sophisticated operations research models. The report was passed along to the company's marketing management with a recommendation to implement the recommended actions as soon as possible. Upon reading the report, the marketing manager claimed that the recommendations were highly unrealistic and completely unworkable. He further stated that the department personnel lacked the understanding and technical ability to implement the MS proposal. Discuss the problems highlighted in this situation. What should top management do to deal with these problems and to prevent their recurrence in the future?

12.6. "The builder of formal models can make his or her greatest contribution by helping others to be more explicit about the assumptions they are making and by assisting in developing a suitable test for a particular model." Comment.

A | MATHEMATICS FOR MARKETING MODELS

A wide range of researchers with an equally wide range of skills have made important contributions to the marketing models area. The breadth of mathematical coverage in the models in our literature is, indeed, vast, and there is no way even to sketch that breadth in a single short appendix. We do not intend or pretend to be complete here; rather, we have selected a potpourri of topics and results that marketing modelers use frequently and assume their readers are aware of. We also provide some useful references for readers who wish to go into greater depth.

MISCELLANY: A GRABBAG OF ELEMENTARY TOPICS

Geometric Series. Define

$$S_n = a + ar + ar^2 + ar^3 + \ldots + ar^n \tag{A.1}$$

or

$$S_n = \sum_{j=0}^{n} ar^j = a\,\frac{1 - r^{n+1}}{1 - r} \tag{A.2}$$

and

$$\lim_{n\to\infty} S_n = \frac{a}{1 - r}, \quad \text{for} \quad |r| < 1 \tag{A.3}$$

Binomial Expansion.

$$(a + b)^n = \sum_{j=0}^{n} \binom{n}{j} a^j b^{n-j} \tag{A.4}$$

where

$$\binom{n}{j} = \frac{n!}{j!(n - j)!}$$

are called *binomial coefficients.*

Expansion of Partial Fractions.   Any quotient $g(x)/f(x)$ of a polynomial $g(x)$ of degree m and a polynomial $f(x)$ of degree $n > m$, without common roots can be expressed as a sum of n *partial fractions* corresponding to the roots x_k of $f(x) = 0$ as follows:

$$\frac{g(x)}{f(x)} = \sum_k \left[\frac{b_{k1}}{(x - x_k)} + \frac{b_{k2}}{(x - x_k)^2} + \ldots + \frac{b_{km_k}}{(x - x_k)^{m_k}} \right] \tag{A.5}$$

where m_k = multiplicity of the kth root of $f(x) = 0$. (This result is important in solving differential equations—see the mathematics of optimization section).

Exponential-Trigonometric Relationships.

$$e^{iz} = \cos z + i \sin z \tag{A.6}$$

where $i = \sqrt{-1}$.

Gamma Function.

$$\Gamma(z) = \int_0^\infty e^{-t}\, t^{z-1}\, dt \,(z > 0)$$

$$\Gamma(1/2) = \sqrt{\pi}, \quad \Gamma(1) = 1 \qquad \text{(A.7)}$$

$$\Gamma(n + 1) = n\Gamma(n)$$

$$\Gamma(n) = (n - 1)! \qquad \text{for } n \text{ integer}$$

Beta Function.

$$B(p, q) = \frac{\Gamma(p)\Gamma(q)}{\Gamma(p + q)}$$

$$= \int_0^1 t^{p-1}(1 - t)^{q-1}\, dt \quad p,q > 0 \qquad \text{(A.8)}$$

See DeGroot (1987), Edwards and Penney (1990), and Mizrahi and Sullivan (1986) for further developments.

SOME IMPORTANT STATISTICAL DISTRIBUTIONS FREQUENTLY USED IN MARKETING MODELS

In this section,

$E(X)$ = expected value of the random variable
$\mathrm{Var}(X)$ = variance of the random variable
$p(X)$ = probability function (discrete random variables)
$f(X)$ = density function (continuous random variables)

Bernoulli Distribution. (often used as likelihood of a purchase event or in more general terms, a "success")

$$p(X) = p^X(1 - p)^{1-X}, \quad X = 0, 1$$

$$p = \text{probability of event} \qquad \text{(A.9)}$$

$$E(X) = p$$

$$\mathrm{Var}\,(X) = p(1 - p)$$

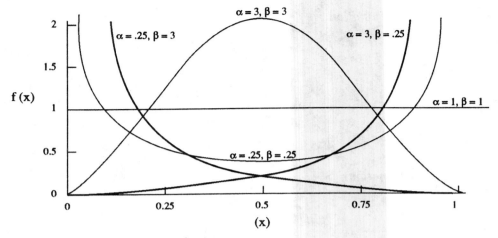

EXHIBIT A.1   (a) Beta distribution.

Beta Distribution.   (often used as a mixing distribution for probability of purchase)

$$f(x) = \frac{\Gamma(\alpha + \beta)}{\Gamma(\alpha)\Gamma(\beta)} X^{\alpha-1}(1 - X)^{\beta-1}, \qquad 0 \le X \le 1$$

$$E(X) = \frac{\alpha}{\alpha + \beta} \tag{A.10}$$

$$\text{Var}(X) = \frac{\alpha\beta}{(\alpha + \beta)^2(\alpha + \beta + 1)}$$

See Exhibit A.1(a).

Binomial Distribution.   (a sum of n Bernoulli random variables)

$$p(X) = \binom{n}{X} p^X(1 - p)^{n-X}, \quad X = 0, \ldots, n$$

$$0 \le p \le 1 \tag{A.11}$$

$$E(X) = np$$

$$\text{Var}(X) = np(1 - p)$$

Cauchy Distribution.   (the ratio of two independent normal random variables)

$$f(X) = \frac{1}{b\pi} \left\{ \left[\frac{(X - a)}{b} \right]^2 + 1 \right\} \quad -\infty \le X \le +\infty \tag{A.12}$$

where

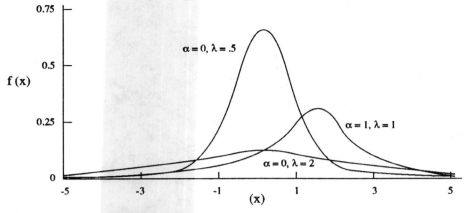

EXHIBIT A.1 (b) Cauchy distribution.

a = median
b = scale parameter

This is a symmetric distribution whose moments about the median do not exist. See Exhibit A.1(b).

Chi-Squared Distribution. (sum of squares of v standard normal variates)

$$f(X) = \frac{X^{(v-2)/2} \, e^{-X/2}}{2^{v/2} \, \Gamma(v/2)}, \qquad 0 \le X \le +\infty$$

$$v = \text{shape parameter (degrees of freedom)} \qquad \textbf{(A.13)}$$

$$E(X) = v$$

$$\text{Variance} = 2v$$

Exponential Distribution. ("memoryless" process distribution)

$$f(X) = \lambda e^{-\lambda X}, \quad 0 \le X \le +\infty$$

$$\lambda = \text{scale parameter} \qquad \textbf{(A.14)}$$

$$E(X) = \frac{1}{\lambda}$$

$$\text{Var}(X) = \left(\frac{1}{\lambda}\right)^2$$

See Exhibit A.1(c).

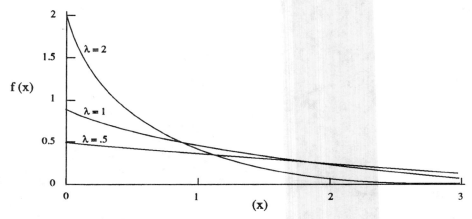

EXHIBIT A.1   (c) Exponential distribution.

Extreme Value Distribution.   (asymptotic distribution of the smallest of a set of random variables; reversal of the sign of X gives the distribution of the largest)

$$f(X) = \left[\frac{1}{b}\right] e^{[(X-a)/b]} e^{-e^{[(X-a)/b)]}}, \quad -\infty \leq X \leq +\infty$$

a, b = parameters (a = mode)   **(A.15)**

$E(X) = a + b\Gamma'(1)$ where $\Gamma'(1) = -0.57721$, the first derivative of the gamma function at $n = 1$

$$\mathrm{Var}(X) = \frac{b^2\pi^2}{6}$$

See Exhibit A.1(d).

F Distribution.   (the ratio of two independent chi-squared distributions)

$$f(X) = \frac{\Gamma[(v + w)/2] \cdot V \frac{v}{2} \cdot W \frac{w}{2} \cdot X^{(v-2)/2}}{\Gamma\left(\frac{v}{2}\right) \cdot \Gamma\left(\frac{w}{2}\right) \cdot [w + vX]^{(v+w)/2}}, \quad 0 \leq X \leq +\infty \quad \textbf{(A.16)}$$

v, w = parameter (degrees of freedom for numerator and denominator chi square distribution respectively).

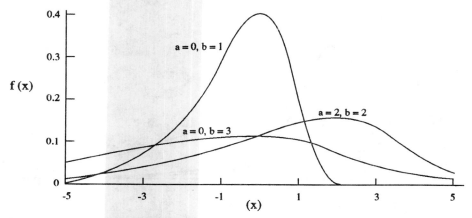

EXHIBIT A.1   (d) Extreme value distribution.

$$E(X) = \frac{w}{(w-2)}, \quad w > 2$$

$$\mathrm{Var}(X) = \frac{2w^2(v+w-2)}{v(w-2)^2(w-4)}$$

See Exhibit A.1(e).

Gamma Distribution.   (a sum of c exponential random variables for c integer)

$$f(X) = \frac{\lambda^c X^{c-1} e^{-\lambda X}}{\Gamma(c)}, \quad 0 \le X \le +\infty \tag{A.17}$$

EXHIBIT A.1   (e) F distribution.

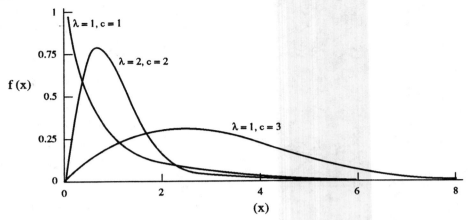

EXHIBIT A.1 (f) Gamma distribution.

$$\lambda, c = \text{parameters}, \quad \lambda > 0, c > 0$$

$$E(X) = \frac{c}{\lambda}$$

$$\text{Var}(X) = \frac{c}{\lambda^2}$$

Note that

- If $c = 1$, gamma reduces to the exponential distribution.
- If c is an integer, the distribution is known as an Erlang distribution.
- If $2c$ is an integer, then the gamma is also an χ^2 distribution with $2c$ degrees of freedom.

See Exhibit A.1(f).

Geometric Distribution. (a sequence of Bernoulli trials up to the first "success")

$$p(X) = p(1 - p)^{X-1}, \quad X = 1, 2, \ldots$$

$$p = \text{Bernoulli parameter} \tag{A.18}$$

$$E(X) = \frac{1}{p}$$

$$\text{Var}(X) = \frac{(1 - p)}{p^2}$$

Hypergeometric Distribution. (the number of successes drawn in a sample of size n from a population of size N with S successes in the N-population)

$$p(X) = \frac{\binom{S}{n}\binom{N-S}{n-X}}{\binom{N}{n}}, \max[0, n-N+S] \le X \le \min[S, n] \quad \textbf{(A.19)}$$

N = population size

S = number of successes in total population

n = sample size

$$E(X) = n\frac{S}{N}$$

$$\text{Var}(X) = \frac{(nS/N)(1 - S/N)(N-n)}{(N-1)}$$

Logistic Distribution. (derived in random utility likelihood of purchase models when the error term is extreme value):

$$f(X) = \frac{e^{-(X-a)/k}}{k[1 + e^{[-(X-a)/k]^2}]}, \qquad -\infty \le X \le +\infty$$

a, k = parameters $\qquad\qquad\qquad\qquad$ **(A.20)**

$$E(X) = a$$

$$\text{Var}(X) = \frac{k^2\pi^2}{3}$$

See Exhibit A.1(g).

Log-Normal Distribution. (random variable whose logarithm is normal)

$$f(X) = \frac{1}{X\sigma(2\pi)^{1/2}} e^{[-[\log(X/m)]^2/2\sigma^2]}, \qquad +\infty \le X \le -\infty$$

m, σ^2 = parameters (the mean and variance of log X, respectively) **(A.21)**

$$E(X) = me^{(\sigma^2/2)}$$

$$\text{Var}(X) = \frac{m^2 e^{(\sigma^2/2)}}{e^{\sigma^2/2} - 1}$$

See Exhibit A.1(h).

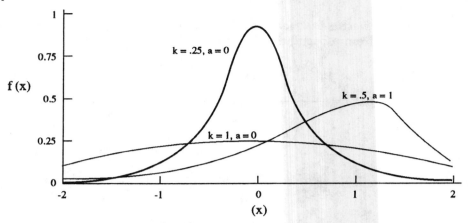

EXHIBIT A.1 (g) Logistic distribution.

Multinomial Distribution. (the multivariate extension of the binomial distribution)

$$p(X_1, \ldots, X_k) = n! \prod_{i=1}^{k} \left(\frac{p_i^{X_i}}{X_i!} \right) \tag{A.22}$$

$$p_i = \text{probability of event } i, \, i = 1, \ldots, k, \quad \sum_{i=1}^{k} p_i = 1$$

Note: The multinomial distribution derives from n independent trials, each of which can take one of k independent outcomes with probability p_i, $i = 1, \ldots, k$. It is often used to describe the distribution of purchases across a set of brands.

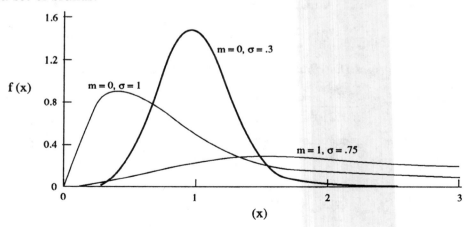

EXHIBIT A.1 (h) Log-normal distribution.

Negative Binomial Distribution.   (the number of failures before the bth success in a sequence of Bernouilli trials)

$$p(X) = \binom{b + X - 1}{X} p^b (1 - p)^X, \quad 0 \le X \le +\infty, \text{ an integer} \quad \textbf{(A.23)}$$

$p =$ Bernouilli success probability

$b =$ number of (pre-specified) successes

$$E(X) = \frac{b(1 - p)}{p}$$

$$\text{Var}(X) = \frac{b(1 - p)}{p^2}$$

Note that:

- If $b = 1$, the distribution is geometric.
- A Poisson random variable with a gamma mixing (heterogeneity) distribution yields a negative binomial distribution.

Normal Distribution.   (used frequently to model an error distribution)

$$f(X) = \frac{1}{\sigma(2\pi)^{1/2}} e^{[-(X - u)]^2 / 2\sigma^2]}, \quad -\infty \le X \le +\infty$$

$u, \sigma =$ parameters, $\quad \sigma > 0$ $\quad\quad$ **(A.24)**

$$E(X) = u$$

$$\text{Var}(X) = \sigma^2$$

See Exhibit A.1(i).

Pascal Distribution.   (the number of trials up to and including the bth success in a sequence of Bernoulli trials)

$$p(X) = \binom{X - 1}{X - b} p^b (1 - p)^{X - b}, \quad b \le X \le +\infty \quad \textbf{(A.25)}$$

$p =$ Bernoulli probability

$b =$ number of pre-specified successes.

$$E(X) = \frac{b}{p}$$

$$\text{Var}(X) = \frac{b(1 - p)}{p^2}$$

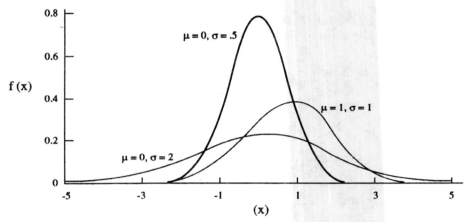

EXHIBIT A.1   (i) Normal distribution.

Poisson Distribution   (the number of arrivals—purchases—in a fixed time interval when interarrival times are exponentially distributed)

$$p(X) = \frac{\lambda^X e^{-\lambda}}{X!}, \quad X = 0, 1, \ldots, +\infty \tag{A.26}$$

λ = (exponential) arrival rate parameter

$E(X) = \lambda$

$\mathrm{Var}(X) = \lambda$

Student's t Distribution.   (the ratio of a standard normal to an independent chi-squared distribution with v degrees of freedom)

$$f(X) = \frac{\{\Gamma[(v + 1)/2]\}[1 + (X^2/v)]^{-(v+1)/2}}{(\pi v)^{1/2}\,\Gamma(v/2)}, \quad -\infty \le X \le +\infty$$

v = shape parameter, degrees of freedom, a positive integer   **(A.27)**

$E(X) = 0$

$$\mathrm{Var}(X) = \frac{v}{(v - 2)}, \quad v > 2$$

See Exhibit A.1(j).

Uniform Distribution.   (used to model the likelihood of an event over a range, when that event is equally likely throughout the range)

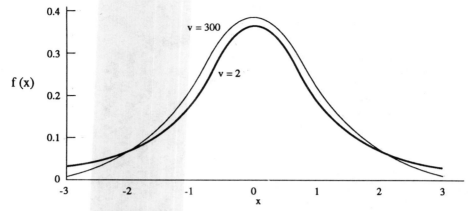

EXHIBIT A.1 (j) Student's t distribution.

$$f(X) = \frac{(X - a)}{b}, \quad a \le X \le a + b \qquad \text{(A.28)}$$

a = lower bound on range (parameter)

b = length of range (parameter).

$$E(X) = a + \frac{b}{2}$$

$$\text{Var}(X) = \frac{b^2}{12}$$

Weibull Distribution.   (a generalized form of the exponential distribution)

$$f(X) = cX^{c-1} \lambda^c e^{-(X\lambda)^c}, \quad 0 \le X \le +\infty \qquad \text{(A.29)}$$

c = shape parameter

λ = scale parameter

$$E(X) = \frac{\Gamma[(c + 1)/c]}{\lambda}$$

$$\text{Var}(X) = \frac{\Gamma[(c + 2)/c] - \{\Gamma[(c + 1)/c]\}^2}{\lambda^2}$$

Note that

• When $c = 1$, the Weibull reduces to the exponential distribution.

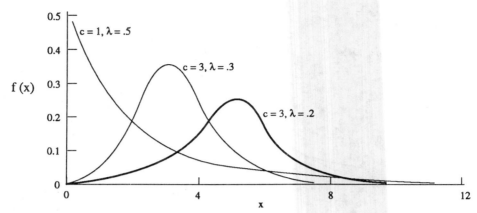

EXHIBIT A.1   (k) Weibull distribution.

• When $c = 2$, the distribution is often known as the Raleigh distribution.

See Exhibit A.1(k).

For further developments see Arnold (1990), Bain and Engelhardt (1989), DeGroot (1987), and Walpole and Myers (1989).

MIXING DISTRIBUTIONS AND HETEROGENEITY

In marketing models, especially those models of individual buyer behavior, researchers often assume that each member of a population purchases according to a given probability of purchase model, but that individuals vary according to some parameters (life-style, past purchase behavior, tastes, etc.).

If such individual differences can be handled directly (by measuring lifestyle, preference data, and the like) those variables are used directly in the purchase model. Often, the researcher may have only a short purchase sequence at the individual level and no other data about the individual. In these cases, the researcher may develop a *conditional* probability of purchase model, where the conditioning is on one or more parameters not directly observable but assessed to vary across the population.

For example,

$p(\text{purchase } A|k)$ = conditional probability of purchase of individual i given parameter k_i.

$f(k)$ = distribution of the parameter k across the population (i.e., a *mixing distribution*).

To get the unconditional probability of purchasing the brand, k has to be integrated out:

$$p(\text{purchase } A) = \int_k p(\text{purchase } A|k) \, f(k) \, dk$$

EXAMPLE

Suppose we have a two-brand market, with brands A and B and that

$$p(A|k) = c\left(\frac{\Pi_B}{\Pi_A + \Pi_B}\right)^k \tag{A.30}$$

where

$$\Pi_A, \Pi_B = \text{prices of the brands}$$
$$k = \text{price sensitivity parameter}$$
$$c = \text{scale parameter}$$

Suppose also we assume a mixing distribution:

$$k = \begin{cases} 1 \text{ with probability } 0.8 \\ 2 \text{ with probability } 0.2 \end{cases}$$

Then

$$p(A) = p(A|k = 1)p(k = 1) + p(A|k = 2)p(k = 2) \tag{A.31}$$

$$= c\left[0.8\left(\frac{\Pi_B}{\Pi_A + \Pi_B}\right) + 0.2\left(\frac{\Pi_B}{\Pi_A + \Pi_B}\right)^2\right]$$

EXAMPLE

Assume that a two-brand market is made up of Bernoulli customers (i.e., everyone has an individual probability of purchasing each of the two brands) but that those probabilities vary across the population. Suppose we use the beta distribution as a mixing distribution (a popular and flexible distribution often used for this purpose), observe the n purchase occasions and note r purchases of brand 1. If we want to estimate the (posterior) distribution of p given the (prior) mixing distribution and our observations we proceed as follows:

$$f(p|\alpha, \beta) = k_1 p^{\alpha-1}(1 - p)^{\beta-1} \qquad \text{(A.32)}$$

(prior, mixing distribution)

$$p(r|n, p) = k_2 p^r (1 - p)^{n-r} \qquad \text{(A.33)}$$

$r = 0, \ldots, n$ (binomial likelihood distribution)

Noting that by Bayes's theorem, the posterior distribution of p is proportional to the prior times the likelihood, we get (posterior):

$$f(p|n, r, \alpha, \beta) = k_3 p^{\alpha+r-1}(1 - p)^{\beta+n-r-1} \qquad \text{(A.34)}$$

In the foregoing equation, we see that the posterior distribution of p has the same functional form as the prior—it is also beta in form (with two additional parameters that must be estimated). A distribution of this sort is called a "natural conjugate distribution"—where the prior and the posterior have the same functional form. Another natural conjugate set of distributions is normal-prior (mixing) and normal likelihood.

In many stochastic models, one aims to estimate those values of α and β (and other parameters) that provide an empirical frequency distribution of purchase (purchase sequences strings) that best matches up with what equation (A.34) above would predict.

For example, in purchase strings of length 3, (Bernoulli purchasing) one can have 0, 1, 2 or 3 purchases of a brand. If we denote these as N_1, N_2, N_3 and N_4, then, across the population

$$N_1 + N_2 + N_3 + N_4 = N \text{ (population size)}.$$

The expected value of p from the distribution in equation (A.34) is

$$E(p|n, r) = \frac{\alpha + r}{\alpha + \beta + n}. \qquad \text{(A.35)}$$

So, for $n = 3$, we get

$$E_3 = E(p|r = 3) = \frac{\alpha + 3}{\alpha + \beta + 3}$$

$$E_2 = E(p|r = 2) = \frac{\alpha + 2}{\alpha + \beta + 2}$$

$$E_1 = E(p|r = 1) = \frac{\alpha + 1}{\alpha + \beta + 1}$$

$$E_0 = E(p|r = 0) = \frac{\alpha}{\alpha + \beta}.$$

One can then use one of several estimation procedures (maximum likelihood, minimum chi square) to estimate those values of α and β that match the observed frequencies (N_i) with those expected frequencies derived from the likelihood and the mixing distribution (E_i).

The issue of assessing and evaluating heterogeneity of a population is subtle, as individuals may differ in both the choice process they use (the brand selection model), as well as in their tastes and other characteristics. It is quite possible that what appears to be a higher order stochastic process (observed at the market level) is the result of a simple individual process confounded by population heterogeneity.

EXAMPLE

Assume we have a market with two brands (A and B) and that the buying population is made up of two subpopulations (I and II). Assume also that there are five times as many II's as I's; that is, p(customer in I) = 1/6 if a customer is randomly chosen from the population. Further assume that these subpopulations are homogeneous with given and constant (but different) probabilities of purchasing each of the brands:

$$p(A|I) = 0.6 \quad p(A|II) = 0.06 \qquad \textbf{(A.36)}$$

If we sample from this population, what is the probability that brand A will be purchased? This probability can be calculated as

$$p(A) = p(A|I)p(I) + p(A|II)p(II) \qquad \textbf{(A.37)}$$

$$= (0.6)(1/6) + (0.06)(5/6) = 0.15$$

Now let us consider the probability that the population that buys A on a given purchase repeats it on the next purchase:

$$p(A \text{ on } 2 | A \text{ on } 1) = \frac{p(A_2 \text{ and } A_1)}{p(A_1)}$$

$$p(A_2 \text{ and } A_1) = p(A_2 A_1 | I) p(I) + p(A_2 A_1 | II) p(II)$$

$$= (0.6)^2 (1/6) + (0.06^2)(5/6) = 0.063 \qquad \textbf{(A.38)}$$

With equations (A.37) and (A.38) we get $p(A_2 | A_1) = 0.063/0.15 = 0.42$! Now compare $p(A_1) = 0.15$ to $p(A_2 | A_1) = 0.42$. Thus, in this example, the purchase of A on a given occasion apparently increases the probability that the brand will be purchased next. The increase is real, but the cause is due to selective selection (i.e., the spurious effect of heterogeneity) rather than learning.

For further developments see French (1986), Raiffa and Schlaifer (1961), Ross (1989), Winkler and Hays (1975), and Winkler (1972).

MATHEMATICS OF OPTIMIZATION

Mean Value Theorem. The *mean value theorem* states that *if* $f(x)$ is continuous on an interval $a < x < b$, then there exists a number $\bar{x}$ such that

$$\frac{[f(b) - f(a)]}{(b - a)} = f'(\bar{x}), \quad a < \bar{x} < b \qquad \textbf{(A.39)}$$

Exhibit A.2 gives the geometric interpretation of this theorem, which is that there is at least one point in the interval between a and b where the curve has the same slope as the line segment connecting the points $[a, f(a)]$ and $[b, f(b)]$.

Taylor Series Expansion. Taylor's theorem states that if a function $f(x)$ and its first $n + 1$ derivatives are continuous in the interval $a \le x \le b$, then for $a < x_0 < b$, the nth order Taylor series expansion of $f(x)$ around the point x_0 is

$$f(x) = f(x_0) + \sum_{m=1}^{n} \frac{(x - x_0)^m}{m!} f^m(x_0) + R_{n+1} \qquad \textbf{(A.40)}$$

where

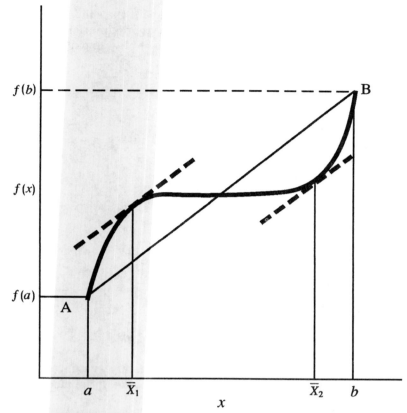

EXHIBIT A.2   The Mean Value Theorem states that at least one point between a and b must have the same slope as the line connecting point A and point B. Here there are two: $\overline{X}_1$ and $\overline{X}_2$.

$$f^i = \frac{d^i f}{dx^i}$$

$$R_n = \frac{(x - x_0)^n}{n!} f^n(\bar{x}), \quad \text{for some } a \le \bar{x} < b$$

Note that if $x_0 = 0$, equation (A.40) becomes

$$f(x) = f(0) + f'(0)x + \frac{f''(0)}{2!} x^2 + \frac{f'''(0)}{3!} x^3 + \cdots + R_n. \tag{A.41}$$

As n gets larger, R_n gets small in general so that any curve can be approximated well in the neighborhood of a point by a polynomial of sufficiently high order. In the absence of a theory about the shape of a curve, this theorem provides justification for a polynomial approximation.

Taylor's theorem for several variables expanded around the origin $(0, \ldots, 0)$ is

$$f(x_1, x_2, \ldots, x_n) = f(0, \ldots, 0) + \sum_{i=1}^{n} \frac{\partial f}{\partial x_i}\Big|_0 x_i$$

$$+ \frac{1}{2!} \sum_{i=1}^{n} \sum_{j=1}^{n} \frac{\partial^2 f}{\partial x_i \partial x_j}\Big|_0 x_i x_j + \cdots$$

$$+ \frac{1}{3!} \sum_{i=1}^{n} \sum_{j=1}^{n} \sum_{k=1}^{n} \frac{\partial^3 f}{\partial x_i \partial x_j \partial x_k}\Big|_0 x_i x_j x_k + \cdots \qquad \textbf{(A.42)}$$

$$+ \cdots$$

$$+ \cdots$$

$$+ R_m$$

For $n = 2$, this reduces to

$$f(x_1, x_2) = a_0 + a_1 x_1 + a_2 x_2 + a_3 x_1^2 + a_4 x_1 x_2 + a_5 x_2^2 + R_3 \qquad \textbf{(A.43)}$$

where the a_i's correspond to the appropriately evaluated constants or partial derivatives in equation (A.41). If a_3 and a_5 are 0, the model reduces to a linear model with interactions (see Appendix C).

Concavity and Convexity. A function $f(x)$ is *concave* on $a \leq x \leq b$ if for all $0 \leq t \leq 1$ and for any $a \leq x_1 \leq x_2 \leq b$

$$tf(x_1) + (1 - t)f(x_2) \leq f(tx_1 + (1 - t)x_2) \qquad \textbf{(A.44)}$$

Geometrically, Exhibit A.3 shows that if a function is (strictly) concave, i.e., the inequality < replaces $\leq$ in equation A.44), a line segment connecting any two points on the curve falls strictly below the curve.

A function is said to be *convex* if the inequality in equation (A.44) is reversed.

A necessary and sufficient criterion for a twice differentiable function to be (strictly) concave is for $f''(x) = d^2f/dx^2 < 0$ for all x in its domain. Again, if $f''(x) > 0$, the function is (strictly) convex in the region.

The extension of (A.44) to several variables is: $f(x_1, \ldots, x_n)$ is (strictly) concave if:

$$tf(x^*) + (1 - t)f(x^0) < f(tx^* + (1 - t)x^0) \qquad \textbf{(A.45)}$$

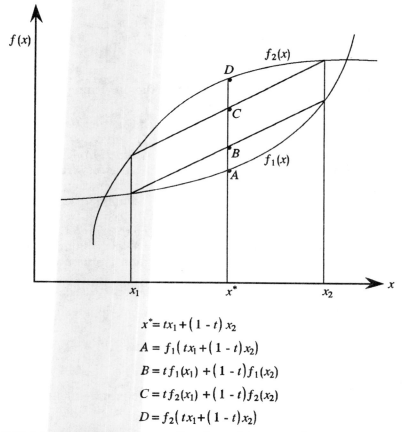

$$x^* = t x_1 + (1 - t) x_2$$

$$A = f_1(t x_1 + (1 - t) x_2)$$

$$B = t f_1(x_1) + (1 - t) f_1(x_2)$$

$$C = t f_2(x_1) + (1 - t) f_2(x_2)$$

$$D = f_2(t x_1 + (1 - t) x_2)$$

EXHIBIT A.3   Concave and convex functions: f_1 is convex because $B > A$; f_2 is concave because $D > C$.

for all $0 \leq t \leq 1$ and any pair of points $x^* = (x_1^*, \ldots, x_n^*)$ and $x^0 = (x_1^0, \ldots, x_n^0)$ in the domain of x. The analogous condition for the second derivative condition is that the Hessian matrix must be negative definite, where the Hessian matrix is the matrix of second-order partial derivatives:

$$H = \begin{bmatrix} \dfrac{\partial^2 f}{\partial x_1^2} & \dfrac{\partial^2 f}{\partial x_1 \partial x_2} & \cdots & \dfrac{\partial^2 f}{\partial x_1 \partial x_n} \\ \vdots & \cdots & \cdots & \vdots \\ \dfrac{\partial^2 f}{\partial x_n x_1} & \cdots & \cdots & \dfrac{\partial^2 f}{\partial x_n^2} \end{bmatrix} \qquad \textbf{(A.46)}$$

A matrix is **negative definite** if its principal minors alternate in sign, beginning with negative:

$$f_{11} < 0, \quad \begin{vmatrix} f_{11} & f_{12} \\ f_{21} & f_{22} \end{vmatrix} > 0; \quad \begin{vmatrix} f_{11} & f_{12} & f_{13} \\ f_{21} & f_{22} & f_{23} \\ f_{31} & f_{32} & f_{33} \end{vmatrix} < 0 \cdots (-1)^n |H| > 0 \qquad \textbf{(A.47)}$$

where $f_{ij} = \partial^2 f / \partial x_i \partial x_j$ and $|H|$ refers to the determinant of H.

Quasi-concave Functions. A real-valued function $f(x)$ with a convex domain $X \subset R_n$ is defined to be *quasi-concave* if for any $x_1, x_2 \in X$ and any $k \in (0, 1)$, $f(kx_1 + (1 - k)x_2) \geq \min\{f(x_1,), f(x_2)\}$. A function f is strictly quasi-concave if the inequality is strict. Strictly quasi-concave functions are unimodal, but they can be convex, concave, or even a combination of the two. Of course, both strict concavity and strict convexity imply strict quasi-concavity.

The attractiveness of quasi-concavity comes from the fact that it is a weaker assumption than concavity and at the same time it has the property that every local maximum is also a global maximum. And strict quasi-concavity guarantees that the global maximum is unique.

Unconstrained Maxima and Minima. If $f(x)$ is twice differentiable and attains its maximum at x^* on $a < x < b$, from the mean value theorem (equation A.39), we get

$$f(x) - f(x^*) = f'(\bar{x})(x - x^*) \qquad \textbf{(A.48)}$$

for some $\bar{x}$ between x and x^*. Since x^* maximizes f, the left side of (A.48) must be ≤ 0, so

$$f'(\bar{x})(x - x^*) \leq 0 \qquad \textbf{(A.49)}$$

Thus f' must be ≥ 0 when $x < x^*$ and $f' \leq 0$ when $x > x^*$ so

$$f'(x^*) = 0 \qquad \textbf{(A.50)}$$

Also for x^* to be a maximum, it must be larger than functional values around it (above any line segment connecting any two points around it), so $f(x)$ must be concave or $f''(x) < 0$. For a local minimum, $f(x)$ must be convex and $f'(x)$ must $= 0$ as well.

Analogously, for a function of several variables all first partial derivatives must be zero and the function must be (strictly) concave (the Hessian must be negative definite).

Equality-Constrained Optimization. Consider the problem of finding the maximum or the minimum of a function $f(x_1, \ldots, x_n)$, subject to certain restrictions on the values of $x_1, \ldots, x_n$:

$$\text{Maximize(minimize)} f(x_1, \ldots, x_n) \tag{A.51}$$

subject to

$$g_1(x_1, \ldots, x_n) = b_1$$
$$\vdots$$
$$g_m(x_1, \ldots, x_n) = b_m$$

where $m < n$.

The classical approach for handling this problem is with Lagrange multipliers. The procedure starts by formulating the composite function, the *Lagrangian*:

$$L(x_1, \ldots, x_n, \lambda_1, \ldots, \lambda_m) = f(x_1, \ldots, x_n) + \Sigma \, \lambda_i \, [g_i(x_1, \ldots, x_n) - b_i] \tag{A.52}$$

where the new variables $\lambda_1, \ldots, \lambda_m$ are called *Lagrange multipliers*. The key thing to observe from equation (A.51) is that for all permissible values of $x_1, \ldots, x_n$, $g_i(x_1, \ldots, x_n) - b_i = 0$ for all i. Thus $L(x_1, \ldots, x_n, \lambda_1, \ldots, \lambda_m) = f(x_1, \ldots, x_n)$, and if $(x_1^*, \ldots, x_n^* \, \lambda_1^*, \ldots, \lambda_m^*)$ is a critical point (local or global optimum) of equation (A.52), then $x_1^*, \ldots, x_n^*$ is a corresponding critical point of the original problem.

Thus the Lagrange multiplier method reduces to analyzing (A.52) by the procedure suggested above for unconstrained functions. The $m + n$ partial derivatives are set equal to zero:

$$\frac{\partial L}{\partial X_j} = \frac{\partial f}{\partial X_j} - \sum_{i=1}^{m} \lambda_i \frac{\partial g_i}{\partial X_j} = 0, \quad j = 1, 2, \ldots, n \tag{A.53}$$

$$\frac{\partial L}{\partial \lambda_i} = g_i(x_1, \ldots, x_n) - b_i = 0, \quad i = 1, \ldots, m \tag{A.54}$$

and the critical points are derived by solving equations (A.53) and (A.54) for $x_1, \ldots, x_n$ and $\lambda_1, \ldots, \lambda_m$. Note that equation (A.54) gives the constraints in the original equations, so only permissible solutions are considered.

Although the Lagrange multiplier method is a neat procedure conceptually, it suffers from computational difficulties. It is often difficult or impossible to solve equations (A.53) and (A.54), and the solutions, when found, are often large in number, or infinite, making evaluation of the results difficult. Nevertheless, for certain small problems, the approach can sometimes be used successfully.

EXAMPLE _____

Assume that a company sells in two territories, and the estimated demand functions are, respectively,

$$Q_1 = 6X_1^{1/2} \tag{A.55}$$

$$Q_2 = 3X_2^{1/2} \tag{A.56}$$

Territory 1 shows twice the response to promotional-marketing expenditures (X_1) as territory 2, although in both cases there are diminishing marginal returns. The total costs of selling in the two territories are assumed to be

$$C_1 = 60 + 4Q_1 + X_1 \tag{A.57}$$

$$C_2 = 28 + 5Q_2 + X_2 \tag{A.58}$$

Prices in these markets are $p_1 = \$7$ and $p_2 = \$9$, and profit for the firm in a terrory is calculated as:

$$\text{Revenue} - \text{costs} = PQ(X) - C(Q(X)) \tag{A.59}$$

Assuming a promotional budget of $65,000 (i.e., $X_1 + X_2 = 65$), how much should be spent in each territory?

To solve this problem we form the Lagrangian profit function:

$$
\begin{aligned}
L &= (7 - 4)6X_1^{1/2} - 60 - X_1 + (9 - 5)3X_2^{1/2} \\
&\quad - 28 - X_2 + \lambda(65 - X_1 - X_2) \\
&= 18X_1^{1/2} - 60 - X_1 + 12X_2^{1/2} - 28 - X_2 \\
&\quad + \lambda(65 - X_1 - X_2)
\end{aligned}
\tag{A.60}
$$

Then we find the partial derivatives of L in equation (A.60) with respect to X_1, X_2, and λ and set each of them equal to zero:

$$\frac{\partial L}{\partial X_1} = 9X_1^{-1/2} - 1 - \lambda = 0 \tag{A.61}$$

$$\frac{\partial L}{\partial X_2} = 6X_2^{-1/2} - 1 - \lambda = 0 \tag{A.62}$$

$$\frac{\partial L}{\partial \lambda} = 65 - X_1 - X_2 = 0 \qquad (A.63)$$

Setting equations (A.61) and (A.62) equal to each other, we have

$$9X_1^{-1/2} = 6X_2^{-1/2} \qquad (A.64)$$

Solving equation (A.63) for X_2 and substituting it into equation (A.64), we find that it becomes

$$9X_1^{-1/2} = 6(65 - X_1)^{-1/2} \qquad (A.65)$$

Solving equation (A.65) for X_1^*, we find $X_1^* = \$45$ (this figure and the following dollar figures are in thousands of dollars). Thus territory 1 receives $45 and territory 2 receives the remaining $20. According to equation (A.60), this allocation of the $65 will generate total profits of $21.40. Solving (A.61) for λ gives $\lambda = \$0.34$, showing that a unit increase in the promotional budget will add $0.34 to profit.

See Anton (1987) and Stirling (1987) for further developments.

Linear Inequality Constrained Optimization

Linear Programming. A linear program is a problem with a linear objective function subject to linear constraint. The linearity of the problem prevents a solution by classical methods earlier, because the objective function is neither strictly concave nor strictly convex and has an optimum at an extreme point of its feasible region. This extreme-point property leads to the solution procedures. A form of the linear program problem is

$$\text{Maximize} \sum_{i=1}^{n} a_i x_i \qquad (A.66)$$

Subject to

$$\sum_{i=1}^{n} b_{ij} x_i \le c_j, \quad j = 1, \ldots, \quad m \; x_i \ge 0$$

Methods for solving such problems are generally of two types: they either begin with a feasible extreme point (a point on the boundary of the feasible region) and move around the boundary, or they begin with an internal point and "project" toward the boundary.

A good, contemporary review of optimization methods can be found in Nemhauser, Kan, and Todd (1989), reviewing this and other procedures.

Integer and Mixed-Integer Programming.   In linear programming and in the classical approaches, the functions were assumed to be continuous and differentiable. In many marketing problems only certain (integer) values are permitted for some (mixed integer) or all (pure integer) of the variables. Rounding off a solution to, say, a linear programming approximation can give answers that are not close to optimal, and it may not be clear whether it is better to round up or round down. Special algorithms (and theory) have been developed to handle such problems.

Four types of problems that occur frequently in marketing that can be characterized by integer or mixed-integer programming formulation are described below.

Either-or Constraints.   Frequently, one of two restrictions must hold, but not necessarily both. For example, one of two warehouses (each with holding-cost schedules) will be used for storing product in transit: warehouse A charges $3 per unit of product 1 and $2 per unit of product 2, while in warehouse B the charges are reversed. Furthermore, we have an inventory-cost spending limit of $2,000. These two constraints can be formulated separately:

$$3X_1 + 2X_2 \le 2{,}000 \tag{A.67}$$

$$2X_1 + 3X_2 \le 2{,}000 \tag{A.68}$$

For only one of these constraints to hold at a time, we introduce the $0 - 1$ variable y and the very large positive number M and append them to equations (A.67) and (A.68) to form

$$3X_1 + 2X_1 \le 2{,}000 + yM \tag{A.69}$$

$$2X_1 + 3X_2 \le 2{,}000 + (1 - y)M \tag{A.70}$$

Here if $y = 1$, constraint (A.68) holds and if $y = 0$, constraint (A.69) holds.

k out of K Constraints.   The idea above is extended to the situation in which k out of K constraints hold:

$$g_1(X_1, \ldots, X_n) \le b_1 + My_1$$

$$\vdots \tag{A.71a}$$

$$g_k(X_1, \ldots, X_n) \le b_K + My_K$$

$$\sum_{i=1}^{K} y_i = K - k \tag{A.71b}$$

$$y_i = 0 \text{ or } 1 \text{ for all i} \tag{A.71c}$$

Constraints (A.71b) and (A.71c) force k out of the K constraints in equation (A.71a) to hold while the others are ineffective.

Functions with K Possible Values. Suppose a given function (perhaps the possible levels of production capacity of a plant with multiple production lines) is required to take on any one of K discrete values:

$$g(X_1, \ldots, X_n) = b_1 \text{ or } b_2 \text{ or } \ldots \text{ or } b_k \tag{A.72}$$

Equation (A.72) can be written as an integer programming constraint:

$$g(X_1, \ldots, X_n) = \sum_{i=1}^{K} b_i y_i$$

$$\sum_{i=1}^{K} y_i = 1 \tag{A.73}$$

$$y_i = 0 \quad \text{or } 1$$

Fixed-Charge Problem. A situation that comes up frequently in marketing, especially in distribution planning, is the fixed-charge problem, in which there is a fixed charge for a production facility (as well as a variable charge if it is used) and no charge otherwise. If we let X_i denote the amount of production or use of the jth facility, we might have a cost function that looks like

$$C_j(X_j) = \begin{cases} b_j + d_j X_j & \text{if } X_j > 0 \\ 0 & \text{otherwise} \end{cases} \tag{A.74}$$

Then if our original objective function was to minimize

$$C(X_1, \ldots, X_n) = \sum_{j=1}^{n} C_j(X_j) \tag{A.75}$$

subject to constraint (A.74), it can be replaced by minimizing

$$C(X_1, \ldots, X_n) = \sum_{j=1}^{n} b_j y_j + d_j X_j \tag{A.76}$$

$$X_j - My_j \leq 0, \quad j = 1, \ldots, n \tag{A.77}$$

$$y_j = 0 \text{ or } 1, \quad j = 1, \ldots, n \tag{A.78}$$

Constraint (A.76) is needed to ensure that $y_j = 1$ rather than zero whenever facility j is used ($X_j > 0$).

Some of the most popular methods used to solve integer programming problems employ the divide-and-conquer approach. The idea is that if, in the unrestricted linear program, y does not equal zero or one, define two new problems, one with $y_j = 0$ and another with $y_j = 1$ and then solve each of these problems separately. Much of the theory of solving integer-programming problems is based on clever solutions to such problems. (See Nemhauser, Kan and Todd, 1989).

Nonlinear Programming Problems. Many key decision problems in marketing have a relatively complicated, nonlinear structure. There are classes of nonlinear programming problems that often arise in marketing analyses that are inherently simpler to solve than others. The general, nonlinear-programming problem is

$$\text{Maximize } f(X_1, \ldots, X_n)$$

Subject to

$$g_1(X_1, \ldots, X_n) \leq b_1 \tag{A.79}$$

$$\vdots$$

$$g_m(X_1, \ldots, X_n) \leq b_m$$

Two special mathematical programming problems that often arise in marketing are separable and quadratic programming problems.

Separable Programming. An objective function is separable when it can be written as a sum of separate terms, each of which involves only a single variable:

$$f(X_1, \ldots, X_n) = f_1(X_1) + \cdots + f_n(X_n) \tag{A.80}$$

To develop an approximate solution to such a problem, it can be reduced to a linear programming problem by approximating each $f_j(X_j)$ with a piecewise linear function. The procedure guarantees a unique optimal solution if each $f_j(X_j)$ is concave (for a maximization problem) or convex (for a minimization problem).

Quadratic Programming. Quadratic programming refers to the maximization of a quadratic objective function subject to linear constraints:

$$\text{Maximize } f(X_1, \ldots, X_n) = \Sigma c_j X_j + 1/2 \, \Sigma\Sigma q_{jk} X_j X_k$$

subject to: **(A.81)**

$$\sum_{j=1}^{n} a_{ij} X_j \le b_i, \quad i = 1, 2, \ldots, m$$

$$X_j \ge 0$$

Powerful solution procedures similar to the simplex method have been developed for the special quadratic programming case where the objective function in equation (A.81) is concave. For f to be concave,

$$\Sigma\Sigma q_{jk} X_j X_k \ge 0 \tag{A.82}$$

for all feasible values of $X_1, \ldots, X_n$. This condition is equivalent to the condition that the q_{jk} be elements of a negative semidefinite matrix.

Quadratic programming is often employed when a quadratic objective function is used to approximate a more complex functional form.

More General, Nonlinear Programming Methods. As with general integer programming methods, the general nonlinear programming problem is inherently a difficult problem. General solution procedures are not always successful; special insight into the structure of the problem is often required in order to choose a solution strategy.

Again, Nemhauser, Kan, and Todd (1989) provide a good overview of the most recent approaches. Also see Bazaraa and Shetty (1979) and Luenberger (1984).

Multiple-Objective Optimization. Often a problem may have more than one objective. The different objectives may be of equal importance, or, at least, it may be difficult for the decision maker to compare the importance of one objective with another. The utility-theory–based approach (Appendix C) has been applied in this area. An alternative approach is known as the Pareto optimality approach. In certain cases if the decision variables are subject to linear constraints, the alternatives can be evaluated as described in the paragraphs that follow.

We seek a feasible point X^* that dominates all other feasible points in the sense that there is no other feasible Y^* at which all objectives are at least as good as X^* and at which at least one objective value is better. Such a point X^* is termed a Pareto optimum, and the set of points $\{X\}$ that satisfy this condition are called the efficient frontier. Exhibit A.4 illustrates this concept: points A, B, and C correspond to Pareto optima for the problem. The problem

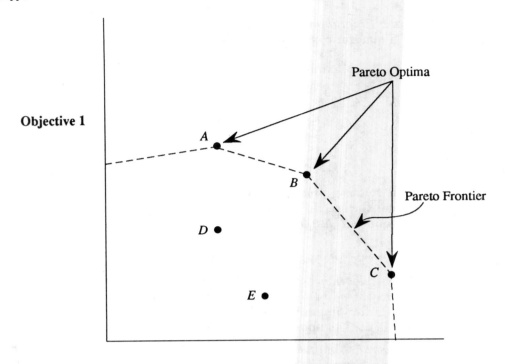

EXHIBIT A.4 The Pareto optimum approach to multiple-criteria problems.

of finding Pareto optima can be put into a linear-programming framework. (See Nemhauser, Kan and Todd, 1989, and Cohen, 1978.)

Optimal-Control Problems. Most of the problems presented so far have focused on choosing values of variables to maximize an objective function subject to restrictions (constraints): these are mathematical programming problems.

Optimal-control problems occur when the problem is to choose time paths for certain variables, called control variables [advertising rate, say, $X = X(t)$], from a given feasible control set. The choice of time paths for the control variables leads, through a set of differential equations called the equations of motion, to time paths for various variables describing the system called state variables (sales rates, for example). Time paths of the control variables are chosen to maximize an objective functional (e.g., profit). (Note that a function is defined over variables while a functional is defined over other functions.)

The simplest optimal-control problem is one of selecting a control function, $u(t)$, $t_0 \leq t \leq t_1$ to

$$\text{Maximize} \int_{t_0}^{t_1} f[t, x(t), u(t)] \, dt \tag{A.83}$$

Subject to

$$\dot{x}(t) = g[t, x(t), u(t)] \tag{A.84}$$

where

$$\dot{x} = \frac{dx}{dt}$$

and

$$t_0, t_1, x(t_0) = x_0 \text{ fixed} \quad \text{and} \quad x(t_1) \text{ free}$$

EXAMPLE

In marketing, most optimal control problems emerge when one is studying the profit-maximizing time path of one or more marketing instruments. For example, Horsky and Simon (1983) study the optimal advertising policy when sales are driven according to the following equation (see Chapter 10):

$$\dot{Q}(t) = [N - Q(t)][\alpha + \beta \ln(A(t)) + \gamma Q(t)] \tag{A.85}$$

where

$$Q(t) = \text{cumulative sales by } t$$

$$\dot{Q}(t) = \frac{dQ(t)}{dt} = \text{sales rate}$$

$$N = \text{ultimate sales (market potential)}$$

$$A(t) = \text{advertising rate}$$

$$\alpha, \beta, \gamma = \text{constants (assumed known)}.$$

They form a profit function as follows:

$$\Pi = \int_0^\infty [g\dot{Q}(t) - A(t)]e^{-\theta t}\,dt \qquad\qquad \text{(A.86)}$$

where

g = gross margin exclusive of advertising
θ = cost of capital

To find $A(t)$ that maximizes (A.86) subject to (A.85) and some initial and terminal condition is an optimal-control problem: a dynamic system with one static variable $(Q(t))$ and one control variable $(A(t))$. Using solution methods based on Pontryagin's (1962) maximum principal, the authors are able to characterize the time path of $A(t)$ as declining over time.

Most marketing applications of control theory are similar to the foregoing—the results are normally qualitative, providing insight into the structure of an optimal policy as opposed to being quantitative (providing a mechanism for providing specific levels of the control). See Kamien and Schwartz (1981) for a thorough treatment of optimal control in management applications.

Other Optimization Procedures

While we have addressed a number of optimization procedures that have seen applications in marketing, there are a number of others, as follows.

Dynamic programming can be used to solve multi-stage problems in both continuous and discrete space. If a problem

- requires a sequence of decisions to be made
- has a number of stages, each of which has a number of associated states, only one of which can be operant at the stage
- enters a state at stage k as a function of where it is at stage $k - 1$ and the decision only

then it may be amenable to a dynamic programming approach. The idea behind the approach is to use the system's lack of memory—called separability—to devise a sequence of simpler optimal solutions that lead to the overall optimal solution (Ravindran, Phillips, and Solberg, 1987).

Optimization Under Uncertainty. The approaches just outlined have generally assumed that all variables and parameters are known with certainty. A number of modeling approaches have attempted to relax that consideration these include

• *stochastic programming,* where some of the parameters of the mathematical program are assumed to be random variables. Here, the objective function may become a random variable and (normally) its expected value is maximized, and constraints are frequently expanded to take on all possible values of the (now stochastic) parameters (see Ravindran, Phillips and Solberg, 1987).

• *chance constrained programming,* where the constraints do not have to hold with certainty but only with some probability (see Schrage, 1987).

• *stochastic control theory,* where the equation of motion of the dynamic system are not known with certainty (see Ross, 1983).

LINEAR DIFFERENTIAL EQUATIONS

Many marketing problems deal with rates (sales rates, advertising rates, etc.) and, as such, are frequently formulated as differential equations. We will deal here with first-order linear differential equations.

A first-order linear, non-homogeneous differential equation has the following form:

$$\frac{dy}{dt} + a(t)y = b(t) \tag{A.87}$$

Associated with (A.87) is another differential equation obtained by replacing $b(t)$ by 0:

$$\frac{dy}{dt} + a(t)y = 0 \tag{A.88}$$

which is called the *reduced or homogeneous* equation. The homogeneous solution is important because of the following:

Result: The general solution to (A.87) (y) is the sum of the general solution to (A.88) (y_c) plus any particular solution to (A.87) (y_p).

To illustrate, if we want to solve:

$$\frac{dy(t)}{dt} + ay(t) = bt \tag{A.89}$$

we first solve

$$\frac{dy}{dt} + ay = 0 \tag{A.90}$$

as follows:

$$\int \frac{dy}{y} = \int - a \, dt$$

$$\ln y = -at + c \tag{A.91}$$

or

$$y = ke^{-at}$$

where

$$k = e^c$$

We call the solution in (A.91), the complementary solution, or y_c. To get a particular solution, y_p, we might guess that

$$y_p = c_1 t + c_2 \tag{A.92}$$

Substituting (A.92) into (A.89) yields

$$c_1 + a(c_1 t + c_2) = bt \tag{A.93}$$

Because (A.93) must hold *for all* t, (A.93) must be an identity—that is, coefficients of all powers of t (t^0 and t^1) must vanish identically. Thus, we have:

$$(c_1 + ac_2) + (ac_1 - b)t = 0 \tag{A.94}$$

implying

$$c_1 + ac_2 = 0 \tag{A.95}$$

and

$$ac_1 - b = 0$$

resulting in

$$c_1 = \frac{b}{a} \quad \text{and} \quad c_2 = -\frac{b}{a^2} \tag{A.96}$$

or

$$y_p = \frac{bt}{a} - \frac{b}{a^2} \tag{A.97}$$

and

$$y = y_c + y_p = ke^{-at} + \frac{bt}{a} - \frac{b}{a^2} \tag{A.98}$$

The method for generating y_p is called the *method of undetermined coefficients.*

Note that (A.98) has an undetermined constant, k, to be determined. An initial or boundary condition is required to assess k. If $y(0) = 0$, then

$$0 = k - \frac{b}{a^2} \quad \text{or} \quad k = \frac{b}{a^2}$$

and

$$y = \frac{b}{a} e^{-at} + \frac{bt}{a} - \frac{b}{a^2}. \tag{A.99}$$

To solve (A.87) in general we proceed similarly. To get the complementary solution, y_c, we solve:

$$\frac{dy}{dt} + a(t)y = 0 \tag{A.100}$$

or

$$\frac{dy}{y} = -a(t)$$

so

$$\ln y = -\int a(t)\, dt + c$$

or

$$y_c = ke^{-\int a(t)dt} \tag{A.101}$$

To obtain the complete solution to (A.100) we then seek a particular solution, y_p, to add to (A.101). If elementary functions are used, that particular solution will have the following form:

(a) If

$$b(t) = k_1 \, e^{k_2 t}$$

then

$$y_p = c_1 e^{k_2 t}$$

(b) If

$$b(t) = \sum_{i=0}^{I} k_i t^i$$

then

$$y_p = \sum_{i=0}^{I} c_i t^i$$

(c) If

$$b(t) = k_1 \, \sin(k_2 t) + k_3 \, \cos(k_4 t)$$

then

$$y_p = c_1 \, \sin(k_2 t) + c_2 \, \cos(k_4 t)$$

(d) If

$$b(t) = b_1(t) + b_2(t) + b_3(t)$$

then

$$y_p(t) = y_p^1(t) + y_p^2(t) + y_p^3(t)$$

The cases just given, while apparently quite restrictive, cover a surprisingly wide range of marketing applications, which is why the method of undetermined coefficients gets used widely.

EXAMPLE _____

The Vidale-Wolfe (1957) model is specified as follows:

$$\frac{dQ}{dt} = \frac{rX(V - Q)}{V} - \lambda Q \tag{A.102}$$

where

$$
\begin{aligned}
Q &= \text{sales volume} \\
\frac{dQ}{dt} &= \text{change in sales at } t \\
X &= \text{total market volume} \\
r &= \text{sales-response constant} \\
\lambda &= \text{sales-decay constant}
\end{aligned}
$$

If $X = 0$, (A.102) reduces to

$$\frac{dQ}{dt} = -\lambda Q \tag{A.103}$$

so

$$Q = k_0 e^{-\lambda t} \tag{A.104}$$

where

$$k_0 = Q(0).$$

If $X = $ constant, we get (rearranging terms)

$$\frac{dQ(t)}{dt} + \left(\frac{rX}{V} + \lambda\right)Q = rX \tag{A.105}$$

We can find that

$$y_c = k_1\, e^{-(rX/V + \lambda)t} \tag{A.106}$$

and using the method of undetermined coefficients we let $y_p = c$ in (A.105) and get

$$c = \frac{rX}{(rX/V) + \lambda} = \frac{V}{1 + (\lambda V/rX)} \qquad \textbf{(A.107)}$$

so

$$y = y_c + y_p = k_1\, e^{-(rX/V + \lambda)t} + \frac{V}{1 + (\lambda V/rX)} \qquad \textbf{(A.108)}$$

Letting $Q(0) = Q_0$ in (108) yields

$$Q(t) = \frac{V}{1 + (\lambda V/rX)}\,[1 - e^{-(rX/V + \lambda)t}] + Q_0 e^{-(rX/V + \lambda)t} \qquad \textbf{(A.109)}$$

A Pair of First-Order Linear Differential Equations.   Consider the system of two linear differential equations (with constant coefficients):

$$\frac{dx}{dt} = a_1 x(t) + b_1 y(t) + p(t) \qquad \textbf{(A.110a)}$$

$$\frac{dy}{dt} = a_2 x(t) + b_2 y(t) + g(t) \qquad \textbf{(A.110b)}$$

where we seek to find $x(t)$ and $y(t)$. Again, the solution to (A.110a) and (A.110b) is found as a solution to the homogeneous equations related to (A.110) plus a particular solution to the equations.

The homogeneous equations related to (A.110) are

$$\frac{dx}{dt} = a_1 x + b_1 y \qquad \textbf{(A.111a)}$$

$$\frac{dy}{dt} = a_2 x + b_2 y \qquad \textbf{(A.111b)}$$

A method of solving (A.111) is to reduce that pair to a single, second order linear differential equation. Differentiating (A.111a) with respect to t yields

$$\frac{d^2 x}{dt^2} = a_1 \frac{dx}{dt} + b_1 \frac{dy}{dt} \qquad \textbf{(A.112)}$$

Rewriting (A.111a) we get

$$y = \frac{1}{b_1} \left[\frac{dx}{dt} - a_1 x \right] \tag{A.113}$$

and using (A.113) in (A.111b) yields

$$\begin{aligned}
\frac{dy}{dt} &= a_2 x + b_2 \left[\frac{1}{b_1} \left(\frac{dx}{dt} - a_1 x \right) \right] \\
&= \left[a_2 - \frac{b_2 a_1}{b_1} \right] x + \frac{b_2}{b_1} \frac{dx}{dt}
\end{aligned} \tag{A.114}$$

Using (A.114) in (A.112) yields

$$\frac{d^2 x}{dt^2} - (a_1 + b_2) \frac{dx}{dt} + (a_1 b_2 - a_2 b_1) x = 0 \tag{A.115}$$

To solve such a second-order, linear homogeneous equation with constant coefficients

$$\frac{d^2 x}{dt^2} + c_1 \frac{dx}{dt} + c_2 x = 0 \tag{A.116}$$

we form the "characteristic equation" (by substituting r for $d^n x / dt^n$)

$$r^2 + c_1 r + c_2 = 0 \tag{A.117}$$

and then three cases emerge:

Case a: The roots of (A.117) are real and distinct ($r_1 \neq r_2$):

$$x(t) = k_1 e^{r_1 t} + k_2 e^{r_2 t} \tag{A.118}$$

Case b: The roots of (A.117) are real and repeated (both $= r$):

$$x(t) = k_1 e^{rt} + k_2 t e^{rt} \tag{A.119}$$

Case c: The roots are a complex conjugate pair ($r = a \pm bi$, $i = \sqrt{-1}$):

$$x(t) = k_1 e^{at} \cos bt + k_2 e^{at} \sin bt \tag{A.120}$$

Using the appropriate solution from (A.118–A.120) for the characteristic equation associated with (A.115) provides $x_c(t)$. To obtain $y_c(t)$, note that from (A.113) we get

$$y_c(t) = \frac{(dx/dt - a_1 x)}{b_1} \tag{A.121}$$

Using the solution for x, (and hence dx/dt) in (A.121) will provide the solution.

Methods analogous to those for the method of undetermined coefficients can be used to solve for $x_p(t)$ and $y_p(t)$ and, in general, two conditions—$x(0)$ and $y(0)$—will be needed to evaluate the constants.

Most differential equation applications in marketing have been either a single or a system of linear first-order differential equations.

The area of differential equations is an area of current excitement given the recent discoveries about the quite unusual behavior of (even quite simple) nonlinear dynamic systems. Much of this work is being referred to as "chaos theory." (See Devaney, 1990, and Thompson and Stewart, 1986, for a treatment of this subject.)

There are many fine, comprehensive texts dealing with ordinary differential equations such as Birkhoff and Rota (1989), McCann (1982), and Rice and Strange (1989).

B | OBJECTIVES AND UTILITIES

Objectives and utilities are pervasive, if often implicit, in marketing models. The consumer behavior models we develop in Chapter 2 differ significantly in their assumptions about how consumers process information and make "decisions." When we refer to a firm or a consumer making a decision, we implicitly assume that the following conditions hold:

- There are one or more decision makers.
- There are decision variables that the decision maker can control—advertising level, product to buy, and so on.
- Depending on the decision, the outcomes differ in their value to the decision maker.
- There may be constraints on these decisions.
- There may be noncontrollable aspects of the decision.

The appendix outlines some approaches to defining utility or value, both at the individual and the organizational level.

DECISION MAKERS AND OBJECTIVES

We must distinguish between organizational objectives and individual objectives. Organizational objectives depend on the type of organization: for profit, not for profit, and public sector. For a for-profit organization, given perfect capital markets whose stockholders can diversify their portfolios, the appropriate corporate objective is to maximize discounted long-run profits when the discount rate is the risk-adjusted cost of capital for the organization. For a nonprofit organization, the objective could be to break even subject to fulfilling its mission. Thus, a nonprofit theater group like the Yale Repertory Theater tries to break even while presenting the kinds of plays and attracting the kinds of audiences specified in its charter. For regulated public sector organizations, the objectives might be specified by the regulatory agency, and typically those objectives require the organization to break even while providing efficiency and equity. For example, the U.S. Postal Service is required to break even while keeping its rates for a standard letter affordable to all.

Regardless of the type of organization, the notion of profit is central to the organization's objectives. The profit from an action in any time period is the difference between the revenues and cost from that action in that time period. Costs can be variable or fixed, the former varying with quantity sold, the latter not varying with quantity sold. Since fixed costs change only for the decision to produce or not produce the product, they don't play a role in determining the contribution-maximizing quantity to sell. Once the contribution-maximizing quantity has been determined, then fixed cost must be considered to see if the maximum contribution covers fixed cost or not. If the former condition holds, then the product should be produced and sold at the contribution-maximizing level of the action; if the latter condition holds, then the product should not be produced at all.

For example, consider a firm trying to decide on the profit-maximizing price level for its product. Price will determine the quantity sold, D, as a function of price, p, that in turn will determine the variable cost in producing and selling the product. Let v denote the variable cost per unit. There are also fixed costs, F, involved in the production and selling of the product, but these are unaffected by the price level. To determine the profit-maximizing price level, the firm should maximize the contribution, C:

$$C = (p - v)D(p) \qquad \text{(B.1)}$$

with respect to p. Once the contribution-maximizing price level has been determined, say, p^*, then the firm can check whether the net profit, NP,

$$NP = (p^* - v)D(p^*) - F \qquad \text{(B.2)}$$

is positive or not, to decide if it should produce the good at all.

The time period over which the profit-maximizing analysis is done determines what actions are possible and what are not, and this, in turn, determines what costs are relevant to consider and what costs are irrelevant. Irrelevant costs are also called sunk costs. For example, a firm may buy advertising time on television for the entire year at the beginning of the year, and the advertising costs are then irrelevant for any decisions taken during the year. In general, more costs become relevant as the time period for analysis lengthens. For example, a consumer goods firm may contemplate withdrawing a product from a product line with which it shares some costs. Over one year, whether the product is withdrawn or not, the other products in the line will be produced, so costs such as advertising for the entire product line, common management costs, and so on, are irrelevant. But over five years, the entire product line could be withdrawn, and for that decision, all these costs are relevant.

We often talk loosely about a firm's objective being to maximize "profit," perhaps as defined earlier. However, not only is this statement vague, but there is no consensus that even if it were properly defined, it would be true. Companies are groups of individuals who may have personal objectives as well as corporate ones. Certainly, their value systems may differ. Furthermore, companies may wish to pursue single or multiple goals. Current profit is an appealing and frequently stated goal and has the additional advantage of providing an easily quantified objective function to guide policy determination. Yet the use of this criterion has been criticized for years (Berle and Means, 1932; Kaplan, Dirlam, and Lanzillotti, 1958; Simon, 1952). Criticisms have centered on its neglect of long-term effects, alternative goals, multiple decision makers, and risk. In the sections that follow, we introduce the concept of risk and suggest how to handle multiple objectives and multiple decision makers.

INCORPORATING RISK: ASSESSING UTILITY FUNCTIONS

The approach just suggested assumes that the resulting profit streams are known with certainty But this is seldom the case. A firm may have a choice of investing in a project that will lose $50,000 if it fails and make $70,000 if it succeeds with equal likelihood, or of investing in an alternative that is almost certain to return $10,000 on the same investment. These alternatives both return $10,000 on average (i.e., have an expected return of $10,000), but the first is riskier (has higher variance) than the other. Utility theory has been developed to address situations involving trade-offs and risks.

Suppose X_1 and X_2 have probability distributions $f_1(X_1)$ and $f_2(X_2)$. Then X_1 is preferred to X_2 if and only if $E_1(u(X_1)) > E_2(u(X_2))$, where E_1 and E_2 are the expected values of the utility function, with respect to f_1 and f_2, respectively. For example, if f_1 is characterized by discrete possible outcomes $X_{11}, \ldots, X_{1n}$ with probabilities $p_{11}, \ldots, p_{1n}$, and f_2 is characterized similarly by $X_{21}, \ldots, X_{2m}$ with probabilities $p_{21}, \ldots, p_{2m}$, then f_1 is preferred to f_2 if

$$\sum_{i=1}^{n} u(X_{1i})p_{1i} > \sum_{j=1}^{m} u(X_{2j})p_{2j} \tag{B.3}$$

Adding a constant or multiplying by a positive constant will still yield a utility function. That is, if

$$u(X_1) > u(X_2) \tag{B.4}$$

then

$$a + bu(X_1) > a + bu(X_2) \tag{B.5}$$

Now let us assess a decision maker's utility function for profits from an investment, which has two possible outcomes, $0 and $1,000,000. By the statement given (i.e., a and b are arbitrary in equation B.5), we can set $u(1,000,000) = 100$ and $u(0) = 0$. To aid in determining the function u, we introduce the concept of a lottery, denoted by

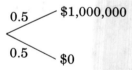

which represents a 0.5 chance of receiving $1,000,000 and a 0.5 chance of receiving nothing. Then the first question to the decision maker is how much he would be willing to sell this lottery for. This amount is called the certainty monetary equivalent (CME) of the lottery. Suppose he said $400,000. That means he is indifferent between $400,000 and a 50:50 chance of getting $1,000,000. Mathematically,

$$u(400,000) = 0.5u(0) + 0.5u(1,000,000) = 50 \tag{B.6}$$

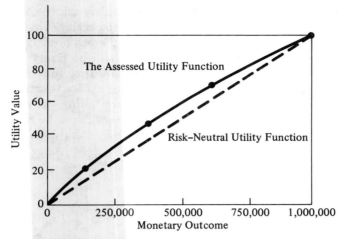

EXHIBIT B.1 The assessed (risk-averse) utility function.

which represents one point on his utility function. To assess other points, we ask the decision maker what his CME is for

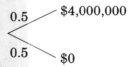

Suppose it is $180,000. Then,

$$u(180,000) = 0.5u(0) + 0.5u(400,000) = 25 \qquad \textbf{(B.7)}$$

Similarly, we ask him what his CME is for

Suppose it is $180,000. Then,

If the answer is 650,000, then

$$u(650,000) = 0.5u(1,000,000) + 0.5u(400,000) = 75 \qquad \textbf{(B.8)}$$

Our initial conditions plus equations (B.6)–(B.8) give us the utility function plotted in Exhibit B.1.

One can always proceed with the steps just outlined. However, it is useful to get an idea of the shape of the utility curve. A simple characteristic that many utility curves have is monotonicity, that is, $u(X_i) > u(X_j)$ if $X_i > X_j$. This condition should hold for most profit-related measures. (But what if profit beyond a certain level would be likely to trigger government action? How might that affect the firm's utility function?)

A second prevalent characteristic of utility functions is attitude toward risk. If the decision maker always prefers taking the monetary equivalent of the average payoff of a lottery to the lottery itself, he is said to be risk-averse. That is, he prefers a certain payment of $(X_1 + X_2)/2$ to any lottery of the form

If a person is *risk-averse,* his utility function must be concave, that is, a line segment connecting any two points on the utility curve lies below the curve, or

$$u((X_1 + X_2)/2) > 1/2 \, u(X_1) + 1/2 \, u(X_2).$$

He is *risk-neutral* if

$$u((X_1 + X_2)/2) = 1/2u(X_1) + 1/2u(X_2), \qquad \text{for all } X_1 \text{ and } X_2$$

And he is *risk-prone* if

$$u((X_1 + X_2)/2) < 1/2u(X_1) + 1/2u(X_2)$$

A measure of risk aversion, $r(X)$, is

$$r(X) = -\frac{u''(X)}{u'(X)} = -\frac{d}{dx}[\log u'(X)] \qquad \textbf{(B.9)}$$

This function can be used as follows:

1. If r is positive for all X, then u is concave and the decision maker is risk-averse.

2. If $r = 0$ for all X, then u is linear and the decision maker is risk-neutral.

3. If r is negative for all X, then u is convex and the decision maker is risk-prone.

If $r(X)$ is constant for all X, then the decision maker is constantly risk-averse. In other words, the decision maker is equally risk-averse no matter what the monetary outcome. If the decision maker is constantly risk-averse, then his utility function has to be of the form

$$u(X) = k_1 + k_2 e^{-cx} \tag{B.10}$$

where $c > 0$, $k_2 < 0$ and k_1 is arbitrary.

For a fuller discussion of assessment of single attribute utility functions, see Keeney and Raiffa (1976) and Farquhar (1984).

MULTIPLE-GOAL FORMULATIONS: SINGLE DECISION MAKER

Although profit is an overriding goal of some firms, it is not the only factor that an organization considers when trying to decide among alternative plans of action.

Consider the following sample of statements that businesspeople make:

"We want to achieve the greatest sales at the least cost."

"We want to keep down inventory costs and maximize sales."

"We want to design the best possible product in the shortest time."

If we have a set of n objectives, $Z_1, Z_2, ..., Z_n$, all of which cannot be simultaneously maximized by any one conceivable plan, how can these goals be operationalized in such a way as to provide an unambiguous ranking of alternative plans?

There are several approaches to this problem. One is to assign all but one of the objectives to constraints, so that management optimizes one criterion (a profit measure) while satisficing on others (e.g., a market-share restriction might be that share must not drop below 12%). Another approach is the goal programming approach, where targets for each objective are set and a loss function—the differences between the target and actual performance, summed over objectives—is minimized.

We sketch a consistent approach to the multicriteria problem, relying on multiattribute utility theory. As with the single-attribute development, the approach incorporates risk naturally (see Keeney and Raiffa, 1976, for a more detailed account).

A logical first step in evaluating a multiple-objective function with a utility-based approach is to assess utility functions for each of the individual objectives. The procedure developed earlier is useful for this step. Here we deal with two objectives only and sketch extensions to more than two.

To proceed (in fact, to determine if assessing a single-attribute utility function is a well-defined operation), we need the concept of utility independence. Assume that we have two objectives: (1) to maximize Y, a market-share measure, and (2) to maximize Z, a measure of profitability. Let us further assume that we wish to explore Y and Z at values (y, z) in the following ranges:

$$10\% \leq y \leq 40\% \quad \text{and} \quad \$1 \text{ million} \leq z \leq \$5 \text{ million} \qquad \textbf{(B.11)}$$

Thus there are upper and lower bounds on the values of the utility function $u(y, z)$ that we wish to assess.

Now we can begin asking lottery questions of the following sort "If your profit is fixed at $25 million throughout, what is your certainty equivalent for a 50:50 gamble yielding market shares of 20% and 30%?" Suppose the answer is 24%, so that the decision maker is indifferent between

$$\text{(24\%, \$25 million)} \text{ and} \quad \begin{array}{l} {}^{0.5}\diagup \text{ 30\%, \$25 million} \\ {}_{0.5}\diagdown \text{ 20\%, \$25 million} \end{array}$$

Next we ask the same question with profit fixed at, say, $30 million. Would the certainty equivalent value for market share shift from 24%? According to Keeney and Raiffa (1976, p. 226),"in a surprisingly large number of contexts, it does not shift." We formalize this statement in the following definition:

DEFINITION: Y is utility-independent of Z when conditional preferences for lotteries on Y, given any value of Z, do not depend on the particular level of Z.

Utility independence of Y with respect to Z implies that

$$u(y, z) = g(z) + h(z)u(y) \qquad \textbf{(B.12)}$$

Note that Y can be utility-independent of Z and not vice versa. All cases are possible: neither holds, one holds without the other, or both hold.

Two conditions that simplify our search for utility-function forms are mutual utility independence and additive independence.

Mutual Utility Independence.   If Y and Z are mutually utility independent, then $u(y, z)$ can be represented by the *multilinear form.*

$$u(y, z) = k_1 u_y(y) + k_2 u_z(z) + k_3 u_y(y)u_z(z) \qquad \textbf{(B.13)}$$

The coefficient k_3 in equation (B.13) measures the interrelationship between the objectives. For $k_3 > 0$ the objectives complement each other; for $k_3 < 0$, the objectives are substitutes. When $k_3 = 0$, we have the special case of an additive utility function.

Additive Independence.   If Y and Z are mutually utility-independent and if there are some values of Y and Z such that the decision maker is indifferent between the two lotteries,

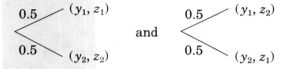

and where $u(y_1, z_1)$ is not equal to either $u(y_1, z_2)$ or $u(y_2, z_1)$, then

$$u(y, z) = k_1 u_y(y) + k_2 u_z(z) \tag{B.14}$$

The conditions and procedures for more than two objectives are generalizations of what is presented here. The process of checking for types of independence, specifying the form, and assessing utility functions is a relatively straightforward process after some practice. If utility independence does not hold, Keeney and Raiffa (1976) suggest some transformations and approximations that can be used. Alternatively, the joint utility function can be assessed over a sample of points in the space of alternatives and a curve-fitting technique can be used to approximate it.

MULTIPLE DECISION MAKERS

Rarely is a single individual solely responsible for specifying the objectives of an organization. Rather, the setting of organizational goals and objectives is a group decision, involving several individuals.

Theoretically, a group should be considered an entity with its own utility function. Hence, in a manner similar to the foregoing procedures, the group should select a course of action that maximizes its expected utility function. In other words, it should choose alternative a_j from set $\{a_1, \ldots, a_n\}$ that maximizes

$$E_j[u_G(c)] = \sum_{i=1}^{m} u_G(c_i) p_j(c_i) \tag{B.15}$$

where

$$c \qquad = (c_1, \ldots, c_m) = \text{possible consequences}$$

$p_j(c_i) = $ likelihood of consequence c_i occurring following action (alternative) a_j

$u_G \qquad = $ group utility function

This issue of assessing group utility functions has been investigated by numerous researchers. Most of the work has concerned ordinal social-welfare functions. Arrow (1963) proved that, in general, there is no procedure for obtaining a group ordering of alternatives consistent with five reasonable assumptions. This result has been used to conclude that knowledge about group structures (hierarchy, dictatorship, power levels, communication patterns, etc.) is required for development of a group-welfare function.

For cardinal utilities the group's decision problem is concerned with both the existence and the specification of $u_G = u_G(u_1, \ldots, u_n)$ where $u_1, \ldots, u_n$ represent the individual utility functions of the group members.

Harsanyi (1955) developed conditions for a group utility function to be a weighted average of individual group members' utility functions:

$$u_G = \sum_i \lambda_i \mu_i \tag{B.16}$$

The key condition is that if each individual within a group is indifferent between two alternatives (with associated probability distributions), the group as a whole must also be indifferent to them.

Keeney and Kirkwood (1975) developed a more general form that follows from relaxing Harsanyi's conditions somewhat. They present two conditions that say, in essence, that if only one or two people in the group care about what happens (are not indifferent between alternatives), then they should decide what to do. These conditions imply a group utility function of the form

$$u_G = \sum_{i=1}^{n} \lambda_i u_i + \sum_{\substack{i=1 \\ j>i}}^{n} \lambda_{ij} u_i u_j + \cdots + \lambda_{12\ldots n} u_1 \ldots u_n \tag{B.17}$$

Note that for two individuals equation (B.17) reduces to

$$u_G = \lambda_1 u_1 + \lambda_2 u_2 + \lambda_3 u_1 u_2 \tag{B.18}$$

This form is the multilinear form introduced in equation (B.13); Keeney and Kirkwood (1975) replace "attributes" with "decision participants" and specify conditions that are equivalent to utility independence. Eliashberg and Winkler (1981) explored the risk-sharing and group decision-making implications of utility functions (B.16) and (B.18).

Keeney and Kirkwood's (1975) assumptions seem reasonable. However, the estimation of the parameters $\{\lambda_i\}$ requires a group decision that may not easily be resolved. (See Wilson, Lilien, and Wilson, (1991), for an example of decision participant weight estimation.) In addition, there may be disagreement among group members about the likelihood of various consequences occurring (the subjective probabilities).

Another Perspective.   The bulk of the material above has been based on classical utility theory. A variety of studies, however, demonstrate that people often do not behave in accordance with the principles of that theory (for a good overview, see Hogarth, 1987). Among the problems that Hogarth notes are that people have different risk attitudes toward gains and losses, so logically identical situations lead to different choices depending on how the outcomes are framed (as gains or losses). In particular, people are more sensitive to losses than to gains, and the reference point, or status quo, while possibly arbitrary, matters.

A model that has been proposed to address these decision-making realities is prospect theory (Kahneman and Tversky, 1979). Prospect theory has a value function and a decision-weight function, where the latter captures the weights attached to choice probabilities. In practice a typical value function in prospect theory evaluates actions as deviations from a reference point, with that function being steeper for losses than for gains and steeper the closer one is to the reference point. The decision-weight function normally overweights small probabilities and underweights high probabilities.

While prospect theory and other approaches (Einhorn and Hogarth's, 1985, ambiguity model, for example) have attempted to address apparent inconsistencies and irrationalities in human decision making, they do not claim roles as proper prescriptive devices. Although behavior that violates the axioms of utility theory has been termed "irrational," Hogarth (1987, p. 108) asks "to what extent is such irrational behavior unreasonable?" His answer is that the psychological principles leading to such behavior are pervasive and powerful and that it would be unwise to ignore them. The prescription is to frame problems in multiple ways when developing utility functions, or "Frame or be framed" as Hogarth says.

The implication of this discussion is that, while there are powerful, utility-theory based tools available to help determine objectives and values, one needs explicitly to consider human frailties, biases, limited information processing capabilities, and difficulties in dealing with risk and uncertainty when using those tools.

C | AGGREGATE MARKET RESPONSE MODELS

To the craftsman with only a hammer, the entire world looks like a nail. But give that craftsman a screwdriver, and think of what new opportunities emerge!

So it is with marketing models. We seem to have linear model experts, log-linear model specialists, those whose world abounds in logistic curves, and the like. Our view is that familiarity with a wide range of functional forms is essential training to prevent "response model myopia" in the marketing modeler.

There have been a number of excellent expositions on aggregate market response that the readers should consider: Hanssens, Parsons, and Schultz (1990) provide a thorough, integrated treatment of aggregate response models in marketing, with emphasis on econometric and time-series analysis. A concise but surprisingly thorough treatment of the process of choosing and testing aggregate market response models can be found in an article by Saunders (1987). Naert and Leeflang (1978) provide a useful organization and catalog of marketing models as well.

In this appendix, we will attempt to link marketing phenomena with common mathematical representation of those phenomena.

TAXONOMY OF MODELS

There are a large number of dimensions that can be used to characterize marketing models. The ones we will use are the following:

Mathematical form. Is the model linear? Nonlinear but linearizable? Inherently nonlinear?

Static/dynamic. Does the model deal with a flow of actions and responses over time or does it represent a static snapshot?

Deterministic/probabilistic. Nothing is known with certainty. Whether a deterministic model is used as an approximation or a stochastic model is used explicitly is a matter of model-building style.

Aggregate versus individual. Individual response can be modelled and then aggregated to the market level or total market response can be modeled directly.

Level of demand. Models can deal with the sales of a brand, the sales of the product class or the market share of the brand.

Exhibit C.1 depicts these major elements and provides some examples. In this appendix, we will deal with aggregate market models only. (See Chapter 2 for a development of individual response models.)

NONCOMPETITIVE MARKET RESPONSE PHENOMENA

A simple market response function describes how two variables (e.g., sales and advertising) are related in the absence of competitive response. In a review of the literature, Saunders (1987, pp. 17–18) summarizes propositions about the shape of the relationship, where "effect" may be sales (or awareness or any other appropriate measure of response) and "effort" is the level of the marketing instrument. (For conciseness, we consider only positive effects; a "price reduction" is, then, a positive price stimulus.)

P1. Effect is zero when effort is zero.

P2. There is a linear relationship between effect and effort.

P3. There are decreasing returns to scale of effort.

P4. There is a level of effect that cannot be exceeded (saturation).

P5. There are increasing returns to scale of effort.

P6. There are first increasing and then decreasing returns to scale with effort (S-shaped).

P7. There is a level of effort that must be exceeded before there is any effect (threshold).

P8. There is a level of effort beyond which effect declines (supersaturation).

P9. There are systematic variations in response of the following sort:

Dimension	Examples
1. Mathematical Form	
Linear in parameters and variables	$Q = a_0 + a_1 X$
Nonlinear in variables, linear in parameters	$Q = a_0 + a_1 X + a_2 X^2$
Nonlinear in parameters, linearizable	$Q = a_0 X_1^{a_1} X_2^{a_2}$
Inherently nonlinear	$Q = a_0 (1 - e^{-a_1 x})$
2. Dynamic Effects	
Discrete time	$Q_1 = a_0 + a_1 X_t + \lambda Q_{t-1}$
Continuous time	$\dfrac{dQ}{dt} = \dfrac{r X (V - Q)}{V} - \lambda Q$
3. Uncertainty	
Deterministic	$Q = a_0 + a_1 X$
Deterministic with stochastic error	$Q = a_0 + a_1 X + \varepsilon$
Inherently stochastic	$p = f$ (past purchase behavior)
4. Level of Aggregation	
Individual	$p = f$ (past behavior, marketing variables)
Segment or market	$Q_i = a_0 + a_i X$
5. Level of Demand	
Product class	$V = f$ (demographic trends, total marketing spending)
Brand sales	$Q = S V$
Market share	$S = \dfrac{us}{us + them}$

EXHIBIT C.1 Dimensions of model development

- Asymmetry, when the market responds differently to increases and decreases in the marketing instrumental

- Cross-sectional variation, where segments of the market respond differently

- Brand to brand variation

- Temporal variation, where market response, or marketing instrument ffectiveness, varies over time

• Interactions, where the level of response depends on the level of other marketing-mix elements

Shapes corresponding to propositions 1–8 are displayed in Exhibit C.2.

A Brief Catalog of One-Variable Mathematic Forms

In this section, we model quantity sold, Q (the "effect") as a static function of some marketing variables. We analyze several static respond models, and the process we follow is as follows. For $Q = f(X)$ we determine

1. What is $f(0)$? $\lim\limits_{x \to \infty} f(x)$?:	What does this function say about sales (Q) at low/high levels of marketing effort (X)?
2. What is the form of $f'(X)$? (Are there points $X_1 \ldots X_i$, where $f'(X_i) = 0$? What is $f'(0)$?	How does the sales rate change with X? Are there maximum/minimum levels of sales possible? What is the change in sales when X is first applied?
3. Is there a point where $f''(X) = 0$?	Is there a point of inflection (change from concave to convex response) that yields an S-shape?

Step 1 sets the endpoint of the curve; steps 2 and 3 guide the progress of the curve from start ($X = 0$) to finish ($X \to \infty$). Exhibit C.3 summarizes the forms we discuss next along with some of their properties.

Linear Model

$$Q = a + bX \qquad\qquad (C.1)$$

The linear model is widely used and has several appealing characteristics:

Classical econometric methods are appropriate for parameter estimation.
The model is easy to visualize and understand.
Locally, at least, the model can approximate many more complicated functions quite well.

It has the following problems:

It assumes constant returns to scale everywhere.
It has no upper bound on Q.
It has poor normative implications.

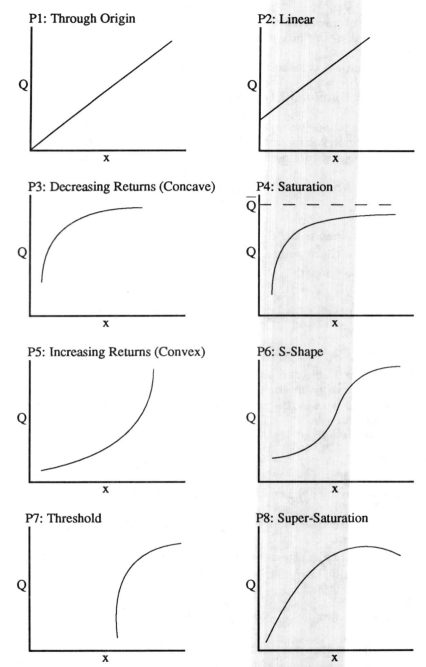

EXHIBIT C.2 Pictorial representation of Saunders's response model propositions.

	Shape	Marginal Response where X = 0 or minimum value	Bounds/Asymptote $X \to 0$	$X \to \infty$
A. Linear: **1. Simple Linear:** $Q = a + bX,\ b > 0$	linear	b	a	unbounded
B. Linear Parameters/ non-linear Variables **2. Power Series:** $Q = a + bX + cX^2 + \ldots$	various	b	a	
3. Fractional Root $Q = a + bX^c$ (c known) i. $b > 0,\ c > 1$	convex	0	a	unbounded
ii. $b > 0,\ 0 < c < 1$	concave	∞	a	unbounded
iii. $b < 0,\ c < 0$ $X > \left(\dfrac{-b}{a}\right)^{-1/c}$	concave	$cb\left[\dfrac{-a}{b}\right]^{(1-c)/c}$ at $X = \left[\dfrac{-b}{a}\right]^{-1/c}$	0 at $X = \left[\dfrac{-b}{a}\right]^{-1/c}$	a
4. Semilog: $Q = a + b\ln X,$ $X > e^{-a/b}$	concave	$be^{a/b}$ when $X = e^{-a/b}$	0 at $X = e^{-a/b}$	unbounded
5. Multiplicative $Q = aX^b,\ b > 0$ (b unknown)	various	a, for b = 1 0, for b < 1 ∞, for b > 1	0	unbounded
6. Exponential $Q = ae^{bX},\ b > 0$	convex	ab	a	unbounded

EXHIBIT C.3   Single-Variable Response Models

	Shape	Marginal Response where X = 0 or minimum value	Bounds/Asymptote	
			$X \rightarrow 0$	$X \rightarrow \infty$
7. Log Reciprocal $Q = e^{a-b/X}, \; b > 0$	S- Shape	0	0	e^a
C. Nonlinear:				
8. Modified Exponential $Q = a\left(1 - e^{-bX}\right) + c,$ $a, b, c > 0$	concave	ab	c	$a + c$
9. Logistic $Q = \dfrac{a}{1 + e^{\{b+cX\}}} + d$ $a, b, c > 0$	S- Shape	$\dfrac{ace^{-b}}{\left(1 + e^{-b}\right)^2}$	$\dfrac{a}{\left(1 + e^{-b}\right)} + d$	$a + d$
10. Gompertz $Q = ab^{c^X} + d$ $\left(a > 0, \; 1 > b > 0, \; c < 1\right)$	S- Shape	$ab\ln b\ln c$	$ab + d$	$a + d$
11. Adbudg $Q = b + (a - b)\dfrac{X^c}{d + X^c}$ $a, b\,c, d > 0$	S- Shape $c > 1$ concave $c < 1$	0, for c > 1 ∞, for c < 1	b	a

EXHIBIT C.3 (continued)

Specifically, on this last point, note that $dQ/dX = b$. Thus, if the contribution margin (assumed constant, for the moment) is m for the product, then the marginal profit from an additional unit of spending is bm. If $bm > 1$, more should be spent on that marketing activity (without limit); if $bm < 1$, less should be spent (until spending ceases). Clearly, this model is of limited global use for decision making, but locally, at least, the model suggests whether a spending increase or decrease might be recommended.

Linear models have seen wide use, historically in marketing, they readily handle propositions P1 and P2.

Models 3.2–3.4 are linear in parameters while including non-linear variables.

Power Series Model.   If we are uncertain what the relationship, f, is between X and Q_1 a power series model of the form

$$Q = a + bX + cX^2 + dX^3 + \cdots \tag{C.2}$$

can approximate any smooth relationship. Depending on how closely we wish to approximate f, we may be satisfied with a quadratic form, a cubic form, and so on.

The power series model may fit well within the range of the data but will normally behave badly (becoming unbounded) outside the data range.

Some examples of the use of power series models in marketing are Frank (1966) and Little and Lodish (1966). In varying forms with varying parameter values the model handles properties $P1$, $P2$, $P3$, $P5$, $P6$ and $P8$.

Fractional Root Model.   The fractional root model

$$Q = a + bX^c \text{ (with } c \text{ known)} \tag{C.3}$$

has a simple but quite flexible form. As Exhibit C.3 indicates, there are combinations of parameters that give increasing, decreasing and (with $c = 1$) constant returns to scale. When $c = \frac{1}{2}$, the model is called the *square root model;* when $c = -1$, it is called *the reciprocal model,* which asymptotes to the value a. (Note that some authors use the term "fractional root model" only when $1 > c > 0$. We use the term more widely here.)

Various forms of the fractional root model have been used by Naert and Leeflang (1978) and Winer (1980a, b). It handles proposition P1, P2, P3, P4, and P5 depending on the selection of parameter values.

Semilog Model.   With functional form

$$Q = a + b \ln X \tag{C.4}$$

the semilog model handles situations where constant percentage increases in marketing effort result in constant absolute increases in sales. Lambin (1969), Carroll, Green, and DeSarbo (1979), Wildt (1977), and Simon (1982) have used this model in marketing. It handles propositions P3 and P7. Models 3.5–3.7 are linearizable via a log transformation.

Multiplicative Model.   We handle the multiplicative model here

$$Q = aX^b \tag{C.5}$$

separately from the fractional root model in that this model normally takes on several marketing mix elements (with the exponent b not known) while the fractional root model normally handles a single-response variable and its exponent is assumed known. As with the fractional root model, the multiplicative model admits various shapes. Lambin (1972b) and Ryans and Weinberg (1979) have used this model. With appropriate parameter values, it can deal with proposition P1, P2, P3, and P5.

Exponential Model.   The exponential model

$$Q = ae^{bx} \tag{C.6}$$

characterizes situations where there are increasing returns to scale (for $b > 0$); however, it is most widely used as a price-response function for $b < 0$ (i.e., increasing returns to decreases in price) when Q approaches 0 with X large. This model has been used by Parsons (1974) and Cowling and Cubbin (1971). It handles property P5.

Log Reciprocal Model.   The log-reciprocal model has the form

$$Q = e^{a - b/X} \qquad \text{or} \qquad \log Q = a - \frac{b}{X} \tag{C.7}$$

This model has an S-shape, with increasing returns for $X < 1/2b$. Bemmaor (1984) and Brown and Tucker (1961) have reported using it. It handles properties P4 and P6.

Models 8–11 are inherently nonlinear; thus they require either outside knowledge of some parameters or nonlinear estimation procedures for calibration. Indeed, as all these models have saturation levels, the parameters dealing with that saturation are often far outside the range of data anyway, and best estimates are made judgmentally or from other sources.

Modified Exponential Model.   The modified exponential model has the following form:

$$Q = a(1 - e^{-bx}) + c \tag{C.8}$$

It has an easily seen saturation level ($a + c$) and shows decreasing returns to scale. It has seen wide use in marketing: Buzzell (1964), Shakun (1965), Little and Lodish (1969), Sexton (1970), Holthausen and Assmus (1982), and Rangan (1987). The model admits proportions P3 and P4.

Logistic Model. Of the S-shaped models used in marketing, the logistic is perhaps the most common:

$$Q = \frac{a}{1 + e^{-(b+cX)}} + d \qquad \text{(C.9)}$$

This model has a saturation level $(a + d)$ and has a region of increasing returns followed by decreasing return to scale; it is symmetric around $d + a/2$. Naert and Leeflang (1978) and Johansson (1979) report uses of this model. This model is linearized via the logit transformation:

$$\ln\left(\frac{(Q-d)/a}{1 - (Q-d)/a}\right) = b + cX \qquad \text{(C.10)}$$

An alternative form of equation (C.10) that is often used replaces the right-hand side of equation (C.10) with $b + c \ln X$ to yield a non-symmetric S-shaped relationship. This model can admit propositions P1, P4 and P6.

Gompertz Model. Another S-shaped function is the Gompertz model:

$$Q = ab^{c^x} + d \qquad \text{(C.11)}$$
$$a > 0, \quad 1 > b > 0, c < 1$$

To linearize equation (C.11) we take logarithms twice to yield.

$$\ln[\ln(Q - d) - \ln a] = X \ln c + \ln \ln b \qquad \text{(C.12)}$$

Equation (C.12) shows that the Gompertz model represents a situation in which the growth increments in the logarithms are declining by a constant proportion, c. Both the Gompertz and logistic curves operate between a lower bound and an upper asymptote; the Gompertz curve involves a constant ratio of successive first differences of log Q while the logistic curve involves a constant ratio of successive first differences of $1/Q$.

Naert and Leeflang (1978) report the use of this model; it admits propositions P1, P4, and P6.

ADBUDG Model. The ADBUDG model, popularized by Little (1970) has the form

$$Q = b + (a - b)\frac{X^c}{d + X^c} \qquad \text{(C.13)}$$

The model is S-shaped for $c > 1$ and concave for $0 < c < 1$ and is bounded between b (lower) and a (upper). This model has been used frequently when judgmental calibration is called for (Little, 1970; Fudge and Lodish, 1977; Lodish et al., 1988). Johansson (1979) uses a different functional form that is algebraically equivalent to the ADBUDG model. The model can admit properties P1, P3, P4, and P6.

Interactions

The previous section dealt with response models of one variable. When multiple marketing-mix variables are considered their interactions should be accounted for. As Saunders (1987, p. 39) points out, interactions are usually treated in one of three ways: (1) by assuming they do not exist, (2) by assuming that they are multiplicative, and (3) by assuming they are multiplicative and additive. Assuming that we have two variables X_1 and X_2 with individual response functions $f(X_1)$ and $g(X_2)$, then assumption (1) leads us to

$$Q = af(X_1) + bg(X_2) \tag{C.14}$$

Assumption (2) gives us

$$Q = af(X_1)g(X_2) \tag{C.15}$$

and assumption (3) gives us

$$Q = af(X_1) + bg(X_2) + cf(X_1)g(X_2) \tag{C.16}$$

In practice, when multiple marketing-mix elements are involved, researchers generally resort to one of the following two forms: the (full) linear interactive form or the multiplicative form.

The full linear interactive model (for two variables) takes the following form:

$$Q = a + bX_1 + cX_2 + dX_1X_2 \tag{C.17}$$

Note here that $\partial Q/\partial X_1 = b + dX_2$, so that sales response to instrument 1 is affected by the level of variable 2.

The multiplicative form is as follows:

$$Q = aX_1^b X_2^c \tag{C.18}$$

Here $\partial Q/\partial X_1 = aX_1^{b-1}X_2^c$, so the response at any point is a function of the level of all mix variables. Note that

$$e_{Q,X_1} = \frac{\partial Q}{\partial X_1} \frac{X_1}{Q} = b \tag{C.19}$$

and similarly for c; thus b and c represent the (constant) elasticities of instruments 1 and 2.

There are a number of more general forms of interaction. For example, Hanssens, Parsons, and Schultz (1990, pp. 42–43) suggest the translog (transcendental logarithm model), which takes the following form:

$$\ln Q = a + b \ln X_1 + c(\ln X_1)^2 + d \ln X_1 \ln X_2 + f \ln X_2 + g(\ln X_2)^2 \quad \textbf{(C.20)}$$

The translog form provides a (quadratic) approximate to any continuous function; in general, the elasticities vary with the entire marketing mix:

$$e_{Q,X_1} = b + 2c \ln X_1 + d \ln X_2$$

A special case of this model is the multiplicative nonhomogeneous model (with a and $f = 0$ in equation C.20). (See Jagpal, Sudit, and Vinod, 1979; Jagpal, 1981.) The multiplicative model equation (C.18) emerges if, in addition, $d = 0$.

Other forms of interaction have been suggested by Balachandran and Gensch (1974) and Corstjens and Doyle (1979). However, our current lack of theory regarding the form of interaction combined with the usual lack of reliable data that allows us to distinguish between forms of interaction suggests that the simpler (linear interaction or multiplicative) forms are to be preferred for most applications.

DYNAMIC EFFECTS

Response to marketing actions does not always take place immediately. The effect of an ad campaign does not end when that campaign is over; the effect, or part of it, will remain perceptible for some future time. Many customers purchase more than they can consume of a product during a short-term price promotion. This action leads to inventory buildup and a lowering of sales in subsequent periods. Furthermore, the effect of that sales promotion will clearly depend on how much inventory buildup occurred in past periods (i.e., how much potential buildup is left). If customers stocked up on brand A cola last week, a new promotion this week is likely to be less productive than one in which a long period existed since the last such promotion).

"Carryover effects" is the general term used to describe the influence of a current marketing expenditure on sales in future periods. Several types of carryover effects can be distinguished. One type, the *delayed-response effect*, arises from delays that occur between the time marketing dollars are spent and the time induced purchases occur. This response is especially evident in industrial markets, where the delay, especially for capital equipment, can be a year or more. Another type of effect, the *customer-holdover effect*, arises from new customers created by the marketing expenditures, who remain customers for many subsequent periods. Their later purchases should be credited to some extent to the earlier expenditures. Some percentage of the new customers will be retained each period; this situation gives rise to the notion of the *customer retention rate* and its converse, the *customer decay rate* (also called attrition or erosion rate).

A third form of delayed response is *hysteresis,* the asymmetry in sales buildup compared to sales decline. For example, sales may rise quickly when an advertising program begins and then remain the same or decline slowly when the program is completed.

New trier effects, in which sales reach a peak before settling down to steady state, are common for frequently purchased products, where many customers try the product but only a few become regular users. Chapter 10 deals with this phenomenon in more detail.

Stocking effects after a deal or sales promotion occur when the promotion not only attracts new customers but encourages existing customers to "stockup" or "buyahead." The stocking effect often leads to a sales "trough" in the period following the promotion. Exhibit C.4 illustrates these phenomena.

The dynamics of market response have been modeled in discrete time versions and continuous-time versions. We deal with these in turn.

Discrete-Time Models

For simplicity in this section we deal with linear dynamic models involving a single marketing variable. The activity X and the response variable Q will be subscripted by the discrete-time interval t. Conceptually, the problem we face is the following: Q_t will be affected not only by X_t but by X_{t-1}, X_{t-2}, and so on. The equation for Q_t can thus be written as:

$$Q_t = a_0 + a_1 X_t + a_2 X_{t-1} + a_3 X_{t-2} + \ldots \qquad \text{(C.21)}$$

Due to a variety of data and estimation problems, most models posit some relationship among the a_i's. The most common one develops as follows: assume that the effects of $\{X_t\}$ on Q decays with time in a consistent way—that is, it loses a constant proportion of its influence each time period. This assumption is equivalent to

$$\frac{a_{i+1}}{a_i} = \lambda, \qquad \text{for all } i \qquad \text{(C.22)}$$

Using equation (C.22), we get

$$\frac{a_2}{a_1} = \lambda, \qquad \frac{a_3}{a_1} = \frac{a_2}{a_1}\frac{a_3}{a_2} = \lambda \cdot \lambda = \lambda^2$$

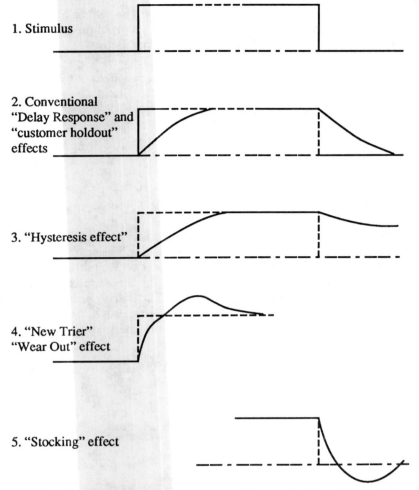

1. Stimulus

2. Conventional "Delay Response" and "customer holdout" effects

3. "Hysteresis effect"

4. "New Trier" "Wear Out" effect

5. "Stocking" effect

EXHIBIT C.4 Dynamic marketing responses. (*Source:* Sauders, 1987, p. 33.)

and, in general,

$$\frac{a_i}{a_1} = \lambda^{i-1} \qquad \text{or} \qquad a_i = a_1\lambda^{i-1} \qquad \text{(C.23)}$$

Now we can rewrite equation (C.21) as

$$Q_t = a_0 + a_1X_t + a_1\lambda X_{t-1} + a_1\lambda^2 X_{t-2} + \ldots \qquad \text{(C.24)}$$

which has only three unknowns: a_0, a_1, and λ.

But equation (C.24) still depends on the whole history, X_t, X_{t-1}, ..., so our truncation problem still is with us. This problem can be solved by lagging equation (C.24) one period and multiplying it by λ:

$$\lambda Q_{t-1} = \lambda a_0 + \lambda a_1 X_{t-1} + \lambda^2 a_1 X_{t-2} + \dots \qquad \text{(C.25)}$$

Subtracting equation (C.25) from equation (C.24) yields

$$Q_t - \lambda Q_{t-1} = a_0(1 - \lambda) + a_1 X_t$$

or

$$Q_t = a^* + \lambda Q_{t-1} + a_1 X_t \qquad \text{(C.26)}$$

where $a^* = a_0(1 - \lambda)$. This procedure, attributed to Koyck (1954), is often referred to as the Koyck transformation. Estimation problems are now greatly reduced, with but three parameters and two variables.

Note that the parameters λ and a_1 give measures of the short- and long-term effects of marketing instrument X. Clearly, a_1 measures the short-term effect of X from equation (C.21). Now suppose $X_t = X$ for a long time and that $Q_t = Q$; that is, that sales stabilize. Then equation (C.26) becomes

$$Q = a^* + \lambda Q + a_1 X$$

or

$$Q - \lambda Q = a^* + a_1 X$$

or

$$Q = \frac{a^*}{1 - \lambda} + \frac{a_1}{1 - \lambda} X \qquad \text{(C.27)}$$

Thus $a_1/(1 - \lambda)$ measures the long-term effect of marketing instrument X. The term $1/(1 - \lambda)$ is often called the long-run marketing-expenditure multiplier.

We can also look at elasticities

$$e_{QX} = \frac{dQ}{dX} \cdot \frac{X}{Q} \qquad \text{(C.28)}$$

Note that from our discussion, $dQ_t/dX_t = a_1$, which yields

$$e_{QX} = a_1 \frac{X}{Q} \tag{C.29}$$

Finally, another useful concept is that of long-run elasticity (at a level of marketing spending X):

$$e_{Q\infty X} = \frac{a_1 X}{Q_\infty (1 - \lambda)} \tag{C.30}$$

This equation follows by differentiating equation (C.27) with respect to X to obtain dQ/dX.

There are several problems with this model. First, there are estimation problems because the model in reduced form equation (C.27) results from calculating the difference between two equations separated by one period. The error terms for this model are then autocorrelated. (A form of this model that posits relationship C.26 directly with nonautocorrelated errors is known as a *partial adjustment model*).

Second, this (geometrically declining) set of effects will not handle all the delay phenomena described earlier. Bass and Clarke (1972), Lambin (1972b), and Montgomery and Silk (1972) use a modified form of geometric lag structure where the decline takes place at the jth period. Alternatively the Pascal (negative binomial) distribution can be used to characterize lagged effects,

$$Q_t = a + \sum_{i=1}^{m} b_i X(t - i + 1) \tag{C.31}$$

where

$$b_i = \frac{(r + i - 1)!(1 - h)^r h^i}{(r - 1)!i!}, \qquad i = 0, 1, 2, \ldots$$

and where $0 < h < 1$ and r is a positive integer. When $r = 1$, b_i reduces to the geometric lag structure.

Recent advances in time series analysis, that is, transfer function methods, have permitted the estimation of more general lead and lag structures, where the data specify the market dynamics. Hannsens, Parsons, and Schultz (1990, Ch. 4) give a detailed development of this approach.

Saunders (1987, p. 37) summarizes the literature on lags and concludes "the simple expressions (current effects, direct lag, partial adjustment and autoregressive current effects models) are as good as the more complex ones."

The "autoregressive current effects model" he refers to has the following form:

$$Q_t = a + bA_t + b\lambda A_{t-1} + \lambda S_{t-1} \tag{C.32}$$

One concludes from the current research and methodology in this area that, in contrast to the best thinking of a decade or so ago, one should avail oneself of transfer function methods wherever possible and use the direct lag expression form (C.21) until we have better theory available to specify the appropriate lag structure.

Continuous-Time Models

Discrete-time models are most often used operationally due to the fact that data are normally collected over discrete intervals (weeks, months, quarters, and the like). However, continuous time models afford superior methods of analysis (primarily differential equation methods) and are therefore valuable tools for developing policy implications.

Perhaps the most widely studied of the dynamic models is the one introduced in 1957 by Vidale and Wolfe and reviewed in Appendix A. Other classical dynamic models have included those of Nerlove and Arrow (1962), Sethi's (1973) logarithm model, and the models of Deal (1979) and Kimball (1957), which address competitive market dynamics. Chapter 11 on diffusion models reviews a number of dynamic models in continuous time.

MODELING DEMAND AT DIFFERENT LEVELS

Market-Share and Product-Class Sales

Implicitly to this point we have assumed that (product) sales result directly from marketing activities. However, as Naert and Leeflang (1978, Ch. 8) point out, response models in marketing can be distinguished by the way they handle demand: (1) product-class sales models, (2) brand sales models, and, (3) market-share models. Note that the three types of models are definitially related as

$$Q = SV \tag{C.33}$$

where

Q = brand sales

$$V = \text{product-class sales}$$
$$S = \text{market share}$$

Note that from equation (C.33) we get

$$\frac{\partial Q}{\partial X} = S \frac{\partial V}{\partial X} + V \frac{\partial S}{\partial X} \tag{C.34}$$

and multiplying both sides of equation (C.34) by X/Q yields

$$\frac{X}{Q} \frac{\partial Q}{\partial X} = \frac{XS}{Q} \frac{\partial V}{\partial X} + \frac{XV}{Q} \frac{\partial S}{\partial X} \tag{C.35}$$

or

$$e_Q = e_V + e_S \tag{C.36}$$

where e is the elasticity with respect to X. Equation (C.36) gives us the very important result: brand elasticity with respect to marketing instrument X (e_Q) is the sum of the elasticity of the product class (e_V) plus the elasticity of market share (e_S).

Naert and Leeflang (1978, pp. 152–153) decompose these quantities further as

$$e_V = e_{V_T,X} + r_{X_c} e_{V_T,X_c} \tag{C.37}$$

and

$$e_S = e_{S_T,X} + r_{Xc} e_{S_T,X_c} \tag{C.38}$$

where

$e_{V_T,X}$ = direct product-class sales elasticity with respect to X

e_{V_T,X_c} = product-class sales elasticity derived from competitive spending, X_c

r_{X_c} = reaction elasticity of X_c in response to marketing activity X

X_c = competitive marketing spending

and where $e_{S_T,X}$ and e_{S_T,X_c} are defined similarly for market-share elasticity. If more than one competitor responds with more than one instrument (i.e., firm A increases advertising, B responds with a price cut, C combines an advertising reaction with a promotion, etc.), then expressions (C.37) and (C.38) expand accordingly. Equations (C.36–C.38) can be summarized as follows:

$$\text{Sales elasticity} = \text{Share effect} + \text{market size effect} \tag{C.39}$$

$$\text{Share effect} = \text{Direct effect} + \text{competitive response effect} \tag{C.40}$$

$$\text{Market size} = \text{Direct effect} + \text{competitive response effect} \tag{C.41}$$

The algebra of equations (C.39) to (C.41) suggests that additional insight can be gained by studying sales as the product of market-share and product-class sales. This is especially true in markets where some marketing instruments (price, say) might affect product-class sales more than share while for others (promotion, say) the reverse might be true.

In addition, product-class sales normally incorporate environmental, trend and seasonal variables that can and should be omitted when studying market share.

Product-Class Sales Models

Consumer-demand theory, as developed in economics, has produced a large number of product-class–sales models. The usual approach is to hypothesize a form for a utility function and to look for the utility-maximizing allocation of consumer budgets over a number of products. However, these product classes are often too broadly defined for marketing use. (See Barten, 1977, Brown and Deaton, 1972, and Theil, 1975, 1976.)

In marketing, most models for product-class demand use time-series data and explain demand by environmental variables and aggregate values of marketing variables. Environmental variables include population size, income, weather, and prices and availability of complementary products and/or substitutes. Aggregation of marketing variables usually means product-class (total) advertising expenditures, total number of retail outlets, average market price, and so on.

As an example of this type of modeling, consider the study by Lambin (1970) in which he estimated the demand function for per capita consumption of a food product:

$$\frac{V_t}{N_t} = a_0\left(\frac{Y_t}{N_t}\right)^{a_1} t^{a_2} R_t^{-a_3} K_t^{-a_4} \qquad \textbf{(C.42)}$$

where

V_t = product-class sales
N_t = population size
Y_t = private disposable income
t = time
R = rainfall
K_t = general price index at time t

Equation (C.42) shows per capita market demand going up with disposable income and down with rainfall and increases in the general price trend. The results also show a positive trend in product-class sales.

Market-Share Models

By definition, market share for brands in a product class must sum to one. This constraint is not satisfied by many simple functional forms. For example, consider a two-brand market with brands 1 and 2 and a single marketing instrument X. At first glance the following model looks reasonable:

$$S_{1t} = \lambda_1 S_{1t-1} + g_1 \frac{X_{1t}}{X_{1t} + X_{2t}}$$

and (C.43)

$$S_{2t} = \lambda_2 S_{2t-1} + g_2 \frac{X_{2t}}{X_{1t} + X_{2t}}$$

where

S_{1t} = market share of brand 1 at time t

X_{1t} = advertising spending of brand 1 at time t

Model equation (C.43) says that market share for brand 1 is some fraction of last period's share (g_1) and is affected by the current share of marketing effort $[X_{1t}/(X_{1t} + X_{2t})]$. For shares to sum to one with this model structure, the following conditions are required (Naert and Bultez, 1973):

$$\lambda_1 = \lambda_2 = \lambda$$
$$g_1 = g_2 = g \qquad \text{(C.44)}$$
$$\lambda + g = 1$$

But these conditions are not desirable because they imply that different brands respond in exactly the same way to changes in the marketing instrument. Furthermore, the multiplicative analogy of equation (C.43), $S_t = S_{t-1}^\lambda X_t^g$, leads to even more problems because there are no restrictions on the parameters that can ensure that market shares sum to one. Therefore these models, while simple and understandable, do not satisfy the conditions of model consistency (here market share can be greater than one, less than zero, and, across brands, can sum to something other than one) and must be treated cautiously in practice.

A class of models that does satisfy both range (falling in the zero-to-one region) and sum constraints and that deals with competing brands in a disaggregate form are attraction models, where the attraction of a brand depends on its marketing mix. Essentially, these models say: our share = us/ (us + them).

If we allow S_i to represent market share of brand i and A_i the attraction of brand i, the general attraction model can be defined as

$$S_i = \frac{A_i}{\displaystyle\sum_{j=1}^{I} A_j} \tag{C.45}$$

$i = 1, \ldots, I$, the number of brands in the market

From equation (C.45) it is clear that as long as the $\{A_i\}$ are nonnegative, all S_i are greater than zero and less than one and that $\Sigma_{i=1}^{I} S_i = 1$. Bell, Keeney, and Little (1975) and Barnett (1976) develop the conditions under which a function, such as that in equation (C.45), can be expected to be observed; the conditions are intuitively plausible and are an extension of the range- and-sum-constraint arguments. It must be noted that, in general, each A_i is made up of the components of that brand's marketing mix and could have differential effects for different brands. In addition, brand i's advertising could be included in brand j's attractiveness (most likely, but not always, in a negative way, especially with an "our brand versus their brand" advertising campaign); this type of specification is not ruled out with an attraction model.

Several forms of attraction functions, A_i, have been proposed; the two most common are

the *multiplicative competitive-interaction model (MCI)*:

$$A_i = e^{a_i} \prod_{k=1}^{K} X_{k_i}^{b_k} e_i \tag{C.46}$$

and the *multinomial logit model (MNL)*:

$$A_i = \exp\left(a_i + \sum_{k=1}^{K} b_k X_{ki} + e_i\right) \tag{C.47}$$

where

a_i = constant influence of brand i,

e_i = error term

Both models (C.46) and (C.47) can be linearized for parameter estimation by applying a log-centering transformation as follows:

The full MCI model has the following form:

$$S_i = \frac{e^{a_i} \prod_{k=1}^{K} X_{ki}^{b_k} e_i}{\sum_{j=1}^{I} \left(a_j \prod_{k=1}^{K} X_{kj}^{b_k} e_j \right)} \tag{C.48}$$

Taking logs of both sides of (C.48), yields (C.49):

$$\log S_i = a_i + \sum_{k=1}^{K} b_k \log X_{ki} + \log e_i$$
$$- \log \left[\sum_{j=1}^{I} \left(a_j \prod_{k=1}^{K} X_{kj}^{b_k} e_j \right) \right] \tag{C.49}$$

Summing the i equations ($i = 1, ..., I$) and dividing by I yields

$$\log \tilde{S} = \tilde{a} + \sum_{k=1}^{K} b_k \log \tilde{X}_k + \log \tilde{e}$$
$$- \log \left[\sum_{j=i}^{I} \left(a_j \prod_{k=1}^{K} X_{kj}^{b_k} e_j \right) \right] \tag{C.50}$$

where $\tilde{S}$, $\tilde{X}_k$, and $\tilde{e}$ are the geometric means of S_i, X_{ki} and e_i, respectively. Subtracting equation (C.50) from equation (C.49) yields

$$\log \left(\frac{S_i}{\tilde{S}} \right) = a_i^* + \sum_{k=1}^{K} b_k \log \left(\frac{X_{ki}}{\tilde{X}_k} \right) + e_i^* \tag{C.51}$$

where

$$a_i^* = a_i - \tilde{a}$$
$$e_i^* = \log(e_i / \tilde{e}_i)$$

Equation (C.51) is linear in parameters a_i^* ($i = 1, ..., I$) and b_k ($k = 1, ..., K$) and is amenable to estimation. Similarly, for the MNL model we obtain

$$\log \left(\frac{S_i}{\tilde{S}} \right) = a_i^* + \sum_{k=1}^{K} b_k (X_{ki} - \tilde{X}_k) + (e_i - \tilde{e}) \tag{C.52}$$

where a_i^* is as earlier, and $\bar{X}_k$ and $\bar{e}$ are the arithmetic means of X_{ki} and e_i, respectively.

Cooper and Nakanishi (1988) provide a thorough treatment of these market-share models and others derived from more general attractiveness functions. In particular, they demonstrate how model extensions can accommodate differential effects (brand A's advertising is more effective than brand B's) and cross-competitive effects (A's advertising affects B's differently than it affects brand C).

In this "fully extended" form, a brand's attractiveness is a function of the brand's actions *plus* all of the other brands' actions.

While these appear to be compelling reasons to use attraction models to deal with market share, they are clearly more cumbersome to work with than simpler additive or multiplicative models with share as the dependent variable (multivariate extensions of equations (C.1), (C.5), and (C.6), for example).

In addition they contain many parameters relative to the size of many data samples. Hence, linear or multiplicative market-share models are often used in practice.

As a result, a series of comparative studies on the predictive power of attractive versus linear or multiplicative market-share models have been undertaken (Naert and Weverbergh, 1981, 1985; Brodie and de Kluyver, 1984; Ghosh, Neslin, and Shoemaker, 1984; Leeflang and Reuyl, 1984). The results are mixed: some support attraction models, others do not. Cooper and Nakanishi (1988, p. 31) argue for attraction models as follows: "we do not believe that predictive accuracy is the only important criteria for judging the value of a model. We would rather find the answer in the *construct validity* [italics theirs] (i.e., intrinsic meaningfulness) of those models." On balance, we support Cooper and Nakanishi on the use of attraction models.

OTHER MODELING ISSUES

Individual versus Aggregate Models. Market-response models can be classified by whether they model total market behavior directly or indirectly through individual behavior models, that are then aggregated to determine market response. In physics these classifications are analogous to macroscopic and microscopic perspectives: in "processes involving heat phenomena, the macroscopic point of view is given by thermodynamics and the microscopic one by the atomic theory of heat" (Resnick and Halliday, 1960, p. 488).

Models of aggregate response can be constructed in one of two ways. First, models of individual consumer behavior can be added together to form a model of aggregate (either market or market-segment) response. The probabilistic properties of the aggregate models are then derived from the properties of the individual component models. Second, a model of aggregate behavior can be postulated directly, having its own component of response uncertainty, and applied to aggregate data. The characteristics of the aggregate model are obtained directly in this case. The wide availability of scanner-type data (at the individual level) along with theories relating individual response models to aggregate market response (see Blattberg and Jeuland, 1981) has led to increased interest in models of individual buyer behavior and methods for aggregation. Chapter 2 develops this theme in more detail.

Stochastic/Deterministic Models.   The models we have introduced thus far have been primarily deterministic in nature. However, models of behavioral phenomena may be probabilistic (stochastic) in nature. Thus the marketing modeler may set up a system of equations that either does or does not include probabilistic elements.

Models may be classified as follows:

Deterministic
Deterministic with stochastic error
Inherently stochastic

The choice of model type depends more on the user and the application than on any philosophical understanding of the workings of markets. Whether behavior is really stochastic ["there is a stochastic element in the brain" (Bass, 1974, p. 2)] or whether it is indeed predictable in exact terms is irrelevant from an operational standpoint. Any model capable of making exact predictions would be hopelessly complex, and the data requirements would be enormous: a complete history of all past actions by all individuals involved, all choices available, and a complete picture of the environment would be required. Therefore deterministic models are used as approximations, with the stochastic elements omitted for simplicity.

Thus, models can be built that are either deterministic or probabilistic. Probabilistic models generally fall into two categories: deterministic with stochastic error or inherently stochastic. The choice of model type will be influenced by the type of data available, the use to which the model is to be put, and the preferences of the model builder.

Coefficient Variation.   We seem to treat most of our marketing models as if their coefficients will have values that are fixed over time. Yet advertising programs wear out, the environment shifts, consumers become bored, and so on—for a wide range of reasons, coefficients should be expected to vary over time.

Coefficient variation has been addressed in marketing models in two ways: if the parameters follow a random process, parameter variation is called *stochastic*. If, on the other hand, parameter variation can be linked to time, environmental or other observable variations, that variation is called *systematic*.

Wildt and Winer (1983) provide a review of the literature on stochastic parameter variation, when that process is autoregressive. Hanssens, Parsons, and Schultz (1990) and Saunders (1987) provide reviews of the literature on systematic variation in coefficients. Both conclude that much synthesis is needed to specify properly, a priori, the form that systematic variation is likely to take in marketing models.

Other Phenomena.   Earlier sections of this appendix discussed various forms of asymmetry. Other forms of asymmetry occur across segments, territories, and brands. For example, cross-sectional variation to sales effort is at the heart of sales force allocation models, whether that variation be at the account level (Lodish, 1971b), territory level (Beswick and Cravens, 1977), or the market segment or product level (Lodish, 1976).

Much of the work of Cooper and Nakanishi (1988) demonstrates brand-to-brand variation in response when those brands are in the same market.

CHOOSING AND EVALUATING A MATHEMATICAL FORM

The model forms reviewed in this chapter present a number of trade-offs. One model form is not better than another. Rather, the situation and the model's use need to be considered. Although there are a number of useful criteria for model selection, here are three that can be generally used:

1. *Theoretical soundness.* Is there an empirical or theoretical reason to believe a model should have certain characteristics? Is an S-shape appropriate? Is there an upper bound on sales? If the answers to these questions are yes, a linear model is inappropriate, and the set of possible functional forms is restricted.

2. *Descriptive soundness.* Does the model fit the data well (better than competing models)? In essence, this criterion addresses the question of goodness of fit to historical or judgmental data.

3. *Normative soundness.* Two models may fit equally well, but one may produce normative suggestions that are unreasonable. Therefore, a third criterion for model-form selection deals with finding a model that produces decision-making guidelines that are believable.

In addition, models need to be adapted to the use and user and should incorporate a level of detail that is consistent with the availability of data.

For example, an individual response model will require data at the individual level for calibration.

When one is selecting a model, the three criteria can be summarized as one question: "Does this model make sense for this situation?" That is, does the model have the right form, theoretically, empirically, and normatively? If the answers are all yes, then the model is appropriate.

D | MODEL CALIBRATION

For a model to be concrete, it must be calibrated: values must be assigned to the model's parameters (the unknowns). In this appendix we outline key approaches to this problem. At one extreme, calibration encompasses a classical statistical estimation procedure. At the other extreme, a parameter or set of parameters may be selected judgmentally. In the sections that follow we present three basic approaches to the calibration process: (1) objective procedures, (2) subjective procedures, and (3) Bayesian procedures, which blend objective and subjective procedures.

OBJECTIVE PARAMETER ESTIMATION

In this section, we first sketch linear regression procedures and extend them to multiple regression. We then show how generalized least squares can be used to handle problems of heteroscedasticity and autocorrelation. These procedures are appropriate for estimating parameters of linear or linearizable models. Estimation procedures for nonlinear models are handled next. We then deal with models in which the dependent variable is a probability value (an unobserved value). Finally, we discuss issues in multiple-equation modeling and estimation, including causal- or structural-equation modeling.

Simple Linear Regression Model

Suppose we observe sales levels $\{Q_i\}$ and advertising intensities $\{X_i\}$ in a number of markets, where i refers to market area. Let us assume a linear model is appropriate here. In addition, we are unlikely to model sales so simply with 100% accuracy, so a disturbance or error term is used to account for the deviation of the observed level of Q_i from its expected value. This discussion leads to the following model structure:

$$Q_i = a_0 + a_1 X_i + \varepsilon_i \tag{D.1}$$

where

$$
\begin{aligned}
Q_i &= \text{sales in region } i \\
X_i &= \text{advertising intensity in } i \\
a_0, a_1 &= \text{unknown parameters} \\
\varepsilon_i &= \text{random disturbance}
\end{aligned}
$$

We assume the following:

1. The X_i are measured without error.
2. For a given value of X_i the variation in Q_i can be explained by a probability distribution, $f(Q_i| X_i)$, with the same variance σ^2 for all X_i.
3. The values of Q_i are statistically independent (i.e., large sales in one region do not tend to affect sales in other regions).
4. The mean values of our observations, $E(Q_i)$, lie on the straight line

$$E(Q_i) = a_0 + a_1 X_i \tag{D.2}$$

Exhibit D.1 illustrates these relationships.

Then the problem we face is the estimation of a_0 and a_1. A frequently used approach is the least-squares solution, where we estimate the values of a_0 and a_1 ($\hat{a}_0$ and $\hat{a}_1$) that minimize the sum of squared (observed) deviations of the Q_i from their minimize mean values, $a_0 + a_1 X_i$:

Find a_0 and a_1 to minimize

$$\Sigma(Q_i - a_0 - a_1 X_i)^2 \tag{D.3}$$

Solving equation (D.3) results in

$$\hat{a}_0 = \sum_{i=1}^{I} \frac{Q_i}{I} - \hat{a}_1 \overline{X} \tag{D.4}$$

Objective Parameter Estimation

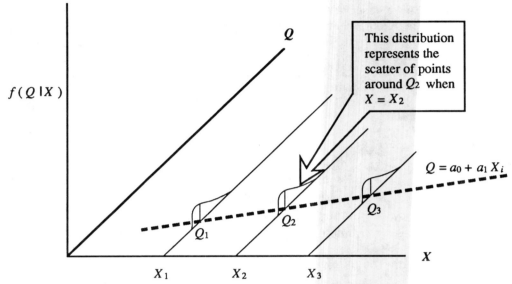

EXHIBIT D.1 The assumptions of the simple linear regression model.

and

$$\hat{a}_1 = \frac{\sum\limits_{i=1}^{I} (X_i - \overline{X})(Q_i - \overline{Q})}{\sum\limits_{i=1}^{I} (X_i - \overline{X})^2}$$

where

$$\overline{X} = \frac{\Sigma X_i}{I} \tag{D.5}$$

A major justification for using the least-squares estimates in equations (D.4) and (D.5) is the *Gauss-Markov theorem*: within the class of linear, unbiased estimators, the least-squares estimators have minimum variance (are most efficient).

There are several properties desirable in estimators: they should be unbiased, efficient, consistent, and best normal.

Unbiased. An unbiased estimator is one that, on the average, is equal to its true value: $\hat{a}_1$, is unbiased if

$$E(\hat{a}_1) = a_1 \tag{D.6}$$

Efficiency.   We might wish to compare several estimators, some more biased perhaps and others spread out around their mean. Consider how an estimator $\hat{a}_1$ is spread out around its true value a_1. The most common measure of this property is the *mean-squared error (MSE)*:

$$MSE = E(\hat{a}_1 - a_1)^2 \tag{D.7}$$

The *MSE* is a measure of both variance and bias; since

$$MSE = \sigma^2 + bias^2$$

Then, for any two estimators $\hat{a}_1$ and a_1^*, the relative efficiency of $\hat{a}_1$ relative to a_1^* is

$$\frac{MSE(a_1^*)}{MSE(\hat{a}_1)} \tag{D.8}$$

Consistency.   A consistent estimator is one that is concentrated in a narrower and narrower range around its target as the sample size gets larger. Formally, $\hat{a}_1$ is consistent if, for any $\delta > 0$

$$\text{Prob}(|\hat{a}_1 - a_1| < \delta) \to 1 \text{ as the sample size} \to \infty \tag{D.9}$$

It can be shown that an estimator whose $MSE \to 0$ as the sample size increases is consistent (although the converse does not hold).

Best Asymptotically Normal (BAN).   An estimator is best asymptotically normal if the following conditions hold:

1. Its distribution is approximately normal when its sample size gets large.

2. It is a consistent estimator.

3. No other consistent, normal estimator is more efficient (has a lower *MSE*).

To use these characteristics of estimators, we must make assumptions about the distribution of the error term ε. Assume that the characteristics of the product and the marketplace that affect Q (other than advertising) are large in number and essentially independent of one another and that no single excluded effect is dominant. In this case the central limit theorem suggests that the distribution of the error term is likely to be approximately normal with mean zero (by construction) and variance σ^2:

$$f_\varepsilon(\varepsilon) = \frac{1}{\sqrt{2\pi}\sigma} \, e^{-1/2(\varepsilon/\sigma)^2} \qquad \textbf{(D.10)}$$

We introduce here another estimation concept, that of maximum-likelihood estimation.

Likelihood Function.   The likelihood function of n random variables, $Q_1, \ldots, Q_n$, is the joint probability density function of those variables, $f(Q_1, \ldots, Q_n; a_0, a_1)$, considered to be some function of the parameters a_0, and a_1. In particular, if the $\{Q_i\}$ are independent and identically distributed, then the likelihood function is

$$f(Q_1, \ldots, Q_n; a_0, a_1) = f_Q(Q_1; a_0, a_1) \ldots f_Q(Q_n; a_0, a_1) \qquad \textbf{(D.11)}$$

That is, the likelihood function is the product of the individual probability densities.

This function gives the relative likelihood that a particular sample $(Q_1, \ldots, Q_n)$ could have been generated by a probability distribution with parameters a_0 and a_1. The principle of maximum-likelihood estimation is to choose parameter values that maximize this likelihood.

Maximum-Likelihood Estimator.   If the likelihood function is

$$L(a_0, a_1) = f(Q_1, \ldots, Q_n; a_0, a_1) \qquad \textbf{(D.12)}$$

then the $\hat{a}_0$ and $\hat{a}_1$ that maximize the value of the likelihood function are the maximum-likelihood estimates of a_0 and a_1.

Under fairly general conditions, maximum-likelihood estimators are the most efficient estimators in large samples, consistent, and best asymptotically normal. What these conditions mean is that, in general, if we have fairly large samples, not only can we do no better than the maximum-likelihood estimators in terms of estimator variance and bias, but we even know the distribution of the parameter estimators (normal) and can make probability statements about their statistical significance. In addition, in a normal regression model (errors being normal), the maximum-likelihood estimates of the parameters are identical to the least-squares estimates.

Multiple Linear Regression

In many situations there will be two or more independent variables that influence the variable of interest, Q in our case. The multiple linear equation analogous to equation (D.1) is

$$Q = a_0 + a_1 X_1 + a_2 X_2 + \cdots + a_K X_K + \varepsilon \qquad \textbf{(D.13)}$$

where

$$X_1 \qquad\qquad = \text{advertising}$$
$$X_2 \qquad\qquad = \text{price (etc.)}$$
$$a_0, a_1, a_2, \ldots, a_K = \text{parameters to be estimated}$$
$$\varepsilon \qquad\qquad = \text{stochastic error term, with mean zero and standard deviation } \sigma$$

We will assume for the moment that assumptions 1–4 from the previous section hold here as well.

In general, it is easier to describe and present the multiple regression model in matrix form

$$Q_j = \boxed{\begin{array}{cccc} 1 & X_{j1} & X_{j2} \ldots X_{jK} \end{array}} \begin{bmatrix} a_0 \\ a_1 \\ \vdots \\ a_K \end{bmatrix} + \varepsilon_j \tag{D.14}$$

If we stack all Q observations into a column vector, we get

$$Q = Xa + \varepsilon$$

or

$$\begin{bmatrix} Q_1 \\ \vdots \\ Q_J \end{bmatrix} = \begin{bmatrix} 1 & X_{11} & \ldots & X_{1K} \\ & \cdots\cdots\cdots\cdots \\ & \cdots\cdots\cdots\cdots \\ & \cdots\cdots\cdots\cdots \\ 1 & X_{J1} & \ldots & X_{JK} \end{bmatrix} \begin{bmatrix} a_0 \\ \vdots \\ a_K \end{bmatrix} + \begin{bmatrix} \varepsilon_1 \\ \vdots \\ \varepsilon_J \end{bmatrix} \tag{D.15}$$

Again we assume that $\{\varepsilon_i\}$ are independent errors with mean zero and variance σ^2, so

$$E(\varepsilon) = 0 \tag{D.16}$$

and the covariance matrix of $\boldsymbol{\varepsilon}$ is

$$\text{cov}(\boldsymbol{\varepsilon}) = E(\varepsilon\,\varepsilon') = \sigma^2 \mathbf{I} \tag{D.17}$$

or

$$\text{cov}(\boldsymbol{\varepsilon}) = \begin{bmatrix} E(\varepsilon_1\varepsilon_1) \ldots E(\varepsilon_1\varepsilon_J) \\ \cdots\cdots\cdots \\ E(\varepsilon_J\varepsilon_1) \ldots E(\varepsilon_J\varepsilon_J) \end{bmatrix} = \begin{bmatrix} \sigma^2 & 0 & \ldots & 0 \\ 0 & \sigma^2 & \ldots & 0 \\ \cdots\cdots\cdots \\ 0 & \ldots & 0 & \sigma^2 \end{bmatrix}$$

Note that the ε distribution is, in fact, the $\boldsymbol{Q}$ distribution translated onto a mean of zero—the only difference between the ε and $\boldsymbol{Q}$ distributions is their mean values:

$$E(\mathbf{Q}) = \mathbf{Xa} \tag{D.18}$$

$$\text{cov}(\mathbf{Q}) = \sigma^2\mathbf{I} \tag{D.19}$$

Now in the multiple-variable case (as in the single-variable case), we consider minimizing the sum of squared deviations. In matrix form this condition becomes

$$\text{Minimize } (\mathbf{Q} - \mathbf{Xa})'(\mathbf{Q} - \mathbf{Xa}) \tag{D.20}$$

Using principles of matrix multiplication and differentiation, we obtain

$$\hat{\mathbf{a}} = (\mathbf{X'X})^{-1}\mathbf{X'Q} \tag{D.21}$$

By the Gauss-Markov theorem, $\hat{\boldsymbol{a}}$ is the best linear unbiased estimator of $\boldsymbol{a}$. Under the additional assumption that the $\{\varepsilon_i\}$ are normally distributed, equation (D.21) represents the maximum-likelihood estimator of $\boldsymbol{a}$, with the properties already described.

Key properties of the distribution of $\hat{\boldsymbol{a}}$ used in testing hypotheses about model parameters are

$$E(\hat{\mathbf{a}}) = \mathbf{a} \tag{D.22}$$

(i.e., the estimators are unbiased) and

$$\text{cov}(\hat{\mathbf{a}}) = \sigma^2(\mathbf{X'X})^{-1} \tag{D.23}$$

Relaxing the Assumptions: Generalized Least Squares. Marketing data and the associated marketing models often do not satisfy the neat assumptions needed for optimality of the ordinary least-squares (OLS) approach. The most common problems seen in building multiple-variable marketing models are

(1) heteroscedasticity, where the disturbance terms do not have the same variance; (2) autocorrelation, where the disturbance terms are not independent; and (3) multicollinearity, where two or more of the independent variables are related. The first two can be handled by a single procedure known as *generalized least squares (GLS)*.

If equation (D.17) does not hold, then, in general,

$$\text{cov}(\varepsilon) = \begin{vmatrix} \sigma_{11} & \sigma_{12} & \sigma_{1J} \\ \multicolumn{3}{c}{\cdots\cdots\cdots} \\ \sigma_{J1} & \cdots & \sigma_{JJ} \end{vmatrix} = \sigma^2 \Omega^* = \Omega \tag{D.24}$$

where Ω is a positive definite, symmetric, $J \times J$ matrix of full rank. Now we introduce the matrix, $\mathbf{V}$:

$$\mathbf{V'V} = \Omega^{*-1} \quad \text{or} \quad (\mathbf{V'V})^{-1} = \Omega^* \tag{D.25}$$

If we go back to equation (D.15) and premultiply by V, we get

$$\mathbf{VQ} = \mathbf{VXa} + \mathbf{V\varepsilon} \tag{D.26}$$

After substitution and some matrix manipulations, we obtain

$$E[(\mathbf{V\varepsilon})(\mathbf{V\varepsilon})'] = \sigma^2 \mathbf{I} \tag{D.27}$$

This equation means that the disturbance term in the transformed model, equation (D.26), satisfies the standard least-squares regression conditions. Then applying the least-squares procedure to equation (D.26) yields

$$\hat{\mathbf{a}} = (\mathbf{X'} \Omega^{-1} \mathbf{X})^{-1} \mathbf{X'} \Omega^{-1} \mathbf{Q} \tag{D.28}$$

which is known as the generalized least-squares estimator of **a**. Note that in the special case where $\Omega = \sigma^2 \mathbf{I}$, equation (D.28) reduces to equation (D.21), the ordinary least-squares estimator. (For an example of the use of GLS in marketing, see Franke and Wilcox, 1987.)

Two special cases frequently arise in marketing analysis. The first is common in analyses of cross-sectional data where the assumption of homoscedasticity (all disturbance terms having the same variance) is often violated. In the model $Q = a_0 + a_1 X$, it might be reasonable for $\sigma^2 = g(X)$; that is, the amount of error around the sales figure might increase with larger levels of advertising (and hence sales). In this case,

$$\Omega = \begin{array}{|ccc|} \hline \sigma_1^2 & \cdots & 0 \\ \vdots & \cdots & \\ 0 & \cdots & \sigma_j^2 \\ \hline \end{array} \qquad \text{(D.29)}$$

Because the Ω matrix is diagonal,

$$\Omega^{-1} = \begin{array}{|ccc|} \hline \dfrac{1}{\sigma_1^2} & \cdots & 0 \\ & \cdots & \\ 0 & \cdots & \dfrac{1}{\sigma_j^2} \\ \hline \end{array} \qquad \text{(D.30)}$$

and the least-squares solution to equation (D.26) turns out to be

$$\text{Minimize} \sum_{j=1}^{J} \left(\frac{Q_j - \mathbf{X}_j\mathbf{a}}{\sigma_j} \right)^2 \qquad \text{(D.31)}$$

where X_j is the jth row of matrix X. Equation (D.31) is identical to the least-squares criterion, except for the $\{\sigma_j^2\}$ in the denominator. These weights give rise to the term *weighted least squares (WLS)*, a special case of generalized least squares.

A second problem that frequently arises in analysis of time-series data is serially correlated error. In this situation let us index the observations on Q by t to suggest temporal effects. Each row of our equation looks like

$$Q_t = \mathbf{X}_t\mathbf{a} + \varepsilon_t, \qquad t = 1, \ldots, T \qquad \text{(D.32)}$$

or

$$\mathbf{Q} = \mathbf{X}\mathbf{a} + \varepsilon$$

For purposes of illustration we assume that the $\{\varepsilon_t\}$ are no longer independent of one another but are related in a simple autoregressive scheme:

$$\varepsilon_t = \rho\varepsilon_{t-1} + v_t, \qquad t = \ldots, -2, -1, 0, 1, 2, \ldots \qquad \text{(D.33)}$$

where $|\rho| < 1$. Here the disturbances $\{v_t\}$ are assumed to have the usual characteristics:

$$E(\mathbf{v}) = \mathbf{0} \qquad \qquad \text{(D.34)}$$

$$\text{cov}(\mathbf{v}) = \sigma^2 \mathbf{I} \qquad \qquad \text{(D.35)}$$

In this case $E(\mathbf{\varepsilon}) = \mathbf{0}$, but $E(\varepsilon\ \varepsilon')$ is

$$\text{cov}(\mathbf{\varepsilon}) = \mathbf{\Omega} = \frac{\sigma^2}{1-\rho^2} \begin{bmatrix} 1 & \rho & \rho^2 & \cdots & & \cdot \\ \rho & 1 & \rho & \cdots & & \cdot \\ \rho^2 & \rho & 1 & \cdots & & \cdot \\ \rho^3 & \rho^2 & \rho & \cdots & & \cdot \\ \vdots & \vdots & \vdots & & \ddots & \vdots \\ & \cdot & & \cdot & & 1. \end{bmatrix} \qquad \text{(D.36)}$$

Note that

$$\mathbf{\Omega}^{-1} = \frac{1}{\sigma^2} \begin{bmatrix} 1 & -\rho & \cdots\cdots\cdots & & 0 \\ -\rho & 1+\rho^2 & & & \vdots \\ \vdots & & \ddots & & \vdots \\ \vdots & & 1+\rho^2 & & \vdots \\ \vdots & & & \ddots & \vdots \\ \vdots & & & 1+\rho^2 & -\rho \\ 0 & \cdots\cdots\cdots & & -\rho & 1 \end{bmatrix} \qquad \text{(D.37)}$$

and substitution of equation (D.37) into equation (D.28) yields the GLS solution.

In the preceding discussion we have assumed that $\mathbf{\Omega}$ is known. This is rarely the case, and we usually must rely on sample information to estimate $\mathbf{\Omega}$. For the case of heteroscedasticity, the data must be segregated into m groups that are more or less homogeneous, with n_j observations in each group, such that $\Sigma_{j=1}^{m} n_j = J$.

A useful procedure is to use ordinary least squares to estimate $\hat{a}_0, \ldots, \hat{a}_K$ and to use the residuals from this regression to estimate $\hat{\sigma}_j, j = 1, \ldots, m$:

$$\hat{\sigma}_j = \sum \frac{\left(Q_j - \sum_{l=1}^{K} \hat{a}_l X_{lj} \right)}{n_j}, \qquad \text{for } j = 1, \ldots, m \qquad \text{(D.38)}$$

where the summation is over those observations (i) in group n_j.

The estimates from equation (D.38) can then be substituted into equation (D.31) to obtain the generalized (or weighted) least-squares solution. See Kristensen (1984) for an approach to the problem of heteroscedasticity.

For the case of the first-order autoregressive scheme, an estimation approach is often required to estimate p. One direct approach is to estimate ρ as

$$\hat{\rho} = \frac{\sum\limits_{t=2}^{T} \hat{\varepsilon}_t \hat{\varepsilon}_{t-1}}{\sum\limits_{t=2}^{T} \hat{\varepsilon}_t^{\,2}} \tag{D.39}$$

where $\{\hat{\varepsilon}_t\}$ are estimated from ordinary least squares in the original equation. Note that equation (D.29) produces the least-squares estimate of $\hat{\rho}$ from equation (D.33). The value of $\hat{\rho}$ can be included in equation (D.37), which, in turn, is substituted into equation (D.28) to estimate a. (See Simon, 1982, and Vanhonacker, 1984, for applications of this approach and Wittink, 1983, for a review of approaches to autocorrelation in marketing models.)

Marketing models often face data that are gathered across geographic areas (or products) and over time. In these cases the disturbance terms may be cross-sectionally heteroscedastic and timewise autoregressive. For approaches to this problem, see Moriarty (1975), Moriarty and Salamon (1980), and Bass and Wittink (1975).

A third problem that is common in multiple regression models is *multicollinearity*. This situation occurs if two or more variables are significantly related to one another. Therefore if X_1 is advertising and X_2 is selling, and the firm budgets 9 dollars of selling for every dollar of advertising multicollinearity occurs, as shown in the following $\mathbf{X}$ matrix:

$$\mathbf{X} = \begin{bmatrix} 1 & X_{11} & 9X_{11} & X_{31} \ldots \\ 1 & & & \\ 1 & & & \\ \vdots & \vdots & \vdots & \vdots \\ 1 & X_{1J} & 9X_{1J} & X_{3J} \ldots \end{bmatrix} \tag{D.40}$$

Multicollinearity is reflected in the X_2 column, which is a multiple of the X_1 column (i.e., the columns are linearly dependent).

The result of multicollinearity is some very large values in the inverse matrix $(X'X)^{-1}$. Because $\sigma^2(X'X)^{-1}$ is the covariance matrix of $\hat{a}$, large variances and wide confidence intervals for the values of a result. In these circumstances it is difficult to establish that Q is influenced by any particular independent variable. When two (or more) variables are so related, the influence of one is easily attributable to another.

Multicollinearity is most often handled in one of three ways:

1. Eliminating some independent variables
2. Reducing the independent variables to a smaller number of principal components
3. Using RIDGE regression

Eliminating Variables. If two variables are meant to measure the same thing or, computationally, turn out to be linearly related, then the model loses nothing by eliminating one of the variables. When appropriate variables to eliminate are not apparent, a common procedure is principal components.

Principal Components. Principal components is a technique for reexpressing the X's with a smaller number of Y variables that are linear combinations of the X's. These new Y variables are orthogonal (and therefore have no multicollinearity problems) and capture as much of the variation in the X's as possible, with the first Y capturing the most variation, the second Y capturing the maximum remaining, and so on.

The main difficulty with this approach is that the effects of truly important independent variables can be lost in among the principal components, which are selected for their ability to explain the X's and therefore may not be the best set for explaining Q. A good alternative approach is to have important explanatory variables retained in their original form, with variables of lesser importance grouped as principal components.

RIDGE Regression. To retain all the independent variables in their original form we can adjust the data matrix to stabilize the model coefficients. Multicollinearity exists when $\mathbf{X'X}$ has large off-diagonal elements and relatively small diagonal elements. RIDGE regression deals with this problem directly by augmenting the main diagonal of $\mathbf{X'X}$ with the addition of a matrix $\mathbf{D}$, which has positive diagonal elements and zeros elsewhere. The RIDGE regression estimate then becomes

$$\hat{\mathbf{a}} = (\mathbf{X'X} + \mathbf{D})^{-1}\mathbf{X'Q} \qquad \textbf{(D.41)}$$

When multicollinearity is present, these estimators are much more stable than the OLS estimators. But the procedure introduces bias. Therefore for the RIDGE estimators to be superior to the OLS estimators, the elements of $\mathbf{D}$ must be chosen to minimize the bias. (See Hoerl and Kennard, 1970, for details and Erickson, 1981, Ofir and Khuri, 1986, and Shipchandler and Moore, 1988, for marketing applications.)

Thus the general linear regression model is a widely used estimation procedure in marketing. Under fairly general conditions GLS estimators provide estimators that have minimum variance among unbiased linear estimators. They are also maximum likelihood estimators if the error terms are normally distributed.

The procedures outlined here apply to any of the models in the last chapter that are either *linear, linear in the parameters,* or *linearizable.* However, they rely on a fairly large number of observations for estimation precision because standard errors contract with the square root of sample size. Furthermore, the least-squares criterion is sensitive to extreme points. If a few unusual or outlying points exist, they may greatly affect the parameter estimates, and "robust regression" procedures—bounded-loss functions and others—may be more appropriate.

Finally, these procedures do not apply to models that are inherently nonlinear or to models with binary dependent variables. These models are treated next.

Parameter Estimation for Nonlinear Models

When a least-squares approach is applied to the estimation of parameters for nonlinear models, the resulting equations may be difficult to solve for unique values. Two approaches can be used: numerical solution or iterative application of least squares with a Taylor series approximation to the original series.

EXAMPLE

Suppose we assume that sales go up with advertising, although nonlinearly, and that there is a base level of sales the firm would see even if advertising were zero. In this case we might model sales as

$$Q = a_0 + a_1 X^{a_2} + \varepsilon \qquad \textbf{(D.42)}$$

It can easily be seen that equation (D.42) cannot be directly transformed to a linear form. However, least-squares estimates can still be justified with the maximum-likelihood argument, and a normally distributed error term ε in equation (D.42) might be a reasonable assumption. Then the problem is to find a_0, a_1, and a_2 to

$$\text{Minimize } W = \Sigma(Q_i - a_0 - a_1 Xi^{a_2})^2 \qquad \textbf{(D.43)}$$

The procedure here is the same as that of a linear model. We take derivatives of equation (D.43) with respect to the parameters and set those derivatives equal to zero. (We must check second derivatives more carefully now because nonlinear models may lead us to local optima.)

$$\frac{\partial W}{\partial a_0} = \Sigma\, 2(-1)(Q_i - a_0 - a_1 Xi^{a_2}) = 0 \tag{D.44a}$$

$$\frac{\partial W}{\partial a_1} = \Sigma\, 2(-Xi^{a_2})(Q_i - a_0 - a_1 Xi^{a_2}) = 0 \tag{D.44b}$$

$$\frac{\partial W}{\partial a_2} = \Sigma\, 2(a_1 Xi^{a_2} \ln a_2)(Q_i - a_0 - a_1 Xi^{a_2}) = 0 \tag{D.44c}$$

Given values of $\{Q_i\}$ and $\{X_i,\}$ equation (D.44) must be solved for a_0, a_1, and a_2. The difficulty is that they are nonlinear, and even a single nonlinear equation may be difficult to solve. Moreover, there may no longer be a unique solution to the equations; therefore each set of values would have to be plugged into equation (D.43) to see which minimized W. Because of these analytical difficulties, an iterative, numerical computer routine is usually used to solve such problems.

A number of powerful computer-based methods have been developed for this problem, some using second-order series expansions of the functions, some providing numerical estimates of the derivatives, and others permitting constraints on the parameters. Many are readily available as standard computer packages.

Parameter Estimation for Binary Dependent Variables

Throughout this section we have assumed that the dependent variable of interest was a single, observable marketing variable, such as sales. But a class of very useful marketing models, individual choice models, presented in Chapter 2, have a 0–1 type of dependent variable. For example, we often observe consumer purchasing response as a 0–1 variable (bought the brand or not); an underlying probability model may be generating this (observed) 0–1 response.

Suppose we feel that individual probability of purchase p would increase with advertising exposure. To model this relationship, we might use the logit model, with

$$Y = \begin{cases} 1, & \text{if purchase is made} \\ 0, & \text{otherwise} \end{cases} \tag{D.45}$$

$$p = \text{probability that } Y = 1 \tag{D.46}$$

$$x = \text{advertising level}$$

and

$$p = \frac{1}{1 + e^{-(a_0 + a_1 x)}} \tag{D.47}$$

or

$$\log \frac{p}{1 - p} = a_0 + a_1 x \tag{D.48}$$

It appears that equation (D.48) can be used to estimate a_0 and a_1 by ordinary least squares. But if we use the original buy/not-buy data (0–1 responses) to replace p in equation (D.48), $\log [p/(1 - p)]$ is undefined.

An appropriate approach here is that of maximum likelihood. Assume we had only one observation Y_1 associated with X_1. The probability that $Y_1 = 1$, called p_1, is given by equation (D.47); the probability of $Y_1 = 0$ is simply $1 - p_1$. We can combine these two cases in a (Bernoulli) distribution function:

$$p(Y_1) = p_1^{Y_1}(1 - p_1)^{1-Y_1} \tag{D.49}$$

Note that p_1 is a function of a_0 and a_1 from equation (D.48). In like manner, we can get

$$p(Y_1, \ldots, Y_n) = p(Y_1) \ldots p(Y_n) \tag{D.50}$$

$$= \prod_{i=1}^{n} p_i^{Y_i}(1 - p_i)^{1-Y_i} \tag{D.51}$$

Although equation (D.51) looks like a complicated expression, in fact, it is only a function of two parameters, a_0 and a_1. Equation (D.51) is the *likelihood function* for this sample of n observations, and because it is a function of a_0 and a_1, we denote it as $L(a_0, a_1)$.

As in the previous section on nonlinear optimization, the values of a_0 and a_1 that maximize $L(\cdot)$ must be developed numerically. Many standard computer packages include numerical routines for the linear logit model. As indicated earlier, these maximum-likelihood estimates are best asymptotically normal, and, as such, most computer routines automatically provide standard errors of the estimates. (See Malhotra, 1984, for a review of the logit model and its use in marketing.)

Although this section has been framed in terms of the logit model, as long as the purchase events are independent of one another, equation (D.51) holds for any assumed equation for p_i.

Other, less widely used methods include least squares with constraints (when probabilities are observed or observations are aggregated to get input estimates of probabilities), discriminant analysis, and entropy maximization (where parameters are found to maximize the system randomness subject, usually, to market share constraints). Maximum likelihood seems to be the prevailing procedure of choice, at the moment, however, providing consistent, robust results in a wide range of reported applications (Bunch and Batsell, 1989).

Multiple-Equation Problems and Solutions

In the preceding sections we assumed that the requirements of a single-equation model held at least roughly, that is, that the direction of causality between Q and X is clear and that X is not measured with error. If either X is measured with error or our single equation is an integral part of a larger equation system, then OLS coefficient estimates will be biased and inconsistent.

To get an idea of what is going on here, assume that both sales and advertising are measured with some error:

$$Q = Q^T + \varepsilon \qquad \textbf{(D.52)}$$

$$X = X^T + \mu \qquad \textbf{(D.53)}$$

where Q^T and X^T represent true values of Q and X, respectively. For simplicity, suppose further that

$$Q^T = a_0 + a_1 X^T \qquad \textbf{(D.54)}$$

that is, true sales and true advertising are related to one another in a perfect linear manner. Substituting equations (D.52) and (D.53) into equation (D.54) yields

$$Q = a_0 + a_1 X + \omega \qquad \textbf{(D.55)}$$

where

$$\omega = \varepsilon - a_1 \mu \qquad \textbf{(D.56)}$$

Even if errors ε and μ are mutually independent and serially independent with constant variances, the assumptions for least squares do not apply because ω is not independent of X. It can be shown (Johnston, 1984) that the least-squares estimator of a_1, ($\hat{a}_1$), is biased:

$$E(\hat{a}_1) = a_1 \left(\frac{1}{1 + (\sigma_\mu^2/\sigma_X^2)} \right) \qquad \textbf{(D.57)}$$

What equation (D.57) says is that if the variance of the error in measuring X (advertising, say) is 10% of the variation observed in the analysis, then straightforward least squares would underestimate a_1 by about 10% even in very large samples. In single-equation situations, this problem is often handled through the introduction of *instrumental variables*, variables that are related to the X's but that are uncorrelated with the error term ε. Other approaches include grouping observations to get estimates of the level of error and the so-called classical approach, relying on strong assumptions about the error terms (Johnston, 1984).

We bring up the problem of correlation between error and independent variables here because it occurs when an equation to be estimated is part of a whole system of simultaneous equations. Such equation systems occur in marketing models when the direction of causality is unclear or when a series of (brand-specific) market-share equations must be consistent. As an example, consider the dilemma faced by the marketing analyst who believes that advertising (X) and level of distribution (D) affect sales (Q), but advertising in his firm is set at a fixed percentage of sales. These two relationships can be described as

$$Q = a_0 + a_1 X + a_2 D + \varepsilon_1 \qquad \text{(D.58)}$$

$$X = b_0 + b_1 Q + \varepsilon_2 \qquad \text{(D.59)}$$

If we substitute equation (D.59) into equation (D.58), we get

$$Q = \frac{a_0 + a_1 b_0}{1 - a_1 b_1} + \frac{a_2}{1 - a_1 b_1} D + \frac{\varepsilon_1 + a_1 \varepsilon_2}{1 - a_1 b_1} \qquad \text{(D.60)}$$

Equation (D.60) clearly shows that Q and ε_2 are correlated, as in the errors-in-variables case described earlier. Similarly, it can be shown that ε_1 and X are correlated. Thus if we apply OLS to either equation (D.58) or (D.59), our estimates will be biased and inconsistent. A variety of methods have been suggested for handling these problems, of which the simplest to apply is two-stage least squares (2SLS).

The idea behind 2SLS is to purge Q of its dependency on ε_2. This is accomplished by replacing Q by $\hat{Q}$, which resembles Q but is independent of ε_2 (i.e., an instrumental variable). To find $\hat{Q}$, regress Q on D,

$$\hat{Q} = c_0 + c_1 D \qquad \text{(D.61)}$$

Because, by assumption, D is independent of ε_2, this linear function will be independent of ε_2 as well. This step is the first stage of 2SLS: regress each endogenous (dependent) variable against all related exogenous (independent) variables.

The second stage of 2SLS simply substitutes equation (D.61) into equation (D.59) to get

$$X = b_0 + b_1 \hat{Q} + \varepsilon_3 \qquad \textbf{(D.62)}$$

We can now apply OLS to equation (D.62), which leads to consistent estimators because $\hat{Q}$ is uncorrelated with the (adjusted) error term ε_3.

An additional problem in multiple-equation estimation concerns *identification*. In terms of our original objectives, which were to estimate a_0, a_1, a_2, b_0, and b_1, we have produced consistent estimates of b_0 and b_1. But what of a_0, a_1, and a_2? Comparing equations (D.60) and (D.61), we find we have established the following relationships:

$$\hat{c}_0 = \frac{a_0 + a_1 b_0}{1 - a_1 b_1} \qquad \textbf{(D.63)}$$

$$\hat{c}_1 = \frac{a_2}{1 - a_1 b_1} \qquad \textbf{(D.64)}$$

In equations (D.63) and (D.64) we have two equations but three unknowns. In such circumstances we say that the equation is underidentified. This is a critical point for multiple-equation systems: an equation can be underidentified (as is equation D.58), just identified (as is equation D.59), or overidentified. A condition that must be satisfied for an equation to be identified is called the order condition. This condition relates the number of excluded exogeneous (independent) variables (m_0) to the number of included endogenous (dependent variables, q). There are three cases:

1. If $m_0 < q - 1$, the equation is *underidentified*, or unidentified, and the coefficients of the original equation cannot be estimated.

2. If $m_0 = q - 1$, the equation is *exactly identified*, and the coefficients can be estimated exactly.

3. If $m_0 > q - 1$, the equation is *overidentified* because more equations are available than are necessary to estimate the coefficients.

In equation (D.58), $q = 3$ (including the constant), and in equation (D.59), $q = 2$. In both cases $m_0 = 1$. Then by the rule just given, equation (D.58) is unidentified, while equation (D.59) is just identified. This simple order condition is usually a good indicator of the identifiability of each equation in a multiple-equation system. (See Fisher, 1966, for treatment of this issue.)

There are many other methods for estimating coefficients in multiple-equation systems. These methods usually fall into two categories: (1) limited-information methods and (2) full-information methods. Limited-information methods address one equation in the system at a time and include 2SLS and limited-information maximum likelihood. Full-information methods estimate all system coefficients simultaneously and include three-stage least squares and full-information maximum likelihood. Although full-information methods may, on the surface, appear superior, they are much more sensitive to model misspecification (including or excluding incorrect variables or functional relationships) than are limited-information methods. The limited-information methods insulate estimation of any equation from specification errors committed in other equations: "in an economic world where (the dependent variables) depend on a large number of other variables in the economy, the more one reduces the model size in order to provide theoretical and mathematical simplicity . . . the greater may be the risk of mis-specification; accordingly, the more one might prefer 2SLS" (Wonnacott and Wonnacott, 1979, p. 520).

Finally, 2SLS has been applied to a large number of marketing studies reported in the literature, including Cowling and Cubbin (1971), Albach (1979), Bass and Parsons (1969), Lambin, Naert, and Bultez (1975), and Lambin (1976).

Causal Models and Unobserved Variables

In the model systems we have reviewed, the associations between variables can be either empirical or causal. When the relationships are causal, the model is called a *structural-equation model*. All the variables in these models are assumed to represent a single, theoretical construct and are usually assumed to be measured without error. From a marketing standpoint such an assumption is very limiting; in many contexts, especially where perceptual or psychological variables are included, single indicators are unlikely to capture all the richness of the theoretical construct and may well be measured with error.

Within the context of linear systems of equations and subject to restrictions imposed by the necessities of identification, hypothetical constructs, called unobserved variables, can be included and estimated in structural-equation models. For example, an unobserved variable may be preference for a brand, where the measurement of preference is a scale of 1–10 or a paired comparison with another brand.

Ideally, one would like to use a modeling-and-estimation procedure that directly measures the degree of correspondence between unobservable constructs and measurements, the level of error in those measurements, the level of error in equations, and the relationship between the observable constructs themselves. These measurements and diagnostics can all be achieved in a linear causal-modeling framework, provided that the system is linear and identified, that there are multiple measurements of at least some of the unobservable variables in the model, and that errors are approximately normal.

Structural-equation models are popularly represented in causal diagrams with the following conventions (Bagozzi, 1979b):

$$y = \beta x \quad \leftrightarrow \quad x \overset{\beta}{\to} Y$$

$$y = \beta x + \mu \quad \leftrightarrow \quad x \overset{\beta}{\to} Y \overset{\mu}{\swarrow}$$

$$y = \beta_1 x_1 + \beta_2 x_2 + \beta_3 x_3 + \mu \quad \leftrightarrow \quad \begin{matrix} x_1 \searrow \\ x_2 \to Y \overset{\mu}{\swarrow} \\ x_3 \nearrow \end{matrix}$$

□ = observed variable

○ = theoretical construct

EXAMPLE

Consider a model in which one theoretical construct B causes another, A. Both A and B are operationalized by two variables– each, measured with error.

Exhibit D.2 shows the associated causal diagram, which yields the following structural equation:

$$A = \gamma B + \phi \tag{D.65}$$

and the following four equation relating observables to unobservables:

$$Y_1 = \lambda_1 A + \varepsilon_1 \tag{D.66a}$$

$$Y_2 = \lambda_2 A + \varepsilon_2 \tag{D.66b}$$

$$X_1 = \lambda_1' B + \delta_1 \tag{D.66c}$$

$$X_2 = \lambda_2' B + \delta_2 \tag{D.66d}$$

In terms of available information, the variables Y_1, Y_2, X_1, and X_2 provide four variances and six covariances. Assuming the variances of A and B are standardized, there are nine parameters to be estimated.

These parameters can be related to the observed variances and covariances as follows:

$$\text{cov}(X_1 X_2) = \lambda_1' \lambda_2 \tag{D.67a}$$

$$\text{cov}(X_2 Y_2) = \lambda_2' \gamma \lambda_2 \tag{D.67b}$$

and so on.

With ten relations among nine unknowns, the system is overiden-

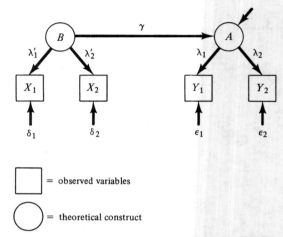

EXHIBIT D.2 Example of a causal model where one theoretical variable causes a second, each operationalized by two indicators.

tified. Bagozzi (1979b, pp. 109–110) describes a study using a model such as that here, where attitudes (affect) toward the church (B) affect behavioral intentions (A). B is operationalized by two scale measurements, as is A.

Jöreskog's development (1969, 1970, 1973, 1974) of a maximum-likelihood approach to estimate and test causal models addresses the issue of measurement errors and unobservables directly. In general, a causal model may be represented as a set of recursive or simultaneous linear structural equations,

$$\mathbf{aN} = \mathbf{bM} + \mathbf{\Theta} \qquad \textbf{(D.68)}$$

where

$\mathbf{N}$ = m x 1 vector of true, unobservable dependent variables
$\mathbf{M}$ = n x 1 vector of true, unobservable independent variables
$\mathbf{a}$ = m x m matrix of parameters
$\mathbf{b}$ = m x n matrix of parameters
$\mathbf{\Theta}$ = vector of random residuals

Equation (D.68) represents the relationship among the variables $\mathbf{N}$ through the parameters in $\mathbf{a}$ and their relationship to the true independent variables

M through the parameters in **b**. The unobserved theoretical constructs, **M** and **N**, are related to the observations as follows,

$$Y = \mu_Y + \Lambda_Y N + \epsilon \qquad \text{(D.69a)}$$

$$X = \mu_X + \Lambda_X M + \delta \qquad \text{(D.69b)}$$

where

Y	=	vector of observed dependent variables
X	=	vector of observed independent variables
μ_x, μ_y	=	mean vectors for X and Y
Λ_x, Λ_y	=	matrices of regression or factor coefficients
ϵ, δ	=	errors in measurement (also known as unique factors in X and Y

In Jöreskog's development, the errors in these relationships are assumed to have a multivariate normal distribution. Under this assumption a maximum-likelihood procedure, LISREL (Jöreskog and Sörbom, 1986), is available to perform the estimation. However, although it is the most popular estimation procedure, LISREL suffers from the problems of full-information methods—sensitivity of the whole system to misspecification. Fornell and Bookstein (1982), in a marketing context, compare the LISREL approach to a partial least-squares (PLS) approach, which is not sensitive to the multinormality assumption. Bagozzi (1979b) provides a thorough description of the causal-modeling approach, describing several applications in marketing.

Causal modeling has seen wide applicability in the social sciences, and its use in marketing research is maturing. Indeed, the November 1982 issue of the *Journal of Marketing Research* is devoted to causal modeling. The approach is useful for testing a linear theory and for describing the relationships in a behavioral system. However, the linearity and multinormality restrictions limit the use of the approach for calibrating response models (Babakus, Ferguson, and Jöreskog, 1987).

SUBJECTIVE PARAMETER ESTIMATION

Data for many marketing situations are either not available at all or not available soon enough for decision making. The econometric approach, characterized by some as "looking forward through a rear-view mirror" (a remark attributed to Robert Shlaiffer of Harvard), implicitly assumes that historical data will be a good indication of responses in the future. In many demand situations this assumption may be a reasonable one; in others, it corresponds to a risky leap of faith. (See Stobaugh and Yergin, 1979, for a critique of this assumption in the area of energy demand.) Econometric, data-based models are best suited for interpolative tasks, estimating responses within the range and the time period of the collected data; extensions beyond the data base, whether in time or in space (such as assuming that an advertising-response parameter is valid at double the highest observed level of spending), may be difficult to justify. Thus econometric models are limited by their data and by the fact that parameters and model structure are usually assumed fixed throughout the period of calibration.

But decision makers have been making decisions based on their experience for a long time and will continue to do so in the future. These decisions make implicit assumptions about response parameters. The purpose of subjective estimation then is to elicit judgments from decision makers and quantify them (turn them into model parameters). Subjective estimation is not necessarily inferior to objective estimation and may be clearly superior in many cases, especially when objective data are subject to significant biases or errors. Surely a market manager working closely with a product amasses a great amount of valuable information about it.

There are two fundamental problems in gathering and using subjective data. The first concerns methods of obtaining useful estimates for the decision model from a single expert (consultant, company executive, etc.). The second concerns the problem of pooling the estimates of two or more experts when there may be some divergence of opinion (the consensus problem).

Single-Assessor Model Calibration. Little (1970) introduced the concept of decision calculus for formally incorporating managerial judgment in the calibration task for marketing models. A large number of models based on decision calculus have been proposed and implemented (see Chakravarti, Mitchell, and Staelin, 1979, for a review), suggesting the impact the approach has had on the field.

Decision-calculus model calibration structures a manager's experience into a formal model that is then used in subsequent decision making. Support for this mode of thinking comes from several sources. The research of Bowman (1963), Kunreuther (1969), and others has shown that a quantitative procedure formulated from an individual's previous decisions may outperform his future decisions. Theoretically, this result occurs through the analytical systemization of past experience in the model. A second source of support comes from the work of Armstrong (1985) and of Brown (1969), who discuss the principle of decomposition. They report that predictions can be improved by first decomposing a complex problem into a series of simpler prediction problems that are more relevant to the respondent and then recombining these estimates to predict desired outcomes.

There are at least four major categories of judgmental information obtainable from a single assessor that might be important to a marketing analyst. First, he might need a *point estimate* of the value of some independent variable or coefficient, such as a size-of-market estimate or a unit-cost figure. Second, he might need a *sales-response function*—that is, an indication of how the expert feels sales would vary with variations in the level of one or more marketing factors. Third, he might need estimates of the *uncertainty* surrounding parameter estimates, function estimates, or key events. Finally, he might need a set of *ratings* and/or *weights* to assign to certain variables in his model.

The emerging view is that combining judgments can improve estimation results, but different experts will normally provide different subjective estimates, which must be combined into a single response. There are two methods for combining subjective judgments: analyst selected and group selected.

Analyst-Selected Pooling Methods. A frequently used method for combining individual estimates is to have the analyst do it with some justifiable procedure.

Winkler (1968) distinguishes four logical bases for developing combining weights:

1. Assign equal weights to the estimates if there is no further indicator of the relative expertness of each expert.

2. Assign weights that are proportional to someone's subjective ranking or rating of the experts' relative competence.

3. Assign weights that are proportional to the experts' self-ratings of their competence.

4. Assign weights that are proportional to the past predictive accuracy of the various experts.

There is no one best method of determining weights; the analyst must rely on his or her experience in using different procedures. (See Winkler, 1986, and Clemen and Winkler, 1986, for further discussion and critique and Bordley, 1982, for conditions under which a multiplicative rule is appropriate.)

Group-Selected Pooling Methods. If the group itself is asked to resolve its differences, there are two common ways to do this: cooperatively or by the Delphi method.

In a cooperative group, questions or differences are discussed openly, and the group continues discussion until a single collective answer is reached. This procedure is subject to bandwagon effects, hierarchical managerial effects, and issues of power politics. (See Dalkey and Helmer, 1963, for elaboration.)

It was partially in response to these problems that the Delphi method was developed. The method has three key features: (1) *anonymous response*, in which opinions and assessments are obtained formally but anonymously;

(2) *interaction and controlled feedback*, in which interaction is brought about by a systematic exercise conducted in several interactions with controlled feedback between rounds; and (3) *statistical group response*, where group opinion is an aggregate of individual opinions in the final round. These procedures are designed to mitigate the impact of dominant individuals, irrelevant comments, and group pressure toward conformity.

Several experiments have shown that the Delphi method does, in fact, produce good results (see Jolson and Rossow, 1971, and Martino, 1983). Another interesting application of the Delphi method, performed by well-known model builders and aimed at evaluating the likelihood of managers accepting a number of marketing models, is found in Larréché and Montgomery (1977).

The judgmental assessment of response is not without controversy. In laboratory work Chakravarti, Mitchell, and Staelin (1981) found that subjects using the ADBUDG model made worse decisions than those who did not. Little and Lodish (1981) argue that subjects in a laboratory experiment rarely have access to certain kinds of information, such as supplemental background knowledge of the dynamics of the particular market. They conclude that

> A main thrust of the decision calculus concept is to capture useful information from the manager's rich knowledge of the marketing environment and blend it into decision making [Chakravarti, Mitchell, and Staelin, 1981], coming from experiments that show the manager to be a mediocre data processor, tend to display a desire to replace him or her with a competent econometric package. We are happy to support formal statistical methods whenever valid inferences can be made from the data, but we are oriented toward the overall management process and see judgmental calibration as plugging an important gap in problem solving.   *(Little and Lodish, 1981, p. 28)*

McIntyre (1982) and McIntyre and Currim (1982) also provide evaluation and support for the judgmental calibration approach, but Wright and Anderson (1989) show some disturbing experimental evidence that expertise may lead to judgmental bias. Finally, Beach and Barnes (1987) review the literature here and conclude that much of evidence on judgmental bias supports Little and Lodish's (1981) conclusion that such experiments may not be appropriately applied to managers in situations they are familiar with.

The Beach and Barnes (1987) study refers to the vast literature on biases in judgment and decision making that has emerged in the last several decades. Hogarth (1987) provides an excellent review showing how individual biases, recent events, and extraneous information can affect subjective estimates. While the literature in the area appears mixed, there do exist conditions under which experts can provide good estimates. Drawing from Phillips (1987), an emerging set of guidelines includes the following:

1. *Expertise matters.* While the vast majority of research studies have demonstrated biases using student-judges, true experts fare better. (See

Little and Lodish, 1981, Larréché and Moinpour, 1983, and Lodish et al., 1988.)

2. *Use multiple assessors.* It appears that groups can do better than even the best single assessor (Armstrong, 1985).

3. *Training helps.* Feedback on the quality of past calibration makes individuals aware of their biases and helps them overcome them (Lichtenstein and Fischoff, 1980; Murphy and Dean, 1984).

4. *The type of questioning matters.* For example, ask individuals to think of the highest (lowest) value imaginable and work backward to get a probability distribution. Individuals consistently overstate their confidence and need to have the possibility set expanded (Hershey, Kunreuther, and Schoemaker, 1982; Armstrong, 1985).

5. *Iterate and incorporate redundancy.* This permits the weeding out of inconsistent judgments.

6. *Decompose.* People are better at judging simple things; computers/models are excellent at putting those things together.

These results are consistent with those of Bunn and Wright (1991), who provide a good review of the circumstances under which judgmental forecasts outperform statistical forecasting procedures. In particular, they confirm that experts do well in their domain of expertise when the problem is properly decomposed for them. (Asking them to estimate trial and repeat rates separately rather than asking for a direct estimate of market share, for example.)

BLENDING JUDGMENTAL AND EMPIRICAL DATA: BAYESIAN ESTIMATION

The procedures for estimation just presented were either purely data-based (objective) or subjective. However, these can be viewed as extreme cases. In many situations some field data and some judgmental data are available. These two types of information can be combined and logically incorporated into an estimation procedure. Such types of analyses are usually called Bayesian analyses.

We noted earlier that a likelihood function is the relative probability of observing a sample given (or as a function of) specific parameter values. To this idea we add the distinction of prior and posterior distributions. A *prior distribution* is a probability distribution of the parameter(s) *before* observing any data. This distribution is our judgmental assessment about the value of the system's parameters. A *posterior distribution* is an update of the prior distribution *after* observing the data, combining objective and subjective information.

Suppose we go back to our sales and advertising model,

$$Q = a_0 + a_1 X \tag{D.70}$$

where we are most interested in the advertising-response parameter a_1. Furthermore, suppose that either through past experience with this product or through judgment, management provides a prior distribution on the response parameter a_1 that is normal with mean a_{10} and variance σ_{10}^2. Therefore the prior distribution of a_1 is $N(a_{10}, \sigma_{10}^2)$.

Assume further that our sample provides an estimator of a_1 (perhaps by least squares), call it a_1, with mean a_1 and variance $\sigma^2/\Sigma(X_i - \overline{X})^2$ (*where a_1 is the population mean and σ^2 is the error variance*). If we use the notation

$$V^2 = \frac{1}{n} \Sigma(X_i - \overline{X})^2 \tag{D.71}$$

we can denote the variance of $\hat{a}_1$ as $\sigma^2/V^2/n$, where n is the sample size. So assuming normality again, we have

$$\hat{a}_1 \sim N\left(a_1, \frac{\sigma^2/V^2}{n}\right) \tag{D.72}$$

To derive a posterior distribution, we apply Bayes's rule, which states that

Posterior distribution $\propto$ prior distribution $\times$ likelihood function $\tag{D.73}$

where $\propto$ means "is proportional to" (see Raiffa and Schlaifer, 1961). In addition, the normal distributions of the prior and the likelihood functions provide what is referred to as a natural conjugate process, producing a normal posterior distribution. This natural conjugate process allows a closed-form result for the posterior distribution that is also normal:

$$\text{Posterior distribution of } a_1 \sim N\left(\frac{n_0 a_0 + n\hat{a}_1}{n_0 + n}, \frac{\sigma^2/V^2}{n_0 + n}\right) \tag{D.74}$$

where

$$n_0 = \frac{\sigma^2/V^2}{\sigma_{10}^2} \tag{D.75}$$

The term n_0 is known as the pseudosample size because the effect of bayesian

95% Bayesian Confidence Interval	95% Classical Confidence Interval
$a_1 = \dfrac{n_0 \hat{a}_{10} + n\hat{a}_1}{n_0 + n} \pm 1.96 \sqrt{\dfrac{\sigma^2/V^2}{n_0 + n}}$	$a_1 = \hat{a}_1 \pm 1.96 \sqrt{\dfrac{\sigma^2/V^2}{n}}$

EXHIBIT D.3 A Classical and a Bayesian confidence interval around the regression coefficient a_1

regression on our parameter estimates is to add a pseudosample of size n_0 to our actual sample.

In general, Bayesian estimates have smaller variance than classical estimates and yield mean values that are compromises between the classical regression estimates and the means of the prior distributions. We compare Bayesian and classical 95% confidence intervals in Exhibit D.3.

Formal Analysis.   Repeating equation (D.15), we get

$$Q = Xa + \varepsilon \qquad (D.76)$$

Assume we now have a set of prior estimates of a, say, $\hat{a}_0$. These estimates will have mean a if they are unbiased:

$$E(\hat{a}_0) = a \qquad (D.77)$$

With uncertainty in the prior,

$$\hat{a}_{j0} = a_{j0} + \varepsilon_0 \qquad (D.78)$$

where ε_0 is the error term for the jth estimate. Then the prior covariance matrix is

$$E(\varepsilon_0 \varepsilon_0') = \Phi \qquad (D.79)$$

In matrix form we can write equation (D.78) as

$$a_0 = Ia_0 + \varepsilon_0 \qquad (D.80)$$

Combining equation (D.76) with equation (D.80) yields

$$
\left[\begin{array}{c} Q \\ \hline a_0 \end{array}\right]
=
\left[\begin{array}{c} X \\ \hline I \end{array}\right] a
+
\left[\begin{array}{c} \varepsilon \\ \varepsilon_0 \end{array}\right]
\qquad (D.81)
$$

or

$$\mathbf{Q}^* = \mathbf{YA} + \boldsymbol{\varepsilon}^*$$

with

$$E(\boldsymbol{\varepsilon}^*\boldsymbol{\varepsilon}^{*\prime}) = \begin{bmatrix} \sigma^2\mathbf{I} & 0 \\ 0 & \Phi \end{bmatrix} \tag{D.82}$$

Thus the Bayesian estimate of **a** can be calculated from equation (D.81) by generalized least squares. In particular, when there is no assumed covariation between the prior estimates of **a**, formulas (D.30) and (D.31) hold, giving weighted least-squares estimators for the parameters. The weights reflect the compromise between the prior and the likelihood functions. A look at equation (D.81) shows that Bayesian regression is equivalent to adding observations to the data matrix from the prior distribution, the number of such observations being determined by the precision (level of confidence) of the prior distribution.

The use of Bayesian procedures in marketing is particularly appropriate when little data are available, but comparable data (other studies, past products) should provide a guide for developing priors. For examples of developing priors in the new product forecasting area see Lilien, Rao, and Kalish (1981); Rao and Yamada (1988); and Sultan, Farley, and Lehmann (1990). Also see Farley and Lehmann (1986) for discussion of the meta-analysis approach for developing priors for market-response parameters.

E | GAME THEORY CONCEPTS

The recent focus on competition in marketing models has led to much interest in the concept and methods of noncooperative game theory. We review the main concepts here.

Noncooperative game theory is a theory about how firms or individuals behave in competitive situations. (We will assume we are dealing with firms from here on.) A competitive situation arises when firms with conflicting interests are interdependent, but are unable to collude explicitly. Interdependence means that the consequences to a firm of taking an action depend not just on that firm's action, but also on the actions of its competitors. Conflicts of interest mean that the firms differ in what they would like each of them to do. Finally, inability to collude explicitly means that the firms are unable to enter into enforceable binding agreements. For example, Coca-Cola and Pepsi are in a competitive situation with respect to their advertising because (1) Coca-Cola's advertising affects Pepsi's market share and Pepsi's advertising affects Coca-Cola's market share, (2) each would like *only* the other to stop its advertising, and (3) any explicit agreement between the two firms would be illegal under the Sherman Antitrust Act.

RATIONALITY, INTELLIGENCE, AND RULES OF THE GAME

Game theory assumes that the competitors are rational and intelligent. Competitors are *rational* if they make decisions by maximizing their subjective expected "utility." (For risk-neutral firms—firms whose "utility" functions are linear in profits—this means maximizing expected profits.) When faced with uncertainty, rational firms form subjective estimates of the probability of uncertain events·and use these estimates to compute the expected utilities of different actions. Firms are *intelligent* if they recognize that their competitors are rational. Intelligent firms can reason from their competitors' points of view. Only in some trivial cases, where each firm has a dominant mode of behavior—a mode of behavior that maximizes the firm's expected utility *regardless* of what the other firms do—can the requirement of intelligence be relaxed.

Rules of the game means a complete description of the game including (1) the number of competitors, (2) their feasible sets of actions at every juncture in the game, (3) their utilities (profits) for each combination of moves, (4) the sequence of moves, and (5) the structure of information about moves (who knows what? when?). A *game of complete information* is one in which the rules of the game are common knowledge among the firms. Every firm knows the rules, every firm knows that every other firm knows the rules, every firm knows that the other firms know that it knows the rules, and so on. In contrast, a *game of incomplete information* is one in which the rules of the game are not common knowledge among the firms. In such games, the firms differ in the information they possess at the start of the game. Most real-world games are games of incomplete information either because firms differ in their knowledge of the environment or because they do not know the motivations or capabilities of their competitors.

STRATEGIC AND EXTENSIVE FORM REPRESENTATIONS

Once a game has been specified, we can distinguish between moves (or actions) and strategies. A *pure strategy* (or *"strategy"* for short hereafter) is a plan of action. It specifies what the firm will do (what move the firm will make) as a function of what the firm knows (about environmental events or about the other firms' previous moves) at every juncture in the game. A *mixed strategy* is a probability distribution on the firm's feasible set of pure strategies. In other words, by choosing a mixed strategy, a firm is really choosing a randomization device and the strategy played will depend on the outcome of the randomization. Thus, every pure strategy is also a mixed strategy—one that assigns a probability of one to that (pure) strategy and zero to the other pure strategies.

To see the difference between moves and strategies consider the following game.

Two airlines, A and B, serve a given route. A is the price leader—it moves first—

and chooses between two moves, the ticket prices $200 and $300; B, the follower, observes A's move, then chooses between $200 and $300.

A's strategies are the same as its moves—$200 and $300—because it does not observe anything before it moves. B has four strategies (it had two moves): (1) choose $300 regardless of what A chooses, (2) choose $200 regardless of what A chooses, (3) choose $300 if A chooses $300, otherwise choose $200, and (4) choose $200 if A chooses $300, otherwise choose $300. Notice how each strategy of B specifies what it will do in every possible state of its information—every move A might make. A strategy, because it is a plan of action, can be delegated to an agent. All the agent has to do is follow the plan embodied in the strategy. The concept of strategies makes it possible to represent games compactly in what is called the "strategic form representation" of a game.

A *strategic form representation* of the game (also called a "normal form representation") consists of sets of possible strategies, one for each firm, and the payoffs to each firm for each combination of strategies. An important feature of such a representation is that even though the firms may move sequentially in the game, they "play" their strategies simultaneously, that is, without observing their competitors' strategies. If firms could observe their competitors' strategies before they played their own strategy, they could develop a new strategy—a "superstrategy"—conditioned on the strategy they observe. The only way to avoid this regression is to have the strategies played simultaneously.

The more detailed description of a game from which the strategic form is derived and which makes explicit the flow of moves and information—often represented as a "game tree"— is called an *extensive form representation*. Exhibit E.1 is the extensive form representation of the airline pricing game. Games in extensive form have *imperfect information* if some firm at some stage does not know what move some other firm or "nature" made earlier in the game. (Contrast this with games of incomplete information where the uncertainty is about the rules of the game. A game of imperfect information could be a game of complete information if the structure of information about the moves is common knowledge at the start of the game.) For example, if in the airline pricing game both firms were to move simultaneously, or even at different times as long as they do not know each other's moves, we would have a game of imperfect information. Exhibit E.1 is an extensive form representation of this game; the framed box around the nodes 1 and 2 indicates that firm B does not know—when it makes its move—whether it is at node 1 (i.e., whether A chose $200) or at node 2 (i.e., whether A chose $300). (We also could have drawn the game tree for this simultaneous-move game with B moving "first" and A not observing B's move.) This could still be a game of complete information if it were common knowledge at the start of the game that at nodes 1 and 2 B would not know what move A made earlier.

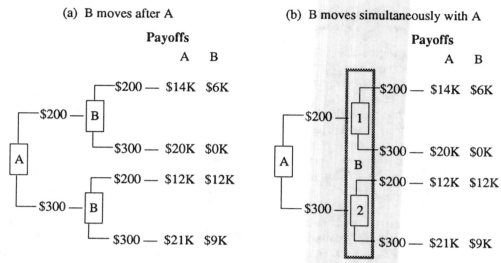

(a) B moves after A   (b) B moves simultaneously with A

EXHIBIT E.1   Extensive form representation of a pricing game.

Nash Equilibrium

Definition.   Nash equilibrium is the central concept of noncooperative game theory (Nash, 1950). It is a prediction about how rational and intelligent firms will compete. The definition is as follows. A *Nash equilibrium* is a specification of strategies (pure or mixed) for each firm such that no firm would change its strategy *unilaterally*. In other words, for each firm, its strategy in the equilibrium is a best response to the others' strategies in the equilibrium, where "goodness" of a strategy is determined by the firm's utility function.

For an illustration of a Nash equilibrium, let us go back to the airline example. Each firm moves simultaneously (i.e., without knowledge of the other firm's move), choosing one of two prices—$200 or $300 (Exhibit E.1). Exhibit E.2 shows the strategic form representation of the game. Because the firms move simultaneously, the firms' strategies and moves are the same. The payoffs are represented as pairs of numbers (*a*, *b*), *a* to the row firm (firm A), *b* to the column firm (firm B). Clearly, each firm prefers a higher payoff to a lower payoff.

The configuration of the payoffs shows that both firms are better off if both priced at $300 rather than $200, but if B thinks that A is going to price at $300, it is best off pricing at $200. That is, the pair of strategies ($300, $300) is not an equilibrium because there is an incentive for some firm to change its strategy unilaterally. Similarly, the strategy pairs ($200, $300) and ($300, $200) are not equilibria. The pair ($200, $200) is an equilibrium because either firm moving to $300 with the other firm pricing at $200 hurts the mover.

B's Strategies

	$200	$300
$200	$14K, $6K	$20K, $0K
$300	$12K, $12K	$21K, $9K

A's Strategies

The first number in each cell is A's payoff; the second number is B's payoff.

EXHIBIT E.2   Strategic form representation of a pricing game.

There is a subtle change in the equilibrium if we change the rules of the pricing game so that one firm, say, A, assumes the role of a price leader (Exhibit E.1). Then the equilibrium is A chooses the strategy $200, B chooses the strategy "charge $200 regardless of what A charges." (A Nash equilibrium in a leader-follower game is also called a Stackelberg equilibrium.) Why is this an equilibrium? If B is going to choose $200 regardless of A's move, it is optimal for A to choose $200, and if A is going to choose $200, B does best by choosing $200. Notice that B never gets to use the part of its equilibrium strategy that calls for it to choose $200 if A chooses $300—because A does not choose $300 in equilibrium. However, it is the presence of this part of B's strategy that makes A choose $200 in the equilibrium. The outcome of this leader-follower game is the same as the outcome of the simultaneous move game—the price pair ($200, $200). This is not a general phenomenon, however; we subsequently examine examples in which leadership confers definite advantages to the leader.

Game theorists give two arguments for why rational and intelligent firms would use equilibrium strategies. First, a rational firm would by definition choose its strategy as a best response to the strategies it assumes for the others. Then, because the firm is also intelligent, it must not assume strategies for the other firms that are not themselves best responses to some strategy of the given firm (after all, the other firms are rational, too). The other justification of a Nash equilibrium views the essence of competition as the absence of binding agreements. Any agreement reached under competition must therefore be self-enforcing. A self-enforcing agreement must not provide any firm the incentive to break the agreement unilaterally. The equilibrium does that.

In addition to these "philosophical" arguments supporting the Nash equilibrium, there is an extensive body of empirical evidence (Plott, 1982).

B's Strategies

	Use A's technology	Use B's technology
Use A's technology	2, 1	0, 0
Use B's technology	0, 0	1, 2

A's Strategies

EXHIBIT E.3 Efficiency of Nash equilibrium in a technology game.

Efficiency. The pricing game illustrates a basic dilemma of competition: the Nash equilibrium gives each firm a payoff that is less than what it could get from some other pair of strategies, namely, ($300, $300). In other words, the equilibrium outcome is inefficient for the two firms—there is an alternative assignment of strategies that will make both firms better off. If binding agreements were possible and enforceable, then the firms would never agree to inefficient outcomes. But, without such agreements, competition leads inexorably to a less desirable outcome for both firms. This is, however, not a general feature of noncooperative games. The game illustrated in Exhibit E.3 has three equilibria, of which two are pure-strategy equilibria yielding the outcomes (2, 1) and (1, 2) and the third is a mixed-strategy equilibrium with each firm choosing its own technology with probability 2/3 and its opponent's technology with probability 1/3. To compute a mixed-strategy equilibrium we use the proposition that each firm's randomization must make the *other* firm indifferent among the strategies that it uses with positive probability. Thus, when B plays the mixed strategy (2/3, 1/3), A's expected payoff from each of its pure strategies is 2/3. Similarly, with A playing (2/3, 1/3), B is indifferent between its pure strategies. Clearly, both pure-strategy equilibria are efficient, but the mixed-strategy equilibrium which gives each firm an expected payoff of 2/3 is not.

Existence. Games that have a finite number of strategies always have an equilibrium. Often a pure-strategy equilibrium will not exist in a finite game, but then there will be a mixed-strategy equilibrium. Exhibit E.4 describes an advertising game with no equilibrium in pure strategies. There are two firms, a leader and a challenger, the leader being the firm with the dominant market share. Each firm must decide where to advertise, in medium 1 or medium 2. The payoffs reflect the leader's inclination to keep some distance from the challenger—if the latter advertises in medium 1, the lender would rather

Leader's Strategies

	Advertise in medium 1	Advertise in medium 2
Challenger's Strategies Advertise in medium 1	1, 0	0, 1
Advertise in medium 2	0, 1	1, 0

EXHIBIT E.4 An advertising game without a pure-strategy Nash equilibrium.

advertise in medium 2, and vice versa—and the challenger's preference for conferring legitimacy to its brand by advertising alongside the leader. The only equilibrium is a mixed-strategy equilibrium with both the challenger and the leader randomizing 50:50 between "advertise in medium 1" and "advertise in medium 2."

For infinite games—games with an infinite number of strategies—the existence of equilibria is more difficult to resolve. See Dasgupta and Maskin (1986a, b) for a discussion.

Perfectness.   Consider a competitive situation in which an incumbent firm (A) faces entry by another firm (B). The entrant moves first, deciding whether to enter or not. If the entrant does not enter, the incumbent does not respond; if the entrant enters, however, the incumbent must decide whether to "fight" the entry (say, by cutting prices) or to "acquiesce" to the entry (say, by pricing at the duopoly equilibrium prices). The extensive form of this game is shown in Exhibit E.5. The payoffs capture the idea that it is best for the entrant to enter if it can be assured of a peaceful response, whereas if entry should provoke fighting it is better not to enter. For the incumbent, it is best that the entrant not enter at all, but if entry were to occur it is best to acquiesce rather than fight. There are two pure-strategy equilibria in this game. One of them has the entrant playing "do not enter" and the incumbent playing "if entrant enters, fight." The other pure equilibrium has the entrant playing "enter" and the incumbent playing "if entrant enters, acquiesce." How should the firms play? Clearly equilibrium alone does not provide adequate guidance here, yet the second equilibrium seems more compelling because the first equilibrium is sustained by a spurious threat. In the first equilibrium, the entrant does not enter because it thinks the incumbent would fight, but the incumbent would not fight if it were confronted with entry. Faced with entry the incumbent is better off acquiescing.

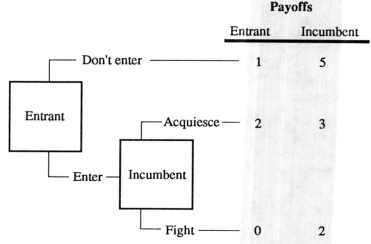

EXHIBIT E.5 The entry game.

Selten (1975) has proposed a strengthening of the equilibrium concept that would rule out equilibria sustained by spurious threats. The strengthening criterion is called "subgame perfectness" and is based on the idea of subgames. Essentially, a subgame of a game in extensive form is any "game" starting from some node of the original game. An equilibrium is subgame perfect if for every subgame the equilibrium strategies restricted to the subgame continue to form an equilibrium. In the entry game, the node at which the incumbent moves starts a subgame. The first equilibrium, restricted to this subgame, has the incumbent fighting, but this is not an equilibrium strategy in this subgame—it is better for the incumbent to acquiesce than fight when faced with entry. Thus, the first equilibrium is not subgame perfect. The second equilibrium is subgame perfect. Applying the criterion of subgame perfectness, we are able to identify a unique solution to the entry game: the entrant enters and the incumbent acquiesces.

Consider now an example from Kreps and Wilson (1982) in which even subgame perfectness does not help in identifying a unique solution for a game. Exhibit E.6 depicts a game with two firms in which firm 1 moves first, choosing among three moves L, R, and A. Firm 2 cannot move if 1 chooses A, but if A is not chosen, firm 2 can choose between ℓ and r. The key feature of the game—indicated by the framed box—is that firm 2 does not know, when it has the move, whether firm 1 moved L or R.

One pure equilibrium of this game has 1 choosing A and 2 choosing "if not A, then r." This equilibrium is trivially subgame perfect; the game has no subgames. (The "subgames" starting from nodes m and n are not really subgames because 2 does not know whether it is at m or n and so its payoffs are not well defined at those nodes.) However, this equilibrium is not very

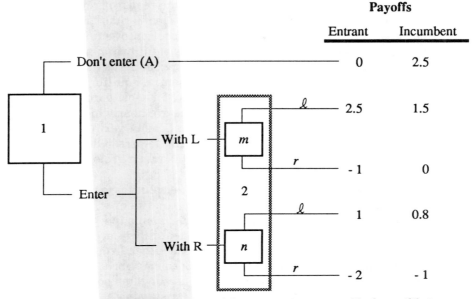

Payoffs

	Entrant	Incumbent
Don't enter (A)	0	2.5
ℓ	2.5	1.5
r	-1	0
ℓ	1	0.8
r	-2	-1

EXHIBIT E.6   An advertising game without a pure-strategy Nash equilibrium.

appealing because if 2 gets to move, surely it would be better off choosing ℓ over r regardless of whether it is at m or n. Realizing this, shouldn't firm 1 not simply pick L, which yields 2.5 (with the expected ℓ from firm 2) instead of the zero it gets by playing A? In other words, the equilibrium with 1 playing L and 2 playing ℓ (if not A) seems better than the equilibrium with 1 playing A, but not on the criterion of subgame perfectness—both equilibria are subgame perfect.

A second, stronger, refinement of the equilibrium concept due to Kreps and Wilson (1982) takes care of the problem with subgame perfectness. This refinement is called "sequential rationality." An equilibrium is *sequentially rational* if at every juncture in the game each firm's subsequent strategy (as specified by the equilibrium) is optimal with respect to some assessment of the probabilities of all uncertain events, including any preceding, unobserved, moves of the other firms. (An equilibrium that is sequentially rational is called a "*sequential equilibrium.*") It is clear that the equilibrium with firm 1 moving L is sequentially rational (no assessment of probabilities by 2 about 1's previous move—whether it was L or R—will make ℓ suboptimal) whereas the equilibrium with 1 moving A is not sequentially rational (no assessment of probabilities by 2 can support the r that it threatens if 1 were not to choose A).

A third concept of perfectness (Selten, 1975), called "trembling-hand perfectness," is stronger than sequential rationality. We do not get into the rather technical definition of this concept here; the reader is referred to Selten (1975) and Kreps and Wilson (1982). The main idea is that "good" equilibria should be robust to slight "trembles" in the execution of equilibrium strategies—a firm may make a mistake in playing its equilibrium strategy.

The relation among the three concepts of perfectness is that every trembling-hand perfect equilibrium is a sequential equilibrium and every sequential equilibrium is subgame perfect; also, for most games, sequential equilibria and trembling-hand perfect equilibria are nearly identical. The sequential equilibrium has the advantage that it is easily verifiable, but, more important, it provides a natural extension of single-person decision theory to multi-person competition—it makes explicit the crucial role of firms' beliefs in sustaining an equilibrium.

The problem of identifying a unique solution for a game is by no means resolved. In fact, it is very likely that it may never be. As an example of a "difficult" game in this respect, consider again the game in Exhibit E.3. It has two pure equilibria. The two pure equilibria are mirror images of each other—one favors one firm, the other the other firm—and the real question is who should get the better bargain? Both equilibria are trembling-hand perfect (and hence sequentially rational and subgame perfect as well). One could say that the mixed-strategy equilibrium stands out in this case and should in fact be played. Apart from the realism of firms choosing randomized strategies, the main drawback of the mixed-strategy equilibrium is that it is inefficient in comparison with either of the pure-strategy equilibria; both firms would be better off with either pure equilibrium. Therefore, if we must choose between the two pure equilibria, we must do it on the basis of some external consideration not in the existing structure of the game. Such an external consideration might be that this particular competitive episode between the two firms is but one in an ongoing larger game, the unique equilibrium of which calls for firm A (B) to compromise in this episode.

For a more complete introduction to the methods as well as the concepts of game theory, see Rasmusen (1989) and for assessment of its value/limitations see Aumann (1987) and Rubinstein (1991).

BIBLIOGRAPHY

AAKER, DAVID A. (1973), "Toward a Normative Model of Promotional Decision Making," *Management Science,* Vol. 19, no. 6 (February), pp. 593–603.

AAKER, DAVID A. (1975), "ADMOD: An Advertising Decision Model," *Journal of Marketing Research,* Vol. 12 (February), pp. 37–45.

AAKER, DAVID A. (1988), *Developing Business Strategies,* 2nd ed. New York: John Wiley.

AAKER, DAVID A. and JAMES M. CARMAN (1982), "Are You Overadvertising?" *Journal of Advertising Research,* Vol. 22, no. 4 (August/September), pp. 57–70.

AAKER, DAVID A. and JOHN G. MYERS (1987), *Advertising Management,* 3rd ed. Englewood Cliffs, N.J.: Prentice Hall.

ABELL, DEREK F. and J. S. HAMMOND (1978), "Strategic Windows," *Journal of Marketing,* Vol. 42 (July), pp. 21–26.

ABELL, DEREK F. and J. S. HAMMOND (1979), *Strategic Marketing Planning.* Englewood Cliffs, N.J.: Prentice Hall.

ABRAHAM, MAGID M. and LEONARD M. LODISH (1987a), "Reply," *Marketing Science,* Vol. 6, no. 2 (Spring), pp. 152–153.

ABRAHAM, MAGID M. and LEONARD M. LODISH (1987b), "PROMOTER: An Automated Promotion Evaluation System," *Marketing Science,* Vol. 6, no. 2 (Spring), pp. 101–123.

ABRAHAM, MAGID M. and LEONARD M. LODISH (1989a), "Fact-Based Strategies for Managing Advertising and Promotion Dollars: Lessons from Single Source Data," Working paper #89–006, Marketing Department, The Wharton School of the University of Pennsylvania (February).

ABRAHAM, MAGID M. and LEONARD M. LODISH (1989b), "PROMOTIONSCAN: A System for Improving Promotion Productivity for Retailers and Manufacturers Using Scanner Store and Household Panel Data," Working paper #89–007, Marketing Department, The Wharton School of the University of Pennsylvania (February).

ABREU, D., D. PEARCE, and E. STACHETTI (1985), "Optimal Cartel Equilibria with Imperfect Monitoring," *Journal of Economic Theory,* Vol. 39, pp. 251–269.

ACHABAL, DALE D., WILPEN L. GORR, and VIJAY MAHAJAN (1982), "MULTILOC: A Multiple Store Location Decision Model," *Journal of Retailing,* Vol. 58, no. 2 (Summer), pp. 5–25.

ACHENBAUM, ALVIN A. (1964), "The Purpose of Test Marketing." In R. M. Kaplan, ed., *The Marketing Concept in Action.* Chicago: American Marketing Association.

ACHROL, RAVI S., TORGER REVE, and LOUIS W. STERN (1983), "The Environment of

Marketing Channel Dyads: A Framework for Comparative Analysis," *Journal of Marketing,* Vol. 4, no. 4 (Fall), pp. 55–67.

ACHROL, RAVI S. and LOUIS W. STERN (1988), "Environmental Determinants of Decision Making Uncertainty in Marketing Channels," *Journal of Marketing Research,* Vol. 25, no. 1 (February), pp. 36–50.

ACITO, FRANK and RONALD D. ANDERSON (1986), "A Simulation Study of Factor Score Indeterminacy," *Journal of Marketing Research,* Vol. 23 (May), pp. 111–118.

ACKOFF, RUSSELL L. (1962), *Scientific Method: Optimizing Applied Research Decisions.* New York: John Wiley.

ADAM, D. (1958), Les Reactions du Consommoteur Devant le Prix. Paris: Sedesp.

ADAMS, W. and J. YELLEN (1976), "Commodity Bundling and the Burden of Monopoly," *Quarterly Journal of Economics,* Vol. 90, pp. 475–498.

Advertising Age (September 27, 1989), p. 1.

AGARWAL, MANOJ (1988), "An Empirical Comparison of Traditional Conjoint and Adaptive Conjoint Analysis," Working paper #88–140, School of Management, State University of New York at Binghamton.

AGARWAL, MANOJ K. and PAUL E. GREEN (1991), "Adaptive Conjoint Analysis versus Self-Explicated Models: Some Empirical Results," *International Journal of Research in Marketing,* Vol. 8, no. 2 (June), pp. 141–146.

AGGARWAL, SUMER (1973), "A Critique of 'The Distribution Simulator' by M. M. Connors et al.," *Management Science,* Vol. 20, no. 4, pt. 1 (December), pp. 482–486.

AGOSTINI, M. M. (1961), "How to Estimate Unduplicated Audiences," *Journal of Advertising Research,* Vol. 1, no. 3 (March), pp. 11–14.

AJZEN, ICEK and MARTIN FISHBEIN (1980), Understanding Attitudes and Predicting Social Change. Englewood Cliffs, NJ: Prentice Hall.

ALBA, JOSEPH W. and AMITAVA CHATTOPAD-

HYAY (1985), "Effects of Context and Part-Category Cues on Recall of Competing Brands," *Journal of Marketing Research,* Vol. 22 (August), pp. 340–349.

ALBA, JOSEPH W. and AMITAVA CHATTOPA-DHYAY (1986), "Salience Effects in Brand Recall," *Journal of Marketing Research,* Vol. 23 (November), pp. 363–369.

ALBA, JOSEPH W. and J. WESLEY HUTCHINSON (1987), "Dimensions of Consumer Expertise," *Journal of Consumer Research,* Vol. 13, pp. 411–454.

ALBACH, HORST (1979), "Market Organization and Pricing Behavior of Oligopolistic Firms in the Ethical Drugs Industry," *KYKLOS,* Vol. 32, no. 3, pp. 523–540.

ALBERTS, WILLIAM W. (1989), "The Experience Curve Doctrine Reconsidered," *Journal of Marketing,* Vol. 53 (July), pp. 36–49.

ALLAIRE, YVAN (1973), "The Measurement of Heterogeneous Semantic, Perceptual and Preference Structures," Ph.D. thesis, Massachusetts Institute of Technology, Cambridge.

ALLEN, CHRIS T. and THOMAS J. MADDEN (1985), "A Closer Look at Classical Conditioning," *Journal of Consumer Research,* Vol. 12 (December), pp. 301–335.

ALPAR, P. (1991), "Knowledge-Based Modeling of Marketing Managers' Problem Solving Behavior," *International Journal of Research in Marketing,* Vol. 8, no. 1, pp. 5–16.

AMEMIYA, TAKESHI (1981), "Qualitative Response Models: A Survey," *Journal of Econometric Literature,* Vol. 19 (December), pp. 1483–1583.

ANDERSON, CARL R. and FRANK T. PAINE (1978), "PIMS: A Reexamination," *Academy of Management Review,* no. 3 (July), pp. 602–612.

ANDERSON, JAMES C. (1985), "A Measurement Model to Assess Measurement Specific Factors in Multiple Informant Research," *Journal of Marketing Research,* Vol. 22, no. 1 (February), pp. 86–92.

ANDERSON, JAMES C. and JAMES A. NARUS (1984), "A Model of the Distributor's Perspective of Distributor-Manufacturer Working Relationships," *Journal of Marketing,* Vol. 48, no. 4 (Fall), pp. 62–74.

ANDERSON, PAUL (1979), "The Marketing Management/Finance Interface." In N. Beckwith, M. Houston, R. Mittelstaedt, K. B. Monroe, and S. Ward, eds., *1979 AMA Educator Conference Proceedings,* pp. 325–329. Chicago: American Marketing Association.

ANDERSON, PAUL (1981), "Marketing Investment Analysis." In J. N. Sheth, ed., *Research in Marketing,* Vol. 4, pp. 1–38. Greenwich, Conn.: JAI Press.

ANDERSON, PAUL (1983), "Marketing, Scientific Progress, and Scientific Method," *Journal of Marketing,* Vol. 47 (Fall), pp. 18–31.

ANDERSON, PAUL and TERRY M. CHAMBERS (1985), "A Reward Measurement Model of Organization Buying Behavior," *Journal of Marketing,* Vol. 49, no. 1 (Spring) pp. 7–23.

ANDERSON, RALPH E. (1973), "Consumer Dissatisfaction: The Effect of Disconfirmed Expectancy on Perceived Product Performance," *Journal of Marketing Research,* Vol. 10 (February), pp. 38–44.

ANSARI, A. (1986), "Strategies for the Implementation of JIT Purchasing," *International Journal of Physical Distribution and Materials Management,* Vol. 16, no. 3, p. 9.

ANTLE, R. and A. SMITH (1986), "An Empirical Investigation of the Relative Performance Evaluation of Corporate Executives," *Journal of Accounting Research,* Vol. 24, pp. 1–39.

ANTON, HOWARD (1987), *Elementary Linear Algebra,* 5th ed. New York: John Wiley & Sons.

APPEL, VALENTINE (1971), "On Advertising Wear-out," *Journal of Advertising Research,* Vol. 11 (February), pp. 11–14.

APPLEBAUM, WILLIAM (1966), "Methods for Determining Store Trade Areas, Market Penetration, and Potential Sales," *Journal of Marketing Research,* Vol. 3 (May), pp. 127–141.

APPLEBAUM, WILLIAM (1968), "Survey of Store

Location by Retail Chains." In C. Kornblau, ed., *Guide to Store Location Research.* Reading, Mass.: Addison-Wesley.

ARMSTRONG, J. SCOTT (1986), "The Ombudsman: Research on Forecasting: A Quarter Century Review," 1960–1984, *Interfaces,* Vol. 16, no. 1 (January/February), pp. 89–109.

ARMSTRONG, J. SCOTT (1985), *Long Range Forecasting: From Crystal Ball to Computer,* 2nd ed. New York: John Wiley.

ARNOLD, STEVEN F. (1990), *Mathematical Statistics.* Englewood Cliffs, N.J.: Prentice Hall.

ARORA, RAJ (1982), "Validation of an S-O-R Model for Situation, Enduring, and Response Components of Involvement," *Journal of Marketing Research,* Vol. 19 (November), pp. 505–516.

ARORA, RAJ (1985), "Consumer Involvement: What It Offers Marketing Strategy," *International Journal of Advertising,* Vol. 4, pp. 119–130.

ARROW, KENNETH J. (1963), *Social Choice and Individual Values,* 2nd ed. New York: John Wiley.

ASSAEL, HENRY and GEORGE S. DAY (1968), "Attitudes and Awareness as Predictors of Market Share," *Journal of Advertising Research,* Vol. 8, no. 4 (December), pp. 3–10.

ASSMUS, G. (1975), "NEWPROD: The Design and Implementation of a New Product," *Journal of Marketing,* 39 (January), pp. 16–23.

ASSMUS, GERT, JOHN U. FARLEY, and DONALD R. LEHMANN (1984), "How Advertising Affects Sales: Meta-analysis of Econometric Results," *Journal of Marketing Research,* Vol. 21 (February), pp. 65–74.

AUMANN, R. (1987), "What is Game Theory Trying to Accomplish?" In K. J. Arrow and S. Honkapohja, eds., *Frontiers of Economics.* Oxford: Blackwell.

AXELROD, JOEL N. (1968), "Attitude Measures That Predict Purchase," *Journal of Advertising Research,* Vol. 8 (March), pp. 3–17.

AXELROD, ROBERT (1980a), "Effective Choice

in the Prisoner's Dilemma," *Journal of Conflict Resolution,* Vol. 24 (March), pp. 3–25.

AXELROD, ROBERT (1980b), "More Effective Choice in the Prisoner's Dilemma," *Journal of Conflict Resolution,* (September), pp. 379–403.

AYKAC, A., M. CORSTJENS, D. GAUTSCHI, and I. HOROWITZ (1989), "Estimation Uncertainty and Optimal Advertising Decisions," *Management Science,* Vol. 35, no. 1 (January), pp. 42–50.

BABAKUS, EMIN, CARL E. FERGUSON, JR., and KARL G. JÖRESKOG (1987), "The Sensitivity of Confirmatory Maximum Likelihood Factor Analysis to Violations of Measurement Scale and Distributional Assumptions," *Journal of Marketing Research,* Vol. 24 (May), pp. 222–228.

BAGOZZI, RICHARD P. (1978), "Marketing as Exchange: A Theory of Transactions in the Marketplace," *American Behavioral Scientist,* Vol. 21 (April), pp. 535–556.

BAGOZZI, RICHARD P., ed. (1979a), *Sales Management: New Developments from Behavioral and Decision Model Research.* Cambridge, Mass.: Marketing Science Institute.

BAGOZZI, RICHARD P. (1979b), *Causal Models in Marketing.* New York: John Wiley.

BAGOZZI, RICHARD P. (1980), "Performance and Satisfaction in an Industrial Salesforce: An Examination of their Antecedents and Simultaneity," *Journal of Marketing,* Vol. 44 (Spring), pp. 65–77.

BAGOZZI, RICHARD P. (1982), "A Field Investigation of Causal Relations Among Cognitions, Affect, Intentions and Behavior," *Journal of Marketing Research,* Vol. 19 (November), pp. 562–584.

BAGOZZI, R. P. and A. J. SILK (1983), "Recall, Recognition and the Measurement of Memory for Print Advertisements," *Marketing Science,* Vol. 2, no. 2 (Spring), pp. 95–134.

BAIN, JOE S. (1956), *Barriers to Competition.* Cambridge, Mass.: Harvard University Press.

BAIN, LEE J. and MAX ENGELHARDT (1989), *Introduction to Probability and Mathematical Statistics.* Boston: PWS-Kent.

BAIN, JOE S. (1968), *Industrial Organization,* New York: Wiley and Sons.

BALACHANDRAN, V. and DENNIS H. GENSCH (1974), "Solving the 'Marketing Mix' Problem Using Geometric Programming," *Management Science,* Vol. 21, no. 2 (October), pp. 160–170.

BALAKRISHNAN, P. V. and JEHOSHUA ELIASHBERG (1990), "A New Analytical Process Model of Two-Party Interorganizational Negotiation: Theoretical Implications and Empirical Findings," Working paper, The Wharton School of the University of Pennsylvania (August).

BALASUBRAMANIAN, SIVA K. and V. KUMAR (1990), "Analyzing Variations in Advertising and Promotional Expenditures: Key Correlates in Consumer, Industrial, and Service Markets," *Journal of Marketing,* Vol. 54, no. 2 (April), pp. 57–68.

BALDERSTON, F. E. (1958), "Communication Networks in Intermediate Markets," *Management Science,* Vol. 4 (January), pp. 154–171.

BALIGH, HELMY and LEON E. RICHARTZ (1967), *Vertical Market Structures.* Boston: Allyn & Bacon.

BARBOSA, L. C. and R. G. HIRKO (1980), "Integration of Algorithmic Aids into Decision Support Systems," *MIS Quarterly* (March), pp. 1–12.

BARNETT, ARNOLD L. (1976), "More on a Market Share Theorem," *Journal of Marketing Research,* Vol. 13 , pp. 104–109.

BARTEN, A. P. (1977), "The Systems of Consumer Demand Functions Approach: A Review," *Econometrica,* Vol. 45, pp. 23–51.

BASS, F. (1969a), "A New Product Growth Model for Consumer Durables," *Management Science,* Vol. 15 (January), pp. 215–227.

BASS, F. (1969b), "A Simultaneous Equation Regression Study of Advertising and Sales of Cigarettes," *Journal of Marketing Research,* Vol. 6, pp. 291–300.

BASS, F. (1974), "The Theory of Stochastic Preference and Brand Switching," *Journal of Marketing Research,* Vol. 11, pp. 1–20.

BASS, F. (1980), "The Relationship Between Diffusion Rates, Experience Curves, and Demand Elasticities for Consumer Durable Technological Innovations," *Journal of Business,* Vol. 53 (July), pp. 551–567.

BASS, FRANK M. and ALAIN V. BULTEZ (1982), "A Note on Optimal Strategic Pricing of Technological Innovations," *Marketing Science,* Vol. 1 (Fall), pp. 371–378.

BASS, FRANK M. and D. G. CLARKE (1972), "Testing Distributed Lag Models of Advertising Effects," *Journal of Marketing Research,* Vol. 9, pp. 298–308.

BASS, FRANK M., ABEL P. JEULAND, and GORDON P. WRIGHT (1976), "Equilibrium Stochastic Choice and Market Penetration Theories: Derivation and Comparisons," *Management Science,* Vol. 22 (June), pp. 1051–1063.

BASS, FRANK M. and ROBERT P. LEONE (1983), "Temporal Aggregation, the Data Interval Bias and Empirical Estimation of Bimonthly Relations from Annual Data," *Management Science,* Vol. 29, no. 1 (January), pp. 1–11.

BASS, FRANK M. and ROBERT P. LEONE (1986), "Estimating Micro Relationships from Macro Data: A Comparative Study of Two Approximations of the Brand Loyal Model Under Temporal Aggregation," *Journal of Marketing Research,* Vol. 23 (August), pp. 291–297.

BASS, FRANK M. and LEONARD J. PARSONS (1969), "A Simultaneous Equation Regression Analysis of Sales and Advertising," *Applied Economics,* Vol. 1, pp. 103–124.

BASS, F. and R. RAO (1983), "Equilibrium Dynamic Pricing of New Products in Oligopolies: Theory and Evidence," Working Paper, University of Chicago.

BASS, FRANK M. and W. WAYNE TALARZYK (1972), "An Attitude Model for the Study of Brand Preference," *Journal of Marketing Research,* Vol. 9 (February), pp. 93–96.

BASS, FRANK M., MOSHE GIVON, MANOHAR U. KALWANI, DAVID REIBSTEIN, and GORDON P. WRIGHT (1984), "An Investigation into the Order of the Brand Choice Process," *Marketing Science,* Vol. 3, no.4 (Fall), pp. 267–287.

BASS, FRANK M. and DICK R. WITTINK (1975), "Pooling Issues and Methods in Regression Analysis with Examples in Market Research," *Journal of Marketing Research,* Vol. 12, pp. 414–425.

BASS, FRANK ET AL., EDS. (1961), *Mathematical Models and Methods in Marketing.* Homewood, Ill.: Richard D. Irwin.

BASU, AMIYA K. and RAJEEV BATRA (1988), "ADSPLIT: A Multi-Brand Advertising Budget Allocation Model," *Journal of Advertising,* Vol. 17, no. 1, pp. 44–51.

BASU, AMIYA K. and GURUMURTHY KALYANARAM (1990), "On the Relative Performance of Linear Versus Nonlinear Compensation Plans," *International Journal of Research in Marketing,* Vol. 7, nos. 2, 3, pp. 171–178.

BASU, A., R. LAL, V. SRINIVASAN, and R. STAELIN (1985), "Salesforce Compensation Plans: An Agency Theoretic Perspective," *Marketing Science,* Vol. 4 (Fall), pp. 267–291.

BATSELL, RICHARD R. and JOHN C. POLKING (1985), "A New Class of Market Share Models," *Marketing Science,* Vol. 4, no. 3 (Summer), pp. 177–198.

BAUMOL, W. (1972), *Economic Theory and Operations Analysis.* Englewood Cliffs, N.J.: Prentice Hall.

BAUMOL, WILLIAM J. and EDWARD A. IDE (1956), "Variety in Retailing," *Management Science,* Vol. 3 (October), pp. 93–101.

BAWA, KAPIL and ROBERT W. SHOEMAKER (1987), "The Effects of a Direct Mail Coupon on Brand Choice Behavior," *Journal of Marketing Research,* Vol. 24 (November), pp. 370–376.

BAYER, JUDY and RACHEL HARTER (1991), " "Miner," "Manager," and "Researcher": Three Modes of Analysis of Scanner Data," *International Journal of Research in Marketing,* Vol. 8, no. 1, pp. 17–27.

BAYER, J., S. LAWRENCE, and J. KEON (1988), "PEP: An Expert System for Promotion Marketing. In E. Turban and P. R. Watkins, eds., *Applied Expert Systems,* pp. 121–141. Amsterdam: North-Holland.

BAYUS, BARRY L. (1987), "Forecasting Sales of New Contingent Products: An Application to the Compact Disk Market," *Journal of Product Innovation Management,* Vol. 4 (December), pp. 243–255.

BAYUS, BARRY L. (1988), "Accelerating the Durable Replacement-Cycle with Marketing Mix Variables," *Journal of Product Innovation Management,* Vol. 5, no. 3 (September), pp. 216–226.

BAZARAA, MOKHTAR S. and C. M. SHETTY (1979), *Nonlinear Programming: Theory and Algorithms.* New York: John Wiley.

BEACH, L. CHRISTENSEN-SZLANSKI and V. BARNES (1987), "Assessing Human Judgment: Has It Been Done, Can It Be Done, Should It Be Done?" In G. Wright and P. Ayton, eds., *Judgmental Forecasting,* pp. 49–62. New York: John Wiley.

BEARDEN, WILLIAM O. and MICHAEL J. ETZEL (1982), "Reference Group Influence on Product and Brand Purchase Decisions," *Journal of Consumer Research,* Vol. 9 (September), pp. 183–194.

BEARDEN, WILLIAM O. and JESSE E. TEEL (1983), "Selected Determinants of Consumer Satisfaction and Complaint Reports," *Journal of Marketing Research,* Vol. 20 (February), pp. 21–28.

BECHTEL, GORDON G. (1990), "Share-Ratio Estimation of the Nested Multinomial Logit Model," *Journal of Marketing Research,* Vol. 27 (May), pp. 232–237.

BECKWITH, NEAL E., and D. R. LEHMANN (1975), "The Importance of Halo Effects in Multi-attribute Attitude Models," *Journal of Marketing Research,* Vol. 12 (August), pp. 265–275.

BELL, DAVID E., RALPH L. KEENEY, and JOHN D. C. LITTLE (1975), "A Market Share Theorem," *Journal of Marketing Research,* Vol. 12, pp. 136–141.

BEMMAOR, ALBERT C. (1984), "Testing Alternative Econometric Models on the Existence of Advertising Threshold Effect," *Journal of Marketing Research,* Vol. 21 (August), pp. 298–308.

BEN-AKIVA, MOSHE and STEVEN R. LERMAN (1985), *Discrete Choice Analysis: Theory and Application to Travel Demand.* Cambridge: Massachusetts Institute of Technology Press.

BENSOUSSAN, A., ALAIN BULTEZ, and PHILIPPE NAERT (1978), "Leader's Dynamic Marketing Behavior in Oligopoly," *TIMS Studies in the Management Sciences,* Vol. 9, pp. 123–145.

BERKOWITZ, M. K. and G. H. HAINES (1982), "Predicting Demand for Residential Solar Heating: An Attribute Method," *Management Science,* Vol. 28, no. 7 (July), pp. 717–727.

BERLE, ADOLPH A., JR., and GARDINER C. MEANS (1932), *The Modern Corporation and Private Property.* New York: Macmillan.

BESANKO, DAVID and WAYNE L. WINSTON (1990), "Optimal Price Skimming by a Monopolist Facing Rational Consumers," *Management Science,* Vol. 36, no. 5 (May) pp. 555–567.

BEST, ROGER J. and GEORGE C. HOZIER, JR. (1980), "Relating Market Share Behavior to the Main and Interactive Components of a Firm's Marketing Mix." In D. Montgomery and D. Wittink, eds., *Marketing Measurement and Analysis.* Cambridge, Mass.: Marketing Science Institute.

BESWICK, C. A. (1973), "An Aggregate Multistage Decision Model for Sales Force Management," Ph.D. thesis, University of Tennessee, Knoxville.

BESWICK, C. A. (1977), "Allocating Selling Effort via Dynamic Programming," *Management Science,* Vol. 23, no. 7 (March), pp. 667–678.

BESWICK, C. A., and D. W. CRAVENS (1977), "A Multistage Decision Model for Salesforce Management," *Journal of Marketing Research,* Vol. 14 (May), pp. 135–144.

BETANCOURT, R. and D. GAUTSCHI (1988), "The Economics of Retail Firms," *Managerial and Decision Economics,* Vol. 9, pp. 133–142.

BETANCOURT, R. and D. GAUTSCHI (1990), "Demand Complementarities, Household Production, and Retail Assortments,"

Marketing Science, Vol. 9, no. 2 (Spring), pp. 146–161.

BETTMAN, JAMES R. (1971), "The Structure of Consumer Choice Processes," *Journal of Marketing Research,* Vol. 8 (November), pp. 465–471.

BETTMAN, JAMES R. (1979), *An Information Processing Theory of Consumer Choice.* Reading, Mass.: Addison-Wesley.

BETTMAN, J. R., N. CAPON, and J. R. LUTZ (1975), "Cognitive Algebra in Multiattribute Attitude Models," *Journal of Marketing Research,* Vol. 12, pp. 151–164.

BIEHAL, GABRIEL J. (1983), "Consumers' Prior Experiences and Perceptions in Auto Repair Choice," *Journal of Marketing,* Vol. 47 (Summer), pp. 82–91.

BIGGADIKE, E. R. (1976), *Corporate Diversification: Entry Strategy and Performance,* Harvard University Press, Cambridge, MA.

BIMM, E. B. and A. D. MILLMAN (1978), "A Model for Planning TV in Canada," *Journal of Advertising Research,* Vol. 18, no. 4 , pp. 43–48.

BIRKHOFF, GARRETT and GIAN-CARLO ROTA (1989), *Ordinary Differential Equations,* 4th ed. New York: John Wiley.

BLACKBURN, J. D., and K. J. CLANCY (1983), "LITMUS: An Evolutionary Step in New Product Planning Models From Marketing Plan Evaluation to Marketing Plan Generation," *Advances and Practices of Marketing Science,* F. Zufryden, ed., (The Institute of Management Sciences, Providence, R.I.)

BLACKMAN, A. WADE, JR. (1974), "The Market Dynamics of Technological Substitutions," *Technological Forecasting and Social Change,* Vol. 6, no. 1 pp. 41–63.

BLACKMAN, A. WADE, JR., E. J. SELIGMAN, and G. C. SOLGLIERO (1973), "An Innovation Index Based Upon Factor Analysis," *Technological Forecasting and Social Change,* Vol. 4, pp. 301–316.

BLASKO, VINCENT J., and CHARLES H. PATTI (1984), "The Advertising Budgeting Practices of Industrial Marketers," *Journal of Marketing,* Vol. 48, no. 4 (Fall), pp. 104–110.

BLATTBERG, ROBERT C. (1987), "Reply," *Marketing Science,* Vol. 6, no. 2 (Spring), pp. 154–155.

BLATTBERG, ROBERT C., GARY D. EPPEN, and JOSHUA LIEBERMAN (1981), "A Theoretical and Empirical Evaluation of Price Deals for Consumer Non-Durables," *Journal of Marketing,* Vol. 45, no. 1 (Winter), pp. 116–129.

BLATTBERG, ROBERT C. and JOHN GOLANTY (1978), "Tracker: An Early Test Market Forecasting and Diagnostic Model for New Product Planning," *Journal of Marketing Research,* Vol. 15 (May), pp. 192–202.

BLATTBERG, ROBERT C. and ABEL P. JEULAND (1981), "A Micro-Modeling Approach to Investigate the Advertising-Sales Relationship," *Management Science,* Vol. 27, no. 9 (September), pp. 988–1004.

BLATTBERG, ROBERT C. and ALAN LEVIN (1987), "Modelling the Effectiveness and Profitability of Trade Promotions," *Marketing Science,* Vol. 6, no. 2 (Spring), pp. 124–146.

BLATTBERG, ROBERT C. and SCOTT A. NESLIN (1989), "Sales Promotion: The Long and the Short of It," *Marketing Letters,* Vol. 1, no. 1, pp. 81–97.

BLATTBERG, ROBERT C. and SCOTT A. NESLIN (1990), *Sales Promotion: Concepts, Methods, and Strategies.* Englewood Cliffs, N.J.: Prentice Hall.

BLATTBERG, ROBERT C. and KENNETH J. WISNIEWSKI (1989), "Price-Induced Patterns of Competition," *Marketing Science,* Vol. 8, no. 4, pp. 291–309.

BLATTBERG, ROBERT C. and KENNETH J. WISNIEWSKI (1988), "Modelling Store-Level Scanner Data," Marketing Working Paper #43. University of Chicago.

BLOOM, DEREK, ANDREA JAY, and TONY TWYMAN (1977), "The Validity of Advertising Pretests," *Journal of Advertising Research,* Vol. 17, no. 2 (April), pp. 7–16.

BODNAR JUDITH, PETER DILWORTH, and SALVATORE IACONO (1988), "Cross-Sectional Analysis of Residential Telephone Subscription in Canada," *Information Economics and Policy,* Vol. 3, pp. 359–378.

BOLTON, P. and G. BONANNO (1988), "Vertical Restraints in a Model of Vertical Differentiation," *Quarterly Journal of Economics,* Vol. 103, no. 3 (August), pp. 555–570.

BONANNO, G. and J. VICKERS (1988), "Vertical Separation," *Journal of Industrial Economics,* Vol. 36 (March), pp. 257–266.

BOND, R. S., and D. F. LEAN (1977), "Sales Promotion and Product Differentiation in Two Prescription Drug Markets," *Economic Report* (February), Federal Trade Commission.

BONOMA, THOMAS V., VICTORIA L. CRITTENDEN, and ROBERT J. DOLAN (1988), "Can We Have Rigor and Relevance in Pricing Research." In T. M. Devinney, *Issues in Pricing: Theory and Research,* Chap. 15. Lexington, Mass.: Lexington Books.

BOOZ, ALLEN and HAMILTON (1982), *New Products Management for the 1980s.* New York: Authors.

BORCH, K. (1962), "Equilibrium in a Reinsurance Market," *Econometrica,* Vol. 30 (July), pp. 424–444.

BORDLEY, ROBERT F. (1982), "A Multiplicative Formula for Aggregating Probability Assessments," *Management Science,* Vol. 28, no. 10 (October), pp. 1137–1148.

BOSTON CONSULTING GROUP (1970), *Perspectives on Experience.* Boston: Authors.

BOULDING, WILLIAM (1990), "Commentary on "Unobservable Effects and Business Performance: Do Fixed Effects Matter?" *Marketing Science,* Vol. 9, no. 1 (Winter), pp. 88–91.

BOWER, JOHN (1963), "Net Audiences of U.S. and Canadian Magazines: Seven Tests of Agostini's Formula," *Journal of Advertising Research* (March), pp. 13–21.

BOWERSOX, D. J., O. K. HELFERICH, E. J. MARIEN, P. GILMOUR, M. L. LAWRENCE, F. W. MORGAN, and R. T. ROGERS (1972), *Dynamic Simulation of Physical Distribution Systems.* East Lansing: Michigan State University Business Studies.

BOWMAN, E. H. (1963), "Consistency and Optimality in Managerial Decision Making," *Management Science,* Vol. 9 (January), pp. 310–321.

BOWMAN, RUSSELL (1986), "Sales Promotion: The 1985 Annual Report," *Marketing and Media Decisions* (July), pp. 1770–1774.

BOYD, HARPER W., JR., and MICHAEL L. RAY (1971), "What Big Agency Men in Europe Think of Copy Testing Methods," *Journal of Marketing Research,* Vol. 8 (May), pp. 219–223.

BRANDER, J. A. and A. ZHANG (1990), "Market Conduct in the Airline Industry: An Empirical Investigation," *The Rand Journal of Economics,* 21 (Winter), pp. 567–583.

BRAUN, M. A. and V. SRINIVASAN (1975), "Amount of Information as a Determinant of Consumer Behavior Toward New Products," Reprint Series, Report No. 220. Stanford University.

BRESNAHAN, T. (1987), "Competition and Collusion in the American Automobile Industry: The 1955 Price War," *Journal of Industrial Economics,* Vol. 35, pp. 457–482.

BRETSCHNEIDER, STUART I. and VIJAY MAHAJAN (1980), "Adaptive Technological Substitution Models," *Technological Forecasting and Social Change,* Vol. 18 (October), pp. 129–139.

BROADBENT, SIMON (1984), "Modeling with Ad Stock," *Journal of the Market Research Society,* Vol. 26 (October), pp. 295–312.

BROADBENT, SIMON (1989a), "Point of View: What Is a 'Small' Advertising Elasticity?" *Journal of Advertising Research,* Vol. 29, no. 4 (August/September), pp. 37–39.

BROADBENT, SIMON (1989b), "A 'Small' Advertising Elasticity: A Rejoinder and Some Conclusions," *Journal of Advertising Research* (August/September), p. 44.

BRODIE, RODERICK and CORNELIUS A. DE KLUYVER (1984), "Attraction Versus Linear and Multiplicative Market Share Models: A Empirical Evaluation," *Journal of Marketing Research,* Vol. 21 (May), pp. 194–201.

BROWN, A. A. and A. DEATON (1972), "Surveys in Applied Economics: Models of Consumer Behavior," *The Economic Journal,* Vol. 82, pp. 1145–1236.

BROWN, A. A., F. T. HULSWIT, and J. D. KETTELLE (1956), "A Study of Sales Operations," *Operations Research Quarterly*, Vol. 4 (June), pp. 296–308.

BROWN, D. B. and M. R. WARSHAW (1965), "Media Selection by Linear Programming," *Journal of Market Research*, Vol. 2 (February), pp. 83–88.

BROWN, ROBERT G. (1973), "A Model for Measuring the Influence of Promotion on Inventory and Consumer Demand," *Journal of Marketing Research* (November), pp. 380–389.

BROWN, ROBERT G. (1974), "Sales Response to Promotions and Advertising," *Journal of Advertising Research* (August), pp. 33–39.

BROWN, R. V. (1969), *Research and the Credibility of Estimates*. Cambridge, Mass.: Harvard University Press.

BROWN, S. and D. SIBLEY (1986), *The Theory of Public Utility Pricing*. Cambridge: Cambridge University Press.

BROWN, STEPHEN W. and TERESA A. SWARTZ (1989), "A Gap Analysis of Professional Service Quality," *Journal of Marketing*, Vol. 53 (April), pp. 92–98.

BROWN, W. M. and TUCKER, W. T. (1961), "Vanishing Shelf Space," *Atlantic Economic Review*, Vol. 9, pp. 9–13.

BUCKNELL, ROGER W. (1982), "The Product-Timing 'Window,'" *Industrial Marketing*, 69 (May), pp. 62–64.

BULOW, J. (1982), "Durable Goods Monopolists," *Journal of Political Economy*, Vol. 90, pp. 314–332.

BULTEZ, A. V. and P. A. NAERT (1979), "Does Lag Structure Really Matter in Optimizing Advertising Expenditures?" *Management Science*, Vol. 25 (May), pp. 454–465.

BULTEZ, A. V. and P. A. NAERT (1988a), "When Does Lag Structure Really Matter . . . Indeed?" *Management Science*, Vol. 34, no. 7 (July), pp. 909–916.

BULTEZ, A. V. and P. A. NAERT (1988b), "S.H.A.R.P.: Shelf Allocation for Retailers' Profit," *Marketing Science*, Vol. 7, no. 3 (Summer), pp. 211–231.

BUNCH, DAVID S. and RICHARD R. BATSELL (1989), "A Monté Carlo Comparison of Estimators for the Multinomial Logit Model," *Journal of Marketing Research*, Vol. 26, (February), pp. 56–68.

BUNGE, MARIO (1967), *Scientific Research: The Search for Information*. New York: Springer-Verlag.

BUNN, DEREK and GEORGE WRIGHT (1991), "Interaction of Judgmental and Statistical Forecasting Methods: Issues and Analysis," *Management Science*, Vol. 37, no. 5 (May), pp. 501–518.

BURGER, P. C., H. GUNDEE and R. LAVIDGE (1981), "COMP: A Comprehensive System for the Evaluation of New Products," *New Product Forecasting: Models and Applications*, Y. Wind, V. Mahajan and R. Cardozo, eds., Lexington Books, Lexington, MA.

BURKE, RAYMOND R. (1991), "Reasoning with Empirical Marketing Knowledge," *International Journal of Research in Marketing*, Vol. 8, no. 1, pp. 75–90.

BURKE, RAYMOND R., ARVIND RANGASWAMY, JERRY WIND, and JEHOSHUA ELIASHBERG (1990), "A Knowledge-Based System for Advertising Design," *Marketing Science*, Vol. 9, no. 3, pp. 212–229.

BURKE MARKETING SERVICES (1984), "BASES: Introduction, Services, Validation, History," Cincinnati, OH: Burke Marketing Services.

BUSS, W. C. (1981), "A Comparison of the Predicative Performance of Group-Preference Models." In Ken Bernhardt, ed., *AMA Educators' Conference Proceedings*, 47, pp. 174–177. Chicago: American Marketing Association.

BUTLER, D. H. and B. F. BUTLER (1971), "Hendrodynamics: Fundamental Laws of Consumer Dynamics," New York: The Hendry Corporation.

BUZZELL, R. D. (1964), *Mathematical Models and Marketing Management*. Boston: Harvard University, Division of Research.

BUZZELL, ROBERT (1966), "Competitive Behavior and Product Life Cycles." In J. S. Wright and J. L. Goldstucker, eds., *New*

Ideas for Successful Marketing. Chicago: American Marketing Association.

BUZZELL, ROBERT D. (1990), "Commentary on 'Unobservable Effects and Business Performance,'" *Marketing Science,* Vol. 9, no. 1 (Winter), pp. 86–87.

BUZZELL, ROBERT D. and PAUL W. FARRIS (1976), "Industrial Marketing Costs," Working paper, Marketing Science Institute, Cambridge, Mass. (December).

BUZZELL, ROBERT D. and BRADLEY T. GALE (1987), *The PIMS Principles,* p. 28. New York: The Free Press.

CAMPBELL, NIGEL D. G., JOHN L. GRAHAM, ALAIN JOLIBERT, and HANS GUNTHER MEISSNER (1988), "Marketing Negotiations in France, Germany, the United Kingdom, and the United States," *Journal of Marketing,* Vol. 52, no. 2 (April), pp. 49–62.

CANNON, HUGH (1987), "A Theory-Based Approach to Optimal Frequency," *Journal of Media Planning* (Fall), pp. 33–44.

CANNON, HUGH and NORMAN GOLDRING (1986), "Another Look at Effective Frequency," *Journal of Media Planning* (Fall), pp. 29–36.

CAPON, NOEL, "Product Life Cycle," Harvard Business School, Case no. 579-872.

CAPON, NOEL, J. U. FARLEY, and S. HOENIG (1990), "Determinants of Financial Performance: A Meta-Analysis," *Management Science,* Vol. 36, no. 19 (October), pp. 1143–1159.

CARDOZO, RICHARD N. (1983), "Modeling Organizational Buying as a Sequence of Decisions," *Industrial Marketing Management,* Vol. 12, pp. 75–81.

CARDOZO, RICHARD N. and DAVID K. SMITH, JR. (1983), "Applying Financial Portfolio Theory to Product Portfolio Decisions: An Empirical Study," *Journal of Marketing,* Vol. 4 (Spring), pp. 110–119.

CARDOZO, RICHARD and YORAM WIND (1980), "Portfolio Analysis for Strategic Product Market Planning," Working paper, The Wharton School of the University of Pennsylvania.

CARLSON, J. G. (1961), "How Management Can Use the Improvement Phenomenon,"

California Management Review, Vol. 3, no. 2, pp. 83–94.

CARLSON, J. G. (1973), "Cubic Learning Curves: Precision Tools for Labor Estimating," *Manufacturing Engineering and Management,* Vol. 71, no. 5, pp. 22–25.

CARMAN, J. M. (1966), "Brand Switching and Linear Learning Models," *Journal of Advertising Research,* Vol. 6 (June), pp. 23–31.

CARPENTER, GREGORY S. (1987), "Modeling Competitive Marketing Strategies: The Impact of Marketing-Mix Relationships and Industry Structure," *Marketing Science,* Vol. 6, no. 2 (Spring), pp. 208–221.

CARPENTER, GREGORY S. (1989), "Perceptual Position and Competitive Brand Strategy in a Two-Dimensional, Two-Brand Market," *Management Science,* Vol. 35, no. 9 (September), pp. 1029–1044.

CARPENTER, GREGORY S., LEE G. COOPER, DOMINIQUE M. HANSSENS, and DAVID F. MIDGLEY (1988), "Modeling Asymmetric Competition," *Marketing Science,* Vol. 7, no. 4 (Fall), pp. 393–412.

CARPENTER, G. and D. LEHMANN (1985), "A Model of Marketing Mix, Brand Switching, and Competition," *Journal of Marketing Research,* Vol. 22 (August), pp. 318–329.

CARROLL, J. D. and J. J. CHANG (1964), "A General Index of Nonlinear Correlation and Its Applications to the Interpretation of Multidimensional Scaling Solutions," *American Psychologist,* Vol. 19, pp. 540–549.

CARROLL, J. D., P. E. GREEN, and W. S. DE-SARBO (1979), "Optimizing the Allocation of Fixed Resources: A Simple Model and Its Experimental Test," *Journal of Marketing,* Vol. 43, no. 1, pp. 51–57.

CARROLL, V. P., A. G. RAO, H. L. LEE, A. SHAPIN, and B. L. BAYUS (1985), "The Navy Enlistment Marketing Experiment," *Marketing Science,* Vol. 4, no. 4 (Fall), pp. 352–374.

CASTORE, CARL H., KEVIN PETERSON, and THOMAS A. GOODRICH (1971), "Risky Shift: Social Value or Social Choice? An Alternative Model," *Journal of Person-*

ality and Social Psychology, Vol. 20, no. 3, pp. 487–494.

CATTIN, PHILIPPE and DICK R. WITTINK (1982), "Commercial Use of Conjoint Analysis: A Survey," *Journal of Marketing,* Vol. 46 (Summer) pp. 44–53.

CELSI, RICHARD L. and JERRY C. OLSON (1988), "The Role of Involvement in Attention and Comprehension Processes," *Journal of Consumer Research,* Vol. 15 (September), pp. 210–224.

CHAKRAVARTI, D. (1981), "Judgment Based Marketing Decision Models: Problems and Possible Solutions," *Journal of Marketing,* Vol. 45, No. 4 (Fall), pp. 13–23.

CHAKRAVARTI, D., A. A. MITCHELL, and R. STAELIN. (1979), "Judgmental Based Marketing Decision Models: An Experimental Investigation," *Management Science,* Vol. 25 (March), pp. 251–263.

CHAMBERLAIN, E. (1957), *The Theory of Monopolistic Competition.* Cambridge, Mass.: Harvard University Press.

CHAPMAN, RANDALL G. and RICHARD STAELIN (1982), "Exploiting Rank Ordered Choice Set Data Within the Stochastic Utility Model," *Journal of Marketing Research,* Vol. 19 (August), pp. 288–301.

CHARNES, A., W. W. COOPER, J. K. DEVOE, D. B. LEARNER, and W. REINECKE (1968), "A Goal Programming Model for Media Planning," *Management Science,* Vol. 14 (April), pp. 431–436.

CHATFIELD, C. and G. J. GOODHARDT (1973), "A Consumer Purchasing Model with Erlang Inter-Purchase Times," *Journal of the American Statistical Association* (December), pp. 828–835.

CHATTERJEE, KALYAN (1982), "Incentive Compatibility in Bargaining Under Uncertainty," *Quarterly Journal of Economics,* Vol. 97, pp. 717–726.

CHATTERJEE, KALYAN (1986), "The Theory of Bargaining." In L. Samuelson, ed., *Microeconomic Theory,* pp. 159–194. Boston: Kluwer-Nijhoff.

CHATTERJEE, KALYAN and W. F. SAMUELSON (1983), "Bargaining Under Incomplete Information," *Operations Research,* Vol. 31, pp. 835–851.

CHATTERJEE, RABIKAR and JEHOSHUA ELIASHBERG (1990), "The Innovation Diffusion Process in a Heterogeneous Population: A Micromodeling Approach," *Management Science,* Vol. 36, no. 9 (September), pp. 1057–1074.

CHOFFRAY, JEAN-MARIE (1981), "A Normative Methodology to Support Corporate Diversification Decisions," Paper presented at the Intensive Advanced Course in Marketing—Corporate Diversification and the Management of the Industrial Innovation Process, European Institute for Advanced Studies in Management, Brussels, November.

CHOFFRAY, JEAN-MARIE (1990), "Intelligent Marketing Systems." Working draft, University of Liége.

CHOFFRAY, JEAN-MARIE and GARY L. LILIEN (1978), "Assessing Response to Industrial Marketing Strategy," *Journal of Marketing,* Vol. 42, no. 2 (April) pp. 20–31.

CHOFFRAY, JEAN-MARIE and GARY L. LILIEN (1980), *Market Planning for New Industrial Products.* New York: John Wiley.

CHOFFRAY, JEAN-MARIE and GARY L. LILIEN (1982), "DESIGNOR: A Decision Support Procedure for Industrial Product Design," *Journal of Business Research,* Vol. 10, no. 2 (September), pp. 185–197.

CHOFFRAY, JEAN-MARIE and GARY L. LILIEN (1986), "A Decision Support System for Evaluating Sales Prospects and Launch Strategies for New Industrial Products," *Industrial Marketing Management,* Vol. 15, pp. 75–85.

CHOI, S. CHAN, WAYNE S. DESARBO, and PATRICK T. HARKER (1990), "Product Positioning Under Price Competition," *Management Science,* Vol. 36, no. 2 (February), pp. 175–199.

CHOW, G. C. (1967), "Technological Change and the Demand for Computers," *American Economic Review,* Vol. 57, no. 5 (December), pp. 1117–1130.

CHU, W. (1990), "Demand Signalling and Screening in Channels of Distribution," Working Paper, Massachusetts Institute of Technology, Cambridge.

CHURCHILL, GILBERT A., JR., NEIL M. FORD,

STEVEN W. HARTLEY, and ORVILLE C. WALKER, JR. (1985), "The Determinants of Salesperson Performance: A Meta-analysis," *Journal of Marketing Research,* Vol. 22 (May), pp. 103–118.

CHUSSIL, J. (1984), "PIMS: Fact or Folklore—Our Readers Reply," *Journal of Business Strategy* (Spring), pp. 90–96.

CLARKE, DARRYL G. (1976), "Economic Measurement of the Duration of Advertising Effects on Sales," *Journal of Marketing Research,* Vol. 18, pp. 345–357.

CLARKE, DARRAL G. (1987), *Marketing Analysis and Decision Making: Text and Cases.* Redwood City, Calif.: Scientific Press.

CLAXTON, JOHN D., JOSEPH N. FRY, and BERNARD PORTIS (1974), "A Taxonomy of Prepurchase Information Gathering Patterns," *Journal of Consumer Research,* Vol. 1 (December), pp. 35–42.

CLAYCAMP, H. J. and L. E. LIDDY (1969), "Prediction of New Product Performance: An Analytic Approach," *Journal of Marketing Research,* 6 (November), pp. 414–420.

CLAYCAMP, HENRY J. and C. W. MCCLELLAND (1968), "Estimating Reach and the Magic of K," *Journal of Advertising Research,* Vol. 8 (June), pp. 44–51.

CLEMEN, R. T. and R. L. WINKLER (1986), "Combining Economic Forecasts," *Journal of Business and Economic Statistics,* Vol. 4 (in press).

CLOPTON, STEPHEN W. (1984), "Seller and Buying Firm Factors Affecting Industrial Buyers' Negotiation Behavior and Outcomes," *Journal of Marketing Research,* Vol. 21, no. 1, February, pp. 39–53.

COCKS, DOUGLAS L. and JOHN R. VIRTS (1975), "Market Diffusion and Concentration in the Ethical Pharmaceutical Industry," Internal Memorandum, Eli Lilly & Co.

COHEN, JARED L. (1978), *Multiobjective Programming and Planning.* Boston: Academic Press.

COLLEY, RUSSEL H. (1975), *Defining Advertising Goals for Measured Advertising Results.* New York: Association of National Advertisers.

COLLINS, R. H. (1984), "Portable Computers: Applications to Increase Salesforce Productivity," *Journal of Personal Selling & Sales Management,* (November), pp. 75–79.

COLLINS, R. H. (1985), "Microcomputer Systems to Handle Sales Leads: A Key to Increase Salesforce Productivity," *Journal of Personal Selling and Sales Management* (May), pp. 77–83.

COLLINS, R. H. (1986), "Sales Training: A Microcomputer Based Approach," *Journal of Personal Selling and Sales Management* (May), pp. 71–76.

COLLINS, R. H. (1987), "Salesforce Support Systems: Potential Applications to Increase Productivity," *Journal of the Academy of Marketing Science,* Special Issue, Vol. 15, no. 2 (Summer)

COLLOPY, FRED and J. SCOTT ARMSTRONG (1989a), "Rule Based Forecasting," Case Western Reserve/Weatherhead School of Management Working Paper #89–14, Cleveland, Ohio.

COLLOPY, FRED and J. SCOTT ARMSTRONG (1989b), "Toward Computer-Aided Forecasting Systems." In G. R. Widemeyer, ed., *DSS 89 Transactions,* Vol. 9, pp. 103–119. Providence, R.I.: TIMS College on Information Systems.

COLOMBO, RICHARD A. and DONALD G. MORRISON (1989), "A Brand Switching Model with Implications for Marketing Strategies," *Marketing Science,* Vol. 8, no. 1, (Winter), pp. 89–99.

COMER, J. M. (1974), "ALLOCATE: A Computer Model for Sales Territory Planning," *Decision Sciences,* Vol. 5 (July), pp. 323–338.

CONLISK, J., E. GERSTNER, and J. SOBEL (1984), "Cyclic Pricing by a Durable Goods Monopolist," *Quarterly Journal of Economics,* Vol. 99, pp. 489–505.

CONNORS, M. M., C. CORAY, C. J. CUCCARO, W. K. GREEN, D. W. LOW, and H. M. MARKOWITZ (1972), "The Distribution System Simulator," *Management Science,* Vol. 18, no. 8 (April), pp. B425-B453.

COOKE, ERNEST and BEN EDMUNDSON (1963), "Computer Aided Product Investment Decisions." In T. Greer, ed., *Increasing*

Marketing Productivity and Conceptual and Methodological Foundations of Marketing. Chicago: American Marketing Association.

COOPER, LEE G. (1988), "Competitive Maps: The Structure Underlying Asymmetric Cross-elasticities," *Management Science,* Vol. 34 (June), pp. 96–108.

COOPER, LEE G. and MASAO NAKANISHI (1988), *Market-Share Analysis.* Norwell, Mass.: Kluwer.

COOPER, ROBERT G. (1979), "The Dimensions of Industrial New Product Success and Failure," *Journal of Marketing,* 43 (Summer), pp. 93–103.

CORFMAN, KIM (1991), "Perceptions of Relative Influence: Formation and Measurement," *Journal of Marketing Research,* Vol. 28 (May), pp. 125–136.

CORFMAN, KIM and SUNIL GUPTA (1991), "Mathematical Models of Group Choice," New York University, Working draft.

CORFMAN, KIM and DONALD R. LEHMANN (1987), "Models of Comparative Group Decision-Making and Relative Influence," *Journal of Consumer Research,* Vol. 14, (June), pp. 1–13.

CORSTJENS, M. (1981), "A Model for Optimizing Retail Space Allocations," *Management Science,* Vol. 27, no. 7 (July), pp. 822–833.

CORSTJENS, M. (1983), "A Dynamic Model for Strategically Allocating Retail Space," *Journal of the Operational Research Society,* Vol. 34, no. 10, pp. 943–951.

CORSTJENS, M. and PETER DOYLE (1979), "Channel Optimization in Complex Marketing Systems," *Management Science,* Vol. 25, no. 10 (October), pp. 1014–1025.

CORSTJENS, M. and PETER DOYLE (1981), "A Model for Optimizing Retail Space Allocations," *Management Science,* Vol. 27, no. 7 (July), pp. 822–833.

CORSTJENS, MARCEL L. and DAVID A. GAUTSCHI (1983), "Formal Choice Models in Marketing," *Marketing Science,* Vol. 2, no. 1 (Winter), pp. 19–56.

CORSTJENS, MARCEL and DAVID WEINSTEIN (1982), "Optimal Strategic Business Unit Portfolio Analysis." In A. Zoltners, ed., *Marketing Planning Models, TIMS Studies in the Management Sciences,* Vol. 18, pp. 141–160. New York: North-Holland.

CORT, STANTON G., DAVID R. LAMBERT, and PAULA L. GARRET (1982), "Frequency in Business-to-Business Advertising—A State-of-the-Art Review," Paper presented at the 4th Annual Business Advertising Research Conference, April 21, 1982. New York: The Advertising Research Foundation.

COUGHLAN, ANNE T. and SUBRATA K. SEN (1989), "Salesforce Compensation: Theory and Managerial Implications," *Marketing Science,* Vol. 8, no. 4 (Fall), pp. 324–342.

COUGHLAN, A. and B. WERNERFELT (1989), "On Credible Delegation by Oligopists: A Discussion of Distribution Channel Management," *Management Science,* Vol. 35, no. 2 (February), pp. 226–239.

COURSEY, DON L. (1985), "A Normative Model of Behavior Based upon an Activity Hierarchy," *Journal of Consumer Research* (June), pp. 64–73.

COURSEY, DON L. (1988), "Preference Trees, Preference Hierarchies, and Consumer Behavior," *Journal of Consumer Research,* Vol. 15 (December), pp. 407–409.

COWLING, K. and J. CUBBIN (1971), "Price, Quality and Advertising Competition: An Econometric Investigation of the United Kingdom Car Market," *Economica,* Vol. 38 (November), pp. 378–394.

COX, WILLIAM, JR. (1967), "Product Life Cycles as Marketing Models," *Journal of Business,* Vol. 40 (October), pp. 375–384.

CRAIG, C. S. and A. GHOSH (1985), "Maximizing Effective Reach in Media Planning." In *AMA Educator's Proceedings,* pp. 178–182. Chicago: American Marketing Association.

CRAVENS, DAVID W. (1979), "Salesforce Decision Models: A Comparative Assessment." In R. Bagozzi, ed., *Sales Management: New Developments from Behavioral and Decision Model Research,* pp. 310–324. Cambridge, Mass.: Marketing Science Institute.

CURRIM, IMRAN S. (1982), "Predictive Testing of Consumer Choice Models Not Subject to Independence of Irrelevant Alternatives," *Journal of Marketing Research,* Vol. 19 (May), pp. 208–222.

CURRIM, IMRAN S. and RAKESH K. SARIN (1989), "Prospect Versus Utility," *Management Science,* Vol. 35, no. 1 (January), pp. 22–41.

CURRIM, IMRAN and LINDA G. SCHNEIDER (1991), "A Taxonomy of Consumer Purchase Strategies in a Promotion-Intensive Environment," *Marketing Science,* Vol. 10, no. 2 (Spring), pp. 91–110.

CURRY, DAVID J., MICHAEL B. MENASCO and JAMES W. VAN ARK (1991), "Multiattribute Dyadic Choice: Models and Tests," *Journal of Marketing Research,* Vol. 28 (August), pp. 259–267.

CURRY, DAVID J. and PETER C. RIESZ (1988), "Prices and Price/Quality Relationships: A Longitudinal Analysis," *Journal of Marketing,* Vol. 52 (January), pp. 36–51.

DAGANZO, CARLOS (1979), *Multinomial Probit.* New York: Academic Press.

DALAL, S. R. and R. W. KLEIN (1988), "A Flexible Class of Discrete Choice Models," *Marketing Science,* Vol. 7, no. 3 (Summer), pp. 232–251.

DALAL, S. R., J. C. LEE, and D. J. SABAVALA (1984), "Prediction of Individual Buying Behavior: A Poisson-Bernoulli Model with Arbitrary Heterogeneity," *Marketing Science,* Vol. 3, no. 4 (Fall), pp. 352–367.

DALKEY, NORMAN C. and OLAF HELMER (1963), "An Experimental Application of the Delphi Method to the Use of Experts," *Management Science,* Vol. 9 (April), pp. 458–467.

DANAHER, PETER (1991), "A Canonical Expansion Model for Multivariate Media Exposure Distributions: A Generalization of the Duplication of Viewing Law," *Journal of Marketing Research,* Vol. 28 (August), pp. 361–367.

DANAHER, PETER J. (1989), "An Approximate Log-Linear Model for Predicting Magazine Audiences," *Journal of Marketing Research,* Vol. 26 (November), pp. 473–479.

DASGUPTA, P. and E. MASKIN (1986a), "The Existence of Equilibrium in Discontinuous Economic Games. Part 1: Theory," *Review of Economic Studies,* Vol. 53, pp. 1–26.

DASGUPTA, P. and E. MASKIN (1986b), "The Existence of Equilibrium in Discontinuous Economical Games. Part 2: Applications," *Review of Economic Studies,* Vol. 53, pp. 27–41.

DAVIS, J. H. (1973), "Group Decision and Social Interaction: A Theory of Social Decision Schemes," *Psychological Review,* Vol. 80, no. 2 (March), pp. 97–125.

DAVIS, J. H., J. L. COHEN, J. HORNIK, and K. RISSMAN (1970a), "Dyadic Decision as a Function of the Frequency Distribution Describing the Preferences of Members' Constituencies," *Journal of Personality and Social Psychology,* Vol. 26, no. 2, pp. 178–195.

DAVIS, JAMES H., J. A. HORNIK, and JOHN P. HORNSETH (1970b), "Group Decision Schemes and Strategy Preferences in a Sequential Response Task," *Journal of Personality and Social Psychology,* Vol. 15, no. 4, pp. 397–408.

DAVIS, JAMES H., R. A. HOPPE, and JOHN P. HORNSETH (1968), "Risk-Taking: Task, Response Pattern and Grouping," *Organizational Behavior and Human Performance,* Vol. 3, pp. 124–142.

DAVIS, OTTO A. and JOHN U. FARLEY (1971), "Allocating Sales Force Effort with Commissions and Quotas," *Management Science,* Vol. 18, no. 4, pt. 2 (December), pp. 55–63.

DAY, GEORGE (1986), *Analysis for Strategic Market Decisions.* St. Paul, Minn.: West.

DAY, GEORGE (1981a), "The Product Life Cycle: Analysis and Applications Issues," *Journal of Marketing,* Vol. 45, no. 4 (Fall), pp. 60–67.

DAY, GEORGE and D. B. MONTGOMERY (1983), "Diagnosing the Experience Curve," *Journal of Marketing,* Vol. 47 (Spring), pp. 44–58.

DAY, GEORGE S. and TERRY DEUTSCHER (1982),

"Attitudinal Predictions of Choices of Major Appliance Brands," *Journal of Marketing Research,* Vol. 19 (May), pp. 192–198.

DAY, GEORGE S., ALLAN D. SHOCKER, and RAJENDRA K. SRIVASTAVA (1979), "Consumer-Oriented Approaches to Identifying Product Markets," *Journal of Marketing,* Vol. 43, no. 4 (Fall), pp. 8–19.

DAY, RALPH L. (1963), "Linear Programming in Media Selection," *Journal of Advertising Research* (June), pp. 40–44.

DEAL, KENNETH R. (1979), "Optimizing Advertising Expenditures in a Dynamic Duopoly," *Operations Research,* Vol. 27 (July/August), pp. 682–692.

DEARDEN, JAMES A. and GARY L. LILIEN (1990), "On Optimal Salesforce Compensation in the Presence of Production Learning Effects," *International Journal of Research in Marketing,* Vol. 7, No. 2, 3 (December), pp. 179–188.

DEGROOT, MORRIS H. (1987), *Probability and Statistics,* 2nd ed. Reading, Mass.: Addison-Wesley.

DEGROOT, MORRIS H. (1970), *Optimal Statistical Decisions.* New York: McGraw-Hill.

DELLA BITTA, ALBERT J., KENT B. MONROE, and JOHN M. MCGINNIS (1981), "Consumer Perceptions of Comparative Price Advertisements," *Journal of Marketing Research,* Vol. 18 (November), pp. 416–427.

DESARBO, WAYNE S. and DONNA L. HOFFMAN (1987), "Constructing MDS Joint Spaces from Binary Choice Data: A Multidimensional Unfolding Threshold Model for Marketing Research," *Journal of Marketing Research,* Vol. 24 (February), pp. 40–54.

DESARBO, WAYNE S. and VITHALA R. RAO (1986), "A Constrained Unfolding Methodology for Product Positioning," *Marketing Science,* Vol. 5, no. 1 (Winter), pp. 1–19.

DESHMUKH, S. D. and S. D. CHICKTE (1977), "Dynamic Investment Strategies for a Risky R & D Project," *Journal of Applied Probability* 14, (March), pp. 144–152.

DESHPANDE, ROHIT and GERALD ZALTMAN (1987), "A Comparison of Factors Affecting the Use of Marketing Information in Consumer and Industrial Firms," *Journal of Marketing Research,* Vol. 24 (February), pp. 114–118.

DEVANEY, ROBERT L. (1990), *Chaos, Fractals, and Dynamics: Computer Experiments in Mathematics.* Reading, Mass.: Addison-Wesley.

DEVINNEY, T. (1987), "Entry and Learning," *Management Science,* Vol. 33, pp. 706–724.

DEVINNEY, T. (1988a), "Economic Theory and Pricing Behavior: A General Framework." In T. M. Devinney, ed., *Issues in Pricing: Theory and Research,* Chap. 1. Lexington, Mass.: Lexington Books.

DEVINNEY, T. (1988b), "Price, Advertising, and Scale as Information-Revelation Mechanisms in Product Markets." In T. M. Devinney, ed., *Issues in Pricing: Theory and Research,* Chap.3. Lexington, Mass.: Lexington Books.

DHALLA, NARIMAN and SONIA YUSPEH (1976), "Forget the Product Life Cycle Concept," *Harvard Business Review,* Vol. 54 (January/February), pp. 102–112.

DHEBAR, A. and S. OREN (1985), "Optimal Dynamic Pricing for Expanding Networks," *Marketing Science,* Vol. 6 (Winter), pp. 1–22.

DHEBAR, ANIRUDH, SCOTT A. NESLIN, and JOHN A. QUELCH (1987), "Developing Models for Planning Retailer Sales Promotions: An Application to Automobile Dealerships," *Journal of Retailing,* Vol. 63, no. 4 (Winter), pp. 333–364.

DIAMOND, DANIEL S. (1968), "A Quantitative Approach to Magazine Advertisement Format Selection," *Journal of Marketing Research* (November), pp. 376–387.

DIAMOND, WILLIAM T. (1963), *Distribution Channels for Industrial Goods.* Columbus: Ohio State University Press.

DICK, ALAN, DIPANKAR CHAKRAVATI, and GABRIEL BIEHAL (1990), "Memory-Based Inferences During Consumer Choice," *Journal of Consumer Research,* Vol. 17 (June), pp. 82–93.

DICKSON, PETER R. (1983), "Distributor Portfolio Analysis and the Channel Dependence Matrix: New Techniques for Understanding and Managing the Channel," *Journal of Marketing,* Vol. 4, no. 3 (Summer), pp. 35–44.

DILLON, WILLIAM R., ROGER CALENTONE and PARKER WORTHING (1979), "The New Product Problem: An Approach for Investigating Product Failures" *Management Science,* Vol. 25, (December), pp. 1184–1196.

DILLON, WILLIAM R., DONALD G. FREDERICK, and VANCHAI TANGPANICHDEE (1982), "A Note on Accounting for Sources of Variation in Perceptual Maps," *Journal of Marketing Research,* Vol. 19 (August), pp. 302–311.

DIXIT, A. (1979), "A Model of Duopoly Suggesting a Theory of Entry Barriers," *The Bell Journal of Economics,* Vol. 10, no. 1 (Spring), pp. 20–32.

DOBSON, GREGORY and SHLOMO KALISH (1988), "Positioning and Pricing a Product Line," *Marketing Science,* Vol. 7, no. 2 (Spring), pp. 107–125.

DOCKNER, E. (1985), "Optimal Pricing in a Dynamic Duopoly Game Model," *Zeitschrift für Operations Research,* Series B.

DOCKNER, E. and S. JÖRGENSEN (1988a), "Optimal Pricing Strategies for New Products in a Dynamic Oligopoly," *Marketing Science,* Vol. 7, no. 4 (Fall), pp. 315–334.

DOCKNER, E. and S. JÖRGENSEN (1988b), "Optimal Advertising Policies for Diffusion Models of New Product Innovation in Monopolistic Situations," *Management Science,* Vol. 34, no. 1 (January), pp. 119–130.

DODDS, W. and K. MONROE (1985), "The Effect of Brand and Price Information on Subjective Product Evaluations." In E. Hirschman and M. Holbrook, eds., *Advances in Consumer Research,* Vol. 12, pp. 85–90. Provo, Utah: Association for Consumer Research.

DODSON, JOE A., JR., and EITAN MULLER (1978), "Models of New Product Diffusion Through Advertising and Word-of-Mouth," *Management Science,* Vol. 24 (November), pp. 1568–1578.

DODSON, JOE A., JR., ALICE M. TYBOUT, and BRIAN STERNTHAL (1978), "Impact of Deals and Deal Retractions on Brand Switching," *Journal of Marketing Research,* Vol. 15 (February), pp. 72–81.

DOLAN, R. (1987), "Quantity Discounts: Managerial Issues and Research Opportunities," *Marketing Science,* Vol. 6 (Winter), pp. 1–22.

DOLAN, ROBERT J. (1981), "Models of Competition: A Review of Theory and Empirical Evidence." In B. Enis and K. Roering, eds., *Review of Marketing,* pp. 224–234. Chicago: American Marketing Association.

DOLAN, ROBERT J. and ABEL P. JEULAND (1981), "Experience Curves and Dynamic Demand Models: Implementation for Optimal Pricing Strategies," *Journal of Marketing,* Vol. 45, no. 1 (Winter), pp. 52–73.

DOLAN, ROBERT J., ABEL P. JEULAND, and EITAN MULLER (1986), "Models of New Product Diffusion: Extension to Competition Against Existing and Potential Firms over Time." In V. Mahajan and Y. Wind, eds., *Innovation Diffusion Models of New Product Acceptance.* Cambridge, Mass.: Ballinger.

DOMENCICH, T. A. and DANIEL McFADDEN (1975), *Urban Travel Demand: A Behavioral Analysis.* Amsterdam: North-Holland.

DOMINGUEZ, LUIS and RICHARD W. OLSHAVSKY (1981), "Information Processing Analysis of a Stochastic Model of Brand Choice," *Journal of Business Research,* Vol. 9, pp. 39–48.

DONNELLEY MARKETING (1988), *10th Annual Survey of Promotional Practices.* Stamford, Conn.: Donnelley Marketing.

DOYLE, PETER and JOHN SAUNDERS (1985), "The Lead Effect of Marketing Decisions," *Journal of Marketing Research,* Vol. 22 (February), pp. 54–65.

DOYLE, PETER and JOHN SAUNDERS (1990), "Multiproduct Advertising Budgeting," *Marketing Science,* Vol. 9, no. 2 (Spring), pp. 97–113.

DRUMWRIGHT, M. and R. J. DOLAN (1989), "An Experimental Test of the Effects of Bundling," Working paper, Harvard Business School, Cambridge, Mass.

DUBIN, JEFFREY A. (1986), "A Nested Logit Model of Space and Water Heat System Choice," *Marketing Science,* Vol. 5, no. 2 (Spring), pp. 112–124.

DUNN, THEODORE F. and RUTH ZIFF (1974), "PREP: A New Copy Testing System," *Journal of Advertising Research,* Vol. 14 (October), pp. 53–59.

DUTTA, BIPLAB K. and WILLIAM R. KING (1980), "A Competitive Scenario Modeling System," *Management Science,* Vol. 26, no. 3 (March), pp. 261–273.

EASINGWOOD, CHRISTOPHER J. (1973), "Heuristic Approach to Selecting Sales Regions and Territories," *Operations Research Quarterly,* Vol. 24, no. 4 (December), pp. 527–534.

EASINGWOOD, CHRISTOPHER J., VIJAY MAHAJAN, and EITAN MULLER (1983), "A Nonuniform Influence Innovation Diffusion Model of New Product Acceptance," *Marketing Science,* Vol. 2 (Summer), pp. 273–296.

EASTLACK, J. O. and A. G. RAO (1986), "Modelling Response to Advertising and Price Changes for 'V-8' Cocktail Vegetable Juice," *Marketing Science,* Vol. 5, no. 3 (Summer), pp. 245–259.

EASTLACK, J. O. and A. G. RAO (1989), "Advertising Experiments at the Campbell Soup Company," *Marketing Science,* Vol. 8, no. 1 (Winter), pp. 57–71.

EASTON G. and ARAUJO, L. (1986), "Networks, Bonding and Relationships in Industrial Markets," *Industrial Marketing and Purchasing,* Vol. 1, no. 1, pp. 8–25.

EBBINGHAUS, HERMANN (1902), *Grundzuge der Psychologie.* Leipzig: Viet.

EDELMAN, FRANZ (1965), "Art and Science of Competitive Bidding," *Harvard Business Review* (July/August), pp. 53–66.

EDWARDS, C. H., JR., and DAVID E. PENNEY (1990), *Calculus and Analytic Geometry,* 3rd ed., Vols. I and II. Englewood Cliffs, N.J.: Prentice-Hall.

EHRENBERG, A. S. C. (1965), "An Appraisal of Markov Brand Switching Models," *Journal of Marketing Research,* Vol. 2, pp. 347–363.

EHRENBERG, A. S. C. (1972), *Repeat-Buying: Theory and Applications.* Amsterdam: North-Holland.

EHRENBERG, A. S. C. (1981), *Data Reduction.* London: John Wiley.

EHRENBERG, A. S. C. (1988), *Repeat Buying: Facts, Theory and Data,* 2nd ed. New York: Oxford University Press.

EHRENBERG, ANDREW S. C., GERALD J. GOODHARDT, and T. PATRICK BARWISE (1990), "Double Jeopardy Revisited," *Journal of Marketing,* Vol. 54, no. 3 pp. 82–91.

EIN-DOR, PHILLIP and ELI SEGEV (1981), *A Paradigm for Management Information Systems.* New York: Praeger.

EINHORN, H. J. and R. M. HOGARTH (1985), "Ambiguity and Uncertainty in Probabilistic Inference," *Psychological Review,* Vol. 92, pp. 433–461.

EINHORN, HILLEL, ROBIN HOGARTH, and ERIC KLEMPNER (1977), "Quality of Group Judgment," *Psychological Bulletin,* Vol. 84, no. 1, pp. 158–172.

EISENHARDT, K. (1985), "Control: Organizational and Economic Approaches," *Management Science,* Vol. 31, pp. 134–149.

ELIASHBERG, JEHOSHUA (1980), "Consumer Preference Judgments: An Exposition with Empirical Applications," *Management Science,* Vol. 26, no. 1 (January), pp. 60–77.

ELIASHBERG, JEHOSHUA and R. CHATTERJEE (1985), "Analytical Models of Competition with Implications for Marketing: Issues, Findings and Outlook," *Journal of Marketing Research,* Vol. 22 (August), pp. 237–261.

ELIASHBERG, JEHOSHUA and R. CHATTERJEE (1986), "Stochastic Issues in Innovation Diffusion Models." In V. Mahajan and Y. Wind, eds., *Innovation Diffusion Models of New Product Acceptance,* pp. 151–202. Cambridge, Mass.: Ballinger.

ELIASHBERG, JEHOSHUA and J. HAUSER (1985), "A Measurement Error Approach for Modelling Consumer Risk Preferences,"

Management Science, Vol. 31, no. 1 (January), pp. 1–25.

ELIASHBERG, JEHOSHUA and K. HELSEN (1988), "Cross Country Diffusion Processes and Market Entry Timing," Working paper, Marketing Department, The Wharton School of the University of Pennsylvania.

ELIASHBERG, JEHOSHUA and A. P. JEULAND (1986), "The Impact of Competitive Entry in a Developing Market upon Dynamic Pricing Strategies," *Marketing Science,* Vol. 5 (Winter), pp. 20–36.

ELIASHBERG, JEHOSHUA, STEPHEN A. LATOUR, ARVIND RANGASWAMY, and LOUIS W. STERN (1986), "Assessing the Predictive Accuracy of Two Utility-Based Theories in a Marketing Channels Negotiation Context," *Journal of Marketing Research,* Vol. 23, no. 2 (May), pp. 101–110.

ELIASHBERG, JEHOSHUA and DONALD A. MICHIE (1984), "Multiple Business Goals Sets as Determinants of Marketing Research," *Journal of Marketing Research,* Vol. 21, no. 1 (February), pp. 75–88.

ELIASHBERG, JEHOSHUA and THOMAS S. ROBERTSON (1988), "New Product Preannouncing Behavior: A Market Signaling Study," *Journal of Marketing Research,* Vol. 25 (August), pp. 282–292.

ELIASHBERG, JEHOSHUA and R. STEINBERG (1987), "Marketing-Production Decisions for an Industrial Channel of Distribution," *Management Science,* Vol. 33, no. 8 (August), pp. 981–1000.

ELIASHBERG, JEHOSHUA, C. TAPIERO, and J. WIND (1987), "Diffusion of New Products in Heterogeneous Populations: Incorporating Stochastic Coefficients," Working paper #87–003, The Wharton School of the University of Pennsylvania.

ELIASHBERG, JEHOSHUA and R. L. WINKLER (1981), "Risk Sharing and Group Decision Making," *Management Science,* Vol. 27, no. 11, pp. 1221–1235.

ELROD, TERRY (1988), "Choice Map: Inferring a Product-Market Map from Panel Data," *Marketing Science,* Vol. 7, no. 1 (Winter), pp. 21–40.

EMERY, F. (1970), "Some Psychological Aspects of Price." In B. Taylor and G. Willis, eds., *Pricing Strategy,* pp. 98–111. Princeton, N.J.: Brandon Systems.

ENGEL, JAMES F. and MARTIN R. WARSHAW (1964), "Allocating Advertising Dollars by Linear Programming,"*Journal of Advertising Research,* Vol. 4 (September), pp. 42–48.

ENGELBRECHT-WIGGANS, RICHARD (1980), "Auctions and Bidding Models: A Survey," *Management Science,* Vol. 26, no. 2 (February), pp. 119–142.

ENGLAND, J. L. (1975), "Linear Learning Models for Two-Party Negotiations," *Journal of Conflict Resolution,* Vol. 19, pp. 682–707.

ERICKSON, GARY M. (1981), "Using Ridge Regression to Estimate Directly Lagged Effects in Marketing," *Journal of the American Statistical Association,* Vol. 76, no. 376 (December), pp. 766–773.

ERICKSON, GARY M. (1985), "A Model of Advertising Competition," *Journal of Marketing Research,* Vol. 22 (August), pp. 297–304.

ESKIN, GERALD J. (1985), "Tracking Advertising and Promotion Performance with Single Source Data," *Journal of Advertising Research,* Vol. 25, no. 1 , pp. 31–39.

ESKIN, G. J. (1973), "Dynamic Forecasts of New Product Demand Using a Depth of Repeat Model," *Journal of Marketing Research* 10 (May), pp. 115–129.

ESKIN, GERALD J. and PENNY H. BARON (1977), "Effects of Price and Advertising in Test Market Experiments," *Journal of Marketing Research,* Vol. 14 (November), pp. 499–508.

FADER, PETER S. and JOHN R. HAUSER (1987), "Implicit Coalitions in a Generalized Prisoner's Dilemma," Working paper #88–017 (October), Harvard Business School, Cambridge, Mass.

FARLEY, JOHN U. (1964), "An Optimal Plan for Salesmen's Compensation," *Journal of Marketing Research,* Vol. 1 (May), pp. 39–43.

FARLEY, JOHN U. and DONALD R. LEHMANN (1986), *Meta-analysis in Marketing:*

Generalization of Response Models. Lexington, Mass.: Lexington Books.

FARQUHAR, PETER H. (1984), "Utility Assessment Methods," *Management Science,* Vol. 30, no. 11 (November), pp. 1283–1300.

FARQUHAR, PETER H. and VITHALA R. RAO (1976), "A Balance Model for Evaluating Subsets of Multiattributed Items," *Management Science,* Vol. 22 (January), pp. 528–539.

FARRIS, PAUL W. and MARK S. ALBION (1980), "The Impact of Advertising on the Price of Consumer Products," *Journal of Marketing,* Vol. 44, no. 3 (Summer), pp. 17–35.

FARRIS, PAUL W. and ROBERT D. BUZZELL (1976), "Relationship Between Changes in Industrial Advertising and Promotion Expenditures and Changes in Market Share," Working paper #76–119, Marketing Science Institute, Cambridge, Mass. (December).

FARRIS, PAUL W. and ROBERT D. BUZZELL (1979), "Why Advertising and Promotional Costs Vary: Some Cross Sectional Analyses," *Journal of Marketing,* Vol. 43, no. 4 (Fall), pp. 112–122.

FARRIS, PAUL W. and ROBERT D. BUZZELL (1980), "A Comment on Modeling the Marketing Mix Decision for Industrial Products," *Management Science,* Vol. 26, no. 1 (January), pp. 97–100.

FAULHABER, G. R. and J. L. PANZAR (1977), "Optimal Two-Part Tariffs with Self-selection," Bell Laboratories Economic Discussion Paper #4.

FEDER, GERSHON and GERALD T. O'MARA (1982), "On Information and Innovation Diffusion: A Bayesian Approach," *American Journal of Agricultural Economics,* Vol. 64 (February), pp. 145–147.

FEICHTINGER, GUSTAV, ALFRED LUHMER, and GERHARD SORGER (1988), "Optimal Price and Advertising Policy for a Convenience Goods Retailer," *Marketing Science,* Vol. 7, no. 2 (Spring), pp. 187–201.

FERN, EDWARD F. and JAMES R. BROWN (1984), "The Industrial/Consumer Marketing Dichotomy: A Case of Insufficient Justification," *Journal of Marketing,* Vol. 48, no. 1 (Spring), pp. 68–77.

FERSHTMAN, CHAIM, VIJAY MAHAJAN, and EITAN MULLER (1990), "Marketshare Pioneering Advantage: A Theoretical Approach," *Management Science,* Vol. 36, no. 8 (August), pp. 900–918.

FESTINGER, LEON (1957), *A Theory of Cognitive Dissonance.* Evanston, Ill.: Row Peterson.

FINKBEINER, CARL T. and PATRICIA J. PLATZ (1986), "Computerized Versus Paper and Pencil Methods: A Comparison Study," Paper presented at the Association for Consumer Research Conference, Toronto (October).

FINN, A. (1988), "Print Ad Recognition Readership Scores: An Information Processing Perspective, " *Journal of Marketing Research,* Vol. 25, no. 2 (May), pp. 168–177.

FISHBEIN, MARTIN (1963), "An Investigation of Relationship Between Beliefs About an Object and the Attitude Toward the Object," *Human Relations,* Vol. 16, pp. 233–240.

FISHBEIN, MARTIN (1967), "Attitude and Prediction of Behavior." In M. Fishbein, ed., *Readings in Attitude Theory and Measurement,* pp. 477–492. New York: John Wiley.

FISHBEIN, MARTIN and L. AJZEN (1975), *Belief. Attitude, Intention and Behavior.* Reading, Mass.: Addison-Wesley.

FISHER, FRANK M. (1966), *The Identification Problem in Econometrics.* New York: McGraw-Hill

FISHER, J. C. and R. H. PRY (1971), "A Simple Substitution Model of Technological Change," *Technological Forecasting and Social Change,* Vol. 3, pp. 75–88.

FITZROY, PETER T. (1976), *Analytic Methods for Marketing Management.* New York: McGraw-Hill.

FOGELMAN-SOULIE, F., B. MUNIER, and M. F. SHAKUN (1983), "Bivariate Negotiations as a Problem of Stochastic Terminal Control," *Management Science,* Vol. 29, no. 7, pp. 840–55.

FOGG, C. D. and J. W. ROKUS (1973), "A Quantitative Method for Structuring A Profitable Salesforce," *Journal of Marketing,* Vol. 37, no. 3 (July), pp. 8–17.

FOLKES, VALERIE S. (1988), "Recent Attribution Research in Consumer Behavior: A Review and New Directions," *Journal of Consumer Research,* Vol. 14 (March), pp. 548–565.

FORBIS, J. L. and N. T. MEHTA (1979), "Economic Value to the Customer," McKinsey Staff Paper, pp. 1–10, McKinsey & Co. Chicago (February).

FORD, D. (1980), "The Development of Buyer-Seller Relationships in Industrial Markets," *European Journal of Marketing,* Vol. 14, nos. 5 and 6, pp. 75–88.

, FORD, D., H. HAKANSSON, and J. JOHANSSON (1986), "How Do Companies Interact?" *Industrial Marketing and Purchasing,* Vol. 1, no. 1, pp. 26–41.

FORD, NEIL M., ORVILLE C. WALKER, JR., and GILBERT A. CHURCHILL, JR. (1981), "Differences in the Attractiveness of Alternative Rewards Among Industrial Salespeople: Additional Evidence," Working paper, Marketing Science Institute, Cambridge, Mass.

FORNELL, CLAES and FRED L. BOOKSTEIN (1982), "Two Structural Equation Models: LISREL and PLS Applied to Consumer Exit-Voice Theory," *Journal of Marketing Research,* Vol. 19 (November), pp. 440–452.

FORSYTH, RICHARD, ed. (1984), *Expert Systems.* New York: Chapman and Hall.

FOTHERINGHAM, A. STEWART (1988), "Consumer Store Choice and Choice Set Definition," *Marketing Science,* Vol. 7, no. 3 (Summer), pp. 299–310.

FOURT, LOUIS A. and JOSEPH W. WOODLOCK (1960), "Early Prediction of Market Success for New Grocery Products," *Journal of Marketing,* Vol. 24 (October), pp. 31–38.

FRANK, RONALD E. (1962), "Brand Choice as a Probability Process," *Journal of Business,* Vol. 35 (January), pp. 43–56.

FRANK, RONALD E. (1966), "Use of Transformations," *Journal of Marketing Research,* Vol. 3, pp. 247–253.

FRANKE, GEORGE and GARY WILCOX (1987), "Alcoholic Beverage Advertising and Consumption in the United States, 1964–1984," *Journal of Advertising,* Vol. 16, no. 3, pp. 22–30.

FRASER, CYNTHIA and JOHN W. BRADFORD (1983), "Competitive Market Structure Analysis: Principal Positioning of Revealed Substitutabilities," *Journal of Consumer Research,* Vol. 10, (June), pp. 5–30.

FRASER, CYNTHIA and JOHN W. BRADFORD (1984), "Competitive Market Structure Analysis: A Reply," *Journal of Consumer Research,* Vol. 11 (December), pp. 842–847.

FRAZIER, GARY L. (1983), "On The Measurement of Interfirm Power in Channels of Distribution," *Journal of Marketing Research,* Vol. 20, no. 2 (May), pp. 158–166.

FRAZIER, GARY L. and JOHN O. SUMMERS (1984), "Interfirm Influence Strategies and Their Application Within Distribution Channels," *Journal of Marketing,* Vol. 48, no. 3 (Summer), pp. 43–55.

FRAZIER, GARY L. and JOHN O. SUMMERS (1986), "Perceptions of Interfirm Power and Its Use Within a Franchise Channel of Distribution," *Journal of Marketing Research,* Vol. 23, no. 2 (May), pp. 169–176.

FRENCH, SIMON (1986), *Decision Theory: An Introduction to the Mathematics of Rationality.* Chichester, West Sussex, England: Ellis Horwood Limited

FREY, ALBERT WESLEY (1955), *How Many Dollars for Advertising?* New York: Ronald Press.

FRIEDMAN, J. (1971), "A Noncooperative Equilibrium for Supergames," *Review of Economic Studies,* Vol. 28, pp. 1–12.

FUDENBERG, D. and J. TIROLE (1983a), "Learning-by-Doing and Market Performance," *Bell Journal of Economics,* Vol. 14, pp. 522–530.

FUDENBERG, D. and J. TIROLE (1983b), "Capital as a Commitment: Strategic Investment in Continuous Time," *Journal of Economic Theory,* Vol. 31, pp. 227–250.

FUDGE, W. K. and L. M. LODISH (1977), "Evaluation of the Effectiveness of a Model Based Salesman's Planning System by Field Experimentation," *Interfaces,* Vol. 8, no. 1, pt. 2 (November), pp. 97–106.

FULGONI, G. M. (1987), "The Role of Advertising—Is There One?" Presentation at 33rd Annual Conference of the Advertising Research Foundation.

GABOR, A. and C. W. J. GRANGER (1966), "Price as an Indicator of Quality: Report on an Inquiry," *Economica,* Vol. 33, no. 129 (February), pp. 43–70.

GALPER, MORTON (1979), "Communication Spending Decisions for Industrial Products: A Literature Review," Working paper, Marketing Science Institute, Cambridge, Mass.

GARDNER, YEHUDI A. and BURLEIGH B. COHEN (1966), "ROP Color and Its Effect on Newspaper Advertising," *Journal of Marketing Research,* Vol. 3 (November), pp. 365–371.

GASKI, JOHN F. (1984), "The Theory of Power and Conflict in Channels of Distribution," *Journal of Marketing,* Vol. 48, no. 3 (Summer), pp. 9–29.

GASKI, JOHN F. and JOHN R. NEVIN (1985), "The Differential Effects of Exercised and Unexercised Power Sources in a Marketing Channel," *Journal of Marketing Research,* Vol. 22, no. 2 (May), pp. 130–142.

GATIGNON, HUBERT (1984), "Toward a Methodology for Measuring Advertising Copy Effects," *Marketing Science,* Vol. 3, no. 4 (Fall), pp. 308–326.

GATIGNON, HUBERT, ERIN ANDERSON, and KRISTIAAN HELSEN (1989), "Competitive Reactions to Market Entry: Explaining Interfirm Differences," *Journal of Marketing Research,* Vol. 26, no. 1 (February), pp. 44–55.

GATIGNON, HUBERT, JEHOSHUA ELIASHBERG, and THOMAS S. ROBERTSON (1989), "Modeling Multinational Diffusion Patterns: An Efficient Methodology," Working paper, The Wharton School of the University of Pennsylvania.

GATIGNON, HUBERT and THOMAS S. ROBERTSON (1989), "Technology Diffusion: An Empirical Test of Competitive Effects,"

Journal of Marketing, Vol. 53, no. 1 (January), pp. 35–49.

GAUTSCHI, DAVID A. (1981), "Specification of Patronage Models for Retail Center Choice," *Journal of Marketing Research,* Vol. 18 (May), pp. 162–174.

GAUTSCHI, DAVID A. and M. CORSTJENS (1979), "Retail Patronage Models: An Empirical Testing of Specification and Trip Heterogeneity Issues." In J. P. Leonardi, ed., *Proceedings of the Sixth International Research Seminar in Marketing,* Senoinque, France. Aix en Provence.

GAUVIN, STÉPHANE, GARY L. LILIEN and KALYAN CHATTERJEE (1990), "The Impact of Information and Computer Based Training on Negotiators' Performance," *Theory and Decision,* 23, pp. 331–354.

GENERAL ELECTRIC COMPANY (1980), "Price-Share-Margin Computer Model." Internal memorandum.

GENSCH, DENNIS H. (1973), *Advertising Planning.* New York: Elsevier.

GENSCH, DENNIS H. (1979), "The Traveling Salesman's Subtour Problem," *AIIE Transactions,* Vol. 10, no. 4 (January), pp. 362–370.

GENSCH, DENNIS H. (1984), "Targeting the Switchable Industrial Customer," *Marketing Science,* Vol. 3, no. 1 (Winter), pp. 41–54.

GENSCH, DENNIS H. (1985), "Empirically Testing a Disaggregate Choice Model for Segments," *Journal of Marketing Research,* Vol. 22 (November), pp. 462–467.

GENSCH, DENNIS H. (1987), "Empirical Evidence Supporting the Use of Multiple Choice Models in Analyzing a Population," *Journal of Marketing Research,* Vol. 24 (May), pp. 197–207.

GENSCH, DENNIS, NICOLA ARERSA, and STEVEN P. MOORE, (1990), "A Choice Modelling Market Information System That Enabled ABB Electric to Expand Its Market Share," *Interfaces,* Vol. 20, no. 1 (January/February), pp. 6–25.

GENSCH, DENNIS H. and RAJSHEKHAR G. JAVALGI (1987), "The Influence of Involvement on Disaggregate Attribute Choice Models," *Journal of Consumer Research,* Vol. 14 (June), pp. 71–82.

GENSCH, DENNIS H. and W. W. RECKER (1979), "The Multinominal, Multiattribute Logit Choice Model," *Journal of Marketing Research,* Vol. 16 (February), pp. 124–132.

GENSCH, DENNIS H. and JOSEPH A. SVESTKA (1984), "A Maximum Likelihood Hierarchical Disaggregate Model for Predicting Choice of Individuals," *Journal of Mathematical Psychology,* Vol. 28, pp. 160–178.

GEOFFRION, ARTHUR M. (1975), "A Guide to Computer Assisted Methods of Distribution Systems Planning," *Sloan Management Review,* Vol. 16, no. 2 (Winter), pp. 17–38.

GEOFFRION, A. M. and G. W. GRAVES (1974), "Multicom modity Distribution System Design by Benders Decomposition," *Management Science,* Vol. 20, no. 5 (January), pp. 822–844.

GEOFFRION, ARTHUR M. and RICHARD F. POWERS (1980), "Facility Location Is Just the Beginning," *Interfaces,* Vol. 10, no. 2 (April), pp. 22–30.

GEOFFRION A. and J. J. VANROY (1979), "Caution: Common Sense Planning Methods Can Be Hazardous to Your Corporate Health," *Sloan Management Review,* Vol. 20 (Summer), pp. 31–42.

GERSTNER, EITAN and JAMES HESS (1987), "Why Do Hot Dogs Come in Packs of 10 and Buns in 8s or 12s? A Demand Side Investigation," *Journal of Business,* 60 (October), pp. 491–518.

GERSTNER, EITAN and DUNCAN HOLTHAUSEN (1986), "Profitable Pricing When Markets Overlap," *Marketing Science,* 5, (Winter), pp. 55–69.

GESSNER, GUY, WAGNER A. KAMAKURA, NARESH K. MALHOTRA, and MARK E. ZMIJEWSKI (1988), "Estimating Models with Binary Dependent Variables: Some Theoretical and Empirical Observations," *Journal of Business Research,* Vol. 16, no. 1, pp. 49–65

GHOSH, AVIJIT and C. SAMUEL CRAIG (1983), "Formulating Retail Location Strategy in a Changing Environment," *Journal of Marketing,* Vol. 47, no. 3 (Summer), pp. 56–68.

GHOSH, AVIJIT and C. SAMUEL CRAIG (1986), "An Approach to Determining Optimal Locations for New Services," *Journal of Marketing Research,* Vol. 23, no. 4 (November), pp. 354–362.

GHOSH, AVIJIT and SARAH L. McLAFFERTY (1982), "Locating Stores in Uncertain Environments: A Scenario Planning Approach," *Journal of Retailing,* Vol. 58, no. 4, (Winter), pp. 5–22.

GHOSH, AVIJIT, SCOTT NESLIN, and ROBERT SHOEMAKER (1984), "A Comparison of Market Share Models and Estimation Procedures," *Journal of Marketing Research,* Vol. 21 (May), pp. 202–210.

GIDDINGS, F. H. (1924), *The Scientific Study of Human Society.* Chapel Hill: University of North Carolina Press.

GIVON, MOSHE (1984), "Variety Seeking Through Brand Switching," *Marketing Science,* Vol. 3 (Winter), pp. 1–22.

GIVON, MOSHE and DAN HORSKY (1978), "Market Share Models as Approximators of Aggregate Heterogeneous Brand Choice Behavior," *Management Science,* Vol. 26 (September), pp. 43–56.

GIVON, MOSHE and DAN HORSKY (1979), "Application of a Composite Stochastic Model of Brand Choice," *Journal of Marketing Research,* Vol. 16, pp. 258–267.

GIVON, MOSHE and DAN HORSKY (1990), "Untangling the Effects of Purchase Reinforcement and Advertising Carryover," *Marketing Science,* Vol. 9, no. 2, (Spring), pp. 171–187.

GLAZE, R. and C. B. WEINBERG (1979), "A Sales Territory Alignment Program and Account Planning System." In R. Bagozzi, ed., *Sales Management: New Developments from Behavioral and Decision Model Research.* Cambridge, Mass.: Marketing Science Institute.

GOLDISH, LOUIS H., "Figures Do Lie: Real-Life Lessons for Technical Marketing Research," Technical Marketing Associates: Framingham, MA.

GOLDMAN, M. B., H. E. LELAND, and D. S. SIBLEY (1984), "Optimal Nonuniform Pricing," *Review of Economic Studies,* Vol. 51 (April), pp. 305–320.

GOODHARDT, G. J. and A. S. C. EHRENBERG (1967), "Conditional Trend Analysis: A Breakdown by Initial Purchasing Level," *Journal of Marketing Research,* Vol. 4 (May), pp. 155–162.

GOODWIN, STEPHEN and MICHAEL ETGAR (1980), "An Experimental Investigation of Comparative Advertising: Impact of Message Appeal, Information Load and Utility of Product Class," *Journal of Marketing Research,* Vol. 17 (May), pp. 187–202.

GRASS, ROBERT C. (1968), "Satiation Effects of Advertising," 14th Annual Conference, Advertising Research Foundation, New York, New York.

GREEN, E. and R. PORTER (1984), "Non-Cooperative Collusion Under Imperfect Price Information," *Econometrica,* Vol. 52, pp. 87–100.

GREEN, H. L. and W. APPLEBAUM (1975), "The Status of Computer Applications to Store Location Research." Paper delivered at the Seventy-first Annual Meeting of the Association of American Geographers, Milwaukee, Wisconsin (April 23).

GREEN, PAUL E. (1975), "Marketing Applications of MDS: Assessment and Outlook," *Journal of Marketing,* Vol. 39 (January), pp. 24–31.

GREEN, PAUL E. (1984), "Hybrid Models for Conjoint Analysis: An Expository Review," *Journal of Marketing Research,* Vol. 21 (May), pp. 155–159.

GREEN, PAUL E., STEPHEN M. GOLDBERG, and MILA MONTEMAYOR (1981), "A Hybrid Utility Estimation Model for Conjoint Analysis," *Journal of Marketing,* Vol. 45 (Winter), pp. 33–41.

GREEN, PAUL E. and ABBA M. KRIEGER (1989), "Recent Contributions to Optimal Product Positioning and Buyer Segmentation," *European Journal of Operational Research,* Vol. 41, pp. 127–141.

GREEN, PAUL E. and ABBA M. KRIEGER (1991), "Modeling Competitive Pricing and Market Share: Anatomy of a Decision Support System," *Journal of the European Operational Research Society* (forthcoming).

GREEN, PAUL E., ABBA M. KRIEGER, and MA-NOJ K. AGARWAL (1991), "Adaptive Conjoint Analysis: Some Caveats and Suggestions," *Journal of Marketing Research,* Vol. 28, no. 2 (May), pp. 215–222.

GREEN, PAUL E., VIJAY MAHAJAN, STEPHEN M. GOLDBERG, and PRADEEP K. KEDIA (1984), "A Decision-Support System for Developing Retail Promotional Strategy," *Journal of Retailing,* Vol. 59, no. 3 (Fall), pp. 116–143.

GREEN, PAUL E. and VITHALA R. RAO (1972), *Applied Multidimensional Scaling.* New York: Holt, Rinehart and Winston.

GREEN, PAUL E. and V. SRINIVASAN (1978), "Conjoint Analysis in Consumer Research: Issues and Outlook," *Journal of Consumer Research,* Vol. 5 (September 1978), pp. 103–123.

GREEN, PAUL E. and V. SRINIVASAN (1990), "Conjoint Analysis in Marketing Research: New Developments and Directions," *Journal of Marketing,* Vol. 54, no. 4 (October), pp. 3–19.

GREEN, PAUL E. and DONALD S. TULL (1975), *Research for Marketing Decisions,* 3rd ed. Englewood Cliffs, N.J.: Prentice Hall.

GREEN, PAUL E. and Y. WIND (1973), *Multi-Attribute Decisions in Marketing.* Hinsdale, Ill.: Dryden Press.

GREENWALD, ANTHONY G. and CLARK LEAVITT (1984), "Audience Involvement in Advertising: Four Levels," *Journal of Consumer Research,* Vol. 11 (June), pp. 581–592.

GRETHER, E. T. (1983), "Regional-Spatial Analysis in Marketing," *Journal of Marketing,* Vol. 47, no. 4 (Fall), pp. 36–43.

GROSS, IRWIN (1972), "The Creative Aspects of Advertising," *Sloan Management Review,* Vol. 14 (Fall), pp. 83–109.

GROSSMAN, S. J. and O. D. HART (1983), "An Analysis of the Principal-Agent Problem," *Econometrica,* Vol. 51 (January), pp. 7–45.

GROVER, RAJIV and V. SRINIVASNAN (1987), "A Simultaneous Approach to Market Segmentation and Market Structuring," *Journal of Marketing Research,* Vol. 24 (May), pp. 139–153.

GUADAGNI, PETER M. and JOHN D. C. LITTLE (1983), "A Logit Model of Brand Choice Calibrated on Scanner Data," *Marketing Science,* Vol. 2, no. 3 (Summer), pp. 203–238.

GUADAGNI, PETER M. and JOHN D. C. LITTLE (1987), "When and What to Buy: A Nested Logit Model of Coffee Purchase," Working Paper #1919–87, Sloan School of Management, Massachusetts Institute of Technology, Cambridge, Mass. (August).

GUPTA, SUNIL (1988), "Impact of Sales Promotion on When, What, and How Much to Buy," *Journal of Marketing Research,* Vol. 25 (November), pp. 342–355.

GUPTA, SUNIL (1989), "Modeling Integrative, Multiple Issue Bargaining," *Management Science,* Vol. 35, no. 7.

GUPTA, SUNIL (1990), "Testing the Emergence and Effect of the Reference Outcome in an Integrative Bargaining Situation," *Marketing Letters,* Vol. 1, no. 2, pp. 103–112.

GUPTA, S. and Z. A. LIVNE (1988), "Resolving Conflict Situations with a Reference Outcome: An Axiomatic Model," *Management Science,* Vol. 34, no. 11, pp. 1303–1314.

HAAS, ROBERT W. (1989). *Industrial Marketing Management: Text and Cases,* 4th ed. Boston: Kent.

HAGERTY, MICHAEL R. and DAVID A. AAKER (1984), "A Normative Model of Consumer Information Processing," *Marketing Science,* Vol. 3, no. 3 (Summer), pp. 227–246.

HAINES, G. (1964), "A Theory of Market Behavior After Innovation," *Management Science,* Vol. 10 (July), pp. 634–658.

HAINES, GEORGE H. (1974), "Process Models of Consumer Decision Making." In G. D. Hughes and M. L. Ray, eds, *Buyer/Consumer Information Processing.* Chapel Hill: University of North Carolina Press.

HAINES, G. (1984), "A Theory of Market Behavior After Innovation," *Management Science,* Vol. 10 (July), pp. 634–658.

HAKANSSON, HAKAN, ed. (1982), *International Marketing and Purchasing of Industrial Goods: An Interaction Approach.* Chichester, England: John Wiley.

HAKANSSON, HAKAN and BJORN WOOTZ (1979), "A Framework of Industrial Buying and Selling," *Industrial Marketing Management,* Vol. 8, pp. 28–39.

HALEY, RUSSELL L. (1978), "Sales Effects of Media Weight," *Journal of Advertising Research,* Vol. 18, pp. 9–18.

HANSON, WARD and R. KIPP MARTIN (1990), "Optimal Bundle Pricing," *Management Science,* Vol. 36, no. 2, pp. 155–174.

HANSSENS, DOMINIQUE M. (1980), "Marketing Response, Competitive Behavior, and Time Series Analysis," *Journal of Marketing Research,* Vol. 17 (November), pp. 470–485.

HANSSENS, DOMINIQUE M. and BARTON A. WEITZ (1980), "The Effectiveness of Industrial Print Advertisements Across Product Categories," *Journal of Marketing Research,* Vol. 17 (August), pp. 294–306.

HANSSENS, DOMINIQUE M., LEONARD J. PARSONS, and RANDALL L. SCHULTZ (1990), *Market Response Models: Econometric and Time Series Analysis.* Boston: Kluwer.

HARARY, F. and B. LIPSTEIN (1962), "The Dynamics of Brand Loyalty: A Markovian Approach," *Operations Research,* Vol. 10, pp. 19–40.

HARMAN, PAUL and DAVID KING (1985), *Expert Systems.* New York: John Wiley.

HARRELL, STEPHEN G. and ELRNER D. TAYLOR (1981), "Modeling the Product Life Cycle for Consumer Durables," *Journal of Marketing,* Vol. 45, no. 4 (Fall), pp. 68–75.

HARRIS, M. and A. RAVIV (1979), "Optimal Incentive Contracts with Imperfect Information," *Journal of Economic Theory,* Vol. 20, pp. 231–259.

HARSANYI, J. C. (1955), "Cardinal Welfare, Individualistic Ethics and Interpersonal Comparison of Utility," *Journal of Political Economy,* Vol. 63, pp. 309–321.

HARSHMAN, RICHARD A., PAUL E. GREEN, YORAM WIND, and MARGARET E. LUNDY (1982), "A Model for the Analysis of

Asymmetric Data in Marketing Research," *Marketing Science,* Vol. 1, no. 2 (Spring), pp. 205–242.

HART, O. and B. HOLMSTROM (1987), "The Theory of Contracts." In T. Bewley, ed., *Advances in Economic Theory,* Fifth World Congress. New York: Cambridge University Press.

HARTUNG, P. H. and J. C. FISHER (1965), "Brand Switching and Mathematical Programming in Market Expansion," *Management Science,* Vol. 11 (August), pp. B231-B243.

HAUSER, JOHN R. (1978), "Testing the Accuracy, Usefulness, and Significance of Probabilistic Choice Models: An Information Theoretic Approach," *Operations Research,* 26 (May/June), pp. 406–421.

HAUSER, JOHN R. (1984), "Consumer Research to Focus R&D Projects," *Journal of Product Innovation and Management,* Vol. 2, pp. 70–84.

HAUSER, JOHN R. (1986), "Agendas and Consumer Choice," *Journal of Marketing Research,* Vol. 23 (August), pp. 199–212.

HAUSER, JOHN R. (1988), "Competitive Price and Positioning Strategies," *Marketing Science,* Vol. 7, no.1 (Winter), pp. 76–91.

HAUSER, JOHN R. and STEVEN P. GASKIN (1984), "Application of the 'DEFENDER' Consumer Model," *Marketing Science,* Vol. 3, no.4 (Fall), pp. 327–351.

HAUSER, JOHN R. and F. S. KOPPELMAN (1979), "The Relative Accuracy and Usefulness of Alternative Perceptual Mapping Techniques," *Journal of Marketing Research,* Vol. 14, no. 3 (November), pp. 495–507.

HAUSER, JOHN R., JOHN H. ROBERTS, and GLEN L. URBAN (1983), "Forecasting Sales of a New Durable." In Fred S. Zufryden, ed., *Advances and Practices of Marketing Science Management,* pp. 115–128. Providence, R.I.: The Institute of Management Science.

HAUSER, JOHN R. and STEVEN M. SHUGAN (1980), "Intensity Measures of Consumer Preference," *Operations Research,* Vol. 28, no. 2 (March/April), pp. 278–320.

HAUSER, JOHN R. and STEVEN M. SHUGAN (1983), "Defensive Marketing Strategies," *Marketing Science,* Vol. 3 (Fall), pp. 327–351.

HAUSER, JOHN R. and GLEN L. URBAN (1977), "A Normative Methodology for Modeling Consumer Response to Innovation," *Operations Research,* Vol. 25, no. 4 (July/August), pp. 579–619.

HAUSER, JOHN R. and GLEN L. URBAN (1979), "Assessment of Attribute Importances and Consumer Utility Functions: Von Neuman-Morganstern Theory Applied to Consumer Behavior," *Journal of Consumer Research,* Vol. 5 (March), pp. 251–262.

HAUSER, JOHN R. and GLEN L. URBAN (1986), "The Value Priority Hypotheses for Consumer Budget Plans," *Journal of Consumer Research,* Vol. 12 (March), pp. 449–462.

HAUSER, JOHN R. and BIRGER WERNERFELT (1988), "Existence and Uniqueness of Price Equilibria in DEFENDER," *Marketing Science,* Vol. 7, no. 1 (Winter), pp. 92–93.

HAUSER, JOHN R. and BIRGER WERNERFELT (1990), "An Evaluation Cost Model of Consideration Sets," *Journal of Consumer Research,* Vol. 16 (March), pp. 393–408.

HAUSER, JOHN R. and KENNETH J. WISNIEWSKI (1982a), "Dynamic Analysis of Consumer Response to Marketing Strategies," *Management Science,* Vol. 28, no. 5 (May), pp. 455–486.

HAUSER, JOHN R. and KENNETH J. WISNIEWSKI (1982b), "Application, Predictive Test, and Strategy Implications for a Dynamic Model of Consumer Response," *Marketing Science,* Vol. 1, no. 2 (Spring), pp. 143–179.

HAX, ARNOLDO (1975), "A Comment on 'The Distribution System Simulator,'" *Management Science,* Vol. 21, no. 2 (October), pp. 233–236.

HAX, ARNOLDO C. and NICOLAS S. MAJLUF (1982), "Competitive Cost Dynamics: The Experience Curve," *Interfaces,* Vol. 12, no. 5 (October), pp. 50–61.

HAYES-ROTH, FREDERICK, DONALD A. WATER-

MAN, and DOUGLAS B. LENAT, eds. (1983), *Building Expert Systems.* Reading, Mass.: Addison-Wesley.

HELSON, H. (1964), *Adaptation-Level Theory.* New York: Harper & Row.

HENDON, DONALD W. (1973), "How Mechanical Factors Affect Ad Perception," *Journal of Advertising Research,* Vol. 13, no. 4, pp. 39–46.

HERBIG, PAUL A. (1991), A Cusp Catastrophe Model of the Adoption of an Industrial Innovation," *Journal of Product Innovation Management,* Vol. 8, no. 2 (June), pp. 127–137.

HERSHEY, JOHN C., HOWARD C. KUNREUTHER, and PAUL J. H. SCHOEMAKER (1982), "Sources of Bias in Assessment Procedures for Utility Functions," *Management Science,* Vol. 28, no. 8 (August), pp. 936–954.

HESKETT, JAMES L. (1977), "Logistics—Essential to Strategy," *Harvard Business Review* (November/December), pp. 85–96.

HESS, S. W. and S. A. SAMUELS (1971), "Experiences with a Sales Districting Model: Criteria and Implementation," *Management Science,* Vol. 18, no. 4, pt. 2 (December), pp. 41–54.

HIEBERT, L. DEAN (1974), "Risk, Learning and the Adoption of Fertilizer Responsive Seed Varieties," *American Journal of Agricultural Economics,* Vol. 56 (November), pp. 764–768.

HINKLE, CHARLES L. (1965), "The Strategy of Price Deals," *Harvard Business Review* (July/August), pp. 75–84.

HIRSCHMAN, ELIZABETH C. (1981), "Retail Research and Theory." In B. Enis and K. Roering, eds., *Review of Marketing,* pp. 120–133. Chicago: American Marketing Association.

HLAVAC, T. E., JR., and J. D. C. LITTLE (1970), "A Geographic Model of an Urban Automobile Market." In D. Montgomery and G. L. Urban, eds., *Applications of Management Sciences in Marketing.* Englewood Cliffs, N.J.: Prentice Hall.

HODOCK, CALVIN J. (1980), "Copy Testing and Strategic Positioning," *Journal of Advertising Research,* Vol. 20 (February), pp. 33–38.

HOERL, ARTHUR E. and ROBERT W. KENNARD (1970), "Ridge Regression: Applications to Non-Orthogonal Problems," *Technometrics,* Vol. 12, no. 7 (February), pp. 69–81.

HOFMANS, PIERRE (1966), "Measuring the Cumulative Net Coverage of Any Combination of Media," *Journal of Marketing Research* (August), pp. 269–278.

HOFFMAN, DONNA L. and GEORGE R. FRANKE (1986), "Correspondence Analysis: Graphical Representation of Categorical Data in Marketing Research," *Journal of Marketing Research,* Vol. 23 (August), pp. 213–227.

HOGARTH, ROBIN (1987), *Judgment and Choice,* 2nd ed. New York: John Wiley.

HOLBROOK, MORRIS B., and D. V. HOLLOWAY (1984), "Marketing Strategy and the Structure of Aggregate, Segment-Specific, and Differential Preferences," *Journal of Marketing,* Vol. 48 (Winter), pp. 62–67.

HOLBROOK, MORRIS B., WILLIAM L. MOORE, and RUSSELL S. WINER (1982), "Constructing Joint Spaces from Pick-Any Data: A New Tool for Consumer Analysis," *Journal of Consumer Research,* Vol. 9 (June), pp. 99–105.

HOLMSTROM, B. (1979), "Moral Hazard and Observability," *Bell Journal of Economics,* Vol. 10, pp. 74–91.

HOLMSTROM, B. and P. MILGROM (1987), "Aggregation and Linearity in the Provision of Intertemporal Incentives," *Econometrica,* Vol. 55, no. 2 (March), pp. 303–320.

HOLMSTROM, B. and J. TIROLE (1989), "The Theory of the Firm," R. Schmalensee and R. D. Willing, eds., *Handbook of Industrial Organization,* Vol. 1. New York: Elsevier Science Publishers.

HOLTHAUSEN, DUNCAN M., JR., and GERT ASSMUS (1982), "Advertising Budget Allocation Under Uncertainty," *Management Science,* Vol. 28, no. 5 (May), pp. 487–499.

HORSKY, DAN (1976), "An Empirical Analysis of the Optimal Advertising Policy," *Management Science,* Vol. 23, (June), pp. 1037–1049.

HORSKY, DAN (1977), "Market Share Response to Advertising: An Example of Theory Testing," *Journal of Marketing Research,* Vol. 14, pp. 10–21.

HORSKY, DAN (1990), "A Diffusion Model Incorporating Product Benefits, Price, Income and Information," *Marketing Science,* Vol. 9, no. 4 (Fall), pp. 342–365.

HORSKY, DAN and KARL MATE (1988), "Dynamic Advertising Strategies of Competing Durable Good Producers," *Marketing Science,* Vol. 7, no. 4 (Fall), pp. 356–367.

HORSKY, DAN and PAUL NELSON (1989), "New Brand Positioning and Pricing in an Oligopolistic Market," Working paper, University of Rochester, Rochester, N.Y.

HORSKY, DAN and M. R. RAO (1984), "Estimation of Attribute Weights from Preference Comparisons," *Management Science,* Vol. 30, no. 7, pp. 801–822.

HORSKY, DAN and LEONARD S. SIMON (1983), "Advertising and the Diffusion of New Products," *Marketing Science,* Vol. 2 (Winter) pp. 1–10.

HOTELLING, H. (1929), "Stability in Competition," *Economic Journal,* Vol. 39, pp. 41–57.

HOWARD, JOHN A. (1989), *Consumer Behavior in Marketing Strategy.* Englewood Cliffs, N.J.: Prentice Hall.

HOWARD, JOHN A. and JAGDISH N. SHETH (1969), *The Theory of Buyer Behavior.* New York: John Wiley.

HUBER, GEORGE P. (1981), "The Nature of Organizational Decision Making and the Design of Decision Support Systems," *MIS Quarterly* (June), pp. 1–10.

HUBER, JOEL and JOHN MCCANN (1982), "The Impact of Inferential Beliefs on Product Evaluations," *Journal of Marketing Research,* Vol. 19 (August), pp. 324–333.

HUDSON, C. L. (1971), "Buying-Selling: Greater Integration in the Seventies," *Industrial Marketing Management,* Vol. 1, no. 1, pp. 59–79.

HUFF, DAVID L. (1962), "Determination of Inter-Urban Retail Trade Areas," Los Angeles: University of California, Real Estate Research Program.

HUFF, DAVID L. (1963), "A Probabilistic Analysis of Consumer Spatial Behavior." In W. S. Decker, ed., *Emerging Concepts in Marketing.* Chicago: American Marketing Association.

HUFF, DAVID L. (1964), "Defining and Estimating a Trading Area," *Journal of Marketing,* Vol. 28 (July), pp. 34–38.

HUFF, DAVID L. and ROLAND T. RUST (1984), "Measuring the Convenience of Market Areas," *Journal of Marketing,* Vol. 49, no. 1 (Winter), pp. 68–74

HUGHES, G. DAVID (1974), "The Measurement of Beliefs and Attitudes." In R. Ferber, ed., *The Handbook of Marketing Research,* pp. 3.16–3.43. New York: McGraw-Hill.

HUSTAD, THOMAS P., CHARLES S. MAYER, and THOMAS W. WIPPLE (1975), "Consideration of Context Differences in Product Evaluation and Market Segmentation," *Journal of the Academy of Marketing Science,* Vol. 3 (Winter), pp. 34–47.

HUTCHINSON, J. WESLEY (1986), "Discrete Attribute Models of Brand Switching," *Marketing Science,* Vol. 5, no.4 (Fall), pp. 350–371.

HUTT, MICHAEL D. and THOMAS W. SPEH (1989), *Business Marketing Management,* 3rd ed. Chicago: Dryden Press.

HUXLEY, THOMAS H. (1953), "Education Value of Natural History Sciences." In P. P. Wiener, ed., *Readings in Philosophy of Science.* New York: Scribner.

INFORMATION RESOURCES INC. (1985), "ASSESSOR-FIT: The Next Generation" (Chicago, IL: Information Resource).

INTERMARCO, Ltd. (1971), *Advertising Planning by Media-Planex.* London: Author.

IVES, B. and M. H. OLSON (1984), "User Involvement and MIS Success: A Review of Research," *Management Science,* Vol. 30 (May), pp. 586–603.

JACOBSON, ROBERT (1990a), "Unobservable Effects and Business Performance," *Marketing Science,* Vol. 9, no. 1 (Winter), pp. 74–85.

JACOBSON, ROBERT (1990b), " 'Unobservable Effects and Business Performance,' Reply to the Comments of Boulding and

Buzzell," *Marketing Science,* Vol. 9, no. 1 (Winter), pp. 92–95.

JAGPAL, HARSHARANJEET S. (1981), "Measuring Joint Advertising Effects in Multiproduct Firms," *Journal of Advertising Research,* Vol. 21, no. 1, pp. 65–69.

JAGPAL, HARSHARANJEET S., EPHRAIM F. SUDIT, and HRISHIKESH D. VINOD (1979), "A Model of Sales Response to Advertising Interactions," *Journal of Advertising Research,* Vol. 19 (June), pp. 41–47.

JAIN, DIPAK C., VIJAY MAHAJAN, and EITAN MULLER (1989), "Innovation Diffusion in the Presence of Supply Restrictions," Working paper, Cox School of Business, Southern Methodist University, Dallas, Tex.

JAIN, DIPAK C. and KALYAN RAMAN (1990), "Using Stochastic Calculus to Model Uncertainty in Dynamic Systems," J. Sheth, ed. *Research in Marketing,* Vol. 10, JAI Press Inc., Greenwich, CN.

JAIN, DIPAK C. and RAM C. RAO (1990), "Effect of Price on the Demand for Durables: Modeling, Estimation and Findings," *Journal of Business and Economic Statistics,* Vol 8 No. 2 (April), pp. 163–170.

JEULAND, ABEL P. (1978), "Brand Preference over Time: A Partially Deterministic Operationalization of the Notion of Variety-Seeking," *Proceedings,* Educators' Conference, Series No. 43. Chicago: American Marketing Association.

JEULAND, ABEL P. (1979), "Brand Choice Inertia as One Aspect of the Notion of Brand Loyalty," *Management Science,* Vol. 25 (July), pp. 671–682.

JEULAND, ABEL P., FRANK BASS, and GORDON WRIGHT (1980), "A Multibrand Stochastic Model Compounding Heterogeneous Erlang Timing and Multinomial Choice Processes," *Operations Research,* Vol. 28, no. 2 (March/April), pp. 255–277.

JEULAND, ABEL P. and ROBERT J. DOLAN (1982), "An Aspect of New Product Planning: Dynamic Pricing," In A. A. Zoltners, ed., *Marketing Planning Models,* pp. 1–21, TIMS Studies in the Management Sciences, Vol. 18; New York: North-Holland.

JEULAND, ABEL P. and CHARKRAVARTHI NARASIMHAN (1985), "Dealing—Temporary Price Cuts—by Seller as a Buyer Discrimination Mechanism," *Journal of Business,* Vol. 58, no. 3, pp. 295–308.

JEULAND, ABEL P. and S. SHUGAN (1983), "Managing Channel Profits," *Marketing Science,* Vol. 2 (Summer), pp. 239–272.

JOHANSSON, J. K. (1979), "Advertising and the S-Curve: A New Approach," *Journal of Marketing Research,* Vol. 16 (August), pp. 345–354.

JOHN, GEORGE and TORGER REVE (1982), "The Reliability and Validity of Key Informant Data from Dyadic Relationships in Marketing Channels," *Journal of Marketing Research,* Vol. 19, no. 4 (November), pp. 517–524.

JOHN, GEORGE and BARTON WEITZ (1989), "Salesforce Compensation: An Empirical Investigation of Factors Related to Use of Salary Versus Incentive Compensation," *Journal of Marketing Research,* Vol. 26 (February), pp. 1–14.

JOHNSON, ERIC J. and JOHN W. PAYNE (1985), "Effort and Accuracy in Choice," *Management Science,* Vol. 31, no.4 (April), pp. 395–414.

JOHNSON, ERIC J. and J. EDWARD RUSSO (1984), "Product Familiarity and Learning New Information," *Journal of Consumer Research,* Vol. 11 (June), pp. 542–550.

JOHNSON, JAMES E. and DONALD F. WOOD (1986), *Contemporary Physical Distribution and Logistics,* 3rd ed. New York: Macmillan.

JOHNSON, MICHAEL D. (1984), "Consumer Choice Strategies for Comparing Noncomparable Alternatives," *Journal of Consumer Research,* Vol. 11 (December), pp. 741–753.

JOHNSON, MICHAEL D. (1986), "Modeling Choice Strategies for Noncomparable Alternatives," *Marketing Science,* no. 1 (Winter), pp. 37–54.

JOHNSON, MICHAEL D. (1988), "Comparability and Hierarchical Processing in Multialternative Choice," *Journal of Consumer Research,* Vol. 15 (December), pp. 303–314.

JOHNSON, MICHAEL D. (1989), "The Differential Processing of Product Category and Noncomparable Choice Alternatives," *Journal of Consumer Research,* Vol. 16, no. 3 (December), pp. 300–308.

JOHNSON, RICHARD M. (1974), "Tradeoff Analysis of Consumer Values," *Journal of Marketing Research,* Vol. 11 (May), pp. 121–127.

JOHNSON, RICHARD M. (1975), "A Simple Method for Pairwise Monotone Regression," *Psychometrika,* Vol. 40 (June), pp. 163–168.

JOHNSON, RICHARD M. (1987), "Adaptive Conjoint Analysis." In *Sawtooth Software Conference on Perceptual Mapping, Conjoint Analysis, and Computer Interviewing,* pp. 253–265. Ketchum, Idaho: Sawtooth Software.

JOHNSON, RICHARD M. (1991), "Comment on 'Adaptive Conjoint Analysis: Some Caveats and Suggestions,'" *Journal of Marketing Research,* Vol. 28, no. 2 (May), pp. 223–225.

JOHNSTON, JACK (1963), *Statistical Cost Analysis.* New York: McGraw-Hill.

JOHNSTON, J. (1984), *Econometric Methods,* 3rd ed. New York: McGraw-Hill.

JOLSON, M. A. and G. L. ROSSOW (1971), "The Delphi Process in Marketing Decision Making," *Journal of Marketing Research,* Vol. 8, pp. 443–448.

JONES, CHARLES (1985), "Strategic Issues in New Product Introduction" *Journal of Advertising Research* 25, (April/May), pp. 11–13.

JONES, J. PHILIP (1986), *What's in a Name,* Lexington, Mass.: Lexington Books.

JONES, J. M. (1973), "A Composite Heterogeneous Model for Brand Choice Behavior," *Management Science,* Vol. 19 (January), pp. 499–509.

JONES, J. MORGAN and CHRISTOPHER J. RITZ (1987), "Incorporating Distribution into New Product Diffusion Models," Working paper, Marketing Department, University of North Carolina, Chapel Hill.

JONES, J. M. and F. S. ZUFRYDEN (1981), "Relating Deal Purchases and Consumer Characteristics to Repeat Purchase Probability," *Journal of the Marketing Research Society,* Vol. 23, pp. 84–99.

JONES, J. M. (1982), "An Approach for Assessing Demographic and Price Influences on Brand Purchase Behavior," *Journal of Marketing,* Vol. 46 (Winter), pp. 36–46.

JÖRESKOG, K. (1969), "A General Approach to Confirmatory Maximum Likelihood Factor Analysis," *Psychometrica,* Vol. 34, pp. 183–202.

JÖRESKOG, K. (1970), "A General Method for the Analysis of Covariance Structures," *Biometrika,* Vol. 57, pp. 239–251.

JÖRESKOG, K. (1973), "A General Method for Estimating A Linear Structural Equation System." In A. Goldberger and O. D. Duncan, *Structural Equations in the Social Sciences,* pp. 85–112. New York: Academic Press.

JÖRESKOG, K. (1974), "Analyzing Psychological Data by Analysis of Covariance Matrices." In R. Atkinson, D. H. Krantz, R. D. Lucet, and P. Suppes, eds., *Contemporary Developments in Mathematical Psychology,* pp. 1–56. San Francisco: W. H. Freeman.

JÖRESKOG, K. and DAG SÖRBOM (1979), *Advances in Factor Analysis and Structural Equation Models.* Cambridge, Mass.: Abt Books.

JÖRESKOG, K. and DAG SÖRBOM (1986), *LISREL VI: Analysis of Linear Structural Relationships by Maximum Likelihood, Instrumental Variables and Least Squares Methods,* 4th ed. Mooresville, Ind.: Scientific Software.

KAHN, BARBARA E. and THERESE A. LOUIE (1988), "The Effects of Price Promotions on Brand Choice Behavior," Working Paper, Anderson School of Management, UCLA.

KAHN, BARBARA E. and THERESE A. LOUIE (1990), "The Effect of Retraction of Price Promotions on Brand Choice Behavior for Variety Seeking and Last-Purchase-Loyal Customers," *Journal of Marketing Research,* Vol. 27 (August), pp. 279–298.

KAHN, BARBARA E., MANOHAR U. KALWANI, and DONALD G. MORRISON (1986a), "Measuring Variety-Seeking and Reinforcement Behaviors Using Panel Data," *Journal of Marketing Research,* Vol. 23 (May), pp. 89–100.

KAHN, BARBARA E., DONALD G. MORRISON, and GORDON P. WRIGHT (1986b), "Aggregating Individual Purchases to the Household Level," *Marketing Science,* Vol. 5, no. 3 (Summer), pp. 260–268.

KAHNEMAN, DANIEL and AMOS TVERSKY (1979), "Prospect Theory: An Analysis of Decision Under Risk," *Econometrica,* Vol. 47 (March), pp. 263–291.

KALISH, SHLOMO (1983), "Monopolist Pricing with Dynamic Demand and Production Costs," *Marketing Science,* Vol. 2, no. 2 (Spring), pp. 135–159.

KALISH, SHLOMO (1985), "A New Product Adoption Model with Price, Advertising, and Uncertainty," *Management Science,* Vol. 31, no. 12 (December), pp. 1569–1585.

KALISH, SHLOMO (1988), "Pricing New Products from Birth to Decline: An Expository Review." In T. M. Devinney, ed., *Issues in Pricing: Theory and Research,* Chap. 6. Lexington, Mass.: Lexington Books.

KALISH, SHLOMO and GARY L. LILIEN (1986a), "A Market Entry Timing Model for New Technologies," *Management Science,* Vol. 32 (February), pp. 194–205.

KALISH, SHLOMO and GARY L. LILIEN (1986b), "Applications of Innovation Diffusion Models in Marketing." In Vijay Mahajan and Yoram Wind, eds., *Innovation Diffusion Models of New Product Acceptance.* Cambridge, Mass.: Ballinger.

KALISH, S. and P. NELSON (1991), "Can Monetary Utilities Be Measured and Other Related Issues," *Marketing Letters,* (forthcoming).

KALISH, SHLOMO and SUBRATA K. SEN (1986), "Diffusion Models and the Marketing Mix for Single Products." In Vijay Mahajan and Yoram Wind, eds., *Innovation Diffusion Models of New Product Acceptance.* Cambridge, Mass.: Ballinger.

KALWANI, MANOHAR U. (1979), "The Entropy Concept and the Hendry Partitioning Approach" Working Paper, Sloan School, MIT.

KALWANI, M. U. and D. G. MORRISON (1977), "A Parsimonious Description of the Hendry System," *Management Science,* Vol. 23, pp. 467–477.

KALWANI, MANOHAR U. and ALVIN J. SILK (1980), "Structure of Repeat Buying for New Packaged Goods," *Journal of Marketing Research,* Vol. 18 (August), pp. 316–322.

KAMAKURA, WAGNER A. and SIVA K. BALASUBRAMANIAN (1987), "Long-Term Forecasting with Innovation Diffusion Models: The Impact of Replacement Purchase," *Journal of Forecasting,* Vol. 6, no. 1, pp. 1–19.

KAMAKURA, WAGNER A. and SIVA K. BALASUBRAMANIAN (1988), "Long-Term View of the Diffusion of Durables," *International Journal of Research in Marketing,* Vol. 5, pp. 1–13.

KAMAKURA, WAGNER A. and RAJENDRA K. SRIVASTAVA (1984), "Predicting Choice Shares Under Conditions of Brand Interdependence," *Journal of Marketing Research,* Vol. 21 (November), pp. 420–434.

KAMAKURA, WAGNER A. and RAJENDRA K. SRIVASTAVA (1986), "An Ideal-Point Probabilistic Choice Model for Heterogeneous Preferences," *Marketing Science,* Vol. 5, no. 3 (Summer), pp. 199–218.

KAMIEN, M. and NANCY L. SCHWARTZ (1972), "Timing of Innovations under Rivalry," *Econometrica* 40 (January), pp. 43–60.

KAMIEN, M. and NANCY L. SCHWARTZ (1981), *Dynamic Optimization: The Calculus of Variations and Optimal Control in Economics and Management.* New York: North-Holland.

KAMIN, HOWARD (1988), "Why Not Use Single Source Measurements Now?" *Journal of Media Planning* (Spring), pp. 27–31.

KANNON, P. K. and G. P. WRIGHT (1991), "Modeling and Testing Structural Markets: A Nested Logit Approach," *Marketing Science,* Vol. 10, no. 1 (Winter), pp. 58–82.

KAPLAN, A. D. H., JOEL B. DIRLAM, and ROBERT F. LANZILLOTTI (1958), *Pricing in Big*

Business. Washington, D.C.: Brookings Institution.

KARAKAYA, FAHRI and MICHAEL J. STAHL (1989), "Barriers to Entry and Market Entry Decisions in Consumer and Industrial Goods Markets," *Journal of Marketing,* Vol. 53, no. 2 (April), pp. 80–91.

KASSARJIAN, HAROLD H. and WALTRAUB M. KASSARJIAN (1979), "Attitudes Under Low Commitment Conditions." In John C. Mahoney and Bernard Silverman, eds., *Attitude Research Plays for High Stakes.* Chicago: American Marketing Association.

KASULIS, JACK J., ROBERT F. LUSCH, and EDWARD F. STAFFORD (1979), "Consumer Acquisition Patterns for Durable Goods," *Journal of Consumer Research,* Vol. 6, (June), pp. 47–57.

KATAHIRA, HOTAKA (1990), "Perceptual Mapping Using Ordered Logit Analysis," *Marketing Science,* Vol. 9, no. 1 (Winter), pp. 1–17.

KEEFER, DONALD L., F. BECKLEY SMITH, JR., and HARRY B. BACK (1991), "Development and Use of a Modeling System to Aid a Major Oil Company in Allocating Bidding Capital," *Operations Research,* Vol. 39, no. 1, pp. 28–41.

KEEN, PETER G. W. (1981), "Value Analysis: Justifying Decision Support Systems," *MIS Quarterly* (March), pp. 1–15.

KEEN, PETER G. W. and MICHAEL S. SCOTT MORTON (1978), *Decision Support Systems: An Organizational Perspective.* Reading, Mass.: Addison-Wesley.

KEENEY, RALPH L. and CRAIG W. KIRKWOOD (1975), "Group Decision Making Using Cardinal Social Welfare Functions," *Management Science,* Vol. 22, no. 4 (December), pp. 430–437.

KEENEY, R. L. and G. L. LILIEN (1987), "New Industrial Product Design and Evaluation Using Multiattribute Value Analysis," *Journal of Product Innovation Management,* Vol. 4, no. 3 (September), pp. 185–198.

KEENEY, RALPH L. and HOWARD RAIFFA (1976), *Decisions with Multiple Objectives: Pref-erences and Value Tradeoffs.* New York: John Wiley.

KELLER, K. (1987), "Memory Factors in Advertising: The Effect of Advertising Retrieval Cues on Brand Evaluations," *Journal of Consumer Research,* Vol. 14 (December), pp. 316–333.

KELLER, KEVIN L. and RICHARD STAELIN (1989), "Assessing Biases in Measuring Decision Effectiveness and Information Overload," *Journal of Consumer Research,* Vol. 15 (March), pp. 504–508.

KEMENY, J. G. and L. J. SNELL (1962), "Preference Ranking: An Axiomatic Approach." In J. G. Kemeny and L. J. Snell, eds., *Mathematical Models in the Social Sciences,* pp. 9–23. New York: Ginn.

KENG, KAU AU and A. S. C. EHRENBERG (1984), "Patterns of Store Choice," *Journal of Marketing Research,* Vol. 21 (November), pp. 399–409.

KEON, JOHN W. and JUDY BAYER (1986), "An Expert System Approach to Sales Promotion Management," *Journal of Advertising Research,* Vol. 26, no. 3, pp. 19–28.

KERIN, ROGER, VIJAY MAHAJAN, and P. RAJAN VARADARAJAN (1990), *Strategic Market Planning.* Reading, Mass.: Allyn & Bacon.

KIMBALL, GEORGE E. (1957), "Some Industrial Applications of Military Operations Research Methods," *Operations Research,* Vol. 5 (April), pp. 201–204.

KINBERG, YORAM and AMBAR G. RAO (1978), "Branch Bank Expansion Planning." New York University, Working paper.

KING, MALCOLM and ALAN MERCER (1991), "Distributions in Competitive Bidding," *Journal of the Operational Research Society,* Vol. 42, no. 2 (February), pp. 151–155.

KLAHR, D. (1969), " A Monte Carlo Investigation of the Statistical Significance of Kruskal's Non-Metric Scaling Procedure," *Psychometrica,* Vol. 34, no. 3 (September), pp. 319–330.

KLINGMAN, DARWIN, NANCY PHILLIPS, DAVID STEIGER, ROSS WIRTH, and WARREN YOUNG (1986), "The Challenges and

Success Factors in Implementing an Integrated Products Planning System for Citgo," *Interfaces,* Vol. 16, no. 3 (May/June), pp. 1–19.

KLINGMAN, DARWIN, NANCY PHILLIPS, DAVID STEIGER, ROSS WIRTH, and WARREN YOUNG (1987), "The Successful Deployment of Management Science Throughout Citgo Petroleum Corporation," *Interfaces,* Vol. 17, no. 1 (January/February), pp. 4–25.

KOHLI, RAJEEV and R. SUKUMAR (1990), "Heuristics for Product-Line Design Using Conjoint Analysis," *Management Science,* Vol. 36, no. 12 (December), pp. 1464–1478.

KOHLI, RAJEEV and VIJAY MAHAJAN (1991), "A Reservation Practice Model for Optimal Pricing of Multiattribute Products in Conjoint Analysis," *Journal of Marketing Research,* Vol. 28 (August), pp. 347–354.

KOTLER, PHILIP (1965), "Computerized Media Planning: Techniques, Needs, and Prospects." In *Occasional Papers in Advertising.* Urbana, Ill.: American Academy of Advertising.

KOTLER, PHILIP (1971), *Marketing Decision Making: A Model Building Approach.* New York: Holt, Rinehart and Winston.

KOYCK, L. M. (1954), *Distributed Lags and Investment Analysis.* Amsterdam: North-Holland.

KRAPFEL, ROBERT E., JR. (1982), "An Extended Interpersonal Influence Model of Organizational Buyer Behavior," *Journal of Business Research,* Vol. 10, no. 2, pp. 147–157.

KREPS, D. and J. SCHEINKMAN (1983), "Quantity Precommitment and Bertrand Competition Yield Cournot Outcomes," *Bell Journal of Economics,* Vol. 14, pp. 325–337.

KREPS , D. P. and R. WILSON (1982), "Sequential Equilibria," *Econometrica,* Vol. 50, pp. 863–894.

KRIEWALL, MARY ANN ODEGAARD (1980), "Modeling Multi-person Decision Processes on a Major Consumption Decision," unpublished dissertation, Stanford University, Stanford, Calif.

KRISHNAMURTHI, LAKSHMAN (1981), "Modeling Joint Decision Making Through Relative Influence," unpublished dissertation, Stanford University, Stanford, Calif.

KRISHNAMURTHI, LAKSHMAN (1988), "Conjoint Models of Family Decision Making," *International Journal of Research in Marketing,* Vol. 5, pp. 185–198.

KRISHNAMURTHI, LAKSHMAN, JACK NARAYAN, and S. P. RAJ (1986), "Intervention Analysis of a Field Experiment to Assess the Buildup Effect of Advertising," *Journal of Marketing Research,* Vol. 23 (November), pp. 337–345.

KRISHNAMURTHI, LAKSHMAN and S. P. RAJ (1985), "The Effect of Advertising on Consumer Price Sensitivity," *Journal of Marketing Research,* Vol. 22 (May) pp. 119–129.

KRISHNAMURTHI, LAKSHMAN and S. P. RAJ (1988), "A Model of Brand Choice and Purchase Quantity Price Sensitivities," *Marketing Science,* Vol. 7, no. 1 (Winter), pp. 1–21.

KRISHNAMURTHI, LAKSHMAN and S. P. RAJ (1991), "An Empirical Analysis of the Relationship Between Brand Loyalty and Consumer Price Elasticity," *Marketing Science,* Vol. 10, no. 2 (Spring), pp. 172–183.

KRISTENSEN, KAI (1984), "Hedonic Theory, Marketing Research, and the Analysis of Complex Goods," *International Journal of Research in Marketing,* Vol. 1, no. 1, pp. 17–36.

KRUGER, MICHAEL W. (1987), "Steps Toward Mastering Trade Promotions, Commentary," *Marketing Science,* Vol. 6, no. 2 (Spring), pp. 147–149.

KRUGMAN, HERBERT E. (1972), "Why Three Exposures May Be Enough," *Journal of Advertising Research,* Vol. 12 (December), pp. 11–14.

KUEHN, ALFRED A. (1962), "Consumer Brand Choice—A Learning Process?" *Journal of Advertising Research,* Vol. 2 (December), pp. 10–17.

KUEHN, ALFRED A. and A. C. ROHLOFF (1967a), "Evaluating Promotions Using a Brand Switching Model." In P. Robinson, *Promotional Decisions Using Mathematical*

Models, pp. 50–85. Reading, Mass.: Allyn & Bacon.

KUMAR, K. RAVI and D. SUDHARSHAN (1988), "Defensive Marketing Strategies: An Equilibrium Analysis Based on Decoupled Response Function Models," *Management Science,* Vol. 34, no.7 (July), pp. 805–815.

KUNREUTHER, HOWARD (1969), "Extensions of Bowman's Theory of Scientific Decision-making," *Management Science,* Vol. 15 (April), pp. B415-N439.

KURITSKY, A. P., J. D. C. LITTLE, A. J. SILK, and E. S. BASSMAN (1982), "The Development, Testing and Execution of a New Marketing Strategy at AT&T Long Lines," *Interfaces,* Vol. 12, no. 6 (December), pp. 22–37.

LACKMAN, C. L. (1978), "Gompertz Curve Forecasting: A New Product Application," *Journal of the Market Research Society,* Vol. 20 (January), pp. 45–47.

LaForge, RAYMOND W. and DAVID W. CRAVENS (1985), "Empirical and Judgment-Based Sales-Force Decision Models: A Comparative Analysis," *Decision Sciences,* Vol. 16, no. 2 (Spring), pp. 177–195.

LaForge, RAYMOND W., DAVID W. CRAVENS, and GIPSIE B. RANNEY (1984), "Comparative Evaluation of Empirical Response Functions in Sales Management Decision Making," *Journal of Business Research,* Vol. 12, pp. 377–391.

LaForge, RAYMOND W., CHARLES W. LAMB, JR., DAVID W. CRAVENS and WILLIAM C. MONCRIEF, III (1989), "Improving Judgment Based Salesforce Decision Model Applications," *Journal of the Academy of Marketing Sciences,* Vol. 17, No. 2 (Spring), pp. 167–177.

LAL, RAJIV (1982), "A Theory of Compensation Plans," unpublished doctoral dissertation, Graduate School of Industrial Administration, Carnegie-Mellon University, Pittsburgh, Penn.

LAL, RAJIV (1986), "Delegating Pricing Responsibility to the Salesforce," *Marketing Science,* Vol. 5, no. 2 (Spring), pp. 159–168.

LAL, RAJIV (1988), "A Theory of Manufacturer Trade Deals and Retail Price Promotions," Working paper, Stanford University, Stanford, Calif. (May).

LAL, RAJIV (1990), "Improving Channel Coordination Through Franchising," *Marketing Science,* Vol. 9 (Fall), pp. 299–318.

LAL, RAJIV and V. SRINIVASAN (1988), "Salesforce Compensation Plans: A Dynamic Perspective," Research paper No. 999, Stanford University, Graduate School of Business, Stanford, Calif. (June).

LAL, R., D. OUTLAND, and R. STAELIN (1990), "Salesforce Compensation Plans: An Empirical Test of the Agency Theory Framework," Working paper, Fuqua School of Business, Duke University, Durham, N.C.

LAMBERT, Z. V. (1968), *Setting the Size for the Sales Force.* University Park: Pennsylvania State University Press.

LAMBIN, JEAN-JACQUES (1969), "Measuring the Profitability of Advertising: An Empirical Study," *Journal of Industrial Economics,* Vol. 19, pp. 86–103.

LAMBIN, JEAN-JACQUES (1970), *Modeles et Programmes de Marketing.* Paris: Presses Universitaires de France.

LAMBIN, JEAN-JACQUES (1972a), "A Computer On-Line Marketing Mix Model." *Journal of Marketing Research,* Vol. 11 (May), pp. 119–126.

LAMBIN, JEAN-JACQUES (1972b), "Is Gasoline Advertising Justified?" *Journal of Business,* Vol. 45, pp. 585–619.

LAMBIN, JEAN-JACQUES (1976), *Advertising, Competition and Market Conduct in Oligopoly over Time.* Amsterdam: North-Holland.

LAMBIN, JEAN-JACQUES, PHILLIPPE NAERT, and ALAIN BULTEZ (1975), "Optimal Marketing Behavior in Oligopoly," *European Economic Review,* Vol. 6, pp. 105–128.

LAMBKIN, MARY and G. S. DAY, "Evolutionary Processes in Competitive Markets: Beyond the Product Life Cycle," *Journal of Marketing,* Vol. 53 (July 1989), pp. 4–20.

LANCASTER, KELVIN (1966), "A New Approach to Consumer Theory," *Journal of Political Economy,* pp. 132–157.

LANCASTER, KELVIN (1979), *Variety, Equity and Efficiency.* New York: Columbia University Press.

LANCASTER, KENT M. and THOMAS C. MARTIN (1988), "Estimating Audience Duplication Among Consumer Magazines," *Journal of Media Planning* (Fall), pp. 22–28.

LANE, W. J. (1980), "Product Differentiation in a Market with Endogenous Sequential Entry," *The Bell Journal of Economics,* Vol. 11, no. 1 (Spring), pp. 237–260.

LANE, W. J. and S. N. WIGGINS (1981), "Quality Uncertainty, Repeat Purchases and First Entrant Advantages," Working Paper, Texas A&M University.

LARRÉCHÉ, JEAN-CLAUDE and REZA MOINPOUR (1983), "Managerial Judgment in Marketing: The Concept of Expertise," *Journal of Marketing Research,* Vol. 20 (May), pp. 110–121.

LARRÉCHÉ, JEAN-CLAUDE and DAVID B. MONTGOMERY (1977), "A Framework for the Comparison of Marketing Models: A Delphi Study," *Journal of Marketing Research,* Vol. 14, no. 4 (November), pp. 487–498.

LARRÉCHÉ, JEAN-CLAUDE and V. SRINIVASAN (1981), "STRATPORT: A Decision Support System for Strategic Planning," *Journal of Marketing,* Vol. 45, no. 4 (Fall), pp. 39–52.

LARRÉCHÉ, JEAN-CLAUDE and V. SRINIVASAN (1982), "STRATPORT: A Model for the Evaluation and Formulation of Business Portfolio Strategies," *Management Science,* Vol. 28, no. 9 (September), pp. 979–1001.

LATTIN, JAMES (1984), "A Model of Balanced Choice Behavior," Working paper, Graduate School of Business, Stanford University, Stanford, Calif.

LATTIN, JAMES M. (1987), "A Model of Balanced Choice Behavior," *Marketing Science,* Vol. 6, no. 1 (Winter), pp. 48–65.

LATTIN, JAMES M. (1988), "The Impact of Store Brands on the Nature of Manufacturer's Trade Deals and Retail Price Promotion," Working paper, Stanford University, Stanford, Calif. (January).

LATTIN, JAMES M. and RANDOLPH E. BUCKLIN (1989), "Reference Effects of Price and Promotion on Brand Choice Behavior," *Journal of Marketing Research,* Vol. 26 (August), pp. 299–310.

LATTIN, JAMES M. and LEIGH MCALISTER (1985), "Using a Variety-Seeking Model to Identify Substitute and Complementary Relationships Among Competing Products," *Journal of Marketing Research,* Vol. 22 (August), pp. 330–339.

LATTIN, JAMES M. and JOHN H. ROBERTS (1989), "Modeling the Role of Risk-Adjusted Utility in the Diffusion of Innovation," Research paper 1019, Graduate School of Business, Stanford University, Stanford, Calif. (October).

LAUGHLIN, PATRICK R. and P. CHRISTOPHER EARLEY (1982), "Social Combination Models, Persuasive Arguments Theory, Social Comparison Theory, and Choice Shift," *Journal of Personality and Social Psychology,* Vol. 42, no. 2, pp. 273–280.

LAURENT, GILLES and JEAN-NÖEL KAPFERER (1985), "Measuring Consumer Involvement Profiles," *Journal of Marketing Research,* Vol. 22 (February), pp. 41–53.

LAVIDGE, ROBERT J. and GARY A. STEINER (1961), "A Model for Predictive Measurement of Advertising Effectiveness," *Journal of Marketing* (October), pp. 59–67.

LAWLESS, MICHAEL W. and ROBERT J. FISHER (1990), "Sources of Durable Competitive Advantage in New Products," *Journal of Product Innovation Management,* Vol. 7, no. 1 (March), pp. 35–44.

LAWRENCE, R. J. (1975), "Consumer Brand Choice: A Random Walk?" *Journal of Marketing Research,* Vol. 12, pp. 314–324.

LAYMAN, P. L. (1986), "Computers Find Growing Use in Marketing of Chemicals," *Chemical and Engineering News* (July 21), pp. 9–13.

LAZEAR, EDWARD P. (1986), "Retail Pricing and Clearance Sales," *The American Economic Review,* Vol. 76, no. 1 (March), pp. 14–32.

LEARNER, D. (1961), "Mathematical Programming for Better Media Selection," Paper delivered at the 1961 Regional Convention, American Association of Advertising Agencies, New York.

LEARNER, D. B. (1965). "DEMON New Product Planning: A Case History" *Commentary* 7, (October).

LEAVITT, CLARK (1962), "The Application of Perception Psychology to Marketing." In Charles H. Hindersman, ed., *Marketing Precision and Executive Action*, pp. 430–437. Chicago: American Marketing Association.

LECKENBY, J. D. and K-H. JU (1989), "Advances in Media Decision Models." In J. Leigh and C. Martin, eds., *Current Issues & Research in Advertising*, Issue 2. Ann Arbor: University of Michigan, Division of Research.

LECKENBY, JOHN D. and SHIZUE KISHI (1984), "The Dirichlet Multinomial Distribution as a Magazine Exposure Model," *Journal of Marketing Research*, Vol. 21 (February), pp. 100–106.

LEE, T. C., G. JUDGE, and A. ZELLNER (1970), *Estimating the Parameters of the Markov Probability Model from Aggregate Time Series Data*. Amsterdam: North-Holland.

LEEFLANG, PETER S. H. and ANNE BOONSTRA (1982), "Some Comments on the Development and Application of Linear Learning Models," *Management Science*, Vol. 26, no. 11 (November), pp. 1233–1246.

LEEFLANG, P. S. H. (1974), *Mathematical Models in Marketing*. Stenfert Kroese: Leiden.

LEEFLANG, P. S. and J. C. REUYL (1984), "On the Predictive Power of Market Share Attraction Models," *Journal of Marketing Research*, Vol. 21 (May), pp. 211–215.

LEHMANN, DONALD R. (1971a), "Television Show Preference: Application of A Choice Model," *Journal of Marketing Research*, Vol. 8 (February), pp. 47–55.

LEHMANN, DONALD R. and KIM P. CORFMAN (1989), "The Importance of Others' Welfare: A Model and Application to the Bargaining Relationship," Working paper No. 89-AV-2 (April), Columbia Business School, Columbia University, New York.

LEIGH, T. W., DAVID B. MACKAY, and JOHN O. SUMMERS (1984), "Reliability and Validity of Conjoint Analysis and Self-Explicated Weights: A Comparison," *Journal of Marketing Research*, Vol. 21 (November), pp. 456–462.

LENK, PETER J. and AMBAR G. RAO (1987), "Forecasting the Effect of an Environmental Change on Marketing Performance: An Intervention Time-Series Approach," *International Journal of Forecasting*, Vol. 3, pp. 463–478.

LENK, PETER J. and AMBAR G. RAO (1990), "New Models From Old: Forecasting Product Adoption by Hierarchical Bayes Procedures," *Marketing Science*, Vol. 9, no. 1, pp. 42–53.

LEVITT, THEODORE (1965), "Exploit the Product Life Cycle" *Harvard Business Review* 43 (November/December), pp. 81–94.

LEONE, ROBERT P. (1987), "Forecasting the Effect of an Environmental Change on Marketing Performance: An Intervention Time Series Approach" *International Journal of Forecasting*, Vol. 3, pp. 463–478.

LICHTENSTEIN, S. and B. FISCHHOFF (1980), "Training for Calibration," *Organizational Behavior and Human Performance*, Vol. 26, pp. 149–171.

LIEBERMAN, M. (1984), "The Learning Curve and Pricing in the Chemical Processing Industry," *Rand Journal of Economics*, Vol. 15, pp. 213–228.

LIEBERMAN, MARVIN, B. and DAVID B. MONTGOMERY (1988), "First Mover Advantages," *Strategic Management Journal*, Vol. 9, pp. 41–48.

LILIEN, GARY L. (1974a), "A Modified Linear Learning Model of Buyer Behavior," *Management Science*, Vol. 20 (March), pp. 1027–1036.

LILIEN, GARY L. (1974b), "An Application of a Modified Linear Learning Model of Buyer Behavior," *Journal of Marketing Research*, Vol. 11 (August), pp. 279–285.

LILIEN, GARY L. (1975), "Model Relativism: A

Situational Approach to Model Building," *Interfaces*, Vol. 5, pp. 11–18.

LILIEN, GARY L. (1978), *A Study of Industrial Marketing Budgeting Descriptive Analysis—Final Report*. Cambridge: Massachusetts Institute of Technology Press (February).

LILIEN, GARY L. (1979), "Advisor 2: Modeling the Marketing Mix for Industrial Products," *Management Science*, Vol. 25, no. 2 (February), pp. 191–204.

LILIEN, GARY L. (1980), "Reply to Farris and Buzzell's Comment on ADVISOR 2 Paper," *Management Science*, Vol. 26, no. 1 (January), pp. 101–105.

LILIEN, GARY L. (1983), "A Descriptive Model of the Trade-Show Budgeting Decision Process," *Industrial Marketing Management*, Vol. 12, no. 1 (February) pp. 25–29.

LILIEN, GARY L. and AMBAR G. RAO (1976), "A Model for Allocating Retail Outlet Building Resources across Market Areas," *Operations Research*, Vol. 24 (January/February), pp. 1–14.

LILIEN, GARY L., AMBAR G. RAO, and SHLOMO KALISH (1981), "Bayesian Estimation and Control of Detailing Effort in a Repeat Purchase Environment," *Management Science*, Vol. 27, no. 5 (May), pp. 493–507.

LILIEN, GARY and DAVID WEINSTEIN (1984), "An International Comparison of the Determinants of Industrial Marketing Expenditures," *Journal of Marketing* (Winter), pp. 46–53.

LILIEN, GARY L. and M. ANTHONY WONG (1984), "An Exploratory Investigation of Structure of the Buying Center in the Metalworking Industry," *Journal of Marketing Research*, Vol. 21 (February), pp. 1–11.

LILIEN, GARY L. and EUNSANG YOON (1988), "An Exploratory Analysis of the Dynamic Behavior of Price Elasticity over the Product Life Cycle: An Empirical Analysis of Industrial Chemical Products." In T. M. Devinney, ed., *Issues in Pricing: Theory and Research*, Chap. 12. Lexington, Mass.: Lexington Books.

LILIEN, GARY L. and EUNSANG YOON (1989), "Determinants of New Industrial Product Performance: A Strategic Re-Examination of the Empirical Literature," *IEEE Transactions on Engineering Management*, Vol. 36 (February), pp. 3–10.

LILIEN, GARY L. and EUNSANG YOON (1990), "The Timing of Competitive Market Entry: An Exploratory Study of New Industrial Products," *Management Science*, Vol. 36, no. 5 (May), pp. 568–585.

LITTLE, JOHN D. C. (1966), "A Model of Adaptive Control of Promotional Spending," *Operations Research*, Vol. 14, pp. 1075–1097.

LITTLE, JOHN D. C. (1970), "Models and Managers: The Concept of A Decision Calculus," *Management Science*, Vol. 16, pp. B466-B485.

LITTLE, JOHN D. C. (1975), "BRANDAID: A Marketing Mix Model, Part I: Structure; Part II: Implementation," *Operations Research*, Vol. 23, pp. 628–673.

LITTLE, JOHN D. C. (1979a), "Decision Support Systems for Marketing Managers," *Journal of Marketing*, Vol. 43, no. 3 (Summer), pp. 9–27.

LITTLE, JOHN D. C. (1979b), "Aggregate Advertising Models: The State of the Art," *Operations Research*, Vol. 27, no. 4 (July/August), pp. 629–667.

LITTLE, JOHN D. C. (1986), "Comment on 'Advertising Pulsing Policies for Generating Awareness for New Products,'" *Marketing Science*, Vol. 5, no. 2 (Spring). pp. 107–108.

LITTLE, JOHN D. C. (1988), "Cover Story: An Expert System to Find the News in Scanner Data," Sloan School, MIT Working Paper.

LITTLE, JOHN D. C. (1990), "Information Technology in Marketing," Working paper #1860-87, revised, Sloan School of Management, Massachusetts Institute of Technology, Cambridge (September).

LITTLE, JOHN D. C. and LEONARD M. LODISH (1966), "A Media Selection Model and Its Optimization by Dynamic Programming," *Industrial Management Review*, Vol. 8 (Fall), pp. 15–23.

LITTLE, JOHN D. C. and LEONARD M. LODISH (1969), "A Media Planning Calculus," *Operations Research*, Vol. 17 (January/February), pp. 1–35.

LITTLE, JOHN D. C. and LEONARD M. LODISH (1981), "Commentary on 'Judgment Based Marketing Decision Models,'" *Journal of Marketing*, Vol. 45, no. 4 (Fall), pp. 24–29.

LIU, L. and D. HANSSENS (1981), "A Bayesian Approach to Time-Varying Cross-sectional Regression Models, "*Journal of Econometrics*, Vol. 15, pp. 341–356.

LOCKE, JAMES L. (1984), "Automatic Order Entry," *Industrial Management and Data Systems* (August), pp. 20–22.

LODISH, LEONARD M. (1971a), "Considering Competition in Media Planning," *Management Science*, Vol. 17 (February), pp. B293–306.

LODISH, LEONARD M. (1971b), "CALLPLAN: An Interactive Salesman's Call Planning System," *Management Science*, Vol. 18, no. 4, pt. 2 (December), pp. 25–40.

LODISH, LEONARD M. (1974), "'Vaguely Right' Approach to Sales Force Allocations," *Harvard Business Review*, Vol. 52 (January/February), pp. 119–124.

LODISH, LEONARD M. (1975), "Sales Territory Alignment to Maximize Profit," *Journal of Marketing Research*, Vol. 12 (February), pp. 30–36.

LODISH, LEONARD M. (1976), "Assigning Salesmen to Accounts to Maximize Profit," *Journal of Marketing Research*, Vol. 13 (November), pp. 440–444.

LODISH, LEONARD M. (1980), "A User Oriented Model for Sales Force Size, Product and Market Allocation Decisions," *Journal of Marketing*, Vol. 44 (Summer), pp. 70–78.

LODISH, LEONARD M. (1981), "Experience with Decision Calculus Models and Decision Support Systems." In R. Schultz and A. Zoltners, eds., *Marketing Decision Models*, pp. 165–182. New York: North-Holland.

LODISH, LEONARD M. (1982), "A Marketing Decision Support System for Retailers," *Marketing Science*, Vol. 1, no. 1 (Winter), pp. 31–56.

LODISH, LEONARD M., ELLEN CURTIS, MICHAEL NESS, and M. KERRY SIMPSON (1988), "Sales Force Sizing and Deployment Using a Decision Calculus Model at Syntex Laboratories," *Interfaces*, Vol. 18, no. 1 (January/February), pp. 5–20.

LONG, J. SCOTT (1983), "Confirmatory Factor Analysis," *Quantitative Applications in the Social Sciences*, Series No. 33. Beverly Hills, Calif.: Sage Publications.

LONGMAN, KENNETH A. (1968), "Remarks on Gross' Paper," *Proceedings of the 13th Annual Conference of the Advertising Research Foundation*. New York: Advertising Research Foundation.

LOUVIERE, JORDAN J. and DAVID A. HENSHER (1983), "Using Discrete Choice Models with Experimental Design Data to Forecast Consumer Demand for a Unique Cultural Event," *Journal of Consumer Research*, Vol. 10 (December), pp. 348–361.

LOUVIERE, JORDAN J. and GEORGE WOODWORTH (1983), "Design and Analysis of Simulated Consumer Choice or Allocated Experiments: An Approach Based on Aggregate Data," *Journal of Marketing Research*, Vol. 20 (November), pp. 350–367.

LUBATKIN, MICHAEL and MICHAEL PITTS (1983), "PIMS: Fad or Folklore," *Journal of Business Strategy*, Vol. 3 (Winter), pp. 38–44.

LUBATKIN, MICHAEL and MICHAEL PITTS (1985), "PIMS and the Policy Perspective," *Journal of Business Strategy*, (Summer), pp. 88–92.

LUCAS, HENRY C., JR. (1978), "The Evolution of an Information System: From Key-Man to Every Person," *Sloan Management Review*, Vol. 20 (Winter), pp. 39–52.

LUCAS, HENRY C., MICHAEL J. GINZBERG, and RANDALL L. SCHULTZ (1990), *Information Systems Implementation: Testing a Structural Model*. Norwood: NJ: Ablex.

LUCAS, HENRY C., C. B. WEINBERG, and K. CLOWES (1975), "Sales Response as a Function of Territorial Potential and Sales Representative Workload," *Jour-*

nal of Marketing Research, Vol. 12 (August), pp. 298–305.

LUCE, R. DUNCAN (1959), Individual Choice Behavior. New York: John Wiley.

LUENBERGER, DAVID G. (1984), Linear and Nonlinear Programming, Reading, Mass.: Addison-Wesley.

LUSCH, ROBERT F. and JAMES R. BROWN (1982), "A Modified Model of Power in the Marketing Channel," Journal of Marketing Research, Vol. 19, no. 3 (August), pp. 312–323.

LUTZ, RICHARD J. and JAMES R. BETTMAN (1977), "Multiattribute Models in Marketing: A Bicentennial Review." In A. Woodside, J. Sheth, and P. Bennett, eds., Consumer and Industrial Buying Behavior, pp. 137–149. New York: North-Holland.

LYNCH, JOHN G., JR. (1985), "Uniqueness Issues in the Decompositional Modeling of Multiattribute Overall Evaluations: An Information Integration Perspective," Journal of Marketing Research, Vol. 22 (February), pp. 1–19.

LYNCH, JOHN G., JR. and THOMAS SRULL (1982), "Memory and Attentional Factors in Consumer Choice: Concepts and Research Methods," Journal of Consumer Research, Vol. 9 (June), pp. 18–37.

MCAFEE, R. P. and J. MCMILLAN (1987), "Auctions," Journal of Economic Literature, Vol. 25, pp. 699–738.

MCALISTER, LEIGH (1982), "A Dynamic Attribute Satiation Model of Variety-Seeking Behavior," Journal of Consumer Research, Vol. 9 (September), pp. 141–150.

MCALISTER, LEIGH, MAX H. BAZERMAN, and PETER FADER (1986), "Power and Goal Setting in Channel Negotiations," Journal of Marketing Research, Vol. 23, no. 3 (August), pp. 228–236.

MCALISTER, LEIGH and EDGAR PESSEMIER (1982), "Variety Seeking Behavior: An Interdisciplinary Review," Journal of Consumer Research, Vol. 9 (December), pp. 311–322.

MCBRIDE, RICHARD D. and F. S. ZUFRYDEN (1988), "An Integer Programming Approach to the Optimal Product Line Se-

lection Problem," Marketing Science, Vol. 7, no. 2 (Spring), pp. 126–140.

MCCALL, J. and B. WARRINGTON (1984), Marketing by Agreement. London: John Wiley.

MCCANN, JOHN M. (1974), "Market Segment Response to the Marketing Decision Variables," Journal of Marketing Research, Vol. 11 (November), pp. 399–412.

MCCANN, JOHN M. (1986), The Marketing Workbench. New York: Dow-Jones-Irwin.

MCCANN, JOHN M. and JOHN P. GALAGHER (1988), "The Future of Marketing Systems: From Information to Knowledge Systems," Working paper, Duke University, Durham, N.C.

MCCANN, JOHN M., WILLIAM G. LAHTI, and JUSTIN HILL (1991), "The Brand Manager's Assistant: A Knowledge-Based System Approach to Brand Management," International Journal of Research in Marketing, Vol. 8, no. 1, pp. 51–73.

MCCANN, ROGER C. (1982), Introduction to Ordinary Differential Equation. New York: Harcourt Brace Jovanovich.

MCDONALD, COLIN (1971), "What Is the Short-Term Effect of Advertising?" Special Report No. 71–142, Marketing Science Institute, Cambridge, Mass. (February).

MCFADDEN, D. (1976), "Quantal Choice Analysis: A Survey," Annals of Economic and Social Measurement, (May), pp. 363–369.

MCFADDEN, DANIEL (1978), "Modelling the Choice of Residential Location." In A. Karlquist et al., eds., Spatial Interaction Theory and Residential Location. Amsterdam: North-Holland.

MCFADDEN, DANIEL (1980), "Econometric Models for Probabilistic Choice Among Products," Journal of Business, Vol. 53, no. 3, pt. 2 (July), pp. 513–530.

MCFADDEN, DANIEL (1986), "The Choice Theory Approach to Market Research," Marketing Science, Vol. 5, no.4 (Fall), pp. 275–297.

MCFADDEN, DANIEL (1991), "Advances in Computation, Statistical Methods and Testing of Discrete Choice Models,"

Marketing Letters, Vol. 2, no. 3 (August), pp. 215–230.

McGuire, T. and R. Staelin (1983), "An Industry Equilibrium Analysis of Downstream Vertical Integration," *Marketing Science,* Vol. 2 (Spring), pp. 161–192.

McGuire, T. and R. Staelin (1986), "Channel Efficiency, Incentive Compatibility, Transfer Pricing, and Market Structure: An Equilibrium Analysis of Channel Relationships." In Louis P. Bucklin, ed., *Research in Marketing,* Vol. 8. Greenwich, Conn.: JAI Press.

McGuire, William (1976), "A Bibliography of TV Copy Research," Unpublished manuscript, Advertising Research Foundation, New York.

McIntyre, Shelby H. (1982), "An Experimental Study of the Impact of Judgment-Based Marketing Models," *Management Science,* Vol. 28, no. 1 (January), pp. 17–33.

McIntyre, Shelby H. and Imran S. Currim (1982), "Evaluating Judgment-Based Marketing Models: Multiple Measures, Comparisons and Findings." In A. A. Zoltners, ed., *Marketing Planning Models,* pp. 185–207. *TIMS Studies in the Management Sciences,* Vol. 18. New York: North-Holland.

McKay, David B., Richard W. Olshavsky, and Gerald Sentell (1975), "Cognitive Maps and Spatial Behavior of Consumers," *Geographical Analysis,* Vol. 7, No. 1 (January), pp. 19–34.

McKay, David B. and Joseph L. Zinnes (1986), "A Probabilistic Model for the Multidimensional Scaling of Proximity and Preference Data," *Marketing Science,* Vol. 5, no. 4 (Fall), pp. 325–344.

Maffai, R. B. (1960a), "Brand Preference and Simple Markov Processes," *Operations Research,* Vol. 8, pp. 210–218.

Maffai, R. B. (1960b), "Planning Advertising Expenditures by Dynamic Programming Methods," *Industrial Management Review,* Vol. 1 (December), pp. 94–100.

Magat, Wesley A., John M. McCann, and Richard C. Morey (1986), "When Does Lag Structure Really Matter in Optimizing Advertising Expenditures," *Management Science,* Vol. 32, no. 2 (February), pp. 182–193.

Magat, Wesley A., John M. McCann, and Richard C. Morey (1988), "Reply to 'When Does Loag Structure Really Matter . . . Indeed?'" *Management Science,* Vol. 34, no. 7 (July), pp. 917–918.

Mahajan, Vijay, Paul S. Green, and Stephen M. Goldberg (1982), "A Conjoint Model for Measuring Self and Cross Price/Demand Relationships," *Journal of Marketing Research,* Vol. 19 (August), pp. 334–342.

Mahajan, Vijay, Charlotte H. Mason, and V. Srinivasan (1986), "An Evaluation of Estimation Procedures for New Product Diffusion Models." In Vijay Mahajan and Yoram Wind, eds., *Innovation Diffusion Models of New Product Acceptance.* Cambridge, Mass.: Ballinger.

Mahajan, Vijay and Eitan Muller (1979), "Innovation Diffusion and New Product Growth Models in Marketing," *Journal of Marketing,* Vol. 43 (Fall), pp. 55–68.

Mahajan, V. and E. Muller (1982), "Innovation Behavior and Repeat Purchase Diffusion Model," Proceedings, American Marketing Educators Conference (AMA: Chicago, IL), pp. 456–460.

Mahajan, Vijay and Eitan Muller (1986a), "Advertising Pulsing Policies for Generating Awareness for New Products," *Marketing Science,* Vol. 5, no. 2 (Spring), pp. 86–106.

Mahajan, Vijay and Eitan Muller (1986b), "Reflections on Advertising Pulsing Policies for Generating Awareness for New Products," *Marketing Science,* Vol. 5, no. 2 (Spring), pp. 110–111.

Mahajan, Vijay, Eitan Muller, and Frank M. Bass (1990), "New Product Diffusion Models in Marketing: A Review and Directions for Research," *Journal of Marketing,* Vol. 54 (January), pp. 1–26.

Mahajan, Vijay, Eitan Muller, and Roger A. Kerin (1984), "Introduction Strategy for New Products with Positive and Negative Word-of-Mouth," *Management Science,* Vol. 30 (December), pp. 1389–1404.

Mahajan, Vijay, Eitan Muller, and Sub-

HASH SHARMA (1984), "An Empirical Comparison of Awareness Forecasting Models of New Product Acceptance," *Marketing Science,* Vol. 3 (Summer), pp. 179–197.

MAHAJAN, VIJAY, EITAN MULLER, and RAJENDRA SRIVASTAVA (1990), "Determination of Adopter Categories by Using Innovation Diffusion Models," *Journal of Marketing Research,* Vol. 27 (February), pp. 37–50.

MAHAJAN, VIJAY and ROBERT A. PETERSON (1978), "Innovation Diffusion in a Dynamic Potential Adopter Population," *Management Science,* Vol. 24 (November), pp. 1589–1597.

MAHAJAN, VIJAY and ROBERT A. PETERSON (1979), "First-Purchase Diffusion Models of New-Product Acceptance," *Technological Forecasting and Social Change,* Vol. 15, pp. 127–146.

MAHAJAN, VIJAY and SUBHASH SHARMA (1986), "Simple Algebraic Estimation Procedure for Innovation Diffusion Models of New Product Acceptance," *Technological Forecasting and Social Change,* Vol. 30 (December), pp. 331–346.

MAHAJAN, VIJAY, SUBHASH SHARMA, and RICHARD A. BETTES (1988), "The Adoption of the M-Form Organizational Structure: A Test of the Imitation Hypothesis," *Management Science,* Vol. 34, no. 10 (October), pp. 1188–1201.

MAHAJAN, VIJAY, S. SHARMA and R. KERIN (1988), "Assessing Market Penetration Opportunities and Saturation Potential for Multi-Store, Multi-Market Retailers," *Journal of Retailing,* Vol. 64, no. 3 (Fall), pp. 315–333.

MAHAJAN, VIJAY, S. SHARMA and D. SRINIVAS (1985), "An Application of Portfolio Analysis for Identifying Attractive Retail Locations," *Journal of Retailing,* 61 (Winter), pp. 19–34.

MAHAJAN, VIJAY and JERRY WIND (1985), "Integrating Financial Portfolio Analysis with Product Portfolio Models." In Thomas and Gardner, eds., *Strategic Marketing and Management,* pp. 195–212. New York: John Wiley.

MAHAJAN, VIJAY and YORAM WIND (1986), *Innovation Diffusion Models of New Product Acceptance.* Cambridge, Mass.: Ballinger.

MAHAJAN, VIJAY and YORAM WIND (1988), New Product Forecasting Models: Directions for Research and Implementation," *International Journal of Forecasting,* Vol. 4, pp. 341–358.

MAHAJAN, VIJAY, YORAM WIND, and JOHN W. BRADFORD (1982), "Stochastic Dominance Rules for Product Portfolio Analysis." In A. A. Zoltners, ed., *Marketing Planning Models, TIMS Studies in the Management Sciences,* Vol. 18. New York: North-Holland, pp. 161–183.

MAHAJAN, VIJAY, YORAM WIND, and SUBHASH SHARMA (1983), "An Approach to Repeat Purchase Diffusion Models." In Patrick E. Murphy et al., eds., *AMA Proceedings,* Series 49. Chicago: American Marketing Association, pp. 442–446.

MALHOTRA, NARESH K. (1982), "Information Load and Consumer Decision Making," *Journal of Consumer Research,* Vol. 8 (March), p. 419–430.

MALHOTRA, NARESH K. (1984), "The Use of Linear Logit Models in Marketing Research," *Journal of Marketing Research,* Vol. 21 (February), pp. 20–31.

MALHOTRA, NARESH K. (1986), "An Approach to the Measurement of Consumer Preferences Using Limited Information," *Journal of Marketing Research,* Vol. 23 (February), pp. 33–40.

MALHOTRA, NARESH K. (1987), "Validity and Structural Reliability of Multidimensional Scaling," *Journal of Marketing Research,* Vol. 24 (May), pp. 164–173.

MALHOTRA, NARESH K., ARUN K. JAIN, and CHRISTIAN PINSON (1988), "The Robustness of MDS Configurations in the Case of Incomplete Data," *Journal of Marketing Research,* Vol. 25 (February), pp. 95–102

MANNIX, ELIZABETH A., LEIGH L. THOMPSON, and MAX H. BAZERMAN (1989), "Negotiation in Small Groups," *Journal of Applied Psychology,* Vol. 74, no. 3, pp. 508–517.

MANRAI, AJAY K. and PRABHAKANT SINHA (1989), "Elimination-by-Cutoffs," *Mar-*

keting Science, Vol. 8, no. 2 (Spring), pp. 133–152.

MANSFIELD, EDWIN (1961), "Technical Change and the Rate of Imitation," *Econometrica,* Vol. 29, no. 4 (October), pp. 741–765.

MANSFIELD, EDWIN (1968), *Industrial Research and Technological Innovation.* New York: W. W. Norton.

MANSFIELD, EDWIN (1979), *Microeconomics: Theory and Applications.* New York: W. W. Norton.

MARCH, J. G. (1966), "The Power of Power" In D. Easton, ed., *Varieties of Political Theory,* pp. 39–70. Englewood Cliffs, N.J.: Prentice Hall.

MARCUS, M. LYNNE (1983), "Power, Politics, and MIS Implementation," *Communications of the ACM,* Vol. 26 (June), pp. 430–44.

MARTINO, JOSEPH P. (1983), *Technological Forecasting for Decision Making.* New York: Elsevier.

MARTINOTT, R. T. (1987), "The Traveling Salesman Goes High Tech," *Chemical Week,* (June 10), pp. 22–24.

MASON, CHARLOTTE H. (1990), "New Product Entries and Product Class Demand," *Marketing Science,* Vol. 9, no. 1 (Winter), pp. 58–73.

MASSY, W. F. (1969), "Forecasting the Demand for New Convenience Products" *Journal of Marketing Research* 6 (November), pp. 405–412.

MASSY, WILLIAM F. (1971), "Statistical Analysis of the Relationship Between Variables." In D. A. Aaker, ed., *Multivariate Analysis in Marketing: Theory and Application.* Belmont, Calif.: Wadsworth.

MASSY, W. F., D. B. MONTGOMERY, and D. G. MORRISON (1970), *Stochastic Models of Buying Behavior.* Cambridge: Massachusetts Institute of Technology Press.

MATTSSONS, L. G. (1973), Systems Selling as a Strategy in Industrial Markets," *Industrial Marketing Management,* Vol. 3, no. 2, pp. 107–120.

MAZIS, MICHAEL B. and OLLI T. AHTOLA (1975), "A Comparison of Four Multi-Attribute Models in the Prediction of Consumer

Attitudes," *Journal of Consumer Research,* Vol. 2 (June), pp. 38–52.

MEIDAN, ARTHUR (1982), "Optimizing the Number of Industrial Salespersons," *Industrial Marketing Management,* Vol. 11, pp. 63–74.

METHERINGHAM, R. A. (1964), "Measuring the Net Cumulative Coverage of a Print Campaign," *Journal of Advertising Research,* Vol. 4, no. 4 (December), pp. 23–28.

MEYER, MARC H. and EDWARD D. ROBERTS (1986), "New Product Strategy in Small Technology-Based Firms: A Pilot Study," *Management Science,* Vol. 32 (July), 806–821.

MEYER, ROBERT J. and ARVIND SATHI (1985), "A Multiattribute Model of Consumer Choice During Product Learning," *Marketing Science,* Vol. 4, no 1 (Winter), pp. 41–61.

MICKWITZ, GOSTA (1959), *Marketing and Competition.* Helsingfors, Finland: Central Tryckeriet.

MIDGLEY, D. F. (1976), "A Simple Mathematical Theory of Innovative Behavior," *Journal of Consumer Research,* Vol. 3 (June), pp. 31–41.

MIDGLEY, DAVID F. (1983), "Patterns of Interpersonal Information Seeking for the Purchase of a Symbolic Product," *Journal of Marketing Research,* Vol. 20 (February), pp. 74–83.

MIDGLEY, D. F. and G. R. DOWLING (1978), "Innovativeness: The Concept and its Measurement," *Journal of Consumer Research,* Vol. 4, no. 4 (March), pp. 229–247.

MILGROM, P. and J. ROBERTS (1982), "Limit Pricing and Entry Under Incomplete Information: An Equilibrium Analysis," *Econometrica,* Vol. 50, pp. 443–460.

MILLER, D. W. and M. K. STARR (1960), *Executive Decisions and Operations Research.* Englewood Cliffs, N.J.: Prentice Hall.

MILLER, K. S. (1968), *An Introduction to the Calculus of Finite Differences and Difference Equations.* New York: Henry Holt.

MITCHELL, ANDREW A., J. EDWARD RUSSO, and DICK R. WITTINK (1991), "Issues in the Development and Use of Expert Systems for Marketing Decisions," *International Journal of Research in Marketing,* Vol. 8, no. 1, pp. 41–50.

MIZRAHI, ABE and MICHAEL SULLIVAN (1986), *Calculus and Analytic Geometry,* 2nd ed. Belmont, Calif.: Wadsworth.

MONAHAN, GEORGE E. (1984), "A Pure Birth Model of Optimal Advertising with Word-of-Mouth," *Marketing Science,* Vol. 3, no. 2 (Spring), pp. 169–178.

MONAHAN, G. (1987), "The Structure of Equilibria in Market Share Attraction Models," *Management Science,* Vol. 33, no.2 (February).

MONAHAN, GEORGE E. and KOFI O. NTI (1988), "Optimal Pricing and Advertising for New Products with Repeat Purchases." In T. M. Devinney, ed., *Issues in Pricing: Theory and Research,* Chap. 7. Lexington, Mass.: Lexington Books.

MONROE, K. (1971a), "Psychophysics of Prices: A Reappraisal," *Journal of Marketing Research,* Vol. 8, pp. 248–250.

MONROE, K. (1971b), "The Information Content of Prices: A Preliminary Model for Estimating Buyer Response," *Management Science,* Vol. 17, pp. B519-B532.

MONROE, K. B. (1990), *Pricing: Making Profitable Decisions,* 2nd ed. New York: McGraw-Hill.

MONROE, K. and J. CHAPMAN (1987), "Framing Effects on a Buyers' Subjective Product Evaluations." In P. Anderson and M. Wallendorf, eds., *Advanced in Consumer Research,* Vol. 14. Provo, Utah: Association for Consumer Research.

MONROE, K. B. and A. J. DELLA BITTA (1978), "Models for Pricing Decisions," *Journal of Marketing Research,* Vol. 15 (August), pp. 413–428.

MONROE, KENT and W. DODDS (1988), "A Research Program for Establishing the Validity of the Price-Quality Relationship," *Journal of the Academy of Marketing Science,* Vol. 16 (Spring), pp. 151–168.

MONROE, KENT B. and TRIDIB MAZUNDAR (1988), "Pricing Decision Models: Recent Developments and Research Opportunities." In T. M. Devinney, ed., *Issues in Pricing: Theory and Research,* Chap. 16. Lexington, Mass.: Lexington Books.

MONROE, K. and ANDRIS A. ZOLTNERS (1979), "Pricing the Product Line During Periods of Scarcity," *Journal of Marketing,* Vol. 43, no. 3 (Summer), pp. 49–59.

MONTGOMERY, DAVID B. (1969), "A Stochastic Response Model with Application to Brand Choice," *Management Science,* Vol. 15, pp. 323–337.

MONTGOMERY, D. B. and A. J. SILK (1972), "Estimating Dynamic Effects of Marketing Communications Expenditures," *Management Science,* Vol. 18 (June), pp. B485-B501.

MONTGOMERY, D. B., A. J. SILK, and C. E. ZARAGOZA (1971), "A Multiple-Product Sales Force Allocation Model," *Management Science,* Vol. 18, no. 4, pt. 2 (December), pp. 3–24.

MONTGOMERY, DAVID B. and V. SRINIVASAN (1989), "An Improved Method for Meta Analysis with Application to New Product Diffusion Models," Working paper, Graduate School of Business, Stanford University, Stanford, Calif.

MONTGOMERY, DAVID B. and GLEN L. URBAN (1969), *Management Science in Marketing.* Englewood Cliffs, N.J.: Prentice Hall.

MOORE, WILLIAM L. and DONALD R. LEHMANN (1982), "Effects of Usage and Name on Perceptions of New Products," *Marketing Science,* Vol. 1, no. 4 (Fall), pp. 351–370.

MOORE, WILLIAM L. and DONALD R. LEHMANN (1989), "A Paired Comparison Nested Logit Model of Individual Preference Structures," *Journal of Marketing Research,* Vol. 26, no. 4 (November), pp. 420–428.

MOORE, WILLIAM L. and RICHARD J. SEMENIK (1988), "Measuring Preference with Hybrid Conjoint Analysis: The Impact of a Different Number of Attributes in the Master Design," *Journal of Business Research,* Vol. 16, pp. 261–274.

MOORE, WILLIAM L. and RUSSELL S. WINER (1987), "A Panel-Data Based Method for

Merging Joint Space and Market Response Function Estimation," *Marketing Science,* Vol. 6, no. 1 (Winter), pp. 25–42.

MOORTHY, K. S. (1984), "Market Segmentation, Self-selection, and Product Line Design," *Marketing Science,* Vol. 3 (Fall), pp. 288–305.

MOORTHY, K. S. (1985), "Using Game Theory to Model Competition," *Journal of Marketing Research,* Vol. 22 (August), pp. 262–282.

MOORTHY, K. S. (1987), "Managing Channel Profits: Comment," *Marketing Science,* Vol. 6 (Fall), pp. 375–379.

MOORTHY, K. S. (1988), "Product and Price Competition in a Duopoly," *Marketing Science,* Vol. 7, no. 2 (Spring), pp. 141–168.

MOORTHY, K. S. (1990), "Theoretical Modeling in Marketing." Working Paper, University of Rochester, Rochester, N.Y.

MOORTHY, K. S. and I. P'NG (1991), "Market Segmentation, Cannibalization, and the Timing of Product Introductions," *Management Science,* forthcoming.

MORE, ROGER A. (1984), "Timing of Market Research in New Product Situations" *Journal of Marketing* 48 (Fall), pp. 84–94.

MORIARTY, MARK M. (1975), "Cross-Sectional, Time-Series Issues in the Analysis of Marketing Decision Variables," *Journal of Marketing Research,* Vol. 12 (May), pp. 142–150.

MORIARTY, MARK M. (1985), "Retail Promotional Effects on Intra- and Interbrand Sales Performance," *Journal of Retailing,* Vol. 61 (Fall), pp. 27–48.

MORIARTY, MARK M. and URSULA MORAN (1990), "Managing Hybrid Marketing Systems," *Harvard Business Review* (November/December), pp. 146–155.

MORIARTY, MARK M. and GERALD SALAMON (1984), "Estimation and Forecast Performance of a Multivariate Time Series Model of Sales," *Journal of Marketing Research,* Vol. 27 (November), pp. 558–564.

MORIARTY, MARK M. and ROBERT E. SPEKMAN (1990), "An Empirical Investigation of the Information Sources Used During the Industrial Buying Process," *Journal of Marketing Research,* Vol. 21, no. 2 (May), pp. 137–147.

MORIARTY, ROWLAND T. and JOHN E. G. BATESON (1982), "Exploring Complex Decision Making Units: A New Approach," *Journal of Marketing Research,* Vol. 19 (May), pp. 182–191.

MORRIS, MICHAEL H., WILBUR W. STANTON, and ROGER J. CALANTONE (1985), "Measuring Coalitions in the Industrial Buying Center," *Journal of the Academy of Marketing Science,* Vol. 13, no. 4 (Fall), pp. 18–39.

MORRISON, DONALD G. (1966), "Testing Brand Switching Models," *Journal of Marketing Research,* Vol. 3, pp. 401–409.

MORRISON, DONALD G. (1979), "Purchase Intentions and Purchase Behavior," *Journal of Marketing,* Vol. 43, no. 2 (Spring), pp. 65–74.

MORRISON, DONALD G., RICHARD D. H. CHEN, SANDRA L. KARPIS, and KATHRYN E. BRITNEY (1982), "Modeling Retail Customer Behavior at Merrill Lynch," *Marketing Science,* Vol. 1, no. 2 (Spring), pp. 123–141.

MORRISON, DONALD G. and A. PERRY (1970), "Some Data Based Models for Analyzing Sales Fluctuations," *Decision Sciences,* Vol. 1, pp. 258–274.

MORRISON, DONALD G. and DAVID C. SCHMITTLEIN (1981), "Predicting Future Random Events Based on Past Performances," *Management Science,* Vol. 27, pp. 1006–1023.

MORRISON, DONALD G. and DAVID C. SCHMITTLEIN (1988), "Generalizing the NBD Model for Customer Purchases: What Are the Implications and Is It Worth the Effort?" *Journal of Business and Economic Statistics,* Vol. 6, no. 2 (April), pp. 145–159.

MURPHY, A. H. and H. DEAN (1984), "Impacts of Feedback and Experience on the Quality of Subjective Probability Forecasts: Comparison of Results from the First and Second Years of the Zierikyce

Experiment," *Monthly Weather Review,* Vol. 112, no. 3, pp. 413–423.

Mussa, M. and S. Rosen (1978), "Monopoly and Product Quality," *Journal of Economic Theory,* Vol. 18, pp. 301–317.

Myers, James H. (1976), "Benefit Structure Analysis: A New Tool for Product Planning," *Journal of Marketing,* Vol. 40 (October), pp. 23–32.

Naert, Philippe and Alain V. Bultez (1973), "Logically Consistent Market Share Models," *Journal of Marketing Research,* Vol. 10, pp. 334–340.

Naert, Philippe and Alain V. Bultez (1975), "A Model of a Distribution Network Aggregate Performance," *Management Science,* Vol. 21, no. 10 (June), pp. 1102–1112.

Naert, Philippe and Peter Leeflang (1978), *Building Implementable Marketing Models.* Leiden: Martinus Nijhoff.

Naert, Philippe and M. Weverbergh (1981), "On the Predictive Power of Market Share Attraction Models," *Journal of Marketing Research,* Vol. 18 (May), pp. 146–153.

Naert, Philippe and M. Weverbergh (1985), "Market Share Specification, Estimation, and Validation: Toward Reconciling Seemingly Divergent Views," *Journal of Marketing Research,* Vol. 22 (November), pp. 453–467.

Nagle, T. (1987), *The Strategy and Tactics of Pricing.* Englewood Cliffs, N.J.: Prentice Hall.

Nakanishi, M. (1973), "Advertising and Promotion Effects on Consumer Response to New Products" *Journal of Marketing Research* 10 (August), pp. 242–249.

Nakanishi, Masao and Lee G. Cooper (1974), "Parameter Estimation for a Multiplicative Competitive Interaction Model—Least Squares Approach," *Journal of Marketing Research,* Vol. 11 (August), pp. 303–311.

Nakanishi, M. and James R. Bettman (1974), "Attitude Models Revisited: An Individual Level Analysis" *Journal of Consumer Research* 1, (December), pp. 20–21.

Nalebuff, B. and J. Stiglitz (1983), "Prizes and Incentives: Toward a General Theory of Compensation and Competition," *Bell Journal of Economics,* Vol. 13, pp. 21–43.

Naples, M. J. (1979), *Effective Frequency.* New York: Association of National Advertisers.

Narasimhan, Chakravarthi (1984), "A Price Discrimination Theory of Coupons," *Marketing Science,* Vol. 3, no. 2 (Spring), pp. 128–147.

Narasimhan, Chakravarthi (1988), "Competitive Promotional Strategies," *Journal of Business,* Vol. 61 (October), pp. 427–449.

Narasimhan, Chakravarthi (1989), "Incorporating Consumer Price Expectations in Diffusion Models," *Marketing Science,* Vol. 8, no. 4 (Fall), pp. 343–357.

Narasimhan, Chakravarthi and Subrata K. Sen (1983), "New Product Models for Test Market Data," *Journal of Marketing,* Vol. 47 (Winter) pp. 11–24.

Narayana, Chem L. and Rom J. Markin (1975), "Consumer Behavior and Product Performance: An Alternative Conceptualization," *Journal of Marketing,* Vol. 39 (October), pp. 1–6.

Nash, J. (1950), "Equilibrium Points in n-Person Games," *Proceedings of the National Academy of Sciences,* Vol. 36, pp. 48–49.

Nedungadi, Prakash (1990), "Recall and Consumer Consideration Sets: Influencing Choice Without Changing Brand Evaluations," *Journal of Consumer Research,* Vol. 17, no. 3 (December), pp. 263–276.

Nelson, Richard (1958), *The Selection of Retail Locations.* New York: F. W. Dodge Corporation.

Nemhauser, G. L., A. G. Rinooy Kan, and M. J. Todd, eds. (1989), *Optimization.* New York: North-Holland.

Nerlove M. and K. J. Arrow (1962), "Optimal Advertising Policy Under Dynamic Conditions," *Econometrica,* Vol. 29 (May), pp. 129–142.

Neslin, Scott A. (1990), "A Market Response

Model for Coupon Promotions," *Marketing Science,* Vol. 9, no. 2 (Spring), pp. 125–145.

NESLIN, SCOTT A. and LEONARD GREENHALGH (1983), "Nash's Theory of Cooperative Games as a Predictor of the Outcomes of Buyer-Seller Negotiations: An Experiment in Media Purchasing," *Journal of Marketing Research,* Vol. 30 (November), pp. 368–379.

NESLIN, SCOTT A. and LEONARD GREENHALGH (1986), "The Ability of Nash's Theory of Cooperative Games to Predict the Outcomes of Buyer-Seller Negotiations: A Dyad-Level Test," *Management Science,* Vol. 32, no. 4 (April), pp. 480–498.

NESLIN, SCOTT A., CAROLINE M. HENDERSON, and JOHN A. QUELCH (1985), "Consumer Promotions and the Acceleration of Product Purchases," *Marketing Science,* Vol. 4 (Spring), pp. 147–165.

NESLIN, SCOTT A. and ROBERT W. SHOEMAKER (1983), "A Model for Evaluating the Profitability of Coupon Promotions," *Marketing Science,* Vol. 2, no. 4 (Fall), pp. 361–388.

NOOTEBOOM, BART (1989), "Diffusion, Uncertainty and Firm Size," *International Journal of Research in Marketing,* Vol. 6, pp. 109–128.

NORTON, JOHN A. and FRANK M. BASS (1987), "A Diffusion Theory Model of Adoption and Substitution for Successive Generations of High Technology Products," *Management Science,* Vol. 33 (September), pp. 1069–1086.

OFIR, CHEZY and ANDRÉ KHURI (1986), "Multicollinearity in Marketing Models: Diagnostics and Remedial Measures," *International Journal of Research in Marketing,* Vol. 3, no. 3, pp. 181–205.

OGILVY and MATHER RESEARCH DEPARTMENT (1965), *An Experimental Study of the Relative Effectiveness of Three Television Dayparts.* New York: Authors.

OHMAE, K. (1985), *Triad Power.* New York: The Free Press.

OI, W. Y. (1971), "A Disneyland Dilemma: Two-Part Tariffs for a Mickey Mouse Monopoly," *Quarterly Journal of Economics,* Vol. 85, pp. 77–90.

OLANDER, F. (1970), "The Influence of Price on the Consumer's Evaluation of Products and Purchases." In B. Taylor and G. Willis, eds., *Pricing Strategy.* Princeton, N.J.: Brandom Systems Press, pp. 50–69.

OLIVER, R. and B. WEITZ (1989), "The Effects of Risk Preference, Perceived Uncertainty, and Incentive Compensation on Salesperson Motivation," Working paper, The Wharton School of Business, University of Pennsylvania.

OLIVER, R. and R. WINER (1987), "A Framework for the Formulation and Structure of Consumer Expectations: Review and Propositions," *Journal of Economic Psychology,* Vol. 9, pp. 469–499.

OLSON, JEROME A. and SEUNGMOOK CHOI (1985), "A Product Diffusion Model Incorporating Repeat Purchases," *Technological Forecasting and Social Change,* Vol. 27, pp. 385–397.

ORDOVER, J. and G. SALONER (1989), "Predation, Monopolization and Antitrust." In R. Schmalensee and R. Willig, eds., *Handbook of Industrial Organization.* Amsterdam: North-Holland.

OREN, SHMUEL S. and RICK G. SCHWARTZ (1988), "Diffusion of New Products in Risk-Sensitive Markets," *Journal of Forecasting,* Vol. 7 (October/December), pp. 273–287.

OREN, SHMUEL, STEPHEN SMITH, and ROBERT WILSON (1984), "Pricing a Product Line," *Journal of Business,* Vol. 57, no. 1, pt. 2, pp. S73-S110.

OSTLUND, LYMAN E., KEVIN J. CLANCY, and RAKESH SAPRA (1980), "Inertia in Copy Research," *Journal of Advertising Research,* Vol. 20, no. 1 (February), pp. 17–23.

PAPATLA, PURUSHOTTAM and LAKSHMAN KRISHNAMURTHI (1991), "A Probit Model of Choice Dynamics," *Marketing Science,* forthcoming.

PARFITT, J. H. and B. J. K. COLLINS (1968), "Use of Consumer Panels for Brand Share Prediction," *Journal of Marketing Research,* Vol. 5 (May), pp. 131–146.

PARKER, BARNETT R. and V. SRINIVASAN (1976), "A Consumer Preference Approach to the

Planning of Rural Primary Health Care Facilities," *Operations Research,* Vol. 24 (September/October), pp. 991–1025.

PARRY, MARK and FRANK M. BASS (1990), "When to Lead or to Follow? It Depends," *Marketing Letters,* Vol. 1, no. 3 (November), pp. 187–198.

PARSONS, LEONARD J. (1974), "An Econometric Analysis of Advertising, Retail Availability and Sales of a New Brand," *Management Science,* Vol. 20, no. 6, pp. 938–947.

PARSONS, LEONARD J. (1975), "The Product Life Cycle and Time Varying Advertising Elasticities," *Journal of Marketing Research,* Vol. 12, no. 3 (August), pp. 476–480.

PARSONS, LEONARD J. and RANDALL SCHULTZ (1976), *Marketing Models and Econometric Research.* New York: North-Holland.

PATTI, C. H. and V. J. BLASKO (1981), "Budgeting Practices of Big Advertisers," *Journal of Advertising Research,* Vol. 21 (December), pp. 23–29.

PATTON, W. E., C. E. PUTO and R. H. KING (1986), "Which Buying Decisions Are Made By Individuals and Not By Groups," *Industrial Marketing Management,* 15, pp. 129–138.

PEDRICK, JAMES H. and FRED K. ZUFRYDEN (1991), "Evaluating the Impact of Advertising Media Plans: A Model of Consumer Purchase Dynamics Using Single-Source Data," *Marketing Science,* Vol. 10, no. 2 (Spring), pp. 111–130.

PEKELMAN, DOV and SUBRATA SEN (1979), "Improving Prediction in Conjoint Measurement," *Journal of Marketing Research,* Vol. 16 (May), pp. 211–220.

PERREAULT, WILLIAM D., JR., and FREDERICK A. RUSS (1976), "Physical Distribution in Industrial Purchase Decisions," *Journal of Marketing,* Vol. 40 (April), pp. 3–10.

PESSEMIER, EDGAR A. (1966), *New Product Decisions: An Analytical Approach.* New York: McGraw-Hill.

PESSEMIER, EDGAR A. (1976), "Market Structure Analysis of New Product and Market Opportunities," *Journal of Contemporary Business* (Spring), pp. 35–67.

PESSEMIER, EDGAR (1978), "Stochastic Properties of Changing Preferences," *American Economic Review,* Vol. 68, no. 2, pp. 380–385.

PESSEMIER, EDGAR A., PHILIP BURGER, RICHARD TEACH, and DOUGLAS TIGER (1971), "Using Laboratory Brand Preference Scales to Predict Consumer Brand Purchases," *Management Science,* Vol. 17 (February), pp. B371-B385.

PETER, PAUL J. and WALTER R. NORD (1982), "A Clarification and Extension of Operant Conditioning Principles in Marketing," *Journal of Marketing* 46 (Summer), pp. 102–107.

PETERSON, ROBERT A. and V. MAHAJAN (1978), "Multi-Product Growth Models." In J. Sheth, ed., *Research in Marketing,* Vol. 1, pp. 201–232. Greenwich, Conn.: JAI Press.

PETTY, RICHARD E. and JOHN T. CACIOPPO (1986), *Communication and Persuasion.* New York: Springer-Verlag.

PHILLIPS, LAWRENCE D. (1987), "On the Adequacy of Judgmental Forecasts." In G. Wright and P. Ayton eds. *Judgmental Forecasting,* pp. 11–30. New York: John Wiley.

PLOTT, C. R. (1982), "Industrial Organization Theory and Experimental Economics," *Journal of Economic Literature,* 20, pp. 1485–1527.

POLLI, R. and V. COOK (1969), "Validity of the Product Life Cycle," *The Journal of Business,* Vol. 42, no. 4 (October), pp. 385–400.

PONTRYAGIN, L. S. (1962), *The Mathematical Theory of Optimal Processes.* New York: John Wiley.

PORTER, MICHAEL E. (1980), *Competitive Strategy: Techniques for Analyzing Industries and Competitors.* New York: Macmillan.

PORTER, MICHAEL E. (1985), *Competitive Advantage: Creating and Sustaining Superior Performance.* New York: The Free Press.

PRASAD, KANTI V. and L. WINSTON RING (1976),

"Measuring Sales Effects of Some Marketing Mix Variables and Their Interactions," *Journal of Marketing Research,* Vol. 13 (November), pp. 391–396.

PRINGLE, LEWIS G., R. DALE WILSON and EDWARD I. BRODY (1982), "NEWS: A Decision-Oriented Model for New Product Analysis and Forecasting."

PRINGLE, LEWIS G., R. DALE WILSON and EDWARD I. BRODY (1984), "Issues in Comparing the Awareness Component of New Product Models," *Marketing Science,* Vol. 3 (Summer), pp. 203–205.

PRUITT, D. G. (1981), *Negotiation Behavior.* New York: Academic Press.

PUNJ, G. N. and R. STAELIN (1978), "The Choice for Graduate Business Schools," *Journal of Marketing Research,* Vol. 15 (November), pp. 588–598.

PUNJ, GIRISH N. and RICHARD STAELIN (1983), "A Model of Consumer Information Search Behavior for New Automobiles," *Journal of Consumer Research,* Vol. 9 (March), pp. 366–380.

QUALLS, WILLIAM, RICHARD W. OLSHAVSKY, and RONALD E. MICHAELS (1981), "Shortening of the PLC—An Empirical Test," *Journal of Marketing,* Vol. 45, no. 4 (Fall), pp. 76–80.

RAIFFA, HOWARD (1982), *The Art and Science of Negotiation.* Cambridge, Mass.: Harvard University Press.

RAIFFA, HOWARD and ROBERT SCHLAIFER (1961), *Applied Statistical Decision Theory.* Boston: Colonial Press.

RAJU, J., V. SRINIVASAN, and R. LAL (1990), "The Effects of Brand Loyalty on Competitive Price Promotion Strategies," *Management Science,* Vol. 36, no. 3 (March), pp. 276–304.

RAM, SADHA and SUNDARESAN RAM (1988), "INNOVATOR: An Expert System for New Product Launch Decisions," *Applied Artificial Intelligence,* Vol. 2, pp. 129–148.

RAM, SUNDARESAN and SUDHA RAM (1989), "Expert Systems: An Emerging Technology for Selecting New Product Winners," *Journal of Product Innovation Management,* Vol. 6, no. 2 (June), pp. 89–98.

RAMANUJAM, V. and N. VENKATRAMAN (1984), "An Inventory and Critique of Strategy Research Using the PIMS Data Base," *Academy of Management Review,* Vol. 9, pp. 138–151.

RAMOND, CHARLES (1976), *Advertising Research: The State of the Art.* New York: Association of National Advertisers.

RANGAN, V. KASTURI (1987), "The Channel Design Decision: A Model and an Application," *Marketing Science,* Vol. 6 (Spring), pp. 156–174.

RANGAN, V. KASTURI, ANDRIS A. ZOLTNERS, and ROBERT J. BECKER (1986), "The Channel Intermediary Selection Decision: A Model and an Application," *Management Science,* Vol. 32, no. 9 (September), pp. 1114–1122.

RANGASWAMY, ARVIND, RAYMOND BURKE, JERRY WIND, and JEHOSHUA ELIASHBERG, (1987), "Expert Systems for Marketing," Report No. 87–107, *Marketing Science Institute,* Cambridge, Mass.

RANGASWAMY, ARVIND, JEHOSHUA ELIASHBERG, RAYMOND R. BURKE, and JERRY WIND (1989), "Developing Marketing Expert Systems: An Application to International Negotiations," *Journal of Marketing,* Vol. 53 (October), pp. 24–39.

RANGASWAMY, ARVIND, BARI A. HARLAM, and LEONARD M. LODISH, (1991), "INFER: An Expert System for Automatic Analysis of Scanner Data," *International Journal of Research in Marketing,* Vol. 8, no. 1, pp. 29–40.

RANGASWAMY, ARVIND, PRABHAKANT SINHA, and ANDRIS ZOLTNERS (1990), "An Integrated Model Based Approach for Sales Force Restructuring," *Marketing Science,* Vol. 9, no. 4 (Fall), pp. 279–298.

RANGASWAMY, ARVIND and YORAM WIND (1991), "Information Technology in Marketing." In Allen Kent and James G. Williams, eds., *Encyclopedia of Microcomputers,* Vol. 9. New York: Marcel Dekker, Inc., (November) pp. 67–83.

RAO, AMBAR G. (1978), "Productivity of the Marketing Mix: Measuring the Impact of Advertising and Consumer and Trade Promotions on Sales," Paper presented at ANA Advertising Research Workshop, New York.

RAO, AMBAR G. and GARY L. LILIEN (1972), "A System of Promotional Models," *Management Science,* Vol. 19, no. 2 (October), pp. 152–160.

RAO, AMBAR G. and P. B. MILLER (1975), "Advertising/Sales Response Functions," *Journal of Advertising Research,* Vol. 15, pp. 7–15.

RAO, AMBAR G. and MELVIN F. SHAKUN (1972), "A Quasi-Game Theory Approach to Pricing," *Management Science,* Vol. 18, no. 15 (January), pp. 110–123.

RAO, AMBAR G. and MELVIN F. SHAKUN (1974), "A Normative Model of Negotiations," *Management Science,* Vol. 20, no. 10, pp. 1364–1375.

RAO, AMBAR G. and MASATAKA YAMADA (1988), "Forecasting with a Repeat Purchase Diffusion Model," *Management Science,* Vol. 34 (June), pp. 734–752.

RAO, RAM C. (1988), "Strategic Pricing in Durables under Competition." In T. M. Devinney, ed., *Issues in Pricing: Theory and Research,* Chap. 9. Lexington, Mass.: Lexington Books.

RAO, RAM C. (1990a), "The Impact of Competition on Strategic Marketing Decisions." In G. Day, B. Weitz, and R. Wensley, eds., *The Interface of Marketing and Strategy.* Greenwich, Conn.: JAI Press.

RAO, RAM C. (1990b), "Compensating Heterogeneous Salesforces: Some Explicit Solutions," *Marketing Science,* Vol. 9, no. 4 (Fall), pp. 319–341.

RAO, RAM C. (1991), "Pricing and Promotions in Asymmetric Duopolies," *Marketing Science,* Vol. 10, no. 2 (Spring), pp. 131–144.

RAO, RAM C. and FRANK BASS (1985), "Competition, Strategy and Price Dynamics: A Theoretical and Empirical Investigation," *Journal of Marketing Research,* Vol. 22, pp. 283–296.

RAO, V. and D. GAUTSCHI (1982), "The Role of Price in Individual Utility Judgments: Development and Empirical Validation of Alternative Models." In L. McAlister, ed., *Choice Models for Buyer Behavior.* Greenwich, Conn.: JAI Press, pp. 57–80.

RAO, V. and DARIUS SABAVALA (1981), "Some Issues in the Construction of Models for Marketing Decisions." In J. Sheth, ed., *Research in Marketing,* Vol. 4, 251–272. Greenwich, Conn.: JAI Press.

RAO, V. R. and J. H. STECKEL (1991), "A Polarization Model for Describing Group Preferences," *Journal of Consumer Research,* Vol. 18, no. 1 (June), pp. 108–118.

RAPOPORT, A. (1966), *Two-Person Game Theory.* Ann Arbor: University of Michigan Press.

RASMUSEN, E. (1989), *Games and Information: An Introduction to Game Theory.* New York: Basil Blackwell.

RATCHFORD, BRIAN T. and G. STOOPS (1991), "An Econometric Model of a Retail Firm," *Managerial and Decision Economies,* (forthcoming).

RAVINDRAN, A., DON T. PHILLIPS, and JAMES J. SOLBERG (1987), *Operations Research: Principles and Practices.* New York: John Wiley.

REEDER, R. R., E. G. BRIERTY and B. H. REEDER (1987), *Industrial Marketing: Analysis, Planning and Control.* Englewood Cliffs, N.J.: Prentice Hall.

REIBSTEIN, DAVID J. and HUBERT GATIGNON (1984), "Optimal Product Line Pricing: The Influence of Elasticities and Cross-elasticities," *Journal of Marketing Research,* Vol. 21 (August), pp. 259–267.

REIBSTEIN, DAVID J. and PHILLIS A. TRAVER (1982), "Factors Affecting Coupon Redemption Rates," *Journal of Marketing,* Vol. 46 (Fall), pp. 102–113.

REINITZ, R. C. (1968), "A Sales Forecasting Model for Gasoline Service Stations," private correspondence.

RESNICK, ROBERT and DAVID HALLIDAY (1960), *Physics,* Part 1. New York: John Wiley.

REY, P. and J. TIROLE (1986a), "Vertical Restraints from a Principal-Agent Viewpoint." In L. Pellegrini and S. Reddy, eds., *Marketing Channels: Relationships and Performance.* Lexington, Mass.: Lexington Books.

REY, P. and J. TIROLE (1986b), "The Logic of

Vertical Restraints," *American Economic Review,* Vol. 76, pp. 921–939.

RHODES, R. (1977), "What AdTel Has Learned: Six Recommendations for Increased Payout from Television Advertising Research," Paper presented at the Advertising Research Conference, American Marketing Association, New York (March).

RICE, BERNARD J. and JERRY D. STRANGE (1989), *Ordinary Differential Equations with Applications,* 2nd ed. Pacific Grove, Calif.: Brooks/Cole.

RICE, MARSHALL D. (1988a), "Estimating the Reach and Frequency of Mixed Media Advertising Schedules," *Journal of the Market Research Society,* Vol. 30, no. 4 (October), pp. 439–451.

RICE, MARSHALL D. (1988b), "A Practical Method for Estimating Reach and Frequency of Mixed Media," *Journal of Media Planning* (Fall), pp. 29–39.

RICHARDSON, R. J. (1979), "A Territory Realignment Model—MAPS," Paper presented at the New Orleans ORSA/TIMS Meeting (May).

RINK, DAVID R. and JOHN E. SWAN (1979), "Product Life Cycle Research: A Literature Review," *Journal of Business Research,* Vol. 7, no. 3 (September), pp. 219–242.

ROBERTS, JOHN H. and JAMES M. LATTIN (1991), "Development and Testing of a Model of Consideration Set Composition," *Journal of Marketing Research,* Vol. 28 (November).

ROBERTS, JOHN and GARY L. LILIEN (1992), "Explanatory and Predictive Models of Consumer Behavior." In J. Eliashberg and G. L. Lilien, eds., *Handbook of OR/MS in Marketing.* New York: Elsevier, (forthcoming).

ROBERTS, JOHN and GLEN L. URBAN (1988), "Modeling Multiattribute Utility, Risk, and Belief Dynamics for New Consumer Durable Brand Choice," *Management Science,* Vol. 34, no. 2 (February), pp. 167–185.

ROBEY, DANIEL (1984), "Conflict Models in Implementation Research." In Randal L. Schultz and Michael Ginzberg, eds.,

Management Science Implementation, Greenwich, Conn.: JAI Press, pp. 89–105.

ROBINSON, BRUCE and CHET LAKHANI (1975), "Dynamic Price Models for New-Product Planning," *Management Science,* Vol. 21, no. 10 (June), pp. 1113–1122.

ROBINSON, MIKE (1985), "A Logit Model of the All Electric Residence Decision," *Review of Regional Economics and Business,* (October), pp. 17–20.

ROBINSON, P. J. (1981), "A Comparison of Pretest Market New Product Forecasting Models," *New Product Forecasting: Models and Applications,* Y. Wind, V. Mahajan and R. Cardozo, eds., (Lexington Books: Lexington, MA).

ROBINSON, W. T. (1988a), "Sources of Market Pioneering Advantages: The Case of Industrial Goods Industries," *Journal of Marketing Research,* Vol. 25 (February), pp. 87–94.

ROBINSON, W. T. (1988b), "Marketing Mix Response to Entry," *Marketing Science* (Fall), pp. 368–385.

ROBINSON, W. T. and C. FORNELL (1985), "Sources of Market Pioneer Advantages in Consumer Goods Industries," *Journal of Marketing Research,* Vol. 12, pp. 305–306.

ROGERS, E. M. (1983), *Diffusion of Innovations,* 3rd ed. New York: The Free Press.

ROHLFS, J. (1974), "A Theory of Interdependent Demand for a Communication Service," *Bell Journal of Economics and Management Science,* Vol. 5 (Spring), pp. 16–37.

ROSHWALB, IRVING (1975), "How Much Is an Ad Test Worth?" *Journal of Advertising Research,* Vol. 15, no. 1 (February), pp. 17–23.

ROSS, S. (1973), "The Economic Theory of Agency: The Principal's Problem," *American Economic Review,* Vol. 63, pp. 134–139.

ROSS, SHELDON M. (1979), "Stochastic Control Theory and Stochastic Differential Systems," *Series, Lecture Notes in Control and Information Sciences,* Vol. 16. Stanford, CA: Stanford University.

ROSS, SHELDON M. (1983), *Introduction to Sto-*

chastic Dynamic Programming. New York: Academic Press.

ROSS, SHELDON M. (1989), *Introduction to Probability Models,* 4th ed. New York: Academic Press.

ROSSITER, JOHN R. (1981), "Predicting Starch Scores," *Journal of Advertising Research,* Vol. 21, no. 5 (October), pp. 63–68.

ROSSITER, JOHN R., LARRY PERCY, and ROBERT J. DONOVAN (1991), "A Better Advertising Planning Grid," *Journal of Advertising Research,* Vol. 31, No. 5 (Oct./Nov.), pp. 11–21.

ROSSITER, JOHN R. and LARRY PERCY (1987), *Advertising and Promotion Management.* New York: McGraw-Hill.

ROTH, A. E. (1979), "Axiomatic Models of Bargaining," *Lecture Notes in Economics and Mathematical Systems,* 170. New York: Springer-Verlag

ROTH, ALVIN, E. (1985), "Towards a Focal Point Theory of Bargaining." In A. E. Roth, ed. *Game Theoretic Models of Bargaining.* Cambridge: Cambridge University Press.

ROTHCHILD, MICHAEL L. (1979), "Advertising Strategies for High and Low Involvement Situations." In John Maloney and Bernard Silverman, eds., *Attitude Research Plays for High Stakes,* Chicago: American Marketing Association, pp. 74–93.

ROTHKOPF, MICHAEL (1991), "On Auctions with Withdrawable Winning Bids," *Marketing Science,* Vol. 10, no. 1 (Winter), pp. 40–57.

RUBINSTEIN, A. (1991), "Comments on the Interpretation of Game Theory," *Econometrica,* Vol. 59, no. 4 (July), pp. 909–924.

RURNELT, RICHARD P. and ROBIN WENSLEY (1980), "In Search of the Market Share Effect," Working paper, University of California at Los Angeles.

RUST, ROLAND (1986), *Advertising Media Models: A Practical Guide.* Lexington, Mass.: Lexington Books.

RUST, ROLAND T. and NARAS V. EECHAMBADI (1989), "Scheduling Network Television Programs: A Heuristic Audience Flow Approach to Maximizing Audience Share," *Journal of Advertising,* Vol. 18, no. 2, pp. 11–18.

RUST, ROLAND T., MARY R. ZIMMER, and ROBERT P. LEONE (1986), "Estimating the Duplicated Audience of Media Vehicles in National Advertising Schedules," *Journal of Advertising,* Vol. 15, no. 3, pp. 30–37.

RYAN, M. J., E. H. BONFIELD, and MORRIS B. HOLBROOK (1982), "Decision-Specific Conflict in Organizational Buying Behavior," *Journal of Marketing,* Vol. 46, no. 2 (Summer), pp. 62–68.

RYANS, A. B. and C. B. WEINBERG (1979), "Sales Territory Response," *Journal of Marketing Research,* Vol. 16 (November), pp. 453–465.

RYANS, A. B. and C. B. WEINBERG (1987), "Territory Sales Response Models: Stability over Time," *Journal of Marketing Research,* Vol. 24 (May), pp. 229–233.

SAATY, THOMAS L. and LUIS G. VARGAS (1982). *The Logic of Priorities.* Boston: Kluver.

SAGHAFI, MASSOUD M. (1988), "Optimal Pricing to Maximize Profits and Achieve Market-Share Targets for Single-Product and Multiproduct Companies." In T. M. Devinney, ed., *Issues in Pricing: Theory and Research,* Chap. 11. Lexington, Mass.: Lexington Books.

SALES and MARKETING MANAGEMENT (1986), "Portables for Salespeople a $2 Billion Market," (June), pp. 87–88.

SALES and MARKETING MANAGEMENT (1987), "From the Bytes of Babes comes Sales Force Automation," (June), pp. 92–94.

SALOP, STEVEN and JOSEPH STIGLITZ (1977), "Bargains and Ripoffs: A Model of Monopolistic Competitive Price Dispersion," *Review of Economic Studies,* Vol. 4, pp. 493–510.

SALOP, STEVEN and JOSEPH STIGLITZ (1982), "The Theory of Sales: A Simple Model of Equilibrium Price Dispersion with Identical Agents," *The American Economic Review,* Vol. 72, no. 3 (December), pp. 1121–1130.

SASIENI, MAURICE W. (1971), "Optimal Advertising Expenditures," *Management Sci-*

ence, Vol. 18, no. 4, pt. 2 (December), pp. 64–72.

SASIENI, MAURICE W. (1981), "Pricing and Advertising for Profit," *Paper presented at Pennsylvania State University,* University Park (October).

SASIENI, MAURICE W. (1989), "Sales Commission for Multiproduct Sales Forces," *IMA Journal of Mathematics Applied in Business & Industry,* Vol. 2, pp. 17–23.

SAUNDERS, JOHN (1987), "The Specification of Aggregate Market Models," *European Journal of Marketing,* Vol. 21, no. 2, pp. 1–47.

SCHERER, F. (1980), *Industrial Market Structure and Economic Performance,* 2nd ed. Skokie, Ill.: Rand McNally.

SCHMALENSEE, R. (1982), "Product Differentiation Advantages of Pioneering Brands," *American Economic Review,* Vol. 72 (June), pp. 159–180.

SCHMALENSEE, R. (1984), "Gaussian Demand and Commodity Bundling," *Journal of Business,* Vol. 57, pp. S211-S230.

SCHMITTLEIN, DAVID C. and DONALD G. MORRISON (1983), "Prediction of Future Random Events with the Condensed Negative Binomial Distribution," *Journal of the American Statistical Association,* Vol. 78, pp. 449–456.

SCHMITTLEIN, DAVID C., DONALD G. MORRISON, and RICHARD COLOMBO (1987), "Counting Your Customers: Who Are They and What Will They Do Next?" *Management Science,* Vol. 33, no. 1 (January), pp. 1–24.

SCHMITZ, JOHN D., GORDON D. ARMSTRONG, and JOHN D. LITTLE (1990), "CoverStory: Automated News Finding in Marketing." In Linda Bolino, ed., *DSS Transactions.* Providence R.I.: TIMS College on Information Systems (May).

SCHNAARS, STEVEN P. (1986), "When Entering Growth Markets, Are Pioneers Better than Poachers?" *Business Horizons,* Vol. 29 (March/April), pp. 2–36.

SCHONBERGER, RICHARD J. (1980), "MIS Design: A Contingency Approach," *MIS Quarterly,* (March), pp. 13–20.

SCHRAGE, LINUS E. (1987), *LINDO.* Redwood City, Calif.: Scientific Press.

SCHULTZ, DON E. and MARTIN P. BLOCK (1986), "Empirical Estimation of Advertising Response Functions," *Journal of Media Planning,* (Fall), pp. 17–24.

SCHULTZ, DON E. and WILLIAM A. ROBINSON (1982), *Sales Promotion Management.* Chicago: Crain.

SCHULTZ, RANDALL L. (1984), "The Implementation of Forecasting Models," *Journal of Forecasting,* Vol. 3 (January/March), pp. 43–55.

SCHULTZ, RANDALL L. and MICHAEL J. GINZBERG, eds. (1984), *Management Science Implementation.* Greenwich, Conn.: JAI Press.

SCHULTZ, RANDALL L., MICHAEL J. GINZBERG, and HENRY C. LUCAS, JR. (1984), "A Structural Model of Implementation." In Randall L. Schultz and Michael J. Ginzberg, eds., *Management Science Implementation,* pp. 55–87. Greenwich, Conn.: JAI Press.

SCHULTZ, R. L. and M. D. HENRY (1981), "Implementing Decision Models." In R. Schultz and A. A. Zoltners, eds., *Marketing Decision Models,* pp. 275–296. New York: North-Holland.

SCHULTZ, RANDALL L. and DENNIS P. SLEVIN (1983), "The Implementation Profile," *Interfaces,* Vol. 13, pp. 87–92.

SCHULTZ, RANDALL L. and DENNIS P. SLEVIN (1979), "Introduction: The Implementation Problem." In Robert Doktor, Randall L. Schultz, and Dennis P. Sleven, eds., *The Implementation of Management Science,* pp. 1–15. Amsterdam: North-Holland.

SCHUMANN, M., PATRICIA A. GONGLA, KYOUNG-SANG LEE and J. GENE SAKAMOTO (1987), "BUSINESS STRATEGY ADVISOR: An Expert System Implementation," Paper presented at the IBM Los Angeles Scientific Center.

SCITOVSKY, T. (1944–45), "Some Consequences of the Habit of Judging Quality by Price," *Review of Economic Studies,* Vol. 12, pp. 100–105.

SCOTT, CAROL A. (1976), "The Effects of Trial

Incentives on Repeat Purchase Behavior," *Journal of Marketing Research,* Vol. 13 (August), pp. 263–269.

SCOTT, CAROL A. and ALICE M. TYBOUT (1979), "Extending the Self-perception Explanation: The Effect of Cue Salience on Behavior." In William L. Wilkie, ed., *Advances in Consumer Behavior,* Vol. 6, Ann Arbor, Mich.: Association for Consumer Research. pp. 50–54.

SCOTT, CAROL A. and RICHARD F. YALCH (1980), "Consumer Response to Initial Trial: A Bayesian Analysis," *Journal of Consumer Research,* Vol. 7 (June), pp. 32–41.

SEGAL, M. and D. B. WEINBERGER (1977), "Turfing," *Operations Research,* Vol. 25, no. 3 (May/June), pp. 367–386.

SELIGMAN, DANIEL (1956), "How Much for Advertising?" *Fortune* (December), pp. 120–126.

SELTEN, R. (1975), "Re-examination of the Perfectness Concept for Equilibrium Points in Extensive Games," *International Journal of Game Theory,* Vol. 4, pp. 25–55.

SESHADRI, S., K. CHATTERJEE and G. L. LILIEN (1991), "Multiple Source Procurement Competitions," *Marketing Science,* Vol. 10, no. 3 (Summer), pp. 246–263.

SETHI, SURESH P. (1973), "Optimal Control of the Vidale-Wolfe Advertising Model," *Operations Research,* Vol. 21, no. 4 (July/August), pp. 998–1013.

SEWALL, MURPHY A. and DAN SAREL (1986), "Characteristics of Radio Commercials and Their Recall Effectiveness," *Journal of Marketing,* Vol. 50, no. 1 (January), pp. 52–60.

SEXTON, DONALD E., JR. (1970), "Estimating Marketing Policy Effects on Sales of a Frequently Purchased Product," *Journal of Marketing Research,* Vol. 7 (August), pp. 338–347.

SHAKED, A. and J. SUTTON (1982), "Relaxing Price Competition Through Product Differentiation," *Review of Economic Studies,* Vol. 49, pp. 3–13.

SHAKUN, MELVIN F. (1965), "Advertising Expenditures in Coupled Markets—A Game-Theory Approach," *Management Science,* Vol. 11 (February), pp. B42–47.

SHANKER, R. J., R. E. TURNER, and A. A. ZOLTNERS (1975), "Sales Territory Design: An Integrated Approach," *Management Science,* Vol. 22, no. 3 (November), pp. 309–320.

SHAPIRO, ARTHUR (1976), "Promotional Effectiveness at H. J. Heinz," *Interfaces,* Vol. 6, no. 2 (February), pp. 84–86.

SHARIF, M. N. and K. RAMANATHAN (1981), "Binomial Innovation Diffusion Models with Dynamic Potential Adopter Population," *Technological Forecasting and Social Change,* Vol. 20, no. 1 (August) pp. 63–87.

SHARIF, M. N. (1982), "Polynomial Innovation Diffusion Models," *Technological Forecasting and Social Change,* Vol. 21, pp. 301–323.

SHARMA, SUBHASH and D. D. ACHABAL (1982), "STEMCOM: An Analytical Model for Marketing Control," *Journal of Marketing.* Vol. 46 (Spring), pp. 104–113.

SHARMA, SUBHASH and RICHARD M. DURAND (1980), "Using the Linear Learning Model to Represent Variety-Seeking Behavior," *Proceedings,* Educators' Conference, Series No. 46. Chicago: American Marketing Association, pp. 148–151.

SHAW, RICHARD W. and SUSAN A. SHAW (1986), "Late Entry, Market Share and Competitive Survival: The Case of Synthetic Fibers," *Management and Decision Economics* 5 (June), pp. 72–79.

SHERIF, M. and C. HOVLAND (1961), *Social Judgment.* New Haven, Conn.: Yale University Press.

SHETH, JAGDISH N. (1973a), "Brand Profiles from Beliefs and Importances," *Journal of Advertising Research,* Vol. 13 (February), pp. 37–42.

SHETH, JAGDISH N. (1973b), "A Model of Industrial Buyer Behavior," *Journal of Marketing,* Vol. 37 (October), pp. 50–56.

SHETH, JAGDISH N. (1974), *Models of Buyer Behavior: Conceptual, Quantitative, and Empirical.* New York: Harper & Row.

SHIFLETT, S. (1979), "Toward a General Model

of Small Group Productivity," *Psychological Bulletin,* Vol. 86, pp. 69–79.

SHIPCHANDLER, ZOHER E. and JAMES S. MOORE (1988), "Examining the Effects of Regression Procedures on the Temporal Stability of Parameter Estimates in Marketing Models," *Journal of the Academy of Marketing Science,* Vol. 16 (Fall), pp. 79–87.

SHOCKER, ALLAN D., MOSHE BEN AKIRA, BRUNO BOCCARA and PRAKASH NEDUNGADI, "Consideration Set Influences on Consumer Decision-Making and Choice: Issues, Models, and Suggestions" *Marketing Letters* Vol. 2, no. 3 (August), pp. 181–198.

SHOCKER, ALLAN D. and V. SRINIVASAN (1974), "A Consumer-Based Methodology for the Identification of New Product Ideas," *Management Science,* Vol. 20, no. 6 (February), pp. 921–937.

SHOCKER, ALLAN D. and V. SRINIVASAN (1979), "Multi-attribute Approaches for Product Concept Evaluation and Generation: A Critical Review," *Journal of Marketing Research,* Vol. 16 (May), pp. 159–180.

SHOCKER, ALLAN D., ANTHONY J. ZAHORIK, and DAVID W. STEWART (1984), "Competitive Market Structure Analysis: A Comment on Problems," *Journal of Consumer Research,* Vol. 11 (December), pp. 836–847.

SHOEMAKER, ROBERT W. (1979), "An Analysis of Consumer Reactions to Product Promotions." In O. C. Ferrell, S. W. Brown, and C. W. Lamb, Jr., eds., *Conceptual and Theoretical Developments in Marketing,* Chicago: American Marketing Association. pp. 244–248.

SHOEMAKER, ROBERT W. (1986), "Comment on 'Dynamics of Price Elasticity and Brand Life Cycles: An Empirical Study,'" *Journal of Marketing Research,* Vol. 23 (February), pp. 78–82.

SHOEMAKER, ROBERT W., KENNETH G. HARDY, and HERBERT F. MACKENZIE (1989), "Measuring and Evaluating Sales Promotions from the Manufacturer and Retailer Perspectives," Conference Summary, Report No. 89–102, Marketing Science Institute, Cambridge, Mass. (January).

SHOEMAKER, ROBERT W. and F. R. SHOAF (1977), "Repeat Rates of Deal Purchases," *Journal of Advertising Research,* Vol. 17 (April), pp. 47–53.

SILK, ALVIN J. (1977), "Test-Retest Correlations and the Reliability of Copy Testing," *Journal of Marketing Research,* Vol. 14 (November), pp. 476–486.

SILK, ALVIN J. and MANOHAR U. KALWANI (1982), "Measuring Influence in Organizational Purchase Decisions," *Journal of Marketing Research,* Vol. 19 (May), pp. 165–181.

SILK, ALVIN J. and GLEN L. URBAN (1978), "Pre-Test Market Evaluation of New Packaged Goods: A Model and Measurement Methodology," *Journal of Marketing Research,* Vol. 15 (May), pp. 171–191.

SIMON, HERBERT A. (1952), "A Behavioral Model of Rational Choice," *Quarterly Journal of Economics,* Vol. 89, pp. 99–118.

SIMON, HERMANN (1978), "An Analytical Investigation of Kotler's Simulation Model," *Management Science,* Vol. 24, No. 14 (October), pp. 1462–1473.

SIMON, HERMANN (1979), "Dynamics of Price Elasticity and Brand Life Cycles: An Empirical Study," *Journal of Marketing Research,* Vol. 16, no. 4 (November), pp. 439–452.

SIMON, HERMANN (1982), "ADPULS: An Advertising Model with Wearout and Pulsation," *Journal of Marketing Research,* Vol. 19 (August), pp. 352–363.

SIMON, HERMANN (1989), *Price Management.* New York: North Holland.

SIMON, HERMANN and KARL-HEINZ SEBASTIAN (1987), "Diffusion and Advertising: The German Telephone Campaign," *Management Science,* Vol. 33, no. 4 (April), pp. 451–466.

SIMON, HERMANN and MICHAEL THIEL (1980), "Hits and Flops Among German Media Models," *Journal of Advertising Research,* Vol. 20, no. 6 (December), pp. 25–29.

SIMON, JULIAN L. and JOHAN ARNDT (1980), "The Shape of the Advertising Function," *Journal of Advertising Research,* Vol. 20 (August), pp. 11–28.

SIMONSON, ITAMAR (1990), "The Effect of Purchase Quantity and Timing on Variety-Seeking Behavior," *Journal of Marketing Research,* Vol. 27 (May), pp. 150–162.

SIMULMATICS CORPORATION (1962), *Simulmatics Media-Mix, Technical Description.* New York: Simulmatics Corp.

SINGER, E. (1968), *Antitrust Economics: Selected Legal Cases and Economic Models.* Englewood Cliffs, N.J.: Prentice Hall.

SINGH, JAGDIP (1988), "Consumer Complaint Intentions and Behavior: Definitional and Taxonomical Issues," *Journal of Marketing,* Vol. 52 (January), pp. 93–107.

SKINNER, B. F. (1938), *The Behavior of Organisms: An Experimental Analysis.* New York: Appleton Century Crofts.

SMITH, CLIFFORD W., JR. and ROSS L. WATTS (1984), "The Structure of Executive Compensation Contracts and the Control of Management," Working paper, University of Rochester. Rochester, N.Y. (March).

SOWTER, A. P., A. GABOR, and C. W. J. GRANGER (1971), "The Effect of Price on Choice," *Applied Economics,* Vol. 3, pp. 167–181.

SPEKMAN, ROBERT E. (1979), "Organizational Boundary Behavior: A Conceptual Framework for Investigating the Industrial Salesperson." In R. Bagozzi, ed., *Sales Management: New Developments from Behavioral and Decision Model Research,* Cambridge, Mass.: Marketing Science Institute, pp. 133–144.

SPENCE, A. M. (1981), "The Learning Curve and Competition," *Bell Journal of Economics,* Vol. 12, pp. 49–70.

SPENGLER, J. (1950), "Vertical Integration and Anti-Trust Policy," *Journal of Political Economy,* Vol. 58 (August), pp. 347–352.

SPRAGUE, RALPH H., JR. (1980), "A Framework for the Development of Decision Support Systems," *MIS Quarterly,* (December), pp. 1–26.

SRINIVASAN, V. (1981), "An Investigation of the Equal Commission Rate Policy for a Multi-product Salesforce," *Management Science,* Vol. 27, no. 7 (July), pp. 731–756.

SRINIVASAN, V. (1982), "Comments on the Role of Price in Individual Utility Judgments, Choice Models for Buyer Behavior." Greenwich, Conn.: JAI Press.

SRINIVASAN, V. (1988), "A Conjunctive-Compensatory Approach to the Self-explication of Multiattributed Preferences," *Decision Sciences,* Vol. 19, no. 2 (Spring), pp. 295–305.

SRINIVASAN, V. and A. D. SHOCKER (1973), "Linear Programming Techniques for Multidimensional Analysis of Preferences," *Psychometrika,* Vol. 38, no. 3 (September), pp. 337–369.

SRINIVASAN, V. and HELEN A. WEIR (1988), "A Direct Aggregation Approach to Inferring Microparameters of the Koyck Advertising-Sales Relationship from Macro Data," *Journal of Marketing Research,* Vol. 25 (May), pp. 145–156.

SRINIVASAN, V., P. VANDEN ABEELE, and I. BUTAYE (1989), "The Factor Structure of Multidimensional Response to Marketing Stimuli: A Comparison of Two Approaches," *Marketing Science,* Vol. 8, no. 1 (Winter), pp. 78–88.

SRIVASTAVA, RAJENDRA K., M. I. ALPERT, and A. D. SHOCKER (1984), "A Customer-Oriented Approach for Determining Market Structures," *Journal of Marketing,* Vol. 48 (Spring), pp. 32–45.

SRIVASTAVA, RAJENDRA K., VIJAY MAHAJAN, SRIDHAR N. RAMASWAMI, and JOSEPH CHERIAN (1985), "A Multi-attribute Diffusion Model for Forecasting the Adoption of Investment Alternatives for Consumers," *Technological Forecasting and Social Change,* Vol. 28 (December), pp. 325–333.

STANLEY, T. and M. SEWALL (1976), "Image Inputs to a Probabilistic Model: Predicting Retail Potential," *Journal of Marketing,* Vol. 40 (July), pp. 48–53.

STARCH, DANIEL (1966), "How Does Shape of Ads Affect Readership?" *Media/Scope,* Vol. 10, no. 7 (July), pp. 83–85.

STARK, R. M. and M. H. ROTHKOPF (1979), "Competitive Bidding: A Comprehensive Bibliography," *Operations Research,* Vol. 27, pp. 364–390.

STECKEL, JOEL H. (1990), "Committee Decision Making in Organizations: An Experimental Test of the Core," *Decision Sciences,* 21 (Winter), pp. 204–215.

STECKEL, JOEL, KIM P. CORFMAN, DAVID J. CURRY, SUMIL GUPTA, and JAMES SHANTEAU, (1991) "Prospects and Problems in Modeling Group Decisions" *Marketing Letters,* Vol. 2, no. 3 (August), pp. 231–240.

STECKEL, JOEL H., DONALD R. LEHMANN and KIM P. CORFMAN (1988), "Estimating Probabilistic Choice Models from Sparse Data: A Method and an Application to Groups," *Psychological Bulletin,* Vol. 103, no. 1, pp. 131–139.

STEFFLRE, VOLNEY J. (1971), *New Products and New Enterprises: A Report of an Experiment in Applied Social Science.* Irvine: University of California (March).

STEIN, M. O., R. V. AYERS, and A. SHAPENESO (1975), "A Model for Forecasting the Substitution of One Technology for Another," *Technological Forecasting and Social Change,* Vol. 7 (February), pp. 57–79.

STEINBERG, M. and R. E. PLANK (1987), "Expert Systems: The Integrative Sales Management Tool of the Future," *Journal of the Academy of Marketing Science,* Special Issue, Vol. 15, no. 2 (Summer), pp. 55–62.

STERN, LOUIS W. and ABEL L. EL-ANSARY (1977), *Marketing Channels.* Englewood Cliffs, N.J.: Prentice Hall.

STERN, LOUIS W. and ABEL L. EL-ANSARY (1988), *Marketing Channels,* 3rd ed. Englewood Cliffs, N. J.: Prentice Hall.

STEWART, DAVID N. and JOAN BLACKWELL (1980), "Media Decision Models: A Review and Evaluation," Paper presented at the TIMS/ORSA Meeting, Washington, D.C. (May).

STEWART, DAVID N. and DAVID H. FARSE (1986), *Effective Television Advertising: A Study of 1000 Commercials.* Lexington, Mass.: Lexington Books.

STEWART, DAVID W. (1989), "Measures, Methods, and Models in Advertising Research," *Journal of Advertising Research,* Vol. 29, no. 3 (June/July), pp. 54–60.

STEWART, M. (1990), "Was STAT Scan Really an Advance on AMTES?" *ADMAP* (April), pp. 32–35.

STIGLER, GEORGE (1952), *The Theory of Price,* rev. ed. New York: Macmillan.

STIGLER, GEORGE (1963), "A Note on Block Booking," reprinted in *Organization of Industry.* Chicago: Chicago University Press.

STIRLING, DAVID S. G. (1987), *Mathematical Analysis.* Chichester, West Sussex, England: Ellis Horwood Limited, distributed by Halsted Press, New York.

STOBAUGH, ROBERT and DANIEL YERGIN, eds. (1979), *Energy Future.* New York: Random House.

STOCK, JAMES R. and DOUGLAS M. LAMBERT (1987), *Strategic Logistics Management,* 2nd ed. Homewood, Ill: Richard D. Irwin.

STOETZEL, J. (1954), "Le prix comme limite." In P. L. Reynaud, ed., *La Psychologie Economique.* Paris: Librairie Marcel Riviere.

STOETZEL, J. (1970), "Psychological/Sociological Aspects of Price." In B. Taylor and G. Willis, eds., *Pricing Strategy,* Princeton, N.J.: Brandon Systems. pp. 70–74.

STOKEY, N. (1979), "Intertemporal Price Discrimination," *Quarterly Journal of Economics,* Vol. 93, pp. 355–371.

STOKEY, N. (1981), "Rational Expectations and Durable Goods Pricing," *Bell Journal of Economics,* Vol. 12, pp. 112–128.

STONEMAN, P. (1981), "Intra-Firm Diffusion, Bayesian Learning and Profitability," *Economic Journal,* Vol. 91 (June), pp. 375–388.

STRANG, ROGER A., ROBERT M. PRENTICE, and ALDEN G. CLAYTON (1975), *The Relationship Between Advertising and Promotion in Brand Strategy.* Cambridge, Mass.: Marketing Science Institute.

STRUSE, RUDOLPH W., III (1987), "Approaches to Promotion Evaluation: A Practitioner's Viewpoint, Commentary," *Marketing Science,* Vol. 6, no. 2 (Spring), pp. 150–151.

SUDHARSHAN, D., JENOLD H. MAY, and ALLAN D. SHOCKER (1987), "A Simulation Comparison of Methods for New Product Location," *Marketing Science,* Vol. 6, no. 2 (Spring), pp. 182–201.

SUJAN, M. (1985), "Consumer Knowledge: Effects on Evaluation Strategies Mediating Consumer Judgments," *Journal of Consumer Research,* Vol. 12, pp. 31–46.

SULTAN, FAREENA, JOHN U. FARLEY, and DONALD, R. LEHMANN (1990), "A Meta-analysis of Applications of Diffusion Models," *Journal of Marketing Research,* Vol. 27 (February), pp. 70–78.

SULTAN, R. (1975), "Pricing in the Electrical Oligopoly," Division of Research, Harvard Graduate School of Business Administration, Cambridge, Mass.

SWAN, JOHN E. and LINDA JONES COMBS (1976), "Product Performance and Consumer Satisfaction: A New Concept," *Journal of Marketing Research,* Vol. 13 (April), pp. 25–33.

SWINYARD, W. R. and M. L. RAY (1977), "Advertising Selling Interactions: An Attribution Theory Experiment," *Journal of Marketing Research,* Vol. 14, pp. 509–516.

TANNY, S. M. and N. A. DERZKO (1988), "Innovators and Imitators in Innovation Diffusion Modeling," *Journal of Forecasting,* Vol. 7 (October/November), pp. 225–234.

TAUBER, EDWARD M. (1977), "Forecasting Sales Prior to Test Market," *Journal of Marketing,* Vol. 41 (January), pp. 80–84.

TAYLOR, THAYER C. (1987), "Hewlett Packard Gives Sales Reps a Competitive Edge," *Sales and Marketing Management,* (February), pp. 36–41.

TELLIS, GERARD J. (1986), "Beyond the Many Faces of Price: An Integration of Pricing Strategies," *Journal of Marketing,* 50 (October), pp. 146–160.

TELLIS, GERARD J. (1987), "Consumer Purchasing Strategies and the Information in Retail Prices," *Journal of Retailing,* Vol. 63, no. 3 (Fall), pp. 279–297.

TELLIS, GERARD J. (1988), "The Price Elasticity of Selective Demand: A Meta-analysis of Econometric Models of Sales," *Journal of Marketing Research,* Vol. 25 (November), pp. 331–341.

TELLIS, GERARD J. (1989), "Point of View: Interpreting Advertising and Price Elasticities," *Journal of Advertising Research* (August/September), pp. 40–43.

TELLIS, GERARD J. and BIRGER WERNERFELT (1987), "Competitive Price and Quality Under Asymmetric Information," *Marketing Science,* Vol. 6, no. 3 (Summer), pp. 240–253.

TELSER, L. G. (1962), "The Demand for Branded Goods as Estimated from Consumer Panel Data," *Review of Economics and Statistics,* Vol. 44, pp. 300–324.

TELSER, L. G. (1980), "A Theory of Self-enforcing Agreements," *Journal of Business,* Vol. 53, no. 1, pp. 27–44.

THALER, RICHARD (1985), "Mental Accounting and Consumer Choice," *Marketing Science,* Vol. 4, no. 3 (Summer), pp. 199–214.

THEIL, HENRI (1975), *Theory and Measurement of Consumer Demand,* Vol. 1. New York: North-Holland.

THEIL, HENRI (1976), *Theory and Measurement of Consumer Demand,* Vol. 2. New York: North-Holland.

THIETART, R. and R. VIVAS (1984), "An Empirical Investigation of Success Strategies for Business Along the Product Life Cycle," *Management Science,* Vol. 30, no. 12 (December), pp. 1405–1423.

THOMAS, ROBERT J. (1984), "Bases of Power in Organizational Buying Decisions," *Industrial Marketing Management,* Vol. 13, pp. 209–217.

THOMPSON, GERALD L. and JINN-TSAIR TENG (1984), "Optimal Pricing and Advertising Policies for New Product Oligopoly Models," *Marketing Science,* Vol. 3, no. 2 (Spring), pp. 148–168.

THOMPSON, J. M. T. and H. B. STEWART (1986), *Nonlinear Dynamics and Chaos.* New York: John Wiley.

THOMPSON, LEIGH L., ELIZABETH A. MANNIX, and MAX H. BAZERMAN (1988), "Group Negotiation: Effects of Decision Rule, Agenda, and Aspiration," *Journal of Personality and Social Psychology,* Vol. 54, pp. 86–95.

THOMPSON, PATRICK and THOMAS NOORDEWIER (1988), "Effects of Consumer-Oriented Sales Promotions on Durable

Goods: The Case of Domestic Automobile Sales," Working paper, College of Business, The Ohio State University, Columbus.

THORELLI, HANS B. and STEPHEN C. BURNETT (1981), "The Nature of Product Life Cycles for Industrial Goods Businesses," *Journal of Marketing,* Vol. 45, no. 4 (Fall), pp. 97–108.

TORGERSON, WARREN S. (1958), *Theory and Method of Scaling.* New York: John Wiley.

TOTTEN, JOHN C. and MARTIN BLOCK (1987), *Analyzing Sales Promotion: Text and Cases.* Chicago: Commerce Communications.

TRODAHL, VERLING C. and ROBERT L. JONES (1965), "Prediction of Newspaper Advertisement Readership," *Journal of Advertising Research,* Vol. 5 (March), pp. 23–27.

TSE, DAVID K. and PETER C. WILTON (1988), "Models of Consumer Satisfaction Formation: An Extension," *Journal of Marketing Research,* Vol. 25 (May), pp. 204–212.

TULL, D., R. BORING, and M. GONSIOR (1964), "The Relationship of Price and Imputed Quality," *Journal of Business,* Vol. 37, pp. 186–191.

TULL, DONALD S., VAN R. WOOD, DALE DUHAN, TOM GILLPATRICK, KIM R. ROBERTSON, and JAMES G. HELGESON (1986), "'Leveraged Decision Making in Advertising: The Flat Maximum Principle and Its Implications," *Journal of Marketing Research,* Vol. 23 (February), pp. 25–32.

TURNBULL, P. W. and J. P. VALLA, eds. (1986), *Strategies for International Industrial Marketing.* London: Croom Helm.

TVERSKY, AMOS (1972), "Elimination by Aspects: A Theory of Choice," *Psychological Review,* Vol. 79, pp. 281–299.

TVERSKY, AMOS and DANIEL KAHNEMAN (1974), "Judgment Under Uncertainty: Heuristics and Biases," *Science,* Vol. 185, pp. 1124–1131.

TWEDT, DIK W. (1952), "A Multiple Factor Analysis of Advertising Readership," *Journal of Applied Psychology* (June), pp. 207–215.

TYBOUT, ALICE M. and CAROL A. SCOTT. (1983), "Availability of Well-Defined Internal Knowledge and the Attitude Formation Process: Information Aggregation versus Self-Perception," *Journal of Personality and Social Psychology,* Vol. 44, pp. 474–479.

UHL, J. (1970), "Consumer Perception of Retail Food Price Changes," Paper presented at the First Annual Meeting of the Association for Consumer Research, New York.

UNIVERSITY OF LONDON ATLAS COMPUTING SERVICE (1972), *DYNAMO—Media Scheduling Suite of Programs.* University of London: Atlas Computing Service.

URBAN, GLEN L. (1969), "A Mathematical Modeling Approach to Product Line Decisions," *Journal of Marketing Research,* Vol. 6 (February), pp. 40–47.

URBAN, GLEN L. (1970), "SPRINTER Mod III: A Model for the Analysis of New Frequently Purchased Consumer Products," *Operations Research,* Vol. 18 (September/October), pp. 805–853.

URBAN, GLEN L. (1974), "Building Models for Decision-Makers," *Interfaces,* Vol. 4, no. 3 (May), pp. 1–11.

URBAN, GLEN L. (1975a), "National and Local Allocation of Advertising Dollars," *Journal of Marketing Research,* Vol. 15, no. 6, pp. 7–16.

URBAN, GLEN L. (1975b), "PERCEPTOR: A Model for Product Positioning," *Management Science,* Vol. 21, no. 8 (April), pp. 858–871.

URBAN, G. L., T. CARTER, S. GASKIN, and Z. MUCHA (1986), "Market Share Rewards to Pioneering Brands: An Empirical Analysis and Strategic Implications," *Management Science,* Vol. 32, pp. 645–659.

URBAN, GLEN L., and GURUMURTHY KALYANARAM (1990) "Dynamic Effects of the Order of Entry on Market Share, Trial Penetration, and Repeat Purchases for Frequently Purchased Consumer Goods," Working paper #3207–90, Sloan School of Management, M.I.T., Cambridge.

URBAN, GLEN L. and JOHN R. HAUSER (1980),

Design and Marketing of New Products. Englewood Cliffs, N.J.: Prentice Hall.

URBAN, GLEN L., JOHN R. HAUSER, and NIKHILESH DHOLAKIA (1987), *Essentials of New Product Management.* Englewood Cliffs, N.J.: Prentice Hall.

URBAN GLEN L., JOHN R. HAUSER, and JOHN H. ROBERTS (1990), "Prelaunch Forecasting of New Automobiles," *Management Science,* Vol. 36, no. 4, pp. 401–421.

URBAN, G., P. L. JOHNSON, and J. R. HAUSER (1984), "Testing Competitive Market Structures," *Marketing Science,* Vol. 3, no. 2 (Spring), pp. 83–112.

URBAN GLEN L. and GERALD M. KATZ (1983), "Pre-Test-Market Models: Validation and Managerial Implications," *Journal of Marketing Research,* Vol. 20 (August), pp. 221–234.

URBANY, JOEL E., PETER R. DICKSON, and WILLIAM L. WILKIE (1989), "Buyer Uncertainty and Information Search," *Journal of Consumer Research,* Vol. 156, no. 2 (September), pp. 208–215.

URBANY, JOEL E., THOMAS J. MADDEN, and PETER R. DICKSON (1989), "All's Not Fair in Pricing: An Initial Look at the Dual Entitlement Principle," *Marketing Letters,* Vol. 1, no. 1, pp. 17–25.

VANDEN ABEELE, PIET, ELS GIJSBRECHTS, and MARC VANHUELE (1990), "Specification and Empirical Evaluation of a Cluster-Asymmetry Market Share Model," *International Journal of Research in Marketing,* Vol. 7, pp. 223–247.

VANHONACKER, WILFRIED R. (1984), "Estimation and Testing of a Dynamic Sales Response Model with Data Aggregated over Time: Some Results for the Autoregressive Current Effects Model," *Journal of Marketing Research,* Vol. 21 (November), pp. 445–455.

VANHONACKER, WILFRIED R. (1990), "Estimating Dynamic Response Models When the Data Are Subject to Different Temporal Aggregation," *Marketing Letters,* Vol. 1, no. 2 (June), pp. 125–138.

VAN HORNE, J. C. (1980), *Financial Management and Policy,* 5th ed. Englewood Cliffs, N.J.: Prentice Hall.

VARIAN, HAL R. (1980), "A Model of Sales," *The American Economic Review,* Vol. 70, no. 4 (September), pp. 651–659.

VIDALE, H. L. and H. B. WOLFE (1957), "An Operations Research Study of Sales Response to Advertising," *Operations Research,* Vol. 5, pp. 370–381.

VYAS, N. and A. G. WOODSIDE (1986), "Micro Analysis of Supplier Choice Strategies: Industrial Packaging Materials." In *Industrial Marketing: An American Perspective.* New York: Springer Verlag.

WAGNER, HARVEY M. (1980), "Research Portfolio for Inventory Management and Production Planning Systems," *Operations Research,* Vol. 28, no. 3 (May/June), pp. 445–475.

WAGNER, UDO and ALFRED TAUDES (1986), "A Multivariate Polya Model of Brand Choice and Purchase Incidence," *Marketing Science,* Vol. 5, no. 3 (Summer), pp. 219–244.

WAID, C., D. F. CLARK, and R. L. ACKOFF (1956), "Allocation of Sales Effort in the Lamp Divisions of the General Electric Company," *Operational Research Quarterly,* Vol. 4 (December), pp. 629–647.

WALPOLE, RONALD E. and RAYMOND H. MYERS (1989), *Probability and Statistics for Engineers and Scientists,* 4th ed. New York: Macmillan.

WASSERMAN, STANLEY and DAWN IACOBUCCI (1986), "Statistical Analysis of Discrete Relational Data," *British Journal of Mathematical and Statistical Psychology,* Vol. 39, pp. 41–64.

WASSERMAN, STANLEY and DAWN IACOBUCCI (1988), "Sequential Social Network Data," *Psychometrika,* Vol. 53, no. 2 (June), pp. 261–282.

WEBSTER, FREDERICK E., JR. (1984), *Industrial Marketing Strategy,* 2nd ed. New York: Wiley.

WEBSTER, FREDERICK E., JR., and YORAM WIND (1972a), "A General Model for Understanding Organizational Buying Behavior," *Journal of Marketing,* Vol. 36 (April), pp. 12–19.

WEBSTER, FREDERICK E., JR., and YORAM WIND (1972b), *Organizational Buying Behav-*

ior. Englewood Cliffs, N.J.: Prentice Hall, 1972.

WEINBERG, CHARLES B. (1975), "An Optimal Commission Plan for Salesmen's Control Over Price," *Management Science,* Vol. 21 (April), pp. 937–943.

WEISS, DOYLE L. (1968), "Determinants of Market Share," *Journal of Marketing Research,* Vol. 5 (August), pp. 290–295.

WEISS, DOYLE L., CHARLES B. WEINBERG, and PIERRE M. WENDAL (1983), "The Effects of Serial Correlation and Data Aggregation on Advertising Measurement," *Journal of Marketing Research,* Vol. 20 (August), pp. 268–279.

WEITZ, B. A. (1981), "Effectiveness in Sales Interactions: A Contingency Framework," *Journal of Marketing,* Vol. 45 (Winter), pp. 85–103.

WEITZ, BARTON (1985), "Introduction to Special Issue on Competition in Marketing," *Journal of Marketing Research,* Vol. 22 (August), pp. 229–236.

WELLAN, DEE M. and ANDREW S. C. EHRENBERG (1990), "A Case of Seasonal Segmentation," *Marketing Research,* (June), pp. 11–13.

WELLS, WILLIAM D., CLARK LEAVITT, and MAUREEN MCCONNELL (1971), "A Reaction Profile for TV Commercials," *Journal of Advertising Research,* Vol. 11, no. 2 (December), pp. 11–17.

WENSLEY, ROBIN (1982), "PIMS and BCG: New Horizons or False Dawn?" *Strategic Management Journal,* Vol. 3, pp. 147–158.

WENZEL, WILFRIED and ROLF SPEETZEN (1987), "How Much Frequency Is Enough?" *Journal of Media Planning* (Spring), pp. 5–16.

WERNERFELT, B. (1985), "The Dynamics of Prices and Market Share over the Product Life Cycle," *Management Science,* Vol. 31, pp. 928–939.

WERNERFELT, B. (1986), "A Special Case of Dynamic Pricing," *Management Science,* Vol. 32, no. 12, (December), pp. 1562–1566.

WESTBROOK, ROBERT A. (1987), "Product/Consumption-Based Affective Re-

sponses and Postpurchase Processes," *Journal of Marketing Research,* Vol. 24 (August), pp. 258–270.

WHITTEN, I. T. (1979), "Brand Preference in the Cigarette Industry and the Advantage of Early Entry," Federal Trade Commission, Bureau of Economics (June).

WIERENGA, B. (1974), *An Investigation of Brand Choice Processes.* Rotterdam: Rotterdam University Press.

WIERENGA, B. (1990), "The First Generation of Marketing Expert Systems," Working series paper #90–009, Department of Marketing, Rotterdam School of Management, Erasmus University.

WILDT, ALBERT R. (1974), "Multi-firm Analysis of Competitive Decision Variables," *Journal of Marketing Research,* Vol. 11 (February), pp. 50–62.

WILDT, ALBERT R. (1976a), "On Evaluating Market Segmentation Studies and the Properties of R^2," *Management Science,* Vol. 22 (April), pp. 904–908.

WILDT, ALBERT R. (1976b), "The Empirical Investigation of Time Dependent Parameter Variation in Marketing Models." In *Educators' Proceedings.* Chicago: American Marketing Association.

WILDT, ALBERT R. (1977), "Estimating Models of Seasonal Marketing Response Using Dummy Variables," *Journal of Marketing Research,* Vol. 14, no. 1 (February), pp. 34–41.

WILDT, ALBERT R. and JOHN M. MCCANN (1980), "A Regression Model for Market Segmentation Studies," *Journal of Marketing Research,* Vol. 17 (August), pp. 335–340.

WILDT, ALBERT R. and RUSSELL S. WINER (1983), "Modeling and Estimation in Changing Market Environments," *Journal of Business,* Vol. 56 (July), pp. 365–388.

WILKIE, WILLIAM L. and EDGAR A. PESSEMIER (1973), "Issues in Marketing's Use of Multi-attribute Models," *Journal of Marketing Research,* Vol. 10 (November), pp. 428–441.

WILLIAMSON, O. (1975), *Markets and Hierar-*

chies: Analysis and Antitrust Implications. New York: The Free Press.

WILLIAMSON, O. (1986), *The Economic Institutions of Capitalism.* New York: The Free Press.

WILLIG, R. (1978), "Pareto-Superior Nonlinear Outlay Schedules," *Bell Journal of Economics,* Vol. 9, pp. 56–69.

WILSON, AUBREY (1969), "Industrial Market Research in Britain," *Journal of Marketing Research,* Vol. 6 (February), pp. 15–28.

WILSON, DAVID T., H. L. MATTHEWS, and J. W. HARVEY (1975), "An Empirical Test of the Fishbein Behavioral Intention Model," *Journal of Consumer Research,* Vol. 1, pp. 39–48.

WILSON, ELIZABETH, J., GARY L. LILIEN, and DAVID T. WILSON (1991), "Developing and Testing a Contingency Paradigm of Group Choice in Organizational Buying," *Journal of Marketing Research,* Vol. 27, (November), pp. 452–466.

WILSON, R. DALE (1980), "A Model Testing Procedure for Evaluating the Influence of Short-Term Promotions on Patterns of Consumer Behavior: Literature Review and Methodology." In R. Leone, ed., *Proceeding, Special Interest Conference on Market Measurement and Analysis, Proceedings,* Providence, R.I.: The Institute of Management Science. pp. 54–69.

WILSON, R. DALE, LARRY M. NEWMAN, and MANOJ HASTAK (1979), "On the Validity of Research Methods in Consumer Dealing Activity: An Analysis of Timing Issues." In Neil Beckwith et al., ed., *Educators' Conference Proceedings,* Chicago: American Marketing Association. pp. 41–46.

WIND, J., P. E. GREEN, D. SHIFFLET, and M. SCARBROUGH (1989), "Courtyard by Marriott: Designing a Hotel Facility with Consumer-Based Marketing Models," *Interfaces,* Vol. 19, no. 1, pp. 25–47.

WIND, YORAM (1973), "A New Procedure for Concept Evaluation," *Journal of Marketing,* Vol. 37 (October), pp. 2–11.

WIND, YORAM (1976), "Preference of Relevant Others and Individual Choice Models,"

Journal of Consumer Research, Vol. 3 (August), pp. 50–57.

WIND, YORAM (1981a), "Marketing-Oriented Strategic Planning Models." In R. Schultz and A. A. Zoltners, eds., *Marketing Decision Models,* New York: North-Holland, pp. 207–250.

WIND, YORAM (1981b), "Marketing and Corporate Strategy: Problems and Perspectives," Paper presented at the 13th Annual Albert Wesley Frey Lecture, The University of Pittsburgh (March).

WIND, YORAM and HENRY CLAYCAMP (1976), "Planning Product Line Strategy: A Matrix Approach," *Journal of Marketing,* Vol. 40 (January), pp. 2–9.

WIND, YORAM, VIJAY MAHAJAN, and DONALD J. SWIRE (1983), "An Empirical Comparison of Standardized Portfolio Models," *Journal of Marketing,* Vol. 47 (Spring), 89–99.

WIND, YORAM and THOMAS S. ROBERTSON (1983), "Marketing Strategy: New Directions for Theory and Research," *Journal of Marketing,* Vol. 47 (Spring), pp. 12–25.

WIND, YORAM and THOMAS L. SAATY (1980), "Marketing Applications of the Analytic Hierarchy Process," *Management Science,* Vol. 26, no. 7 (July), pp. 641–658.

WINER, B. J. (1980a), "A Longitudinal Model to Decompose the Effects of an Advertising Stimulus on Family Consumption," *Management Science,* Vol. 26, no. 1, pp. 78–85.

WINER, B. J. (1980b), "Estimation of a Longitudinal Model to Decompose the Effect of an Advertising Stimulus on Family Consumption," *Management Science,* Vol. 26, no. 5, pp. 471–482.

WINER, RUSSELL S. (1985), "A Price Vector Model of Demand for Consumer Durables: Preliminary Developments," *Marketing Science,* Vol. 4, pp. 74–90.

WINER, RUSSELL S. (1986), "A Reference Price Model of Brand Choice for Frequently Purchased Products," *Journal of Consumer Research,* Vol. 13 (September), pp. 250–256.

WINER, RUSSELL S. (1988), "Behavioral Perspective on Pricing: Buyers' Subjective Perceptions of Price Revisited." In T. M. Devinney, ed., *Issues in Pricing: Theory and Research,* Chap. 2. Lexington, Mass.: Lexington Books.

WINER, RUSSELL S. and WILLIAM L. MOORE (1989), "Evaluating the Effects of Marketing-Mix Variables on Brand Positioning," *Journal of Advertising Research,* Vol. 29, no. 1 (February/March), pp. 39–45.

WINKLER, ROBERT L. (1972), *Introduction to Bayesian Inference and Decision,* New York: Holt, Rinehart and Winston.

WINKLER, ROBERT L. (1968), "The Consensus of Subjective Probability Distributions," *Management Science,* Vol. 15, pp. B61-B75.

WINKLER, ROBERT L. (1986), "Expert Resolution," *Management Science,* Vol. 32, no. 3 (March), pp. 298–303.

WINKLER, ROBERT L. and WILLIAM L. HAYS (1975), *Statistics: Probability, Inference, and Decision,* 2nd ed. New York: Holt, Rinehart and Winston.

WITTINK, DICK R. (1977), "Exploring Territorial Differences in the Relationship Between Marketing Variables," *Journal of Marketing Research,* Vol. 14, pp. 145–155.

WITTINK, DICK R. (1983), "Autocorrelation and Related Issues in Applications of Regression Analysis," Working paper, Johnson Graduate School of Management, Cornell University, Ithaca, N.Y. (October).

WITTINK, DICK R., MICHAEL J. ADDONA, WILLIAM J. HAWKES, and JOHN C. PORTER (1987), "SCAN-PRO: A Model to Measure Short-Term Effects of Promotional Activities on Brand Sales, Based on Store-Level Scanner Data," Working paper, Johnson Graduate School of Management, Cornell University, Ithaca, N.Y.

WITTINK, DICK R. and PHILIPPE CATTIN (1989), "Commercial Use of Conjoint Analysis: An Update," *Journal of Marketing,* 53 (July), pp. 91–96.

WOLFE, H. B., J. R. BROWN, and G. C. THOMPSON (1962), *Measuring Advertising Results.* Studies in Business Policy, No. 102, New York: The Conference Board. pp. 62–68.

WONNACOTT, RONALD J. and THOMAS H. WONNACOTT (1979), *Econometrics,* 2nd ed. New York: John Wiley.

WOODSIDE, ARCH G. and GERALD L. WADDLE (1975), "Sales Effects of In-Store Advertising," *Journal of Advertising Research,* Vol. 15 (June), pp. 29–34.

WRIGHT, P. L. (1974), "The Harassed Decision Maker: Time Pressures, Distractions, and the Use of Evidence," *Journal of Applied Psychology,* Vol. 59 (October), pp. 555–561.

WRIGHT, PETER (1980), "Message-Evoked Thoughts: Persuasion Research Using Thought Verbalizations," *Journal of Consumer Research,* Vol. 7 (September), pp. 151–175.

WRIGHT, PETER L. and FREDERICK BARBOUR (1977), "Phased Decision Strategies: Sequels to an Initial Screening." In Martin Starr and Milan Zeleny, eds., *Multiple Criteria Decision Marking,* North-Holland *TIMS Studies in the Management Sciences,* No. 6, Amsterdam: North-Holland. pp. 91–109.

WRIGHT, W. F. and U. ANDERSON (1989), "Effects of Situational Familiarity and Financial Incentive on Use of Anchoring and Adjustment Heuristic for Probability Assessment," *Organizational Behavior and Human Decision Processes,* Vol. 44, pp. 68–82.

XIE, J. and M. SIRBU (1991), "Duopolistic Dynamic Demand and Strategic Pricing in the Presence of Network Externalities," Paper presented at the ORSA/TIMS Joint National Meeting, Philadelphia.

YAMANAKA, JIRO (1962), "The Prediction of Ad Readership Scores," *Journal of Advertising Research,* Vol. 2 (March), pp. 18–23.

YANKELOVICH, SKELLY and WHITE, INC. (1981), "LTM Estimating Procedures" in *New Product Forecasting: Models and Applications,* Y. Wind, V. Mahajan and R. Cardozo, eds. (Lexington Books: Lexington, MA).

YELLE, L. E. (1979), "The Learning Curve: Historic Review and Comprehensive

Survey," *Decision Sciences,* Vol. 10 (April), pp. 302–327.

YOON, EUNSANG and GARY L. LILIEN (1985), "New Industrial Product Performance: The Impact of Market Characteristics and Strategy," *Journal of Product Innovation Management,* Vol. 3 (September), pp. 134–144.

YOUNG, SHIRLEY (1972), "Copy Testing Without Magic Numbers," *Journal of Advertising Research,* Vol. 12, no. 1 (February), pp. 3–12.

YOUNG, WILLIAM J. (1987), "Have Computers Revolutionized Sales Management?" *Management Review,* (April), pp. 54–55.

ZAICHKOWSKY, JUDITH LYNNE (1985), "Measuring the Involvement Construct," *Journal of Consumer Research,* Vol. 12 (December), pp. 341–352.

ZALTMAN, G. and M. WALLENDORF (1979), *Consumer Behavior: Basic Findings and Management Implications.* New York: John Wiley.

ZEITHAML, V. (1986), "Defining and Relating Price, Perceived Quality, and Perceived Value," Working paper, Marketing Science Institute, Cambridge, Mass.

ZIELSKI, HUBERT A. (1959), "The Remembering and Forgetting of Advertising," *Journal of Marketing,* Vol. 23 (January), pp. 239–243.

ZIELSKI, HUBERT A. (1986), "Comment on 'Advertising Pulsing Policies for Generating Awareness for New Products,'" *Marketing Science,* Vol. 5, no. 2 (Spring), p. 109.

ZOLTNERS, ANDRIS A. (1976), "Integer Programming Models for Sales Territory Alignment to Maximize Profit," *Journal of Marketing Research,* Vol. 13 (November), pp. 426–430.

ZOLTNERS, ANDRIS A. (1979), "A Unified Approach to Sales Territory Alignment." In R. Bagozzi, ed., *Sales Management: New Developments from Behavioral and De-*

cision Model Research, Marketing Science Institute, Cambridge, Mass., pp. 360–376.

ZOLTNERS, ANDRIS A. and J. A. DODSON (1983), "A Market Selection Model for Multiple End-Use Products," *Journal of Marketing,* Vol. 47 (Spring), pp. 76–88.

ZOLTNERS, ANDRIS A. and KATHY S. GARDNER (1980), "A Review of Sales Force Decision Models," Working paper, Northwestern University, Evanston, Ill. (July).

ZOLTNERS, ANDRIS A. and P. SINHA (1980), "Integer Programming Models for Sales Resource Allocation," *Management Science,* Vol. 26, no. 3 (March), pp. 242–260.

ZOLTNERS, ANDRIS A. and PRABHAKANT SINHA (1983), "Sales Territory Alignment: A Review and Model," *Management Science,* Vol. 29, no. 11, November, pp. 1237–1256.

ZOLTNERS, ANDRIS A., PRABHAKANT SINHA, and P. S. C. CHONG (1979), "An Optimal Algorithm for Sales Representative Time Management," *Management Science,* Vol. 25, no. 12 (December), pp. 1197–1207.

ZUFRYDEN, FRED S. (1978), "An Empirical Evaluation of a Composite Heterogeneous Model of Brand Choice and Purchase Timing," *Management Science,* Vol. 24, pp. 761–773.

ZUFRYDEN, FRED S. (1986), "Multibrand Transition Probabilities as a Function of Explanatory Variables: Estimation by a Least-Squares-Based Approach," *Journal of Marketing Research,* Vol. 23 (May), pp. 177–183.

ZUFRYDEN, FRED S. (1987), "A Model for Relating Advertising Media Exposures to Purchase Incidence Behavior Patterns," *Management Science,* Vol. 33, no. 10 (October), pp. 1253–1266.

ZUFRYDEN, FRED S. (1989), "How Much Should Be Spent for Advertising a Brand?" *Journal of Advertising Research,* Vol. 29, no. 2 (April/May), pp. 24–34.

EXHIBIT CREDITS

Exhibit 2.7   A. S. C. Ehrenberg, 1972, *Repeat Buying: Theory and Applications*. Computations of theoretical switching levels using the Ehrenberg (1972) model, Elsevier Science Publishers B. V. Amsterdam.

Exhibit 2.8   Alfred A. Kuehn, "Consumer Brand Choice—A Learning Process?" in *Journal of Advertising Research,* Vol. 2 (December), 1962, pp. 10–17, Advertising Research Foundation.

Exhibit 2.9   Barbara E. Kahn, Manohar U. Kalwani and Donald G. Morrison, "Measuring Variety-Seeking and Reinforcement Behaviors Using Panel Data. Reprinted from *Journal of Marketing Research,* Vol. 23 (May), pp. 89–100, 1986, published by the American Marketing Association.

Exhibit 2.10   Reprinted by permission of the publisher from "Diffusion Uncertainty and Firm Size" by Bart Nooteboom, *International Journal of Research in Marketing,* Vol. 6, p. 120, copyright 1989 by Elsevier Science Publishers B. V. Amsterdam.

Exhibit 2.11   John R. Hauser and Birger Wernerfelt, "An Evaluation Cost Model of Consideration Sets." Reprinted from *Journal of Consumer Research,* 16 (March), p. 394, 1990, published by the American Marketing Association.

Exhibit 2.13   Michael R. Hagerty and David A. Aaker, "A Normative Model of Consumer Information Processing." Reprinted from *Marketing Science,* Vol. 3, No. 3 (Summer), 1984, p. 232, published by The Institute of Management Sciences.

Exhibit 2.15   William L. Moore and Russell S. Winer, "A Panel-Data Based Method for Merging Joint Space and Market Response Function Estimation." Reprinted from *Marketing Science,* Vol. 6, No. 1 (Winter), 1987, p. 31, published by The Institute of Management Sciences.

Exhibit 2.16   Glen L. Urban and John R. Hauser, *Design and Marketing of New Products,* 1980, p. 191, published by Prentice Hall.

Exhibit 2.17   Glen L. Urban and John R. Hauser, *Design and Marketing of New Products,* 1980, pp. 200–205, published by Prentice Hall.

Exhibit 2.18   John R. Hauser and Steven M. Shugan, "Intensity Measures of Consumer Preference." Reprinted from *Operations Research,* Vol. 28, No. 2 (March/April), 1980, p. 303, published by The Institute of Management Sciences.

Exhibit 2.19   J. Scott Long, "Confirmatory Factor Analysis," *Quantitative Applications in the Social Sciences,* Series No. 33, 1983, p. 14, published by Sage Publications, Inc.

Exhibit 2.20   Richard P. Bagozzi, "A Field Investigation of Causal Relations Among Cognitions, Affect, Intentions and Behavior." Reprinted from *Journal of Marketing Research,* Vol. 19 (November), p. 578, 1982, published by the American Marketing Association.

Exhibit 2.21   Glen L. Urban and John R. Hauser, *Design and Marketing of New Products,* 1980, p. 274, published by Prentice Hall.

Exhibit 2.26   Glen L. Urban and John R. Hauser, *Design and Marketing of New Products,* 1980, p. 92, published by Prentice Hall.

Exhibit 2.27   William O. Bearden and Jesse E. Teel, "Selected Determinants of Consumer Satisfaction and Complaint Reports." Reprinted from *Journal of Marketing Research,* Vol. 20 (February), 1983, p. 22, published by the American Marketing Association.

Exhibit 2.28   James M. Lattin and Leigh McAlister, "Using a Variety-Seeking Model to Identify Substitute and Complementary Relationships Among Competing Products." Reprinted from *Journal of Marketing Research,* Vol. 22, 1985, p. 334, published by the American Marketing Association.

Exhibit 2.30   John Roberts and Glen L. Urban, "Modeling Multiattribute Utility, Risk, and Belief Dynamics for New Consumer Durable Brand Choice." Reprinted from *Management Science,* Vol. 34, No. 2 (February), 1988, p. 18, published by The Institute of Management Sciences.

Exhibit 3.1   Jagdish N. Sheth, "A Model of Industrial Buyer Behavior." Reprinted from the *Journal of Marketing,* Vol. 37 (October), 1973, p. 51, published by the American Marketing Association.

Exhibit 3.2   Frederick E. Webster, Jr., and Yoram Wind, *Organizational Buying Behavior,* 1972, p. 15. Published by Prentice Hall.

Exhibit 4.6   Reprinted with permission of Lexington Books, an Imprint of Macmillan, Inc. from *Issues in Pricing: Theory and Research,* Chap. 3 "Price, Advertising, and Scale as Information-Revelation Mechanisms in Product Markets," T. M. Devinney, Editor. Copyright © 1988 by Lexington Books.

Exhibit 4.8   Reprinted with permission of Lexington Books, an Imprint of Macmillan, Inc. from *Issues in Pricing: Theory and Research,* Chap. 3, "Price, Advertising, and Scale as Information-Revelation Mechanisms in Product Markets," T. M. Devinney, Editor. Copyright © 1988 by Lexington Books.

Exhibit 4.9   Gerard J. Tellis, "Beyond the Many Faces of Price: An Integration of Pricing Strategies." Reprinted from the *Journal of Marketing,* 50 (October), 1986, p. 148, published by the American Association.

Exhibit 5.7   Paul E. Green and Donald S. Tull, *Research for Marketing Decisions,* 3rd ed., 1975, p. 644, published by Prentice Hall.

Exhibit 5.8   Glen L. Urban and John R. Hauser, *Design and Marketing of New Products,* 1980, p. 256, published by Prentice-Hall.

Exhibit 5.9   Glen L. Urban, "PERCEPTOR: A Model for Product Positioning." Reprinted from *Management Science,* Vol. 21, No. 8 (April), 1975 p. 867, published by The Institute of Management Sciences.

Exhibit 6.1   John D. C. Little, "Aggregate Advertising Models: The State of the Art." Reprinted from *Operations Research* Vol. 27, No. 4 (July/August), 1979, p. 637, published by The Institute of Management Sciences.

Exhibit 6.2	John D. C. Little, "Aggregate Advertising Models: The State of the Art." Reprinted from *Operations Research* Vol. 27, No. 4 (July/August), 1979, pp. 629–667, published by The Institute of Management Sciences.
Exhibit 6.3	John D. C. Little, "Aggregate Advertising Models: The State of the Art." Reprinted from *Operations Research* Vol. 27, No. 4 (July/August), 1979, pp. 629–667, published by The Institute of Management Sciences.
Exhibit 6.5	Robert C. Grass, "Satiation Effects on Advertising" *14th Annual Conference, Advertising Research Foundation,* 1968, Advertising Research Foundation.
Exhibit 6.6	McDonald, Colin (1971), "What Is the Short-Term Effect of Advertising? Cambridge, MA, *Marketing Science Institute,* Report No. 71-142 (February).
Exhibit 6.11	Vijay Mahajan and Eitan Muller, "Advertising Pulsing Policies for Generating Awareness for New Products." John D. C. Little, "Aggregate Advertising Models: The State of the Art." Reprinted from *Marketing Science,* Vol. 5, No. 2 (Spring), 1986, p. 92, published by The Institute of Management Sciences.
Exhibit 6.13	Ambar G. Rao and P. B. Miller, "Advertising/Sales Response Functions," *Journal of Advertising Research,* Vol. 15, 1975, p. 13, Advertising Research Foundation.
Exhibit 6.14	A. P. Kuritsky, J. D. C. Little, A. J. Silk and E. S. Bassman, "The Development, Testing and Execution of a New Marketing Strategy at AT&T Long Lines." Reprinted from *Interfaces,* Vol. 12, No. 6 (December), 1982, p. 28, published by The Institute of Management Sciences.
Exhibit 6.15	A. P. Kuritsky, J. D. C. Little, A. J. Silk and E. S. Bassman, "The Development, Testing and Execution of a New Marketing Strategy at AT&T Long Lines." Reprinted from *Interfaces,* Vol. 12, No. 6 (December), 1982, p. 29, published by The Institute of Management Sciences.
Exhibit 6.17	John D. C. Little and Leonard M. Lodish, "A Media Planning Calculus." Reprinted from *Operations Research,* Vol. 17 (January/February), 1969, p. 12, published by The Institute of Management Sciences.
Exhibit 7.3	Reprinted with permission of Kluwer Academic Publishers, Robert C. Blattberg and Scott A. Neslin (1989), "Sales Promotion: The Long and the Short of It," *Marketing Letters,* Vol. 1, No. 1, pp. 81–89.

Exhibit 7.4   Reprinted with permission of Kluwer Academic Publishers, Robert C. Blattberg and Scott A. Neslin (1989), "Sales Promotion: The Long and the Short of It," *Marketing Letters,* Vol. 1, No. 1, pp. 81–89.

Exhibit 7.5   Reprinted with permission of Kluwer Academic Publishers, Robert C. Blattberg and Scott A. Neslin (1989), "Sales Promotion: The Long and the Short of It," *Marketing Letters,* Vol. 1, No. 1, pp. 81–97.

Exhibit 7.8   Ambar G. Rao and Gary L. Lilien, "A System of Promotional Models." Reprinted from *Management Science,* Vol. 19, No. 2 (October), 1972, p. 159, published by The Institute of Management Sciences.

Exhibit 7.9   John D. C. Little, "BRANDAID: A Marketing Mix Model, Part I: Structure; Part II: Implementation." Reprinted from *Operations Research,* Vol. 23, 1975, p. 641, published by The Institute of Management Sciences.

Exhibit 7.10   John D. C. Little, "Aggregate Advertising Models: The State of the Art." Reprinted from *Operations Research,* Vol. 27, No. 4, (July/August), 1979, p. 641, published by The Institute of Management Sciences.

Exhibit 7.11   Robert C. Blattberg and Alan Levin, "Modelling the Effectiveness and Profitability of Trade Promotions." Reprinted from *Marketing Science,* Vol. 6, No. 2 (Spring), 1987, p. 127, published by The Institute of Management Sciences.

Exhibit 7.12   Robert C. Blattberg and Alan Levin, "Modelling the Effectiveness and Profitability of Trade Promotions." Reprinted from *Marketing Science,* Vol. 6, No. 2 (Spring), 1987, p. 128, published by The Institute of Management Sciences.

Exhibit 7.13   Robert C. Blattberg and Alan Levin, "Modelling the Effectiveness and Profitability of Trade Promotions." Reprinted from *Marketing Science,* Vol. 6, No. 2 (Spring), 1987, p. 137, published by The Institute of Management Sciences.

Exhibit 8.1   David B. Montgomery and Glen L. Urban, *Management Science in Marketing,* 1969, p. 244, published by Prentice Hall.

Exhibit 8.3   R. J. Shanker, R. E. Turner and A. A. Zoltners, "Sales Territory Design: An Integrated Approach." Reprinted from *Management Science,* Vol. 22, No. 3 (November), 1975, p. 319, published by The Institute of Management Sciences.

Exhibit 8.5   C. A. Beswick and D. W. Cravens, "A Multistage Decision Model for Salesforce Management." Reprinted from the *Journal of Marketing Research,* Vol. 14 (May), 1977, p. 136, published by the American Marketing Association.

Exhibit 9.2   Michael D. Hutt and Thomas W. Speh, "The Channel-design Process," *Business Marketing Management,* 3rd ed., 1989, p. 393, Dryden Press.

Exhibit 9.3   Robert W. Haas, *Industrial Marketing Management: Text and Cases*, 4th edition (Boston: PWS-KENT Publishing Company, 1989), p. 239.

Exhibit 9.8   Gary L. Lilien and Ambar G. Rao, "A Model for Allocating Retail Outlet Building Resources Across Market Areas." Reprinted from *Operations Research,* Vol. 24, (January-February), 1976, p. 6, published by The Institute of Management Sciences.

Exhibit 9.9   Arthur M. Geoffrion and Richard F. Powers, "Facility Location Is Just the Beginning." Reprinted from *Interfaces,* Vol. 10, No. 2 (April), 1980, p. 24, published by The Institute of Management Sciences.

Exhibit 10.4   E. M. Rogers, *Diffusion of Innovations,* 3rd ed., 1983, p. 24, published by The Free Press.

Exhibit 10.5   Louis A. Fourt and Joseph W. Woodlock, "Early Prediction of Market Success for New Grocery Products." Reprinted from the *Journal of Marketing,* Vol. 24 (Oct.), 1960, pp. 33–34, published by the American Marketing Association.

Exhibit 10.6   Reprinted by permission of the publisher from "A Simple Substitution Model of Technological Change," by J. C. Fisher and R. H. Pry, *Technological Forecasting and Social Change,* Vol. 3, pp. 75–88. Copyright 1971 by Elsevier Science Publishing Co., Inc.

Exhibit 10.7   F. Bass, "A New Product Growth Model for Consumer Durables." Reprinted from *Management Science,* Vol. 15 (January), 1969, pp. 217–218, published by The Institute of Management Sciences.

Exhibit 10.8   F. Bass, "A New Product Growth Model for Consumer Durables." Reprinted from *Management Science,* Vol. 15 (January), 1969, pp. 219, published by The Institute of Management Sciences.

Exhibit 10.11   J. H. Parfitt and B. J. K. Collins, "Use of Consumer Panels for Brand Share Prediction." Reprinted from the *Journal of Marketing Research,* Vol. 5 (May), 1986, pp. 132–133, published by the American Marketing Association.

Exhibit 10.12   Alvin J. Silk and Glen L. Urban, "Pre-Test Market Evaluation of New Packaged Goods: A Model and Measurement Methodology." Reprinted from the *Journal of Marketing Research,* Vol. 15 (May), 1978, p. 173, published by the American Marketing Association.

Exhibit 10.13   Alvin J. Silk and Glen L. Urban, "Pre-Test Market Evaluation of New Packaged Goods: A Model and Measurement Methodology." Reprinted from the *Journal of Marketing Research,* Vol. 15 (May), 1978, p. 174, published by the American Marketing Association.

Exhibit 10.14   Reprinted by permission of the publisher from "New Product Forecasting Models: Directions for Research and Implementation," by Vijay Mahajan and Yoram Wind, 1988, *International Journal of Forecasting,* Vol. 4, pp. 341–358. Copyright 1988 by Elsevier Science Publishing Co., Inc.

Exhibit 11.1   Yoram Wind and Thomas S. Robertson, "Marketing Strategy: New Directions for Theory and Research." Reprinted from the *Journal of Marketing,* Vol. 47 (Spring), 1983, p. 16, published by the American Marketing Association.

Exhibit 11.2   George S. Day, Allan D. Shocker and Rajendra K. Srivastava, "Consumer-Oriented Approaches to Identifying Product Markets." Reprinted from the *Journal of Marketing,* Vol. 43, No. 4 (Fall), 1979, p. 11, published by the American Marketing Association.

Exhibit 11.6   Reprinted with permission of The University of Chicago Press. R. Polli, and V. Cook (1969), "Validity of the Product Life Cycle," *The Journal of Business,* Vol. 42, No. 4 (October), pp. 385–400.

Exhibit 11.7   Derek F. Abell and J. S. Hammond, *Strategic Marketing Planning,* 1979, p. 109, published by Prentice Hall.

Exhibit 11.8   L. E. Yelle, 1979, "The Learning Curve: Historic Review and Comprehensive Survey," *Decision Sciences,* Vol. 10 (April), p. 304, published by The Decision Sciences Institute at Georgia State University.

Exhibit 11.9   William W. Alberts, "The Experience Curve Doctrine Reconsidered." Reprinted from the *Journal of Marketing,* Vol. 53 (July), 1989, p. 40.

Exhibit 11.19   Chaim Fershtman, Vijay Mahajan and Eitan Muller, "Marketshare Pioneering Advantage: A Theoretical Approach." Reprinted from *Management Science,* Vol. 36, No. 8 (August), 1990, pp. 905, published by The Institute of Management Sciences.

Exhibit 11.20   Robert D. Buzzell and Bradley T. Gale, *The PIMS Principles,* 1987, p. 274, published by The Free Press.

Exhibit 11.21   Adapted with permission of The Free Press, a Division of Macmillan, Inc. from *The PIMS Principles* by Robert D. Buzzell and Bradley T. Gale. Copyright © 1987 by The Free Press.

Exhibit 11.22   Reprinted by permission of the publisher from "Marketing-Oriented Strategic Planning Models," by Yoram Wind, *Marketing Decision Models,* R. Schultz and A. Zoltners, eds., pp. 207–250. Copyright 1981 by Elsevier Science Publishing Co., Inc.

Exhibit 11.24   Yoram Wind and Thomas L. Saaty, "Marketing Applications of the Analytic Hierarchy Process." Reprinted from *Management Science,* Vol. 26, No. 7 (July), 1980, p. 650, published by The Institute of Management Sciences.

Exhibit 11.26   Yoram Wind and Thomas L. Saaty, "Marketing Applications of the Analytic Hierarchy Process." Reprinted from *Management Science,* Vol. 26, No. 7 (July), 1980, p. 651, published by The Institute of Management Sciences.

Exhibit 12.1   John D. C. Little, "Decision Support Systems for Marketing Managers." Reprinted from the *Journal of Marketing,* Vol. 43, No. 3 (Summer), 1979, p. 10, published by the American Marketing Association.

Exhibit 12.2   Leonard M. Lodish, "Experience with Decision Calculus Models and Decision Support Systems," *Marketing Decision Models,* R. Schultz and A. Zoltners, eds., pp. 165–182. Reprinted by permission of the publisher, copyright 1981 by Elsevier Science Publishing Co., Inc.

Exhibit 12.4   John D. Schmitz, Gordon D. Armstrong and John D. Little, "CoverStory: Automated News Finding in Marketing." Reprinted from *DSS Transactions,* Linda Bolino, ed., 1990, p. 38, published by The Institute of Management Sciences.

Exhibit 12.6   Peter G. W. Keen and Michael S. Scott Morton, *Decision Support Systems: An Organizational Perspective,* © 1978, by Addison-Wesley Publishing Company. Reprinted with permission of the publisher.

Exhibit C.4   MCB University Press Limited, John Saunders, 1987, pp. 1–47, "The Specification of Aggregate Market Models," *European Journal of Marketing,* Vol. 21, No. 2.

NAME INDEX

SUBJECT INDEX

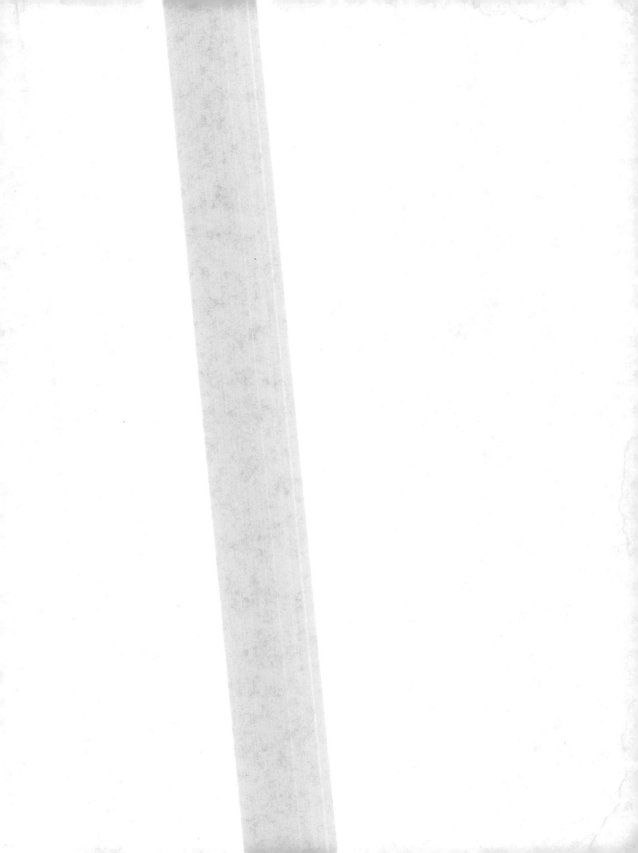